Genreflecting

Recent Titles in Genreflecting Advisory Series

Diana Tixier Herald, Series Editor

Genreflecting

A Guide to Popular Reading Interests

Sixth Edition

Diana Tixier Herald

Edited by Wayne A. Wiegand

Genreflecting Advisory Series
Diana Tixier Herald, Series Editor

LIBRARIES UNLIMITED

U N L I M I T E D

A Member of the Greenwood Publishing Group

Westport, Connecticut • London

Library of Congress Cataloging-in-Publication Data

Herald, Diana Tixier.
  Genreflecting: a guide to popular reading interests. – 6th ed. / by Diana Tixier Herald ; edited
      by Wayne A. Wiegand.
      p. cm. – (Genreflecting advisory series)
  Includes bibliographical references and index.
   ISBN 1-59158-224-5 (alk. paper) – ISBN 1-59158-286-5 (pbk.: alk. paper)
   1. American fiction – Stories, plots, etc. 2. Popular literature – Stories, plots, etc. 3. English
fiction – Stories, plots, etc. 4. Fiction genres – Bibliography. 5. Fiction – Bibliography. 6.
Reading interests. I. Wiegand, Wayne A., 1946- . II. Title. III. Series.
PS374.P63R67 2006
016.813009--dc22   2005030804

British Library Cataloguing in Publication Data is available.

Library of Congress Catalog Card Number: 2005030804
ISBN: 1-59158-224-5
       1-59158-286-5 (pbk.)

First published in 2006

Libraries Unlimited, 88 Post Road West, Westport, CT 06881
A Member of the Greenwood Publishing Group, Inc.
www.lu.com

Printed in the United States of America

The paper used in this book complies with the
Permanent Paper Standard issued by the National
Information Standards Organization (Z39.48–1984).

10 9 8 7 6 5 4 3 2 1

This book is dedicated to the memory of Betty Rosenberg, passionate reader, dedicated teacher, and originator of this guide—an inspiration for all of us.

"Never apologize for your reading tastes."

Betty Rosenberg

Contents

WITHDRAWN

Part II:
The Genres

Acknowledgments

This book would not have been possible without the constant support of Rick Herald.

We would like to thank Libraries Unlimited Acquisitions Editor Barbara Ittner, Production Manager Emma Bailey, and Sharon DeJohn, who not only have done an excellent job of putting this edition of *Genrflecting* together, but throughout have manifested an admirable understanding of the high value millions of public library patrons place on the kinds of reading covered in this book. Like popular fiction readers, they are serious about fun reading, and because of their commitment, readers' advisors across the nation and the world are in their debt.

Part I

Introduction to Popular Reading Interests

Chapter 1

Introduction: "On the Social Nature of Reading"

Wayne A. Wiegand

This introductory chapter has three goals. First, it seeks to outline in a general way the scholarship on the social nature of reading. Second, it attempts to connect this scholarship to another growing body of knowledge that focuses on the existence of a "public sphere," and especially on the concept of "place." Third, it tries to link "reading" and "place" to the world of libraries we've come to know in the first part of the twenty-first century, and to a service in these libraries we now label "readers' advisory."

Reading Together, Manitowoc, Wisconsin, July 1957

It was a family ritual. Every Sunday in the summer of 1957, after an early church service, the Wiegand clan would return to our Manitowoc, Wisconsin, house with Mom's parents to partake of a noon lunch. The routine was well practiced, and firmly grounded in the social habits of the culture that gave our white German American, blue-collar, Protestant family its sense of place and understanding of the world.

Once we entered the house, we divided into two groups. Mom and Grandma quickly went to the kitchen, there to prepare the noontime meal. Dad, Grandpa, my two sisters, and I went to the living room, there to divide up the Sunday edition of the Badger State's major newspaper, the *Milwaukee Journal.* Grandpa took the best chair, Dad the guest chair, my older sister sat on the couch, my younger sister and I sprawled out on the floor. Grandpa went straight to the obituary section, my father to the Home section, my older sister to the Ann Landers column, and my younger sister to the funnies. Being an avid Milwaukee Braves fan, I took the Sports section first. Then began the ritual.

As Grandpa screened the obituaries, he would comment to all in earshot (we didn't always listen) about people he had known in Wisconsin history, and evaluate their contribution to society, at least as he understood it. Grandpa was an FDR Democrat, unforgiving of most Republicans and representatives of the corporate world. Dad, on the other hand, was a McCarthyite Republican. To keep the family peace, he generally didn't say much about politics at these Sunday rituals, except to agree with my grandfather's observations on representatives of the corporate world.

As I lay on the floor with the pages of the Sports section open in front of me I was reading about my hero, Henry Aaron, who with his bat and glove was leading the Milwaukee Braves into the 1957 World Series (which they eventually won). I had three Aarons in my baseball card collection, a hot property in the economy of the eleven-year-old male culture that surrounded me that summer. Often I would raise issues and make points about the Braves with Grandpa and Dad; we all wanted them to win, but we had different ideas on managerial moves, players' behavior, and especially their value to the team's effort.

My younger sister was just beginning to read that summer, but as she combed through the funnies she would attempt to mime the behaviors of others and share from her own reading. Little Lulu, a strip I had recently abandoned because I thought it too childish, was especially attractive to her and occasioned many chuckles. When Grandpa or Dad would ask "What's so funny?" she would take the comics to the inquirer and show him. And usually he would indulge her by laughing too. She then returned to the floor, satisfied that she had shared her reading with the family, just like everybody else in the room.

My older sister, fourteen in 1957, functioned as the connection between the reading community in the living room and the adult female food preparation community in the kitchen. Because at that time our culture worried about the morals of a teenage girl more than those of a teenage boy, I suspect Mom had encouraged my sister to read Ann Landers. All of us learned at an early age that Ann Landers was an authority on social morality and behavior. In fact, we often came home from school to find column clippings taped to our bedroom door, generally on subjects addressing some social transgression we had committed in the recent past.

In good call-and-response fashion my older sister would read from the living room each of the three letters contained in Sunday Ann Landers columns, then wait for the kitchen matriarchy to formulate a response. Immediately Grandma and Mom personalized the problem to particular people in their world, after which they pronounced judgment and waited for my sister to summarize Ann's solution. If the solution matched the judgment emanating from the kitchen, matriarchs assumed that the lesson had been learned. If not, they would quickly inform my older sister why Ann Landers was wrong. While the males in the living room sometimes listened, they commented only on rare occasions. Spheres of influence in our culture were rigidly divided by gender.

Once the meal was ready, members of the living room reading community were called to the table. All of us would drop our self-selected sections of the *Journal* and join the matriarchs in the kitchen, there (quite often) to continue conversations sparked by reading that had taken place the previous half-hour. And while eating, we were as open—and as guarded—about what we had learned as we had been in the living room, even though none of the physical forms of that reading had accompanied us into the kitchen.

Modern Examples of the Social Nature of Reading

For me, this summer 1957 Sunday ritual demonstrates how the family members of one particular culture in a particular place and at a particular time capitalized on the dynamics of the social nature of reading to inform, construct, maintain, debate, and rearrange community in multiple ways. But these kinds of experiences are really timeless, and they happen to everyone. For example, at some time in the past you may have been a participant in one of the following scenarios:

- As a child, you were read to by a parent, grandparent, teacher, or librarian.

- As a parent, grandparent, or librarian, you read to a child.

- As you came across something interesting in your home or workplace reading, you said to your spouse, partner, or colleague, "Hey, listen to this!" after which you proceeded to read something aloud.

- As you came across something interesting on the Web, you forwarded it to several friends or listserv colleagues.

- As you partook of religious rituals with people of the same faith, you all listened to your clergyperson read from a sacred text.

- As you read directional signs in an attempt to find your way around large buildings or cities, you either sought out someone who knew the terrain, or that person approached you because of the confused look on your face.

- As you worked your way through our culture's formal institutions of education, you took classes in which your teachers and professors read to you from the canonical works of civilization; you subsequently quoted from those works to others in your home, workplace, dorm room, perhaps even the library.

- You participated in one of the hundreds of thousands of book clubs—real and virtual—that now meet in living rooms, public libraries, and on the Internet.

- As you saw a stranger on the street with a copy of the same book tucked under her arm that you were reading for your hometown public library "one book/one city" program, you nodded your head in her direction and showed her your copy.

- As you stood in line to get your copy of a best-selling book autographed by a famous author, you discussed the book's contents with the people in front of and behind you. Then you complimented the author on the quality of her work as she scratched out her name in thick blank ink on the title page of your copy. You then showed the autograph to friends and colleagues when you returned to your office, and to your family members when you got home. Ultimately, it found a special place on your bookshelves, from which you removed it on occasion to show dinner guests, all of whom then discussed the book over dinner.

Each of these scenarios is yet another manifestation of the social nature of reading, an essential human behavior that does more to draw people into groups than to separate them from one another. Each also demonstrates that the concept of "solitary reader" is more myth than reality.

Alberto Manguel points out in *A History of Reading* that although the myth has persisted for centuries, reading as a social activity has a much longer history. Even when most people were illiterate a thousand years ago, they were still read to—an example of the social nature of reading. After the invention of moveable type in the mid-fifteenth century, the stories that orally based cultures had accumulated into their folklore found their way into print, where over the centuries they were replicated and modified to meet new social circumstances. Despite the fact that they were often read in solitude, they nonetheless bound people into particular kinds of communities—another manifestation of the social nature of reading. Some reading bound groups by class—dime novels read by factory workers in the late nineteenth-century Midwest. Some reading bound groups by race—the *Chicago Defender* read and shared by African Americans in the early twentieth century segregated South, who obtained copies in the middle of the night when black porters secretly threw them from the moving train on its way to New Orleans; novellas read by Hispanic American migrant workers on the West Coast in the mid-twentieth century. Some reading bound groups by gender—romances read by women in the late twentieth century. All of these kinds of reading, however, demonstrate its essential social nature.

Scholarship on the Social Nature of Reading

As librarians, we recognize the demand for popular fiction, and although we struggle mightily to meet it, we still have a limited understanding of why that demand exists in the first place. To deepen that understanding we have to look outside our own literature, where in the past twenty-five years a growing body of scholarship has emerged that analyzes the subject of reading stories from a variety of perspectives, including literacy studies, reader-response theory, ethnographies of reading, the social history of print, and cultural studies. Reading scholars analyze who reads what stories, and why, by focusing on the complex ways readers from gendered, race, class, and creed-based information cultures use what they read and how they apply that reading in their daily lives. To develop a deeper understanding of how reading functions as a cultural agency and practice in the everyday lives of ordinary people, I recommend a number of titles from this body of scholarship.

One of the pioneering works in this field is Janice Radway's *Reading the Romance: Women, Patriarchy and Popular Literature,* an ethnographic case study that describes the multiple ways in which romances functioned as agents in the everyday lives of a group of women who patronized a particular suburban mall bookstore in the late 1970s. Radway demonstrates how these women used their reading to claim their own mental space and to escape—if only temporarily—the practical demands of being wife and mother. During the past twenty years *Reading the Romance* has gone through two editions, sold tens of thousands of copies, and been assigned as required reading in hundreds of English, history, print culture, and American studies courses across the country.

Benedict Anderson's *Imagined Communities: Reflections on the Origin and Spread of Nationalism* has been equally influential in the scholarship on reading. In the book he argues that people organize themselves into large and small "imagined communities" in order to orient and affiliate with each other. Cultural texts of all kinds function as agents to help construct these imagined communities by providing common sets of experiences, including the reading of shared printed texts. Anderson adds another dimension to the social nature of reading, however. He notes that sometimes this reading takes place in groups, on public property, and in cultural spaces. The feeling of community that individuals sense when filing past an original copy of the Bill of Rights at the National Archives in Washington, D.C., with a group of American strangers is one example of this phenomenon; smiling at drivers in the next lane whose vehicles sport the same political bumper stickers is another.

More recently, Jeremy Rifkin explores another perspective on information and learning that directly relates to the social nature of reading. In *The Age of Access: How the Shift from Ownership to Access Is Transforming Modern Life,* he argues that we are moving from an "age of information" to an "age of access" at the beginning of the twenty-first century, and specifically access to a set of shared "cultural experiences" (Rifkin calls them "webs of meaning") that focus on play more than work. Entertainment, he points out, is the fastest growing industry in the United States, and as the nation moves from industrial to cultural capitalism, a work ethos is slowly giving way to a play ethos. "Play is what people do when they create culture," Rifkin says. "It is the letting free of the human imagination to create shared meanings. Play is a fundamental category of human behavior without which civilization could not exist."[1] Genre fiction fits his definition of cultural play, and everyone reading this chapter knows very well that public libraries lend a lot of people a lot of genre fiction.

If I had to recommend one recently published book that best explores "the social nature of reading," however, it would be Elizabeth Long's *Book Clubs: Women and the Uses of Reading in Everyday Life*. Her first chapter, appropriately titled "The Social Nature of Reading," is a knockout. Here she analyzes reading's capacity to stimulate imagination and construct community through shared meaning. She defines reading as a cultural practice and argues that the modern construction of the solitary reader—much of which is made manifest in the way people are represented as readers in post-Enlightenment art—ignores the thoroughly social base for some kinds of reading. The social nature of reading that enables literacy and encourages the habit of reading, she says, emanates from a social infrastructure that includes shared interpretive frameworks, participation in a set of institutions, and social relations. "Familial reading," she notes, "is both a form of cultural capital and one of the most important determinants of adherence to reading in later life."[2]

Even reading itself is socially framed, she argues. Groups of authorities (like literary critics and teachers at all levels of education) and cultural institutions (like schools and universities) "shape reading practices by authoritatively defining what is worth reading and how to read it." And threaded throughout the act of reading, she notes, are issues of power, privilege, exclusions, and social distinction, all combining in multiple ways so that reading is never "disembodied," never "unsituated."

But Long goes even further. She marries her findings to cultural studies research, which notes that in the free will act of social reading readers "move into and out of the text," and thus "appropriate" (others have even used the word "poach") meaning relevant to their own lives. Thus, because readers can control it, the act of reading becomes pleasurable, empowering, intellectually stimulating, and socially bonding. And it is here that social and cultural acts of defiance—sometimes overt, sometimes covert, sometimes conscious, sometimes subconscious—take place. If authorities at whatever level lack the power to check their reading for an interpretation made legitimate by the dominant cultures, ordinary readers can and do construct their own meanings. Elsewhere Stephen Greenblatt has called this process "self-fashioning;" Barbara Sicherman has called it "self-authorization." Long argues that these processes do not occur in a vacuum, but rather within the boundaries of a social infrastructure where group members mediate their interpretations with each other, their cultures, and their society.

"Imagined communities," "webs of meaning," "appropriate," "poach," "self-fashion," "self-authorize": These words and phrases now function as part of a new vocabulary to explain how reading constructs community, even if the act of reading is done in solitude. And the scholarship on the social nature of reading augments our understanding of why millions of people belong to hundreds of thousands of reading groups and book clubs, many now meeting on the Internet. I think it also helps us understand the increasing number of book festivals in recent years across North America, and the popularity of "one community, one book" and "one campus, one book" reading programs monitored by hundreds of public and academic libraries across the country. Where some see reading primarily as a solitary behavior, Long sees reading primarily as an associational behavior.

Reading and Libraries—Then and Now

History shows that American libraries have done three things exceptionally well in the past century. In no particular order of importance, they have (1) made information accessible to millions of people on a variety of subjects; (2) provided tens of thousands of places where patrons have been able to meet formally as clubs or groups, or informally as citizens or students utilizing a civic institution and cultural agency; and (3) furnished billions of reading materials to billions of people. And in recent years—despite predictions of the demise of libraries and reduction in the number of books they circulate—statistics for each of these categories have held steady or increased. For example, there are 16,180 public library buildings (including branches) in the United States (that's more than McDonald's restaurants); 3,658 academic libraries (hundreds of which have extensive systems with multiple libraries); nearly 100,000 school libraries (public and private); and 11,500 special, armed forces, and government libraries. Every year for the past five academic librarians have answered over 100,000,000 reference questions—more than three times the attendance at college football games. More than 16,000,000 patrons visit academic libraries weekly, and when we annualize that number and add in visits to school and public libraries, the total jumps to 3.5 billion per year, more than twice the attendance at movie theaters in this country. Statistics like these clearly demonstrate that not only is the American library (academic, public, and school) a ubiquitous institution, it is now, and for the last decade has been, a very active civic agency.

Circulation statistics, certainly one manifestation of "reading" in libraries, are equally impressive. For academic libraries, circulation has increased steadily in the past decade to nearly 200,000,000 items per year. For public libraries, per capita circulation increased from 5.6 in 1991 to 6.7 in 2001, and in 2003 it increased another 4 percent. In fact, the Office for Research & Statistics (ORS) of the American Library Association (ALA) estimates that in 2003, 150,000,000 Americans went to a public library to check out a book, and a substantial fraction withdrew scores of books during the year.[3] And public librarians know that large numbers (probably most) of these are genre fiction titles.

These statistics prove conclusively that the American library, whether public, school, or academic, constitutes a major source and site for the act of reading, an essential human behavior librarians of all types have been facilitating and advocating for centuries. Evidence for this conclusion is not hard to find. Scan any ALA Graphics catalog and one will find more than fifty posters with media darlings like Oprah Winfrey, Marion Jones, Yo Yo Ma, and Susan Sarandon, each holding a book with the word "READ" displayed in huge letters at the top. I'll bet scores of these posters line the walls of your own library; perhaps you've put up a few yourself to promote readers' advisory services.

There's also a lot of evidence to demonstrate how libraries foster the social nature of reading. In a survey of 1,500 public libraries serving populations over 5,000 that ALA conducted in 1998, 99.6 percent reported that they hosted other reading-related programs like storytelling, summer reading, and book discussion groups; 82.6 percent said they hosted author presentations and readings, musical and dramatic performances, and creative writing workshops. And statistics from Great Britain I ran across recently reveal that library users who borrow books there are more socially mixed than those who regularly buy them in bookstores—evidence of cultural democracy in action, I would argue.[4]

We also know what library readers expect from librarians. In answer to a question ALA piggybacked onto an omnibus 2001 telephone survey of 1,000 adults about what skills librarians most needed, 76 percent (the highest percentage of any category) said "familiarity with a range of books and authors." The survey also asked what activities people do at public libraries; 92 percent (also the highest percentage of any category) responded: "Borrow books."[5]

Genre Fiction, Libraries, and the Social Nature of Reading

We all know that a substantial fraction of the books circulating out of public libraries by the millions can be categorized as genre fiction, popular literature with story forms that are grouped by shared characteristics and appeal to larger readerships. When looked at through the eyes of their readers, these story forms evoke a variety of responses. They maintain and challenge social realities, help to construct "imagined communities" through "webs of meaning," and facilitate acts of appropriation, poaching, self-fashioning, and self-authorization. But a longer view of history also shows subtle shifts in the details that genre fiction authors build into their story forms. Some of these shifts connect to issues of gender, some to race, some to class, some to age, some to members of a particular generation. Librarians in general, and readers' advisors in particular, are well advised to recognize these shifts; they represent the keys to understanding the complex and multiple connections between the various categories of genre fiction and their readers. That's one of the reasons Libraries Unlimited has to publish new editions of *Genreflecting*; they're made necessary by a set of social dynamics forcing shifts in story forms.

The Library as Place in a Real and Virtual World

Closely connected to understanding the social nature of reading that libraries facilitate is understanding how libraries function as places in the lives of their users, and especially users who read. In *Book Clubs*, Elizabeth Long is particularly critical of Robert Putnam, who in *Bowling Alone: The Collapse and Revival of American Community* hypothesizes that over the last quarter of the twentieth century Americans became increasingly disconnected from family, friends, neighbors, and clubs like the PTA, the Elks, even political parties, thus depriving themselves of opportunities to share the "social capital" so necessary to civic and personal health, and so essential for building strong community bonds. Since about 1970, Putnam says, Americans have largely been "bowling alone." Based on her research, however, Long suggests "Putnam's focus on formal groups may make it difficult for him to see or understand new forms of civic engagement, new ways that our social situations generate social capital."[6]

Let me shift gears here a bit by complicating the word "place." These days one cannot begin to think broadly about "place" without considering the ideas Jurgen Habermas develops in *The Structural Transformation of the Public Sphere: An Inquiry into a Category of Bourgeois Society*. During the eighteenth century, Habermas argues, the growing middle classes sought to influence government actions by assuming control of an emerging "public sphere" of deliberation that eventually found an influential niche between forces exercised by governments and marketplaces. Within this public sphere members of the middle classes developed their own brand of reason, and over time they created their own network of institutions and a series of sites (e.g., newspapers and periodicals, political parties, academic societies, and, I would argue, libraries of all types). In and through these institutions they refined a middle-class–based rationalized discourse into an expression of the "public interest" that governments and markets dared not ignore.

Once Habermas's theory established a foundation for understanding how a series of social and cultural preconditions shaped the public sphere, other scholars began to analyze the institutions and sites where this rationalized discourse has been practiced by multiple communities and groups that have not been primarily concerned either with political ideology or marketplace activities. And it is out of analyses of these institutions and sites that a refined concept of the role of "place" as cultural space has emerged.

Earlier I cited very impressive statistics about the number of times people visit libraries of all types, a number that has increased in the past decade. Why is this phenomenon happening? Perhaps one way to answer this question is to deepen our understanding of the multiple ways people use "library as place." Over the generations millions of patrons have demonstrated their support of the library as a place by visiting it again and again, yet we don't know very much about why they do it. In library and information studies, we have some ideas and beliefs (see, e.g., ALA's "12 Ways Libraries Are Good for the Country"),[7] but little solid evidence based on research to validate these ideas and beliefs. The myriad ways people in libraries "exchange social capital"—a phrase that is so much a part of "public sphere" thinking and yet another dimension to the social nature of reading—have yet to receive adequate attention in our professional literature.

Nor have we adequately explored the role of the library as place in newer cybercommunities of readers. Conversations about books take place on the Internet in multiple settings. Although largely for commercial reasons, Amazon.com solicits reader comments, which we can all read. Other user-friendly Web sites (like Oprah's book club) are designed to encourage readers to feel part of a larger community. And just like the real community that emerges with real book clubs, the virtual community that emerges from virtual book clubs often leads to the kind of intimacy that the social nature of reading makes possible. Long notes that more than face-to-face clubs, online reading groups are organized around special interests in particular story forms. She also cites an observer of these online groups who argues that science fiction, fantasy, crime, and horror readers (among others) are now less likely to find friends willing to share their interests in their own neighborhoods than they are to find them online.

Quietly but efficiently connected to all this cyberactivity surrounding books is the public library—always ready, able, and (within budgetary constraints) willing to supply the reading "sites" on which these self-constructed virtual communities ground themselves. And linking patrons to those "sites" are a series of electronic services that function as a kind of social technology facilitating the social nature of reading, which in turn encourages the formation of interpretive communities, the exchange of social capital, and the same kind of personally empowering self-fashioning and self-authorization mirrored for generations in real reading groups.

When We Don't Know About the Social Nature of Reading and Library as Place

There is a price to be paid for not having a deeper understanding of the social nature of reading and the role library as place plays in enabling it. Two examples will demonstrate; one looks at librarianship from the outside in, the other from the inside out.

In an October 1, 2002, story in the *Tacoma* [WA] *News Tribune,* correspondent Peter Callaghan reports that a local councilman wanted to eliminate local public libraries because "as we see them today" in an Internet age of electronic information, they "are somewhat of a dinosaur . . . too intensive on bricks and mortar." Fellow council members complimented him for thinking "outside the box." Callaghan, however, disagreed. "Let's think inside the box for a moment," he argued, "because it is inside those brick-and-mortar boxes where community lives. Tacoma's 10 libraries are the living rooms of ten neighborhoods. They are places where latchkey kids can feel safe in the afternoons, where people without Internet access at home go online, where parents give their children the gift of reading." The councilman seemed unaware that the library did anything more of value to the local community than provide access to information. Callaghan seemed unaware that the kind of reading and community activities he described taking place at the library had been going on for generations.

In 1996 recipients of a Kellogg grant met in Washington to discuss the future of libraries. There they reviewed a Benton Foundation report on a focus group that identified as its top two public library services (1) "providing reading hours and other programs for children," and (2) "purchasing new books and other printed materials." One member of that same Benton focus group also criticized public libraries for not stocking enough genre fiction titles ("If you want to get the book that everybody is reading right now, it is just not in," she complained). Without knowledge of research on "reading" and "place," however, Kellogg grant recipients seemed unable to tease out the broader significance of the Benton findings, in which I see things like "exchange of social capital" and the "social nature of reading" much in evidence. I also see markers of how the library functions as place in the life of a particular group of users. But what conclusions did Kellogg grant recipients make of these data? They mostly worried that members of the public perceived libraries as warehouses for old books (sort of like that Tacoma councilman). They instead "planned to use the study's findings to take up the challenge of altering public perception" of libraries.[8]

Library in the Life of the User

Here let me come back to a series of points I made earlier. American history demonstrates that for the last century libraries have (1) made information accessible to millions of people on many subjects; (2) provided tens of thousands of places where patrons have been able to meet formally as clubs or groups, or informally as citizens and students utilizing a civic institution and a cultural agency; and (3) furnished billions of reading materials to millions of patrons. As I see it, the social nature of reading is especially facilitated by what libraries have done in the last two categories. But to see this most clearly and in greater detail, we have to think primarily from a "library in the life of the user" perspective, not our traditional "user in the life of the library" perspective. Only then will it become obvious what roles libraries play in the construction of community through the social nature of reading.

Viewed through the eyes of our readers, the "genreflecting" that libraries make possible is an activity that is not only fun but also empowering, intellectually stimulating, and socially bonding.

By taking a "library in the life of the user" perspective, the social roles that the authors and titles listed in this book play as agents in the everyday lives of genre fiction readers become much more transparent and more obviously important—I would argue at least as important as supplying access to information. And because readers' advisors don't want to control what patrons get from their reading of library books (that may be a primary reason they like librarians so much), RAs probably participate in the lives of their readers much more deeply and in many more ways than we now know. The scholarship on the social nature of reading and the concept of public space as a site for the construction of community suggest that the personal touch readers advisors exercise intuitively makes them integral parts of these social dynamics. We also need to remember that access to these communities is by invitation only. When it happens, librarians can be highly complimented, for they've been invited into an exclusive and carefully guarded group. And as long as "advisory" is defined to mean "enabling choice" and not "prescribing better" or "elevating taste," readers' advisors are likely to remain members (and be admitted to more) of these communities.

Readers of this chapter will find that much of what I say here is echoed in the comments of authors in chapter introductions that follow. All of us agree with the late Betty Rosenberg that the reading patrons do for fun is a legitimate area for library professionals to study. We also believe that titles like *Genreflecting* can substantially improve how librarians carry out their professional practice. At the same time, however, all of us seek to deepen understanding of this genre fiction reading phenomenon by asking why people engage in it, what they get from it, and how they use these reading materials and reading experiences in their everyday lives. In short, by using a "library in the life of the user" perspective, we want to place more focus on why the vast majority of library patrons are so *serious* about the "fun" reading libraries provide, and in the process hopefully elevate the importance this professional service has when measured against other professional services that traditionally get much more attention in library education, research, and associational activities. If Jeremy Rifkin is right about the role of cultural play, one can argue persuasively that some of the most important contributions American libraries make to their communities can be found in the access they provide to the materials and the space they make available for play, all of which fosters certain types of learning.

As you use this guide to help determine your genre fiction selections, as you work with library-sponsored book clubs interested in genreflecting, as you hand genre fiction titles across the circulation desk to library readers, I urge you to ask yourself a series of questions:

- To what extent are your genre fiction readers harnessing particular social infrastructures to unite and divide into communities that reflect similar interests, rationalities, and convergent discourses, of which the reading recommended in this book may be only one manifestation?

- To what extent are there issues of power, exclusions, and social distinctions evident in these groupings?

- To what extent are they open with their comments about their reading; to what extent are they guarded? Why?

- To what extent do they "appropriate" or "poach" from the written and oral texts being presented to them, perhaps even engaging in guerrilla tactics (visible and invisible) to dispute the texts they are hearing or reading?

- From the dynamics of social interaction taking place, are there one or more "imagined communities" in evidence where "readers" can be observed "self-fashioning" and "self-authorizing," or exploring similar "webs of meaning?"

All of these questions were relevant in that Manitowoc living room in 1957. Addressing just some of them today will help us understand much more deeply why genre fiction loyalists take their "fun" reading so seriously. It will also help us discover more of the multiple and often invisible ways millions of genre fiction readers across the country continue to enlist libraries as agencies in these everyday social practices and behaviors.

Notes

1. Jeremy Rifkin, *The Age of Access: How the Shift from Ownership to Access Is Transforming Modern Life* (New York: Penguin, 2000), 7, 260.

2. Elizabeth Long, *Book Clubs: Women and the Uses of Reading in Everyday Life* (Chicago: University of Chicago Press, 2003), 9.

3. Unless otherwise indicated, these and other statistics cited in this essay an be found at https://cs.ala.orgyourlibrary.factsandfigures.cfm; http://www.ala.org/ord/plstat_trends.html (both accessed October 20, 2002); and ALA Office for Research and Statistics, "Quotable Facts about American Libraries" (wallet-sized trifold pamphlets) for 1998–1999, 1999–2000, 2000–2001, and 2001–2002.

4. Ibid.

5. Available at http://cs.ala.org@yourlibrary/launchsurvey.cf (accessed April 10, 2001).

6. Robert Putnam, *Bowling Alone: The Collapse and Revival of American Community* (New York: Simon & Schuster, 2000); Long, Book Clubs, 19–20.

7. www.ala.org/ala/alonline/selectedarticles/12wayslibraries.htm (accessed September 22, 2005).

8. "Benton Study: Libraries Need to Work on Message to Public," *Library Journal* 121 (September 1, 1996): 112.

Bibliography

Anderson, Benedict. *Imagined Communities: Reflections on the Origin and Spread of Nationalism.* New York: Verso, 1983.

Augst, Thomas, and Wayne A. Wiegand, eds. *Libraries as Agencies of Culture.* Madison: University of Wisconsin Press, 2001.

Bacon-Smith, Camille. *Science Fiction Culture.* Philadelphia: University of Pennsylvania Press, 1999.

Benedict, Barbara M. *Making the Modern Reader: Cultural Mediation in Early Modern Literary Anthologies.* Princeton, N.J.: Princeton University Press, 1996.

Bird, S. Elizabeth. *For Enquiring Minds: A Cultural Study of Supermarket Tabloids.* Knoxville: University of Tennessee Press, 1992.

Bourdieu, Pierre. *Distinction: A Social Critique of the Judgement of Taste.* London: Routledge, 1986.

Boyarin, Jonathan, ed. *The Ethnography of Reading.* Berkeley: University of California Press, 1992.

Cawelti, John G. *The Six-Gun Mystique Sequel.* Bowling Green, Ohio: Bowling Green State University Press, 1999.

de Certeau, Michel. *The Practice of Everyday Life.* Berkeley: University of California Press, 1984.

Dove, George N. *The Reader and the Detective Story.* Bowling Green, Ohio: Bowling Green State University Press, 1997.

Fish, Stanley. *Is There a Text in This Class? The Authority of Interpretive Communities.* Cambridge: Harvard University Press, 1980.

Habermas, Jurgen. *The Theory of Communication Action.* Vol. I, *Reason and Rationalization of Society.* Boston: Beacon, 1984.

Iser, Wolfgang. *The Act of Reading: A Theory of Aesthetic Response.* Baltimore: Johns Hopkins University Press, 1978.

Jauss, Hans Robert. *Experiences and Literary Hermeneutics.* Minneapolis: University of Minnesota Press, 1982.

Jenkins, Henry. *Textual Poachers: Television Fans & Participatory Culture.* New York: Routledge, 1992.

Long, Elizabeth. *Book Clubs: Women and the Uses of Reading in Everyday Life.* Chicago: University of Chicago Press, 2003.

Mailloux, Steven. *Interpretive Conventions: The Reader in the Study of American Fiction.* Ithaca, N.Y.: Cornell University Press, 1982.

Manguel, Alberto. *A History of Reading.* New York: Viking, 1996.

Munt, Sally R. *Murder by the Book? Feminism and the Crime Novel.* London: Routledge, 1994.

Pustz, Matthew. *Comic Book Culture: Fan Boys and True Believers.* Oxford: University Press of Mississippi, 1999.

Putnam, Robert. *Bowling Alone: The Collapse and Revival of American Community.* New York: Simon & Schuster, 2000.

Radway, Janice. *Reading the Romance: Women, Patriarchy and Popular Literature.* Chapel Hill: University of North Carolina Press, 1991.

Rifkin, Jeremy. *The Age of Access: How the Shift from Ownership to Access Is Transforming Modern Life.* New York: Penguin, 2000.

Rosenblatt, Louis. *Literature as Exploration.* New York: Appleton-Century, 1938.

Smith, Erin A. *Hard-Boiled: Working-Class Readers and Pulp Magazines.* Philadelphia: Temple University Press, 2000.

Tompkins, Jane. *West of Everything: The Inner Life of Westerns.* New York: Oxford University Press, 1992.

Wright, Bradford W. *Comic Book Nation: The Transformation of Youth Culture in America.* Baltimore: Johns Hopkins University, 2001.

Chapter 2

A Brief History of Readers' Advisory

Melanie A. Kimball

Introduction

The establishment of public libraries in the United States in the latter half of the nineteenth century provided ordinary citizens with free reading material, mainly books. Public libraries, over the century and a half since then, have undergone many changes, including the addition of a wide variety of nonprint materials, but books and reading are still at the heart of library services. It naturally follows that providing guidance to readers also remains central to the work of librarians in U.S. public libraries.

The Early Years

One of the most contentious debates in the early years of public libraries in the United States centered on the "fiction problem." Librarians believed that education, not leisure, was the primary mission of the public library.[1] Providing the public with high-quality reading material to further self-education had a prominent place in that mission, but providing fiction did not. Despite this, fiction made up a substantial portion of library circulation statistics in the late nineteenth century, as much as two-thirds in some places.[2] Thus the debate over "give them what they want" versus "give them what they need" began early in the history of the public library.

Librarians subscribed to the belief that it was possible to lead readers from a "lower level" of reading (fiction) to a higher class of literature (nonfiction). This "ladder approach" decreed that novel reading was "desirable when the selection of books read is judicious, and when the practice is indulged in only in moderation."[3] Overwhelmingly, librarians believed that "good" books possessed the power to provide readers with wholesome enlightenment, but that reading sensational fiction could be downright dangerous to the character and morals of the reader.[4] Even more important, librarians saw it as their professional duty to be the arbiters of what constituted "good" reading.[5]

Many articles in library journals discussed how to increase "correct" reading and decrease the number of novels read by patrons. Methods to achieve that aim included careful selection of books for the libraries' collections and distribution to patrons of annotated lists of "the right" books. Further suggestions to improve reading habits included that libraries limit themselves to the purchase of very few novels, that libraries spend less on newer popular fiction in order to purchase duplicate copies of "good books," and that librarians try to attract readers to "good books through personal intervention."[6]

The debate between providing patrons with a high level of reading material and giving them what they wanted (even if what they wanted was lowbrow fiction) has never entirely disappeared. Today's view that the primary work of the librarian is to assist patrons to find useful information through reference assistance rather than providing assistance with leisure reading is very similar. These two distinctive approaches characterize the two main phases in the history of readers' advisory. The first phase began in the 1920s and focused on helping readers improve themselves through systematic reading programs provided by librarians. The second phase, discussed in more depth below, began in the early 1980s; in this phase, instead of the librarian giving suggestions on reading that concentrates on improving the reader, the patron's own reading likes and dislikes are the central concern.

Readers' Advisory, Phase One: Reading with a Purpose

The period immediately following World War I saw improvement in the U.S. economy, an increase in leisure time for adults, an increase in the educational level of the general population, and the establishment of an adult educational movement.[7] Better education resulted in more adults interested in reading during their leisure hours. Many librarians took part in an American Library Association–sponsored program during World War I that guided servicemen in their reading. Librarians were eager to take what they had learned in their work with soldiers and apply it to their everyday jobs.[8] Fiction was more tolerated in the early 1920s than it had been in the previous two decades, but it was still looked upon less favorably than was nonfiction.

> We have ceased to worry about the moral implications of fiction-reading. . . . But the fact remains that we still feel . . . a certain uneasiness over a fifty-five and sixty-five per cent fiction circulation.[9]

The adult education movement provided an opportunity for librarians to use the skills they had developed during the war. The public library was ideally suited to aid adult learners because of its large store of reading material. The formal establishment of a readers' advisory program, and the first use of the term "readers' advisory," occurred between 1922 and 1925, when seven urban public libraries, Detroit, Cleveland, Chicago, Milwaukee, Indianapolis, Cincinnati, and Portland, Oregon, established separate departments devoted to "informal adult education through reading."[10] A specialist readers' advisor met with individual patrons in a location separate from the reference and circulation desks. Following an extensive interview, the advisor prepared a course of reading for the patron based on his or her education level and interests. Generally the list went from lighter reading to more meaty fare, another example of the "ladder" approach to reading. This first phase of readers' advisory was prescriptive in nature; that is, librarians provided the expertise to guide patrons into a directed, systematic program of reading for improvement.

Based in part on the success of the programs at the seven institutions listed above, the American Library Association established the Commission on Library and Adult Education in 1924. The Commission, founded specifically "to study and investigate the role of the public library in adult education" accomplished several things between 1924 and 1926.[11] It published a periodical, *Adult Education and the Library*, with articles on readers' advisory by librarians who specialized in adult education, such as Jennie M. Flexner of the New York Public Library (NYPL). Flexner wrote many articles on readers' advisory as well as a book that detailed the work of readers' advisors at the NYPL.[12] The Commission also produced brochures, available for a charge, in a series called Reading with a Purpose. The brochures, written by subject specialists, covered a wide variety of topics. Between 1925 and 1931 the American Library Association sold 850,000 pamphlets in the series.[13] The Commission also wrote a report of its study of the role of the public library in adult education, *Libraries and Adult Education*. One important finding was that libraries should provide "readers' advisory service to those who wished to pursue their studies alone, rather than in organized groups or classes."[14]

The number of libraries with formal readers' advisory services rose from twenty-five in 1928 to sixty-three advisors in forty-four libraries by 1935.[15] Between 1936 and 1940 readers' advisory changed. The job of readers' advisor became overwhelming as "it became almost impossible for reader's advisors to handle not only the large number of patrons who enlisted in this service, but more especially, the overwhelming burden of background reading which was required."[16] In order to ease the burden on readers' advisors, the duties were spread throughout the staff, and centered on subject specialists, particularly in larger urban libraries.[17]

Useful Information

During World War II, a lack of leisure time contributed to a falling off of interest in systematic programs of reading.[18] As the number of patrons who wanted the services of readers' advisors declined, so did the number of formal programs. Then, in the late 1940s, the Carnegie Foundation funded a study of the public library by a group of social scientists led by Robert D. Leigh from the political science department of the University of Chicago. The resulting report, *The Public Library Inquiry*, suggested that readers' advisory service was no longer the province of a particular group of librarians, but diffused throughout the entire library staff.[19] In addition, the *Inquiry* concluded that the most effective work of public libraries was to provide serious reading and useful information, rather than supplying fiction to readers.[20]

Although it would be incorrect to say that there was no readers' advisory during the period from the late 1940s through the 1970s, it was not as prominent a feature as it had been earlier. Instead, other functions in the library, such as reference work, increased in importance as libraries became centered on providing information and "useful knowledge."[21] The number of articles in professional library literature about readers' advisory dropped off significantly.[22] One of the few articles on the topic was Regan's survey of the field in 1973, which found that out of 126 responses from U.S. public libraries, only 23 still had some form of readers' advisory. Regan concluded that "there is still a sizeable amount of readers' advisory work being done, regardless of how unpublicized its results."[23]

An Emerging Focus on Fiction

Though the formal readers' advisory programs of the 1920s and 1930s focused mainly on didactic programs of reading, readers still wanted to read fiction. An important figure in the development of services to readers of popular fiction was Helen Haines. Haines not only championed the inclusion of fiction in the library, she became one of the preeminent voices to discuss collection development that included strong endorsement of the incorporation of popular contemporary fiction for adults. Her text, *Living with Books: The Art of Book Selection*, was first published in 1935 and widely used as a textbook in library schools, as was the second edition, published in 1950.[24] Haines's work "bridged the gap" between the old idea of readers' advisory that gave readers a course of reading to improve their minds and the gradually emerging definition of readers' advisory as "a patron-oriented library service for adult fiction readers."[25]

The Renaissance of Readers' Advisory: 1980–Present

In the early 1980s, what has been called the "renaissance" of readers' advisory began, although it was more of a complete overhaul than a renaissance. An early indication of this new vision was the publication in 1982 of *Genreflecting* by Betty Rosenberg. Rosenberg's book not only gave readers permission to read whatever they liked (her first law of reading is "never apologize for your reading tastes") , but it provided a new kind of tool for librarians to assist readers to find popular fiction. A second edition of *Genreflecting* appeared in 1986, and other books and articles followed, including *Readers' Advisory Service in the Public Library* (1989) by Joyce Saricks and Nancy Brown and *Book Discussions for Adults: A Leader's Guide* (1992) by Ted Balcom. The new readers' advisor was someone who could recommend fiction reading, especially genre fiction.

Articles in the library literature encouraged librarians to learn about different genres and to familiarize themselves with different authors and types of popular fiction. In particular, librarians were advised to be able to answer a patron's question about finding styles of writing, plot, and characterization similar to those that the patron already liked. Practical methods to help patrons find what they wanted included shelving books by genre rather than by author's last name, purchasing multiple copies of popular titles (even multiple copies of paperback books so there would be adequate numbers of books for readers), and creating pathfinders and reading lists of similar books.

In 1984 a group of Chicago-area librarians established the Adult Reading Round Table (ARRT), which was founded due to "the lack of continuing education available on both the national and local level relevant to . . . readers' advisory service for adults." AART meetings usually lasted for two hours and included a speaker, often a member of the Round Table. In 1985 AART expanded to hold an all-day workshop featuring Betty Rosenberg. Other workshops featuring nationally known speakers such as Sharon Baker, Mary K. Chelton, and Duncan Smith followed.[26] Now in its twentieth year, AART compiles and makes available annotated genre lists, bookmarks, and published genre fiction lists for adults and young adults, and gives the findings of annual studies of particular genres.[27] In response to this grassroots movement, national associations formed the Readers Advisory Committee of the Reference and User Services Association's (RUSA) Collection Development and Evaluation Section (CODES) and the Public Library Association's (PLA) Reader's Advisory Committee.

Research in Reading and Readers' Advisory

As practitioners developed tools and continuing education programs for the new readers' advisors, scholars began to research and write more about readers of popular fiction. In part this was due to an acceptance by academics that popular culture was worthy of study, but also because of a shift in the way that scholars viewed the study of literature. Whereas the text itself had been the central focus of literary studies, an awareness of the reader and the reader's interaction with text became of primary importance. This gave rise to genre studies such as Janice Radway's *Reading the Romance* as well as important research within the LIS scholarly community. The work of Catherine Ross, Mary K. Chelton, and others provides the field of library and information studies with an important research base to accompany the applied work done by librarians.[28]

The 1990s ushered in an era of increasing awareness of and interest in readers' advisory. The rise of the Internet was supposed to bring about the death of the book. Not only did the book survive, it thrived, as evidenced by the increasing popularity of book "superstores" and the success of online booksellers. The Internet also provided a new platform for readers' advisory tools that served readers and librarians alike. Sites such as Amazon.com created a space where users could not only buy a book but read professional reviews as well as comments from other readers. Databases such as NoveList and What Do I Read Next? gave librarians and patrons access to new reference guides to popular fiction. E-mail lists such as Fiction_L provided places for librarians to discuss reading and issues in readers' advisory.[29]

Print publications on popular fiction and articles about readers' advisory also increased in the 1990s and 2000s. *Genreflecting* spun off a readers' series including *Teen Genreflecting* and *Junior Genreflecting*. Other books focused on particular genres such as horror, mystery, and fantasy. In 2000 *Reference and User Services Quarterly* began publishing a regular column on readers' advisory edited by Mary K. Chelton, further evidence of the increasing importance of this topic.

Readers' Advisory and LIS Education

Although the demand for librarians skilled in providing readers' advisory services is very high, the curricula for library schools do not reflect this trend. It is standard in LIS education to provide courses in literature for youth that discuss reading promotion, the fiction genres, and readers' advisory for youth. In fact, those students who want to be school media specialists or youth services librarians are usually required to take such classes. However, it is far less common to see comparable courses for adult readers' advisory, and they often are electives. The prevailing attitude seems to be that services to adults can be covered in courses on reference sources and services and online retrieval. Readers' advisory is considered separate from the reference function. In fact, commonly used textbooks for reference courses, such as the second edition of Richard E. Bopp's and Linda C. Smith's *Reference and Information Services: An Introduction* (1995) and Katz's *Introduction to Reference Work*, 5th ed. (1987) make no mention of readers' advisory at all. The third edition of Bopp and Smith (2001) includes a two-paragraph discussion of readers' advisory in the opening chapter, but it is by no means a thorough introduction to the subject.

Studies of existing readers' advisory services in public libraries found that many librarians did not provide a high quality of service in this area.[30] Moreover, LIS students may not be exposed to courses that will help them gain the necessary skills. A study by the RUSA CODES Readers' Advisory Committee found that only fourteen library schools offered courses in readers' advisory.[31] Another study, by Kenneth D. Shearer and Robert Burgin, concluded that although many ALA–accredited schools offered specific courses in readers' advisory, "most of the programs accredited by the American Library Association do not even expose students to the idea that they can develop a practice devoted to building adult popular collections and encouraging rewarding reading among the general public."[32]

Wayne Wiegand has written articles and presented talks at meetings with library educators in an effort to increase attention on reading studies and their place in library education.[33] Although consistently met with resistance from some educators, there are a growing number of LIS educators who both do research in and teach reading studies. It is to be hoped that with consistent pressure from practitioners and educators working from within, this lack will be redressed soon.

Conclusion

In one form or another, librarians have connected readers with books since the beginning of the modern public library movement. The philosophy, tools, and methods used to advise readers have changed since the early days of the public library. What hasn't changed is that public librarians see it as part of their mission to bring readers and books together. Although public libraries always included fiction in their collections, its presence has proven to be one of the hotly debated issues for librarians since the late nineteenth century. In the past, librarians had an ambiguous relationship with fiction and struggled to define whether their mission was to provide readers with the "right" reading or to give readers what they wanted to read, even if librarians deemed it to be of lesser quality. Today fiction reading is fully acknowledged as an important part of what public libraries provide to their patrons. Providing guidance to readers who want the latest in genre fiction is no longer something that librarians shy away from, but should be central to the work of the public library. Our patrons expect no less.

Notes

1. Robert Ellis Lee, *Continuing Education for Adults Through the American Public Library, 1833–1964* (Chicago: American Library Association, 1966). Lee's book gives a through overview of the "ages" of the public library as an educational agency. References to readers' advisory are scattered throughout the book, but particularly pertinent is chapter IV, "Serving the Individual," which focuses on the period when the term "readers' advisory" first surfaced as a structured program of individualized reading advisement.

2. Charles Francis Adams, "Fiction in Public Libraries and Educational Catalogues," *Library Journal* 4 (1879): 330.

3. Samuel Swett Green. "Sensational Fiction in Public Libraries," *Library Journal* 4 (1879): 346.

4. Ibid., 331.

5. That librarians viewed themselves as experts in directing the public's reading may be seen in such articles as W. E. Foster, "On Aimless Reading and Its Correction," *Library Journal* 4 (1879): 78–80; A. L. Peck ,"What May a Librarian Do to Influence the Reading of a Community?" *Library Journal* 22 (1897): 77–80; Beatrice Winser, "The Encouragement of Serious Reading by Public Libraries," *Library Journal* 28 (1903): 237–38; and Frances L. Rathbone, "A Successful Experiment in Directing the Reading of Fiction," *Library Journal* 32 (1907): 406–8.

6. John Cotton Dana, "The Place of Fiction in the Free Public Library," *Library Journal* 28 (1903): C37.

7. Lee, *Continuing Education for Adults,* 70.

8. Ibid., 46.

9. Charles E. Rush and Amy Winslow, "Encouraging the Use of Adult Non-fiction," *Library Journal* 53 (1928): 291.

10. Lee, *Continuing Education for Adults,* 46.

11. American Library Association, *Libraries and Adult Education* (Chicago: The Association, 1926): 221–46.

12. For a detailed description of the readers' advisory program at the New York Public Library, see *Readers' Advisers at Work* by Jennie M. Flexner and Byron C. Hopkins (New York: American Association for Adult Education, 1941).

13. Lee, *Continuing Education for Adults,* 50–51.

14. Ibid., 50.

15. Ibid., 57–58

16. Lee Regan, "Status of Reader's Advisory Service," *RQ* 12 (1973): 229.

17. Lee, *Continuing Education for Adults,* 59

18. Joyce G. Saricks and Nancy Brown, *Readers' Advisory Service in the Public Library.* 2d ed. (Chicago: American Library Association, 1997), 5.

19. Regan, "Status of Reader's Advisory Service," 230.

20. Wayne Wiegand points out that librarianship's most important professional responsibility became to provide useful information to its constituency, a course of action that influenced not only the practice of the profession on a daily basis, but also the course of library education. See his "Missing the Real Story: Where Library and Information Science Fails the Library Profession," in *Readers' Advisor's Companion,* edited by Kenneth D. Shearer and Robert Burgin, 11 (Englewood, Colo.: Libraries Unlimited, 2001).

21. Ibid.

22. A brief survey of the *Index to Library Literature* showed that for the index of 1936–1939 there were more than twenty articles and multiple references to book reviews under the heading "readers' advisory" (the term changed to "reader guidance" in 1958). The index for 1955–1957 had only twelve references, of which five were in foreign publications, and in 1976–1977 the number of articles had dropped to only four references in English, with a few book reviews and a number of articles in foreign publications.

23. Regan, "Status of Reader's Advisory Service," 230.

24. Robert D. Harlan, "Haines, Helen Elizabeth," in *The Dictionary of American Library Biography* (Englewood, Colo.: Libraries Unlimited, 1978), 225.

25. Saricks and Brown, *Readers' Advisory Service in the Public Library*, 1.

26. Ted Balcom, "The Adult Reading Round Tale: Chicken Soup for Readers' Advisors," *Reference & User Services Quarterly* 41 (2002): 238–43.

27. For more information on the Adult Reading Round Table, its activities, and its publications, visit http://www.aartreads.org.

28. Mary K. Chelton, "Readers' Advisory 101," *Library Journal* (November 1, 2003): 38–39; Mary K. Chelton, "What We Know and Don't Know About Reading, Readers, and Readers Advisory Services," *Public Libraries* (January/February 1999): 42–47; Janice Radway, *Reading the Romance: Women, Patriarchy, and Popular Literature* (University of North Carolina Press, 1984); Catherine Sheldrick Ross, "Readers' Advisory Service: New Directions," *RQ* 30 (1991): 503–18; Catherine Sheldrick Ross, "If They Read Nancy Drew, So What? Series Readers Talk Back," *Library and Information Science Research* 17 (1995): 210–35; Catherine Sheldrick Ross, "Making Choices: What Readers Say About Choosing Books to Read for Pleasure," *Acquisitions Librarian* 25 (2001): 5–21; Catherine Ross and Mary K. Chelton, "Reader's Advisory: Matching Mood and Material," *Library Journal* 126 (2001): 52–53.

29. Paula Wilson, "Readers' Advisory Services: Taking It All Online," *Public Libraries* (November/December 2001): 344–45; Ricki Nordmeyer, "Readers' Advisory Web Sites," *Reference & User Services Quarterly* 41:2 (2001): 139–43; Neal Waytt, "Webwatch," *Library Journal* (September 1, 2002): 32–33.

30. Robert Burgin, "Readers' Advisory in Public Libraries: An Overview of Current Practices," in *Guiding the Reader to the Next Book,* ed. Kenneth Shearer, 71–88 (New York: Neal-Schuman, 1996); Anne K. May, Elizabeth Olesh, Anne Weinlich Miltenberg, and Catherine Patricia Lackner, "A Look at Reader's Advisory Services," *Library Journal* 125, no. 15 (2000): 40–43; Catherine Sheldrick Ross and Patricia Dewdney, "Best Practices: An Analysis of the Best (and Worst) in Fifty-Two Public Library Reference Transactions," *Public Libraries* 33 (September/October 1994): 261–66; Kenneth Shearer, "The Nature of the Readers' Advisory Transaction in Adult Reading," in *Guiding the Reader to the Next Book,* ed. Kenneth Shearer, 1–20 (New York: Neal-Schuman, 1996); Cathleen A. Towey, "We Need to Recommit to Readers' Advisory Services," *American Libraries* 28 (1997): 31.

31. Dana Watson and RUSA CODES Readers' Advisory Committee, "Time to Turn the Page: Library Education for Readers' Advisory Services," *Reference & User Services Quarterly* 40 (2000): 143–46.

32. Kenneth D. Shearer and Robert Burgin, "Partly Out of Sight; Not Much in Mind: Master's Level Education for Adult Readers' Advisory Services," in *The Readers' Advisor's Companion,* ed. Kenneth D. Shearer and Robert Burgin, 24 (Englewood, Colo.: Libraries Unlimited, 2001).

33. Wayne A. Wiegand, "MisReading Library Education," *Library Journal* 122 (1997): 36–38; "Out of Sight and Out of Mind: Why Don't We Have Any Schools of Library and Reading Studies?" *Journal of Library and Information Science Education* 38 (1997): 316–26; "Librarians Ignore the Value of Stories," *Chronicle of Higher Education* 47 (October 27, 2000): B20; "Missing the Real Story: Where Library and Information Science Fails the Library Profession," in *The Readers' Advisor's Companion,* ed. Kenneth D. Shearer and Robert Burgin, 7–14 (Englewood, Colo.: Libraries Unlimited, 2001).

Appendix: A Chronology of Readers' Advisory

1876   Founding of the American Library Association (ALA)

1922   Formal readers' advisory service established at the Detroit Public Library and Cleveland Public Library

1923   Formal readers' advisory service established at the Chicago Public Library and Milwaukee Public Library

1924   Formal readers' advisory service established at the Indianapolis Public Library
       ALA Commission on the Library and Adult Education formed

1925   Formal readers' advisory service established at public libraries in Cincinnati and Portland, Oregon
       Reading with a Purpose pamphlet series begins publication

1935   *Living with Books* by Helen E. Haines published (2d ed. in 1950)

1982   *Genreflecting* by Betty Rosenberg published (multiple editions since)

1984   Adult Reading Round Table (ARRT) formed

1986   *Readers' Advisory Service in the Public Library* by Joyce G. Saricks and Nancy Brown published (2nd ed. in 1997)

2000   Readers' advisory column edited by Mary K. Chelton becomes a regular feature of *Reference & User Services Quarterly*

Chapter 3

The Readers' Advisory Interview

Catherine Sheldrick Ross

Effective readers' advisory work is a matchmaking service. A successful match is made when the reader asks for "a good book to read" and ends up getting reading suggestions for materials likely to be enjoyable. This matchmaking job is tricky because, for any given reader, the concept of the "good book" involves a number of dimensions that go well beyond what may initially be asked for. Relevant factors may include the reader's mood and the context of the intended reading as well as a number of idiosyncratic preferences. Avid pleasure-readers in one study reported overwhelmingly that they choose books according to their mood and what else is happening in their lives: "Short books, easy reads, and old favorites are picked when the reader is busy or under stress."[1]

To make the right match, librarians need to conduct a readers' advisory interview, because readers rarely provide sufficient detail in their initial request. They may request "some good books to read" or ask for a specific genre such as mysteries or history books. The readers' advisor needs a way of finding out what these terms mean to the particular reader. For one, a "well-written" book may mean intricate plotting and fast-paced suspense; for a second reader it may mean good character development; and for a third reader perhaps it means the felicitous use of language, where every paragraph invites reflection, rereading, and savoring. Effective readers' advisors take a nonjudgmental approach that accepts readers' tastes and preferences and doesn't try to change or "improve" them. When the reader asks for a category romance, he or she doesn't want to hear, "Why don't you read a really *good* book like *Jane Eyre* or *Pride and Prejudice*?"

It is now generally recognized that the term "a good book" is relative to the particular reader. Readers may mean a book to match my mood right now, or a book that suits my level of reading ability, or a book that speaks to my particular interests (whether it's horseracing or high fashion or archaeology), or a book written in a style that maximizes the effects I enjoy (e.g., it scares me, comforts me, makes me laugh, makes me cry, lifts my spirits, teaches me something, unsettles my preconceived ideas, or opens my eyes to new possibilities). That's why it doesn't work for a readers' advisor to have the same list of canonical "Good Books" such as *War and Peace* or *Pride and Prejudice* for all readers. Nor does it work for a readers' advisor to recommend his or her own personal favorites to everyone (e.g., "I've just read Yann Martel's *Life of Pi* and it was great; you'll love it.") .

Readers' advisors need to be adept in at least two areas of expertise: first, book knowledge, which involves an understanding of the genres of fiction and nonfiction and their appeal to readers; and second, communication skills, which help readers' advisors find out from readers the kinds of reading experiences they are seeking. This second area of expertise is of course the domain of the readers' advisory interview, which differs less from the reference interview than is sometimes supposed. All interviews are special kinds of conversations, directed intentionally toward some purpose. Both reference interviews and readers' advisory interviews involve collaborative conversations between the library user (who is the expert in the kind of information or reading experience that is wanted) and the information professional (who is the expert in how knowledge is organized, stored, and retrieved).

Often reference interviews fail because the library staff member asks questions relating to the library system such as "Did you check the catalog?", "Do you know the indexing elements?", "Do you want a directory?", or "Have you checked the 282s?"[2] Librarians feel comfortable in this domain, because they are in control. They know all the specialized terms and understand the difference between a biography and a bibliography or between a directory and a dictionary. But users often make mistakes when they are asked to translate their information needs into the unfamiliar vocabulary of the library system. Readers' advisory interviews can similarly fail when the staff member asks questions that relate to classification schemes and literary terms, rather than asking about the kind of experience the reader wants. Such questions as "Do you enjoy thrillers/police procedurals/crime capers?", "Do you like cyberpunk/dystopias/Chick Lit?", "Are you interested in something historical?", or "Do you want escapist fiction?" often go wrong because the reader doesn't share the librarian's understanding of the terms used.

In contrast, in successful readers' advisory (RA) transactions, staff members typically initiate a conversation about books that is designed to get readers talking about their own preferred experiences with books, including favorite books, authors, and genres. In a study of avid readers and how they choose books to read for pleasure,[3] I discovered that the single most important strategy for selection was choosing a book by a known and trusted author. The second was making selections by genre. For readers' advisors, it is also important to discover what readers *don't* like. Although they may sometimes say they will "read anything," they probably won't. One UK investigation of book reading and borrowing[4] reports that readers in the study qualified their "read anything" claim by specifying various categories they would *not* read. Men said they wouldn't read romantic fiction; many, and especially women, said they wouldn't read nonfiction. Others rejected war stories, anything "too violent," or "books which emphasize blood and gore."[5]

To encourage a discussion of the reader's engagement with books, Joyce Saricks and Nancy Brown recommend starting off the RA interview with something like, "Tell me about a book you really enjoyed."[6] Similarly Ross, Nilsen, and Dewdney recommend that readers' advisors intentionally select from questions such as the following[7]:

To get a picture of previous reading patterns:
- So that I can get a picture of your reading interests, can you tell me about a book/author that you've read and really enjoyed?
- What did you enjoy about that book (author/type of book)?
- What do you *not* like and wouldn't want to read?

- What elements do you usually look for in a novel (nonfiction book/biography/travel book)

To determine current reading preferences:
- What are you in the mood for today?

- What have you looked at so far? [to a person who has been looking unsuccessfully for reading material]

- What did you *not* like about these books that you looked at?

- If we could find the perfect book for you today, what would it be like? (What would it be about? What would you like best about it? What elements would it include?)

An effective RA interviewer uses the same communication skills required in the reference interview:
- open questions ("What did you especially like about that particular book?")

- encouragers ("Um-hm, that's interesting. Anything else?")

- reflection of content ("You prefer female detectives but you don't want anything too grisly or violent.")

- summarization ("So it sounds as if you're in the mood for some new mystery authors, especially if they write in a series. Did I get it right?")

- follow-up ("If none of these suggestions pan out, make sure you come back and we can try some other authors.")

When the readers' advisor confirms his or her understanding with a summary such as, "So it sounds like you're in the mood for X," this gives the reader a chance to confirm, correct, or add new information such as, "I like big, fat books," or "I don't read mystery stories by boy authors," or "Did I mention that I really prefer British authors?"

To the reader, this interaction may seem like an ordinary, enjoyable conversation about books. What makes it an interview, however, is that this conversation is directed by an overall purpose—discovering the nature of the reader's engagement with books. The features that the reader chooses to talk about provide important clues to reading tastes and preferences.[8] Open questions such as "What did you enjoy about book X or author Y?" encourage readers to describe the desired reading experience in their own terms. In contrast, closed questions such as "Do you enjoy splatterpunk?" can lead to a response like "What's splatterpunk?", followed by an attempt at a definition and a conclusion like, "Well, if that's what splatterpunk is, then I wouldn't be interested." When readers' advisors listen closely to the words readers use to describe enjoyable books, they are better able to identify which genres would likely suit those readers. Readers who are well-informed about literary terms will often use genre labels themselves to describe their preferences. But even here it's a good idea for the readers' advisor to check out his or her understanding of what the reader means by asking something like, "You've mentioned that you enjoy historical books/fantasy/war stories. Is there a particular book that you've especially enjoyed?"

In *Readers' Advisory Service in the Public Library*, Saricks and Brown refer to features of enjoyable books as "appeal factors," which they identify as pacing, characterization, story line, and frame, or the particular atmosphere or tone that the author constructs.[9]

They urge readers' advisors to pay close attention to clues that reveal which of these appeal factors a particular reader is looking for. For example, does the reader talk about fast-paced action or leisurely description? Does the reader emphasize a single strong character or the complex interweaving of many characters, perhaps through several generations? Does the reader talk about the setting of the book as important, and if so, what settings in time and place does she mention? Does the reader refer to a recently enjoyed book as soothing and comforting, or as challenging and quirky? Are there types of books the reader dislikes and *won't* read? As already noted, readers frequently rule out whole categories of books—no horror or anything too scary, no romances, nothing set on other planets, nothing depressing, not too much description. The ability to listen and distill the essence of what users say about their preferred reading experience is a critical skill that requires practice.

In order to pick up on these clues and interpret them correctly, the readers' advisor needs to know about the various popular genres and subgenres of fiction, the differences among them, and the various satisfactions that each genre offers to readers. Although the reader may not know terms for, say, ten subcategories of romance, he or she may provide clues to his or her genre preferences by saying, "I want something that's a little spicy but I don't like bedhopping," or "I really enjoy Georgette Heyer but I've read all her books," or "I can't remember the name of that book I really liked but it had a high heel on the cover," or "I want a love story that emphasizes Christian values." The readers' advisor can then do the translation work and map the reader's preferences onto the particular genre most likely to provide the appeal factors the reader wants. Seldom is there a single right answer in readers' advisory work—many books could suit the reader. But there are many wrong answers —books that would *not* be appropriate for a particular reader. Matching on a single feature rather than on the overall "feel" of the book can be problematic. Mary K. Chelton points to "the all-time mistake in this regard."[10] A user asked for a read-alike for Alice Sebold's *The Lovely Bones,* and was offered a book on serial killers. The readers' advisor's job is to help narrow choices to a manageable number of suggestions that match the reader's stated interests and tastes. Unlike those earlier readers' advisors, whom Melanie Kimball describes in chapter 2 of this volume as intent on pushing the reader up the reading ladder from light fiction to "serious" works, today's effective readers' advisor is nonjudgmental, values all kinds of reading, and takes the view that the reader, not the librarian, knows best what kind of reading experience is desired.

Notes

1. Catherine Sheldrick Ross, "Making Choices: What Readers Say About Choosing Books to Read for Pleasure," *The Acquisitions Librarian* 25 (2001): 13.

2. Catherine Sheldrick Ross, Kirsti Nilsen, and Patricia Dewdney, *Conducting the Reference Interview* (New York: Neal-Schuman, 2002), 72–73.

3. Ross, "Making Choices," 14.

4. Book Marketing Limited, *Reading the Situation: Book Reading, Buying and Borrowing Habits in Britain* (London: Library and Information Commission, 2000), 145.

5. Ibid.

6. Joyce G. Saricks and Nancy Brown, *Readers' Advisory Service in the Public Library,* 2d ed. (Chicago: American Library Association, 1997), 70.

7. Ross, Nilsen, and Dewdney, *Conducting the Reference Interview.*

8. Duncan Smith, "Talking with Readers: A Competency Based Approach to Readers Advisory Service," *Reference & User Services Quarterly* 40, no. 2 (winter 2000): 135–42.

9. Saricks and Brown, *Readers' Advisory,* 35–55.

10. Mary K. Chelton, "Readers' Advisory 101," *Library Journal* 128, no. 18 (2003): 38–39.

Bibliography

Book Marketing Limited. *Reading the Situation: Book Reading, Buying and Borrowing Habits in Britain.* London: Library and Information Commission, 2000.

Chelton, Mary K. "Readers' Advisory 101." *Library Journal* 128, no. 18 (2003): 38–39.

Ross, Catherine Sheldrick. "Making Choices: What Readers Say About Choosing Books to Read for Pleasure." *The Acquisitions Librarian* 25 (2001): 5–21.

Ross, Catherine Sheldrick, and Mary Kay Chelton. "Reader's Advisory: Matching Mood and Material." *Library Journal* 126, no. 2 (February 1, 2001): 52–55.

Ross, Catherine Sheldrick, Kirsti Nilsen, and Patricia Dewdney. *Conducting the Reference Interview.* New York: Neal-Schuman, 2002.

Saricks, Joyce G., and Nancy Brown. *Readers' Advisory Service in the Public Library.* 2d ed. Chicago: American Library Association, 1997.

Smith, Duncan. "Talking with Readers: A Competency Based Approach to Readers Advisory Service." *Reference & User Services Quarterly* 40, no. 2 (winter 2000): 135–42.

Chapter 4

Serving Today's Reader

Diana Tixier Herald

The American Heritage® Dictionary defines genre as "a category of artistic composition, as in music or literature, marked by a distinctive style, form, or content."[1] Wikipedia, a resource that represents popular consensus, defines genre fiction as "a term for writings by multiple authors that are very similar in theme and style, especially where these similarities are deliberately pursued by authors."[2] The term *genre fiction* is commonly used to discuss works of fiction that fall into the areas of mystery, suspense, thriller, adventure, romance, Western, science fiction, fantasy, and horror.

Books usually described as genre fiction are books that share multiple characteristics and features, allowing them to be categorized as belonging to a specific genre. Those features may include a common setting, for example, the Old West, a distant planet in the future, a historical period on our planet, or a place where magic happens. Stories that share these settings can be classified respectively as Westerns, science fiction, historical fiction, and fantasy. In other cases it is the type of plot premise that stories have in common, for example, boy meets girl, boy loses girl, boy and girl come back together and live happily ever after. Romance fiction generally follows this premise. Crime fiction uses a different type of premise. A person dies under suspicious circumstances, and a detective follows clues until the mystery is solved. We call this story a mystery or detective story. Other genres may not be as formalized as these traditional genres, but nonetheless, the titles within those genres share characteristics that are important to readers. For example, women's fiction generally features a female protagonist, grappling with career or relationship problems within a supportive group of female friends.

Literary, mainstream, or general fiction—all terms used to define what is considered unclassifiable or "nongenre" fiction—can also be considered a genre. However, mainstream fiction is outside the scope of this guide. Nancy Pearl's guides, *Now Read This* (Libraries Unlimited, 1999) and *Now Read This II* (Libraries Unlimited, 2002) are excellent guides to that genre.

It can be said that genre fiction, which tends to be the most popular form of fiction, is the Rodney Dangerfield of literature. These books "get no respect." The definition of genre fiction in Wikipedia cited previously continues:

> *Often as applied to written work the term 'genre' is used pejoratively, suggesting not just similar writings but derivative and generally bad writing . . . the term also suggests writing aimed at a particular audience of readers who are construed as having limited taste. It sometimes connotes a sort of literary 'ghetto' to be contrasted with literature proper.*[3]

One need only check the classics lists in each chapter in part II of this guide to see the fallacy in this thinking. Some of the greatest and most esteemed authors wrote what can be considered "genre fiction"—Jane Austen, Edgar Allan Poe, Stephen Crane, Nathaniel Hawthorne, Alexandre Dumas, Charles Dickens, and the list goes on. In the meantime, while critics, scholars, and even some librarians may strive to "elevate" the tastes of the reading public, readers continue to read what they like.

The roots of genre fiction are in the distant past, when storytellers and bards held audiences enraptured by their tales and ballads of wondrous adventure, larger-than-life heroes and heroines, and magical beasts. In the late nineteenth and early twentieth centuries, publishers and readers began defining genres through works of such authors as Jules Verne, H. G. Wells, and Edgar Allan Poe. Mass marketing of cheap publications in the form of dime novels and periodicals provided fertile ground for many of today's genres to develop. However, genre fiction is also very much tied into contemporary popular culture; with trends and developments in fiction both reflecting and directing current events. Although the literary quality may vary, the thrill of a strong plot, interesting dialogue, and a satisfactory conclusion lead many individuals to read for pleasure.

The Nature of Genre Fiction

Genre fiction is constantly evolving, but its essence remains the same—a tale of heroism in which the characters surmount obstacles to triumph. The scale of the heroism can be as large as a galaxy or as small and intimate as a pair of struggling lovers, but in genre fiction a character is or characters are faced with an obstacle that is overcome through some strength of character, intelligence, or physical attribute. Genre fiction is plot-driven but can also have masterful characterization and graceful prose. Good genre fiction can be and often is characterized as "good storytelling."

Authors of genre fiction tend to be prolific, and often they feature characters who play a continuing role in their works. Characters are so important that often books are referred to by their names rather than by the name of the author or the book's title. Some characters are so popular that biographies have been written about them. This is particularly true in the crime genre, specifically the mystery/detection subgenre, where long-standing series feature favorite detectives solving crime after crime.

Today genre fiction, often criticized for being formulaic and predictable, stretches boundaries while trying to maintain its original appeal. Romance tales include mysteries and murders that take place in futuristic societies. Faerie folk pop up in Westerns, while tales of horror and the occult go for the laughs by incorporating humorous elements. Genreblending has become of such major importance that publishers have created imprints devoted to blends. Tor, voted the best science fiction/fantasy publisher in the prestigious Locus Poll for seventeen years running, added an imprint called Tor Romance that features blends of science fiction and fantasy with romance. Romance giant Harlequin added the Luna imprint to feature romantic stories by major fantasy authors.

Although genreblending can be confounding to the readers' advisor, genre categories continue to be extremely useful in helping readers find the books they will enjoy. Second only to a search by author, readers search for titles by genre. Categorizing fiction by types will never be a science, let alone an exact one. To a large extent, assigning genres is subjective—it is an art. Yet publishers continue to publish genre fiction, and readers continue to read and seek out genre fiction. This is why bookstores arrange much of their stock according to genres. It is also why publishers use genre labels on books and in catalogs. The overwhelming number of books published each year becomes more manageable through genre classification. Whether or not readers are aware of the intricacies, nuances, and language of subgenres, these generally represent titles grouped according to reading tastes. To best serve their patrons, it is essential that librarians, and particularly readers' advisors, familiarize themselves with popular reading interests and genre fiction. With genreblending blurring the lines, that imperative becomes even stronger.

Who Is the Common Reader?

As Wayne Wiegand makes clear in chapter 1, books and common readers are at the heart of the library. But who are the common readers, and what exactly do they want?

Simply put, common readers are people who read. Common readers borrow from the library, or buy, or trade books. They may read e-books or listen to books in various audio formats. They may search for titles via the library's Web site, or they may browse the stacks, or they may order books through Amazon.com. However they access books, common readers read because they enjoy reading, entering another world with more excitement than the mundane, everyday world. These people know the difference between reality and fantasy but choose to enjoy the age-old tradition of storytelling. Common readers can be of any age, any sex, and any intellectual level, and they work in all types of jobs, professions, and careers. They fall into all economic levels of society. Common readers are our public and our customers.

Libraries and Genre Fiction

Earlier editions of *Genreflecting* discussed the controversy over maintaining collections of genre fiction in libraries. Betty Rosenberg cited many articles criticizing popular reading as well as many promoting the library as a community resource for popular fiction. (In chapter 2 Melanie A. Kimball offers an overview of the history of readers' advisory in the public library.) Even now, more than twenty years after publication of the first edition of *Genreflecting*, in which Betty Rosenberg introduced her first law of reading—"never apologize for your reading tastes"—to the public, the controversy continues. The forum may have moved from library periodicals onto the Internet, but a lively exchange still ensued when a librarian asked a newsgroup for opinions regarding the purchase of a "not so good book" because a library user had made requests that it be purchased. Oh, the flames as accusations of censorship and wrong thinking were exchanged! In truth, while the American Library Association has recognized the value of a library's role as "popular reading center," some librarians continue to sniff disdainfully at genre fiction. Fortunately for the millions of library users, more librarians see their community's need for popular reading materials. Although popular fiction collections are not funded in a ratio equivalent to their usage, libraries in the 1990s made efforts to improve access to popular fiction, and that effort continues today.

Several library schools have added readers' advisory classes. Many libraries throughout the United States have staff training and in-service days devoted to learning more about genre fiction and how to help library patrons with their popular reading needs. Librarians extend and share their learning on fiction_L, the readers' advisory listserv hosted by Morton Grove Library.

To further help patrons find genre fiction, easily identifiable genre fiction can be shelved separately in libraries. In many collections, Westerns, mysteries, and science fiction have their own sections or shelves in libraries. Some consider this unfair segregation, but most readers (who know what they like and appreciate easy access) like the chance to browse a manageable segment of the collection and find a number of books from their favorite genre all in one place. In large collections, separate shelving provides access to genre titles and also helps readers navigate the collection. Sharon L. Baker and Karen L. Wallace, who wrote about information overload and fiction classification, suggest that physically separating genre books from the general collection helps users of large collections select books without becoming overwhelmed.[4] In addition to giving browsers a smaller and less intimidating set of books to choose from, it allows them to select from particular genres of interest. Spine labeling by genre is another widely used method to help readers in their quest for books they want to read.

Shelving books by genre does create problems, especially in this era of genreblending. Should a science fiction romance be shelved with science fiction or with romance? Challenges in classification and organization, however, have yet to deter any self-respecting readers' advisory librarian from trying to organize the fiction collection in a manner that helps readers find the books they want. And there's no reason that particular titles might not move from one genre section to another, if they share qualities with more than one genre.

Another improvement is access to genre fiction through the catalog. The GASFD classifications give users points of access for fiction other than merely title and author. Unfortunately, many libraries fail to catalog paperback fiction, which leaves huge segments of the collection read by common readers inaccessible except by serendipity. This presents problems, especially when an author's first several titles are paperback originals followed by hardcover releases. The reader wants early books in the series, but even when the library owns the paperbacks, they can't always be easily found, and there is no way of placing a hold or reserve on them through the public access catalog.

Readers' Advisory Service

Putting people together with the books they want to read is the purpose of a readers' advisory service. Catherine Ross's chapter in this guide (chapter 3) provides valuable instruction and advice on the transaction. Knowing the literature, knowing the reader, and facilitating the meeting of the two are key to being an effective readers' advisor. Knowing the tools—whether online databases such as NoveList and What Do I Read Next? or print tools such as the one in hand—is also essential to effective readers' advisory service.

More than twenty years ago, John Naisbitt, in his best-selling book *Megatrends*, wrote about the importance of becoming "high touch" in a "high tech" world.[5] As libraries become more and more high-tech, readers' advisory is one of the best ways for librarians to maintain a personal relationship with patrons. Readers' advisory may well be the library service that keeps libraries vital in this century as current library users become more sophisticated at using the electronic resources that are moving out of libraries and into homes via personal computers.

A well-armed readers' advisor keeps an arsenal of resources at hand, including bibliographies and booklists in the form of bookmarks or pamphlets that many libraries provide. Bookmarking Web sites, actively participating on listservs, and reading reviews online and in print all build the readers' advisor's knowledge base.

Keeping a reading journal can be extremely helpful. Some librarians prefer to keep the list on index cards in a file, others use a database, and some keep a chronological list in their day planners. A short annotation and an indication of genre and type make the list extremely useful for readers' advisory service and also sharpen the librarian's writing skills. Many libraries maintain Web sites or even notebooks in which staff reviews or annotations are on file, which gives greater access to the information. Even if one does not have the time to write annotations, however, it is very helpful to maintain at least an author/title listing of books read.

Reading plans, scorned by some, are simply ways of mapping out in advance a plan to sample various genres. Several years ago in libraries with a dedication to readers' advisory services (and the staff to support it), novice readers' advisors were assigned a variety of novels to read to become conversant in the different genres. An example of such a reading plan might be to read one book from each genre, then go back through the genres again, this time reading a book by a different author in each genre. Some reading plans were very specific; for example, to read a novel by Dorothy Sayers, followed by a novel by Zane Grey, then one by Isaac Asimov, and finally one by Grace Livingston Hill. A second pass in such a specific plan might call for novels by Raymond Chandler, Max Brand, Robert Silverberg, and Danielle Steel. This ensured that the readers' advisors became familiar with a diversity of authors within each genre. For an advisor who does not read romance, it can be quite eye-opening to read a Bertrice Small novel and an Avalon romance to see the diversity within the genre.

The Readers' Advisor's Companion (Libraries Unlimited, 2002), edited by Kenneth D. Shearer and Robert Burgin, contains a number of enlightening essays written by some of the stars of readers' advisory. The more recent *Nonfiction Readers' Advisory*, edited by Robert Burgin (Libraries Unlimited, 2004), explores how readers' advisory techniques can and should be applied to nonfiction. Titles in the <u>Genreflecting Advisory Series</u> cover in depth specific genres and reading interests that range from adventure and mystery to romance, Christian fiction, and African American literature. For a full list of these titles, visit www.genreflecting.com.

Joyce G. Saricks has written two excellent guides for readers' advisors. *Readers' Advisory Service in the Public Library*, 3d ed. (ALA Editions, 2005) details ways to determine the appeal of a book, so that similar books can be found. It is a must read for anyone striving to perform readers' advisory service with any degree of excellence. In *The Readers' Advisory Guide to Genre Fiction* (ALA Editions, 2001), Saricks tackles genre fiction and popular reading interests.

In her brief chapter "Advising the Reader" in *Romance Fiction: A Guide to the Genre* (Libraries Unlimited, 1999), Kristin Ramsdell shares some effective guidelines for advising readers. She notes that not all readers in need of assistance will ask for it, and libraries should institute passive readers' advisory. Passive readers' advisory includes shelving genre fiction separately, providing booklists and displays, and labeling spines. All these things, though not a substitute for an interview with a good readers' advisor, help readers to find books in the genres they like.

It is virtually impossible to list all the readers' advisory pages now available on the World Wide Web. Many are published by libraries and include book reviews, lists, and links to helpful fiction-related sites. One of the most comprehensive and long-established sites is Overbooked (http://www.overbooked.org/, accessed June 8, 2005), a nonprofit volunteer project by Ann Chambers Theis, collection management administrator of the Chesterfield County (Virginia) Public Library's Collection Management department. The Mid-Continent Public Library Readers' Advisory page (http://www.mcpl.lib.mo.us/readers/, accessed June 8, 2005) is an example of a nicely done library-managed site that provides several helpful lists for its patrons.

Ultimately, the most important skills for readers' advisors are communication skills—and in particular, listening skills. Whether talking face to face, over the phone, or via e-mail, simply asking patrons about a book they enjoyed in the past reveals more about what they might enjoy in the future than all the reference books and reading lists put together.

Publishing Genre Fiction

Genre fiction is popular fiction that publishers continue to publish because it sells. Most of the titles on the weekly best-seller lists (hardcover and paperback) are genre titles. Looking at the *Publishers Weekly* hardcover list in June 2005, there were only two titles in the top fifteen best sellers that were mainstream fiction. They break down as seven crime novels (six featuring series characters), two adventure novels (one cipher thriller and one biothriller), two mainstream novels, and one each in romance, science fiction, historical, and horror. The fourteen fiction titles on the *Publishers Weekly* paperback best-seller list break down as six crime novels, three romance novels, two adventure novels, and one each in science fiction, horror, and women's fiction.

Prolific and popular authors appear regularly—anything they publish, regardless of its quality, will sell. The *Publishers Weekly* number one best seller in both 2003 and 2004 was *The Da Vinci Code* by Dan Brown, a cipher thriller. John Grisham held the number three spot in 2004, a minor change from five years ago when his legal thrillers had garnered the number one spot for four years running.

Genre fiction is published in all formats: hardcover, paperback, audiotape, compact disc, and other digital formats. The publishing industry has seen radical changes in the last couple of years. Giant publishing houses have merged, forming even larger houses. Bantam Doubleday Dell is now part of Random, Inc. Penguin and Putnam have become Penguin Putnam.

As the giants battle it out for supremacy on the best-seller lists by giving staggeringly huge contracts to the top-grossing writers, they seem to be publishing less and less midlist fiction, which, of course, is necessary for the voracious appetites of readers.

At the same time, new technology gives small publishers and self-published authors opportunities never before seen. It is now possible for small publishing houses to make a go of it. Even self-published titles are garnering critical approval. These small presses are becoming a good resource for finding new authors.

Reprint editions and e-books are of particular importance in genre fiction because so many titles go out of print so quickly. Readers often discover a "new" author, often of a series, and find that reprint editions are the only source for finding earlier titles. The large-print publishers have long been a great source for genre fiction reprints in both hardcover and trade paperback. Severn House publishes hardcover reprints of several genres; many are titles that are being published in the United States for the first time. Five Star publishes both reprints and originals in several genres. Online sellers, such as Amazon.com, offer readers more opportunities to purchase used and out-of-print titles.

Gender and Genre Fiction

Women have always written and been featured in genre fiction, but the 1980s saw a tremendous surge in the popularity of the woman's role. By the end of the decade, thrillers featuring women as private investigators or amateur investigators were appearing weekly. Who by now has not heard of V. I. Warshawski or Kinsey Millhone? The 1990s saw an explosion of secondary materials dealing with women in crime fiction, such as the titles *Detecting Women* and *By a Woman's Hand*. Women also gained recognition in science fiction and fantasy and no longer had to resort to male pseudonyms or only their initials. Many readers discovered for the first time that James Tiptree Jr., Andre Norton, Julian May, and C. J. Cherryh were all women. It became more acceptable in those genres for authors to have first names like Margaret, Sherri, or Pamela. Women's fiction has gained prominence as a genre, and "Chick Lit" has become a force in the publishing. These developments are covered in chapter 14.

In the meantime, men are now writing romance fiction. Nicholas Sparks, who is often on the best-seller lists, writes sentimental tales of love. Books about women sleuths written by women writers have become so popular that some male writers have taken to using initials. Joe Konrath, who writes the Jacqueline "Jack" Daniels mysteries as J. A. Konrath, says on his Web site: "I'd like to be judged on the merits of the story, rather than on my Y chromosome."[6]

In the new millennium, genre fiction continues to grow and evolve, which makes it more difficult to define, but also builds excitement in the reading public. In this milieu, the role of the readers' advisor has expanded and become more complex. The core of our role, however, remains the same: As readers' advisors it is important to read and enjoy, and to share information.

Purpose and Scope of This Guide

The primary purpose of this guide is to put books and readers together by helping readers' advisors in libraries, bookstores, and academic institutions find the books their readers will enjoy reading. By offering a structured and detailed overview of genres, it will hopefully help users understand genres and subgenres, and therefore it can also be used as a textbook for courses in genre literature and readers' advisory to discuss popular genres of fiction.

Organization

This edition of *Genreflecting* contains some exciting new features. A chapter contributed by editor Wayne A. Wiegand addresses the social nature of reading, which is vital to our libraries today. Catherine Ross's chapter, "The Readers' Advisory Interview," offers sage advice for practitioners and students on the RA transaction. A brief history of readers' advisory written by Melanie A. Kimball is featured in chapter 2.

Other chapters cover specific genres—historical, Western, crime, adventure, romance, science fiction, fantasy, horror, and, new to this edition, Christian fiction. A final chapter on "emerging genres" covers women's fiction and "chick lit." Introducing each chapter, essays written by notable subject specialists offer overviews of the genres—their characteristics and appeal, their origins and evolution, and current trends. These are followed by descriptions of subgenres and themes and a list of genre classics.

Author names are listed alphabetically. Multiple books by the same author are listed alphabetically below the author's name. In series main entries, titles are listed in alphabetical order unless the books follow a series order. Generally, prequels are listed first and sequels are listed last (unless, of course, the sequel spawns another sequel). Sometimes an author has a recommended order of reading the series that follows neither the interior chronology nor the dates of publication. Even though many series and linked novels are published in order, some are not, so publication dates do not always indicate the best order in which the individual titles should be read. A few authors create related series, and those are listed in an order consistent with the chronology of the books. When both individual books and series are listed below an author's name, the individual books are listed first, in alphabetical order, followed by the series entries.

Bibliographies of popular and current titles and authors are organized by subgenre and theme, according to common reading interests. A topics section at the end of each chapter provides information on resources for more in-depth information on specific facets of the genre. The information varies by chapter depending on the specific character of the genre. Generally bibliographies, critical works, and organizations pertaining to the genre are included, but each chapter, like each genre, has unique characteristics. And finally, each chapter concludes with a section called "D's Picks," a sampling of the genre and personal recommendations by the author.

Scope

Most of the authors represented in this guide are prolific. It is not uncommon for genre authors to write dozens or even hundreds of books. Some authors are actually house names used by publishers or book packagers to put all titles in a series or sequence under one author, while in other instances the author has actually written all those books. An amazing recent trend has been for authors to continue publishing for years after death. An example is V. C. Andrews, who is still wildly prolific, publishing two books in 2004, long after her death. Of course, another author is writing the books published under her name. Lawrence Sanders's <u>McNally series</u> is also posthumous. Some authors are included who have written only a few novels that have made a tremendous impact on their specific genre or who are relatively new and popular or show marked promise.

Title listings are not intended to be all-inclusive but rather exemplary of a writer's work currently in print or widely available in public library collections.

Because the intent of *Genreflecting* is to identify titles enjoyed by today's readers, rather than to provide comprehensive lists of genre fiction published within a certain time frame, titles included are not limited to a specific time range; instead, the focus is on works that are widely available in libraries. Most of the titles were published or reprinted in the last decade. This edition of *Genreflecting* features thousands of new authors and titles published since the last edition was released.

Entries and Annotations

Ideally every title in this guide would be annotated, but that would make the book too large and cumbersome for readers and their advisors to take to the shelves or stacks in search of the next good read. Thus, selected titles are annotated, to illustrate the subgenre or type. Most entries list the author and titles that fit into the subgenre under which they are listed. In order to provide as much coverage as possible but still be concise, some entries (particularly in crime, where many of the entries list the author and the detective) list only the author when that author writes primarily within a specific subgenre.

Symbols are used to indicate the following:

The book/series has received one or more awards, listed in the entry.

🎗 The book is widely known and respected by readers of the genre.

🎬 A movie has been made based on the book.

📖 The book is of interest to those who find language and structure of writing primary appeal factors. This type is frequently used for discussion groups.

TVM A television miniseries has been made based on the book/series.

TVS A television series has been made based on the book/series.

YA Written for young adults but with appeal for adult readers

Suggestions for Use

There are many different ways to access and use the information in *Genreflecting*. Readers' advisors and reference librarians are advised to read through the text and familiarize themselves with the genres and subgenres, as well as with authors and titles within each genre. They can also use the book to fill patron requests for fiction read-alikes. Some readers may even enjoy using this book on their own. Collection development specialists might wish to use the lists as a guide for filling in gaps in the collection or to determine which books might be worth replacing. Librarians have also used previous editions of *Genreflecting* to select titles for displays or for separating genre collections from large general fiction collections.

To find specific authors and titles, refer to that index. When looking for books similar to a known author or title, check the other listings in the specific subgenre section identified by using the author/title index to find where the known author is listed. The table of contents and the subject index can be used to find information on the genres and subgenres. Scholarly materials and reference sources can be found at the end of each essay and by consulting the topics section of each chapter.

Notes

1. *Dictionary of the English Language, Third Edition* (Houghton Mifflin, 1996).

2. http://en.wikipedia.org/wiki/Genre_fiction (accessed June 1, 2005).

3. Ibid.

4. *The Responsive Public Library Collection*, 2d ed. (Libraries Unlimited, 2002).

5. *Megatrends* (Warner Books, 1982).

6. http://www.jakonrath.com/history.html (accessed June 8, 2005).

Bibliography

The American Heritage® Dictionary of the English Language, Third Edition. Houghton Mifflin, 1996.

Baker, Sharon L., and Karen L. Wallace. *The Responsive Public Library Collection*, 2nd ed. Libraries Unlimited, 2002.

Burgin, Robert, ed. *Nonfiction Readers' Advisory.* Libraries Unlimited, 2004.

Heising, Willetta L. *Detecting Women: A Reader's Guide and Checklist for Mystery Series Written by Women.* Purple Moon Press, 1994.

Konrath, J. A., Available at http://www.jakonrath.com/history.html. Accessed June 8, 2005.

Mid-Continent Public Library Readers' Advisory page. Available at http://www.mcpl.lib.mo.us/readers/. Accessed June 8, 2005.

Overbooked. Available at http://www.overbooked.org/. Accessed June 8, 2005.

Ramsdell, Kristin. "Advising the Reader." In *Romance Fiction: A Guide to the Genre.* Libraries Unlimited, 1999.

Saricks, Joyce G. *The Readers' Advisory Guide to Genre Fiction.* ALA Editions, 2001.

———. *Readers' Advisory Service in the Public Library.* 3d ed. ALA Editions, 2005.

Shearer, Kenneth D., and Robert Burgin, eds. *The Readers' Advisor's Companion.* Libraries Unlimited, 2002.

Swanson, Jean, and Dean James. *By a Woman's Hand: A Guide to Mystery Fiction by Women.* Berkley Books, 1994.

Wikipedia: The Free Encyclopedia, Available at http://en.wikipedia.org/wiki/ Genre_fiction. Accessed June 1, 2005.

Part II

The Genres

Chapter 5

Historical Fiction

Essay

R. Gordon Kelly

In recent decades, historical fiction has achieved both critical and commercial success. In light of this resurgent interest, we may well ask: Why do people read historical novels? What do they get from their reading? These are questions about behavior and are best answered by reaching out, through well-designed studies, to actual readers. Few such studies exist, however, whether in history, sociology, literary studies, or popular culture. Surveys of adult book reading, beginning in the 1960s, conclude that people read for pleasure and to become better informed. More specific motives include searching for personal meaning, reading to reinforce or celebrate beliefs or values already held, satisfying a desire to keep up with the reading of friends and colleagues, and wishing to escape. To these generalizations about why people read books, we can add inferences drawn from sources that speak directly to the writing and reading of historical fiction: discussions of their craft by historical novelists, for example, or readers' reactions to historical novels found in reviews or on Internet discussion lists. Renewed interest in historical fiction on the part of novelists and historians alike has created a substantial body of commentary on the aims and possibilities of historical fiction in our multicultural and, some would say, postmodern age.

But what, exactly, is "historical fiction?" "Fiction set in the past" is the generic definition—but how far in the past? Sir Walter Scott, widely regarded as the father of the historical novel, suggested two generations in his subtitle to *Waverley: 'Tis Sixty Years Past* (1814). The Historical Novel Society uses a similar measure today. A novel must be written at least fifty years after the events described, or be set in a time before the author's birth; in short, the historical novel is grounded in research, not personal memory of the events depicted.

The Allure of the Past

Many readers come to historical fiction out of a self-conscious desire to immerse themselves in another world, to travel vicariously in time, to imagine themselves in a radically different setting, or to escape present circumstances, however temporarily. Readers may share with the novelist Stephanie Cowell the feeling of having been born into the wrong century.[1] Willa Cather, according to the literary historian James Woodress, retreated into the historical novel as she, and presumably many of her readers, became increasingly alienated from the culture of the 1920s.[2] Thomas Mallon, critically acclaimed for his novel *Henry and Clara* (1994), describes writing historical fiction as a way to find relief from the (prison) house of self.[3] In all likelihood, he speaks for at least some of his readers. Attempting to explain the renewed interest in the reading and writing of historical fiction in Canada in the last twenty years, Margaret Atwood, too, invokes the notion of "time travel," but suggests that novelists, and presumably their readers, are drawn out of curiosity to the hidden, heretofore unspoken, even taboo aspects of Canada's past. Like other commentators on the renewed popularity of historical fiction, she recognizes the tie to multiculturalism, to the search for one's roots, to an interest in individuals and groups forgotten or marginalized by both history and fiction.[4]

Historical fiction, according to Carol Kammen and others, is more accessible than the writing of professional historians generally. It puts the "story" back in "history" and gives it the narrative often absent in professional social history. Historical novels, Kammen suggests, offer an avenue to local understanding.[5] Looking backward, we—novelists and readers alike—are able to "place ourselves," in Atwood's phrase. A second compelling motive to read historical novels has to do, then, with their potential to teach, to provide a deeper knowledge about the past. Readers come to the historical novel out of a general curiosity about the past as well as out of a more specific interest in the past of their own place, out of a desire to understand how the present came to be, how the group with which they identify has fared, to experience themselves within a larger context of time and human drama. Historical fiction can flesh out the bare bones of history and potentially change readers' settled or conventional views, offering, for example, a sympathetic depiction of Santa Ana at the Alamo (Stephen Harrington's *The Gates of the Alamo*, 1999) or of a woman's decision to remain with her Indian captors (Deborah Larsen's *White*, 2002). But reading for pleasure and reading for knowledge—the constitutive appeals of the historical novel—are distinguishable analytically only up to a point; to explore one's roots via historical fiction surely combines pleasure with knowledge. The same can be said, finally, about immersing oneself in past worlds. Pleasure and knowledge are combined and ultimately indistinguishable.

Readers may also be motivated to read historical fiction to reinforce their values and beliefs. The surging popularity and commercial success of Christian fiction generally and Christian historical fiction in particular in the last ten years is a case in point. Readers also come to books, according to Philip Ennis, in search of personal meaning.[6] For some, novelists and readers alike, the appeal of historical fiction includes its insistence on the contingency of events, on the role of chance in human affairs, and the ways in which lives and events could have turned out differently. This rejection of the inevitability of events also finds expression in recent historical writing such as Joseph Ellis's *Founding Brothers* (2000)—a reminder that historians and historical novelists share a desire to understand the past, to describe it accurately, and to explain change.

Characteristics of Historical Fiction

What readers get from their reading of historical fiction is as much an empirical question as what motivates them to read; and what they get from their reading is closely related to their motives and to their expectations. Both motives and expectations are shaped by prior reading experience—in the formal settings of school and library, for example. For children and young people, after all, the answer to the question, "Why are you reading an historical novel?" is simple: it was assigned. Expectations and motives are among the likely, if variable, consequences of reading and discussing young adult historical novels.

Broadly—and unsurprisingly, given what has already been said—historical fiction provides readers with the pleasures of imaginative immersion in past worlds. The experience is variously characterized as one of authenticity, immediacy, or plausibility. One reviewer of Patrick O'Brian's work marvels at O'Brian's ability to summon up "the shape and texture of a whole era."[7] Alan Furst, the pre-eminent practitioner of the historical espionage novel, is repeatedly praised for the "atmosphere" of his novels. Historical fiction can create, in Thomas Mallon's words, a more "subtly textured time than even good 'social history' does."[8] At its most intense, readers describe the effects of reading as approximating experience itself, as in this response to Howard Bahr's Civil War novel *The Black Flower*: "you can virtually feel the characters' pain and smell the smells that surround them."[9] And they profess reluctance at having to leave such worlds. "I wanted it [*Gone with the Wind*] to go on forever," a reader told the authors of *Voices of Readers: How We Come to Love Books*.[10] Sometimes criticized for his long works, James Michener recalled readers who found them too short: " 'I did not want to quit that vibrant universe,' " one wrote.[11] Critics and historians who are skeptical of historical fiction as a form typically characterize the reading of it as escapist. In his magisterial account, *The Popular Book*, James Hart concluded that the popularity of the historical novel in the United States coincides with periods of doubt, conflict, and uncertainty—the 1890s, for example. Margaret Atwood, however, dismisses the suggestion that nostalgia explains the renewed popularity of the form in Canada. The novels she discusses in her Bronfman Lecture, "In Search of *Alias Grace*," fail to "depict the past as a very soothing place"; they offer neither "escape" nor nostalgia.[12]

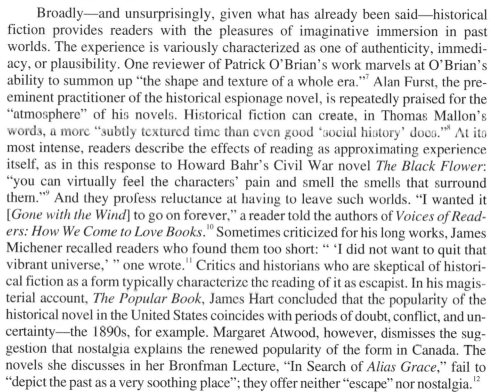

There is nothing controversial in the claim that historical fiction stimulates emotional, even sensory, responses in readers or that these responses are sometimes deeply felt. But can a lie (fiction) be true? Can historical fiction really provide knowledge about the past in addition to delivering pleasure? Many readers and historical novelists make that far more controversial claim. In her seminal study of romance readers, for example, Janice Radway reports "nearly every reader informed me that the novels teach them about far away places and times and instruct them in the customs of other cultures."[13] At least since the 1930s, historical novelists, even those who write the routinely disparaged historical romance—"bodice rippers" in the vernacular—regard extensive research as essential preparation for writing. "Getting things to look right is the historical novelist's paramount task," according to Thomas Mallon, whose archival research for *Henry and Clara* corrected the historical record and unearthed a wealth of neglected material about the couple who shared Lincoln's box on the evening he was shot.[14] In a similar vein, James

Michener urged "ardent research as to facts" and long speculation as to their meaning in preparing to write.[15] More recently, Brian Hall, in a brief afterward to his novel about the Lewis and Clark expedition, *I Should Be Extremely Happy in Your Company*, acknowledges his sources, historiographical and archival, in a conventional bibliographical essay.[16] The result can be absolute fidelity to quotidian detail. In her research for *Alias Grace*, Margaret Atwood found it necessary to recover "now obscure details of daily life" . . . "how to clean a chamber pot . . . the origins of quilt pattern names, and how to store parsnips."[17] Novelists and historians, in the final analysis, are hostage to the same sources—the fragments of the past that exist, for the most part, on paper in the archive. For many readers of historical fiction, the acknowledged contemporary master of quotidian detail is Patrick O'Brian, whose critically acclaimed novels describe the rise of Jack Aubrey through the ranks of the British navy in the late eighteenth and early nineteenth centuries. In addition to a "tremendous" story, one critic writes, the reader sees—and presumably is brought to understand—"the very beginnings of the world we inhabit."[18] No small achievement for an historian, let alone an historical novelist.

Truth and Historical Fiction

Readers of historical novels expect that authors will get the facts right and trust them to do so. For their part, historical novelists, at least since Kenneth Roberts in the 1930s, through James Michener, Marguerite Yourcenar, and Mary Renault, to contemporary writers such as Thomas Mallon, Brian Hall, and Patrick O'Brian, have accepted the obligation entailed by their readers' expectation of factual accuracy and tried to deliver by undertaking the often painstaking, detailed research needed to render, in principle, an authoritative account of past practices, behavior, motives, and so forth. We can say with some confidence, then, that readers can obtain real knowledge of past ways from historical novels.

Nevertheless, there is clearly room for caution and skepticism about this claim. Thomas Mallon, for example, notes that in *Aurora 7* he uses a remark by President John F. Kennedy but attributes it to him a year earlier. The needs of the novelist trumped the scrupulousness of the historian.[19] Mallon's reader can know what Kennedy said but not when he said it. Dee Brown, who won acclaim as an historian for *Bury My Heart at Wounded Knee: An Indian History of the American West* (1971), was several years thereafter the author of an historical novel, *Creek Mary's Blood* (1980), the marketing of which trades on Brown's credentials as an historian. Brown has been accused of seriously distorting the historical record, however, and the favorable reviews of the book strike one historian as pernicious: "[W]ho can appropriately assess the novel? Certainly not a general reading public . . . [or] the high school pop history teachers who already have begun to assign this book as required reading."[20]

A final example. *The Daughter of Time*, Josephine Tey's justly acclaimed historical detective novel, argues that Richard III, Shakespeare's powerful play notwithstanding, was not responsible for the murder of his nephews, whose claim to the throne of England was better than his own. Richard was the victim of Tudor historians with an axe to grind. But Tey ignored documents, available to her at the time, that did not fit her case, and the weight of historical evidence now points to Richard's complicity in the boys' death. Yet Tey's novel remains widely read and persuasive for its apparent reliance on actual historical documents. Historical fiction, we might conclude, conveys accurate information about the past—but only so long as novelistic or ideological imperatives do not subvert the novelist's commitment to hew to the historical record.[21]

What else, besides quotidian detail—"the very shape and texture of a whole era" available in the work of a Patrick O'Brian, for instance—can readers get from historical fiction? Some readers will be drawn to history "itself" as a consequence of reading historical fiction, an outcome encouraged by William Rainbolt, for example, who is both a working historian and the author of *Moses Rose* (1996), an historical novel about a possible survivor of the Alamo.[22] Many, perhaps most young adult historical novels, are written (and assigned in schools) with that outcome in mind. In their *Books That Made a Difference*, Gordon and Patricia Sabine report the early reading that Barbara Tuchman acknowledges as the source of her fascination with history, including Jane Porter's *The Scottish Chiefs* and Doyle's *The White Company*.[23]

C. S. Lewis, the Christian apologist and distinguished English literary historian, famously has suggested that we read to know that we are not alone—not alone, presumably, in the possession of certain beliefs, for example. Historical fiction, according to Thomas Mallon, can encourage in some readers a sense of the contingency of history or a feeling of having been born too late.[24] Stephanie Cowell's powerful sense of belonging elsewhere, of being "possessed by other worlds" must strike some of her readers as a point of shared contact.[25] It is worth noting, finally, that historical fiction overlaps with other genres of popular fiction. Medieval mystery novels, for example, constitute a sizable subgenre. Legions of romance novels, dismissed by their critics as "bodice rippers," conventionally have their settings in seventeenth- and eighteenth-century England. Patrick O'Brian's sea novels and Bernard Cornwell's <u>Sharpe series</u> about an English rifleman in the Napoleonic wars are adventure stories as well as historically authentic fiction. To the appeals of mystery, romance, and adventure, these novels add the hallmark of effective historical fiction—the conviction that one is present in a past world in all of its particularity and quotidian detail.

One of the motives for reading generally, as noted earlier, involves a search for meaning. "The essence of the historical novel," James Michener has written, "is that a writer with current information and attitudes looks back upon events of moment so that he or she can organize such experience and give it meaning." A land does not attain full meaning, he thought, until the artist "externalizes its history and transmutes it into a narrative that sings." Readers of *Centennial* in Nebraska, Wyoming, and Colorado wrote to Michener, saying he had "put into words what they had always felt about their homeland."[26] More broadly, historical fiction can yield an inclusive interpretive framework. In his history of the Chinese secret service, Frederick Wakeman Jr. notes that many recruits came to the service imbued with traditional heroic lore and historical allegories derived from famous historical novels. Similarly, Khachig Tololyan points to the role played by traditional historical narratives in motivating Armenian terrorism.[27] In addition to their close attention to the mundane features of everyday life, historical novels necessarily offer interpretations of historical events and outcomes—that is to say, they are engaged in the larger cultural processes of creating and sustaining meaning on various levels and scales. A man "innocently" agreeing to hold a horse, if that horse is John Wilkes

Booth's, and the novelist is Thomas Mallon, may encourage readers to see themselves as "historical accidents." The reader who takes that inference away from reading *Henry and Clara* gets something more than factually accurate details concerning Lincoln's assassination.

History of Historical Fiction

There is general agreement that the story of the modern historical novel begins with the Waverly novels of Sir Walter Scott. Set in Scotland in the aftermath of the failed Rising of 1745, the novels established the form of the historical novel and demonstrated its potential for commercial success. Scott remained a best-selling author in the United States throughout the nineteenth century. As late as the 1960s, *Ivanhoe* was still a required text in American high schools, as the author can attest from personal experience. In the wake of Scott's American vogue, native authors—notably James Fenimore Cooper—became best-selling historical novelists in their own right. Cooper's *The Spy* (1821), a novel about the American Revolution, launched his career, and in subsequent works his settings included New England during King Philip's War and the Michigan frontier, but he is still best remembered for his five Leatherstocking novels, which took as their subject the frontier, Westward expansion, and the clash of "civilization and savagery." During the 1820s, Cooper was joined by numerous other writers, now largely forgotten, who turned their attention to the nation's New England roots in the aftermath of the War of 1812. Historical novels were one important manifestation of literary nationalism throughout the antebellum period. With the first historical novelists came the first distinguished American historians, George Bancroft and William Hickling Prescott.

From its beginnings in the 1820s, the popularity of historical fiction has ebbed and flowed to the present day—impelled to varying degrees by the questions about national origins and identity that stimulated Cooper and his contemporaries. Another impetus for historical fiction has been regionalism. Southern writers turned to their region's history, beginning in the 1830s with works by William A. Caruthers (*The Cavaliers of Virginia*, 1834, for example), or the prolific William Gilmore Simms (*Guy Rivers*, 1834; *The Yemassee* and *The Partisan,* both 1835, etc.). The emergence of regionalism as a self-conscious literary movement in the 1880s and 1890s encouraged historical fiction about other regions as well: Edward Eggleston's *The Circuit Rider* (1874), set in Indiana, or Harold Frederic's *In the Valley* (1890), set in New York's Mohawk Valley during the French and Indian War.

Popular interest in historical fiction after 1820 drew on other sources than patriotism and regional loyalty, however. Like the travel literature for which there was a large readership in the nineteenth century, historical novels were a "cheap ticket" to exotic lands and times; Cooper's *The Bravo* (1831), set in eighteenth-century Venice, is an early example, and Mary Hartwell Catherwood's *The Romance of Dollard* (1888), set in France's New World colonies, is a later example of popular historical fiction with foreign settings.

The Civil War, like the Revolution and the frontier, gave historical novelists a subject of inexhaustible interest, tapping powerful and persistent regional loyalties as well as questions about national purpose, destiny, and identity. Stephen Crane's *The Red Badge of Courage* (1895) is a canonical work of American literature; it is also an historical novel, and distinguished works about the Civil War continue to be written, for example, Charles Frazier's acclaimed *Cold Mountain* (1998).

In the later nineteenth century, historical fiction enjoyed one of its periods of conspicuous popularity, driven, some have argued, by readers seeking escape from the uncertainty and economic distress of the 1880s and 1890s. Historical fiction could provide temporary respite in difficult times. In addition to economic uncertainty, the late nineteenth century witnessed a crisis of faith as biblical criticism and science, especially Darwinian evolutionism, increasingly challenged traditional religious teachings and the authority of the Bible. Historical novels set in biblical times drew large readerships in the wake of the extraordinary success of *Ben-Hur* (1880), for example, Marie Corelli's *Barrabbus* and Florence Kinglsey's *Titus: A Comrade of the Cross* (both 1894). Enthusiasm for the biblical novel declined after the turn of the century, but it remained a staple of Christian publishing.

In the Depression years of the 1930s, literary criticism, newly professionalized and increasingly housed in the modern university, called on writers to address contemporary problems and attacked writers like Willa Cather who had turned increasingly to historical fiction. Readers, however, flocked to the historical novels of writers like the prolific Kenneth Roberts (e.g. *Rabble in Arms* [1933], *Northwest Passage* [1937]), and made Margaret Mitchell's *Gone With the Wind* (1936) the greatest best seller in American publishing history to that time. The work of Roberts and others reveals an increasing emphasis on historical research and a scrupulous regard for historical detail. Increasingly, historical fiction could be defended as conveying genuine knowledge about the past—in addition to telling a good story.

The centennial of the Civil War and the bicentennial of the nation's birth in the Revolutionary War stimulated the production of historical fiction in the 1960s and throughout the 1970s. John Jakes, for example, achieved enormous popularity with The Kent Family Chronicles, an eight-volume family saga that sold tens of millions of copies and was adapted to television. Distinguished works of historical fiction also found a wide audience at this time, including Gore Vidal's *Lincoln* (1984); William Styron's controversial *The Confessions of Nat Turner* (1967); Jane Gilmore Rushing's *Covenant of Grace* (1982), based on the life of Anne Hutchinson; and Mary Lee Settle's *Blood Tie* (1978), for which she won the National Book Award.

During the last twenty years, historical fiction has received enormous impetus from "multiculturalism," which has focused attention on the marginalized, the neglected, and the historically voiceless. In addition, the legitimacy of historical fiction has been enhanced by the powerful attack mounted from within the historical profession itself on the possibility of objective historical knowledge, on the one hand, and by a newfound interest among philosophers, sociologists, and historians themselves in the techniques of narration—the novelist's stock in trade—on the other. The *Roots* phenomenon and the embrace of narrative as a form of knowledge are international in scope, affecting the writing of historical fiction throughout the Anglo-American world and beyond. At no time in the history of historical fiction has its cognitive potential been greater than at present. Thus it is possible for a novel, Margaret Atwood's *Alias Grace* (1996), to be called "a compelling work of history" and for an historian of the stature of John Demos to undertake a novel, *The Unre-deemed Captive* (1994). Historically distinguished novels published more recently include Brian Hall, *I Should Be Extremely Happy in Your Company* (2003); Bernard Cornwell, *Sharpe's Havoc* (2003); Amy Tan, *The Bonesetter's Daughter* (2001); Tariq Ali, *The Stone Woman* (2001); Louise Erdrich, *The Master Butcher's Singing Club* (2002); Howard Bahr, *The Year of Jubilo* (2000); Patrick O'Brian, *Blue at the Mizzen* (1999); and *Lalita Tademy, Cane River* (2002).

Conclusion

From reading historical novels, readers can and do get sensory and emotional pleasure, reassurance, and a sense of meaning; Historical fiction can stimulate the imagination. None of these outcomes is unique to historical fiction, or even to fiction generally. They are the outcomes of some nonfiction, and, dependably, of Art more broadly. The novel, at its best, is sometimes said to provide us with understanding of the human condition or the human heart. Historical fiction today makes a different and arguably more consequential claim, as we have seen—a claim that ultimately rests on the conviction, or faith, that historical knowledge is attainable at all, whether at the hands of the novelist or the historian. "How do we *know* we know what we think we know?" Margaret Atwood asks.[28] That there is no easy answer to this question has not kept readers from the twin pleasures of historical fiction or writers from the challenge of telling engaging tales about past realities.

Notes

1. *Possessed by the Past,* February 1999, available at http://www.angelfire.com/il/oaparchives/pbtp012899.html (accessed September 4, 2005).

2. "Willa Cather and History," *Arizona Quarterly* 34, no. 3 (1978): 239–54.

3. http://www.picadorusa.com/picador/rgg/henryclaragg.html

4. Margaret Atwood, "In Search of *Alias Grace*: On Writing Canadian Historical Fiction," *American Historical Review* 103, no. 5 (December 1998): 1510.

5. "On Doing Local History," *History News* 58, no. 3 (2003): 3–4.

6. *Adult Book Reading in the United States: A Preliminary Report* (Chicago: National Opinion Research Center, 1965).

7. Richard Snow, *An Author I'd Walk the Plank For,* available at http://www.nytimes.com/books/98/10/18/specials/obrian-plank.html

8. "Writing History/Writing Fiction: A Virtual Conference Session," available at http://www.albany.edu/history/hist_fict/home.htm (accessed August 9, 2004).

9. http://www.militaryhistoryonline.com/bookstore/Bookstore

10. G. Robert Carlson and Anne Sherrill, *Voices of Readers: How We Come to Love Books* (Urbana: NCTE, 1988), 80.

11. Ibid., 48.

12. Atwood, "In Search of *Alias Grace*," 1511.

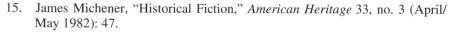

13.   Janice Radway, *Reading the Romance: Women, Patriarchy, and Popular Literature* (Chapel Hill: University of North Carolina Press, 1984), 107.

14.   Thomas Mallon, "Writing Historical Fiction," *American Scholar* 61 (autumn 1992):608.

15.   James Michener, "Historical Fiction," *American Heritage* 33, no. 3 (April/ May 1982): 47.

16.   Brian Hall, "Afterward," in *I Should Be Extremely Happy in Your Company* (New York: Viking, 2003), 413–19.

17.   Atwood, "In Search of *Alias Grace*," 1514.

18.   Snow, *An Author I'd Walk the Plank For.*

19.   Mallon, "Writing Historical Fiction," 605.

20.   Ward Churchill, "The Historical Novel and *Creek Mary's Blood*," *Journal of Ethnic Studies* 12, no. 3 (fall 1984): 119–28.

21.   R. Gordon Kelly, "Josephine Tey and Others: The Case of Richard III," in *The Detective as Historian: History and Art in Historical Crime Fiction*, ed. Ray B. Browne and Laurence A Kreiser Jr., 133–46 (Bowling Green, OH: Bowling Green State University Press, 2000).

22.   "Writing History/Writing Fiction.*"*

23.   Gordon Sabine and Patricia Sabine, *Books That Made a Difference* (Hamden, Conn.: Library Professional Publications, 1983).

24.   Mallon, "Writing Historical Fiction," 610.

25.   Stephanie Cowell, "Possessed by the Past," *Of Ages Past: The Online Magazine of Historical Fiction* 1, no. 2 (February 1999).

26.   Michener, "Historical Fiction," 46.

27.   "Narrative Culture and the Motivation of the Terrorist," in *Texts of Identity*, ed. John Shotter and Kenneth J. Gergen (Palo Alto, Calif.: Sage, 1989).

28.   Atwood, "In Search of *Alias Grace*," 1505.

Bibliography

Atwood, Margaret. "In Search of *Alias Grace*: On Writing Canadian Historical Fiction." *American Historical Review* 103, no. 5 (December 1998): 1503–16.

HistFiction.net—Authors & Books in Historical Fiction (formerly Soon's Historical Fiction Site), http://www.histfiction.net/. (Accessed March 4, 2005).

Kelly, R. Gordon. "Some Readers Reading." In *Mystery Fiction and Modern Life* (Jackson: University Press of Mississippi, 1998); "Historical Fiction." In *Handbook of American Popular Literature*, ed. M. Thomas Inge (Westport, Conn.: Greenwood Press, 1988), 175–96; "Josephine Tey and Others: The Case of Richard III." In *The Detective as Historian: History and Art in Historical Crime Fiction*, ed. Ray B. Browne and Laurence A Kreiser Jr. (Bowling Green, Ohio: Bowling Green State University Press, 2000), 133–46.

Long, Elizabeth. "Women, Reading, and Cultural Authority: Some Implications of the Audience Perspective in Cultural Studies." *American Quarterly* 38 (fall 1986): 591–612.

Mallon, Thomas. "Writing Historical Fiction." *American Scholar* 61 (autumn 1992): 604–10.

Michener, James. "Historical Fiction." *American Heritage* 33, no. 3 (April/May 1982): 44–48.

Peabody, Sue. "Reading and Writing Historical Fiction." *Iowa Journal of Literary Studies* (1989): 29–39; electronically republished at http://www.vancouver.wsu.edu/fac/peabody/histfict.html. Accessed August 9, 2004.

Radway, Janice. *Reading the Romance: Women, Patriarchy, and Popular Literature.* Chapel Hill: The University of North Carolina Press, 1984.

Turner, Joseph W. "The Kinds of Historical Fiction: An Essay in Definition and Methodology." *Genre* 12 (fall 1979): 333–55.

"Writing History/Writing Fiction: A Virtual Conference Session. Available at http://www.albany.edu/history/hist_fict/home.htm. Accessed August 9, 2004.

Themes and Types

Diana Tixier Herald

Historical settings are found in all genres of fiction, from romances, to historical mysteries, to medieval fantasy, to time-travel science fiction. The titles in this chapter may have elements of those other genres, but in these books, the focus is on the historical context. These are what are referred to as "traditional historical novels." Because many readers of historical fiction become enamored of a particular time period or geographic location and search for titles within these parameters, the titles here are organized in chronological and geographical categories. However, when advising readers, it's important to keep in mind that other genre elements come into play as well. There are historical mysteries, historical romances, and historical adventures. For example, a reader who enjoys Margaret Mitchell's romantic *Gone With the Wind*, set during American Civil War times, won't necessarily enjoy Michael Shaara's *The Killer Angels*, a detailed account of the Battle of Gettysburg.

This is a rich and extensive category, and the titles listed are only the tip of the iceberg. Books with U.S. settings are well represented because they seem to be the most commonly published in the United States, followed by books with British settings. For more in-depth coverage consult *Historical Fiction: A Guide to the Genre* by Sarah L. Johnson (Libraries Unlimited, 2005), which combines the geographical and chronological categories with a genre approach that allows readers to find historical fiction in the genres they like such as thrillers, Christian, literary, mystery, and adventure.

Selected Classics

The following authors and titles may be considered classics of historical fiction. Most can be considered literary, and many have received awards. The subgenres are noted in parentheses after the author name or series/book title for those titles listed or annotated elsewhere in the chapter. Additional information, most commonly the geographic area or chronological period, is given at the end of the listing. Additional and more recent classics are listed in the sections that follow.

Aldrich, Bess Streeter.
A Lantern in Her Hand. 1955. Reissued 1994. Nebraska.

Bristow, Gwen.
The Handsome Road. 1938. Civil War.

Cather, Willa. (Western historicals).
Death Comes for the Archbishop. 1927. Reissued 1999. New Mexico.
My Antonia. 1918. Reissued 2005. Nebraska.
O, Pioneers! 1913. Reissued 2004. Nebraska.

Cooper, James Fenimore.

    The Leatherstocking Tales. (colonial America).

        The Pioneers. 1825. Reissued 1991.

        The Last of the Mohicans. 1826. Reissued 2005.

        The Prairie. 1827. Reissued 1987.

        The Pathfinder. 1840. Reissued 1992.

        The Deerslayer. 1841. Reissued 2005.

Crane, Stephen.

    The Red Badge of Courage. 1895. Reissued 2005. A young man in the Civil War.

Dickens, Charles.

    A Tale of Two Cities. 1859. Reissued 2004. French Revolution.

Dumas, Alexandre. (adventure).

    The Count of Monte Cristo. 1845. Reissued 2005. Action and adventure.

    Three Musketeers. 1844–1845. Reissued 2004. Swashbuckling adventure, romance, and even a spy.

Fast, Howard.

    The Immigrants. 1977. Reissued 2000. (family saga). San Francisco—early twentieth century.

    Spartacus. 1951. Reissued 2000. (adventure). Ancient Rome.

Fletcher, Inglis.

    Carolina Chronicles. (saga)

Forester, C. S.

    Hornblower series. Historical sea adventures, listed in the adventure chapter.

Graves, Robert.

    Claudius, the God and His Wife Messalina. 1934. Reissued 1998. (Roman empire).

    I, Claudius. 1934. Reissued 1998. Roman empire.

Hawthorne, Nathaniel.

    The Scarlet Letter. 1850. Reissued 2005. (colonial America).

Heyer, Georgette.

    An Infamous Army. 1937. Reissued in the UK in 2004. (Regency romance/adventure, war). The Battle of Waterloo is central to the story.

    The Spanish Bride. 1940. Reissued 2001. (Regency romance).

Hope, Anthony.

    The Prisoner of Zenda. 1894. Reissued 1999.

Kantor, MacKinlay.

    Andersonville. 1955. Reissued 1993. (American Civil War).]

Kipling, Rudyard.

    Captains Courageous. 1896. Reissued 2005. (sea adventure).

McCullough, Colleen.
> *The Thorn Birds.* 1977. Reissued 1998. Australia. (family saga).

Michener, James.
> *Centennial.* 1974. (epic).

Mitchell, Margaret.
> *Gone With the Wind.* 1939. Reissued 1999. (romance).
>> Classic romantic tale of Scarlett O'Hara, the Civil War, and its aftermath.

Oldenbourg, Zoe.
> *The World Is Not Enough.* 1948. Reissued 1998.
>> The story of a baron and his family in late twelfth-century France.

Orczy, Baroness.
> *The Scarlet Pimpernel.* 1905. Reissued 2005. (adventure and romance). French Revolution.

Renault, Mary.
> *The King Must Die.* 1958. Reissued 1988. (adventure)
>> Greek mythology comes to life in Theseus's Cretan adventure.

> *The Last of the Wine.* 1956. Reissued 2001. Ancient Greece.

Richter, Conrad.
> *Awakening Land.* 1966. Omnibus edition title for the following books:
>> *The Trees.* 1940.
>> *The Fields.* 1946.
>> *The Town.* 1950.

Sabatini, Rafael.
> *Scaramouche: A Romance of the French Revolution.* 1921. Reissued 2005. (adventure, romance).

Scott, Sir Walter.
> *Ivanhoe.* 1820. Reissued 2005. (adventure, military).
>> The battle between the Normans and the Saxons in twelfth-century England.

> *Rob Roy.* 1817. Reissued 2002. (adventure, military). Scottish highlands.
> *Waverley.* 1814. Reissued 1995. (adventure, military).
>> Considered by many to be the first historical novel written.

Seton, Anya.
> *Katherine.* 1962. Reissued 2005. (romance). Mistress, then wife, of John of Gaunt.

Stone, Irving.
> *The President's Lady.* 1951. Reissued 1996. (romance). Rachel and Andrew Jackson.

Styron, William.
>  *The Confessions of Nat Turner.* 1967. Reissued 2002. 1830s slave rebellion in Virginia. Winner of the Pulitzer Prize.

Sutcliff, Rosemary.

Many adult readers of historical fiction were hooked at an early age by the prolific Sutcliff, who wrote dozens of titles for children and young adults. Her series of books about Roman Britain—*The Eagle of the Ninth, The Silver Branch*, and *The Lantern Bearers*—remains popular.

Thane, Elswyth.

<u>Williamsburg series.</u> (family saga). From the American Revolution to World War II.

Thom, James Alexander.

Follow the River. 1983.

The harrowing tale of Mary Ingles's escape from the Shawnee and epic journey home.

Tolstoy, Leo. *War and Peace.* 1889. Reissued 2004. Russian revolution.

Undset, Sigrid.

 Kristin Lavransdatter. 1920–1922. Reissued 2005.

Fourteenth-century Scandinavia, a massive epic in three volumes (*The Bridal Wreath, The Wife*, and *The Cross*). It won the Nobel Prize for Literature in 1928. Different editions have different translators, and the book has been published in one volume and in three separate volumes.

Vidal, Gore.

<u>American Chronicle series.</u>

Burr. 1973. Carefully researched fictional memoir of Aaron Burr.

1876. 1976. Reissued 2000.

Lincoln. 1984.

Empire. 1987. Reissued 2000.

Hollywood. 1990. Reissued 2000.

Washington, D.C. 1967. Reissued 2000.

The Golden Age. 2000.

Prehistoric

The prehistoric epic has become very popular since the 1980 publication of Jean Auel's *Clan of the Cave Bear*, the first in her <u>Earth's Children series</u>. Readers want to know what life was like before our civilization and before there was a written record of how society lived. Often, the stories sweep through history, spanning generations, as well as many pages or even books, in the case of series. The dawn of humanity offers many venues for action-packed adventure and romantic encounters, and it gives room for speculations about what it means to be human, how one might survive in a "primitive" setting, and other philosophical musings.

The settings, often drawn from archaeological and anthropological research, provide a distant and romantic arena for the action. However, even though the settings, costumes, and tools may be scientifically correct, the heroine or hero may exhibit traits and follow social mores belonging more in the late twentieth century than in prehistoric times.

Auel, Jean.

Auel's tremendously successful *Clan of the Cave Bear* and the subsequent series spawned a number of other stories about life in prehistoric times.

Earth's Children series.

Ayla, a Cro-Magnon woman of contemporary sensibilities who was born in the Upper Paleolithic and raised by Neanderthals, domesticates horses and discovers romance.

Clan of the Cave Bear. 1980. Reissued 2002.

The Valley of Horses. 1982. Reissued 2002.

The Mammoth Hunters. 1985.

The Plains of Passage. 1991.

The Shelters of Stone. 2002.

A pregnant Ayla travels with Jondalar and her animal companions to meet Jondalar's people, the people of the Ninth Cave of Zelandonii.

Conley, Robert J.

Conley is a three-time winner of the Spur Award, and is known for writing about Native Americans with insight and authenticity.

Real People series.

The first few books in the series are set in pre-contact America. Other titles in the series are listed in the "Native American" section in the Western chapter.

The Way of the Priests. 1992. Reissued 2000.

The Dark Way. 1993. Reissued 2000.

Cornwell, Bernard.

Stonehenge, 2000 B.C. 2000.

Dann, John R.

"Song Sequence."

Song of the Earth. 2005. Prequel to *Song of the Axe*.

Song of the Axe. 2001. Eurasia, 30,000 B.C.

Gear, W. Michael, and Kathleen O'Neal Gear.

The First North Americans series.

Written by a couple of archaeologists, each title is a stand-alone set at a cusp that decides the future of a culture.

People of the Earth. 1992. Northern Plains, approximately 5000 B.C.

People of the Fire. 1991. Central Rockies and Great Plains, approximately 5000 B.C.

People of the Lakes. 1994. Great Lakes area, approximately A.D. 100.

People of the Lightning. 1995. Florida, approximately thirteenth century.

People of the Masks. 1998. Upstate New York, eleventh century.

People of the Mist. 1997. Approximately fourteenth century, Chesapeake Bay area.

People of the Owl. 2003. Prehistoric Louisiana.

People of the Raven. 2004. Pacific Northwest.

People of the River. 1992. Mississippi Valley, approximately ninth to thirteenth centuries.

People of the Sea. 1993. California, approximately 13,000–10,000 B.C.

People of the Silence. 1996. Twelfth-century Southwest.

People of the Wolf. 1990. Alaska and Northwest Canada, approximately 13,000–10,000 B.C.

People of the Moon. 2005. Eleventh-century Southwest.

Harrison, Sue.

Aleutian trilogy.

Mother Earth, Father Sky. 1990.

Chagak, a young woman who has made an epic journey, comes of age at the end of the last Ice Age, approximately 9,000 years ago.

My Sister the Moon. 1992.

Both of Chagak's sons vie for the love of Kiin.

Brother Wind. 1994.

Kiin and another widow struggle for survival.

Storyteller Trilogy.

Set in the Aleutians in the seventh century B.C., storytellers own stories in times of tribal conflict.

Song of the River. 1997.

Cry of the Wind. 1998.

Call Down the Stars. 2001.

Holland, Cecelia.

Pillar of the Sky. 1985. Reissued 2000.

A tale of the people who built Stonehenge.

Lambert, Joan Dahr.

Circles of Stone. 1997.

The stories of three strong women named Zena in three different prehistoric eras.

Sarabande, William (pseudonym of Joan Lesley Hamilton Cline).

The First Americans.

Series about prehistoric humans crossing a land bridge (called the Bering Strait in modern times) to the Americas.

Beyond the Sea of Ice. 1987.

Corridor of Storms. 1988.

Forbidden Land. 1989.

Walkers of the Wind. 1990.

Sacred Stones. 1991.

Thunder in the Sky. 1992.

Edge of the World. 1993.

Shadow of the Watching Star. 1995.

Face of the Rising Sun. 1996.

Time Beyond Beginning. 1998.

Spirit Moon. 2000.

Shuler, Linda Lay.

> <u>**Time Circle quartet.**</u>
>> Thirteenth-century Southwest North America.
>>
>> *She Who Remembers.* 1988.
>>
>> *Voice of the Eagle.* 1992.
>>
>> *Let the Drum Speak.* 1996.

>> Antelope, one of the Anaszasi's Chosen Ones who can communicate with spirits of her ancestors, travels with her mate, Chomoc, and their baby Skyfeather to the City of the Great Sun.

Ancient Civilizations

Tales set in ancient civilizations provide a sense of lost wonders and settings that seem more exotic than those in eras with well-documented history.

Bradshaw, Gillian.

> *Alchemy of Fire.* 2004. Seventh-century Constantinople.
>
> *The Beacon at Alexandria.* 1986. Resiiued 1994. Fourth century.
>
> *The Bearkeeper's Daughter.* 1987. Byzantine Empire.
>
> *Cleopatra's Heir.* 2002. Ancient Egypt.
>
> *Horses of Heaven.* 1991. Ancient Afghanistan.
>
> *Imperial Purple.* 1988. Byzantine Empire.
>
> *Island of Ghosts.* 1998. A Sarmatian in Roman Britain.
>
> *Render unto Caesar.* 2003. A Greek Alexandrian in Rome.
>
> *The Sand-Reckoner.* 2000. Archimedes.

Diamant, Anita.

> *The Red Tent.* 1997. Biblical.
>> Told from the viewpoint of Jacob's youngest daughter, Dinah.

Durham, David Anthony.

> *Pride of Carthage: A Novel of Hannibal.* 2005.
>> Hannibal's march on Rome, and the second Punic War. A journey tale with gritty, military detail.

Falconer, Colin.

> *Feathered Serpent: A Novel of the Mexican Conquest.* 2002.
>> Cortés's conquest of Mexico focusing on Malinali (La Malinche), the Aztec girl who, sold into slavery upon her father's death, becomes Cortés's interpreter, believing him to be Quetzalcoatl.
>
> *When We Were Gods: A Novel of Cleopatra.* 2000.

Gedge, Pauline.

> *Child of the Morning.* 1977. Reissued 1993. Queen Hatshepsut—ancient Egypt.

George, Margaret.

> *Mary, Called Magdalene.* 2002.
>
> *The Memoirs of Cleopatra: A Novel.* 1997.

Harris, Robert.

Pompeii. 2003.

A young engineer, Marcus Attilius Primus, travels to Pompeii in A.D. 79, only to find that Mount Vesuvius is on the verge of eruption.

Holland, Cecelia.

Valley of the Kings. 1997.

In the 1920s British archaeologist Howard Carter discovers King Tutankhamen's tomb, and then the story moves back 3,500 years in time to the life of the boy king.

Jacq, Christian.

Ramses series.

An epic series about Ramses II, who ruled Egypt for more than sixty years around 1300 B.C.

The Son of Light. 1997.

The Eternal Temple. 1998. Also published as *The Temple of a Million Years.*

The Battle of Kadesh. 1998.

The Lady of Abu Simbel. 1998.

Under the Western Acacia. 1999.

The Stone of Light Series.

Set in a secret village at the end of Ramses's reign.

Nefer the Silent. 2000.

The Wise Woman. 2000.

Paneb the Ardent. 2001.

The Place of Truth. 2001.

Queen of Freedom Trilogy.

Queen Ahotep's story.

The Empire of Darkness: A Novel of Ancient Egypt. 2003.

War of the Crowns. 2004.

The Flaming Sword. 2004.

Jennings, Gary.

Jennings's stories are set in the ancient Aztec civilization of Mexico.

Aztec series.

Aztec. 1980.

Aztec Autumn. 1997.

Aztec Blood. 2001.

McCullough, Colleen.

Masters of Rome series.

The First Man in Rome. 1990.

The Grass Crown. 1993.

Fortune's Favorite. 1995.

Caesar's Women. 1996.

Caesar. 1997.

The October Horse. 2002.

Pressfield, Steven.

Gates of Fire: An Epic Novel of the Battle of Thermopylae. 1998. 480 B.C.
The Virtues of War: A Novel of Alexander the Great. 2004.

Provoost, Anne.

In the Shadow of the Ark. 2004. Translated by John Nieuwenhuizen.
The massive undertaking of the building of Noah's ark.

Smith, Wilbur.

Egyptian Duology. Ancient Egypt.
The River God. 1993.
The Seventh Scroll. 1995.

Middle Ages

Very roughly, the years from A.D. 500 to 1500 may be called the Middle Ages. Readers who enjoy tales of Arthur, Finn MacCool, and Robin Hood may also be interested in titles included in the "Saga, Myth, and Legend" section of the fantasy chapter.

Benson, Ann.

Benson weaves suspenseful tales that feature a historical story paralleling a contemporary one.

Parallel Histories series.

The Plague Tales. 1997.
In fourteenth-century England, a Spanish physician tries to keep the members of the court alive in the face of the plague, while in the twenty-first century a doctor accidentally unleashes the bacillus responsible for the plague on an antibiotic-resistant population.

Burning Road. 1999.

A Spanish physician in fourteenth-century France seeks a cure for the plague in this sequel to *The Plague Tales.*

Thief of Souls. 2002.
In fifteenth-century France, a woman realizes that the disappearances of several boys are connected to Bluebeard, while in twenty-first-century Los Angeles a detective realizes that the disappearances of several boys are the work of a serial killer.

Chevalier, Tracy.

The Lady and the Unicorn. 2004. Fifteenth-century France.
A story of art and love based on the Lady and the Unicorn tapestries that hang today in the Cluny Museum in Paris.

Cornwell, Bernard.

The Last Kingdom. 2005. Ninth-century Vikings.
A Viking warrior, Ragnar the Fearless, battles the kingdoms of England.

<u>Grail Quest.</u> Fourteenth-century England.

Thomas Hookton, an archer who battled in the Hundred Years War, seeks the Holy Grail in an action-packed historical adventure.

The Archer's Tale. 2001.
Vagabond. 2002.
Heretic. 2003.

Dunant, Sarah.

The Birth of Venus. 2003. Fifteenth-century Florence.

Dunnett, Dorothy.

<u>House of Niccolo series.</u>

The adventures of a fifteenth-century merchant prince.

Niccolo Rising. 1986.
The Spring of the Ram. 1988.
Race of Scorpions. 1989.
Scales of Gold. 1994.
The Unicorn Hunt. 1994.
Caprice and Rondo. 1998.
Gemini. 2000.

Eco, Umberto.

The Name of the Rose. 1983. Reissued 1994. ★

Mystery and intrigue set in fourteenth-century Italy. A precursor to the popular cipher thriller.

Follett, Ken.

Pillars of the Earth. 1989. Twelfth-century England. ★

Garwood, Haley Elizabeth.

<u>Warrior Queens series.</u> Each book is a stand-alone title.

Ashes of Britannia. 2000. First-century Britain.
The Forgotten Queen. 1998. Twelfth-century England.
Swords Across the Thames. 1999. Tenth-century England.
Zenobia. 2005. Third-century Palmyra.

Gordon, Noah.

The Last Jew. 2000. Spanish Inquisition.
The Physician. 1986. Eleventh-century. England and Persia.

Holland, Cecelia.

Jerusalem. 1997. The Crusaders in the twelfth-century Holy Land.
The Soul Thief. 2002. Tenth-century Ireland.

Patterson, James, and Andrew Gross.

The Jester. 2003. Twelfth-century France.

Penman, Sharon Kay.

> *Falls the Shadow.* 1988. Simon de Montfort.
>
> *The Reckoning.* 1991. Thirteenth-century Wales.

Peters, Ellis.

> <u>Brother Cadfael mystery series.</u> Twelfth-century Britain.

Seton, Anya.

> *Katherine.* 1954. Reissued 2005. ★
>
> > In England of the fourteenth century, Katherine Swynford and John of Gaunt carried on a long-term love affair.

Vantrease, Brenda Rickman.

> *The Illuminator.* 2005. Fourteenth-century England.

The "Royals"

Kaufman, Pamela.

> *The Book of Eleanor.* 2002. Eleanor of Aquitaine.
>
> > While still in her teens, she married Louis VII of France. After having that marriage annulled, she hoped to wed her beloved Baron Rancon; but instead was kidnapped and forced to marry Henry II of England. Here is the story of a powerful and spirited woman living in twelfth-century Europe.

Penman, Sharon Kay.

> *Here Be Dragons.* 1985. King John of England.
>
> *The Sunne in Splendour.* 1982. King Richard III of England.
>
> <u>Henry II and Eleanor of Aquitaine trilogy.</u> Twelfth-century England.
>
> > So far only two titles in the trilogy have been published.
>
> > *When Christ and His Saints Slept.* 1995.
> >
> > When Henry I died, his daughter (the mother of Henry II) and his nephew battled for the throne.
>
> > *Time and Chance.* 2002.
> >
> > As Henry and Eleanor produce eight children, their lives are filled with conflict.

Exploration, Renaissance

Starting in the fifteenth and sixteenth centuries, varying from place to place, a great change took place in Western civilization as a new focus was put on learning and exploration.

Europe

Chevalier, Tracy.

> *Girl With a Pearl Earring.* 1999. Seventeenth-century Netherlands.
>
> > Sixteen-year-old Griet comes to work as a domestic at the home of Dutch painter Johannes Ver Meer, eventually becoming his assistant and a minor influence on his work.

Cowell, Stephanie.

> *Marrying Mozart.* 2004.
>
>> In eighteenth-century Munich, the young Wolfgang Mozart meets four beautiful and talented sisters—Sophie, Constanze, Josefa, and Aloysia—and becomes forever entangled in their lives.

De Kretser, Michelle.

> *The Rose Grower.* 2000. French Revolution.

Fitzgerald, Penelope.

> *Blue Flower.* 1995. Eighteenth-century Germany. 📖
>
>> The talented Fritz von Hardenberg, who will become one of Germany's greatest Romantic poets, shocks his family when he expresses his wishes to marry a simple twelve-year-old girl, Sophie von Kuhn.

Harrison, Kathryn.

> *Poison.* 1995. Seventeenth-century Spain. 📖

Laker, Rosalind.

> *New World, New Love.* 2002. French Revolution, New Orleans.
>
> *To Dream of Snow.* 2004. Eighteenth-century Russia.

Pérez-Reverte, Arturo.

> *The Fencing Master.* 1989. Reissued 2000. 1860s Spain.

Riley, Judith Merkle.

> *The Serpent Garden.* 1996.
>
>> A touch of the occult in Renaissance France as a widowed painter finds romance while pursued by a diabolical secret society.

Saramago, José.

> *Baltasar and Blimunda.* 1998. Portugal, 1711.

Stone, Irving.

> *The Agony and the Ecstasy.* 1961. Fictionalized biography of Michelangelo. ★

Vreeland, Susan.

> *The Passion of Artemisia.* 2002. Sixteenth-century Italy.

The British Isles

Chevalier, Tracy.

> *Falling Angels.* 2001. Edwardian England.

Cornwell, Bernard.

> **The Richard Sharpe series.**
>
>> Set during the Peninsular War against Napoleon. Titles are listed in the adventure chapter.

Cowell, Stephanie.

> *The Players: A Novel of the Young Shakespeare.* 1997.

Delderfield, R. F.

Swann Family saga. ★

Set in Victorian England over a half–century. Adam Swann returns from service in the Crimea and India to marry, beget a large family, and become successful in business.

God Is an Englishman. 1970. Reissued 1998.
Theirs Was the Kingdom. 1971. Reissued 1999.
Give Us This Day. 1973. Reissued 2001.

Dunnett, Dorothy.

Arguably the most popular writer of historical fiction in the 1990s, Dunnett writes books filled with adventure.

Francis Crawford Lyman series. Sixteenth-century Scotsman. ★

The Game of Kings. 1961.
Queen's Play. 1964.
The Disorderly Knights. 1966.
Pawn in Frankincense. 1969.
The Ringed Castle. 1971.
Checkmate. 1975.

Finney, Patricia.

Gloriana's Torch. 2003. Elizabethan-era spy.

Fowles, John.

The French Lieutenant's Woman. 1969. Reissued 1998. Victorian. 📖 🎬

Pears, Iain.

An Instance of the Fingerpost. 1998. Seventeenth-century murder mystery set in England.

The "Royals"

Biography of royal personages has long been a popular type of publication. Readers find glamour and romance in the lives of royalty—and in these stories they can vicariously experience the life of the privileged and aristocratic elite. Romantic and political intrigues are common. Many historical novels, viewing history from the perspective of various rulers, have been portraits partly based in fact.

Gregory, Philippa.

Tudor series.

The Other Boleyn Girl. 2001.
Love and intrigue in the court of Henry VIII featuring Anne's elder sister, who had an affair with Henry.

The Queen's Fool. 2004.
A young Jewish girl, Hannah, tells the story behind the clash between Queen Mary and Queen Elizabeth.

The Virgin's Lover. 2004.

The passionate and tumultuous early years of the reign of Queen Elizabeth I.

Maxwell, Robin.

Queen Elizabeth I of England Series.

The Secret Diary of Anne Boleyn. 1997.

The Queen's Bastard. 1999.

Virgin: Prelude to the Throne. 2001.

The Wild Irish. 2003.

Queen Elizabeth I meets pirate Grace O'Malley.

Plaidy, Jean.

Jean Plaidy is the pseudonym of romance writer Eleanor Hibbert. Plaidy wrote several histori-cal series that are still popular in libraries. Crown is currently reissuing some of Plaidy's titles under the Three Rivers imprint. Many of her long out-of-print titles are scheduled to be reissued in the near future.

Georgian Saga.

Eleven titles. Started with *The Princess of Celle* (1967) and ended with *Victoria in the Wings* (1972).

The Queens of England Series.

Eleven titles. Started with *Myself the Enemy,* about Henrietta Maria, who married King Charles I (1983), and ended with *The Rose Without a Thorn,* about Catherine Howard, the wife of Henry VIII (published in 1993 and reissued in 2003).

Tudor Novels.

Katharine of Aragon. 1968. Reissued 2005.

Katharine, the Sixth Wife. 1969. Reissued 2005. Katharine Parr.

Victorian Saga.

Began with *The Captive of Kensington Palace* (1976) and ended with *The Widow of Windsor* (1978).

Tannahill, Reay.

Fatal Majesty: A Novel of Mary, Queen of Scots. 1999.

Political intrigue, conspiracy, and the ultimately tragic story of Queen Mary.

Exotic Locales

Exploration resulted in awareness of and experiences in many new lands. Although set in the same time period as titles in the "Exploration, Renaissance" section, the locales in this section are exotic from a Western perspective, which is the point of view generally taken by the authors.

Clavell, James.

Gai-Jin. 1993. Nineteenth-century Japan.

Shogun. 1975. Seventeenth-century Japan. ★ ▬

Falconer, Colin.

> *The Sultan's Harem.* 2004.
>
>> The passions, intrigues, and politics in the palace of sixteenth-century Ottoman sultan Suleyman.

Fletcher, Aaron. Frontier Australia.

> *Outback.* 1997.
> *Outback Legacy.* 1996.
> *Outback Station.* 1991.
> *Walkabout.* 1992.
> *Wallaby Track.* 1994.

Lord, Betty Bao.

> *The Middle Heart.* 1996. China during the Communist Revolution.

Malouf, David.

> Malouf's novels are set in nineteenth-century Australia. Each is a stand-alone title.
>
> *The Conversations at Curlow Creek.* 1996.
> *Remembering Babylon.* 1993.

Mason, Daniel.

> *The Piano Tuner.* 2002. 1880s Burma.
>
>> Mild-mannered Edgar Drake travels from England to exotic and dangerous Burma to tune a valuable grand piano.

McCullough, Colleen.

> *Morgan's Run.* 2000. Eighteenth-century Australia.
> *The Touch.* 2003.
>
>> The story of Alex Kinross, a former Scottish boilermaker who settles in New South Wales and subsequently sends to Scotland for a wife. A family saga, beginning in late nineteenth-century Australia.

Smith, Wilbur.

> **Hal Courtney.**
>
>> Adventure on the high seas.
>>
>> *Birds of Prey.* 1997.
>> Piracy and war in the late seventeenth century off the coast of Africa leave Hal Courtney fatherless and in search of treasure and revenge.
>>
>> *Monsoon.* 1999.
>> Sir Hal, now a privateer and the father of four sons, faces more danger and adventure with the East India Company.

Sundaresan, Indu.

> *The Twentieth Wife.* 2002.
>
>> A novel about the woman for whom the Taj Mahal was built.

Tremain, Rose.

> *The Colour.* 2003. Nineteenth-century New Zealand gold rush.

The Americas

New frontiers and unexplored lands offer a broad canvas for fiction. Frontiers, whether in Australia, the American West, or other locales, provide fertile ground for the clash between "civilization" and the wilderness. The lure of a place far from corrupt cities, crowds, jobs, and schools offers freedom, danger, and excitement. Like many sagas, many of these novels feature families or individuals moving to a new land to seek their fortunes and establish themselves. Thus sagas, as well as many of the books in the "Westerns" chapter, will appeal to readers who enjoy this type of story.

Colonial/Early Settlement/Revolution

Self-reliance and the strength to survive are common traits found in the characters of this type of book. A man (or woman) against nature, hewing out a home and livelihood from the wilderness while battling great odds to survive, is typical. Often conflict arises from the forces of "civilization" trying to take over the wilderness and end the independence of early settlers.

Begiebing, Robert J.

 Rebecca Wentworth's Distraction. 2003.

Rebecca, a twelve-year old orphan, is brilliant, beautiful, and talented but viewed askance by her uncle and others in Boston who perceive her wild, untutored painting style as indicative of insanity. Winner of the Langum Prize.

Carter, Jimmy.

The Hornet's Nest: A Novel of the Revolutionary War. 2003.

The revolutionary war in the South.

Coyle, Harold.

Savage Wilderness. 1997. French and Indian Wars.

"British forces, led by General Edward Braddock, joined by the American colonial militias, and the French aided by their Indian allies, were locked in battle over the great territories of the Ohio valley" (book jacket).

Demos, John.

The Unredeemed Captive: A Family Story From Early America. 1994.

A novel dealing with the French and Indian raid on Deerfield, Massachusetts, in which more than a hundred settlers were marched north to Canada. The focus of this novel is the family of John Williams, especially his daughter Eunice, who stayed with the Indians for the rest of her life.

Donati, Sara.

<u>Bonner Family Saga.</u>

A romantic tale related to James Fenimore Cooper's <u>Leatherstocking Tales,</u> set in eighteenth-century upstate New York. Elizabeth Middleton defies her father's plan to marry her off for his personal gain and falls in love with frontiersman Nathaniel and his wilderness home.

Into the Wilderness. 1998.

Dawn on a Distant Shore. 2000.

Elizabeth and Nathaniel Bonner's married life may be bliss, but it is too short lived when word arrives that Nathaniel's father, Hawkeye, is being held in a Canadian prison, and Nathaniel himself then becomes a prisoner while attempting to free him.

Lake in the Clouds. 2002.

Fire Along the Sky. 2004.

Larsen, Deborah.

The White. 2002.

Mary Jemison was sixteen years old in 1758 when she was kidnapped from southern Pennsylvania by the Shawnee and adopted by a pair of Seneca sisters.

Norman, Diana.

A Catch of Consequence. 2002.

A romantic tale of Makepeace Burke, patriot, fishing one early morning in Boston Harbor, when she fishes a British soldier from the sea.

Taking Liberties. 2004.

Two women, searching for missing loved ones, meet and join forces in Plymouth in the early days of the Revolutionary War.

Robson, Lucia St. Clair.

Mary's Land. 1995. Reissued 2003. Seventeenth-century Maryland.

Shadow Patriots. 2005.

Members of a Quaker community, including a brother and sister, become members of George Washington's Culper spy ring.

Shaara, Jeff.

The Glorious Cause: A Novel of the American Revolution. 2000.

Rise to Rebellion. 2001.

Vidal, Gore.

Burr. 1973. ★

Civil War/Reconstruction/New Nation

The Civil War, events leading up to it, Reconstruction, Westward Expansion, the Gold Rush—the nineteenth century was filled with dramatic and tumultuous events in the Americas. The critical and commercial success of Charles Frazier's *Cold Mountain* in the late 1990s reawakened interest in this time period on the part of readers and publishers. The anniversary of the Lewis and Clark expedition in 2003 and accompanying media attention also resulted in some new historical fiction on this theme.

Atwood, Margaret.

Alias Grace. 1996.

Based on a true story. Grace Marks was convicted of murdering her employer and another person in Canada in 1843.

Bahr, Howard.

The Black Flower: A Novel of the Civil War. 1997.

The Year of Jubilo. 2000.

A Confederate veteran returns home to Cumberland, Mississippi, in the summer of 1865 to a changed world.

Barrett, Andrea.
> *The Voyage of the Narwhal.* 1998. 📖
>> A nineteenth-century Arctic voyage.

Begiebing, Robert J.
> *The Adventures of Allegra Fullerton, or, A Memoir of Startling and Amusing Episodes from Itinerant Life.* 1999.

Brooks, Geraldine.
> *March.* 2005.
>> The story of Mr. March, the absent father of Louisa Alcott's *Little Women*, during the Civil War.

Burke, James Lee.
>> Burke is an acclaimed mystery writer.
>
> *White Doves at Morning.* 2002.
>> Civil War Louisiana, from the Southern perspective.

Cornwell, Bernard.
> <u>**Starbuck Chronicles.**</u>
>> Starbuck is a Northerner in the Confederate Army.
>
>> *Rebel.* 1993.
>> *Copperhead: A Novel of the Civil War.* 1994.
>> *Battle Flag.* 1995.
>> *The Bloody Ground.* 1996.

Dallas, Sandra.
> *The Chili Queen.* 2002. 1860s New Mexico.
>> Winner of the Spur Award.
>
> *The Diary of Mattie Spenser.* 1997. Colorado.

Frazier, Charles.
> *Cold Mountain.* 1997. Civil War, North Carolina. 📖 🎬
>> The journey of Confederate soldier Inman, who, after being wounded, deserts his post to travel home to his true love, Ada. A best seller and winner of the National Book Award.

Gear, W. Michael.
> *The Morning River.* 1997. 1825 Missouri.

Hall, Brian.
> *I Should Be Extremely Happy in Your Company.* 2003. Lewis and Clark expedition.

Harrington, Stephen.
> *The Gates of the Alamo.* 1999.

Jakes, John.
> *Savannah, or, A Gift for Mr. Lincoln.* 2004.

Mallon, Thomas.
> *Henry and Clara*. 1994.
>> A tale of the couple who shared a box with the Lincoln's at Ford's Theater.

Morrison, Toni.
> *Beloved*. 1987. Reissued 2000.
>> The spirit of her murdered child haunts a mother and former slave in post–Civil War Ohio.

Mrazek, Robert J.
> *Unholy Fire: A Novel of the Civil War*. 2003.

Nevin, David.
> *Meriwether: A Novel of Meriwether Lewis and the Lewis & Clark Expedition*. 2004.

> **The American Story.**
>> The early days of the new United States.
>>
>> *1812*. 1996.
>> *Eagle's Cry: A Novel of the Louisiana Purchase*. 2000.
>> *Treason*. 2001. Aaron Burr.

Powell, J. Mark, and L. D. Meagher.
> *The Curse of Cain*. 2005. (adventure and espionage).
>> An honorable young Confederate officer is sent to Washington by Robert E. Lee to foil an assassination plot.

Price, Eugenia.
> A master of Southern romance.

> *The Waiting Time*. 1997.
>> Antebellum Georgia from the viewpoint of a feminist and abolitionist who inherits a plantation and a hundred slaves.

Shaara, Jeff.
> Son of Michael Shaara, the author of *Killer Angels*.
>
> *God and Soldiers*. 1996. Prequel to *Killer Angels* (listed below).
> *Gone for Soldiers: A Novel of the Mexican War*. 2000.
> *The Last Full Measure*. 1998. Sequel to *Killer Angels* (listed below).

Shaara, Michael.
> ★ *Killer Angels*. 1974. Civil War. Pulitzer Proze winner. 📖 ★

Thom, James Alexander.
> *Sign-Talker: The Adventure of George Drouillard on the Lewis and Clark Expedition*. 2000.

Vidal, Gore.
> *Lincoln*. 1984. In Vidal's American Chronicles series.

Wheeler, Richard S.
> *Eclipse*. 2002. Lewis and Clark.

The Twentieth Century

The first half of the twentieth century was filled with notable points in history: the two world wars, the Great Depression, Prohibition, and women's suffrage. Many of the titles in the "West Still Lives" section of the "Westerns" chapter (chapter 6) will be of interest to readers who like this era.

Ali, Tariq.

The Stone Woman. 2001.

Members of a well-born family in the Ottoman Empire at the turn of the century share their stories.

Erdrich, Louise.

The Master Butcher's Singing Club. 2002.

The journey of people who become a family, from Germany at the end of World War I to North Dakota.

Garlock, Dorothy.

Mother Road. 2003.

Route 66 through Oklahoma was the escape route for many hoping to flee the Great Depression.

Tan, Amy.

The Bonesetter's Daughter. 2001.

While her mother is suffering from Alzheimer's, Ruth translates two packets of writing that tell her family's story in the early part of the century in China.

Saga Series

The saga series, spanning decades or centuries, have been around for a long time; but they really took off when a book packager, the late Lyle Engel of Book Creations, started marketing several series that became immensely popular. Sagas and epics are generally lengthier than other historicals, and they offer the reader an opportunity to know the families involved and to become immersed in their lives and times. Most involve a great deal of romance, as well as adventure. Fans of historical sagas should also consult the saga sections in the romance (chapter 9) and Western (chapter 6) chapters.

Anand, Valerie.

<u>Bridges over Time.</u>

A realistic look at medieval English life.

The Proud Villeins. 1990. Eleventh century.
The Ruthless Yeomen. 1993.
Women of Ashdon. 1993.
The Faithful Lovers. 1994. Seventeenth century.
The Cherished Wives. 1996. Eighteenth century.

Cookson, Catherine.

Cookson has written several books and series that follow the pattern of sagas.

Mallen trilogy.

The series began with *The Mallen Streak* (1973), and continued with *The Mallen Girl* (1974) and *The Mallen Lot* (1974). Set in nineteenth-century Northumberland, three generations of a family are seemingly cursed because of past hidden sins. All titles were reissued in 2000.

Tilly Trotter trilogy.

The series is composed of *Tilly* (1980), *Tilly Wed* (1982), *Tilly Alone* (1982). A young woman, outcast in her Tyneside village in the Victorian era because she is perceived as a witch, becomes a mistress, a wife, and a widow, going all the way to America and back in the course of her life. Reissued in 2000 under the British titles *Tilly Trotter, Tilly Trotter Wed*, and *Tilly Trotter Alone*.

De la Roche, Mazo.

The Whiteoak Saga.

Published from 1927, starting with *Jalna,* and ending in 1960 with *Morning at Jalna*, the tales of the Whiteoak family and Jalna, their family estate in Canada, still circulate in some libraries and are frequently the subject of readers' advisory stumpers. *Jalna* was reissued in 2005.

Fletcher, Inglis.

Carolina Chronicles. ★

The early settlement of Coastal Carolina.

Raleigh's Eden. 1940.
Men of Albemarle. 1942.
Lusty Wind for Carolina. 1944.
Toil of the Brave. 1946.
Roanoke Hundred. 1948.
Bennett's Welcome. 1950.
The Queen's Gift. 1952.

Harrod-Eagles, Cynthia.

Morland Dynasty series.

Five hundred years of English history are told through the lives of the Yorkshire Morlands. As of 2005 there were twenty-seven titles in the series, which started with *The Founding* (1980), set in 1443 during the War of the Roses. Three more volumes are planned that will take the Morlands up to World War II. The twenty-seventh volume, *The Restless Sea,* was published in the United Kingdom in 2004 but is not yet for sale in the United States.

Jakes, John.

Charleston. 2002.

The Bell family from the Revolution to the Civil War.

The Kent Family Chronicles. ★

Originally called the American Bicentennial series.

The Bastard. 1974. Reissued in 2004.
The Rebels. 1975.
The Seekers. 1975.

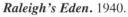

The Furies. 1976.
The Titans. 1976.
The Warriors. 1977.
The Lawless. 1978.
The Americans. 1980.

Lofts, Norah.

The House Trilogy. ★

The adventures of the Reed family of Suffolk, England, are followed from 1496 to the twentieth century.

The Town House: The Building of the House. 1959. Reissued 2000.
The House at Old Vine. 1961. Reissued 2000.
The House at Sunset. 1962. Reissued 2000.

McMurtry, Larry.

Lonesome Dove saga.

Dead Man's Walk. 1995.
Comanche Moon. 1997.
🏵 *Lonesome Dove.* 1985. ★ TVM
A best seller, and winner of the Pulitzer Prize.

The Streets of Laredo. 1993.

Price, Eugenia.

Price wrote several romantic historical sagas, all set in the South.

Georgia trilogy.

Antebellum Georgia.

Bright Captivity. 1991.
Where Shadows Go. 1993.
Beauty from Ashes. 1995.

Savannah quartet.

Antebellum Georgia.

Savannah. 1983. Reissued 1997.
To See Your Face Again. 1985. Reissued 1997.
Before the Darkness Falls. 1987.
Stranger in Savannah. 1989.

Ross, Dana Fuller.

Wagons West series.

Independence!, the first title in the series, was published in 1978 and follows a band of settlers who leave Long Island in 1843 headed for the Oregon Territory. *Celebration!,* the twenty-fourth and final title, was published in 1989. Recurring characters include Whip Holt, a wagonmaster, and his son Toby.

The Holts: An American Dynasty series.

The saga of the Holt family continued, starting with *Oregon Legacy* in 1989.

Smith, Wilbur.

Courtney Family series.

This series starts in 1667, when Sir Francis Courtney and his son Henry "Hal" Courtney are fighting the Dutch off the coast of Africa, and goes through the gold rush of the 1870s, up to the 1970s, following the adventures of the family and the history of Africa.

Birds of Prey. 1997.

Monsoon. 1999. Reissued 2003.

The Blue Horizon. 2003.

When the Lion Feeds. 1989.

The Sound of Thunder. 1966.

A Sparrow Falls. 1977.

The Burning Shore. 1985.

Power of the Sword. 1986.

Rage. 1987.

A Time to Die. 1989.

The Golden Fox. 1990.

Ballantyne family saga.

In 1860 Dr. Robyn Ballantyne returns to Africa with three objectives: to bring Christianity, medicine, and an end to slave trading. This adventure-filled series features the colonial drive for wealth and the conflict between the races while providing a look at Rhodesia's history.

A Falcon Flies. 1980. Also published as *Flight of the Falcon.*

Men of Men. 1983.

The Angels Weep. 1983.

The Leopard Hunts in Darkness. 1984.

Tademy, Lalita.

Cane River. 2002.

A family saga featuring four generations of African American women surviving slavery.

Thane, Elswyth Beebe.

Williamsburg series. ★

A family saga that starts with the American Revolution and goes to World War II. This is often a readers' advisory stumper.

Dawn's Early Light. 1943. Reissued 1996.

Yankee Stranger. 1944.

Ever After. 1945. Reissued 1997.

The Light Heart. 1947. Reissued 1994.

Kissing Cousin. 1948.

This Was Tomorrow. 1951. Reissued 1997.

Homing. 1957. Reissued 1994.

Epics

The epic historical novel covers centuries or even millennia and is focused on a specific geographical location. These large-scale tapestries woven from written words are best typified by James Michener's works.

Delaney, Frank.

Ireland: A Novel. 2005.

Michener, James. ★

Even though Michener has been gone since 1997, readers who love the epic scope of his historical novels keep his books available in libraries and book stores.

Alaska. 1988.
Caribbean. 1989.
Centennial. 1974. Colorado.
Chesapeake. 1978.
The Covenant. 1980. South Africa.
Hawaii. 1959.
Mexico. 1992.
Poland. 1983.
The Source. 1965. The Holy Land.
Texas. 1985.

Rutherfurd, Edward.

The Forest. 2000.
London. 1997.

    The 2,000 years of the city's history, told from the viewpoints of several families.

The Princes of Ireland: The Dublin Saga. 2004.
Russka. 1991.

    Four families and 1,800 years shape the history of Russia.

Sarum. 1987.

    Ten thousand years of history, centered on five families from the Salisbury Plain of England.

Stephenson, Neal.

Baroque Cycle. 📖

    Complex tale of science and scientists in the seventeenth and eighteenth centuries.

Quicksilver. 2003.
The development of calculus.

The Confusion. 2004.
Sea adventures, international intrigue, and alchemy.

The System of the World. 2004.
England's monetary system is at stake among political intrigues in this finale of the Baroque Cycle.

Topics

Bibliographies and Encyclopedias

Adamson, Lynda G. *American Historical Fiction: An Annotated Guide to Novels for Adults and Young Adults*. Oryx Press, 1999.
Lists 3,000 titles. Indexed by author, title, genre, subject, and geographic setting.

———. *World Historical Fiction: An Annotated Guide to Novels for Adults and Young Adults*. Oryx Press, 1998.
Lists over 6,000 titles organized by geographic setting and time period. Extensive indexes. Succinct annotations for each title. Award winners and titles suitable for young adults are listed.

Burgess, Michael, and Jill H. Vassilakos. *Murder in Retrospect: A Selective Guide to Historical Mystery Fiction*. Libraries Unlimited, 2005.

Burt, Daniel S. *What Historical Novel Do I Read Next?* Gale Research, 1997.

Gerhardstein, Virginia Brokaw. *Dickinson's American Historical Fiction*. 5th ed. Scarecrow Press, 1986.
Over 3,000 historical novels covering European colonization to 1984 are annotated and classified.

Hartman, Donald K., and Gregg Sapp. *Historical Figures in Fiction*. Oryx Press, 1994.
Lists 4,200 novels organized by 1,500 significant historical characters.

Johnson, Sarah L. *Historical Fiction: A Guide to the Genre*. Libraries Unlimited, 2005.
Organizes historical fiction by genre and subgenre, as well as setting and time period.

VanMeter, Vandelia L. *America in Historical Fiction: A Bibliographic Guide*. Libraries Unlimited, 1997.
Includes 1,168 annotated entries, focusing on titles that are appropriate for high school students.

Vasudevan, Aruna, and Lesley Henderson, eds. *Twentieth-Century Romance & Historical Writers*. St. James Press, 1994.

Writers' Manuals

Martin, Rhona. *Writing Historical Fiction*. Talman, 1995.

Oliver, Marina. *Writing Historical Fiction: How to Create Authentic Historical Fiction and Get It Published*. Trans-Atlantic, 1998.

Woolley, Persia. *How to Write and Sell Historical Fiction*. Writer's Digest Books, 1997.

Conferences

The **Historical Novel Society** held its first annual conference in London in 2001. Its first North American conference was held in April 2005 in Salt Lake City (http://www.historicalnovelsociety.org).

Awards

Historical novels are frequently considered for and awarded literary prizes. There is one award, however, that is specifically awarded to a work of historical fiction set in the Americas for young adults or children, the Scott O'Dell award. A listing of winners can be found at the Writerswrite.com Web site: http://www.scottodell.com/ (accessed March 4, 2005).

The Historical Short Fiction Prize is a cash award for the best short historical fiction submitted for an annual anthology. It was started in 2005.

The Langum Prize is awarded annually (since 2003) for "Historical fiction set in the American colonial and national periods, that is both excellent fiction and excellent history, and that, to some extent makes a delineation between fiction and history" (http://www.langumtrust.org/histlit.htm, accessed March 21, 2005).

The Bruce Alexander Historical Mystery Award was first awarded in 2004 at the Left Coast Crime conference.

Women Writing the West gives the **Willa Award** in several categories, one of which is historical fiction for women's stories set in the West before contemporary times.

The Romance Writers of America give **Rita Awards** for three categories of romance fiction with historical settings: Best Regency, Best Long Historical, and Best Short Historical.

Online Resources

HistFiction.net—Authors & Books in Historical Fiction (formerly Soon's Historical Fiction Site), http://www.histfiction.net/ (accessed March 4, 2005), lists many authors, some with titles, some with links to Web sites, specific newsgroups, or other locations that have additional information.

The Historical Novel Society, http://www.historicalnovelsociety.org/ (accessed March 4, 2005).

Maiden's Crown, http://www.randomhouse.com/crown/maidenscrown/ (accessed March 4, 2005), provides information on Crown Books (Random House) historical novels.

D's Historical Picks

Donati, Sara.

Dawn on a Distant Shore. **2000.** (Americas—colonial).

In the second book of the Bonner Family saga, Elizabeth and Nathaniel Bonner's married life may be bliss, but it is too short lived, when word arrives that Nathaniel's father, Hawkeye, is being held in a Canadian prison, and Nathaniel himself then becomes a prisoner when attempting to free him.

Sundaresan, Indu.

The Twentieth Wife 2002. (exotic locales).

The life of Mehrunnisa, from her birth in a ragged tent near Qandahar in 1577 while her Persian parents were fleeing the Shah's court, to her wedding to the great Mughal Emperor Jahangir. Along the way, a stroke of good fortune places her father in the royal court in India. Politics and the hidden power of the women of the royal Zenana are illuminated as Mehrunnisa catches the eye of the Empress and informally becomes her companion. Uprisings and conspiracies abound, with danger lurking at every turn.

Vantrease, Brenda Rickman.

The Illuminator. 2005. (middle ages).

In fourteenth-century England, a widow takes in an illuminator and his daughter as she tries to keep her autonomy and home safe from king and church.

Vreeland, Susan.

The Passion of Artemisia. 2002. (exploration/renaissance)

In sixteenth-century Italy, Artemisia Gentileschi, a woman artist, experiences a horrific rape trial during which she is tortured, but with extreme inner strength she continues her career.

Chapter 6

Westerns

Essay

Connie Van Fleet

Some librarians may think the Western, like its archetypical and outdated hero, is pushing up daisies on Boot Hill. For years it seemed that publishers agreed, saddling new Westerns with the "historical" fiction label, hoping to disassociate new releases from the stereotypes and misperceptions that plagued the genre. Readers often identified the Western stories with pulp fiction, B-grade films of the 1930s and 1940s, and television series of the 1950s and 1960s. They recalled all of the old stereotypes: a swaggering John Wayne, a stagecoach surrounded by masked villains, a gunfight on Main Street, a row of Indian warriors on a cliff overlooking a circle of wagon trains. Yet these very images are embedded in our national character and language. We know what it means when an author describes the 1960s Cuban missile crisis as the "high noon of the Cold War," or when it's time to "circle the wagons."

The Western has never been completely forgotten and is now enjoying a periodic resurgence through an expanded "Western literature." This popularity extends to all types of Westerns. Although many baby boomers who drew their heroes from the Saturday matinees and television Westerns of their childhoods still want to see those honest and honorable characters again, in the past two decades the genre has become as open and diverse as the land and people it describes. Today, the Western genre includes titles from Louis L'Amour to Larry McMurtry, from young adult novels by Gary Paulsen to adult series by Tabor Evans.

Definition

Simply put, a Western is a story that takes place in Western North America, often during the latter half of the nineteenth century. The defining element of the Western is its palpable sense of time and place. The American West, with its unending plains, wide deserts, and rugged mountains, provides a physical setting that invites solitude and freedom. It is at once beautiful and unspoiled, redemptive and challenging. Its features reflect both space and timelessness. The vast Western landscape requires physical and mental strength to survive its rigors, but repays that strength with a sense of communion with nature and freedom from artifice. The traditional Western takes place in the frontier era, a time of cowboys and trail towns, Westward expansion and settlement. This physical and temporal environment serves as a "symbolic landscape," a time and place where chaos and order meet, where nature and civilization clash. A "Western" may be set in the modern time, but to be acknowledged as a part of the Western literature oeuvre, it must retain the same nostalgic mood of more traditional work, its feel and plot sometimes rising from the clash between civilized, often oppressive society and the out-of-time and place individual who prefers immediate action to political or social niceties.

Much of the appeal of the traditional Western derives from the adventure and romance of the West and good old-fashioned storytelling. The adventures involve cycles of adrenalin-producing fear, exhilarating success, and quieting rest; the contrast is intense. The reader is engaged, focused, intent upon the outcome, because the outcome is never trivial. Plots spring from the larger-than-life mythical landscape, from the physical environment of the unsettled American West and the sociological context of the frontier psyche. The Western frontier, with its clashes between individuality and society, wilderness and civilization, freedom and capitalism, was rich with thematic opportunities. Justice, survival, and redemption are recurring themes.

In most Westerns, the plot involves an unambiguous conflict with a clear resolution. A protagonist—and there is no doubt about who this is—must overcome an obstacle, whether surviving harsh natural surroundings, redressing evil through personal vengeance or retribution, or defending the weak. Good always survives, even if the good guy doesn't. Although heroes have become more flawed and their inner conflicts more apparent, there is still no doubt as to whom the reader wants to succeed. The protagonist of the Western is self-sufficient and capable. The cowboy, the sheriff, and the pioneer woman all meet obstacles with physical strength, courage, and mental fortitude. Once roused, the protagonist is relentless in pursuit of retribution or justice. With an effort of will, he or she overcomes injury, natural adversity, and weariness. Regardless of inner turmoil or superficial appearance, the Westerner adheres to an internal code of conduct that requires protecting the weak, defending one's honor, and keeping one's word. These elements have been expanded into a modern "Western literature." They have been bent, tweaked, and re-envisioned, but they remain at the heart of what we define as Western writing.

History and Evolution

Most scholars identify *The Last of the Mohicans* (1826) or *The Prairie* (1827) by James Fenimore Cooper as the first Western novel. Cooper's novels portrayed a very complex confrontation between two equally valid societies. The Indians were noble savages, with complex personalities and established cultural values. The novels explored the symbolic conflict between society and individual freedom, peaceful civilization and uncontrolled violence. In 1860, Erastus Beadle and Robert Adams created "dime novels." These popular books—five million sold at a dime each by the end of the Civil War in 1864—featured graphic covers and sensationalized stories of life out West. The dime novels didn't report the West as it existed, but shaped the way it developed, as young cowboys and outlaws used the books to model their behavior.

Even at its origins, however, the Western entered popular culture through both print and performance media. In the late nineteenth century, E. Z. C. Judson produced over 400 stories and dime novels under the pseudonym Ned Buntline. Judson created the Buffalo Bill legend with a series of newspaper articles and a play based on his Buffalo Bill stories. Bill Cody's Buffalo Bill's Wild West show—seen by millions of people throughout the United States and the European continent—included women (who displayed riding and shooting skills) and Indians (who, contrary to contemporary belief, saw an opportunity to reenact an honorable past and to preserve their culture).

Owen Wister established the pattern for the Western in *The Virginian* (1902). His novel marked a return to thematic seriousness and complexity, envisioning the West as a place of moral regeneration and utilizing the individual code of honor as the core of characterization and the impetus for plot development.

Zane Grey, who produced over eighty novels and continued writing into the 1930s, moved Wister's pattern forward. He continued the basic structural elements, building stories around patterns of gradually increasing violence and tension toward the climactic confrontation between the hero and villain. He introduced a hero who was more mysterious and alienated (the heroic gunfighter or outlaw), generally older and a loner, but with a deep yearning to become part of society. Most notably, he brought the landscapes of the West to life, moving them to center stage, using the West as a testing ground of individual strength and cultural ideas. Other influential writers included Ernest Haycox, whose style and characterization set the standard for Western writers and whose work is still in print, W. M. Raine, and B. M. Bower, the first woman Western writer.

The public's enchantment with Westerns followed the genre from print to film in the early 1900s. Beginning with S. Porter's *The Great Train Robbery* (1903), the first silent film to introduce narrative, Westerns became enormously popular, as they blended action, romance, and larger-than-life heroes. Grey's *Riders of the Purple Sage* (1912) appeared on the screen in 1918, the first of over 110 films based on his work. Frederick Faust (Max Brand) published *The Untamed,* the first of his Western novels in 1918, and continues to be known for the storytelling power of his traditional Westerns. He is perhaps best known for *Destry Rides Again* (1930).

While the heroes of the pre-1920 film era were a bit exaggerated, these early films were fairly realistic in story line, dress, action, and scenery. The B-grade motion picture Westerns made by the hundreds between 1920 and 1940 moved away from realism toward a romanticized notion of the Western hero. In 1935, *Tumbling Tumbleweeds*, starring Gene Autry, set the pattern for success: action, comedy in the form of a sidekick, clean living, fancy dress, the cowboy code—and, of course, the cowboy with the guitar. Tex Ritter and Roy Rogers followed. Radio audiences listened to county and western music programs; radio serials, most famously *The Lone Ranger*, hypnotized eager listeners. In print, however, A. B. Guthrie continued the serious and multilayered exploration of the Western myth with *The Big Sky* (1947) and *The Way West*, which received the 1950 Pulitzer Prize.

After mid-century, Louis L'Amour joined Zane Grey as one of America's most popular authors, and ultimately surpassed him in terms of books sold. L'Amour focused on that unsung hero, the common man, and extolled the virtue of honest physical work. He introduced new levels of complexity in his characters and demonstrated himself to be a master storyteller. Well over 85 million copies of L'Amour's novels have been printed; more than sixteen titles were made into films.

In the early 1950s, kids and television Westerns seemed a natural combination. *The Lone Ranger* appeared from 1949 to 1957. For adults, *Gunsmoke* (1956–1975) departed from tradition by placing greater emphasis on relationships and personal conflicts; the tone was often reflective. Other shows featured nontraditional heroes—a gambler (*Maverick*), a hired gun (*Have Gun Will Travel*), and a bounty hunter (*Wanted: Dead or Alive*). Television Westerns reached their peak in 1959, with almost fifty programs appearing in prime time. Westerns were popular into the 1970s, but they did not reach the most desirable demographic: urban, affluent, and middle-aged.

In 1975, Playboy Press gave new meaning to the term "adult" Western with Jake Logan, a tough hero whose adventures were characterized by improbable sexual exploits and a comic twist. In contrast, Don Coldsmith garnered interest in 1980 with the first title in his Spanish Bit Saga, a series of twenty-seven novels that accurately retell the cultural history of the Plains Indians. But it was Larry McMurtry's epic Western *Lonesome Dove* (1985) that won the hearts of readers, and a Pulitzer Prize. Television producers took notice of its popularity, producing four miniseries based on the saga between 1988 and 1996.

The 1990s witnessed a resurgence in the popularity of the Western that continues into the new millennium. All things Southwestern—from art to home décor to fashion—attracted consumer dollars, and New Mexico and Nevada became destinations of choice for both retirees and the young and upwardly mobile. The Western landscape became popular with authors in many genres during this decade. Mystery writers, including J. A. Jance (the JoAnna Brady series), Tony Hillerman (Jim Chee and Joe Leaphorn series), and Robert O. Greer (C. J. Floyd), placed their characters in the modern West. Mainstream authors such as Sherman Alexie, Louise Erdrich, Ivan Doig, Barbara Kingsolver, and Larry McMurtry adopted Western settings. Authors typically associated with other genres also published Westerns: Bill Pronzini (mystery and science fiction), Jane Archer (romance), Trevanian (adventure), and Robert B. Parker (mystery) all produced bona fide Western titles. Larry McMurtry continued to produce Western novels, some giving a new spin on Old West celebrities, some with the flavor of the traditional Western, and some based in the modern West. Elmer Kelton, Loren Estleman, Richard S. Wheeler, and other frankly and unapologetically Western writers contributed new works to what some had thought was the province of dead white guys. Together, these authors expanded the genre into a "Western literature."

More than twenty major Western films were made during the decade, two of which—*Dances with Wolves* (1990), Kevin Costner's sympathetic portrayal of the Sioux, and *Unforgiven* (1992), Clint Eastwood's soul-searching look at Western violence—won Academy Awards for Best Picture. Two new nontraditional Western television series, *Dr.*

Quinn, Medicine Woman and *Walker, Texas Ranger,* premiered on television in 1993. *Crossfire Trail* (2001), based on a book by Louis L'Amour, became the most watched original movie in the history of basic cable. The premiere of *Monte Walsh* (2003), also starring Tom Selleck, was the most watched Friday night program on basic cable, drawing an audience of 18 million over its four showings.

From its inception, the Western as a literary genre has been inextricably bound up with the representation of the West in performance media. Print and performance media reflect and shape each other. Throughout the evolution of both forms, however, the Western has been characterized by variety in quality and approach. To view the Western genre as monolithic in any era is a narrow approach that does a disservice to both Western fans and general readers alike.

The Western Reader

Owen Wister touched a chord with Americans who thought the culture of the East was decaying under the influence of rapidly growing immigrant populations, materialism, and radicalism. In a new preface in the 1911 edition, Wister asserted that *The Virginian* was "an expression of the American faith" under attack by "enemies both in Wall Street and in the Labor Unions." The cowboy was "the last of the freedom-loving Americans."

In contrast to the dirty, crowded, claustrophobic city, the physical setting of the Western is rugged and beautiful, spare and clean. Nature may be brutal or destructive, but it is never deceptive or artificial. The West is a place of moral regeneration, and the themes of Western literature speak to the need for self-transformation—to leave the artificial existence of modern society and somehow, through adversity, freedom, and the forces of nature, to become something purer, more intense, stripped to the essence, uncluttered by superficialities. The land and the work necessary to come to terms with nature serve as a crucible, shaping and forging the protagonist's character; annealing the metal of his being through fire; burning out the impurities created by a modern society removed from its bedrock.

In Westerns, hard work is not a punishment; it is a necessity for survival and an opportunity for redemption. Westerns are not an escape from hard work; they are an escape from the ennui that comes from work that seems meaningless or unchallenging. Much of Louis L'Amour's work revolves around the central theme of work, which invites the reader to identify with the characters and undoubtedly plays a part in his enduring popularity. Diary novels such as *The Diary of Mattie Spenser* (Sandra Dallas) and *One Thousand White Women: The Journals of Mary Dodd* (Jim Fergus) describe the hardships of life on the frontier and give insight into the strength and courage of women pioneers.

Through this work, people define themselves. In the West, actions count more than words. Courage, generosity of spirit, honesty, and the ability to work hard count for more than wealth, lineage, or history. When freed from the constraints of corrupt institutions, devious businessmen, hypocritical politicians, and conditions that force collective dependence instead of self-reliance, individuals can find their best selves. One may argue that they also find acceptance, but it is perhaps freedom from defining oneself in another's terms that is most liberating. While this freedom theme appeals to many readers, it resonates particularly with African Americans. Westerns by African American authors such as Charles Goodman and Hiram King enjoy a growing readership.

The mythical West, with its relative freedom from bureaucracy and society, may be the last bastion of individual empowerment. In the West, a single individual—cowboy, lawman, pioneer woman, or outlaw—may make a difference. Poised between civilization and lawlessness, the Western protagonist must act swiftly and often singly to ensure that good triumphs. No warrants, no lawsuits, no 9/11—just the individual armed with a rigorous moral code, determination, courage, and the skills to back them up.

Finally, the moral theme appeals to readers in an age of complexity and moral ambiguity. In all of the primary Western plot patterns, from the dedicated lawman of the "marshal" story to the bad man turned good (or vice versa) of the "outlaw" story, from the deliverer of retribution in the "revenge story" to the settler in the "ranch story," the story only works insofar as the reader is in sympathy with the protagonist's perspective and understands—and ultimately feels—that any action is justified. For instance, Edward L. Wheeler developed the retribution and revenge pattern through the Deadwood Dick stories as a means of rationalizing his protagonist's violent actions, which were often unilateral and unlawful. This plot device has not only been used to create empathy for fictional characters, but has served to soften and popularize real outlaws such as Frank and Jesse James.

While the strong themes of moral clarity and individual empowerment suggest that the character of the protagonist is an important factor in a book's appeal to readers, in the end it is the consummate storytelling of its writers that accounts for the enduring—and increasing—popularity of Western literature. The best of the Western writers give us a powerful mix of landscape, adventure, character, romance, history, and message.

Characteristics and Types

Within the broader parameters of the genre, readers find great diversity in reading experiences. There are many ways to characterize Western literature. One reader's Western novel may be another's novel of the West or someone else's Western. Some readers regard McMurtry's *Lonesome Dove* as literary fiction, some think of it as one of the best traditional Westerns ever written. Even more ambiguous is classification of McMurtry's *Horseman Pass By*, set in modern (1950s) Texas. The most commonly used classification places novels into three categories: formula Westerns, Western novels, and novels of the West.

Formula Westerns follow a set pattern; they are often series entries that are written to specifications. The author's intent is to reach the widest possible audience with easily accessible entertainment. Typically, formula Westerns are long on dialogue and white space and short on description, characterization, and historical detail. These series are easy to recognize as Westerns because the publishers identify them as such; they're usually produced in paperback, short in length, identified by the leading character's name, and numbered. Many people have come to identify "Western" with this formula. Readers like the predictable endings, the recognizable characters, the consistent style, and the undemanding entertainment in formula Westerns. More recent representatives of this group include adult Western series such as the Slocum series (Jake Logan) and the Christian Battles of Destiny series (Al Lacy).

Western novels fall between formula Westerns and novels of the West. Authors of this subgenre want to entertain with well-written stories about the West. They have no pretensions about writing the great American novel, but they do want to produce work that is well-crafted and original. They want their work to have mass-market appeal, but they don't want to approach it with an assembly line mentality. Western novels will vary in description, depth of characterization, or historical detail, but they typically emphasize good storytelling and have a degree of originality. Resolutions, however, are closed, and although the protagonists may have some failings and self-doubt, it is easy to tell the good guys from the bad.

The Western Writers of America (WWA) was founded in 1953 to bring together authors who wanted to find the middle ground between formula Westerns and mainstream literature. Representative authors, many of whom have received Spur Awards (presented by WWA for "distinguished writing about the West") , include familiar names with mass-market success like Zane Grey, Judy Alter, Frederick Glidden (Luke Short), Louis L'Amour, Elmer Kelton, Ernest Haycox, Loren Estleman, Terry Johnston, and Richard S. Wheeler. Western novel authors who provide a balanced treatment of Native Americans include Don Coldsmith (the Spanish Bit series), Cynthia Haseloff, and Will Henry. David Anthony Durham, Charles Goodman, and Hiram King are among African American authors in this category. Western novels appeal to readers who want to become engaged in a story and appreciate originality and good writing, but nevertheless want to enjoy the recognizable elements of the traditional Western, including identifiable heroes and satisfying endings.

Novels of the West can also be considered mainstream or literary fiction. Although the Western Writers of America defines novels of the West in terms of length (greater than 90,000 words), most are often characterized by sophisticated writing and thematic complexity. Authors in this category take advantage of opportunities presented by the mythic qualities of the Western frontier to create literature that is artistic, multilayered, complex, and often filled with symbolism. They also demonstrate a high degree of originality and historical accuracy. They make their characters fallible and occasionally not very likeable people and force them to confront moral dilemmas and sometimes make poor choices. Resolutions are sometimes ambiguous or unhappy. Authors in this category include Edna Ferber, Wallace Stegner, Cormac McCarthy, Ivan Doig, Willa Cather, Louise Erdrich, Barbara Kingsolver, A. B. Guthrie, and Larry McMurtry. Novels of the West appeal to readers who value writing style and originality and who appreciate complexity. They also appreciate a demanding read and are prepared to put thought and effort into the experience. They are not put off by ambiguity and dislike pat answers and unrealistically happy endings.

Advising the Reader

While these categories provide a broad set of parameters, subject classification is another way to approach Western literature. Arrangement by topic like the one used in this guide has proven effective. Readers' advisors need to consider all facets of the genre.

Readers who want a quick, undemanding read may choose formula Westerns, while those who want to ponder and reflect at length, who enjoy ambiguity and a challenge to received truths, may well prefer mainstream fiction. The majority of Western stories, written by literary artists for popular consumption, will appeal to people who want a well-written genre book, with heroes and heroines who reflect the best of humankind, a landscape that challenges abilities and courage, and a goal worth working and dying for.

More specifically, however, readers' advisors should first be aware that many Western authors are popular years after their deaths. Readers who want "classic" Westerns or who are new to the genre may enjoy authors with well-established reputations. Western readers are also drawn to the genre because they enjoy the mix of adventure, characterization, and great storytelling. Elmer Kelton, Louis L'Amour, Larry McMurtry, and Richard S. Wheeler fit this mold. Readers for whom the lure of the Western is the adventure story will enjoy action-based novels by Max Brand and L'Amour and series Westerns. They may well be pleased with suggestions for other types of adventure novels, particularly those that are historical or character based.

If descriptions of the land are of primary importance for Western readers, Zane Grey is an outstanding choice. If mood is central to a reader's choice, older Westerns tend to be more optimistic; newer Westerns have a bleaker (some would say more realistic) tone. Readers who prefer gentle reads would probably prefer older Westerns, as well as recent Christian series and some young adult novels. Descriptions of violence and death are usually more detailed in newer works. For readers who like character development, books by Larry McMurtry, Loren Estleman, Cynthia Haseloff, and Richard S. Wheeler are sound choices. Point of view is important to some readers as well; many traditional Westerns have an undeniable Anglo perspective. Newer works sensitive to Native American, Hispanic, and African American perspectives are increasingly available.

Western readers for whom historical detail is important will enjoy Don Coldsmith, Sandra Dallas, Willa Cather, or Will Henry. Sagas are perfect for readers who want to become immersed in books that have multiple characters and span generations and eras. Coldsmith's Spanish Bit sagas, L'Amour's Sackett series, McMurtry's series (including the Lonesome Dove saga, the Berrybender series, and the modern Texas series) also fill the bill. These readers may also enjoy some of the historical epics by James Michener, the Kent Family Chronicles by John Jakes, the Australians series by William Stewart Long, or the Australian Destiny series, a Christian saga by Sandy Dengler. In contrast, readers who prefer shorter novels and classic action stories should be guided to Max Brand or Elmer Kelton. They may also enjoy short story collections. (Pronzini has edited a number of these.) Readers who prefer mainstream fiction may well enjoy classic novels of the West by Willa Cather, Edna Ferber, and A. B. Guthrie, or work fitting the category published more recently by Sherman Alexie, Sandra Dallas, Louise Erdrich, Barbara Kingsolver, and Larry McMurtry.

Although subject categories (such as those listed in this book) can be helpful, they constitute a vocabulary that may confuse rather than clarify. It may be much easier for readers' advisors to ask readers what they want a book to be about than to articulate other types of appeal or selection factors. But readers' advisors need to think flexibly before they respond and be prepared to accommodate a number of different reader approaches. Subjects often will appear across genres. For instance, readers who enjoy reading Westerns featuring Native Americans may also want to read historical fiction, crime, or romance novels that focus on this group.

Conclusion

The Western is sometimes viewed as a dying genre, one relegated to a bygone era. But anyone who thinks the Western is dead either isn't paying attention or is imposing personal tastes on other readers. It is true that other forms of genre literature—particularly mystery and romance—enjoy a much greater share of new book sales and fiction circulation. Nevertheless, the traditional Western retains an enduring popularity with a loyal group of devotees. The genre is also drawing in new audiences as it expands and evolves. Western literature has enduring appeal for a growing audience of readers. Older works are read and re-read, and they are continually available in new editions. New authors are affiliating with the genre. Western shelves are no longer filled with the work of authors long deceased. Western literature fills the needs of many readers, some who want the undemanding pleasure of a straightforward adventure story, others who are searching for a more complex reading experience. Professionals who work with readers may want to broaden appeal and increase use by substituting the term "Western literature" when describing today's more complex collections, and locate them all on separate shelving. The effort may result in happy readers, increased circulation, and more efficient use of reader's advisors' time.

The themes of moral regeneration, freedom, and self-reliance that derive from the frontier landscape resonate with contemporary readers, as they have with readers for nearly two centuries. Evocative descriptions of the land, well-drawn characters who overcome obstacles both natural and human, and action-filled narratives combine to engage readers who are drawn to stories that reflect the American experience. For people who want heroes and stories of individual strength and character, Westerns provide them in abundance. Happy trails.

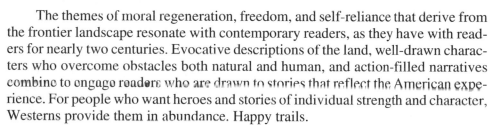

Bibliography

Barnard, Edward S., ed. *Story of the Great American West*. Pleasantville, N.Y.: Reader's Digest Association, 1997.

Cawelti, John G. *Adventure, Mystery, and Romance: Formula Stories as Art and Popular Culture*. Chicago: University of Chicago Press, 1976.

———. *The Six-Gun Mystique Sequel*. Bowling Green, Ohio: Bowling Green State University Popular Press, 1999.

Estleman, Loren D. "Introduction: The New Westward Expansion." In *American West: Twenty New Stories from the Western Writers of America*. New York: Forge, A Tom Doherty Associates Book, 2001.

Etulain, Richard W. "Riding Point: The Western and Its Interpreters." In *The Popular Western: Essays Toward a Definition*, edited by Richard W. Etulain and Michael T. Marsden. Bowling Green, Ohio: Bowling Green University Popular Press, 1974.

George-Warren, Holly. *Cowboy: How Hollywood Invented the Wild West*. Pleasantville, N.Y.: Reader's Digest Association, Inc., 2002.

Henry-Mead, Jean. *Legends in Western Literature: British Western Novelist. J.T. Edson Interview*. Available at www.americanWesternmagazine.com. Accessed July 22, 2004.

Maltin, Leonard, ed. *Leonard Maltin's 2005 Movie Guide*. New York: Plume (Penguin), 2004.

Mort, John. "Writers and Readers Buying Westerns; or, Whatever Happened to Randolph Scott?" *Booklist* 95, no. 13 (March 1, 1999): 1152–53.

Moses, L. C. *Wild West Shows and the Images of American Indians, 1883–1933*. Albuquerque: University of New Mexico Press, 1996.

Nye, Russel. *The Unembarrassed Muse: The Popular Arts in America*. New York: Dial Press, 1970.

Pearl, Nancy. *Now Read This: A Guide to Mainstream Fiction, 1978–1998*. Englewood, Colo.: Libraries Unlimited, 1999.

Rainey, Buck. *The Reel Cowboy: Essays on the Myth in Movies and Literature*. Jefferson, N.C.: McFarland, 1996.

Rosenberg, Betty. *Genreflecting*. Littleton, Colo.: Libraries Unlimited, 1982.

Saricks, Joyce G. *The Readers' Advisory Guide to Genre Fiction*. Chicago: ALA, 2001.

Tompkins, Jane. *West of Everything: The Inner Life of Westerns*. New York: Oxford University Press, 1992.

Wister, Owen. *The Virginian: A Horseman of the Plains.* With a New Afterword by Max Evans. New York: Signet Classic (Penguin Putnam), 2002.

Themes and Types

Diana Tixier Herald

The themes that follow are presented in a roughly chronological order, with mostly traditional Westerns covered in the first seventeen categories. The focus in traditional Westerns is mainly on character types, both of individuals and of groups that journeyed west in the late nineteenth century to garner riches, escape from the lives they had been leading, or make a fresh start in a new land. Stories of the "new West" (twentieth century) are covered in the section "The West Lives On."

Character types generally determine the type of story in the traditional Western. Thus, the stories about law and lawmen will have a strong moral thread, sharply drawn heroes and villains, and themes of justice, and involve shoot-outs or some other use of force to bring about order. Mountain men stories often depict rugged individualists, who survive off the land and adapt to its ways. Survival of ordinary people in extraordinary circumstances is the overarching theme in "Wagons West and Early Settlements." Family and community play central roles as the protagonists battle the natural elements, Indian attacks, and other hardships.

Many older titles are included here, since fans of traditional Westerns often turn to the classics of the genre. Many have been reissued, often by university presses. Others are finding new life in paperback, large print, or audio formats.

Relatively few new Westerns titles are released each year, and although there are not huge waiting lists for Westerns, they circulate steadily, so libraries are wise to hang onto titles in this genre for a long time. Many readers of this genre are retired men who have led active lives, often in physical occupations, and who began reading for pleasure upon retirement. These readers are not easily swayed by glittery covers and novelty, knowing that sometimes the tried and true is the best. (However, it is essential that readers' advisors remember that there are exceptions—the originator of this guide, Betty Rosenberg, a petite librarian and graduate school teacher, was a big fan of the genre.)

Although many of the titles in this chapter were published many years ago, they remain available in public libraries. Some librarians assert that they rarely weed Westerns due to lack of circulation. Rather, the main reason they are removed from library collections is because of deterioration caused by years of repeated use.

Selected Classics

Because so many Western titles can be considered classics, this section focuses on early classic authors who have had a lasting impact on the genre. Some even lived the history on which traditional Westerns are based. Their classic titles as well as others are noted throughout the chapter.

Adams, Andy. (1859–1935).

His *The Log of a Cowboy* (1903) is the classic and authentic story of a trail drive from the Mexican border to Montana.

Brand, Max. (1992–1944).

Pseudonym of Frederick Faust. Brand used thirteen (or more) pseudonyms and wrote 215 Westerns, publishing the first in 1919. His three top sellers (over two million copies) are *Destry Rides Again, Fightin' Fool,* and *Singing Guns.* Twenty-seven of his novels were made into motion pictures. A great many of his titles are currently in paperback, with all of the pseudonyms now appearing as Max Brand.

Burroughs, Edgar Rice. (1875–1950).

Better known for his Tarzan series and science fiction adventures. Two of his Westerns were reprinted in the Gregg Press Western Fiction series: *The War Chief* and *Apache Devil* (both serialized in 1927 and 1928 before publication in book form).

Capps, Benjamin. (1922–).

Several of his books remain in print.

Fergusson, Harvey. (1890–1971).

The native New Mexican was considered a true chronicler of the Spanish Southwest.

Fisher, Vardis. (1895–1968).

Fisher is the subject of *Tiger on the Road: The Life of Vardis Fisher,* a biography by Tim Woodward.

Garfield, Brian. (1939–).

Also known for his adventure novels.

Grey, Zane. (1872–1939).

Between 1903 and his death in 1939 he wrote eighty-nine books, including nonfiction. Over forty of his novels became motion pictures.

Gulick, Bill. (1916–).

Some consider his sense of humor to be his most important contribution to Western fiction.

Guthrie, A. B. (1901–1991).

His *Big Sky* is one of the top-selling Westerns of all time.

Harte, Bret. (1836–1902).

Immortalized the miners, gamblers, and good-hearted fancy ladies of the West of the 1860s in "The Luck of Roaring Camp" and "The Outcasts of Poker Flat."

Haycox, Ernest. (1899–1950).

Haycox is important as a touchstone in the criticism of the Western; his writings, in style and characterization, set standards that have influenced others writing in the genre.

Henry, Will. (1912–).

Also published as Clay Fisher.

Hough, Emerson. (1857–1923).

His *The Covered Wagon* (1922) set a pattern for the Oregon Trail Western.

Johnson, Dorothy M. (1905–1984).

Several of her stories were turned into films, including *A Man Called Horse* and *The Man Who Shot Liberty Valance*.

Kelton, Elmer. (1926–).

His *The Day the Cowboys Quit* (1971) and *The Time It Never Rained* (1973, reissued 1999) were named by the Western Writers of America as two of the "best Western novels of all time."

6

Knibbs, H. H. (1874–1934).

His *The Ridin' Kid from Powder River* (1919) is a classic boy-into-man Western.

L'Amour, Louis. (1908–1988).

When he died, sales of his 101 books, almost all Westerns, were nearing the 200 million mark. Forty-five of his novels were made into movies or television shows. In 1998 he had more than twice as many titles on lists of top fifty best-selling Westerns as any other author. "The Homer of the oaters."—*Time*.

LeMay, Alan. (1899–1964).

LeMay was popular in his time, but his racist depictions of Indians are now passé.

Mulford, Clarence E. (1883–1956).

His *Hopalong Cassidy* (1910) became immortal in a long-running series on the Bar-20 Ranch, appearing in novels, in motion pictures, and on television.

Olsen, Theodore V. (1932-1993)

His *Arrow in the Sun* (1969) was made into the movie *Soldier Blue*.

Raine, William MacLeod. (1871–1954).

He wrote about eighty-five Westerns, his first published in 1908, and they are still being reprinted in large print.

Rhodes, Eugene Manlove. (1869–1934).

"The Hired Man on Horseback" whose romantic Western heroes, frequently at odds with the law, were, as his first book affirmed, *Good Men and True* (1910). Most remember him for *Pasó por Aquí* (1926), with its tag line "We are all decent people." His typical humor is evoked by the compiler W. H. Hutchinson in *The Rhodes Reader: Stories of Virgins, Villains and Varmints* (University of Oklahoma Press, 1957).

Schaefer, Jack. (1907–1991).

His *Shane* (1949) is one of the top-selling Westerns and became a classic motion picture.

Short, Luke. (1908–1975).

In some fifty-seven novels, he covered most of the themes in the genre.

Twain, Mark. (1835–1910).

Twain brought welcome humor to the Western scene in "The Celebrated Jumping Frog of Calaveras County" (1867) and *Roughing It* (1872).

White, Stewart Edward. (1873–1946).

A prolific writer on the Western scene, White is chiefly remembered for *Arizona Nights* (1904), stories of the range, and a trilogy (1913–1915) gathered as *The Story of California.*

Wister, Owen. (1860–1938).

His *The Virginian,* on the best-seller list in 1902 and 1903 and never out of print, set the pattern for the popular cowboy Western, with a hero, a heroine (the schoolmarm), rustlers, a shoot-out at sundown, and other incidents. It gave the genre its classic line: "When you call me that, *smile!*"

Native Americans

The history of indigenous peoples is filled with trials and tribulations, particularly after white settlers arrived in North America. The indigenous characters in books and film have historically been portrayed in stereotypical terms, whether in the disparaging Tonto model or as the "noble savage." The best tales about Native peoples are those told with respect and understanding for their cultures. Many deal with the depredations of the invading culture and the conflict between the two groups. Also included here are titles that deal with Indian captives. Some of the older titles unfortunately evidence the stereotypes found in the early days of the genre.

Readers who enjoy stories about indigenous people may also find many of the titles listed in the "Prehistoric," and "Ancient Civilizations," sections of the historical fiction chapter (chapter 5) of interest.

Arnold, Elliott.

Blood Brother. 1947. ★

Source of the Western motion picture *Broken Arrow.*

Blakely, Mike.

Comanche Dawn. 1998.

Told from the Comanche point of view and set against the historical backdrop of French and Spanish foreign invasion, this well-researched book tells the story of how a courageous warrior named Horseback led the Comanche nation to separate from the Shoshone people.

Blevins, Win.

Stone Song: A Novel of the Life of Crazy Horse. 1995.

Boggs, Johnny.

🎗 *Spark on the Prairie: The Trial of the Kiowa Chiefs.* 2003. Winner of the Western Heritage Award.

Carter, Forrest.

Cry Geronimo. 1978. Also called *Watch for Me on the Mountain.*

Chiaventone, Frederick J.

🎗 *Moon of Bitter Cold.* 2002. Winner of the Western Heritage Award.

Coldsmith, Don.

<u>**The Spanish Bit Saga.**</u>

See the "Sagas" section of this chapter.

Comfort, Will L.

Apache. 1931. Reissued 1986. ★

Conley, Robert J.

Conley writes respectfully and sensitively.

The Actor. 1987.

Back to Malachi. 1987.

Border Line. 1993.

Crazy Snake. 1994.

Incident at Buffalo Crossing. 1998.

Killing Time. 1988.

Medicine War. 2001.

Mountain Windsong: A Novel of the Trail of Tears. 1992.

🏵 *Nickajack.* 1992. Winner of the Spur Award.

Sequoyah. 2002.

Strange Comapany. 1991. Reissued 2002. Winner of the Spur Award.

<u>**Real People series.**</u>

Follows the history of the Cherokee.

The Way of the Priests. 1992.

The Dark Way. 1993.

The White Path. 1993.

The Way South. 1994.

The Long Way Home. 1994.

🏵 *The Dark Island.* 1995. Winner of the Spur Award.

The War Trail North. 1997.

War Woman. 1997.

The Peace Chief. 1998.

Cherokee Dragon. 2000.

Spanish Jack. 2001.

Crawford, Max.

Lords of the Plain. 1985. Reissued 1997.

Fast, Howard.

The Last Frontier. 1941. Reissued 1997. ★

Garcia y Robertson, R.

American Woman. 1998.

Gear, Kathleen O'Neal.

This Widowed Land. 1993.

Glancy, Diane.

Pushing the Bear: A Novel of the Trail of Tears. 1996.

Haseloff, Cynthia.

★ *The Kiowa Verdict.* 1997. Winner of the Spur Award.

Man Without Medicine. 1996.

Henry, Will.

★ *From Where the Sun Now Stands.* 1959. Reissued 2000.

>The 1978 edition has an introduction written by Betty Rosenberg, the originator of *Genreflecting*. Winner of the Spur Award.

Jackson, Helen Hunt.

Ramona. 1884. Reissued 2005. ★

Jones, Douglas C.

★ *Gone the Dreams and Dancing.* 1984. Reissued 2003. Winner of the Spur Award.

La Farge, Oliver.

Laughing Boy. 1929. Reissued 2004. ★

L'Amour, Louis.

Hondo. 1953. Reissued 2004.

O'Brien, Dan.

★ *The Contract Surgeon.* 1999.

>The story of Crazy Horse, told from the viewpoint of an Army surgeon. Winner of the Western Heritage Award.

Patten, Lewis B.

Bones of the Buffalo. 1967. Reissued 2000.

Riefe, Barbara.

Mohawk Woman. 1996.

Schlesier, Karl H.

Josanie's War. 1998.

Smith, C. W.

Buffalo Nickel. 1989.

Stratham, Frances Patton.

Trail of Tears. 1993.

Thom, James Alexander.

Panther in the Sky. 1989.

>Fictionalized account of Chief Tecumseh.

Waldo, Anna Lee.

Sacajawea. 1984.

Welch, James.

Fools Crow. 1986.

>A young Blackfoot comes of age in a realistic portrayal of the Blackfeet in the nineteenth century and their ill-fated contact with the white culture. Written by an author who was Blackfoot and Gros Ventre.

Indian Captives

Popular since colonial times, these tales about individuals captured by Indians who are often adopted into the tribes and about those who search for them have a great appeal. The idea of living inside another culture shows readers a view from an angle that cannot be seen by those completely outside a specific culture or by those on the outside, looking in but able only to experience the culture as an outsider. A captive's view often provides a way of seeing the daily routines of a culture.

Black, Michelle.
An Uncommon Enemy. 2001.

Blake, Michael.
Dances with Wolves. 1988.

Blevins, Win.
Beauty for Ashes. 2004.

Boggs, Johnny D.
The Big Fifty. 2003.

Capps, Benjamin.
A Woman of the People. 1966. Reissued 1999. ★

Eidson, Tom.
The Last Ride. 1995. Reissued as *The Missing* in 2003.

Haseloff, Cynthia.
The Chains of Sarai Stone. 1998.
Changing Trains. 2001.
Satanta's Woman. 1998.

Horsley, Kate.
Crazy Woman. 1992.

Jones, Douglas C.
Season of Yellow Leaf. 1983.

Kelton, Elmer.
Badger Boy. 2001.
The Texas Rifles. 1960. Reissued 2004.

🎗 *Way of the Coyote.* 2001. Winner of the Spur Award.

LeMay, Alan.
The Unforgiven. 1957. Reissued 2000. 🎬 ★

Olsen, Theodore V.
Arrow in the Sun. 1969. ★

Overholser, Stephen.
Shadow Valley Rising. 2002.

Richter, Conrad.

> *The Light in the Forest.* 1953. Reissued 2004. ★ 📖 **YA**

Riefe, Barbara.

> *Desperate Crossing.* 1997.
>
> *The Woman Who Fell from the Sky.* 1994.

Robson, Lucia St. Clair.

> 🎗 *Ride the Wind: The Story of Cynthia Ann Parker and the Last Days of the Comanches.* 1982.
> Winner of the Spur Award.

Wallace, Melanie.

> *Blue Horse Dreaming.* 2003.

Mountain Men

The earliest non-native people to travel the West were the mountain men and trappers, who often took on Indian ways.

Blevins, Win.

> *Charbonneau: Man of Two Dreams.* 1975. ★
>
> *The Misadventures of Silk and Shakespeare.* 1985.
>
> **Rendezvous series.**
>
> > Six volumes are planned that tell the story of Sam Morgan's adventures in the fur trapping trade, starting in the early 1820s when he leaves his home in rural Pennsylvania to head to the Rocky Mountains.
> >
> > 🎗 *So Wild a Dream.* 2003. Winner of the Spur Award.
> >
> > *Beauty for Ashes.* 2004.
> >
> > *Dancing with the Golden Bear.* 2005.

Fergusson, Harvey.

> *Wolf Song.* 1927. Reissued 1981. ★ 🎬
>
> > Although Fergusson did not write the three books that turned into the Followers of the Sun Trilogy as a trilogy, they work well together. The other two titles in the series, *Blood of the Conquerors* (1921) and *In Those Days* (1929), do not deal with mountain men.

Fisher, Vardis.

> 🎗 *Mountain Man.* 1965. Reissued 2000. Winner of the Spur and Western Heritage Awards. ★
> 🎬 *Jeremiah Johnson*
>
> > Based on the true story of "Liver Eating" Johnson.

Guthrie, A. B. ★

> *The Big Sky.* 1947. Reissued 2002.
>
> *These Thousand Hills.* 1956. Reissued 1995.
>
> *The Way West.* 1949. Numerous reissues, most recently 1993.

Johnston, Terry C.

Titus Bass Mountain Man: Prequel series.

Dance on the Wind. 1996.
Buffalo Palace. 1996.
Crack in the Sky. 1997.

Titus Bass: Original trilogy.

Carry the Wind. 1982.
Border Lords. 1985.
One-Eyed Dream. 1988.

Titus Bass: Sequel trilogy.

Ride the Moon Down. 1998.
Death Rattle. 1999.
Wind Walker. 2001.

Johnstone, William W.

Mountain Man series.

The Last Mountain Man. 1984.
Return of the Mountain Man. 1986.
Trail of the Mountain Man. 1987.
Revenge of the Mountain Man. 1988.
Law of the Mountain Man. 1989.
Journey of the Mountain Man. 1988.
War of the Mountain Man. 1990.
Code of the Mountain Man. 1991.
Pursuit of the Mountain Man. 1991.
Courage of the Mountain Man. 1995.
Blood of the Mountain Man. 1996.
Fury of the Mountain Man. 1993.
Rage of the Mountain Man. 1994.
Cunning of the Mountain Man. 1994.
Power of the Mountain Man. 1995.
Spirit of the Mountain Man. 1996.
Ordeal of the Mountain Man. 1996.
Triumph of the Mountain Man. 1997.
Vengeance of the Mountain Man. 1997.
Honor of the Mountain Man. 1998.
Battle of the Mountain Man. 1998.
Pride of the Mountain Man. 1998.
Creed of the Mountain Man. 1999.
Guns of the Mountain Man. 1999.
Heart of the Mountain Man. 2000.
Justice of the Mountain Man. 2000.
Valor of the Mountain Man. 2001.
Warpath of the Mountain Man. 2002.

    Quest of the Mountain Man. 2003.

    Trek of the Mountain Man. 2002.

    Ambush of the Mountain Man. 2003.

    Wrath of the Mountain Man. 2004.

First Mountain Man.

    The First Mountain Man. 1991.

    Blood on the Divide. 1992.

    Absaroka Ambush. 1993.

    Forty Guns West. 1993.

    Cheyenne Challenge. 1995.

    Preacher and the Mountain Caesar. 1995.

    Blackfoot Messiah. 1996.

    Preacher. 2002.

    Preacher's Peace. 2003.

    Preacher's Justice. 2004.

    Preacher's Journey. 2005.

Sherman, Jory.

  The Medicine Horn. 1991. Winner of the Spur Award.

Wagons West and Early Settlement

The westward journey of the nineteenth century, fraught with perils and hazards, placed ordinary people in extraordinary circumstances that tested their grit and endurance. The long and arduous journey from the East was often undertaken by family groups, who faced disease, disaster, and disaffection.

Askew, Rilla.

  The Mercy Seat. 1997. Winner of the Western Heritage Award. 📖

Haycox, Ernest. ★

    The Adventurers. 1954. Reissued 1993.

    The Earthbreakers. 1952. Reissued 1993.

Hough, Emerson.

    The Covered Wagon. 1922. Reissued 2004. ★

Jones, Douglas C.

  Roman Hasford. 1986. Originally published as *Roman.* Winner of the Spur Award.

Lee, Wendi.

    The Overland Trail. 1996.

Riefe, Barbara.

    Against All Odds: The Lucy Scott Mitchum Story. 1997.

Taylor, Robert Lewis.

  The Travels of Jaimie McPheeters. 1958. Winner of the Pulitzer Prize. ★

Wheeler, Richard S.

> *Flint's Gift.* 1997.

>> A newspaperman in an Arizona frontier town.

Merchants and Teamsters

For the West to be opened up, goods and supplies had to be brought in. The enterprising individuals who journeyed West to make a profit were generally a colorful lot, and their broad experience with various individuals in the West offers readers a unique perspective on the times.

Haycox, Ernest.

> *Canyon Passage.* 1945. Reissued 1992. ★ 🎬

>> Mule-train freight line in the Pacific Northwest.

Kelton, Elmer.

> *Bitter Trail.* 1962. Reissued 2002. ★

Wheeler, Richard S.

> *Sierra: A Novel of the California Gold Rush.* 1996.

Mines and Mining

The lure of gold and silver brought many unlikely individuals together and brought out the best and the worst in them. The legends of lost mines and mother lodes drew many individuals to seek their fortunes.

Brand, Max.

> *The Lone Rider.* 1930. Reissued 2005. ★

>> After con-man Billy Newlands weds an heiress fraudulently, he ends up working in a mine.

Champlin, Tim.

> *By Flare of Northern Lights.* 2001.
> *Wayfaring Strangers.* 2000.

Cushman, Dan.

> *In Alaska with Shipwreck Kelly.* 1996. Reissued 2004.

Henry, Will.

> *MacKenna's Gold.* 1963. 🎬

Hodgson, Ken.

> *Fool's Gold.* 2003.
> *God's Pocket.* 2004.

>> As the Gold Rush draws to a close, Milo Goodman buys a saloon in Jarbridge, Nevada.

L'Amour, Louis. ★

> *The Empty Land.* 1969. Reissued in 1999.
> *Milo Talon.* 1981. Reissued 2002.

Nye, Nelson.

> *Death Valley Slim.* 1963. Reissued 2004. ★
> *A Lost Mine Named Salvation.* 1968. Reissued 2003. ★
> *The White Chip.* 1996.
>> A quest for Arizona's fabled Lost Dutchman mine.

Thoene, Brock, and Bodie Thoene.

> *Riders of the Silver Rim.* 1990. (Christian).

Trevanian.

> *Incident at Twenty Mile.* 1998.

Wheeler, Richard S.

> 🎗 *Fool's Coach.* 1989. Winner of the Spur Award.

Law and Lawmen

The frontier was a haven for the lawless, so tales of those who oppose them, trying to impose order on the chaos, take on a great significance.

Bean, Fred, and J. M. Thompson.

> A trilogy featuring gentleman gunner and portraitist Leo LeMat.
>
>> *Ghost Riders.* 2000.
>> *Tombstone.* 2001.
>> *Hell on the Border.* 2002.

Bennett, Dwight.

> *Legend in the Dust.* 1989.

Brandvold, Peter.

> **Ben Stillman series.**
>> Even though Ben Stillman is no longer a lawman, he jumps in to help his new neighbors on the Hi Line of the Montana Territory in this Western mystery series.
>>
>> *Once a Marshall.* 1998.
>> *Once More with a .44.* 2000.
>> *Once a Lawman.* 2000.
>> *Once Hell Freezes Over.* 2001.
>> *Once a Renegade.* 2002.
>> *Once Upon a Dead Man.* 2003.
>> *Once Late with a .38.* 2004.

Brooks, Bill.

> *Leaving Cheyenne.* 1999.
> *Return to No Man's Land.* 2000.

Champlin, Tim.
> *The Tombstone Conspiracy.* 1999.

Clark, Walter Van Tilburg.
> *The Ox-Bow Incident.* 1940. ★
>> A classic tale about mob violence on the American frontier.

Conley, Robert J.
> *The Actor.* 1999.
> **Barjack series.**
>> *Barjack.* 2000.
>> *Broke Loose.* 2000.
>> *The Gunfighter.* 2001.

Cotton, Ralph.
> **Big Iron series.**
>> Featuring Arizona ranger Sam Burrack.
>>
>> *Montana Red.* 1998.
>> *Badlands.* 1998.
>> *Justice.* 1999.
>> *Border Dogs.* 1999.
>> *Misery Express.* 2000.
>> *Blood Rock.* 2001.
>> *Vengeance Is a Bullet.* 2003.
>> *Sabre's Edge.* 2003.

Estleman, Loren D.
> Estleman also writes in the crime genre.
> **Page Murdoch series.**
>> Deputy U.S. Marshall in 1880s Montana territory.
>>
>> *The High Rocks.* 1979.
>> *Stamping Ground.* 1980.
>> *Murdock's Law.* 1982.
>> *The Stranglers.* 1984.
>> *City of Widows.* 1995.
>> *White Desert.* 2000.
>> *Port Hazard.* 2004.

Hackenberry, Charles.
> 🎖 *Friends.* 1993. Winner of the Spur Award.

Hall, Oakley.
> *Warlock.* 1958. Reissued 1996. ★ 🎬

Jones, Douglas C.
> *A Spider for Loco Shoat.* 1997.

Leonard, Elmore.

> Leonard also writes in the crime genre.
>
> *The Law at Randado.* 1954. ★
> *Valdez Is Coming.* 1970. ▦
>> Mexican town constable.

Nesbitt, John D.

> *Red Wind Crossing.* 2003.
>> Clevis always knew that women were trouble, so when Helen caught his eye he knew he was in for it, especially with the deceit and murder in her past.

Paine, Lauran.

> *Cache Cañon.* 1999.
>> When all kinds of crimes start happening around Rock City, Colorado, sheriff Charley Bent suspects three strangers who had recently ridden into town.

Parker, Robert B.

> *Appaloosa.* 2005.

Portis, Charles.

> *True Grit.* 1969. Reissued 2003. ★ ▦

Bad Men and Good

The color of the Stetson does not tell it all. Bad men may have a hidden core of goodness, while those on the side of the law may be evil through and through. Vengeance is a common theme.

Brand, Max.

> *Destry Rides Again.* 1930. Not like the motion picture that took the title. ★ ▦

Carter, Forrest.

> *Gone to Texas.* 1975. Originally published as *The Rebel Outlaw: Josey Wales.* 1973. ▦ *The Outlaw Josey Wales*
> *Josey Wales: Two Westerns.* 1989. Omnibus edition of *Gone to Texas* and *The Vengeance Trail of Josey Wales.*

Champlin, Tim.

> *White Lights Roar.* 2003.
>> When a shipment of rifles disappears, James Whitlaw is blamed, so to find them he teams up with Tommy Gasheen, a volunteer in the Irish Republican Brotherhood, who has his own reasons for wanting the rifles.

Compton, Ralph.

> *Whiskey River.* 1999.

Conley, Robert J.

> *Fugitive's Trail.* 2000.

Doctorow, E. L.

Welcome to Hard Times. 1960.

A shabby Western town in the Dakota territory is summarily destroyed by the bad man from Bodie.

Eidson, Tom.

St. Agnes' Stand. 1994.

Estleman, Loren D.

Bloody Season. 1987.

Tombstone, Arizona, and the OK Corral.

Gun Man. 1985. Reissued 2001.

Grey, Zane.

Lone Star Ranger. 1914. Reissued 2004. ★

Haycox, Ernest.

"Stage to Lordsburg." 1937. ★

The classic short-story Western, source for the original motion picture *Stagecoach.* Can be found in *A Century of Great Western Stories,* edited by John Jakes (2000).

Hirt, Douglas.

A Good Town. 2001.

Matheson, Richard.

🏵 *Journal of the Gun Years.* 1991. Winner of the Spur Award.

Rhodes, Eugene Manlove.

Pasó por Aquí. 1926. ★

Schaefer, Jack.

Shane. 1949. Reissued 2001. ★ 🎬

Svee, Gary D.

🏵 *Sanctuary.* 1990. Reissued 2003. Winner of the Spur Award.

Swarthout, Glendon.

🏵 *The Shootist.* 1975. Winner of the Spur Award. ★ 🎬

Trevanian.

Incident at Twenty Mile. 1998.

Army in the West

The Indian wars and the presence of ex-soldiers in the aftermath of the Civil War brought an often lawless military presence to the West.

Blake, Michael.

Marching to Valhalla. 1996.

An imagined journal of George Armstrong Custer's last seven weeks.

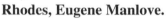

Boggs, Johnny D.

> *Lonely Trumpet.* 2002.

>> When Lieutenant Flipper, the first African American to complete officer training at West Point, is court-martialed for embezzlement in Texas in 1881, Army attorney Captain Merritt Barber, who perceives a conspiracy, will stand against all odds for what is right.

Haycox, Ernest.

> *Border Trumpet.* 1939. ★

Hogan, Ray.

> *Soldier in Buckskin.* 1997.

> *Bugles in the Afternoon.* 1944. Reissued 2003.

O'Brien, Dan.

>  *The Contract Surgeon.* 1999.

>> The story of a friendship between Crazy Horse and surgeon Dr. Valentine McGillicuddy. Winner of the Western Heritage Award.

Short, Luke.

> *Ambush.* 1949. ★

Texas and Mexico

The border country and the American settlement of Mexican lands provide an arena for heroics.

Brown, Sam.

> *The Long Season.* 1987.

Camp, Will.

> *Blood of Texas.* 1996. Winner of the Spur Award.

Chappell, Henry.

> *Blood Kin.* 2004.

>> Isaac Webb joined the Texas Rangers when he was sixteen and the Alamo had just been lost. As more and more settlers arrive in Texas, he attempts to make peace with the Comanche raiders.

Crook, Elizabeth.

> *Promised Lands: A Novel of the Texas Rebellion.* 1995.

Harrigan, Stephen.

> *The Gates of the Alamo.* 2000. Winner of the Spur and Western Heritage Awards.

Kelton, Elmer.

> *After the Bugles.* 1967. Reissued 2004.

>> Young Josh Buckalew lost everything in the Texas war for independence. Now he and friend Ramon Hernandez travel the land, besieged by bandits and criminals, looking for a new start.

Lea, Tom. ★

The Brave Bulls. 1949. Reissued 2002.

The Wonderful Country. 1952. Reissued 2002.

> Martin Brady, seeing his father gunned down in a border town, exacts vengeance and heads south across the border, where he lives for fourteen years until he re-enters Texas in the 1880s.

Long, Jeff.

Empire of Bones. 1993.

Sanders, Leonard.

Star of Empire. 1992.

Wilkinson, D. Marion.

Not Between Brothers: An Epic Novel of Texas. 1996.

Hired Man on Horseback

Cowboys are the quintessential understated Western heroes, but if they had spent their real lives like the cowboys in fiction do, ranching could never have survived.

Adams, Andy.

The Log of a Cowboy. 1903. Reissued 2000. ★

> The classic fictional account of sixteen-year-old Andy Adams, who travels from Texas to Montana, living the cowboy life. Rich in authentic historical detail, with plenty of adventure as well.

Blakely, Mike.

Shortgrass Song. 1994.

> Caleb Holcomb, itinerant musician and cowboy, roams the West in the late 1800s.

Too Long at the Dance. 1996.

> A cowboy troubadour from Texas experiences the range wars and land grabs of the West. A sequel to *Shortgrass Song.*

Borland, Hal.

The Seventh Winter. 1959. ★

Brown, Sam.

The Big Lonely. 1992.
Devil's Rim. 1998.

Grey, Zane.

The Drift Fence. 1933. ★

Kelton, Elmer.

🎗 *The Day the Cowboys Quit.* 1971. ★

> The Canadian River cowboy strike of 1883. Winner of the Spur and Western Heritage Awards.

<u>Hewey Calloway series.</u>

Hewey wants life to continue the way it always has been, but the encroachments of people, fences, and cars are crimping Hewey's cowboy style. The first title is set in the late nineteenth century; the second two titles are set in the first decade of the twentieth century.

Six Bits a Day. 2005. Prequel to the other titles in the series.

🎗 *The Good Old Boys.* 1985. Winner of the Western Heritage Award. 🎞

The Smiling Country. 1998.

Mulford, Clarence E.

Hopalong Cassidy. 1910. ★

Schaefer, Jack.

Monte Walsh. 1963. 🎞

Monte and Chet faced blizzards, outlaws, and rustlers in the ten years they rode the range before hiring on at the Slash Y, but times are changing.

Wister, Owen.

The Virginian. 1902. Reissued 2002. ★ 🎞 **TVS**

Cattle Drives

Driving cattle to a railhead provides the opportunity for adventures involving problems caused by both nature (stampedes, lightning, floods) and humans (rustlers, outlaws, Indians).

Capps, Benjamin.

🎗 *The Trail to Ogallala.* 1964. ★

Bill Scott gets a second chance at being a trail boss on a drive that pushes 3,000 head of cattle from southern Texas to Ogallala, Nebraska. Winner of the Spur Award.

Flynn, Robert.

North to Yesterday. 1967. Winner of the Spur and Western Heritage Awards. ★

Grey, Zane. ★

Trail Driver. 1936. Reissued 1998.

Wilderness Trek. 1944.

An Australian cattle drive.

Kelton, Elmer.

🎗 *The Far Canyon.* 1994. Winner of the Spur Award.

McMurtry, Larry.

🎗 *Lonesome Dove.* 1985. Winner of the Pulitzer Prize and the Spur Award. 📖 **TVM**

Two former Texas Rangers turned horse rustlers, Augustus McCrae and W. F. Call, set out on a cattle drive from Texas to Montana. Still a Western best seller in 2005.

Cattle Kingdoms

Although railroad barons dominated the country in the West, individuals tried to build their own fiefdoms based on huge ranges full of cattle.

Fergusson, Harvey.

Grant of Kingdom. 1950. ★

> The history of a huge Spanish land grant in northern New Mexico as settlers come in, changing the world that former mountain man Jean Ballard found on the grant after he married into the Coronel family and became "el Patron."

Richter, Conrad.

The Sea of Grass. 1936. Reissued 1992. ★

Sherman, Jory.

Grass Kingdom. 1994.

> First in the <u>Barrons of Texas series</u>. Other titles are listed in the "Sagas" section of this chapter.

Range Wars

The battle for free range and to keep the West unfenced provides a scenario rife with possibilities.

Clarke, Richard.

The Homesteaders. 1986. Also published under the author's real name, Lauran Paine.

Grey, Zane.

To the Last Man. 1922. Reissued 2000.

Haycox, Ernest.

Free Grass. 1928.

Hoffman, Lee.

West of Cheyenne. 1969. ★

Johnstone, William W.

Battle of the Mountain Man. 1998.

Vories, Eugene.

Saddle a Whirlwind. 1990.

Sheepmen

Cattlemen were not the only ones who moved West looking for wide-open land, leading to bitter conflicts between those who raised sheep and those who raised cattle.

Doig, Ivan.

Dancing at the Rascal Fair. 1987.

> In 1890 Angus McCaskill, leaves Scotland for Montana, where he homesteads a claim in the Two Medicine River area. This is the first title in Doig's well respected series of Montana books.

Grey, Zane. ★

The Shepherd of Guadaloupe. 1930.

To the Last Man. 1922. Reissued 2000.

Cattlemen versus sheepmen in Arizona.

Laxalt, Robert.

Time of the Rabies. 2000.

In 1920 a coyote attacks an ewe in broad daylight, exposing the fact that rabies is running rampant in the ranching lands outside Carson City. Laxault has written several books and stories that feature the Basque sheep ranchers of Nevada.

Railroads

Ribbons of steel opened up the West to new waves of settlers and opportunists.

Blake, Michael.

The Holy Road. 2001.

In this sequel to *Dances with Wolves* the white man's "holy road," the railroad, wreaks havoc on Comanche life.

Champlin, Tim.

Iron Trail. 1987. Reissued in 2001.

Clamp, Cathy L., and C. T. Adams.

Road to Riches: The Great Railroad Race to Aspen. 2003.

In 1887 the men of the Denver & Rio Grande Railroad raced against those of the Colorado Midland to put in the track that would open up the lucrative route to Aspen.

Grey, Zane.

U. P. Trail. 1918. Reissued in 2002. ★

Johnstone, William W.

Quest of the Mountain Man. 2003.

Spearman, Frank.

Whispering Smith. 1906. ★

Colorado presented some of the most difficult terrain for building a useable railroad route, and when a gang of renegades disrupts the process even more, Smith is sent in to solve the problems.

Buffalo Runners

In just a few years, abundant herds of millions of buffalo were decimated almost to the point of extinction. The best of those engaged in this short-lived but lucrative trade were called runners instead of hunters, as they had to keep on the move because their prey was always roaming.

Estleman, Loren D.

The Hider. 1978. ★

> The last buffalo hunter hunts down the last wild buffalo on the frontier.

Grove, Fred. ★

 The Buffalo Runners. 1968.

> Keith Hayden, seeking adventure, finds all kinds among those who were slaughtering the immense herds of buffalo that darkened the plains in 1876. Winner of the Spur and Western Heritage Awards.

Buffalo Spring. 1967. Reissued in 2002.

Kelton, Elmer.

 Buffalo Wagons. 1958. Reissued 1997. Winner of the Spur Award.

 Slaughter. 1992. ★

> After Nigel Smithwick, British gambler, is thrown from a train in the middle of the desert, he is rescued by Jeff lane, a former Confederate soldier, and the two team up to hunt buffalo and face the Cheyenne. Winner of the Spur Award.

Unromanticized

These Westerns reveal the ugly underbelly of the West, with the patina of a glamorized frontier rubbed away to give a grim, uncompromising view of the area and times.

Dexter, Pete.

Deadwood. 1986. Reissued 2005.

> Shocking and gritty, this tale tells of Wild Bill Hickock, Calamity Jane, and others in the dangerous town of Deadwood. 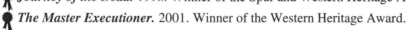 *Wild Bill* **TVS**

Estleman, Loren D.

 Journey of the Dead. 1998. Winner of the Spur and Western Heritage Awards.

 The Master Executioner. 2001. Winner of the Western Heritage Award.

Matthews, Greg.

 Heart of the Country. 1985. Winner of the Western Heritage Award.

McCarthy, Cormac.

Blood Meridian. 1985. 📖

> Desperate and depraved bounty hunters search for Indian scalps on the Texas–Mexico border.

Swarthout, Glendon.

 The Homesman. 1988. Winner of the Spur and Western Heritage Awards.

Picaresque

In this type of story a roguish protagonist, clever and often amoral, is depicted in an episodic series of incidents. Frequently these stories are humorous and satirical.

Berger, Thomas.

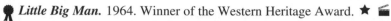 *Little Big Man.* 1964. Winner of the Western Heritage Award. ★ 🎬

> A picaresque tale of a Jack Crabbe, a settler's child raised by the Cheyenne, who experiences all the major events in the history of the West and runs across all the major personalities, including Custer, Wyatt Earp, and Wild Bill Hickock.

The Return of Little Big Man. 1999.

Blevins, Win.

The Rock Child. 1998.

Combs, Harry.

Brules. 1994.

> Gritty tale of mountain man, Indian fighter, and outlaw Cat Brules, by an octogenarian first novelist.

Culp, John H.

The Bright Feathers. 1965. ★

Dallas, Sandra.

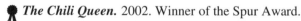 *The Chili Queen.* 2002. Winner of the Spur Award.

> Addie French, the madam at the Chili Queen whorehouse in 1860s New Mexico, takes in mail order bride Emma Roby, who has been abandoned by the man she was to marry. Emma and Addie join forces with bank robber Ned Partner to rob the local bank.

Udall, Brady.

🎗 *The Miracle Life of Edgar Mint.* 2001. Winner of the Spur Award.

Vanderhaeghe, Guy.

The Last Crossing. 2004.

> When a young, well-to-do Englishman goes missing, his father sends his two brothers into the wilds of Indian country to see if they can determine what happened to him and to rescue him if he still lives. They are accompanied on their quest by a diverse group of individuals.

Comedy and Parody

Those who have read extensively in the genre and recognize the unique conventions and traditional devices will derive the most enjoyment from and find the most humor in the following titles.

Brand, Max.

The Gentle Desperado. 1985. ★

Evans, Max.

> *The Rounders.* 1965. Reissued 1983. ★

McNab, Tom.

> *The Fast Men.* 1986.

Pronzini, Bill.

> *The Last Days of Horse-Shy Halloran.* 1987.

Recknor, Ellen.

> 🎗 *Prophet Annie.* 1999. Winner of the Spur Award.

Ross, Ann B.

> *The Pilgrimage.* 1987.

Coming of Age

Traditionally in this genre, coming of age could be described as "boy becomes man," but now protagonists of both genders are experiencing the trials and travails of the journey from childhood to adulthood on a harsh frontier. This is a popular theme in several genres, including science fiction, historical fiction, Christian fiction, fantasy, and mainstream fiction. Readers who like this theme may also enjoy many of the titles written for young adults.

Blakely, Mike.

> *Comanche Dawn.* 1998.
> 🎗 *Summer of Pearls.* 2000.
>> The Great Caddo Lake Pearl Rush of 1874. Winner of the Spur Award.

Blevins, Win.

> *The Misadventures of Silk and Shakespeare.* 1985.

Conley, Robert J.

> 🎗 *The Dark Island.* 1995.
>> Squani, half Indian, half Spanish, confronts his identity. This is part of Conley's <u>Real People series</u>, annotated in the "Native Americans" section of this chapter. Winner of the Spur Award.

Estleman, Loren D.

> *Sudden Country.* 1991. Reissued 2000.

Kelton, Elmer.

> *Pumpkin Rollers.* 1996.

L'Amour, Louis. ★

> *Chancy.* 1968. Reissued 1997.
> 🎗 *Down the Long Hills.* 1968. Reissued 1993. Winner of the Spur Award.

Lansdale, Joe R.

> *The Magic Wagon.* 1986. Reissued 2001.
>
> > When Buster Fogg's family is wiped out by a Texas tornado, he finds refuge with a traveling medicine show run by Billy Bob Daniels, who claims to be Wild Bill Hickock's illegitimate son.

Laxalt, Robert.

> *Dust Devils.* 1997.

Matthews, Greg.

> *The Further Adventures of Huckleberry Finn.* 1983.

McMurtry, Larry.

> *Horseman Pass By.* 1961. Reissued 1992. 🎬 *Hud.*

Reilly, Shauna.

> *Freedom in My Soul.* 1998.

Celebrity Characters

The names of legendary Western personages continue to evoke the spirit of the Wild West.

Alter, Judy.

> *Sundance, Butch and Me.* 2002.
>
> > Etta Place, fleeing her abusive father, ends up in a San Antonio brothel, where she meets the Sundance Kid and joins him and Butch Cassidy on their adventures.

Boggs, Johnny D.

> *East of the Border.* 2004.
>
> > Wild Bill Hickock.
>
> *Law of the Land: A Guns and Gavel Novel.* 2004.
>
> > Billy the Kid.

Brooks, Bill.

> *The Stone Garden : The Epic Life of Billy the Kid.* 2001.

Brown, Dee.

> *Wave High the Banner.* 1999.
>
> > Davy Crockett.

Burns, Walter Noble. ★

> *The Robin Hood of El Dorado.* 1932. Reissued 1999. 🎬
>
> > Joaquin Murieta.
>
> *The Saga of Billy the Kid.* 1926. Reissued 1999.
>
> *Tombstone: An Iliad of the Southwest.* 1927. Reissued 1999. ★
>
> > Wyatt Earp.

Camp, Deborah.
> *Belle Star: A Novel of the Old West.* 1987.

Cole, Judd.
> *The Kinkaid County War.* 1999.
>> Wild Bill Hickock.

Cooke, John Byrne.

> *South of the Border.* 1989.
>> Butch Cassidy and Charlie Siringo; 1919 movie set.

Eickhoff, Randy Lee.
> 🏵 *And Not To Yield: A Novel of the Life and Times of Wild Bill Hickok.* 2004. Winner of the Western Heritage Award.

Eickhoff, Randy Lee, and Leonard C. Lewis.
> *Bowie.* 1998.
>> The legend of Big Jim Bowie.

Estleman, Loren D.
> 🏵 *Aces and Eights.* 1981.
>> Wild Bill Hickock. Winner of the Spur Award.

> *Billy Gashade.* 1997.
>> A sixteen-year-old fleeing the New York draft riots of 1863 becomes a piano player in the West and meets the famous and infamous, including George Armstrong Custer, Billy the Kid, Wild Bill Hickock, Oscar Wilde, and others, over the next several decades.

> *This Old Bill.* 1984.
>> Buffalo Bill Cody.

Fackler, Elizabeth.
> *Billy the Kid: The Legend of El Chivato.* 1995.

Garfield, Brian.
> *Manifest Destiny.* 1989.
>> Teddy Roosevelt in the Badlands.

Irving, Clifford.
> *Tom Mix and Pancho Villa.* 1982.

Kesey, Ken, and Ken Babbs.
> *Last Go Round: A Dime Western.* 1994.
>> John Muir makes an appearance.

McMurtry, Larry.
> *Anything for Billy.* 1988.
>> Billy the Kid.

🎗 *Buffalo Girls.* 1990.

    Calamity Jane. Winner of the Western Heritage Award.

Parker, Robert B.

Gunman's Rhapsody. 2001.

    Wyatt Earp.

Swarthout, Glendon.

The Old Colts. 1985.

    Bat Masterson and Wyatt Earp, now old, get together in 1916.

Wheeler, Richard S.

🎗 *Masterson.* 1999. Winner of the Spur Award.

Zollinger, Norman.

Meridian: A Novel of Kit Carson's West. 1997.

African Americans in the West

Up until recently, cowboys have been most often portrayed as white, but in truth there were many who were Hispanic and black. African American soldiers were seen frequently enough that Native Americans created a name for them, "buffalo soldiers."

Brackett, Leigh.

🎗 *Follow the Free Wind.* 1963. Reissued 2002. Winner of the Spur Award. ★

Burchardt, Bill.

Black Marshal. 1981.

Durham, David Anthony.

Gabriel's Story. 2001.

    Fleeing the disruptions of Reconstruction, fifteen-year-old Gabriel and his mother head west to Kansas to join his stepfather, Solomon, but Gabriel is unhappy and heads to Texas with an ill-fated group.

Evans, Max.

Faraway Blue. 1999.

Fackler, Elizabeth.

Breaking Even. 1998.

    African American sisters in the Southwest.

Goodman, Charles R.

Black Cheyenne. 1993.

Bound by Blood. 1993.

Buffalo Soldier. 1982.

Henry, Will.

One More River to Cross. 1967. ★

Hotchkiss, Bill.

The Medicine Calf: A Novel. 1981.

Black mountain man adopted by Indians.

Jones, Robert F.

Deadville. 1998.

Keaton, Rina.

Revenge of June Daley. 1996.

Kelton, Elmer. ★

Wagontongue. 1972. Reissued 1998.

The Wolf and the Buffalo. 1980.

King, Hiram.

Broken Ranks. 2001.

Dark Trail. 1998.

High Prairie. 1997.

Kluge, P. F.

Season for War. 1984.

African American soldiers go from fighting the Apache in Arizona to the Philippines to fight in the Spanish–American War.

Myers, Walter Dean.

The Righteous Revenge of Artemis Bonner. 1992. **YA**

This humorous, picaresque novel is enjoyed by adults, even though it was written for young teens.

Proctor, George W.

Walks Without a Soul. 1990.

Nate Wagoner hunts the Comanches who killed his baby and kidnapped the rest of his family.

Willard, Tom.

Buffalo Soldiers. 1996.

Former slave Augustus Sharps rises through the Army ranks in the West following the Civil War. This is the first book in the Black Sabre Chronicles, a series about a family of African American military men.

Mormons

All well-defined groups who headed west are subjects of some Westerns. The large group of controversial families traveling with Brigham Young, the extremes of polygamy some practiced, and the activities of the notorious Danites make this group a favorite element in Westerns. Often they are portrayed in a very unflattering light.

Card, Orson Scott.

A Woman of Destiny. 1984.

> Also published as *Saints*. An English family having difficult times converts to Mormonism, and the daughter, Dinah, lives the history of the early life of the church, from a secret marriage to Joseph Smith to the journey west and subsequent polygamous marriage to Brigham Young.

Freeman, Judith.

Red Water. 2002.

> The Mountain Meadows Massacre of 1857, told from the viewpoints of three of the wives of John D. Lee, who was the only individual to be prosecuted and executed for the massacre. Freeman has won awards from the Association for Mormon Letters for her contemporary novels.

Grey, Zane.

Riders of the Purple Sage. 1912. Reissued 2005. ★

> A very negative look at Mormons.

Johnston, Terry C.

Cry of the Hawk. 1993.

> A Confederate soldier who served in the Union Army in the West returns home to discover his family kidnapped by Mormons, and sets out on a violent quest to find them.

Wells, Marian.

The Wedding Dress. 1982. Reissued 1994.

> Christian fiction that aims to expose the wrongness when a young woman discovers that she is not her husband's only wife.

Wormser, Richard.

Battalion of Saints. 1961. ★

> The Mormon Battalion marching to the war with Mexico.

Singular Women

In early Westerns, women played lesser roles than horses and were often depicted stereotypically or in unflattering terms. Fortunately this has changed in recent years, with strong, independent women playing prominent roles.

Alter, Judy.

Cherokee Rose: A Novel of America's First Cowgirl. 1996.

Jessie. 1995.

> A novel about Jessie Benton Freemont.

Libbie. 1994.

> Elizabeth Bacon Custer's fictionalized story.

Mattie. 1988. Winner of the Spur Award.

Bonner, Cindy.

<u>**McDade Cycle series.**</u>

Lily. 1992.

When fifteen-year-old Lily Delony falls for eighteen-year-old Marion Beatty, the youngest brother of a family notorious around McDade, Texas, she doesn't expect to learn that he didn't just look like a bad boy but really was one.

Looking After Lily. 1994.

Haywood Beatty, Marion's older brother, looks after Lily while Marion serves time in prison.

The Passion of Dellie O'Barr. 1996.

The story of Lily's younger sister.

Carroll, Lenore.

One Hundred Girl's Mother. 1998.

A female missionary works with Chinese women in San Francisco.

Charbonneau, Eileen.

Rachel Lemoyne. 1998.

Downing, Sybil.

Fire in the Hole. 1996.

The Ludlow Massacre.

Fackler, Elizabeth.

Badlands. 1996.

Breaking Even. 1998.

African-American sisters in the Southwest.

Texas Lily. 1997.

Ferber, Edna.

Cimarron. 1930. 📖 🎬

Grey, Zane.

Woman of the Frontier. 2000. Published previously in a cut version as *30,000 on the Hoof* (1940).

Kirkpatrick, Jane.

🎗 *A Sweetness to the Soul.* 1995. Winner of the Western Heritage Award.

Lehrer, Kate.

🎗 *Out of Eden.* 1995. Winner of the Western Heritage Award.

Levy, JoAnn.

Daughter of Joy: A Novel of Gold Rush California. 1998.

A young Chinese woman in Gold Rush California.

Recknor, Ellen.

Prophet Annie. **2000.**

> Annie goes to the Arizona Territory to marry a rich old man, who drops dead right after the wedding, leaving her no money and his two elderly relatives. Jonas, even though he is dead, is not gone, and with his information from the beyond, Annie becomes a celebrity as a medium.

Richter, Conrad.

Tacey Cromwell. 1942. ★

Smiley, Jane.

🏵 *The All-True Travels and Adventures of Lidie Newton: A Novel.* 1998. 📖

> The story of a strong young woman who moves with her new husband to the Kansas Territory in the mid-1800s. Winner of the Spur Award.

Stratham, Frances Patton.

Trail of Tears. 1993.

> Features a Cherokee schoolteacher.

Whitson, Stephanie Grace.

Walks the Fire. 1995.

> Has a Christian emphasis.

Williams, Jeanne.

Home Mountain. 1990.

Williamson, Penelope.

Heart of the West. 1995.
The Outsider. 1996.

Romance

Wide-open landscapes, towering mountain ranges, and vivid sunsets make the West a natural setting for romantic fiction. The strong individuals who settled the area also make for engaging romantic leads. The Western setting and heroes have become extremely popular in romance; the sheer abundance of cowboys in romance publishing makes it appear that all American men are cowboys (or at least the good-looking, romantic ones). Readers who like Western romances should also check the romance chapter.

Aldrich, Bess Streeter.

Spring Came on Forever. 1935. ★

Bittner, Rosanne.

> She has more than fifty titles, published as romance. Several are listed in the romance chapter (chapter 9).

Dailey, Janet.

<u>Calder saga.</u>

> Titles are listed in the "Historical Romance, Saga" section of chapter 9.

Durham, Marilyn.

The Man Who Loved Cat Dancing. 1972. ★

Grey, Zane.

The Light of Western Stars. 1942. ★

Kelton, Elmer.

Smiling Country. 1998.

Oke, Janette.

Oke's Christian tales of prairie romance are sometimes read as Westerns, as they deal with life on the western frontier of Canada. Recently reissued titles are listed in the Christian fiction chapter (chapter 13).

Young Adult Westerns

The following Westerns may have been written for teens, but adults enjoy them, too.

Burks, Brian.

Soldier Boy. 1997.

A teenage bare-knuckles boxer enlists in the Army of the West to get away from his promoter after he fails to throw a fight.

Carbone, Elisa.

Last Dance on Holladay Street. 2005.

When her foster parents die, thirteen-year-old Eva Wilkins goes to Denver to find the mother who gave her up at birth, and ends up living in a brothel, where her mother is a prostitute.

Hardeman, Ric.

Sunshine Rider: The First Vegetarian Western. 1998.

Seventeen-year-old Wylie Jackson lands a job as an assistant cook on a cattle drive, taking along his friend's pet cattalo, Roselle.

Hite, Sid.

Stick and Whittle. 2000.

A Civil War veteran and a sixteen-year-old, both named Melvin, find adventure as they travel together from Texas to Kansas.

Ives, David.

Scrib. 2005.

Billy Christmas, known as Scrip, makes his living in the old West by writing letters home for folks who are illiterate, but when someone threatens him he takes his idiosyncratic spelling and looks for other work.

Karr, Kathleen.

The Great Turkey Walk. 1998.

Simon Green, a fifteen-year-old, figures on making his fortune by driving a thousand head of turkeys from Missouri to Denver.

Oh, Those Harper Girls! Or Young and Dangerous. 1992.

Myers, Walter Dean.
The Righteous Revenge of Artemis Bonner. 1992.

Patrick, Denise Lewis.
The Adventures of Midnight Son. 1997.
The Longest Ride. 1999.

Spooner, Michael.
Daniel's Walk. 2001.

> In 1856, fourteen-year-old Daniel LeBlanc joins a westward bound wagon train, walks more than a thousand miles, and suffers intense hardships on the Oregon Trail, all in a quest to find his father.

Stone, Gerald Eugene Nathan.
Rockhand Lizzie. 1999.

> A rollicking picaresque novel set in Arkansas and the Indian Territory begins in 1901 when Lizzie is orphaned shortly before her seventh birthday. Taking up residence with a series of folks she has adventure after adventure.

The West Lives On

The qualities that make Western heroes popular are still inherent in the children of the West today. The following list demonstrates some of the cultural diversity of the region and the changes that have occurred in the twentieth century. Many of the titles listed here are considered mainstream novels, rather than Westerns, and many are literary.

Abbey, Edward.
The Brave Cowboy. 1956.
🎗 *Fire on the Mountain.* 1962. Winner of the Western Heritage Award.
Hayduke Lives! 1989.
The Monkey Wrench Gang. 1975.

Alexie, Sherman.
The Lone Ranger and Tonto Fistfight in Heaven. 1993. 🎬 *Smoke Signals*
Reservation Blues. 1995.
> Native American.

Anaya, Rudolfo.
Albuquerque. 1992.
Bless Me, Ultima. 1972. Reissued 2003.
> Hispanic coming-of-age story set in New Mexico.

Bradford, Richard.
Red Sky at Morning. 1968. Reissued 1999.

> During World War II, a young man from Mobile, Alabama, comes of age in the mountains of northern New Mexico.

So Far from Heaven. 1973.

A Texas executive is taken in by the Tafoya family in a warm, humorous, and very authentic slice-of-life tale about New Mexico in the 1970s.

Dorris, Michael.

A Yellow Raft in Blue Water. 1987. 📖

Native American coming-of-age story set in contemporary times. **6**

Earling, Debra Magpie.

🎗 ***Perma Red.*** 2002.

Reservation life in Perma, Montana, with Louise White Elk, Baptiste Yellow Knife, Charlie Kicking Woman, and others. Winner of the Spur and Willa Awards.

Evans, Max.

Bluefeather Fellini. 1993.

🎗 ***Bluefeather Fellini in the Sacred Realm.*** 1994. Winner of the Western Heritage Award.

The Hi-Lo Country. 1961. Reissued 1998. ★ 🎬

Two ranchers in love with the same woman after returning to New Mexico following World War II. The story is rich in cowboy tradition and the Westerners' love of the land.

Freeman, Judith.

Chinchilla Farm. 1989. Reissued 2003.

A Desert of Pure Meaning. 1996.

🎗 ***Set for Life.*** 1991. Winner of the Western Heritage Award.

Hillerman, Tony.

Many mystery titles featuring Jim Chee and Joe Leaphorn. Native American (Check crime chapter [chapter 7] for lists.)

Hyson, Dick T.

***The Calling.* 1998.**

Native American.

Kelton, Elmer.

🎗 ***The Time It Never Rained.*** 1973. Winner of the Spur and Western Heritage Awards. ★

Ranchers and farmers in Texas during the 1950s have weather worries.

King, Thomas.

Green Grass, Running Water. 1993.

Native American.

Medicine River. 1990.

Kingsolver, Barbara.

Animal Dreams. 1990.

Bean Trees. 1988.

🎗 ***Pigs in Heaven.*** 1993. Winner of the Western Heritage Award.

McCarthy, Cormac.

The Border trilogy.

🎗 *All the Pretty Horses.* 1992. Winner of the Western Heritage and National Book Awards.
The Crossing. 1994.
Cities of the Plain. 1998.

McMurtry, Larry.

The Last Picture Show. 1966. Reissued 1999. 🎬
Texasville. 1988. Reissued 1999. 🎬

Meyers, Kent.

The Work of Wolves. 2004.

A gifted horse trainer, a Lakota working toward a college scholarship, and a German exchange student combine forces to rescue three abused horses.

Owens, Louis.

Bone Game. 1994.
Dark River. 1999.
Nightland. 1996.
The Sharpest Sight. 1992.

Ozeki, Ruth.

All Over Creation. 2003.

Yumi, a Japanese American former hippie, returns home to the large natural seed farm in Idaho where her elderly parents can no longer take care of themselves. It has also become the home of Seeds of Resistance, an anti-biotech group, that is working against a bio-engineered potato. Winner of the Willa Award.

Parks, Mary Anderson.

The Circle Leads Home. 1998.

Native American.

Power, Susan.

The Grass Dancer. 1994.

Native American.

Proulx, Annie.

Bad Dirt: Wyoming Stories 2. 2004. 📖
Close Range: Wyoming Stories. 2000. 📖
That Old Ace in the Hole. 2003. 📖

Bob Dollar leaves Denver to scout for land for the Global Pork Rind corporation in the Texas panhandle.

Salisbury, Ralph.

The Last Rattlesnake Throw. 1998.

Two-Rivers, E. Donald.

Survivor's Medicine. 1998.

Wheeler, Richard S.

The Buffalo Commons. 1998.

Eccentric Variations

The 1990s saw the Western setting finding its way into horror and fantasy as well as mystery and romance. Even though this trend has not continued, the books in this category remain popular with readers and are readily available in many public libraries.

 6

Estleman, Loren D.

🎗 *Journey of the Dead.* 1998. Winner of the Western Heritage Award.

Pat Garret, haunted by the ghost of Billy the Kid, seeks out a Mexican alchemist who is more than 100 years old.

Foster, Alan Dean.

Cyber Way. 1990.

A futuristic, Hillerman-type mystery.

Hays, Clark, and Kathleen McFall.

The Cowboy and the Vampire: A Very Unusual Romance. 1999.

A contemporary Wyoming cowboy must fight for the woman he loves, who just may be the next queen of the vampires.

L'Amour, Louis.

The Haunted Mesa. 1987. ★

A breach in the universe opens parallel worlds.

Murphy, Pat.

Nadya. 1996.

A young female werewolf goes west.

Snyder, Midori.

The Flight of Michael McBride. 1994.

Pursued by evil denizens of Faerie, a railroad baron's son heads west to the end of the tracks.

Sagas

Western sagas tend to take place over several generations and span a huge variety of Western themes.

Bittner, Rosanne.

<u>Savage Destiny series.</u>

Seven volumes filled with romance take Abbie from a young woman in 1845 to a time when her grandson engages in a forbidden affair with a rancher's daughter. Through the Civil War, the coming of the railroads, and conflicts with homesteaders, Abbie loves Lone Eagle. Titles are listed in the romance chapter (chapter 9).

Coldsmith, Don.

The Spanish Bit Saga.

Published in hardcover and reprinted in paperback, it relates the story of the Elk-Dog People of the plains. Listed here in series order.

Trail of the Spanish Bit. 1980.
The Elk-Dog Heritage. 1982. Reissued 2004.
Follow the Wind. 1983.
Buffalo Medicine. 1981. Reissued 2004.
Man of the Shadows. 1983.
Daughter of the Eagle. 1984.
Moon of Thunder. 1985.
The Sacred Hills. 1985.
Pale Star. 1986.
River of Swans. 1986.
Return to the River. 1987.
The Medicine Knife. 1988.
The Flower in the Mountains. 1988.
Trail from Taos. 1989.
Song of the Rock. 1989.
Fort De Chastaigne. 1990.
Quest for the White Bull. 1990.
Return of the Spanish. 1990.
Bride of the Morning Star. 1991.
Walks in the Sun. 1992.
Thunderstick. 1993.
Track of the Bear. 1994.
Child of the Dead. 1995.
Bearer of the Pipe. 1995.
Medicine Hat. 1998.
The Lost Band. 2000.
The Raven Mocker. 2001.
Pipestone Quest. 2004.

Cooke, John Byrne.

🎗 *The Snowblind Moon.* 1984. Winner of the Spur Award.

Doig, Ivan.

Two-Rivers Trilogy.

Dancing at the Rascal Fair. 1987.
🎗 *English Creek.* 1984. Winner of the Western Heritage Award.
Ride with Me, Mariah Montana. 1990.

Modern Montana Trilogy.

Bucking the Sun. 1996.
🎗 *Prairie Nocturne.* 2003. Winner of the Spur Award.
Mountain Time. 1999.

L'Amour, Louis.

Sackett Family series. ★

Seventeen novels; several titles continue to be best-selling Westerns. The series started with *The Daybreakers* in 1959, and unfortunately L'Amour died before writing the seven or eight titles that would have completed the series. L'Amour also wrote a guide to the series titled *The Sackett Companion: The Facts Behind the Fiction* (Bantam, 1988).

McCord, John S.

The Baynes Clan. Reissued in 2002 and 2003 in large print.

Montana Horseman. 1990.

Texas Comebacker. 1991.

Wyoming Giant. 1992.

California Eagles. 1995.

Nevada Tough. 1996.

Kansas Gambler. 1997.

McMurtry, Larry.

Lonesome Dove saga.

Listed in chronological series, not publication, order.

Dead Man's Walk. 1995.

Comanche Moon. 1997.

Lonesome Dove. 1985.

The Streets of Laredo. 1993.

The Berrybender Narratives.

Sin Killer. 2002.

The Wandering Hill. 2003.

By Sorrow's River. 2003.

Folly and Glory. 2004.

Sherman, Jory.

The Barrons series.

Grass Kingdom. 1994.

The Barrons of Texas. 1997.

The Barron Range. 1998.

The Barron Brand. 2000.

The Barron War. 2002.

The Barron Honor. 2005.

Snelling, Lauraine.

Red River of the North series.

Stegner, Wallace.

🎗 *Angle of Repose.* 1971. Winner of the Pulitzer Prize. 📖

Thoene, Brock, and Bodie Thoene.

> Saga of the Sierras.
>> Titles are listed in the Christian fiction chapter (chapter 13).

Zollinger, Norman.

> New Mexico Saga.
>> *Corey Lane.* 1981.
>>
>> ✹ *Rage in Chupadera.* 1991. Winner of the Spur Award.
>>
>> *Not of War Only.* 1994.

Series

One of the curiosities about Western series is that two very divergent styles appear together in them. Many of the inspirational, evangelical, or Christian Westerns appear as series, as do the "adult" Westerns featuring explicit violence and sex.

Bly, Stephen.

> Stuart Brannon series. (Christian).
>> Titles are listed in the Christian chapter (chapter 13).

Combs, Harry.

> *Brules.* 1992.
>> Picaresque, gritty tale of mountain man, Indian fighter, and outlaw Cat Brules, by an octogenarian first novelist.
>
> *The Scout.* 1995.
>> Sequel to the best-selling *Brules.* A third title, *The Legend of the Painted Horse* (1996), although a story about Steven Cartwright (who appeared in the first two novels), is not a Western.

Compton, Ralph.

> Trail Drive series.
>> *Goodnight Trail.* 1992.
>>
>> *Western Trail.* 1992.
>>
>> *Chisholm Trail.* 1993.
>>
>> *Bandera Trail.* 1993.
>>
>> *California Trail.* 1994.
>>
>> *Shawnee Trail.* 1994.
>>
>> *Virginia City Trail.* 1994.
>>
>> *Dodge City Trail.* 1995.
>>
>> The series has been resumed by Dusty Richards, but Ralph Compton's name is still prominent on the covers.
>>
>> *The Abilene Trail: A Ralph Compton Novel.* 2003.
>> *Trail to Fort Smith: A Ralph Compton Novel.* 2004.

Estleman, Loren D.

Page Murdock series.

"A lawless lawman."

The High Rocks. 1979.
Stamping Ground. 1980.
Murdock's Law. 1982.
The Stranglers. 1984.
City of Windows. 1994.
White Desert. 2000.
Port Hazard. 2004.

Evans, Tabor.

Longarm series. (adult). Number 314 was published in 2004.

Fackler, Elizabeth.

Seth Strummer series.

Blood Kin. 1991.
Backtrail. 1993.
Road from Betrayal. 1994.
Badlands. 1996.
Breaking Even. 1998.

Hart, Matthew S.

Cody's Law series.

Gunmetal Justice. 1991.
Die Lonesome. 1991.
Border Showdown. 1991.
Bounty Man. 1992.
Mano a Mano. 1992.
Renegade Trail. 1992.
End of the Line. 1992.
Eagle Pass. 1993.
Prisoners. 1993.
A Gallows Waiting. 1993.
Red Moon's Raid. 1994.
Comanche Code. 1995.

Lacy, Al.

Angel of Mercy series. (Christian).
Battles of Destiny series. (Christian).
Fort Bridger series. (Christian).
Journey of the Stranger series. (Christian).

Lacy, Al, and Joanna Lacy.

Hannah of Fort Bridger series. (Christian).
Mail Order Brides series. (Christian).

Logan, Jake.
> <u>Slocum series.</u> Number 312 was published in 2005. (Adult).

Nelson, Lee.
> <u>Storm Testament series.</u> (Christian).
>> Christian emphasis.

Sharpe, Jon.
> <u>Trailsman series.</u> (adult).
>> Number 279 was published in 2005.

Thompson, David.
> <u>Wilderness series.</u> (adult).
>> Number 45 was published in 2005.

Various Authors.
> <u>Rivers West series.</u>
>> Various Western authors contributed to the series. While they were given numbers, they don't have to be read in sequential order. In fact, Books in Motion, which is publishing the audio versions, numbers them differently than Bantam Books, which originally published them as paperback originals. They are listed here in alphabetical order.
>>
>> *The American River,* by Gary McCarthy. 1992.
>> *The Arkansas River,* by Jory Sherman. 1991.
>> *The Brazos,* by Jory Sherman. 1999.
>> *The Cimarron River,* by Gary McCarthy. 1999.
>> *The Colorado,* by Gary McCarthy. 1990.
>> *The Columbia,* by Jory Sherman.
>> *The Gila River,* by Gary McCarthy. 1996.
>> *The High Missouri,* by Win Blevins. 1994.
>> *The Humboldt River,* by Gary McCarthy. 1996.
>> *The Pecos River,* by Frederic Bean. 1995.
>> *The Powder River,* by Win Blevins. 1990.
>> *The Red River,* by Frederic Bean. 1997.
>> *The Rio Grande*, by Jory Sherman. 1994.
>> *The Russian River,* by Gary McCarthy. 1991.
>> *The Smoky Hill,* by Don Coldsmith. 1989.
>> *The Snake River,* by Win Blevins. 1992.
>> *The South Platte,* by Jory Sherman. 1998.
>> *The Two Medicine River,* by Richard S. Wheeler. 1993.
>> *The Yellowstone,* by Win Blevins. 1988.

Short Stories

Short stories are a good way for readers to sample the writings of various authors and find those they most enjoy. For many years the Western Writers of America released an anthology, and many of these volumes still remain on library shelves.

Brown, Bill. *Reading the West: An Anthology of Dime Westerns*. Bedford Books, 1997.

Estleman, Loren, ed. *American West: Twenty New Stories from the Western Writers of America*. St. Martin's Press, 2001.

Evans, Max, and Candy Moulton, eds. *Hot Biscuits: Eighteen Stories by Women and Men of the Ranching West*. University of New Mexico Press, c2002.

Gorman, Ed, ed. *The Fatal Frontier*. Carroll & Graf, 1997.
    Western stories by crime writers.

———. *Stagecoach*. Berkley, 2003.
    Includes stories by Louis L'Amour, Loren Estleman, Don Coldsmith, Richard Wheeler, Robert Conley, Judy Alter, Robert J. Randisi, and Ed Gorman.

Gorman, Ed, and Martin H. Greenberg, eds. *The Best of the American West: Outstanding Frontier Fiction*. Berkley, 1998.

Greenberg, Martin H., ed. *Great Stories of the American West*. Jove, 1996.

———. *Great Stories of the American West II*. Berkley, 1997.

Jakes, John, and Martin H. Greenberg, eds. *New Trails: Twenty-Three Original Stories of the West from Western Writers of America*. Bantam, 1994.

Kittredge, William, ed. *The Portable Western Reader*. Penguin USA, 1997.

McMurtry, Larry, ed. *Still Wild: Short Fiction of the American West 1950 to the Present*. Simon & Schuster, 2000.

Pronzini, Bill, and Martin H. Greenberg, eds. *Best of the West: Stories That Inspired Classic Western Films*. New American Library, 1986.

———. *Christmas out West*. Doubleday, 1990.

———. *The Western Hall of Fame: An Anthology of Classic Western Stories Selected by the Western Writers of America*. Morrow, 1984.
    These seventeen stories do warrant the "Hall of Fame" label. Includes Haycox's "Stage to Lordsburg" and two classic novellas, Schaefer's *Stubby Pringle's Christmas* and Rhodes's *Pasó por Aquí*.

Randisi, Robert J., ed. *Boot Hill*. Forge, 2002.
    Fifteen new stories.

Stone, Ted, ed. *100 Years of Cowboy Stories*. Red Deer College Press, 1995.

Tuska, Jon, ed. *The American West in Fiction*. Mentor/NAL, 1982.
An interpretive grouping of authors: "The East Goes West" (Mark Twain, Bret Harte, Stephen Crane, Frederic Remington, Owen Wister); "Where West Was West" (Dorothy M. Johnson, Willa Cather, John G. Neihardt, Eugene Manlove Rhodes, Ernest Haycox); "The West of the Storytellers" (Zane Grey, Max Brand, Louis L'Amour, James Warner Bellah, Luke Short); and "The West in Revision" (Elmer Kelton, Will Henry, Benjamin Capps, Walter Van Tilburg Clark, Max Evans). There are bibliographies or suggested further readings, including fiction in three groupings: "Formulary Westerns" (eighteen authors), "Romantic Historical Reconstructions" (sixteen authors), and "Historical Reconstruction" (eighteen authors).

———. *Shadow of the Lariat*. Carroll & Graf, 1995.

———. *The Untamed West*. Dorchester, 2005.
Three short novels: *Black Sheep* by Max Brand, *Cañon Walls* by Zane Grey, and *Showdown on the Hogback* by Louis L'Amour.

———. *The Western Story: A Chronological Treasury*. University of Nebraska Press, 1997.

Tuska, Jon, and Vicki Piekarski, eds. *The Morrow Anthology of Great Western Short Stories*. William Morrow, 1997.

Walker, Dale L., ed. *The Western Hall of Fame Anthology*. Berkley, 1997.
A dozen stories by authors selected by the Western Writers of America.

———. *Westward: A Fictional History of the American West*: *28 Original Stories Celebrating the 50th Anniversary of the Western Writers of America*. Forge, 2003.

Work, James C., ed. *Gunfight! Thirteen Western Stories*. University of Nebraska Press, 1996.

Novella Anthology Series

Tuska, Jon, ed.

Stories of the Golden West.
Five Star Westerns is releasing anthologies that consist of three novellas that up until now have been considered too long for short story anthologies and too short to be published alone. Many of them are by classic Western authors. The sixth volume in the series was published in 2005.

Bibliographies and Encyclopedias

Barton, Wayne. *What Western Do I Read Next?*: *A Reader's Guide to Recent Western Fiction*. Gale, 1998.

Drew, Bernard A. *Western Series and Sequels*. Garland, 1993.
Lists 700 works that have one or more sequels. Includes frontier fiction.

Tuska, Jon, and Vicki Piekarski, eds. *Encyclopedia of Frontier and Western Fiction*. McGraw-Hill, 1983.
More than 300 authors are discussed.

Vinson, James, and D. L. Kirkpatrick, eds. *Twentieth Century Western Writers*. Preface by C. L. Sonnichsen. London: Macmillan, 1982.
A brief biography, bibliography, and critical essay for each of 310 authors.

History and Criticism

Allmendinger, Blake. *Ten Most Wanted: The New Western Literature*. Routledge Kegan Paul, 1998.

Emmert, Scott. *Loaded Fictions: Social Critique in the Twentieth-Century Western*. University of Idaho Press, 1997.

Erisman, Fred, and Richard W. Etulain, eds. *Fifty Western Writers*. Greenwood, 1982.

Tompkins, Jane P. *West of Everything: The Inner Life of Westerns*. Oxford University Press, 1992.

Yates, Norris W. *Gender and Genre: An Introduction to Women Writers of Formula Westerns, 1900–1950*. University of New Mexico Press, 1995.

Organizations

Western Writers of America (http://www.westernwriters.org/). The Western Writers of America has a membership of writers of Western fact and Westerns (fiction). It publishes (since 1953) a monthly journal, *The Roundup*, which includes book reviews and is available for subscription by libraries. At its annual convention, Spur Awards are given in several categories, and the Golden Saddleman Award is given for an "outstanding contribution to the history and legend of the West."

Women Writing the West (http://www.womenwritingthewest.org). This nonprofit organization promotes the women's West through a newsletter, an annual conference, a catalog, and by taking their information on the road to booksellers' conferences.

Awards

The major awards for Westerns are awarded by the Western Writers of America, Women Writing the West, and the Cowboy Hall of Fame.

Spur Awards. The Western Writers of America established the Spur Award in 1953, making it the oldest annual genre fiction award still in existence. When it started, it was awarded in the divisions of novel, historical novel, juvenile, short story, and reviewer. In 1998 the categories were Best Western Novel (under 90,000 words), Best Novel of the West (over 90,000 words), Original Western Paperback, Nonfiction Historical, Nonfiction Contemporary, Nonfiction Biography, Juvenile Fiction, Juvenile Nonfiction, Short Fiction, Short Nonfiction, Story Teller Award (for best illustrated children's literature), Medicine Pipe Bearer Award (Best First Novel), Documentary Screenplay, and Drama Screenplay. At one time there were categories for best TV script and best short subject. The broad categories demonstrate the interest of fans of Westerns in all facets of the Western experience. A list of all winners since the inception of the awards is found at http://www.westernwriters.org/spur_award_history.htm.

Western Heritage Award or the Wrangler Award. The National Cowboy Hall of Fame selects specific works in several different media categories that their judges feel "helped preserve the spirit of the West." The award is called the Western Heritage Award or the Wrangler Award. The books that have won the award for "Outstanding Novel" are listed at http://www.nationalcowboymuseum.org/e_awar_winn.html.

Willa Award. The Willa Award is awarded annually by Women Writing the West to honor women's stories set in the west. For a full list of winners and finalists, see: http://www. womenwritingthewest.org/past_willa.html.

Publishers

Many of the large-type publishers are issuing reprints in both hardcover and paperback. Five Star is publishing approximately thirty-four hardcover traditional Westerns each year, including originals, previously unpublished works by classic authors, and works that originally appeared only in serialized form. Forge is publishing hardcover and paperback originals. Several university presses are also publishing in this area, including University of Nebraska, publisher of *The Collected Stories of Max Brand,* which includes his short fiction in other genres as well. Some university presses, including the University of Oklahoma, are reprinting classic Westerns. Gunsmoke Large Print Westerns publishes three Westerns per month. Thorndike has a large-print Western series, as does Linsford. Roundup and Sagebrush also publish Westerns in large print. Severn House often reprints paperback originals as hardcovers. Leisure publishes sixty paperback Western titles per year, originals and reprints, all set before 1900. A number of religious publishers, including Bethany House, Harvest, Word, Crossways, Multnomah, and Council Press, publish Westerns. Many of the Westerns found on the mass-market racks are reprints.

Online Resources

The National Cowboy Hall of Fame and Western Heritage Center, http://www. cowboyhalloffame.org (accessed February 8, 2005).

The Salt Lake County Library System, http://www.slco.lib.ut.us/spur.htm (accessed February 8, 2005), lists all the Spur Awards from the Western Writers of America.

The Western Writers of America, http://www.westernwriters.org (accessed February 8, 2005).

Women Writing the West, http://www.womenwritingthewest.com (accessed February 8, 2005).

D's Western Picks

Blevins, Win.

So Wild A Dream. **2003.** (mountain men)

> On the day following his eighteenth birthday and the second anniversary of his father's death, Sam Morgan is shocked by the betrothal of his sweetheart to his brother. Seeking solace in the woods he calls Eden, he meets a Delaware named Hannibal MacKye, who advises him to "follow his wild hair." Determining that there is no longer anything for him in Morgantown, Sam heads out on the river, armed with the rifle he inherited from his father, to find adventure. The adventures are endless for a young man in 1822, first on the river, then in the West, where he becomes a mountain man. Along the way he makes friends, fights enemies, and falls in love. The meticulous research based on actual adventures of early nineteenth-century mountain men facing wildfires, capture by the Pawnee, and a 700-hundred-mile solitary trek makes Sam's adventures very real.

Charbonneau, Eileen.

Rachel Lemoyne. **1992.** (singular women).

Rachel, a mixed blood Choctaw, takes a shipment of corn to Ireland during the Great Potato Famine and marries Rare to save his life. Along with her husband and her brother, Atoka, who keeps the traditional ways, they make their way to Oregon in the late 1840s, facing danger and adventure every step of the way.

Dallas, Sandra.

The Chili Queen. **2002.** (singular women)

 6

Addie French, not the name she started life with, has been through much in her life, starting out as an abused child, then becoming a con artist, then a whore; now she owns The Chili Queen parlor house in Nalgitas, New Mexico. What she really wants to do is own a chili restaurant in San Antonio. Her mysterious cook and housekeeper, a former slave named Welcome, may have turned up out of the blue a month ago but has proven to be of more worth than the whores who work at The Chili Queen. The handsome and gallant Ned Partner, a notorious bank robber, frequently makes The Chili Queen home. Emma Roby, a rejected mail order bride, claims to believe The Chili Queen is a respectable ladies' boarding house and moves in, taking Addie's downstairs room. As the four characters come to know each other they fall into planning a bank robbery, in part to avenge an insult to Addie. The 1880s are wild and wooly in this caper within a caper within a con.

Kelton, Elmer.

Texas Rifles. **1960.** (Indian captives).

Sam Houston Cloud, a member of the Texas Rifles discovers one of the young Indian mothers encountered on a raid is really a white woman. She is wrenched from her baby and forced to go back to white civilization, where she cannot adapt because she is worried about her sickly baby, left behind. Sam fights his attraction to her, but when she is rejected by her family he comes through for her, deserting his unit to take her back to the Indians.

Myers, Walter Dean.

The Righteous Revenge of Artemis Bonner. **1992.** (African Americans in the West, young adult).

Young Artemis leaves New York for Tombstone to avenge the death of his uncle, Ugly Ned Bonner. A hilarious quest through the West from Tombstone to Mexico, then to the Alaska Territory and back again in pursuit of the villains, Catfish Grimes and Lucy Featherdip.

Chapter 7

Crime

Essay

Erin A. Smith

By some estimates, crime fiction currently constitutes fully a third of the fiction published in English worldwide.[1] Mysteries were the first mass-market category of fiction in the United States, their audience having been delivered to book publishers already constituted from readers of popular detective magazines in the 1920s and 1930s. The publishing industry has traditionally divided mystery fiction into subgenres: the "cozy," hard-boiled stories, police procedurals, and (sometimes) spy thrillers. Spy thrillers are discussed in this volume under "Spy/Espionage" in chapter 8. The larger catchall category of suspense includes a variety of books that involve crime but do not necessarily have a detective or focus specifically on the solving of the crime. The psychology of the perpetrator is often more important than his or/her identity. Crime/caper stories (as well as some true crime narratives) involve criminals as protagonists, describing their adventurous exploits and the criminal underworld they inhabit.

The "Cozy" or Classical Mystery

The "cozy" or classical mystery is perhaps best exemplified by the works of Agatha Christie and Dorothy Sayers. These stories frequently involve a close, intimate community—a family, a small town, a university. The character of the detective is central to the story's unfolding, and to the book's appeal to readers. In these stories, the detective uses close observation and rational deduction to explain how a crime was committed, identifies the single individual responsible for it, and ultimately restores social order by expelling that individual from the community.

These stories allow readers to engage latent feelings of hostility and violence generated by the repressiveness of families or other institutions. However, they also offer reassurance that we live in a just, rational society in which evil is the result of single individuals rather than corrupt social institutions.[2] These stories are also intellectual puzzles, and some readers enjoy the deductive challenge of solving the crime before the detective does.

The father of the classical detective story is Edgar Allan Poe, whose ratiocinative detective, C. Auguste Dupin, used his powers of deduction to solve three crimes in the 1840s— "Murders in the Rue Morgue" (1841), "The Mystery of Marie-Rogêt" (1842–1843), and "The Purloined Letter" (1844). Arthur Conan Doyle perfected the form in the late nineteenth century with a series of short stories and novellas about Sherlock Holmes, beginning with A Study in Scarlet (1887).

The "Golden Age" of Detective Fiction

The "golden age" of detective fiction refers to the flowering of these classical mysteries (especially in Britain) between the two world wars. British writers such as Agatha Christie, Dorothy Sayers, Josephine Tey, Margery Allingham, Gladys Mitchell, and the Americans John Dickson Carr and S. S. Van Dine created one puzzle mystery after another designed to test the wits of attentive readers. Many of these writers were members of the London Detection Club, whose 1928 "oath" included such guidelines for authors as not withholding clues from readers; avoiding reliance on coincidence, intuition, and hunches rather than reason; and minimizing use of suspect devices like evil twins, conspiracies, and lunatics. The American writing team of Frederick Dannay and Manfred B. Lee, better known as Ellery Queen, left their mark on the era through countless anthologies, reprints, and a magazine that offered prizes to readers who could solve a fictional crime before the solution was presented.

Hard-Boiled Crime Stories

Writers of hard-boiled crime stories such as Dashiell Hammett, Raymond Chandler, and the early Erle Stanley Gardner defined their kind of fiction against the London Detection Club prototype. They saw their fiction as a manly, American, "realistic" reaction against the silly, aristocratic English-country-house fiction written by the likes of Christie and Sayers. Hard-boiled fiction emerged as a subgenre in the 1920s and 1930s in cheap, pulp magazines like Black Mask, Detective Story, and Detective Fiction Weekly, which targeted a mostly working-class, white, male audience. Hard-boiled heroes rely as much on brawn and tough talk as their brains, and the worlds they inhabit are often overrun by systemic crime. These tough-guy detective stories addressed the de-skilling of manual work; the rise of consumer culture; the changing role of women as workers; and the links between class, language, and culture.[3]

Although the faith in a benevolent social order of the classical mysteries is absent, hard-boiled stories often represent the power of a single, exceptional individual to maintain a code of integrity in the face of overwhelming corruption. Pulp magazines folded in the early 1950s, victims of competition from comic books, television, and mass-market paperbacks, but hard-boiled private eyes still appear in the work of Ross Macdonald, Robert B. Parker, John D. MacDonald, Walter Mosley, Sara Paretsky, Sue Grafton, and others.

Although tough guy detectives first appeared in pulp magazines in the 1920s, their literary ancestors can be traced back to the ubiquitous dime novels that circulated in the United States from the 1840s into the early twentieth century. Dime novels were cheap, mass-produced sensation fiction sold to the urban working classes for between 5 and 10 cents. Although they included all kinds of stories of action, adventure, and romance, many of the best known series characters were detectives—Beadle & Adams' Old Sleuth and Street & Smith's Nick Carter, to name a few.

Police Procedurals

The early history of crime stories includes a number of police detectives —Eugène François Vidocq (1827–1828), Émile Gaboriau's M. Lecoq (1868), Georges Simenon's Inspector Maigret (1931)—but police procedurals achieved prominence only in the years following World War II. These stories focused less on the efforts of a single, heroic detective (whether tough or brainy) and more on the plodding, painstaking work of a team of interdependent criminal investigators. Many of the best-known writers—Hillary Waugh, John Creasey, Ed McBain—began writing in the 1950s, although Joseph Wambaugh and others carried the thriving genre into the 1980s and 1990s. Police procedurals have been immensely popular on television, including such programs as *Hill Street Blues, NYPD Blue,* and *Prime Suspect*. These stories demonstrate a faith in the power of patient, well-orchestrated, scientific investigation by loyal members of a team to achieve truth and justice.

Increasing Diversity in Crime Fiction

Since the 1980s, the detectives appearing in crime fiction have become increasingly diverse. Readers and scholars increasingly parse the field by classifying fiction according to the detective's gender, race, religion, sexuality, and regional/national characteristics, diminishing the importance of distinctions between amateurs and professionals, nosy spinsters, cops, and hard-boiled dicks.

For example, in the early 1980s, there were approximately forty professional women private eyes in print. By 1995, there were roughly 400.[4] P. D. James's *An Unsuitable Job for a Woman* (1972) was a feminist touchstone. A small group of female hard-boiled detectives appeared in the late 1970s and early 1980s in the works of Marcia Muller, Sara Paretsky, and Sue Grafton. Paretsky was a founding member of Sisters in Crime, an international organization of authors, publishers, librarians, and fans of women's detective fiction dedicated to reading and advocating for women's mysteries. The organization was, in part, a pressure group opposing pay discrimination by publishers and inequitable reviewing practices to which women authors had been subject. Paretsky was named the 1986 *Ms.* Woman of the Year for her work with the organization.[5]

Lesbian and gay detectives are more prominent as well. Since the 1970s, feminist presses such as Naiad, Seal, and Virago have offered an increasing number of books about lesbian investigators by such writers as Barbara Wilson, Eve Zaremba,

Katherine Forrest, Mary Wings, and Claire McNab. These avowedly feminist presses are driven not only by profits but by a desire for social change. Although the first gay detective appeared in 1966, writers like Joseph Hansen, Michael Nava, Julian Barnes, and Edward Phillips have left their mark on the field since the 1980s. Although over two-thirds of gay and lesbian detective novels are still bought in gay or specialty bookshops, there is some evidence of crossover reading. For example, a number of lesbian writers have begun publishing with mainstream houses or have switched over from small, feminist presses to commercial publishing houses.[6]

Detectives from a variety of ethnic and racial backgrounds crowd the contemporary scene. Stephen Soitos traces the development of African American detectives in *The Blues Detective*.[7] The first African American detective novel was Rudolph Fisher's *The Conjure Man Dies* (1932). Chester Himes wrote about two hard-boiled Harlem cops, Grave Digger Jones and Coffin Ed Johnson, in *When Cotton Comes to Harlem* (1965), *Blind Man with a Pistol* (1969), and eight other novels. Walter Mosley's ongoing series about Easy Rawlins, a working-class Los Angeles detective, began with *Devil in a Blue Dress* (1990), and Barbara Neely's ironically named housekeeper/detective, Blanche White, explores the crimes of black and white society in her series that began with *Blanche on the Lam* (1992).

Perhaps the best-known writer of Native American detective stories is Tony Hillerman, whose Sergeant Joe Leaphorn first appeared in *The Blessing Way* (1970), and whose younger investigator, Jim Chee, first appeared in *People of Darkness* (1980). Although criticized for romanticizing the Navajo, Hillerman is well known for the dense anthropological grounding of his novels in the cultures of the Southwest. Other authors writing about Native American detectives include Linda Hogan, Louis Owens, Jean Hager, and Dana Stabenow.

Although smaller bodies of work, there are crime stories centered in Hispanic communities, Asian American communities, and Jewish neighborhoods. Michael Nava, Marcia Muller, and Alex Abella write detective stories featuring Latino/a detectives. Asian American detective stories have come a long way since Earl Derr Biggers created the first Charlie Chan mystery in 1925. S. J. Rozan writes about detective Lydia Chin, and Chang-Rae Lee uses Henry Park, a Korean American surveillance agent, as the focus of his celebrated 1995 novel, *Native Speaker*. Harry Kemelman explores Jewish identity through a mystery-solving rabbi. Faye Kellerman's serious crime fiction explores the role of orthodox religion in contemporary identity; Kinky Friedman's not-so-serious crime fiction uses Jewish wit.

In the last thirty years, movements for civil rights, women's liberation, and gay liberation have focused attention on the crimes perpetuated against classes of people lacking access to social power. In part, crime stories featuring detectives who are ethnic, female, or gay allow readers to examine questions of social justice in a safe, fictional space, and to think about the ways narratives of identity are constructed. These stories ask not only what equitable treatment of different people might look like, but also just what being black or Jewish, male or female, straight or gay, working-class or professional might mean to an individual, personally and socially.

Crime/Caper Stories

Crime/caper stories focus on crime and the world of criminals rather than the process of detecting who committed the crime and their reasons for doing so. The criminal protagonists of these stories run the gamut from established, wealthy career criminals to petty thieves, burglars, rogues, and drifters who are pushed by circumstances into a life of crime. Although the brains or brawn of detectives are the central concern of detective stories, the cunning of these criminals takes center stage in crime capers. These books include James M. Cain's *The Postman Always Rings Twice* (1934), Michael Crichton's *The Great Train Robbery* (1975), Elmore Leonard's *Get Shorty* (1990), Patricia Highsmith's *The Talented Mr. Ripley* (1966), and such comic adventures as Ken Follett's *Paper Money* (1977) and Mark Childress's *Crazy in Alabama* (1993).

  7

Legal Thrillers

Legal thrillers are a subgenre that has been extraordinarily successful in both print and the movies. Legal thrillers are crime stories featuring a lawyer, law student, or judge as the main character. Although they include some detective work, typically these courtroom dramas involve the ingenuity of the attorney in extricating himself or/herself from a setup or significant legal troubles threatening his or her law firm and personal integrity. That is to say, fast talking and a good legal mind often serve a hero better than plodding, patient detective work. Prominent authors in this genre include David Baldacci, Phillip Margolin, John Grisham, Steve Martini, Richard North Patterson, and Scott Turow.

Postmodern Crime Novels

In recent years, a number of authors have written postmodern crime novels that co-opt the form of the detective story to call into question whether narratives of "truth" or the creation of coherent subjectivities/identities are even possible. These meta-fictional stories undermine the faith in coherent narratives and individual agency at the center of the detective story. Books typically discussed under this rubric are Thomas Pynchon's *The Crying of Lot 49* (1966), Ishmael Reed's *Mumbo Jumbo* (1972), Paul Auster's <u>New York trilogy</u> (1985, 1986, 1986), Barbara Wilson's *Gaudí Afternoon* (1990), and the work of Sarah Schulman (see especially *The Sophie Horovitz Story* [1984]). Umberto Eco and Jorge Luis Borges, in particular, are claimed as appropriators of the form who use it to undermine moral and epistemological certainties.

True Crime

Since the mid-1980s, writers such as Joe McGinness, Ann Rule, Jack Olsen, and Edna Buchanan have made true crime stories increasingly popular. Because these writers market accounts of actual brutal violence and murder, the narratives are often criticized as voyeuristic or sensational. True crime stories often share qualities with the horror genre—dark atmosphere, psychological suspense, and graphic descriptions of heinous events. Some true crime stories are written from the criminal's point of view, but others are told through the eyes of cops, prosecutors, jurors, attorneys, or victims. Many best sellers are written by urban crime reporters, and these stories are part exposé and part ethnography of modern police departments. Others are written by historians, who avoid the guesswork and fictionalizing common in the genre. The tradition of true crime writing can be traced back through Truman Capote's *In Cold Blood* (1965) to the latter part of the nineteenth century. Literary precursors include sensational, broadsheet ballads from the sixteenth century (some featuring verses written by the criminal) and the cheap, ubiquitous "true confessions" printed as pamphlets in the seventeenth and eighteenth centuries. Readers of true crime are generally middle class, with more female book buyers than male, and there is a strong teen market. Few fans of mystery fiction cross over into true crime, although some true crime writers study mysteries as a way to learn the craft of storytelling. Because this volume focuses on fiction, true crime stories are not listed.

The Cultural Work of Modern Detective Novels

Although crime stories have been around a long time, the detective story is a uniquely modern form of narrative. Dorothy Sayers claimed *Oedipus the King* as the first crime story. Others point to such novels as Daniel Defoe's *Moll Flanders* (1722), William Godwin's *Caleb Williams* (1794), Charles Brockden Brown's *Wieland* (1798), Charles Dickens's *Oliver Twist* (1838) and *Bleak House* (1853), and Wilkie Collins's *The Woman in White* (1860) and *The Moonstone* (1868) as early crime novels. With the exception of Poe's ratiocinative detective, however, stories with a detective and the act of detection at the center emerged only in the 1880s. The detective story, then, is a narrative form of complex, modern, industrial capitalist societies. As such, it engages a number of problems at the center of modern, urban life.

First, such complex societies require a profound degree of interdependence. That is to say, one must hand over management of certain aspects of daily life to experts who have the specialized knowledge necessary to manage particular problems. Since it is impossible for a person to be an expert in every field, modern life requires trust in the integrity, skill, and character of others. R. Gordon Kelly claims that detective stories take up the problem of how to "read" both interpersonal cues and the physical world in order to identify situations and individuals worthy of trust.[8]

Second, (post)modernity is characterized by such complexity that a single, coherent narrative cannot accurately represent the world. The problem posed to human consciousness, then, is how to tell a story that gives shape and meaning to a fragmented, incoherent, complicated life. The detective story is concerned with this central problem and offers the fantasy of resolution at the denouement, when the detective presents a narrative of the crime constructed from seemingly random bits of information (clues).[9]

There is a gap, however, between scholarly discussion of crime fiction and the reports of fan-readers of the genre. Literary critics have focused on the denouement of detective novels, where the mystery is solved, the various clues woven together into a seamless and coherent narrative, and social order restored. Such exclusive focus on the form of detective fiction has a number of troubling consequences. First, it privileges formal continuities over differences in subgenre, setting, and protagonist that are of great importance to fan-readers.

Second, it ascribes a monolithic, reactionary politics to detective fiction—that the fiction inevitably recommends an ideology of competitive individualism or that it affirms existing power structures by locating crime in evil individuals rather than corrupt social institutions.

Although there are few studies of mystery readers, one study of white, professional female fans reveals a variety of different ways of reading, many of which have nothing to do with the ending and a great deal to do with characters, language, setting, and other aspects that resonate with readers' everyday lives.[10] Although this study included only women, general surveys typically reveal mystery fans to be well-educated, middle- and upper-middle-class professionals, with slightly more women readers than men.[11]

7

Character

The most important analytic category for fan-readers is character. Fans talk about characters as if they were real people. Many describe a book as "company," and think about reading books about a series detective as spending time with a friend, without any of the demands of human relationships. Readers overwhelmingly prefer protagonists like themselves, detectives whose gender, education, class background, occupation, or life situation resembles their own. The fluid boundary between readers' lives and the stories they choose to read, then, offers opportunities to think through their own concerns while reading, to "try on" ways of being in the world (physically courageous, mouthy, brave) through a protagonist's adventures.

Inevitably, a question about a particular book ("I don't know that one. Tell me about it.") is interpreted as a question about the protagonist. At the close of a response, fans have described the main character's history and personal/professional situation, but have said nothing at all about what happens in the book. If pushed, they will struggle to remember the plot, but most often end with an apology and an explanation, "They all run together." Clearly, the boundaries of the text for readers are not the plot structures that interest scholars, but the subjectivity or personality of the protagonist. Everything about a series character is recalled as a unit, with little memory of which specific texts these details come from.

Settings

Although important, identification with main characters is only one of many ways of reading. Settings loom large for some readers. Reviews of mysteries frequently praise the realism in the descriptions of cities, noting the faithfulness with which authors reproduced the local color of specific neighborhoods and landmarks. Many readers prefer to read books set in places they have lived or visited. Some plan to read local authors while in a new city. Many readers carry around a mental atlas of mysteries, including categories such as "New Orleans mysteries" or "Italian murders." In this way, the books can operate like photographs, inviting readers to remember their own experiences in that place, or like brochures from the travel agent, inviting readers to imagine what visiting or living in such a place might be like.

Other Appeals

Identifications can be multiple, and "good mysteries" are usually those with which readers can find resonances with their own lives. For example, some readers love hard-boiled stories because of the dry, sarcastic "voice" of the detective, regardless of his or her race, gender, profession, etc. One reader enjoyed the interplay of temperaments between an artist and a scientifically minded police detective in one series, since it resonated with her own artist–scientist marriage. Others find they love mysteries that prominently feature a hobby. Gourmet cooks often like mysteries with food in them. Animal lovers frequently choose stories featuring pets.

Plot Structures

Readers, then, are generally less interested in the particular structure of mystery novels than they are in finding characters, scenes, dialogue, and an idiom through which to make sense of their own experience. However, plot structures seem to be important in a paradoxical way. Although almost completely absent from discussion and recall, readers in forced choice surveys rank elements like pace, well-hidden motives, surprises, red herrings, and narrative twists and turns as very important. Readers may choose to be fans of mysteries because of the plot structure, but a good mystery requires other resonances as well. If formal aspects of detective novels are important, the satisfaction they can provide readers is constrained and complicated by the locale, voice, preoccupations, and personalities that inhabit these structures and are enmeshed with the reader's own life circumstances.

Notes

1. Stephen Knight, *Crime Fiction 1800–2000: Detection, Death, Diversity* (New York: Palgrave, 2004), x.

2. John G. Cawelti, *Adventure, Mystery, and Romance: Formula Stories as Art and Popular Culture* (Chicago: University of Chicago Press, 1976), 105.

3. Erin A. Smith, *Hard-Boiled: Working-Class Readers and Pulp Magazines* (Philadelphia: Temple University Press, 2000).

4. Priscilla L. Walton and Manina Jones, *Detective Agency: Women Rewriting the Hard-Boiled Tradition* (Berkeley: University of California Press, 1999), 29.

5. Erin A. Smith, " 'Both a Woman and a Complete Professional': Women Readers and Women's Hard-boiled Detective Fiction," in *Reading Sites: Social Difference and Reader Response,* ed. Patrocinio P. Schweickart and Elizabeth Flynn, 189–220. (New York: Modern Language Association Press, 2004).

6. Smith, *Hard-Boiled,* afterword.

7. Stephen Soitos, *The Blues Detective: A Study of African American Detective Fiction* (Amherst: University of Massachusetts Press, 1996).

8. R. Gordon Kelly, *Mystery Fiction and Modern Life* (Jackson: University Press of Mississippi, 1998).

9. Smith, "Both a Woman," 212.

10. Smith, "Both a Woman."

11.   Winn Dilys, ed. *Murder Ink* (New York: Workman, 1984), 441; Cawelti, *Adventure, Mystery, and Romance,* 105; Kathleen Gregory Klein, *The Woman Detective: Gender & Genre,* 2d ed. (Chicago: University of Illinois Press, 1995), 8.

Bibliography

Cawelti, John G. *Adventure, Mystery, and Romance: Formula Stories as Art and Popular Culture.* Chicago: University of Chicago Press, 1976.

Dilys, Winn, ed. *Murder Ink.* New York: Workman, 1984.

Kelly, R. Gordon. *Mystery Fiction and Modern Life.* Jackson: University Press of Mississippi, 1998.

Klein, Kathleen Gregory. *The Woman Detective: Gender & Genre.* 2d ed. Chicago: University of Illinois Press, 1995.

Knight, Stephen. *Crime Fiction 1800–2000: Detection, Death, Diversity.* New York: Palgrave, 2004.

Reddy, Maureen T. *Traces, Codes, and Clues: Reading Race in Crime Fiction.* New Brunswick, N.J.: Rutgers University Press, 2003.

Smith, Erin A. " 'Both a Woman and a Complete Professional': Women Readers and Women's Hard-boiled Detective Fiction." In *Reading Sites: Social Difference and Reader Response,* ed. Patrocinio P. Schweickart and Elizabeth Flynn, 189–220. New York: Modern Language Association Press, 2004.

———. *Hard-Boiled: Working-Class Readers and Pulp Magazines.* Philadelphia: Temple University Press, 2000.

Soitos, Stephen. *The Blues Detective: A Study of African American Detective Fiction.* Amherst: University of Massachusetts Press, 1996.

Walton, Priscilla L., and Manina Jones. *Detective Agency: Women Rewriting the Hard-Boiled Tradition.* Berkeley: University of California Press, 1999.

Themes and Types

Diana Tixier Herald

Crime fiction, encompassing stories of detection, suspense, legal thrillers, and crime capers, is a huge category and probably the most popular genre in public libraries. Novels of detection tend to be written in series. The detective and the setting are what readers generally seek in books of this type. Suspense tales depend on the unexpected, the plot is of major importance to the readers and the atmosphere, and the feeling one has of impending disaster is also extremely important in this type. Legal thrillers often have recurring characters, but the plot is also a primary consideration. In crime capers, readers are often looking for quirky characters and intricate plotting.

Selected Classics

As one of the most established, plentiful, and diverse genres, Crime claims hundreds of classic titles and authors. The following list is just a sampling of the most prominent and still-popular authors of the genre. With the exceptions of Edgar Allan Poe and Wilkie Collins, the literary predecessors of crime writing (such as Sheridan LeFanu and Charles Dickens) are not listed here, but they are noted in this chapter's essay. Popular detective characters and groundbreaking titles that established new subgenres and themes in the genre are noted when appropriate.

Allingham, Margery. (Albert Campion, aristocrat).

Biggers, Earl Derr. (Charlie Chan series). (police detective).

Brown, Fredric. (Ed and Am Hunter, Chicago).

Cain, James M. *The Postman Always Rings Twice* (1934).

Carr, John Dickson.

Chandler, Raymond. (Philip Marlowe, Los Angeles, hard-boiled). (private detective).

Charteris, Leslie. (Simon Templar, "The Saint," Robin Hood type).

Chesterton, G. K. (Father Brown, Roman Catholic Priest, British). (unofficial detective—ecclesiastical).

Christie, Agatha. (Hercule Poirot, ex-cop; Miss Jane Marple, amateur, cozy). (unofficial detective).

Collins, Wilkie. *The Woman in White*, 1860, and *The Moonstone*, 1868.

Creasey, John. (the honorable Richard Rollison, "The Toff," gentleman burglar, "the poor man's Lord Peter Wimsey") . (police detectives/police procedural).

Crichton, Michael. *The Great Train Robbery.* 1975. (crime/caper).

Doyle, Arthur Conan, Sir. (Sherlock Holmes and Dr. John Watson, cozy).

Ferrars, E. X. (Andrew Basnett, retired professor). (unofficial—academic).

Fisher, Rudolph. *The Conjure Man Dies.* 1932.

Follett, Ken. *Paper Money.* 1977. (crime/caper).

Gaboriau, Émile. (police detective, police procedural).

Gardner, Erle Stanley. Over eighty novels, the first in 1933, celebrate attorney Perry Mason with his aides, Paul Drake and Della Street. Gardner's total was about 103 volumes.

Godwin, William. *Caleb Williams.* 1794.

Hammett, Dashiell. (the Continental Op, Sam Spade, Nick Charles).

Hansen, Joseph. (David Brandstetter, insurance investigator, gay).

Highsmith, Patricia. *The Talented Mr. Ripley,* 1966. (crime/caper); *Strangers on a Train,* 1974 (as well as other books).

Himes, Chester. (Coffin Ed Johnson and Grave Digger Jones, Harlem). *When Cotton Comes to Harlem,* 1965 and *Blind Man with a Pistol,* 1969. (police detective, hard-boiled).

Lockridge, Frances, and **Richard Lockridge.** (Pam and Jerry North). (police detective).

MacDonald, John D. (Travis McGee). (private detective, hard-boiled).

McBain, Ed. (police detective/police procedural, and unofficial detective—lawyer).

Mitchell, Gladys.

Pentecost, Hugh. (Pierre Chambrun, hotel manager).

Poe, Edgar Allan. (C. Auguste Dupin). "Murders in the Rue Morgue," 1841; "The Mystery of Marie-Rogêt," 1842–1843; and "The Purloined Letter," 1844. (historical).

Queen, Ellery. (nom de plume for Frederick Dannay and Manfred B. Lee).

Sayers, Dorothy L. (Lord Peter Wimsey, Montague Egg). (cozy, amateur sleuth).

Simenon, Georges. (police detective/police procedural).

Spillane, Mickey. (Mike Hammer, hard-boiled).

Stewart, Mary. *My Brother Michael.* 1960. (romantic suspense).

Stout, Rex. (Nero Wolfe and Archie Goodwin).

Van Dine, S. S.

Waugh, Hillary. (police detective/police procedural).

Whitney, Phyllis. *Hunter's Green.* 1968 (romantic suspense).

The Detective Story

Tales of detection that involve solving a puzzle, finding the culprit, and bringing him or her to justice are the most popular, or at least the most plentiful, of crime stories. The focus of these stories is on the detective and the process he or she uses to solve the crime. The character of the detective is vital, and series based on detectives keep readers coming back for more. Frequently terms such as *hard-boiled, soft-boiled,* and *cozy* are used to describe the different types within this category.

Hard-boiled, noir, and *Black Mask* are not synonymous in meaning, but they are terms often used together to describe a certain type of mystery. These are mysteries in which the protagonist, usually a male private investigator, working for the most part alone, explores the dark underbelly of a major city while trying to solve the crime. The detective usually has no close personal relationships. The crimes, often depicted in vivid and gory detail, can be described as "gritty." The world of these novels is not a comfortable, orderly place—it is harsh, and only the strong survive. Dialogue is clipped, tough, and even caustic, and the writing is spare, with the focus on atmosphere and action. James Ellroy is currently writing in this vein, and past masters include Raymond Chandler, Dashiell Hammett, and Jim Thompson, all of whose books continue to be read.

Soft-boiled and *cozy* are often used interchangeably, although some argue that soft-boiled falls between hard-boiled and cozy. In this category, although the focus is still on the crime, interpersonal relationships, family and friends, are more important and often play a role in the story. In this type of mystery the community is often smaller or rural as opposed to the urban scenes found in hard-boiled stories. The detective, instead of meeting a series of strangers in pursuit of answers, interacts with people known to him or her. Often the sleuths have no official standing, being amateurs who just seem to be at the right (or perhaps the wrong) place at the right time. The murders often occur "offstage" or, if conducted in full view, are more genteelly described, rather than graphically as in hard-boiled detection.

There are many variations within and between the "hard-boiled" and "cozy" types of mysteries. Gary Niebuhr, author of the award-winning *Make Mine a Mystery* (Libraries Unlimited, 2004), designates a third category, the "traditional," which combines elements of both types. For the purposes of this guide, we limit the major types to two, with further distinction made according to detective types—that is, professional detectives, amateur sleuths.

Today, detective series have virtually become the rule in crime fiction, rather than merely being common. New mysteries frequently identify the sleuth on the cover, even if it is his or her first appearance. Many detective series that start off as paperback originals eventually move into hardcover publication as the sleuth becomes popular and develops a following of readers.

The Professionals

The two major types of professional detectives are the police detective and the private investigator. Until recent years the focus in these novels was completely on the detective and how he or she solved the crime. Now, the detectives have relationships and families that help define them and add multiple levels to the tale of the detective and the crime. However, the detective—his or her persona and how he or she solves the crime—still provides the central appeal and focus of these novels.

Police Detectives

Mysteries involving police detectives often include several characters from a squad or division. Even the series that feature independent sleuths who are on a police force have to work within the constraints imposed by the organization and stay within the law they are trying to uphold. Some of these tales feature one-person po-

lice departments, thus giving the sleuth much in common with independent private investigators.

Frequently the plot will involve several crimes, requiring the detective to work more than one case at a time or to consult on other cases. The stories of police detectives became popular with the rise of organized police forces in the United States, Great Britain, and France.

The best-known type of book featuring police detectives is the police procedural, which often looks as though it could have been taken from a crime blotter. A group of police officers solve crimes as they come up. Joseph Wambaugh and Ed McBain wrote the proto-types in this area.

The detective in the police procedural must function within the rules of the police de-partment; he or she lacks the freedom of the private detective. Although the pattern may vary because of the personality of the detective, most police detectives work as part of a team (as opposed to the private detective, who is often a loner). Two plot patterns are com-mon. One uses a single murder (or several linked murders) or mystery for the basic plot. The other, in effect, uses the police blotter to dictate the story line: Every case followed up by the police station staff is observed in varying degrees, although one case is the focus of detec-tion and, often, the other cases are ingeniously linked to the main crime. Television series such as *NYPD Blue* and *CSI* are good examples of the composite stories and cast of characters found in police procedural novels.

Detection novels featuring police detectives can be either hard-boiled or cozy. The best indication of which category a book falls into is usually the size of the community in which the detective functions. Those set in New York, Los Angeles, and Chicago tend to be more hard-boiled, while those set in places like the fictional Maggody, Arkansas, where Chief Arly Hanks is the sum total of the local police force, deal with more cozy crimes. Time period plays into the mix as well—with the more contemporary stories generally be-ing the most brutal. Thus, the environment, to a great extent, dictates the character of the de-tective and the type of story readers will encounter.

Because readers often recall the name of the character or the setting, the following au-thors are listed by the country to which the police detective belongs. Under the "United States" heading the grouping is by state. The most common type of readers' advisory in-quiry by readers of detection stories it to find the author of a book featuring a detective that the reader liked. Many of the titles by the following authors are quite old but still are read. The characters and notable time periods or places are provided in parentheses after the au-thor name. Sample titles are also given for some authors.

Australia

Cleary, Jon. (Detective Sergeant Scobie Malone, 1970s).

Disher, Garry. (Detective Inspector Hal Challis). Rural Australian hard-boiled police procedural.

McNab, Claire. (Detective Inspector Carol Ashton, lesbian). The first series book was pub-lished in 1988, the sixteenth in 2004.

Upfield, Arthur. (Inspector Napoleon "Bony" Bonaparte, half-aborigine). Twenty-nine nov-els originally published between 1929 and 1962.

Belgium

Freeling, Nicolas. (Henri Castang). The sixteenth and last one was *The Dwarf Kingdom* (1997).

Bosnia

Fesperman, Dan. (Detective Inspector Vlado Petric). *Lie in the Dark,* 1999; *The Small Boat of Great Sorrows,* 2003.

Brazil

Garcia-Roza, Luiz Alfredo. (Inspector Espinosa). Dark police procedurals with deliberate pacing started with *The Silence of the Rain* in 2002. The fourth book is *A Window in Copacabana,* 2005.

Canada

Blount, Giles. (John Cardinal and Lisa Delorme, Algonquin Bay, Ontario).

Craig, Alisa. (Madoc Rhys, Royal Canadian Mounted Police).

Gough, Laurence. (Detectives Jack Willows and Claire Parker, Vancouver).

Jennings, Maureen. (Detective William Murdoch, Toronto, Victorian era).

Reeves, John. (Inspector Andrew Coggin and Sergeant Fred Stemp, Toronto).

Sale, Medora. (Detective Inspector John Sanders, Toronto).

Wood, Ted. (Reid Bennett, Murphy's Harbor, Ontario).

Wright, Eric. (Charlie Salter, Toronto).

Wright, L. R. (Staff Sergeant Karl Aberg, Royal Canadian Mounted Police, British Columbia).

Young, Scott. (Inspector Matteesie, Royal Canadian Mounted Police).

China

Marshall, William. (Yellowthread Street Police Station, Chief Harry Feiffer).

Pattison, Eliot. (Shan Tao Yun, Tibet).

Qiu Xiaolong. (Chief Inspector Chen Cao).

Rotenberg, David. (Zhong Fong, Shanghai Head of Special Investigations).

See, Lisa. (Ministry of Public Security agent Liu Hulan).

Van Gulik, Robert. (Judge Dee, eighth century).

West, Christopher. (Inspector Wang Anzhuang of the Beijing Central Investigations Department).

Egypt

Pearce, Michael. (Gareth Owen, the Mamur Zapt British head of Cairo's secret police).

France

Freeling, Nicolas. (Henri Castang).

Hebden, Mark. (Inspector Evariste Clovis Désiré Pel, Burgundy).

Janes, J. Robert. (Inspectors Jean-Louis St-Cyr of the French police and Hermann Kohler of the German police, World War II occupied France).

McConnor, Vincent. (Francois Vidocq, founder of the Sûreté, nineteenth century).

Simenon, Georges. (Inspector Maigret).

Germany

Savarin, Julian Jay. (Hauptkommissar Jens Muller of the Berlin Police).

Great Britain: Scotland Yard

The legendary detective department of the Metropolitan Police Force of London has an almost mythical standing in detective stories.

Barnard, Robert. (Superintendent Percy Trethowan and Superintendent Sutcliffe).

Butler, Gwendoline. (Inspector Coffin).

Crombie, Deborah. (Superintendent Duncan Kincaid and Sergeant Gemma James).

Grimes, Martha. (Detective Superintendent Richard Jury and amateur Melrose Plant).

Hare, Cyril. (Inspector Mallett).

Harrison, Ray. (Sergeant Bragg and James Morton, London City Police, 1890s).

Heyer, Georgette. (Chief Inspectors Hannasyde and Hemingway).

Hilton, John Buxton. (Inspector Kenworthy).

Hunter, Alan. (Chief Superintendent George Gently).

Inchbald, Peter. (Francis Corti, Art and Antiques Squad).

Innes, Michael. (Inspector, later Sir, John Appleby, and also in retirement).

James, P. D. (Commander Adam Dalgliesh).

Jones, Elwyn. (Detective Chief Superintendent Barlow).

Kenyon, Michael. (Inspector Henry Peckover).

Lawton, John. (Chief Inspector Frederick Troy).

Lemarchand, Elizabeth. (Detective Inspector Tom Pollard and Inspector Gregory Toye).

Lewis, Roy. (Inspector Crow).

Lovesey, Peter. (Sergeant Cribb and Constable Thackeray, nineteenth century).

MacKenzie, Donald. (Detective Inspector Raven, retired).

Marric, J. J. (Commander George Gideon).

Marsh, Ngaio. (Inspector Roderick Alleyn).

Moyes, Patricia. (Chief Superintendent Henry Tibbett and his wife Emmy).

Ormerod, Roger. (Detective Harry Kyle).

Perry, Anne. (Inspector Pitt, nineteenth century).

Selwyn, Francis. (Sergeant Verity, nineteenth century).

Smith, D. W. (Harry Fathers).

Stubbs, Jean. (Inspector Lintott, nineteenth century).

Symons, Julian. (Inspector Bland).

Tey, Josephine. (Inspector Alan Grant).

Todd, Charles. (Inspector Ian Rutledge).

Trow, M. J. (Inspector Sholto Lestrade, nineteenth century).

Wainwright, John. (Chief Inspector Lennox).

Winslow, Pauline. (Superintendent Merle Capricorn and Inspector Copper).

Great Britain Other Than Scotland Yard

Aird, Catherine. (Inspector Sloan).

Anderson, J. R. L. (Chief Constable Pier Deventer).

Ashford, Jeffrey. (Detective Inspector Don Kerry).

Atkins, Meg Elizabeth. (Chief Inspector Henry Beaumont).

Bannister, Jo. (Inspector Liz Graham and Sergeant Cal Donovan).

Barnard, Robert. (Chief Inspector Meredith, Superintendent Ian Dundy).

Beaton, M. C. (Constable Hamish MacBeth, Scotland).

Billingham, Mark. (Inspector Tom Thorne).

Booth, Stephen. (Constable Ben Cooper and Sergeant Diane Fry).

Bowen, Rhys. (Constable Evan Evans, Wales a cozy series).

Burley, W. J. (Chief Superintendent Wycliffe).

Charles, Paul. (Inspector Christy Kennedy).

Cork, Barry. (Angus Straun).

Coward, Mat. (Inspector Don Packham and Constable Frank Mitchell).

Curzon, Clare. (Superintendent Mike Yeadings).

Cutler, Judith. (Det. Sergeant Kate Power, Birmingham).

Davies, Freda. (Inspector Keith Tyrell).

Dexter, Colin. (Chief Inspector Morse, Oxford).

Eccles, Marjorie. (Inspector Gil Mayo).

Ellis, Kate. (Det. Sgt. Wesley Peterson).

Evans, Geraldine. (Detective Inspector Rafferty and Sergeant Llewellyn).

Fraser, Anthea. (Chief Inspector David Webb).

Geddes, Paul. (Ludovic Fender).

George, Elizabeth. (Inspector Thomas Lynley, Sergeant Barbara Havers).

Gilbert, Michael. (Chief Superintendent Charlie Knott, Luke Pagan, Patrick Petrella).

Goodchild, George. (Inspector McLean).

Graham, Caroline. (Chief Inspector Tom Barnaby).

Granger, Ann. (Chief Inspector Markby and former Foreign Service Officer Meredith Mitchell).

Gregson, J. M. (Inspector Percy Peach; Superintendent John Lambert and Sergeant Bert Hook).

Hall, Patricia. (DCI Michael Thackeray).

Harrod-Eagles, Cynthia. (Detective Inspector Bill Slider).

Hart, Roy. (Inspector Roper).

Haymon, S. T. (Detective Inspector Benjamin Jurnet).

Hill, Reginald. (Superintendent Dalziel and Sergeant Pascoe).

Hilton, John Buxton. (Inspector Pickford, Detective Brunt, and Sergeant Nadin, Derbyshire, nineteenth century).

Hunt, Richard. (Detective Chief Inspector Sidney Walsh).

James, Bill. (Chief Superintendent Colin Harpur).

Jardine, Quintin. (DCC Bob Skinner, Edinburgh).

Keating, H. R. F. (Detective Harriet Martens).

Kincaid, M. G. (Sergent Seth Mornay, Scotland).

Knox, Bill. (Colin Thane and Phil Moss, Glasgow; Webb Carrick, Fishery Protection Service).

Longworth, Gay. (Detective Inspector Jessie Driver).

Lovesey, Peter. (Chief Superintendent Peter Diamond).

Maitland, Barry. (Sergeant Kathy Kolla and Chief Inspector Brock).

McGown, Jill. (Detective Chief Inspector Lloyd and Inspector Judy Hall).

McIlvanney, William. (Detective Inspector Laidlaw, Glasgow).

Melville, Jennie. (pseudonym of Gwendoline Butler). (Sergeant Charmian Daniels).

Murray, Stephen. (Alec Stainton).

Neel, Janet. (Inspector John McLeish and Sergeant Bruce Davidson).

Oldham, Nick. (Inspector Henry Christie, Blackpool).

Peters, Ellis. (Detective Inspector George Felse).

Radley, Sheila. (Chief Inspector Douglas Quantrill, Suffolk).

Rankin, Ian. (Inspector John Rebus, Edinburgh). The fourteenth title, *A Question of Blood,* 2004, involves a school shooting.

Rendell, Ruth. (Chief Inspector Wexford and Inspector Borden).

Robinson, Peter. (Chief Inspector Alan Banks).

Ross, Jonathan. (Detective Superintendent George Rogers).

Ruell, Patrick. (pseudonym of Reginald Hill). (Detective Inspector Dog Cicero).

Simpson, Dorothy. (Inspector Luke Thanet, Kent).

Smith, Frank. (Chief Inspector Neil Paget).

Spencer, Sally. (Chief Inspector Woodend).

Stacey, Susannah. (pseudonym of Jill Staynes and Margaret Storey). (Superintendent Bone).

Thomson, June. (Detective Inspector Finch; in U.S. editions, Detective Inspector Rudd).

Turnbull, Peter. (Police Constable Phil Hamilton, Detective Roy Sussock, Glasgow).

Watson, Colin. (Inspector Purbright and Miss Teatime).

Whitehead, Barbara. (Police Inspectors Dave Smart and Bob Southwell, York).

India

Cleverly, Barbara. (Joe Sandilands).

Keating, H. R. F. (Inspector Ghote, Bombay).

Mann, Paul. (Inspector George Sansi).

Ireland

Brady, John. (Inspector Matt Minogue).

Gill, Bartholomew. (Chief Inspector Peter McGarr, Dublin).

Israel

Gur, Batya. (Detective Michael Ohayon, Jerusalem).

Land, Jon. (Palestinian cop Ben Kamal and Israeli government agent Danielle Barnea).

Italy

Browne, Marshall. (Inspector Anders).

Camilleri, Andrea. (Inspector Salvo Montalbano, Sicily).

Dibdin, Michael. (Aurelio Zen).

Hewson, David. (Nic Costa, Rome).

Holme, Timothy. (Achille Peroni, Venice).

Leon, Donna. (Commissario Guido Brunetti, Venice).

Nabb, Magdalen. (Marshal Guarnaccia, Florence).

Pears, Iain. (Flavia di Stefano, Rome, Art Squad).

Williams, Timothy. (Commissario Trotti).

Japan

Melville, James. (Superintendent Otani, Tokyo).

Rowland, Laura Joh. (Sano Ichiro, 17th century).

Luong (Fictional Southeast Asian Kingdom).

Alexander, Gary. (Superintendent Bamsan Kiet).

Netherlands

Baantjer, A. C. (Inspector DeKok).

Freeling, Nicolas. (Inspector Van der Valk).

Van de Wetering, Janwillem. (Detective Grijpstra and Detective Sergeant de Grier).

Puerto Rico

Torres, Steven. (Luis Gonzalo, sheriff of Angustias).

Russia

Kaminsky, Stuart. (Inspector Porfiry Petrovich Rostnikov, Moscow. Series started with *Death of a Dissident* in 1981; the fourteenth book, *Murder on the Trans-Siberian Express,* was published in 2001.

Smith, Martin Cruz. (Chief Homicide Investigator Arkady Renko).

White, Robin. (Gregori Nowek, Siberia).

South Africa

McClure, James. (Lieutenant Tromp Kramer, Afrikaner; Detective Sergeant Zondi, Bantu).

Spain

Jeffries, Roderic. (Inspector Enrique Alverez, Majorca).

Pawel, Rebecca. (Carlos Tejada Alonso Y Leon, a lieutenant in the Guardia).

Serafin, David. (Superintendent Louis Bernal, Madrid).

Wilson, Robert. (Inspector Jefe Javier Falcón, Seville).

Sweden

Edwardson, Åke. (Chief Inspector Erik Winter). *Sun and Shadow,* 2005.

Mankell, Henning. (Inspector Kurt Wallander).

Sjöwall, Maj, and Per Wahlöö. (Martin Beck).

Thailand

Burdett, John. (Detective Sonchai Jitpleecheep).

Turkey

Nadel, Barbara. (Police Inspector Çetin Ikmen).

United States

Alabama

Cook, Thomas H. (Ben Wellman). *Streets of Fire,* 1989.

Kerley, Jack. (Carson Ryder). *The Hundredth Man,* 2004.

Alaska

Jones, Stan. (Nathan Active, state trooper). *White Sky, Black Ice,* 1999; *Shaman Pass,* 2003.

Stabenow, Dana. (Liam Campbell). *Better to Rest,* 2002; *Nothing Gold Can Stay,* 2000.

Arizona

Hillerman, Tony. (Lieutenant Joe Leaphorn and Jim Chee, Navajo Tribal Police). *Skeleton Man,* 2004.

Jance, J. A. (Joanna Brady, Cochise County Sheriff). *Sentenced to Die,* 2005.

Arkansas

Hess, Joan. (Chief Arly Hanks, Maggody). *Muletrain to Maggody,* 2004.

California

Ball, John. (Virgil Tibbs, African-American, Pasadena). *In the Heat of the Night,* 1965. Reissued 2001.

Cannell, Stephen J. (Shane Scully. Los Angeles). *Vertical Coffin,* 2004.

Connelly, Michael. (Detective Harry Bosch, Los Angeles). *The Closers,* 2005.

Cunningham, E. V. (Masao Masuto, Nisei, Beverly Hills). *Case of the Kidnapped Angel,* 1982. Reissued 2001.

Joens, Michael. (Detective Sandra Cameron, Los Angeles). *An Animated Death in Burbank,* 2004.

Kellerman, Faye. (Peter and Rina Lazarus, Los Angeles). *Straight into Darkness,* 2005.

Parker, T. Jefferson. (Merci Rayborn, Orange County). *Black Water,* 2002.

Rosenberg, Nancy Taylor. (Carolyn Sullivan, probation officer, Ventura County). *Sullivan's Justice,* 2005.

Woods, Paula L. (Detective Charlotte Justice, Los Angeles). *Dirty Laundry,* 2003.

Colorado

Doss, James D. (Scott Parris and Charlie Moon, Southwest area and Ute Reservation). *Dead Soul,* 2003.

Florida

Woods, Stuart. (Chief Holly Barker, Orchid Beach). *Orchid Blues,* 2001.

Georgia

Berry, Linda. (Officer Trudy Roundtree). *Death and the Walking Stick,* 2005.

Slaughter, Karin. (Chief Jeffrey Tolliver). *A Faint Cold Fear,* 2004.

Illinois

Bland, Eleanor Taylor. (Marti MacAlister and Vik Jessenovik, Lincoln Prairie). *A Cold and Silent Dying,* 2004.

Holton, Hugh. (Larry Cole, Chicago). *Criminal Element,* 2002.

Kaminsky, Stuart M. (Sergeant Abe Lieberman, a veteran Chicago cop in his sixties).

> The series started with *Lieberman's Folly* in 1990; the eighth book, *The Last Dark Place,* was published in 2004.

Konrath, J. A. (Lieutenant Jacqueline "Jack" Daniels of the Violent Crimes Unit, insomniac).

> The series started in 2004 with *Whiskey Sour;* the second in the darkly humorous series is *Bloody Mary,* 2005.

Iowa

Harstad, Donald. (Carl Houseman, deputy sheriff rural Nation county).

> The series started with *Eleven Days* in 1998. The fifth title is *A Long December,* 2003.

Kansas

Weir, Charlene. (Police Chief Susan Wren, Hampstead).

> The series started with *The Winter Widow* in 1992; the sixth book is *Up in Smoke,* published in 2003.

Louisiana

Burke, James Lee.

> The <u>Dave Robicheaux series</u> started with *The Neon Rain* (1987), and the most recent, the fourteenth in the series, is *Crusader's Cross* (2005). Robicheaux is a Cajun, a sometimes recovering alcoholic, and a police detective on and off, starting off as a homicide detective in New Orleans, leaving the force, moving to Montana, and returning to serve as a cop in New Iberia.

Smith, Julie. (Skip Langdon).

> The series started with *New Orleans Mourning* in 1990; the ninth book featuring this police woman is *Mean Woman Blues,* published in 2003.

Massachusetts

McDonald, Gregory. (Inspector Francis Xavier Flynn, Boston).

> Flynn first appeared in *Confess Fletch.* but the intelligence officer who uses a detective job as a cover first became a series detective in *Flynn* (1977; reissued 2003); *Flynn's World,* the fifth book in the comedic series, was published in 2003.

Parker, Robert B.

> Chief Jesse Stone, a former LAPD cop who moves to a small town named Paradise, is first featured in *Night Passage* (1997). The fourth book in the series is *Stone Cold*, published in 2003.

Michigan

Jackson, Jon A. (Sergeant Mulheisen, Detroit).

The series started in 1977 with *The Diehard*, and Fang Mulheisen is an ex-cop in *No Man's Dog* (2004).

Minnesota

Compton, Jodi. (Sheriff's Detective Sarah Pribek, Minneapolis specializes in missing person cases).

The 37th Hour, published in 2004, is the first in the series, in which Sarah sees her new husband kidnapped. *Sympathy Between Humans* (2005) starts right where the first title left off.

Erickson, K. J. (Marshall "Mars" Bahr).

The series started with *Third Person Singular* in 2001 and is now up to the fourth book. which is *Alone at Night* (2004), in which Mars moves from the Minneapolis Polic Department homicide to the cold case squad.

Gunn, Elizabeth.

The Captain Jake Hines series, set in the northern city of Rutherford, started with *Triple Play* in 1997. The sixth book is *Crazy Eights* (2005).

Monsour, Theresa. (Homicide Detective Paris Murphy).

This gritty series started with *Clean Cut* in 2003. The third title is *Dark Horse* (2005).

Tracy, P. J.

Detectives Leo Magozzi and Gino Rolseth appeared first in *Monkeewrench* in 2003. The third title in this comedic series involving a group of high-tech computer and game programmers is *Dead Run* (2005).

Missouri

Kennett, Shirley.

This series featuring P. J. Gray and Leo Schultz started with *Gray Matter* in 1996. The fourth novel, *Act of Betrayal* (2000), was published under the pseudonym Avery Morgan. A fifth title in the series, *Time of Death,* was published in 2005. P. J., a psychologist and single mom, has been hired by the St. Louis Police Department to use virtual reality techniques in the Computerized Homicide Investigations Project (CHIP) and is teamed up with veteran detective Leo.

Randisi, Robert J.

The Joe Keough series started in 1998 with *Alone with the Dead.* The fifth book, *Arch Angels,* was published in 2004.

Montana

Bowen, Peter.

Gabriel Du Pre, a cattle brand inspector, first appeared in *Coyote Wind* in 1994. The twelfth book in the series is *Stewball* (2005).

New Mexico

Havill, Steven F. (Undersheriff Bill Gastner later Sheriff and Undersheriff Estelle Reyes-Guzman).

Set in Posadas County at the very southern edge of the state. The first in the series was *Heartshot* in 1991; the twelfth book, *Convenient Disposal,* was published in 2004.

Hillerman, Tony. (Lieutenant Joe Leaphorn and Jim Chee, Navajo Tribal Police).

The first title in what has become one of the most loved mystery series of all time was *The Blessing Way* (1970). Hillerman's evocatively described Four Corners setting and respectful depiction of Navajo peoples started a major trend in mysteries. The *Skeleton Man* (2004) is the seventeenth in the series.

McGarrity, Michael. (Chief Kevin Kerney, Santa Fe).

The series started with *Tularosa* in 1996; the ninth book was *Slow Kill,* published in 2004.

New York (New York City unless otherwise noted)

Black, Ethan.

This series featuring Conrad Voort began with *The Broken Hearts Club* in 1999. The fifth book is *At Hell's Gate* (2004).

Charyn, Jerome.

The Isaac Sidel series started with *Blue Eyes* in 1974. *The Isaac Quartet*, an omnibus of the first four titles in the series, was reissued in 2002.

Deaver, Jeffery. (Lincoln Rhyme and Amelia Sachs).

The first title in this series featuring quadriplegic criminologist Lincoln Rhyme, who does not let his injuries incurred in the line of duty stop him from tracking down serial killers with the help of his "eyes and hands," Amelia Sachs, was *The Bone Collector* (1997) 🎬, and the sixth title, *The Twelfth Card,* appeared in 2005.

Fairstein, Linda. (Alexandra Cooper, head of Manhattan's sex crimes unit).

The first title in the series was *Final Jeopardy* (1996). The seventh, *Entombed,* was published in 2005.

Glass, Leslie.

April Woo was introduced in the *Burning Time* (1995). The ninth is *A Clean Kill* (2005).

Jahn, Michael. (Bill Donovan).

The first book was *Night Rituals* (1982), and the ninth, *Murder in Coney Island,* was published in 2003.

Mahoney, Dan.

Detective Brian McKenna was introduced in *Detective First Grade* in 1993 and made his eighth appearance in *Justice* in 2003.

McBain, Ed. (Steve Carella, 87th Precinct).

The benchmark of police procedural series has been going strong for nearly half a century. It started in 1956 with *Cop Hater. Hark!,* the fifty-fourth title, was published in 2004.

Moore, Harker.

Lieutenant James Sakura, a Japanese American homicide detective in Manhattan, appears in *A Cruel Season for Dying* (2003) and *A Mourning in Autumn* (2004).

O'Connell, Carol.

Sergeant Kathleen Mallory, who has been called a sociopath and a homeless street thief, was adopted at age eleven by a cop. She first appeared in *Mallory's Oracle* (2004). *Winter House* (2004) is the eighth in the series.

Stackhouse, Bill.

Chief Ed McAvoy, of Peekamoose Heights, a quiet, sleepy little village in the Catskills, first appeared in *Stream of Death* in 2001. *Wash and Wear* (2003) was the fourth book in the series.

7

Stone, Jonathan.

Julian Palmer is a smart young policewoman who submerses herself in the crimes she is solving. Even though she works for the NYPD, the first novel, *The Cold Truth* (1999), features her internship in upstate Canaanville, the second features a stint Troy, and in the third, *Breakthrough* (2003), she is on maternity leave.

North Carolina

Malone, Michael.

Chief Cuddy Mangum and Lt. Justin Savile are featured in *Uncivil Seasons* (1983, reissued 2002), *Time's Witness* (1989, reissued 2002), and *First Lady* (2001). Otto Penzler called *Uncivil Seasons* "one of the few nearly perfect novels in the history of detective fiction."

Ohio

McInerny, Ralph.

Egidio Manfredi, soon to retire from the Fort Elbow Police Department, is involved in a missing persons case in *Still Life* (2000) and pursues a serial kidnapper/killer in *Sub Rosa* (2001).

Oklahoma

Cooper, Susan Rogers.

Sheriff Milt Kovack, of Prophesy County first appeared in *The Man in the Green Chevy* in 1988. His eighth appearance is in *Lying Wonders* (2003).

Pennsylvania

Constantine, K. C. (Chief of Police Mario Balzic, Detective Ruggerio "Rugs" Carlucci, Rocksburg).

The seventeenth in the Rocksburg series, *Saving Room for Dessert* (2002). features three beat cops. The series started in 1972 with *Rocksburg Railroad Murders*.

Griffin, W. E. B.

The first book in the Badge of Honor series, *Men in Blue*, set in Philadelphia, was originally published in 1988 under the pseudonym John Kevin Dugan. The eighth book in the series is *Final Justice* (2003).

Jones, Solomon.

Philadelphia Detective Kevin Lynch is featured in *The Bridge* (2003), a gritty noir thriller dealing with the kidnapping of a little girl from a notorious housing project.

Tennessee

McCrumb, Sharyn.

Sheriff Spencer Arrowood first appeared in *If Ever I Return, Pretty Peggy-O* (1990), set in Hamelin, Tennessee, in a series that combines past and present mysteries. *Ghost Riders* (2003) is the seventh book.

Villatoro, Marcos McPeek.

Romilia Chacón, a Salvadoran who is now a Nashville homicide cop, appeared first in *Home Killings* (2001), followed by *Minos* (2003).

Texas

Crider, Bill.

This series featuring Sheriff Don Rhodes started with *Too Late to Die* (1986), which won an Anthony Award for best first novel. The twelfth in this humorous series is *Red, White, and Blue Murder* (2003).

Fackler, Elizabeth. (Devon Gray, El Paso).

This series started with *Patricide* in 2000; the third book is *Endless River* (2005).

Moore, Laurie. (Cezanne Martin, Fort Worth).

The Lady Godiva Murder introduced Cezanne Martin, a cop who has just passed the bar exam, in 2002.

Vermont

Mayor, Archer.

The Lieutenant Joe Gunther series, set in Brattleboro, began in 1988 with *Open Season*. The seventeenth book is *St. Alban's Fire* (2005).

Washington

Jance, J. A. (Jonas Piedmont Beaumont, Seattle).

The series started with *Until Proven Guilty* in 1985; the seventeenth book, *Long Time Gone,* was published in 2005.

Pearson, Ridley. (Detective Lou Boldt and police psychiatrist Daphne Matthews, Seattle).

The series started in 1988 with *Undercurrents*. The ninth book is *The Body of David Hayes* (2004).

Wisconsin

Greenlief, K. C. (Sheriff Lark Swenson and Detective Lacey Smith).

> The first book in the series was *Cold Hunter's Moon* (2002). *Death at the Door* (2003) is the second.

Private Investigators

The Private Eye Writers of America, who make it their business to honor excellent work in the genre with their Shamus Awards, define a "private eye" as any mystery protagonist who is a professional investigator, 'but not a police officer or government agent."

The official private detective started out as one of two types—the employee of a large agency or a lone operator—but now is often part of a small one- or two-investigator agency. Dashiell Hammett created two immortal prototypes: the Continental Op, simply identified for his agency and never named, and Sam Spade, a detective who strikes out on his own after his partner is killed in *The Maltese Falcon*. Sam Spade also became the prototype for the hard-boiled private eye, a character often short on morals but long on integrity.

This type of detective is currently most often referred to as a P.I. P.I.s often cross boundaries, break the rules, and are individualistic characters.

Australia

Day, Marele. (Claudia Valentine).
Greenwood, Kerry. (Phryne Fisher 1920s Melbourne).

Bosnia

Fesperman, Dan. (ex-cop Vlado Petric in *The Small Boat of Great Sorrows*, 2003).

Botswana

McCall Smith, Alexander. (Precious Ramotswe, Botswana).

Canada

Engel, Howard. (Benny Cooperman).

France

Black, Cara. (Aimée Leduc).
Blank, Hannah. (Inspector Alphonse Dantan).

Great Britain

Baron, Adam. (Billy Rucker).
Dunant, Sarah. (Hannah Wolfe).
McDermid, Val. (Kate Brannigan).
Staincliffe, Cath. (Sal Kilkenny, Manchester).
Thompson, Christian. (Chris O'Brien).

Tripp, Miles. (John Sampson and Shandy).

Wentworth, Patricia. (Miss Maude Silver).

Ireland

Bruen, Ken. (Jack Taylor).

🎗 *The Guards.* 2003. Winner of the Shamus Award.

Japan

Tasker, Peter. (Kazuo Mori, very hardboiled).

Mexico

Taibo, Paco Ignacio, II. (Hector Belascoaran Shayne).

United States

Alaska

Stabenow, Dana. (Kate Shugak, former district attorney).

Straley, John. (Cecil Younger, Sitka).

California

Barre, Richard. (Wil Hardesty).

Boyle, Alistair. (Gil Yates).

Calder, James. (Bill Damen, Silicon Valley).

Campbell, Robert. (Whistler).

Chang, Leonard. (Allen Choice, San Francisco).

Copper Basil. (Mike Faraday, Los Angeles).

Corpi, Lucha. (Gloria Damasco, Oakland; Justin Escobar and Dora Saldaña).

Crais, Robert. (Elvis Cole).

Dawson, Janet. (Jeri Howard, Oakland).

Dunlap, Susan. (Kiernan O'Shaugnessy, Hollywood).

Gores, Joe. (Neal Fargo, Daniel Kearny Associates, skip-tracing agency).

Grafton, Sue. (Kinsey Millhone).

Grant, Linda. (Catherine Saylor, high-tech P.I., Berkeley).

Greenleaf, Stephen. (John Marshall Tanner, San Francisco).

Kaminsky, Stuart. (Toby Peters, Los Angeles).

Kennealy, Jerry. (Nick Polo).

Kijewski, Karen. (Kat Colorado, private investigator).

Lochte, Dick. (Leo G. Bloodworth, Los Angeles).

Lupoff, Richard A. (insurance investigator Hobart Lindsey and Marvia Plum, police officer).

Macdonald, Ross. (Lew Archer, Santa Barbara).

Mosley, Walter. (Easy Rawlins, Los Angeles).

Muller, Marcia. (Sharon McCone, San Francisco).

Pronzini, Bill. (Nameless detective, San Francisco).

Shannon, John. (Jack Liffey, Los Angeles).

Simon, Roger L. (Moses Wine, Los Angeles).
Singer, Shelley. (Jake Samson and Rosie).

Colorado

Dold, Gaylord. (Mitch Roberts, who never seems to make it home to Colorado).
Ramos, Manuel. (Danny "Moony" Mora; Luis Montez). The first three titles were all reissued in 2004.

District of Columbia

Law, Janice. (Anna Peters).
Pelecanos, George P. (Derek Strange).

Florida

Kaminsky, Stuart M. Lew Fonesca, a depressed process server in Sarasota, formerly an investigator for the District Attorney's office in Chicago, appeared in the first title in 1999; the fourth book, *Denial*, was published in 2005.
Parrish, P. J. (Louis Kincaid).
Sanders, Lawrence. (Archy McNally). The series has been continued by Vincent Lardo.

Illinois

Nelscott, Kris. (Smokey Dalton).
Paretsky, Sara. (V. I. Warshawski).
Raleigh, Michael. (Paul Whelan).
Walker, David J. (Malachy Foley).

Indiana

Lewin, Michael Z. (Albert Samson, Indianapolis).
Tierney, Ronald. (Deets Shanahan).

Iowa

Gorman, Ed. (Sam McCain, Black River Falls, 1950s).

Louisiana

Burke, James Lee. (Dave Robicheaux, an on again off again sometimes cop sometimes P.I.).
Donaldson, D. J. (Dr. Kit Franklin, criminal psychologist, and Chief Medical Examiner Andy Broussard).
Sallis, James. (Lew Griffin).
Smith, Julie. Talba Wallis, African American poet and P.I., was introduced in *Louisiana Hot-Shot* in 2001; the fifth title, *P. I. On a Hot Tin Roof,* was published in 2005.

Maine

Connolly, John. (Charlie Parker, ex-cop).

Maryland

Lippman, Laura. (Tess Monaghan, Baltimore).

Massachusetts

Barnes, Linda. (Carlotta Carlyle; Michael Spraggue, Boston).
Lehane, Dennis. (Patrick Kenzie and Angie Gennaro).
Parker, Robert B. The Spenser series, set in Boston; started with *The Godwulf Manuscript* in 1973. The thirty-first title, *Bad Business,* was published in 2004. *Spenser* was a television show and a couple of made-for-television movies.

Michigan

Estleman, Loren D. (Amos Walker, Detroit).

Minnesota

Sandford, John. (Lucas Davenport). Prey series. In *Mortal Prey*, the thirteenth Prey novel, Lucas goes up against hit woman Clara Rinker from *Certain Prey* (1999), the first Prey book again.

Mississippi

Hegwood, Martin. (Jack Delmas).

Missouri

Lutz, John. (Alo Nudger, St. Louis).

Montana

Crumley, James. (Sughrue and Milo Milodragovitch).
Prowell, Sandra West. (Phoebe Siegel).

New Jersey

Evanovich, Janet. (Stephanie Plum, bounty hunter and former discount lingerie buyer).

New Mexico

Anaya, Rudolfo. (Sonny Baca).
Brewer, Steve. (Bubba Mabry).
Satterthwait, Walter. (Joshua Croft).

New York

Block, Lawrence. (Matthew Scudder).
Chesbro, George C. (Dr. Robert '"Mongo" Frederickson, Ph.D., little person).
Coleman, Reed Farrel. (Moe Prager).

Collins, Michael. (Dan Fortune, one-armed).

Dobyns, Stephen. (Charles Bradshaw, Saratoga).

Eichler, Selma. (Desiree Shapiro).

Friedman, Kinky. (Kinky Friedman).

Fusilli Jim. (Terry Orr).

Hall, Parnell. (Stanley Hastings).

Rozan, S. J. (Lydia Chin and Bill Smith).

🎗 *Reflecting the Sky.* 2001. Winner of the Shamus Award.

Scoppettone, Sandra. (Lauren Laurano).

Simmons, Dan. (Joe Kurtz, Buffalo).

Vachss, Andrew. (Burke).

Ohio

Roberts, Les. (Milan Jacovich).

South Dakota

Adams, Harold. (Carl Wilcox, Depression era).

Tennessee

Womack, Steven. (Harry James Denton, Nashville).

Texas

Riordan, Rick. (Tres Navarre, San Antonio).

Washington (all Seattle).

Emerson, Earl W. (Thomas Black).

Ford, G. M. (Leo Waterman).

Hoyt, Richard. (John Denson).

West Africa

Wilson, Robert. (Bruce Medway, professional "fixer").

Ex-Cops

Former police officers now working as private investigators are featured in a subgenre that offers the best of both major types of sleuths. The investigator has an autonomy and independence that are not possible within the confines of an official law enforcement agency, while at the same time he or she can believably display a knowledge and use of police procedures. The sleuth often still has friends on the force who can give him or her inside information and test results. Some of the following sleuths are also listed in the "Police Detectives" section because they played the role of police detectives in their earlier books.

Barnes, Linda. (Carlotta Carlyle, drives a Boston cab while working as a P.I.).

Block, Lawrence. (Matthew Scudder, a recovering alcoholic).

Burke, James Lee. (Dave Robicheaux).

Connelly, Michael. (Harry Bosch).

Craig, Philip R. (Jeff Jackson).

Daniel, David. (Alex Rasmussen). Third in 2004.

Dunning, John. (Cliff Janeway).

Haddam, Jane. (Gregor Demarkian).

Hamilton, Steve. (Alex McKnight).

Jance, J. A. (Brandon Walker).

King, Jonathon. (Max Freeman).

Krueger, William Kent. (Cork O'Connor).

Langton, Jane. (Homer Kelly, retired homicide detective). The series started with *The Transcendental Murder* (1964); the eighteenth book is *Steeplechase* (2005).

McKevett, G.A. (Savannah Reid).

Raleigh, Michael. (Paul Whelan).

Stroby, Wallace. (Harry Rane).

Swain, James. (Tony Valentine, head of Grift Sense, a gambling consulting company).

Wesley, Valerie Wilson. (Tamara Hayle).

Wishnia, K. J. A. (Filomena Buscarsela).

Woods, Stuart. (Stone Barrington).

Unofficial Detectives

Many novels employ a crime-solving protagonist who has no official standing, either as an officer of the law or as a paid private detective. These are simply individuals who are somehow drawn into the process of solving the crime—whether as an innocent bystander or as a party somehow related to the victim. Cozy novels featuring amateurs predominate; however, hard-boiled noir types also exist.

Hard-Boiled

Many of the hard-boiled detectives who work as private investigators are listed in the ex-cop section. Many of them use only one name.

Child, Lee. (Jack Reacher, former military police).

Hall, James W. (Thorn, Florida).

Blackwater Sound. 2002. Winner of the Shamus Award.

Waiwaiole, Lono. (Wiley, Pacific Northwest).

Amateur Detective, Cozy and Soft-Boiled

Amateur detectives appear everywhere. They may be young or old, single or married, immersed in the community or reluctantly drawn out of solitude. The amateur detective in cozy mysteries is always curious and has a sincere need to help others. The soft-boiled is not as warm and fuzzy but is also not filled with the angst of hard-boiled detectives.

Allbert, Susan Wittig. (China Bayles, herb shop proprietor).

Allyn, Doug. ("Mitch" Mitchell, single mom, café owner).

Atherton, Nancy. (Lori Shepherd, a mom and Aunt Dimity, a ghost—very cozy).

Babson, Marian. (Trixie Dolan and Evangaline Sinclair, aging movie stars).

Bannister, Jo. (Brodie Farrell, single mom who runs a finding agency).

Barrett, Neal, Jr. (Wiley Moss, illustrator; wacky but grisly humor).

Berry, Carole. (Bonnie Indermill, office temp).

Blanc, Nero. (Belle Graham, crossword-puzzle editor).

Blevins, Meredith. (Annie Szabo, widowed writer, and her mother-in-law Madame Mina, a Gypsy).

Brett, Simon. (Carole Seddon; Mrs. Melita Pargeter, amateur).

Cannell, Dorothy. (Ellie Haskell, cozy).

Carvic, Heron. (continued by Hamilton Crane and Hampton Charles). (Miss Seaton, British spinster).

Chittenden, Margaret. (Charlie Plato, co-owner of a country western dance club).

Cockey, Tim. (Hitchcock Sewell, undertaker, Baltimore).

Cooper, Susan Rogers. (E. J. Pugh, romance writing suburban mom).

Dams, Jeanne M. (Dorothy Martin, widow, American living in England).

Fennelly, Tony. (Matt Sinclair, antiques dealer).

Fowler, Earlene. (Benni Harper, curator of folk art museum, California).

Gash, Jonathan. (Lovejoy, antiques dealer).

Gentry, Christine. (Ansel Phoenix, drawer of dinosaurs).

Hammond, Gerald. (Keith Calder, gunsmith, Scotland).

Harris, Charlaine. (Lily Bard, cleaning lady, Arkansas).

Holt, Hazel. (Sheila Malory, British widow). (recently reissued).

Jacobs, Jonnie. (Kate Austen, mom, Marin County, California).

James, Dean. (Simon Kirby-Jones, historian, vampire, and mystery author).

Jorgensen, Christine T. (Stella the Stargazer, astrological advice columnist, Denver).

Kozak, Haley Jane. (Wollie Shelley, greeting card business, Los Angeles).

Lacey, Sarah. (Leah Hunter, tax inspector).

Lathen, Emma. (John Putnam Thatcher, banker).

Lawrence, Martha C. (Elizabeth Chase, psychic).

MacLeod, Charlotte. (Sarah Kelling, amateur).

Malcolm, John. (Tim Simpson, art investment advisor).

Matteson, Stefanie. (Charlotte Graham, seventy-something movie star).

McCrumb, Sharyn. (Elizabeth MacPherson, anthropologist).

Meier, Leslie. (Lucy Stone, mom).

Pickard, Nancy. (Jenny Cain, administrator).

Roberts, Gillian. (Amanda Pepper, English teacher).

Roosevelt, Elliott. (First Lady Eleanor Roosevelt).

Taylor, Phoebe Atwood. (Asey Mayo, New Englander).

Trocheck, Kathy Hogan. (Callahan Garrity, cleaning lady, formerly a cop).

Williams, David. (Mark Treasure, banker).

Wolzien, Valerie. (Susan Henshaw, suburban homemaker).

Psychologists and Psychiatrists

Those who deal with the mind find more than their fair share of crimes that need solving.

Kellerman, Jonathan. (Alex Delaware, psychologist).
Kennett, Shirley. (P. J. Gray, psychological profiler).
Matthews, Alex. (Cassidy McCabe, therapist).
White, Stephen Walsh. (Dr. Alan Gregory, psychologist).

Forensic Scientists

Those who solve mysteries by finding all the clues to be found by working with the human remains have become increasingly popular in a trend that is reflected by television shows such as *CSI.* Whether they are actually digging into the victim or reconstructing a face to seek the identity of a victim of whom only the skull remains, these sleuths become intimately involved with the crime.

Connor, Beverly. (Lindsay Chamberlain, forensic anthropologist).
Cornwell, Patricia D. (Kay Scarpetta, medical examiner).
Deaver, Jeffery. (Lincoln Rhyme, quadriplegic criminologist).
Donaldson, D. J. (Dr. Kit Franklin, criminal psychologist, and Chief Medical Examiner Andy Broussard).
Elkins, Aaron. (Gideon Oliver, forensic anthropologist).
Gerritsen, Tess. (Dr. Maura Isles, medical examiner).
Johansen, Iris. (Eve Duncan, forensic sculptor).
Masters, Priscilla. (Coroner Martha Gunn, Shrewsbury).
Reichs, Kathy. (Tempe Brennan, forensic anthropologist). **TVS** *Bones*
Slaughter, Karin. (Sara Linton, medical examiner).

Lawyers

Lawyers might qualify more as private investigators than as amateurs because they seek to extricate clients from jeopardy; however, their investigations are usually outside of their professional line of duty. In the delicate interface between crime and justice lies the law, and the satisfaction that "justice will be served" is the promise of these novels.

This type of detective story often features scenes of courtroom interrogation in which all is revealed, often dramatically. In some of the following books, the reader is treated to considerable analysis of the law, which can be confusing for U.S. readers when the focus is on British jurisprudence. Jon Breen's bibliography, *Novel Verdicts: A Guide to Courtroom Fiction* (Scarecrow Press, 1999) supplies this background information.

The legal thriller achieved great prominence in the 1990s. Scott Turow, John Grisham, and Steve Martini all made it to the best-seller lists with their crime novels that feature lawyers. However, the legal thriller's emphasis is not necessarily on detection but rather on a crafty attorney's abilities to extricate himself, herself, or others from danger. The legal thriller is covered later in this chapter.

Great Britain

Caudwell, Sarah. (Professor Hilary Tamar, Oxford don, and his inimitable Lincoln's Inn lawyer friends, including two delightful women lawyers, Julia Larwood and Selena Jardine).

Cooper, Natasha. Trish McGuire, a barrister known for arguing child abuse cases, keeps being drawn into cases that connect with her personal life.

Meek, M. R. D. Lennox Kemp may be mild mannered, but he sticks to his cases with dogged persistence.

Mortimer, John. Untidy, middle-aged Horace Rumpole pleads cases at the Old Bailey; he is featured in hundreds of stories.

United States

Burke, James Lee. Billy Bob Holland, transplanted to Montana from Texas, tries to keep his inner violence repressed.

Hall, Parnell. Stanley Hastings is a P.I. who works as an ambulance chaser to drum up clients for a negligence lawyer.

Hensley, Joe L. (Don Robak, a criminal lawyer turned judge).

Jacobs, Jonnie. Kali O'Brien leaves a big San Francisco law firm and moves back to her hometown, which she discovers is just as dangerous and exciting as the city.

Lashner, William. (Victor Carl, an underdog defense attorney).

Maron, Margaret. (Deborah Knott, North Carolina). The series starts when Deborah is running for judge in the *Bootlegger's Daughter* (1992), which won Edgar, Anthony, Agatha, and Macavity Awards.

McInerny, Ralph. (Andrew Broom, a small-town Indiana attorney).

Parker, Barbara. (Gail Connor and Anthony Quintana, Miami lawyers who marry).

Rosenfelt, David. (Andy Carpenter, Paterson, New Jersey, defense lawyer).

Tapply, William G. (Brady Coyne, Boston, low-key and self-reliant).

Wilhelm, Kate. (Barbara Holloway, an attorney who takes on socially important cases in Oregon).

Ecclesiastical

Although those in the clergy usually watch out for the souls of the faithful and those in need, the following sleuths often find themselves investigating people wrongly accused and subsequently discovering the real culprits. These stories usually contain an extra layer of moral turpitude as well as moral resolve. Historical mysteries featuring the clergy are included in the historical mystery section later in this chapter.

Black, Veronica. (Sister Joan, Catholic nun, Cornwall).

Charles, Kate. (Painter Lucy Kingsley and solicitor David Middleton-Brown, Church of England setting).

Coel, Margaret. (Father John O'Malley, Arapaho Indian Reservation, Wyoming).

Greeley, Andrew. (Father Blackie Ryan).

Kemelman, Harry. (Rabbi David Small, New England).

Kienzle, William X. (Father Bob Koesler, Roman Catholic, Detroit).

Manuel, David. (Brother Bartholomew, Faith Abbey, Massachusetts).

McInerny, Ralph. (Father Dowling, Roman Catholic, Chicago area).

O'Marie, Sister Carol Anne. (Sister Mary Helen).

Spencer-Fleming, Julia. (Clare Fergusson, Anglican priest).

Sullivan, Winona. (Sister Cecile, licensed private investigator and nun).

Sumners, Cristina. (Rev. Dr. Kathryn Koerney, Episcopal).

Academic

The professors in the following novels use their scholarly training for crime detection, and not always on the campus. Eccentricity—that obvious characteristic of academics—is present in most.

Bowen, Gail. (Joanne Kilbourne, widowed professor, Saskatchewan, Canada).

Bruce, Leo. (Carolus Deane, schoolteacher, London).

Cross, Amanda. (Dr. Kate Fansler, professor of English).

Elkins, Aaron. (Dr. Gideon Oliver, anthropologist).

Kelly, Nora. (Gillian Adams, professor of history).

McInerny, Ralph. (Roger Knight, Notre Dame).

Swift, Virginia. ("Mustang" Sally Alder, women's history professor, Wyoming).

Taylor, Sarah Stewart. (Sweeney St. George, art history professor).

Truman, Margaret. (Mac Smith, law professor).

Journalists

The investigative reporter may also be considered a private detective (without license). and is often listed as a detective type in critical works on the genre. Books by the following authors illustrate this type of character.

Babson, Marian. (Doug Perkins, PR man, London).

Burke, Jan. (Irene Kelly, Southern California journalist).

D'Amato, Barbara. (Cat Marsala, Chicago reporter).

Hamilton, Denise. (Eve Diamond, Los Angeles).

Pickard, Nancy. (Marie Lightfoot, Florida-based true-crime writer).

Walker, Mary Willis. (Molly Cates, magazine journalist, Texas).

Husband-and-Wife Teams

A combination of considerable charm is a married pair of sleuths. This is teamwork with a dash of romantic tension. The increase in recent years of the importance of relationships in the lives of sleuths is evidenced by the increasing number of paired significant others appearing in the following list.

Allen, Steve. (Steve Allen and Jayne Meadows).

Kellerman, Faye. (Orthodox Jewish housewife Rina Lazarus and her husband, LAPD Detective Sergeant Peter Decker).

MacGregor, T. J. (Quin St. James and Mike McCleary).

Truman, Margaret. (Mac Smith and Annabel Reed).

Wilhelm, Kate. (Charlie Meiklejohn and Constance Leidl).

Human-and-Animal Teams

Americans have a great affection for and fascination with the pets in their lives. Several authors write about human sleuths or animal sleuths working together with the other species. The most famous team is probably that of Qwilleran and his cats KoKo and YumYum, in the series written by Lillian Jackson Braun.

Adamson, Lydia. (Alice Nestleton, cat mysteries).

Baxter, Cynthia. (Jessica Popper, D.V.M., and her dogs Max and Lou).

Benjamin, Carol Lea. (Rachel Alexander, P.I., and her pit bull, Dashiell).

Berenson, Laurien. (Melanie Travis dog fancier series).

Braun, Lilian Jackson. (The Cat Who series, featuring Qwilleran, a human journalist, and KoKo and YumYum, of the Siamese persuasion).

Brown, Rita Mae. (Mary Minor "Harry" Haristeen, postmistress, and feline Sneaky Pie, with occasional assistance from canine Tee Tucker).

Cleary, Melissa. (Jackie Walsh and her shepherd, Jake).

Conant, Susan. (The Dog Lover's series, featuring Holly Winter and Alaskan malamutes Rowdy and Kimi).

Davis, Norbert. (California P.I. Doan and his oversized Great Dane, Carstairs).

Douglas, Carole Nelson. (Midnight Louis series, featuring Las Vegas publicist Miss Temple Barr and Midnight Louie, a studly, big black cat).

Guiver, Patricia. (Delilah Doolittle, British widow, and her Doberman, Watson, California).

Diversity in Detection

A detective's gender, race, ethnicity, and sexual orientation play a major role in how that detective relates to the crime to be solved, as well as to the world in general, and it is a feature many readers seek out A variety of backgrounds bring a wealth of diversity to the detective novel, adding fascinating insights to the unfolding of the characters within. Until recently women were considered an anomaly as crime solvers, but no more. Women as sleuths now seem to make up about half the detectives featured in novels.

Gay and Lesbian

Allen, Kate. (Alison Kane).

Forrest, Katherine V. (LAPD detective Kate Delafield).

Griffith, Nicola. (Aud Torvingen, Norwegian American lesbian ex-cop).

Hart, Ellen. (Jane Lawless, restaurateur).

Herren, Greg. (Scotty Bradley, ex-exotic dancer).

King, Laurie R. (Kate Martinelli, police officer, San Francisco).

Lake, Lori L. (Dez Reilly and Jaylynn Savage, Minnesota police officers).

McDermid, Val. (Lindsay Gordon).

McNab, Claire. (Detective Inspector Carol Ashton).

Nava, Michael. (Henry Rios, lawyer).

Scoppettone, Sandra. (Lauren Laurano).

Sims, Elizabeth. (Lillian Byrd, amateur).

Stevenson, Richard. (Don Strachey, P.I.).

Zubro, Mark Richard. (Paul Turner; Tom Mason and Scott Carpenter).

Black Sleuths

Frankie Y. Bailey's historical and scholarly look at black characters in *Out of the Woodpile: Black Characters in Crime and Detective Fiction* (Greenwood, 1991) includes a directory of black characters in crime and detective fiction, film, and television. A good resource for readers' advisory information on African American crime, suspense, and detection novels is *African American Literature: A Guide to Reading Interests,* edited by Alma Dawson and Connie Van Fleet (Libraries Unlimited, 2004). Paula L. Woods's award-winning anthology *Spooks, Spies and Private Eyes: Black Mystery, Crime, and Suspense Fiction of the 20th Century* (Doubleday, 1995) features original, long-lost, and recent examples of the diversity to be found in tales of crime written by blacks. The following list of books is just a small sampling of detective novels featuring black sleuths.

Ball, John D. (Virgil Tibbs, detective, Pasadena, California, police force).

Bland, Eleanor Taylor. (Marti MacAlister, homicide detective).

DeLoach, Nora. (Mama, a social worker, and her paralegal daughter, Simone Covington, South Carolina).

Edwards, Grace F. (Mali Anderson, ex-cop of NYPD).

Haywood, Gar Anthony. (Aaron Gunner, private investigator, Los Angeles).

Holton, Hugh. (Chicago Police Commander Larry Cole).

Jones, Solomon. (Detective Kevin Lynch, Philadelphia).

McCall Smith, Alexander. (Precious Ramotswe, Botswana).

Mosley, Walter. (Easy Rawlins, private investigator; Fearless Jones).

Neely, Barbara. (Blanche White, a domestic with a keen eye for crime*)*.

Nelscott, Kris. (Smokey Dalton, Chicago, 1960s).

Patterson, James. (Alex Cross, police forensic psychologist).

Sallis, James. (Lew Griffin, at different times in his life).

Smith-Levin, Judith. (police lieutenant Starletta Duvall, Worcester, Massachusetts).

Wesley, Valerie Wilson. (Tamara Hayle, private investigator).

Woods, Paula L. (Charlotte Justice, police officer).

Hispanic Sleuths

Unfortunately, there is not yet a book like Bailey's *Out of the Woodpile* for either Hispanic or Native American crime and detective fiction, but it is likely that publishing in these areas will continue to grow in the next years to meet increasing reader demand.

Anaya, Rudolfo. (Sonny Baca, P.I., Albuquerque).

Burns, Rex. (Gabe Wager, Denver).

Corpi, Lucha. (Gloria Damasco, private investigator, Oakland; Justin Escobar and Dora Saldaña).

Garcia-Aguilera, Carolina. (Lupe Solano, Cuban American, Florida).

🎗 *Havana Heat.* 2000. Winner of the Shamus Award.

Ramos, Manuel. (Luis Montez, lawyer, Denver; Danny "Moony" Mora, PI Denver).

Taibo, Paco Ignacio. (Hector Belascoaran Shayne, Mexico City).

Villatoro, Marcos McPeek. (Romilia Chacón, Salvadoran American, Nashville).

Native American Sleuths

Bowen, Peter. (Gabriel Du Pre, Metis).

Doss, James D. (Charlie Moon, Ute Tribal Police).

Gentry, Christine. (Ansel Phoenix, half-Blackfoot).

Goodweather, Hartley. (Thumps DreadfulWater, Cherokee, ex-cop).

Hager, Jean. (Mitch Bushyhead, police chief; Molly Bearpaw, Native American League).

Hillerman, Tony. (Jim Chee and Joe Leaphorn, Navajo Tribal Police).

Medawar, Mardi Oakley. (Tay-bodal, a Kiowa healer in the 1860s).

Perry, Thomas. (Jane Whitehead, Seneca).

Stabenow, Dana. (Kate Shugak, Aleut).

Thurlo, Aimeé, and David Thurlo. (Agent Ella Clah, Navaho, FBI).

Asian Sleuths

Chang, Leonard. (Allen Choice, Korean American, San Francisco).

Cunningham, E. V. (Masao Masuto, Nisei, Beverly Hills).

Furutani, Dale. (Ken Tanaka, Japanese American; Matsuyama Kaze, seventeenth-century Japan).

Glass, Leslie. (April Woo, Chinese American).

Massey, Sujata. (Rei Shimura, Japanese American English teacher living in Tokyo).

Moore, Harker. (Lieutenant James Sakura, NYPD homicide detective).

Rowland, Laura Joh. (Samurai Sano Ichiro, seventeenth-century Japan).

Rozan, S. J. (Lydia Chin, Chinese American).

Subjects and Themes

Just as many readers of detective fiction prefer a particular type of detective, others seek those stories with a particular background of country, social order, activity, organization, or profession. With the advent of automated catalogs and Library of Congress/OCLC GSAFD fiction subject headings and electronic products like NoveList and What Do I Read Next?, it is now easier to locate mysteries with particular settings or subjects. There is also a guide for selecting titles by locale, Nina King's *Crimes of the Scene: A Mystery Novel Guide for the International Traveler* (St. Martin's Press, 1997).

Following are several of the available anthologies that deal with settings and subjects. A few examples of subject groupings (sports, cookery, bibliomysteries, and art world) are included after the list to show the readers' advisory potential of analysis by type. These anthologies also provide the reader (and the readers' advisor). with a good way to become familiar with previously unknown authors.

Ashley, Mike, ed. *The Mammoth Book of Roman Whodunnits.* Carroll & Graf, 2003.

Bishop, Claudia, and Dean James, ed. *Death Dines In.* Berkley Books, 2004.

Bland, Eleanor Taylor, ed. *Shades of Black: Crime and Mystery Stories by African-American Authors.* Berkley Prime Crime, 2004.

Connelly, Michael, ed. *Murder in Vegas: New Crime Tales of Gambling and Desperation.* Tom Doherty Associates, 2005.

Gorman, Ed, Martin H. Greenberg, and Larry Segriff, eds. *Cat Crimes Through Time.* Carroll & Graf, 1999.

Jakubowski, Maxim, ed. *The Mammoth Book of Comic Crime.* Carroll & Graf, 2002.

Kaminsky, Stuart M., ed. *Mystery Writers of America Presents Show Business Is Murder.* Berkley Prime Crime, 2004.

Morgan, Jill, ed. *Creature Cozies.* Berkley Prime Crime, 2005.

> Featuring cozy stories with pets.

Penzler, Otto, ed. *Dangerous Women.* Mysterious Press, 2005.

Pittman, Joseph, and Annette Riffle, eds. *And the Dying is Easy: All-New Tales of Summertime Suspense.* Signet, 2001.

Spillane, Mickey, and Max Allan Collins, eds. *A Century of Noir: Thirty-Two Classic Crime Stories.* New American Library, 2002.

Sports

The players, owners, and commentators find the final score in settings involving both amateur and high-stakes professional sports.

Coben, Harlan. (Myron Bolitar, sports agent).

Elkins, Charlotte, and Aaron Elkins. (Lee Ofsted, women's professional golf).

Francis, Dick. (jockey, trainer, and others connected with British horse racing).

Gordon, Alison. (Kate Henry, baseball writer, Toronto).

Isleib, Roberta. (Cassie Burdette, golf).

Miles, Keith. (professional golf).

Soos, Troy. (Mickey Rawlings, baseball player in the second decade of the twentieth century).

Cookery

Mm-mm-good. . . . Cooking, food, and dining play major roles in the following selection of mysteries. Some even include recipes!

Bond, Michael. <u>Monsieur Pamplemousse series.</u> The character's dog is Pommes Frites.

Crawford, Isis. (Libby Simmons, caterer and her family members).

Davidson, Diane Mott. (Goldy Bear, caterer, Colorado).

Farmer, Jerrilyn. (Madeline Bean, caterer, Los Angeles).

Laurence, Janet. (Darina Lisle, caterer/cookbook writer).

Myers, Tamar. <u>Pennsylvania Dutch Mystery series</u>, featuring Magdalena Yoder.

Page, Katherine Hall. (Faith Fairchild, gourmet chef).

Pence, Joanne. (Chef Angie Amalfi).

Pickard, Nancy. <u>Eugenia Potter series</u>, originated by Virginia Rich.

Richman, Phyllis. (Chas Wheatley, restaurant critic).

Temple, Lou Jane. (Heaven Lee, restaurateur).

Bibliomysteries

In the following books the amateur sleuths are somehow involved in the world of books, whether as librarians, writers, illustrators, publishers, or booksellers.

Dunning, John. (Cliff Janeway, book collector and expert).

Hall, Parnell.

> *Suspense.* 1998. Stanley Hastings, a reluctant detective, finds himself in the strange and dangerous world of publishing.

Hart, Carolyn G. (Annie Laurance and Max Darling, bookstore owner).

Hess, Joan. (Claire Malloy, bookseller).

James, P. D.

> *Original Sin.* 1995. Adam Dalgliesh and Kate Miskin investigate some mysterious goings-on in England's oldest publishing house.

Jordan, Jennifer. (Mr. and Mrs. Barry Vaughan, writers).

Kaewert, Julie Wallin.

> Her <u>Booklover's Mystery series</u> features British publisher Alex Plumtree, of Plumtree Press, and his American fiance, Sarah. Described by *Publishers Weekly* as "Agatha Christie-meets-Nancy Drew."
>
> > *Unsolicited.* 1994.
> > *Unbound.* 1997.
> > *Unprintable.* 1998.
> > *Untitled.* 1999.
> > *Unsigned.* 2001.
> > *Uncataloged.* 2002.

Kimberly, Alice.

> ***The Ghost and Mrs. McClure.*** 2004.
>
> Penelope Thornton-McClure discovers her Rhode Island bookshop is haunted.

King, Ross.

> ***Ex-Libris.*** 2001.
>
> A seventeenth-century bookseller, Isaac Inchbold, is summoned by Lady Marchamont to find a missing ancient and heretical manuscript, *The Labyrinth of the World*.

Macdonald, Marianne. (Dido Hoare, antiquarian bookseller).

Mosley, Walter. (1950s bookstore owner Paris Minton). <u>Fearless Jones series.</u>

Papazoglou, Orania. (Patience McKenna, writer).

Pérez-Reverte, Arturo.

> ***The Club Dumas.*** 1998.
>
> After he agrees to authenticate a scrap of an old manuscript of *The Three Musketeers*, Spanish book detective Lucas Curso is drawn into a world of occult, murder, and intrigue.

Peters, Elizabeth. (Jacqueline Kirby, librarian/romance writer).

Shankman, Sarah. (Samantha Adams, writer).

Van Gieson, Judith. (archivist Claire Reynier, New Mexico).

Art World

Malcolm, John. (Tim Simpson, art investment advisor).

Muller, Marcia. (Elena Oliverez, art curator).

Pears, Iain. (Jonathan Argyll and Flavia di Stefano).

> <u>Art History Mystery series.</u>

Pérez-Reverte, Arturo.

> ***The Flanders Panel.*** 1996. A tale of art, chess, and a 500-year-old mystery.

Genreblends

Historical Mysteries

Most mystery and detection novels are essentially timeless: Readers simply accept the period backgrounds. One of the fastest-growing subgenres in mystery is the historical, with the nineteenth century and the medieval period being particularly popular. One may only guess at reasons. Perhaps readers of this type like to learn about history at the same time as they read for enjoyment. It has been posited that the appeal lies in the premise that the methods used to solve mysteries during these times were more "primitive" and thus, more natural and intuitive. Historical settings do provide a shadowy and unfamiliar but realistic milieu for tales of detection.

Some readers seek out the nineteenth-century sources of the detective story in Edgar Allan Poe, Wilkie Collins, Sheridan LeFanu, and others who wrote before the creation of Sherlock Holmes. Some mysteries, written as contemporaries, can now be read as historicals. History fans might find the backgrounds as interesting as the plots. More historical mysteries can be found in the "Historical Fiction" chapter (chapter 5).

Alexander, Bruce (pseudonym of Bruce Cook).

His John Fielding series features Sir John Fielding, a blind magistrate who actually did exist in eighteenth-century London.

Blind Justice. 1994.
Murder on Grub Street. 1995.
Watery Grave. 1996.
Person or Persons Unknown. 1997.
Jack, Knave and Fools. 1998.
Death of a Colonial. 1999.
The Color of Death. 2000.
Smuggler's Moon. 2001.
An Experiment in Treason. 2002.
The Price of Murder. 2003.
Rules of Engagement. 2005.

Allen, Conrad.

His Ship Detectives series features George Porter Dillman and Genevieve Masefield, early twentieth-century ship detectives for the Cunard Line.

Murder on the **Lusitania.** 1999.
Murder on the **Mauretania.** 2000.
Murder on the **Minnesota.** 2002.
Murder on the **Caronia.** 2003.
Murder on the **Marmora.** 2004.
Murder on the **Salsette.** 2005.

Banks, T. F.

The Memoirs of a Bow Street Runner series is set in early nineteenth-century London.

The Thief-Taker: Memoirs of a Bow Street Runner. 2001.
The Emperor's Assassin: Memoirs of a Bow Street Runner. 2003.

Barron, Stephanie.

Her Jane Austen Mystery series is set set in England's Regency period and features author Jane Austen as protagonist. These novels will appeal to Austen fans who also have an interest in amateur detection.

Jane and the Unpleasantness at Scargrave Manor. 1996.
Jane and the Man on the Cloth. 1997.
Jane and the Wandering Eye. 1998.
Jane and the Genius on the Place. 1999.
Jane and the Stillroom Maid. 2000.
Jane and the Prisoner on Wool House. 2001.
Jane and the Ghosts on Netley. 2003.
Jane, visiting the ruins of Netley Abbey with her young nephews, is drawn into spying on Sophia Challoner, a widow who may be working against British interests in the Peninsular War.

Jane and His Lordship's Legacy. 2005.

Bowen, Rhys.

The <u>Molly Murphy series</u> takes place in the early 1900s in New York.

> 🎗 *Murphy's Law.* 2001. Winner of the Agatha Award and the Herodotus Award.
> *Death of Riley.* 2002.
> 🎗 *For the Love of Mike.* 2003. Winner of the Anthony Award for Best Historical Novel and the Bruce Alexander Historical Award.
> *In Like Flynn.* 2005.

Brightwell, Emily.

Her <u>Mrs. Jeffries series</u> takes place in Victorian England. The series started with *Mrs. Jeffries and the Inspector* in 1993. The nineteenth title is *Mrs. Jeffries Stalks the Hunter* (2004).

Brown, Molly.

Invitation to a Funeral. 1998. First published in England in 1995. Restoration London.

Aphra Behn, playwright and former spy, investigates the deaths of two brothers, and uncovers a dangerous secret.

Buckley, Fiona.

Her <u>Elizabethan mysteries</u> feature Ursula Blanchard, lady-in-waiting to Queen Elizabeth I. Listed in series order.

> *To Shield the Queen.* 1997.
> *The Doublet Affair.* 1998.
> *Queen's Ransom.* 2000.
> *To Ruin a Queen.* 2000.
> *Queen of Ambition.* 2001.
> *A Pawn for the Queen.* 2002.
> *The Fugitive Queen.* 2003.
> *The Siren Queen.* 2004.

Chisholm, P. F.

His <u>Sir Robert Carey series</u> takes place in sixteenth-century England.

> *A Famine of Horses.* 1995.
> In 1592, Sir Robert is sent to the Scottish Border to take up his duties as Deputy Warden.
>
> *A Season of Knives.* 1996.
> *A Surfeit of Guns.* 1997.
> *A Plague of Angels.* 2000.

Clark, Robert.

Mr. White's Confession. 1998. Minnesota, 1939.

Two young girls have been murdered, and all signs point to the eccentric photographer Mr. White—until police Lieutenant Wesley Horner starts investigating.

Clynes, Michael. (pseudonym of P.C. Doherty).

The Journals of Sir Roger Shallot, featuring Sir Richard Shattot, take place in sixteenth-century Britain. The sixth title was *The Relic Murders* (1998).

Collins, Max Allan.

Featuring private eye Nate Heller, who becomes involved with various notorious cases in the 1930s and 1940s.

> *True Detective.* 1983.
> Nate Heller's first client in Prohibition-era Chicago is Al Capone.
>
> *Angel in Black.* 2001.
> The twelfth Nate Heller mystery takes place in Hollywood.
>
> *Kisses of Death.* 2001.
> A collection of shorter Nathan Heller stories, including a novella featuring Marilyn Monroe.
>
> *Chicago Confidential.* 2002.
> It's 1950, and Heller is back in Chicago in a case involving Frank Sinatra, mobster Sam Giancana, Senator Joe McCarthy, and Jayne Mansfield.

7

Dams, Jeanne.

Her Hilda Johansson series is about an early 1900s Swedish immigrant in Indiana.

> *Death in Lacquer Red.* 1999.
> *Red White and Blue Murder.* 2000.
> *Green Grow the Victims.* 2001.
> *Silence Is Golden.* 2002.

Davis, Lindsey.

The Marcus Didius Falco series features Marcus Didius Falco, a finder in Ancient Rome.

> *The Silver Pigs.* 1989.
> In Falco's first case, he goes to Britain, where he becomes a slave while trying to track down the reason behind the murder of a senator's daughter.
>
> *Ode to a Banker.* 2001.
> Twelfth in the series. Falco is trying to find out who killed Aurelius Chrysippus and if it was his publishing or banking activities that motivated the crime.

> *A Body in the Bath House.* 2002.
> Improvements to his bathhouse create problems for Falco.
>
> *The Jupiter Myth.* 2003.
> *The Accusers.* 2003.
> *Scandal Takes a Holiday.* 2004.
> Falco is looking for a gossip columnist who has gone missing.

> *See Delphi and Die.* 2005. (British publication date. It has not yet been published in the United States.)

Day, Dianne.

Featuring Fremont Jones, an independent career woman in turn-of-the-century San Francisco.

🎗 *The Strange Files of Fremont Jones.* 1995.
In the first book of the series, Fremont Jones goes to San Francisco to start up a type-writing business. Winner of the Macavity Award.

Beacon Street Mourning. 2000.
In the sixth title, Fremont heads home to Boston, where her father is suffering from a wasting disease, and she comes to fear that it may be some kind of poison.

Doherty, P. C.

The Hugh Corbett series.

Satan in St. Mary's. 1986.
Hugh Corbett, a clerk and spy in the court of Edward I, is introduced and investigates a murder.

The Treason of Ghosts. 2000.
The twelfth book in the series sees Hugh on the trail of a serial killer.

Corpse Candle. 2001.
Hugh investigates a locked room mystery in 1303.

Douglas, Carole Nelson.

Her Irene Adler series features American opera singer Irene Adler, the antagonist of Sherlock Holmes, in the Victorian era.

Good Night Mr. Holmes. 1990.
The first book of the series.

Femme Fatale. 2003.
Irene Adler goes to New York in 1889 after Nelly Bly entices her with possible information about her hidden parentage.

Spider Dance. 2004.
Still seeking her mother, Irene finds an international conspiracy and lost treasure.

Dukthas, Ann.

Nicholas Segalla travels through time solving historical mysterie*s.*

In the Time of the Poisoned Queen. 1998. Tudor England.
The Prince Lost to Time. 1995. France, early nineteenth century.
A Time for the Death of a King. 1994. Mary, Queen of Scots.
The Time of Murder at Mayerling. 1996. Nineteenth-century Austria.

Dunn, Carola.

Her Daisy Dalrymple Mystery series contains cozies set in 1920s England.

Death at Wentwater Court. 1994. Reissued 2000.
Daisy, having lost most of the men in her life to World War I or the horrible influenza, takes a magazine job.

Rattle His Bones. 2000.
In her eighth outing, the Honorable Daisy finds a dinosaur-bone– pierced body in the London Natural History Museum.

To Davy Jones Below. 2001.
Daisy and Scotland Yard inspector Alex Fletcher take a cruise to the United States for their honeymoon.

The Case of the Murdered Muckraker. 2002. Tenth in the series.

Mistletoe and Murder. 2002.

Die Laughing. 2004.

A Mourning Wedding. 2004.

A pregnant Daisy tries to solve a murder at a country house party.

Fall of a Philanderer. 2005. The fourteenth in the series.

Emerson, Kathy Lynn.

Her Elizabethan-era mysteries feature Susanna, Lady Appleton, a headstrong herbalist.

Face Down in the Marrow-Bone Pie. 1997.

Face Down upon an Herbal. 1998.

Face Down Among the Winchester Geese. 1999.

Face Down Beneath the Eleanor Cross. 2000.

Face Down Under the Wych Elm. 2000.

Face Down Before the Rebel Hooves. 2001.

Face Down Across the Western Sea. 2002.

Face Down Below the Banqueting Hall. 2005.

The Diana Spaulding Mystery series features journalist Diana Spaulding in late nineteenth-century New York.

Deadlier Than the Pen. 2004.

Spaulding investigates the murder of two fellow journalists, and runs into horror author Damon Bathory.

Furutani, Dale.

The Samurai Mystery series, set in seventeenth-century Japan, features Matsuyama Kaze.

🎗 *Death at the Crossroads.* 1997. Winner of the Anthony Award.

Jade Palace Vendetta. 1999.

Kill the Shogun. 2000.

Gordon, Alan.

Medieval Mysteries.

An Antic Disposition: A Medieval Mystery. 2004.

This fifth title is a thirteenth-century telling of a story about a prince of Denmark.

Grace, C. L. (pseudonym of P. C. Doherty).

The Kathryn Swinbrooke series features a medieval physician in fifteenth-century Canterbury.

A Shrine of Murders: Being the First of the Canterbury Tales of Kathryn Swinbrooke, Leech, and Physician. 1993.

In the first installment of the series Kathryn looks for a poisoner.

Saintly Murders. 2001.

In the fourth book in the series, Kathryn takes on an infestation of rats, both rodents and humans.

A Maze of Murders. 2002.

An unsavory knight is beheaded in a maze.

A Feast of Poisons. 2004.

Now a wife, Kathryn is once again investigating poisonings.

Granger, Pip.

Featuring Zelda Fluck in London in the 1940s.

Hall, Robert Lee.

Featuring Benjamin Franklin in the late eighteenth century.

Hambly, Barbara.

Featuring Ben January in 1830s New Orleans.

Harper, Karen.

Featuring sleuthing done by Elizabeth I.

Kaminsky, Stuart M.

Featuring Toby Peters, private eye, Hollywood, in the 1940s, in a series in which actual motion picture stars are characters (e.g., John Wayne, Charlie Chaplin).

Kilian, Michael.

The Harrison Raines Civil War Mystery series features Virginia gentleman and secret Pinkerton agent Harrison "Harry" Raines.

King, Laurie R.

Her Mary Russell series features Sherlock Holmes's apprentice, later his wife, in the early twentieth century.

The Game. 2004. Seventh book, published in 2004.

Lawrence, Margaret.

Her Hannah Trevor series features Hannah Trevor, a midwife in eighteenth-century Maine who is drawn into solving mysteries following the American Revolution.

Hearts and Bones. 1996.
Blood Red Roses. 1997.
The Burning Bride. 1998.
The Iceweaver. 2000.

Linscott, Gillian. (Nell Bray, English suffragette).

Linscott won the CWA's Ellis Peters Historical Dagger 2000 and the Herodotus Award for Best International Historical Mystery Novel.

The Perfect Daughter. 2000. Ninth in the series.
Dead Man Riding. 2002. Tenth in the series.
Blood on the Wall. 2004.

McMillan, Ann.

Civil War mysteries.

Dead March. 1998.
Angel Trumpet. 1999.

Civil Blood. 2001.

Chickahominy Fever. 2003.

Meyers, Maan.

These books feature the obtuse and bumbling Sheriff Pieter Tonneman, New Amsterdam (New York), in the seventeenth century.

The Dutchman. 1992.

Newman, Sharan.

The Catherine LeVendeur Mystery series features Catherine and Edgar in twelfth-century Europe. This couple travels!

Death Comes as Epiphany. 1993.

The Devil's Door. 1994.

The Wandering Arm. 1995.

Strong as Death. 1996.

Cursed in the Blood. 1998.

The Difficult Saint. 1999.

To Wear the White Cloak. 2000.

Heresy. 2002.

Outcast Dove. 2003.

The Witch in the Well. 2004.

Paige, Robin.

Sir Charles Sheridan series.

Death at Bishops Keep. 1994.

Kathryn Ardleigh, an American writer of penny-dreadfuls, meets amateur sleuth Sir Charles Sheridan in this first book of the series.

Death at Rottingdean. 1999. Fifth in the series.

Death at Whitechapel. 2000.

Death at Epsom Downs. 2001.

Death at Dartmoor. 2002.

Death at Glamis Castle. 2003.

Death in Hyde Park. 2004.

Death at Blenheim Palace. 2005.

In 1903, while Lord Charles and Kate are visiting the hereditary home of the Dukes of Marlborough, both a maid and a mistress go missing.

Parry, Owen.

The Abel Jones mystery series is set in American in the 1860s. Winner of the Hammett Award and the Herodotus Award.

Faded Coat of Blue. 1999.

Shadows of Glory. 2000.

Call Each River Jordan. 2001.

Honor's Kingdom. 2002.

Bold Sons of Erin. 2003.

Pears, Iain.

>*An Instance of the Fingerpost*. 1998. Restoration England.
>
>In Oxford, Dr. Robert Groves is found dead, apparently the victim of poisoning; and a young woman is accused. Then four witnesses tell conflicting stories about what they saw, but only one reveals the truth.

Penman, Sharon Kay.

>Her Medieval Mystery series features Justin de Quincy.
>
>>*The Queen's Man.* 1996.
>>
>>Justin, discovering he was not a poor foundling taken in by the powerful bishop of Chester but rather the man's unacknowledged bastard, sets out to make his way in the world, and ends up solving mysteries while in the employ of Queen Eleanor of Aquitaine.
>>
>>*Cruel as the Grave.* 1998.
>>
>>*Dragon's Lair.* 2003.
>>
>>*Prince of Darkness.* 2005.

Pérez-Reverte, Arturo.

>*The Fencing Master.* 1998.
>
>In nineteenth-century Spain, fencing master Don Jaime Astarloa leads a dull life teaching a dying art—until he meets a mysterious woman with an uncanny skill at swordplay.

Perry, Anne.

>Her Thomas and Charlotte Pitt series takes place in London in the nineteenth century.
>
>>*The Cater Street Hangman.* 1979.
>>
>>Inspector Thomas Pitt and the socially privileged Charlotte Ellison meet and start their crime-solving partnership.
>>
>>*The Whitechapel Conspiracy.* 2001. Twenty-first in the series.
>>
>>*Southampton Row.* 2002.
>>
>>*Seven Dials.* 2003.
>>
>>*Long Spoon Lane.* 2005.
>
>Her William Monk series is about an amnesiac Victorian police detective who later turns private investigator.
>
>>*The Face of a Stranger.* 1990.
>>
>>A carriage accident leaves Monk with no memory.
>>
>>*Slaves of Obsession.* 2000.
>>
>>Monk and his wife Hester travel to the United States and into the Civil War.
>>
>>*A Funeral in Blue.* 2001.
>>
>>*Death of a Stranger.* 2002.
>>
>>Monk regains his memory.
>>
>>*The Shifting Tide.* 2004.

Peters, Elizabeth.

>The Amelia Peabody series.
>
>>*Crocodile on the Sandbank.* 1975.
>>
>>Amelia Peabody, Victorian Egyptologist, is introduced.

He Shall Thunder in the Sky. 2000.
This twelfth book in the series takes place in the winter of 1914–1915.

Lord of the Silent. 2001.
The Golden One. 2002.
Children of the Storm. 2003.
Guardian of the Horizon. 2003.
The Serpent on the Crown. 2005.
In this seventeenth installment, Emerson is asked to dispose of a golden statue that the late owner's widow thinks is cursed.

Robb, Candace.

Her <u>Owen Archer series</u> takes place in fourteenth-century England.

The Apothecary Rose. 1993.
A Spy for the Redeemer. 2002. Seventh in the series.
The Cross-Legged Knight. 2003.

Robinson, Lynda S.

Her <u>Lord Meren series</u> takes place in ancient Egypt in the fourteenth century B.C.

Murder in the Place of Anubis. 1994.
Lord Meren, the "eyes and ears" of Pharaoh Tutankhamun, seeks a murderer who desecrated the Place of Anubis.

Slayer of Gods. 2001.
In the sixth title in the series, Lord Meren investigates Nefertiti's death.

Rowland, Laura Joh.

Her <u>Sano Ichiro series</u> features Samurai Sano Ichiro in seventeenth-century Japan.

Shinju. 1994.
The Samurai's Wife. 2000. Fifth in the series.
Black Lotus. 2001.
The Pillow Book of Lady Wisteria. 2002.
The Dragon King's Palace. 2003.
The Perfumed Sleeve. 2004.

Satterthwait, Walter.

His books feature Pinkerton detective Phil Beaumont and his British partner, Jane Turner, in 1920s Paris.

Masquerade. 1998.
A murder investigation with Gertrude Stein, Ernest Hemingway, Pablo Picasso, and other lost generation luminaries lurking on the periphery.

Saylor, Steven.

His <u>Roma Sub Rosa series</u> features Gordanius the Finder in ancient Rome.

Roman Blood. 1991.
Gordanius the Finder is introduced.

> ### *Last Seen in Massilia.* 2000.
> In the eighth title in the series, Gordanius is in Marseilles in on a personal quest to learn the truth about his missing son.
>
> ### *A Mist of Prophecies.* 2002.
> ### *The Judgement of Caesar.* 2004.
> In the tenth title in the series, Gordanius is in Alexandria, as are Caesar, Cleopatra, and Ptolemy.
>
> ### *A Gladiator Dies Only Once: The Further Investigations of Gordianus the Finder.* 2005.
> A collection of nine stories featuring Gordianus.

Sedley, Kate.

> Her <u>Roger the Chapman series</u> features a fifteenth-century peddler cum amateur detective.
>
> ### *Death and the Chapman.* 1991.
> In 1471, realizing he had no vocation, Roger leaves the monastic life and becomes a traveling peddler.
>
> ### *The Goldsmith's Daughter.* 2001.
> This tenth entry in the series sees Roger and his wife traveling to London for the royal wedding of King Edward IV's four-year-old son; Roger is asked to clear the king's favorite mistress of a murder charge.
>
> ### *The Lammas Feast.* 2002.
> ### *Nine Men Dancing.* 2003.
> ### *The Midsummer Rose.* 2004.
> ### *The Burgundian's Tale.* 2005.

Futuristic Mysteries

In direct counterpoint to historical mysteries are those set in the future. These novels often have the same appeal of an exotic setting in a place unreachable, except through story. Futuristic mysteries are also listed in the science fiction chapter (chapter 10), and mysteries with fantasy settings can be found in the fantasy chapter (chapter 11).

Bizarre Blends

A recent trend in the crime genre involves some unlikely detectives, most notably vampires and dinosaurs. For example, Eric Garcia's <u>Dinosaur Mafia series</u> features dinos who went into hiding, disguised as humans.

Cunningham, Elaine.

> ### *Shadows in the Darkness.* 2004.
> The dark world of Faerie merges with our world.

Driver, Lee.

> The <u>Chase Dagger Mystery series</u> features Chase Dagger, who not only has a shapeshifter for an assistant, he also has a way of becoming involved in mysteries where the paranormal has had an influence.
>
> ### *The Good Die Twice.* 1999.

Full Moon, Bloody Moon. 2000.

The Unseen. 2004.

Elrod, P. N.

The Vampire Files series features Jack Fleming, private investigator and vampire, in 1930s Chicago. *The Vampire Files,* an omnibus of the first three titles, was published in 2003.

Bloodlist. 1990.

When reporter Jack Fleming wakes up dead and a vampire, he sets out discover who killed him.

Lady Crymsyn. 2000.

The ninth book in the series sees Jack finally having enough money to open his nightclub, but he finds a murdered corpse in a wall.

Cold Streets. 2003.

Jack is out to rescue a kidnap victim.

A Song in the Dark. 2005.

Garcia, Eric.

His Dinosaur Mafia Mystery series features Vincent Rubio, a hard-boiled Los Angeles private investigator and dinosaur in disguise.

Anonymous Rex. 2000.

Casual Rex. 2001.

Hot And Sweaty Rex. 2004.

Harris, Charlaine.

Her Southern Vampire Mysteries features psychic waitress Sookie Stackhouse.

Dead Until Dark. 2001.

Living Dead in Dallas. 2002.

Club Dead. 2003.

Dead to the World. 2004.

Dead as a Doornail. 2005.

Suspense

Even though crime-solving and detection are common elements in novels of suspense, the emphasis is not so much on "who done it" but on why it was done. The psychology of the perpetrator of the crime takes center stage in these stories, and dark atmospheres are commonplace. Unlike novels of detection, where the series sleuth has become the norm, in suspense, the series is the exception rather than the rule.

Often in novels of suspense, the reader knows the identity of the perpetrator early on, but must keep reading to find out what happens next. The reader often feels a sense of impending doom. Many of the books listed under "Legal Thriller" are also novels of suspense.

Abrahams, Peter.

> *Their Wildest Dreams.* 2003.
> *The Tutor.* 2002.

Andrews, Russell.

> *Aphrodite.* 2003.

Bayer, William.

> *The Dream of the Broken Horses.* 2002.

Blauner, Peter.

> *The Last Good Day.* 2003.

Case, John.

> *The Eighth Day.* 2003.
> *The Murder Artist.* 2004.

Clark, Mary Higgins.

> *Nighttime Is My Time.* 2004.
> A serial killer who calls himself "the Owl," who is also a former classmate of Jean Sheridan's, shows up at the school reunion.
>
> *No Place Like Home.* 2005.
> Liza Barton, who at age ten accidentally shot and killed her mother, has changed her name and made a new life for herself. But when she moves with her husband and son back into her childhood home twenty-four years later, she finds her past is difficult to shed, and someone is out to get her and her family.
>
> *The Second Time Around.* 2003.

Clark, Mary Jane.

> *Nowhere to Run.* 2003.

Coben, Harlan.

> *Just One Look.* 2004.

Cook, Thomas H.

> *The Interrogation.* 2002.
> *Peril.* 2004.

Fielding, Joy.

> *Don't Cry Now.* 1995.
> *The First Time.* 2000.
> *Grand Avenue.* 2001.
> *Kiss Mommy Goodbye.* 1980.
> *Lost.* 2003.
> *Missing Pieces.* 1997.
> *Puppet.* 2005.

Fyfield, Frances.

> *Blind Date.* 1999.
> *Undercurrents.* 2001.

Hogan, Chuck.

> *Prince of Thieves.* 2004.
> A grittily realistic story about a criminal mastermind from a rough Boston neighborhood.

Kellerman, Jonathan.

> *Billy Straight.* 1998.

Koontz, Dean.

> *Life Expectancy.* 2004.

Lehane, Dennis.

> *Mystic River.* 2002.
> *Shutter Island.* 2003.
> When U.S. Marshall Teddy Daniels comes to Shutter Island's Ashecliffe Hospital for the Criminally Insane to investigate the disappearance of a patient, he knows a murderer is on the loose. Then the hurricane hits.

Lewis, Pam.

> *Speak Softly, She Can Hear.* 2005.

Matheson, Richard.

> *Hunted Past Reason.* 2002.

Palmer, Michael.

> Medical suspense that verges on horror.
> > *The Society.* 2004.

Rice, Christopher.

> *Light Before Day.* 2005.

Robotham, Michael.

> *Suspect.* 2005.

Stewart, Leah.

> *Body of a Girl.* 2000.
> One evening Olivia and a couple fellow journalists are talking about how far they have gone to get a story. At the time Olivia has no inkling that she will shortly be going so far over the edge in her quest for the truth in a story she is writing that she may not make it back. Although this is a crime story with plenty of detection it is not a mystery. At its center is not who did it or why it was done, but who the victim really was.

Walker, Mary Willis.

> *All the Dead Lie Down.* 1997.
> *The Red Scream.* 1995.
> *Under the Beetle's Cellar.* 1994.

Walters, Minette.

Acid Row. 2002.
Acid Row, a down-and-out suburban London housing project, goes over the edge when a ten-year-old girl disappears and residents discover that the government has moved a pedophile into their midst.

The Breaker. 1998.
The Dark Room. 1995.
Disordered Minds. 2005.
The Echo. 1997.
Fox Evil. 2002.
The Ice House. 1992.
The Scold's Bridal. 1994.
The Sculptress. 1993.
The Shape of Snakes. 2000.
The Tinderbox. 1999.

Ward, Liza.

Outside Valentine. 2004.

Wilhelm, Kate.

The Good Children. 1999.
Skeletons. 2002.

Serial Killers and Psychopaths

A psychopathic killer pursuing (usually) a woman is as common a plot element in this subgenre as are serial killers. Madness and murder appear in other genres, and some examples are included in the psychological horror section in chapter 12.

Baldacci, David.

Hour Game. 2004.

Case, John.

The Murder Artist. 2004.
When television correspondent Alex Callahan's six-year-old twins are kidnapped, he starts on the treacherous trail to find the horrifyingly twisted predator called "the Pipe."

Connelly, Michael.

Blood Work. 1998.

Dorsey, Tim.

Torpedo Juice. 2005.

Gruber, Michael.

Tropic of Night. 2003.

Gutman, Amy.

The Anniversary. 2003.

Hall, James W.

Body Language. 1998.

Hoffman, Jilliane.

Last Witness. 2005.

Jaffe, Michael.

Loverboy. 2004.

Lindsay, Jeff.

Dexter Morgan, a blood splatter analyst for the Miami Dade Police Department, is also a psycho serial killer.

Darkly Dreaming Dexter. 2004.

Dearly Devoted Dexter. 2005. Sequel to *Darkly Dreaming Dexter.*

Lutz, John.

Night Caller. 2001.

Night Spider. 2003.

Night Watcher. 2002.

Margolin, Phillip.

Sleeping Beauty. 2004.

Prescott, Michael.

In Dark Places. 2004.

Rendell, Ruth.

Adam and Eve and Pinch Me. 2001.

The Rottweiler. 2003.

Sandford, John.

Psychopathic killers appear frequently in his Prey series.

Broken Prey. 2005.

The sixteenth Lucas Davenport novel features a whole slew of serial killers.

Wiltse, David.

Blown Away. 1997.

Romance/Suspense Writers

Romance writers who write suspenseful romances often include more suspense than romance. Many of the following authors are also included in the romance chapter. Five years ago, these authors—specifically Tami Hoag, Karen Robards, Iris Johansen, and Tess Gerritsen—were closely associated with the romance genre, but in the intervening time they have acquired reputations for solid suspense. The combination of suspense and romance adds excitement in both directions for readers.

Brown, Sandra.

Hello, Darkness. 2003.

White Hot. 2004.

Coulter, Catherine.

Her <u>Sherlock and Savitch series</u> includes the following:

The Cove. 1996.
The Maze. 1998.
The Target. 1998.
The Edge. 1999.
Riptide. 2000.
Hemlock Bay. 2001.
Eleventh Hour. 2002.
Blindside. 2003.
Blowout. 2004.
Point Blank. 2005.

Gardner, Lisa.

Alone. 2005.
The Killing Hour. 2003.
The Next Accident. 2001.

Gerritsen, Tess.

The Apprentice. 2002.
Body Double. 2004.
The Sinner. 2003.
The Surgeon. 2001.
Vanish. 2005.

Graham, Heather.

Hurricane Bay. 2002.

Hoag, Tami.

Guilty as Sin. 1996.
Kill the Messenger. 2004.
Night Sins. 1995.

Johansen, Iris.

And Then You Die. 1998.
The Ugly Duckling. 1997.

Her <u>Eve Duncan Series</u> includes the following:

The Face of Deception. 1999.
The Killing Game. 2000.
Body of Lies. 2002.
Blind Alley. 2004.
Countdown. 2005.

Krentz, Jayne Ann.

Her <u>Whispering Springs series</u> features psychic designer Zoe Luce and P.I. Ethan Truax.

Lowell, Elizabeth.

>*Amber Beach.* 1998.
>*The Color of Death.* 2004.
>*Jade Island.* 1999.
>*Pearl Cove.* 2000.

Robards, Karen.

>*Bait.* 2004.
>*The Midnight Hour.* 1999.
>*Whispers at Midnight.* 2003.

Crime/Caper

Crime and its perpetrators, rather than those finding out who did it or even why it was done, provide the focus in the following titles. Some of the protagonists are career criminals, while others may be ordinary folks pushed by circumstances into committing crimes. And while some are charming or even likable, and others are detestable, one trait the diverse rogues all possess is cunning, regardless of social standing, education, economic level, gender, or race.

Many of the following authors write other types of books involving crime. The titles noted are examples of their novels that distinctly involve a caper.

Blincoe, Nicholas.

>*Acid Casuals.* 1997.
>Transsexual assassin Estela Santos has returned to Manchester, England, in this story that is an explosive mix of gangs, car chases, flying bullets, and lots of drugs.

Block, Lawrence.

>*Hit Man.* 1998.
>His Bernard Rhodenbarr series includes lighthearted stories featuring Bernard Rhodenbarr. The series started in 1977 with *Burglars Can't Be Choosers;* the tenth book, published in 2004, is *Burglar on the Prowl.*

Bonfiglioli, Kyril.

>His series of books features the Honorable Charlie Mortdecai.

>>*Don't Point That Thing at Me.* Reissued in 2004.
>>*After You with the Pistol.* Reissued in 2005.

Cannell, Stephen J.

>Cannell created TV's *The Rockford Files.*

>>*King Con.* 1997.
>>Beano X. Bates, the reigning king of the con, pulls a poker con on Joe Rino, Mafia don, that results in his near death at the wrong end of a savagely wielded golf club. As a member of the FBI's 10 Most Wanted list, Beano decamps from the hospital as soon as he regains consciousness, teams up

with a disgruntled prosecutor, and sets out to execute the ultimate con and turn Joe and his brother Tommy against each other.

Dorsey, Tim.

His <u>Serge A. Storm</u> series features a serial killer.

> *Triggerfish Twist.* 2002.
> *Florida Roadkill.* 1999.
> *Hammerhead Ranch Motel.* 2000.
> *The Stingray Shuffle.* 2003.
> *Orange Crush.* 2001.
> *Cadillac Beach.* 2004.
> *Torpedo Juice.* 2005.

Eisler, Barry.

This series of books features John Rain, a Japanese American freelance hit man.

> *Rain Fall.* 2002.
> *Hard Rain.* 2003.
> *Rain Storm.* 2004.

Hiaasen, Carl.

> *Basket Case.* 2002.
> *Lucky You.* 1997.
> *Sick Puppy.* 2000.
> *Skinny Dip.* 2004.
> *Stormy Weather.* 1995.

Leonard, Elmore.

> *Mr. Paradise.* 2002.
> *Pagan Babies.* 2000.
> *Tishomingo Blues.* 2002.

His <u>Chilly Palmer Duet</u> includes:

> *Get Shorty.* 1991. 🎬
> *Be Cool.* 2000. 🎬

Maxim, John R.

His "<u>Bannerman</u>" series includes:

> *The Bannerman Solution.* 1989.
> *The Bannerman Effect.* 1990.
> *Bannerman's Law.* 1991.
> *A Matter of Honor.* 1993.
> *Bannerman's Promise.* 2001.
> *Bannerman's Ghosts.* 2003.

Legal Thriller

The protagonist in this type is usually a lawyer who has gotten into a fix and needs to extricate himself (or herself) through clever use of a superior intellect. There actually is variety within this subgenre, with protagonists ranging from the earnest young attorney who finds out that he is unwittingly representing organized crime to the attorney wrongly accused of murder and duped by those close to her. The hero may also be a young legal student who, as an intellectual exercise, tries to solve murders; but then, because of her theories, ends up as the target of the killers, or an earnest judge who is manipulated into an explosive situation. In this type of story, the focus is not on the solving of a mystery but rather on the thrill of the chase, usually from the point of view of the one being chased!

 7

Aubert, Rosemary.

Her Ellis Portal series features a homeless former judge.

The Feast of Stephen. 1999.
The Ferryman Will Be There. 2001.
Leave Me By Dying. 2003.

Baldacci, David.

The Simple Truth. 1998.
An appeal sent to the Supreme Court starts a string of murders and the exposure of corruption at the highest levels.

Bernhardt, William.

His Ben Kincaid series includes:

Primary Justice. 1991.
Ben Kincaid has always believed in justice, but when he leaves the DA's office for a big firm, he discovers that what is right and what is in the client's best interests are not the same.

Blind Justice. 1992.
Deadly Justice. 1993.
Perfect Justice. 1994.
Cruel Justice. 1996.
Naked Justice. 1997.
Extreme Justice. 1998.
Dark Justice. 1999.
Silent Justice. 2000.
Murder One. 2001.
Criminal Intent. 2002.
Death Row. 2003.
Hate Crime. 2004.
Ben, with a reputation as a defense attorney who fights tirelessly for his clients, refuses to take the case of a notorious bigot accused of a hate crime but ends up getting into the case when his partner, Christina McCall, runs into trouble.

Brandon, Jay.

The Chris Sinclair series includes:

After Image. 2000.

Executive Privilege. 2001.

Silver Moon. 2003.

Grudge Match. 2004.

When San Antonio District Attorney Chris Sinclair discovers that a man he thought was a dirty cop and had prosecuted eight years earlier was really innocent, he sets the ball rolling to have Steve Greerdon pardoned. Someone, though, had executed the perfect frame-up and is not going to be happy about this turn of events.

Compton, David.

Impaired Judgment. 2000.

Paula Candler, a federal judge and the first lady, is above reproach. Her husband won the presidency on their integrity and partnership. It seems impossible that a mafioso, accused of murdering another federal judge, could find something to hold over her head, but Tony Remalli's sleazy lawyer and his sexy private investigator have found something that could conceivably bring down the presidency.

Finder, Joseph.

High Crimes. 1998.

A lawyer takes on the military courts when her husband is accused of a heinous massacre.

Grisham, John.

The Brethren. 2000.

The King of Torts. 2003.

The Last Juror. 2004.

The Partner. 1997.

The Rainmaker. 1995.

The Runaway Jury. 1996.

The Street Lawyer. 1998.

The Summons. 2002.

The Testament. 1999.

Hoffman, Jilliane.

Retribution. 2004.

A Miami prosecutor, working on the case of a serial killer, faces a dilemma when the accused admits that he was the rapist who destroyed her life when she was a promising law student with a different name who had everything going for her.

Horn, Stephen.

In Her Defense. 2000.

Law of Gravity. 2002.

A Justice Department lawyer is in over his head when he is assigned to look into the disappearance of an aide.

Kane, Stephanie.

Her <u>Jackie Flowers</u> series includes:

> ***Blind Spot.*** 2000.
> ***Extreme Indifference.*** 2003.
> ***Seeds of Doubt.*** 2004.
> Jackie Flowers, a dyslexic Denver attorney, takes a client into her home
> while she defends her against charges of kidnapping a child.

Lescroart, John.

His <u>Dismas Hardy series</u> features an ex-cop defense attorney.

> ***Dead Irish.*** 1989.
> ***The Vig.*** 1990.
> ***Hard Evidence.*** 1993.
> ***The 13th Juror.*** 1995.
> ***A Certain Justice.*** 1996.
> ***Guilt.*** 1997.
> ***The Mercy Rule.*** 1998.
> ***Nothing but the Truth.*** 1999.
> ***The Hearing.*** 2001.
> ***The Oath.*** 2002.
> ***The First Law.*** 2003.
> ***The Second Chair.*** 2004.
> ***The Motive.*** 2005.

Margolin, Phillip.

> ***After Dark.*** 1995.
> ***The Associate.*** 2001.
> ***The Burning Man.*** 1996.
> ***Ties that Bind.*** 2003.
> ***The Undertaker's Widow.*** 1998.
> ***Wild Justice.*** 2000.

Martini, Steve.

> ***Critical Mass.*** 1998.
> ***The List.*** 1997.

His <u>Paul Madriani</u> series includes:

> ***Compelling Evidence.*** 1992.
> ***Prime Witness.*** 1993.
> ***Undue Influence.*** 1994.
> ***The Judge.*** 1996.
> ***The Attorney.*** 2000.
> ***The Jury.*** 2001.
> ***The Arraignment.*** 2002.
> ***Double Tap.*** 2005.

Patterson, Richard North.

> *Balance of Power.* 2003.
> *Conviction.* 2005.
> *Degree of Guilt.* 1994.
> *No Safe Place.* 1998.
> *Protect and Defend.* 2000.
> *Silent Witness.* 1997.

Putney, Mary Jo.

> *Twist of Fate.* 2003.

When Val Covington, high-powered corporate attorney, receives a million dollar wind-fall, she decides to go out on her own to work for real justice. Kendra, her paralegal, agrees to join her under the condition that she take on a last-ditch effort to prove the inno-cence of death row inmate Daniel Monroe, who is facing imminent execution. She finds an excellent investigator (and love interest) in Rob Smith, the owner of the remodeled church she rents for office space, who has his own reasons for fighting against the death penalty.

Rosenberg, Nancy Taylor.

> *Buried Evidence.* 2000.
> *Conflict of Interest.* 2002.
> *Trial by Fire.* 1996.

Scottoline, Lisa.

Her <u>Rosato & Associates</u> series is about a woman-powered law firm.

> *Everywhere That Mary Went.* 1994. Reissued 2003.
> ❦ *Final Appeal.* 1997. Reissued 2003. Winner of the Edgar Award.
> *Running from the Law.* 1995.
> *Legal Tender.* 1996.
> *Rough Justice.* 1997.
> *Mistaken Identity.* 1999.
> *Moment of Truth.* 2000.
> *The Vendetta Defense.* 2001.
> *Courting Trouble.* 2002.
> *Dead Ringer.* 2003.
> *Killer Smile.* 2004.

Her <u>Vicki Allegretti</u> series includes:

> *Devil's Corner.* 2005.

Tanenbaum, Robert K.

His <u>Butch Karp and Marlene Ciampi</u> series includes:

> *No Lesser Plea.* 1987.
> *Depraved Indifference.* 1989.
> *Immoral Certainty.* 1991.
> *Reversible Error.* 1992.
> *Material Witness.* 1993.

Justice Denied. 1994.
Corruption of Blood. 1994.
Falsely Accused. 1996.
Irresistible Impulse. 1997.
Reckless Endangerment. 1998.
Act of Revenge. 1999.
True Justice. 2000.
Enemy Within. 2001.
Absolute Rage. 2002.
Resolved. 2003.
Hoax. 2004.

Turow, Scott.

Personal Injuries. 1999.
Reversible Errors. 2002.

So much has been written about the crime genre, it is impossible to list all sources of information here. This is a sample of resources for the curious, a starting point for the ambitious.

Anthology Series

The number of anthology series being published has sharply diminished in recent years. Fortunately there are still two at this writing that are appearing regularly.

Best American Mystery Stories. Edited by a different prominent author each year; in 2004 it was Nelson DeMille. Houghton Mifflin.

World's Finest Mystery and Detective Stories. Edited by Ed Gorman and Martin H. Greenberg. (The fifth collection was published in 2004.) Forge.

Bibliographies and Genre Guides

The following bibliographies and genre guides vary in coverage. Some cover the authors in the genre, some include material on allied genres, some are of secondary works, and several embrace a number of aspects.

Bleiler, Richard. *Reference and Research Guide to Mystery and Detective Fiction.* 2nd ed. Libraries Unlimited, 2004.

Burgess, Michael, and Jill H. Vassilakos. *Murder in Retrospect: A Selective Guide to Historical Mystery Fiction.* Libraries Unlimited, 2005.

Charles, John, Joanna Morrison, and Candace Clark. *Mystery Readers' Advisory: The Librarian's Clues to Murder and Mayhem.* ALA Editions, 2002.

Fischer-Hornung, Dorothea, and Monika Mueller. *Sleuthing Ethnicity: The Detective in Multiethnic Crime Fiction.* Associated University Presses, 2003.

Heising, Willetta L. *Detecting Women: A Reader's Guide and Checklist for Mystery Series Written by Women.* Purple Moon Press, 2000.
Lists women authors who have written mystery series that have had at least two titles published. They are included with a list of titles and a short biographical note. The book includes a glossary, a great list of resources, convention and award information, pseudonyms, geographical settings, types, series characters, and a chronology.

Huang, Jim, ed. *100 Favorite Mysteries of the Century.* Crum Creek Press, 2000.
Selected by the Independent Mystery Booksellers Association.

Hubin, Allen J. *Crime Fiction IV: A Comprehensive Bibliography, 1749–2000.* 4th ed. Battered Silicon Dispatch Box, 2003.
> The most comprehensive bibliography of crime fiction, in its expanded fourth edition. Noted are series detectives and pseudonyms. There are several indexes: author, title, setting, movie, and series characters.

Kelleghan, Fiona, ed. *100 Masters of Mystery and Detective Fiction.* Salem Press, 2001.

Niebuhr, Gary Warren. *Make Mine a Mystery: A Reader's Guide to Mystery and Detective Fiction.* Libraries Unlimited, 2003.
> This multi-award-winning (the Macavity Award for Best Biographical/Critical Mystery Work for 2004 from the Mystery Readers International and the Anthony Award for Best Critical/Non-fiction Work for 2004) readers' advisory resource groups more than 2,500 mystery and detective fiction titles into useable categories.

 7

Pederson, Jay P. *St. James Guide to Crime & Mystery Writers.* 4th ed. St. James Press, 1996. Formerly titled *Twentieth-Century Crime & Mystery Writers.*
> Some 600 writers are given bibliographical and critical coverage. The signed critical essays vary greatly in length and quality.

Saricks, Joyce. *Readers' Advisory Guide to Genre Fiction.* ALA Editions, 2001.

Encyclopedias

Ashley, Mike, comp. *The Mammoth Encyclopedia of Modern Crime Fiction.* Carroll & Graf, 2002.

DeAndrea, William L. *Encyclopedia Mysteriosa: A Comprehensive Guide to the Art of Detection in Print, Film, Radio, and Television.* Macmillan, 1994.

Writers' Manuals

Grafton, Sue, ed. *Mystery Writers of America. Writing Mysteries: A Handbook.* Writer's Digest Books, 2002.

Roth, Martin. *The Crime Writer's Reference Guide.* Michael Wiese Productions, 2003.

Tapply, William G. *The Elements of Mystery Fiction: Writing the Modern Whodunit.* Poisoned Pen Press, 2004.

Van Dine, S. S., "Twenty Rules for Writing Detective Stories." Originally published in *American Magazine* (1928) and subsequently included in the *Philo Vance Investigates Omnibus* (1936), this brief article is available at http://gaslight. mtroyal.ab.ca/vandine.htm.

Associations and Conventions

Associations of mystery and crime writers serve to further the status and publishing of the subgenre as well as the economic welfare of writers. The U.S. and British associations present annual prizes. The prestige of these associations is recognized by publishers, who note an author's prize-winning status in advertisements and on book jackets.

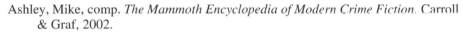

Associations

Crime Writers' Association. This British group was founded in 1953. The "Gold Daggers" are the annual awards. There is a memorial John Creasey First Novel award.

Crime Writers of Canada. Founded in 1982, this group presents Arthur Ellis Awards (named after the traditional pseudonym for Canada's official hangman) in the categories of best novel, best first novel, best true crime book, best short story, and best work of criticism or reference.

International Association of Crime Writers. Founded in 1986, its national chapters present Hammett Awards.

Mystery Writers of America. This U.S. organization was founded in 1945. "Edgars" (Edgar Allan Poe Awards) are presented in several categories at the annual dinner.

Private Eye Writers of America. This U.S. group was established in 1982. The Shamus Award is for outstanding paperback and hardcover novels. The Eye Award is for career achievement.

Sisters in Crime. Formed in 1985 to work for gender equality in crime publishing, this is an international organization, with over 3,600 members in 2005.

Conventions

Bouchercon is the annual Anthony Boucher memorial convention. The first was held in 1969. Anthony Boucher, a pseudonym of William Anthony Parker White, wrote detective and science fiction stories and was notable as a critic and reviewer.

The **International Congress of Crime Writers** held its first congress in London in 1975. The 2004 meeting was in Amsterdam and Antwerp.

Left-Coast Crime awards the Lefty Award for the funniest novel of the previous year. The sixteenth annual convention is scheduled for March 2006 in Bristol, England. The Dilys Award from the Independent Mystery Booksellers Association is also awarded at this conference.

Malice Domestic holds an annual convention celebrating "cozy mysteries" in the Washington, D.C. area. The seventeenth convention was in 2005.

Awards

Agatha Award. Awarded annually at the Malice Domestic Convention, it is named for Agatha Christie, whose works exemplify the traditional (sometimes called cozy) mystery. Winners and finalists are listed at http://www.malicedomestic.org/ agathapast_new.htm (accessed March 25, 2005).

Macavity Awards. Awarded by Mystery Readers International annually at Bouchercon, the World Mystery Convention. A full listing of winners is at http://www.mysteryreaders.org/macavity.html (accessed March 25, 2005).

Anthony Awards. Awarded annually at Bouchercon, the World Mystery Convention by members of the convention.

Edgar Awards. Awarded by the Mystery Writers of America; they are listed at http://www.mysterywriters.org/pages/awards/winners.htm (accessed March 25, 2005).

Online Resources

The plethora of resources on the World Wide Web is overwhelming. The following sites are of particular interest and use to librarians and booksellers. Additional online resources and updates to the links listed here are regularly published on the Genreflecting Web site at http://www.genrefluent.com.

ClueLass, http://www.cluelass.com (accessed March 25, 2005), provides links to many sites of interest to mystery fans. Lists forthcoming titles. The Mysterious Home Page is also found here.

The Gumshoe Site, http://www.nsknet.or.jp/~jkimura (accessed March 25, 2005).

DorothyL, http://www.dorothyl.com/(accessed March 25, 2005), provides subscription information for DorothyL, a very busy listserv for mystery readers and writers.

7

Overbooked, http://www.overbooked.org/genres/mystery/index.html (accessed March 25, 2005), is a volunteer project by Ann Chambers Theis and the Chesterfield County (Virginia). Public Library collection management staff, it features information about awards, bookstores, authors, characters, magazines, organizations, publishers, reviews, reading lists, and new mysteries.

The Thrilling Detective, http://www.thrillingdetective.com/(accessed March 25, 2005).

D's Crime Picks

Cunningham, Elaine.
Shadows in the Darkness. **2004.** (bizarre blends).

GiGi Gellman, young looking for her age, has ended her career with the Providence, Rhode Island, police department under a cloud, blamed for a blood bath in a sting that went wrong. Now as a private investigator she is called on to find a missing teenager, which sends her back to the seamy underside of the city and to Underhill, a "gentlemen's club" that caters to pedophiles. When the owner of Underhill gives her a file on a missing heir he wants her to investigate, she passes it on to her retired mentor, who ends up dead. Delving into both cases, she makes discoveries that lead right back to her own mysterious past.

Goodweather, Hartley. (pseudonym of Thomas King).
DreadfulWater Shows Up. **2003.** (diversity in detection—Native American).

Now living in the town of Chinook adjacent to the Blackfoot Reservation, Thumps DreadfulWater, who is Cherokee and a former California cop, is called in to photograph a murder victim at the luxury resort and casino the tribal band is due to be opening soon. The woman in his life, who is also the tribal leader, asks him to investigate in an attempt to keep her teen son, who was totally opposed to the project, from turning into a suspect. As Thumps investigates, more outsiders visiting Chinook end up dead. This gently humorous mystery with a strong sense of place and realistic characters is a worthy diversion.

King, Jonathon.
🎗 *The Blue Edge of Midnight*. **2002.** (ex-cop).

Max Freeman is living in the Florida Everglades as a hermit. But his peace is destroyed when he is thrust into the limelight and comes under police suspicion when he finds the body of a child who had been kidnapped by a serial killer. Max's tortured past is portrayed through flashbacks that show him shooting and killing a twelve-year-old and arresting a man for murder whom he has come to believe is innocent. Winner of the Edgar Award.

Leon, Donna.

Uniform Justice. **2003.** (police detectives—Italy).

When Commissario Brunetti of the Venice police department is called to an exclusive military academy, he finds that there may be more to the apparent suicide of the son of a reform minded politician. Brunetti's wife adds a philosophical perspective that keeps the story from being hopelessly bleak.

McGarrity, Michael.

Everyone Dies. **2003.** (police detectives—New Mexico).

Santa Fe police chief Kevin Kerney is supposed to be on leave. His wife, Lt. Colonel Sara Brannon, is ready to give birth to their first child at any moment, when he is called back to duty when the city's best known attorney is murdered. The serial killer leaves notes and dead animals threatening Kerney. The pace accelerates as the killer gets closer to Kerney and those he loves. The New Mexico setting alone is well worth the read, but the compelling plot and interesting characters make this a winner.

Rosenfelt, David.

Bury the Lead. **2004.** (unofficial detectives—lawyers).

Andy Carpenter, a northern New Jersey criminal attorney, has no worries what with all the money he's accumulated lately, the Tara foundation that places rescued dogs, and a honey of a girlfriend he cleared in one of his earlier exploits. He has no idea that he is going to end up defending someone who is accused of killing women seemingly at random and lopping the hands off his victims. Andy's pal Vince at the newspaper puts him on a retainer shortly before his star reporter is arrested for the killings. Andy and his crew are likeable, and giggles may turn into guffaws. All is not laughs however, as Andy tries to balance right and wrong, ethics, and fairness.

Chapter 8

Adventure

Essay

Diana Tixier Herald

The adventure story comes in many guises—from swashbuckling tales of pirates on the high seas to contemporary high-tech conspiracy stories, where the existence of the world as we know it is threatened. In fact, some may argue that adventure is a quality or characteristic of literature, rather than a distinct genre. Publishers have not clearly defined it; critics and review journals often treat it as an appendage of other genres (e.g., mystery/suspense); and although some bookstores have separate shelves for action, adventure, or intrigue, this is the exception, rather than the rule. Until late 2004, when The International Thriller Writers was formed at the World Mystery Convention (Bouchercon), the adventure genre had no societies as may be found for romance, science fiction, mystery, and other genres.

Indeed, adventure is often present in many other genres; it marries particularly well with the genres crime, Western, historical fiction, science fiction, and fantasy. However, the pure adventure, a story involving a hero (or heroine) taking risks and overcoming dangers to complete a journey or task, is a form on its own—and in fact, it is probably the oldest recorded genre in existence. *The Epic of Gilgamesh*, first chronicled on clay tablets in the third millennium B.C., tells of the adventures of Gilgamesh, the King of Uruk (located in what is now Iraq), a superhero, two-thirds divine and one-third human, and his quest for immortality. Adventure is also one of the most popular genres today, with exemplary stories, such as those written by Tom Clancy and Michael Crichton, nearly guaranteed a spot on the best-seller lists when they are released.

Definition

Colleen Warner, head librarian of the Popular Culture Library at Bowling Green State University, describes adventure fiction as a form of male romance, "in which the virtuous hero tries, and sometimes fails, to attain the prize."[1] Warner's description provides a good place to start.

The basic elements of the adventure story are simple: a protagonist (either individual or group, usually "virtuous") and a great challenge. That challenge may come in the form of obstacles encountered on a journey, it may be the threat of a villain or group of villains, or it may be the effects of natural disasters. The challenge may be physical, mental, emotional, or any combination thereof. The story form runs the gamut from survival stories, heroic quests, and tales of exploration, to war stories and tales of revenge, intrigue, and espionage. Simply put, an adventure is a story that involves a protagonist (singular or group) who faces adversity and grave danger and actively struggles to overcome them. Yet it is the resulting effect of the story that defines the genre: To be successful, the adventure tale must be told in a way that conveys excitement and allows the reader to vicariously experience the "adventure"—the dangers, the risks, and generally, the triumphs of the story.

Characteristics and Appeals

The satisfying reading experience for the adventure fan is one in which the reader vicariously experiences the story and its sensational impact. Plot line and pacing play important roles in the adventure story, pulling the reader through the story—sometimes at record speeds. Readers sometimes describe these stories as "roller-coaster rides," indicating the thrill and adrenalin rush that accompany them; or likewise as "page-turners"—books too exciting to put down. Sometimes the term "thriller" is used to describe books in this genre.

Danger and fast pacing are essential to the thriller, and all thrillers may be considered adventure stories. However, many adventure stories, such as the seafaring adventures of Patrick O'Brian, employ a more deliberate pacing that nonetheless excites readers, and they qualify as adventure stories.

The protagonist, and the character of the protagonist, in many ways direct the adventure story. Although there are many types of protagonists, from the inexperienced and naive to the seasoned and worldly-wise, protagonists generally fall into two categories:

> There are two kinds of adventurers: those who go truly hoping to
> find adventure and those who go secretly hoping they won't.[2]

In one case, the adventurer is simply caught up in unforeseen circumstances and must work his or her way out, like Jack Forman in Michael Crichton's *Prey,* who stumbles onto a nanotechnological plot for world domination and is the only one available to stop it. The experience of adventure builds the character of a common human being into a hero. In the other case, the adventurer is a superhero of sorts—one with special skills, strengths, or abilities, who makes a profession (paid or unpaid) of heroics. Clive Cussler's Dirk Pitt, with his underwater expertise and constant quests, fits this type.

Almost as important as the protagonist in the adventure tale is the nature of the challenge—the villain, the catastrophe, or the forces that the hero battles. Whether the challenge is a sinking ship, a volcano, vile terrorists, evil Nazis, devious spies, corrupt politicians, greedy businessmen, or depraved doctors, that challenge will in part determine the type of response the protagonist must make. Must brute strength be used? Quick wits? Strategic thinking? Technical expertise? The drama and excitement of the adventure story are accentuated by the strength, force, and evil of the challenge, and usually, the more extreme the challenge, the better the ride. As Michael Gannon explains in his informative guide to the genre:

> The characters (and the reader) can always expect the worst—the main characters (the hero/heroine) can, and usually do, have everything thrown at them as they proceed on their quest, search, or mission . . . without an adversary or obstacle; there can be no adventure.[3]

The spy/espionage novel, a specific and currently popular subgenre of adventure, holds an added appeal of what John Cawelti and Bruce Rosenberg (1987) call "clandestinity,"[4] which can also be found in many thrillers, whether or not they involve traditional spies. Back in the late 1980s, in the long shadows of the Cold War, Vietnam, and Watergate, they wrote:

> We live in a time that has become deeply obsessed with espionage, conspiracy, and other forms of clandestinity.[5]

Today, with international terrorism threatening the safety of the world, the explosion of technology, and issues of privacy and surveillance on the rise, this preoccupation has become even more relevant. The popularity of such subgenres as biothrillers, financial thrillers, and even cipher thrillers speaks to this obsession.

In the adventure novel, good usually triumphs over evil, but sometimes it is difficult to determine who is good and who is evil, particularly in tales of assassination and espionage. Likewise, in many adventure stories "the end justifies the means," with heroes acting in ways not normally considered exemplary. Rules are broken, violence is commonplace, but it is always in service to the greater good.

Settings in adventure stories range from the icy wastelands of polar ice caps and steamy, tropical rainforests to urban metropolises and the interior of a submarine. They may be part of the protagonist's challenge; but if given any prominence in the story, the settings are generally in some sense "extreme." In any case, the hero must always exhibit control of his or her environment in order to succeed at the task at hand.

Weapons, gadgetry, and technical expertise are also important to many adventure stories, particularly in the technothriller and espionage subgenres. The adventure hero must be adept in using whatever means it takes to overcome the challenge, whether it is a machete, a Walther PPK handgun, an Aston Martin missile, or a lethal bowler hat. Sometimes the weapons almost take the role of a character, such as the submarine in Clancy's *Hunt for Red October*. Other high-tech gadgetry performs a more ornamental function, its purpose being to amuse or amaze—a voice transmitter embedded in a fountain pen, shoe phones, cigarette lighters that double as cameras, money clips that encase vials for poison, cars that eject passengers and explode, and cameras that shoot daggers.

Love interest and sexual exploits are also common to the adventure story; however they are not usually center stage. The love interest is often "the prize" the hero receives for the successful completion of his tasks. Of course, sexual favors may be granted along the way, although in many cases, these may simply disguise further dangers. In either case, the characters of the love or lust object (usually women) are not represented in full dimension, but rather in flat or fairly stereotypical terms.

History

The Epic of Gilgamesh has been mentioned as an early adventure tale. Numerous other examples of adventure in ancient literature exist. Consider the heroic tales of *The Kalevala*, *The Ramayana*, *The Odyssey*, and *Beowulf*. In the early nineteenth century, works written by Sir Walter Scott in England (e.g., *Waverly, Rob Roy, Ivanhoe*) and James Fenimore Cooper (*Last of the Mohicans, The Pioneers, The Pathfinder, The Spy*) were wildly popular with readers, mainly for their elements of adventure. Many works of classic literature are still read today as lively adventure stories—Alexandre Dumas's *Three Musketeers* (1844) and *The Count of Monte Cristo*; Robert Louis Stevenson's adventure classics, including *Treasure Island* (1883); and Mark Twain's *Adventures of Huckleberry Finn* (1884).

Male romance (so termed because it was considered the male equivalent genre to romance for females), such as books written by H. Rider Haggard (*King Solomon's Mines,* 1885; *She,* 1887) grew in popularity at the beginning of the twentieth century, and many readers today equate "adventure" with this type of fiction. These stories, often set in wild or "primitive" parts of the world, are filled with combat and villains of all sorts. They commonly feature treasure hunts, lost mines, piracy, and the like. Other adventure authors during this period, typified by Jack London, Edgar Rice Burroughs, and James Oliver Curwood, emphasized survival in nature.

However, for most of the twentieth century, publishers and readers have turned their attention to tales of spies and espionage. These stories add suspense to the adventure tale, thereby purportedly heightening the reading experience. In 1901 Rudyard Kipling published the eponymous *Kim*, a spy story set against the exotic backdrop of India, in which the protagonist refers to his espionage activities as "The Great Game." G. K. Chesterton's *The Man Who Was Thursday: A Nightmare* (1908) featured anarchists and double agents. Nearly a decade later, Joseph Conrad published *Under Western Eyes,* which tells the story of an Englishman living in Czarist Russia and holding a dark secret; and in 1915, John Buchan introduced series character spy and spy-catcher Richard Hannay in the classic *The Thirty-Nine Steps*, later immortalized by Alfred Hitchcock in the film of the same name.

During the 1920s, World War I became the favored setting for novels of espionage. W. Somerset Maugham, who served as a spy during the war, wrote in a subdued, almost dispassionate tone the action adventure *Ashenden: Or the British Agent* (1928), which featured an antihero protagonist and is considered the first realistic spy story. In 1942, the commercial success of the film version of the espionage romance *Casablanca*, written by Michael Curtiz, marked the beginning of the marriage of media for the spy story.

The popularity of spy novels continued throughout the century, rising to great heights during the Cold War of the 1950s, 1960s, and 1970s. Ian Fleming's James Bond series epitomized this subgenre with its urbane spy, futuristic technologies, despicable villains, and alluring but treacherous women. Television series such as *Man from U.N.C.L.E.,* and *Mission Impossible* and an eruption of films, including the James Bond movies, *The Ipcress File*, and *The Spy Who Came in from the Cold*, reflected and reinforced the subgenre's popularity. Don Pendleton's <u>Max Bolan series</u> also burst onto the scene during this time, starting the new paperback category known as "action/adventure." Conspiracy thrillers reflecting real-life espionage activities (e.g., Loren Singer's *The Parallax View* and James Grady's *Six Days of the Condor*) also rose to popularity in the 1970s. Further, spoofs and parodies of the genre made there way into popular culture, with the television series *Man from Uncle* and the film *Our Man Flint*. (More recently, the *Austin Powers* movies have poked fun at the spy story.)

In the 1980s, in response to the profound technological innovations of that decade, the technothriller, an offshoot of the espionage tale that focuses more on technology, emerged, and by the 1990s it had become the most popular subgenre of adventure. Stephen Coonts (with his <u>Jake Grafton</u> novels) and Dale Brown were in demand, but Tom Clancy was king, dominating best-seller lists with such titles as *The Hunt for Red October* (1984) and his <u>Jack Ryan series</u>.

The late twentieth century saw many types of popular thrillers. Martial arts thrillers rose to prominence in the 1970. Also gaining popularity were financial thrillers, such as David Aaron's *Agent of Influence*, which explores the cutthroat tactics of investment bankers; and biothrillers, which featured biological agents as tools of terrorism (e.g., Richard Preston's *The Cobra Event,* 1997).

Recent Trends

As terrorism has increased around the world, and particularly since 9/11, there has been no dearth of stories about terrorists and terrorism. Ward Carroll's *Punk's Wing* (2003) is a case in point. Graphic novels, many of which can be considered "adventure," are a burgeoning field of publishing and reading interest, particularly with younger readers.

However, in 2003 a new subgenre rose to the top. That year Dan Brown's *The Da Vinci Code* occupied the *Publishers Weekly* best0seller list for thirty-nine weeks, positioned as number one best seller for twenty-five of those weeks, and remained on the list through 2004. *The Da Vinci Code* formalized a new adventure subgenre—the cipher thriller. Conspiracies, secrets, clues, and code-cracking feature prominently in these stories. The <u>Left Behind series</u>, another publishing phenomenon of the early twenty-first century, also arguably falls into the cipher thriller category, since it focuses on clues that are hidden in Bible passages. This subgenre has even made it into the movies with *National Treasure* (in which the directions to a treasure trove are deciphered from hidden writing on the back of the Declaration of Independence) and TNT's *The Librarian: Quest for the Spear* (in which a librarian uses his encyclopedic knowledge to decipher clues and reunite three parts of a magic spear).

Advising the Reader

Because adventure is a diverse genre that appeals to a broad range of readers, the readers' advisor must establish, through a readers' advisory interview, what the reader means by the term "adventure," and which types of adventure fiction the reader prefers. Finding titles the reader has previously enjoyed, whether or not they are classified as "adventure" in this guide; and then looking for other titles in the same categories that follow, is the standard way to start, but often more is needed.

The story—its pacing, the complexity of the plot—may be the primary appeal, but the character of the protagonist is also an important factor, with series based on particular heroes common to the genre. For example, Jack Ryan and Dirk Pitt (larger-than-life series characters in Tom Clancy's and Clive Cussler's works) have huge readership followings, as did (and to some extent still does) James Bond. In fact, these characters are so resilient that they sometimes (as in the case of James Bond) outlive their originators, with other authors continuing to write about their escapades. Other readers may prefer heroes they can more closely identify with—regular people who just happen to be thrown in harm's way, such as Louis L'Amour's Joe Mack in *The Last of the Breed*.

Setting can also be a draw—contemporary, historical, urban, exotic locales, at sea, and so on. However, it is important to keep in mind that different novels that share some setting elements may have entirely different stories. For example, Clive Cussler's adventure tales, which involve contemporary oceanography, hold a different appeal than Patrick O'Brian's historical seafaring adventures. Setting involves time and place, as well as atmosphere.

Other considerations include what type of challenge or conflict is involved—natural disasters, war stories, wilderness survival stories, and so on. Many of the title groupings that follow are based on these characteristics. For the reader who has exhausted his or her preferences in the adventure genre, keep in mind that elements of adventure can be found in many other genres (and specific subgenres) as well—particularly in science fiction, fantasy, crime, Westerns, and historical fiction. Militaristic science fiction is a subgenre that is full of adventure and sometimes presents weaponry that appeals to readers of technothrillers. Readers who enjoy political intrigue and espionage often find the suspense subgenre in crime of interest.

Closing

Adventure stories have captured the human imagination since prehistoric times. It is unlikely the genre will disappear, but undoubtedly it will change. The iterations and manifestations we see in this lively genre over the next decade will likely tell an adventure story of their own.

Notes

1. "Extraordinary Collection of Adventure Fiction Now at Bowling Green State University's Popular Culture Library." *Ascribe Higher Education News Service*, May 15, 2002.

2. William Least Heat Moon, *Blue Highways: A Journey into America* (New York: Little, Brown, 1983).

3. Michael B. Gannon, *Blood, Bedlam, Bullets, and Bad Guys: A Reader's Guide to Adventure/Suspense Fiction* (Westport, Conn.: Libraries Unlimited, 2004).

4. John G. Cawelti and Bruce A. Rosenberg. *The Spy Story* (Chicago: University of Chicago Press, 1987).

5. Ibid.

Bibliography

Biederman, Danny. *The Incredible World of Spy-Fi: Wild and Crazy Gadgets, Props, and Artifacts from TV and the Movies.* San Francisco: Chronicle Books, 2004.

Cawelti, John G. *Adventure, Mystery, and Romance: Formula Stories as Art and Popular Culture.* Chicago: University of Chicago Press, 1976.

Cawelti, John G., and Bruce A. Rosenberg. *The Spy Story.* Chicago: University of Chicago Press, 1987.

Gannon, Michael B. *Blood, Bedlam, Bullets, and Bad Guys: A Reader's Guide to Adventure/Suspense Fiction.* Westport, Conn.: Libraries Unlimited, 2004.

Newton, Michael. *How to Write Action Adventure Novels.* Cincinnati: Writer's Digest Books, 1989.

Themes and Types

Diana Tixier Herald

This chapter is arranged in several groupings. The first, which was the dominant type of adventure fiction in the twentieth century, covers tales of spies and espionage. Thrillers—from technothrillers to cipher thillers—currently the most popular type, follow. Survival, a smaller subgenre but one with enduring popularity, covers tales featuring personal survival as well as tales of coping with large-scale disaster. With several movies in the works dealing with the tsunami of December 2004, it is expected to rise in popularity. Exploration, exotic locales, soldiers of fortune, and action/adventure series are grouped together in the "Male Romance" section, followed by "Military and Naval Adventure."

Selected Classics

The classics below fall mainly into two types—male romance and spy/espionage. The former were generally the first to appear, and the predecessors of the genre as a whole. Spy/espionage stories comprised a second wave for the genre and dominated adventure publishing during the twentieth century. More recently, disaster novels, biothrillers, cipher thrillers, and other subgenres have risen to prominence. Although it is still too early to declare classic authors and titles, it is likely we will see many of these recent publications emerge as new classics over the next decade. As in Westerns and science fiction, backlist titles are important in this genre, and multiple reissues can be an indication of forthcoming classic status. Following is a sampling of established classics.

Ambler, Eric. (spy/espionage).

> The Middle East and the Balkans are the settings for Ambler's tales, in which antiheroes and amateurs are unwittingly caught up in a spy network run by scheming spymasters and their sardonic agents. Several of his titles have been reissued since 2000.
>
> *The Intercom Conspiracy.* 1969.
> *The Levanter.* 1972.
> *Mask of Dimitrios.* 1939.

Buchan, John. (male romance, spy/espionage).

> *The Thirty-Nine Steps.* 1915. 🎬
>
> > This book introduces Richard Hannay, spy-catcher and spy, who appears in several of Buchan's novels. *The Thirty-Nine Steps* has one of the greatest, long chase scenes in the genre. It became a classic motion picture, directed by Alfred Hitchcock.

Burroughs, Edgar Rice.

> <u>Tarzan series.</u> (male romance).

Chesterton, G. K.

The Man Who Was Thursday: A Nightmare. 1908. (spy/espionage).

The surreal world of anarchists and double agents.

Childers, Erskine.

The Riddle of the Sands. 1903. (spy/espionage).

Introduced the theme of the German plot to invade England, complete with a British traitor and an amateur hero.

Condon, Richard.

The Manchurian Candidate. 1959. (spy/espionage).

While the book features an international espionage plot, the 2004 film switches the evil entity to a corporation.

Conrad, Joseph.

Heart of Darkness. 1902. (male romance).

The Secret Agent. 1907. (spy/espionage).

The Secret Agent brings in the world of revolutionaries and anarchists.

Under Western Eyes. 1911. (spy/espionage).

Crichton, Michael.

The Andromeda Strain. 1969. (survival-disaster).

A deadly disease from space.

Curwood, James Oliver.

Nomads of the North. 1919. (male romance).

Deighton, Len. (spy/espionage).

Funeral in Berlin. 1964. Reissued 1994.

The Ipcress File. 1962.

Dumas, Alexandre.

The Count of Monte Cristo. 1844–1845. (male romance).

Three Musketeers. 1844. (male romance).

Fleming, Ian. (spy/espionage).

James Bond, 007, the British Secret Service agent, is of course among the immortals of spy/espionage literature. Fleming had experience in naval intelligence during World War I. The first Bond adventure, *Casino Royale* (1953), established 007's flamboyant characteristics. Sex and sadism in an international setting were ingredients for some outrageous adventures with Cold War spies. Linked to Bond is the tag "Licensed to Kill." So popular was the series that the Bond legend has continued beyond the death of its creator. The most recent 007 title is *The Man With the Red Tattoo* (2002), written by Raymond Benson, who has taken over from John E. Gardner.

Follett, Ken. (spy/espionage).

Eye of the Needle. 1978. Reissued 2005.

Forester, C. S.

Horatio Hornblower series. (historical military and naval).

Forsyth, Frederick.

Day of the Jackal. 1971.

Greene, Graham. (spy/espionage).

Greene is generally considered a literary rather than genre fiction author, but he wrote notable spy novels, his first being *The Confidential Agent* (1939), which is no longer widely available. During World War II, Greene was in intelligence and he undoubtedly drew from his experience for the classic parody, *Our Man in Havana*, which reduces the genre to the ridiculous. He also wrote *The Quiet American* (1955), a somber spy novel set in Vietnam in the 1950s. It was made into a movie twice, most recently in 2003, and the book was reissued by Penguin Classics in 2004.

Haggard, H. Rider. (male romance, wild frontiers).

King Solomon's Mines. 1885.

She. 1887. Reissued 1999.

Household, Geoffrey. (spy/espionage).

Rogue Male. 1938.

This is the classic story of the private citizen who undertakes his own spy mission, in this case an assassination, encountering extreme danger and exciting chases.

Hughes, Richard.

A High Wind in Jamaica. 1929. (male romance).

Kipling, Rudyard.

Kim. 1901. (male romance, spy/espionage).

"The Great Game," as Kim calls his spying for British intelligence in India, introduced the exotic background, an aspect that adds greatly to the appeal of the genre. How Kim, as a boy, is trained for his work is described marvelously.

Le Carré, John. (spy/espionage).

Le Carré's experience in the British Foreign Office undoubtedly contributed to his writings. Although most of his older work qualifies as classic, a notable contribution to the genre is

The Spy Who Came in from the Cold. 1963.

This set the classic pattern for the spy as antihero, the pattern of double agents, and the anatomization of the bureaucracy of intelligence headquarters operations.

Levin, Ira.

Boys from Brazil. 1976. Nazis.

London, Jack.

The Sea Wolf. 1904. (male romance).

MacInnes, Helen.

Above Suspicion. 1941. (spy/espionage).

Maugham, W. Somerset.

Ashenden: Or, the British Agent. 1928. (spy/espionage).

> Maugham was an agent during World War I, probably the first of the agents to turn his experience into a novel. He introduces the antihero as agent. His tone is realistic and sardonic, and the outrageous or sensational is toned down to the ordinary.

Oppenheim, E. Phillips.

> Several of Oppenheim's many spy novels survive, being reissued in various electronic formats. His first published novel of international intrigue was issued in 1898, and several more appeared during World War I. He introduced the spy world of elegant high society and exotic European cities; Monte Carlo with its gambling setting was often used.

The Great Impersonation. 1920. (spy/espionage).

Orczy, Baroness.

The Scarlet Pimpernel. 1905. (spy/espionage, historical). 🎬

> The aristocratic fop as a disguise for the highly intelligent agent is here at its most romantic. The theme is introduced of daring rescues from enemy countries, in this case aristocrats saved from the guillotine during the French Revolution.

Sabatini, Rafael. (male romance).

Captain Blood. 1922. Reissued 2004. 🎬

The Sea Hawk. 1915. 🎬

Scott, Sir Walter. (military, historical).

Ivanhoe. 1819. 🎬

Rob Roy. 1817. 🎬

Waverley. 1814.

Stevenson, Robert Louis.

Treasure Island. 1883. (male romance). 🎬

Verne, Jules. (male romance).

> Often credited as the first adventure novelist and the first science fiction writer, Verne wrote fantastic tales that have been reissued countless times, recorded, and made into movies. Titles include:

Around the World in Eighty Days. 1873. 🎬

Journey to the Center of the Earth. 1864. 🎬

The Mysterious Island. 1875. 🎬

20,000 Leagues Under the Sea. 1870. 🎬

Wren, P. C. (male romance).

Beau Geste. 1925. Reissued 1999. 🎬

Spy/Espionage

The spy or secret agent has never been portrayed as a fully respectable figure, but shady dealings and devious personalities make for great reading. The spy character did not become a major figure in literature until the twentieth century, and by the 1990s the character type had all but disappeared from the genre. In the middle part of the century, however, spies in all their various permutations were the epitome of adventure, and many of these titles remain popular with today's readers.

The pattern for this subgenre was set in *The Thirty-Nine Steps* (1915) by John Buchan, *The Man Who Was Thursday: A Nightmare* (1908) by G. K.Chesterton, *The Riddle of the Sands* (1903) by Erskine Childers, *Under Western Eyes* (1911) and *The Secret Agent* (1907) by Joseph Conrad, *Kim* (1901) by Rudyard Kipling, *Ashenden: Or, The British Agent* (1928) by W. Somerset Maugham, *The Great Impersonation* (1920) by E. Phillips Oppenheim, and *The Scarlet Pimpernel* (1905) by Baroness Orczy, all of which were still in print in 2005. Most have also been reissued since 2000.

Spy Novels

The end of the Cold War seemingly sounded the death knell for the spy thriller, with few titles being published in the 1990s, but the twenty-first century saw a small but significant revival with Vintage Crime/Black Lizard publishing reprints and some originals. Severn House is publishing some British novels in the United States that were first published in the United Kingdom decades ago. Forge, an imprint of Tom Doherty and Associates, is also publishing new spy espionage novels, but by and large the following lists of spy books feature the tried and true that still have followings in public libraries.

Allbeury, Ted.

> *Cold Tactics.* 2001. Originally published in Great Britain as *The Twentieth Day of January* in 1981.
>
> *Hostage.* 2004. Originally published in Great Britain as *A Place to Hide* in 1984.
>
> *Rules of the Game.* 2001. Originally published in Great Britain as *A Wilderness of Mirrors* in 1988.

Archer, Jeffrey.

> *The Eleventh Commandment.* 1998.

Bell, Ted.

Hawke series.

> Gorgeous British super-spy Lord Alexander Hawke takes on secret missions for the United States and United Kingdom chasing down terrorists and murderers.
>
> *Hawke.* 2003.
>
> *Assassin.* 2004.

Block, Lawrence.

Block also writes crime novels.

Tanner Series.

> Many of the titles were reissued in the late 1990s. The first title in the series is *The Thief Who Couldn't Sleep* (1966, reissued 1998), and the final is *Tanner on Ice* (1998).

Buckley, William F., Jr.

Blackford Oates Series.

> Featuring CIA operative Blackford Oates, during and after the Cold War. The first title in the series, *Saving the Queen* (1976, reissued 2005), is set in England in 1951. The tenth and final installment is *A Very Private Plot* (1994).

Condon, Richard.

> *The Manchurian Candidate.* **1959.** Reissued 2003. ★ 🎬
>
>> Although the book features an international espionage plot, the 2004 film switches the evil entity to a corporation.

Deighton, Len.

> *Catch a Falling Spy.* 1976. Originally published in Great Britain as *Twinkle, Twinkle, Little Spy.* ★
>
> *Funeral in Berlin.* 1964. Reissued 1994. 🎬
>
> *The Ipcress File.* 1962. ★ 🎬
>
> *Spy Story.* 1974. ★

Finder, Joseph.

> *Extraordinary Powers.* 1994.
>
> *Moscow Club.* 1991.

Follett, Ken.

> Follett wrote a number of spy novels in the late 1970s and 1980s, including *Lie Down with Lions* (1986), *The Man from St. Petersburg* (1982), *Key to Rebecca* (1980), *Triple* (1979), and *Eye of the Needle* (1978), which was reissued in 2005. In following years, the author has turned his pen to other subgenres, most recently the biothriller.

Freemantle, Brian.

> Featuring the disheveled and cranky Charlie Muffin. While most titles in the series are still available in larger library systems, some are out of print and difficult to locate in smaller library collections. To make things even more confusing, they were published with different titles in different English-speaking countries with different copyright dates. As some are rissued in audio or large print format, they may be published under the British rather than the U.S. title. The first in the series was *Charlie Muffin* (1977), also published as *Charlie M.,* and the twelfth was *Kings of Many Castles* (2002).

Furst, Alan.

> Set in Europe during World War II, Furst's novels are rich in historical detail and feature complex plots. (Listed in original publication date order.)
>
> *Night Soldiers.* 1988. Reissued 2002.
>
> *Dark Star.* 1991. Reissued 2002.
>
> *The Polish Officer.* 1995. Reissued 2001.
>
> *Red Gold.* 1999. Reissued 2002.
>
> *Kingdom of Shadows.* 2000.
>
> *Blood of Victory.* 2002.
>
> *Dark Voyage.* 2004.
>
>> A Dutch captain, his merchant vessel, and assorted crew undertake secret missions for the British navy in 1941.

Griffin, W. E. B.

> <u>Men at War series.</u>
>
>> Originally published under the pseudonym Alex Baldwin and reissued between 1998 and 2001.
>
> *The Last Heroes.* 1985. Reissued 1998.

The Secret Warriors. 1986. Reissued 1998.
The Soldier Spies. 1987. Reissued 2000.
Fighting Agents. 1988. Reissued 2001.

Higgins, Jack.

Liam Devlin series. IRA Operative.

The Eagle Has Landed. 1975. Reissued 2000.
Touch the Devil. 1982.
Confessional. 1985.
Eagle Has Flown. 1991.

Sean Dillon series.

Features former hit man and IRA enforcer Sean Dillon, who is always in the middle of the action when there are plots to assassinate the queen, prime minister, or even the president of the United States.

Eye of the Storm. 1992. *Midnight Man*
Thunder Point. 1993.
On Dangerous Ground. 1994
Angel of Death. 1995.
Drink with the Devil. 1996.
The President's Daughter. 1997.
The White House Connection. 1999.
Day of Reckoning. 2000.
Edge of Danger. 2001.
Midnight Runner. 2002.
Bad Company. 2003.
Dark Justice. 2004.

Hunter, Stephen.

The Spanish Gambit. 1985. Reissued in 1997 as *Tapestry of Spies.*

Hynd, Noel.

His books feature FBI Special Agent Thomas Cochrane.

Flowers from Berlin. 1985. Reissued 2000.

James, Bill.

Split. 2002.

Le Carré, John.

Absolute Friends. 2004.

The war in Iraq brings two Cold War agents back into play.

Tailor of Panama. 1996. Reissued 2001.

A satirical tale inspired by Greene's classic *Our Man in Havana.*

Lindsey, David L.

The Color of Night. 1999.

Littell, Robert.

> *Agent in Place.* 1991.
> *The Amateur.* 1981. Reissued 2003.
> *The Company.* 2002.
> *The Debriefing.* 1979. Reissued 2004.
> *The Defection of A. J. Lewinter.* 1973. Reissued 2002.
> *The Once and Future Spy.* 1990. Reissued 2003.

Ludlum, Robert.

The popular series featuring Jason Bourne received a new lease on life with the success of the movie versions, which sent them back onto best-seller lists in 2004. (A film version of *The Bourne Ultimatum* is in production for late 2007/2007 release.) At the behest of Ludlum's estate, Eric Van Lustbader continues the series.

> *The Bourne Identity.* 1980.
> *The Bourne Supremacy.* 1986.
> *The Bourne Ultimatum.* 1990.

Lustbader, Eric Van.

> *The Bourne Legacy.* 2004.
>> Continuation of Ludlum's Bourne series.

Shelby, Philip.

> *Gatekeeper.* 1998.

Silva, Daniel.

> *The Marching Season.* 1999.
> *The Mark of the Assassin.* 1998.

> **Gabriel Allon series.**

Art restorer Gabriel Allon is an undercover Mossad agent.

> *The Kill Artist.* 2000.
> *The English Assassin.* 2002.
> *The Confessor.* 2003.
> *A Death in Vienna.* 2004.
> *Prince of Fire.* 2005.

Thomas, Craig.

> *Firefox.* 1977.
> *A Hooded Crow.* 1992.
> *Last Raven.* 1991.
> *Wild Cat.* 1990.
> *Wild Justice.* 1995.
> *Wolfsbane.* 1978.

Thomas, Ross.

Mac McCorkle and Mike Padillo books. Listed in original publication date order.

> *The Cold War Swap.* 1966. Reissued 2003.
> *Cast a Yellow Shadow.* 1967.
> *Backup Men.* 1971.
> *Twilight at Mac's Place.* 1990. Reissued 2004.

Trevanian.

> *The Eiger Sanction.* 1972. Reissued 2005. ▰
> *Loo Sanction.* 1973.

Woods, Stuart.

> *Deep Lie.* 1986. Reissued 2001.

Women Spies

Female spies appear frequently as secondary characters in many of the older espionage novels; but in each of the following books, a woman is the main character, and four of the women are series characters. Readers searching for strong female protagonists will find them here.

Deverell, Diana.

> *12 Drummers Drumming.* 1998.
> *Night on Fire.* 1999.
>> Kathryn "Casey" Collins works for a terrorist-fighting State Department agency.

Duffy, Margaret.

> **Ingrid Langley and Patrick Gillard.**
>> Novelist Ingrid Langley is married to fellow agent Patrick Gillard in this comedic British series.

> *A Murder of Crows.* 1987.
> *Death of a Raven.* 1988.
> *Brass Eagle.* 1989.
> *Who Killed Cock Robin?* 1990.
> *Rook Shoot.* 1991.
> *Gallows Bird.* 1993.
> *A Hanging Matter.* 2002.
> *Dead Trouble.* 2004.

Eddy, Paul.

> *Flint.* 2000.
>> Inspector Grace Flint, a British undercover cop, loses everything dear to her when a sting operation turns bad, but she gets her chance for revenge years later, when British Intelligence loans her to the FBI.

> *Flint's Law.* 2002.
>> Could undercover agent Grace Flint's new husband be part of the money-laundering scheme she is trotting the globe to stop?

Gilman, Dorothy.

Featuring the beloved and indomitable Mrs. Pollifax, grandmother and CIA agent. The first book in the series appeared in 1966 and the fourteenth in 2000, all with exotic locales. These stories are considered mysteries, as much as novels of espionage.

The Unexpected Mrs. Pollifax. 1966. ▰

The Amazing Mrs. Pollifax. 1970.

The Elusive Mrs. Pollifax. 1971.

A Palm for Mrs. Pollifax. 1973.

Mrs. Pollifax on Safari. 1976.

Mrs. Pollifax and the China Station. 1983.

Mrs. Pollifax and the Hong Kong Buddha. 1985.

Mrs. Pollifax and the Golden Triangle. 1988.

Mrs. Pollifax and the Whirling Dervish. 1990.

Mrs. Pollifax and the Second Thief. 1993.

Mrs. Pollifax Pursued. 1995.

Mrs. Pollifax and the Lion Killer. 1996.

Mrs. Pollifax, Innocent Tourist. 1997.

Mrs. Pollifax Unveiled. 2000.

Hillhouse, Raelynn.

Rift Zone. 2004.

A Cold War thriller featuring Professor Faith Whitney.

Lynds, Gayle.

Ex-CIA agent Liz Sansborough just can't seem to escape her past.

Masquerade. 1996.

The Coil. 2004.

MacInnes, Helen.

Above Suspicion. 1941. ★ ▰

With this book MacInnes began a best-selling line of novels of romantic international intrigue. Her female spy is usually an amateur and often paired romantically with another amateur, all in the most exotic spots in Europe.

Ride a Pale Horse. 1985. MacInnes's twenty-first, and last, novel.

Matthews, Francine.

Cutout. 2001.

O'Donnell, Peter.

Featuring Modesty Blaise, a character who began in the comic strips in 1962 and appeared first in book form in 1965. She is the female equivalent of James Bond.

Silbert, Leslie.

The Intelligencer. 2004.

Time travel between present-day New York and sixteenth-century London, where private eye Kate Morgan discovers the truth behind the death of playwright Christopher Marlowe.

Truman, Margaret.

Murder in the CIA. 1987.

Political Intrigue and Terrorism

Common to this subgenre are many of the characteristics of the spy/espionage and disaster subgenres, including undercover operatives and weapons of mass destruction, frequently with futuristic overtones of science fiction. Agencies such as the CIA are often featured. The ominous threat of terrorism pervades current releases.

Abercrombie, Neil, and Richard Hoyt.
Blood of Patriots. 1996.

Aellen, Richard.
The Cain Conversion. 1993.

Archer, Jeffrey.
The Eleventh Commandment. 1998.
Shall We Tell the President? 1977. Reissued 1987.

Berry, Steve.
The Amber Room. 2003.
The Romanov Prophecy. 2004.

> Miles Lord, an African American lawyer, travels to Moscow in an effort to restore the Romanov dynasty.

Bond, Larry.
Day of Wrath. 1999.
The Enemy Within. 1997.

Coonts, Stephen.
Liars and Thieves. 2004.

Correa, Arnaldo.
Spy's Fate. 2002.

Deutermann, P. T.
Hunting Season. 2001.

Folsom, Allan.
Day of Confession. 1998.

Forsyth, Frederick.

Forsyth penned several best-selling espionage novels in the 1970s, among them *The Day of the Jackal* (1971, reissued 2002) and *The Odessa File* (1972), that hit the best-seller lists and were turned into films. With the demise of the Cold War he turned his hand to historical mysteries, but returned to espionage with *The Avenger* in 2003, a tale of a vigilante who is tracking down an FBI-protected Serbian killer.

Garber, Joseph R.
Whirlwind. 2004.

> An ex-CIA agent, Charlie MacKenzie, comes out of retirement to track down a stolen secret weapon, known as the Whirlwind.

Hunter, Stephen.
> *Point of Impact.* 1993.

Judd, Alan.
> *Legacy.* 2003.

Liu, Aimee.
> *Flash House.* 2003.

Mills, Kyle.
> *Rising Phoenix.* 1997.
> *Sphere of Influence.* 2002.

Morrell, David.
> *Extreme Denial.* 1996.
> *The League of Night and Fog.* 1987. Reissued 2003.
> *The Protector.* 2003.

Nance, John J.
> *Blackout.* 2000.
> *The Last Hostage.* 1998.
> *Medusa's Child.* 1997.

Patterson, Richard North.
> *No Safe Place.* 1999.
>> Senator Kerry Kilcannon is running for president—and for his life, as he is pursued by a crazed right-to-life activist.

Shelby, Philip.
> *By Dawn's Early Light.* 2002.
> *Days of Drums.* 1996.
> *Gatekeeper.* 1998.
> *Last Rights.* 1997.

Stone, Robert.
> *Damascus Gate.* 1998.

Trevanian.
> *Shibumi.* 1979. Reissued 2005.

Whitcomb, Christopher.
> *Black.* 2004.

Thrillers

Often equated with the page-turner because of its fast pacing and high level of suspense, the thriller is currently the most popular subgenre of adventure fiction, with new twists and titles regularly cropping up on best-seller lists. While spies and espionage frequently are evident in these stories, disasters of a natural or man-made type also are popular. Heart-pounding action, nail-biting suspense, and larger-than-life heroes fill their pages.

Cipher Thrillers

The runaway popularity of Dan Brown's *Da Vinci Code* has turned readers' attention to these clever thrillers that involve history and the high-level thinking required to crack codes. Recent films such as *National Treasure* and *The Librarian: Quest for the Spear* illustrate the type.

Bondurant, Matt.

The Third Translation. 2005.

> Egyptologist Walter Rothschild has one week to solve a cryptic reference on an ancient funerary stone.

Brown, Dan.

Angels & Demons. 2000.

The Da Vinci Code. 2003.

> In this runaway best seller, Harvard symbologist Robert Langdon and French cryptologist Sophie Neveu play suspects and detectives in solving the murder of Neveu's grandfather and unraveling a tightly guarded mystery that sheds new light on Western history. A film version is currently in production fro release in 2006.

Deception Point. 2001.

Digital Fortress. 1998.

Caldwell, Ian, and Dustin Thomason.

The Rule of Four. 2004. 📖

> Two college students search for the location of a secret treasure-filled crypt, which has been hidden in a cipher within the pages of an obscure Renaissance text.

Eco, Umberto.

Foucault's Pendulum. 1990. 📖

> What begins as a game for three editors in Milan becomes far too real.

Fasman, Jon.

The Geographer's Library. 2005. 📖

> When journalist Paul Tomm visits his alma mater to write an obituary of an eccentric professor, he stumbles upon a mystery involving fifteen stolen artifacts that may hold the key to eternal life.

Grossman, Lev.

Codex. 2004.

> A young investment banker, seeking a rare book, finds parallels in a computer game.

Monteleone, Thomas F.

Eyes of the Virgin. 2002.

> The clues here are in the stained glass eyes of the Virgin Mary.

Neville, Katherine.

The Eight. 1988.

> Eighteenth-century novices and a 1970s computer wiz seek, through ciphers and other clues, the pieces of Charlemagne's chess set that posses enormous powers.

Perdue, Lewis.

The Da Vinci Legacy. 1983. Reissued 2004.

> Dr. Vance Erikson, a Da Vinci scholar of the Indiana Jones persuasion, discovers that some of the pages in a rare Da Vinci codex were forgeries and is thrust into a worldwide maelstrom of secret societies and assassinations.

Silbert, Leslie.

The Intelligencer. 2004.

> A volume of sixteenth-century espionage documents in ciphered form is the object of an attempted burglary.

Stephenson, Neal.

Cryptonomicon. 1999. 📖

> Cryptology and treasure in two different time lines.

Zafón, Carlos Ruiz.

The Shadow of the Wind. 2004. 📖

Nazis

Nazis, for decades the evil antagonists in many genres, continue to occupy their standard role in today's adventure fiction. Often they are remnants of old Hitlerian plots resurfacing in current times, rather than neo-Nazis. Titles about Nazis can usually be identified by a swastika or the lightning bolt symbol of the SS on the cover.

Anthony, Evelyn.

Codeword Janus. 2003. Originally published in Great Britain as *The Grave of Truth.*

Browne, Marshall.

The Eye of the Abyss. 2003.

> A one-eyed German banker carries on a covert fight against the Nazis in the 1930s.

Deaver, Jeffery.

Garden of Beasts. 2004.

> A Mafia hit man is sent to Berlin in 1936 to take out a high ranking Nazi.

Diehl, William.

27. 1990. Retitled *The Hunt.*

> On the eve of World War II, an ex-bootlegger takes on agent 27, the Third Reich's perfect spy.

Folsom, Allan.

The Day After Tomorrow. 1994.

> Hitler makes a guest appearance.

Gifford, Thomas.

The Wind Chill Factor. 1975.

Nazi survivors plan to resurrect the Reich.

Heywood, Joseph.

Berkut. 1987.

Joyce, Brenda.

The Chase. 2002.

Murder at her husband's birthday party starts a woman on the trail of a Nazi spy and serial killer who has evaded capture for sixty years.

Levin, Ira.

Boys from Brazil. 1976. ★

Llewellyn, Sam.

Maelstrom. 1994.

Modern-day Norwegian Nazis.

Ludlum, Robert.

The Apocalypse Watch. 1995.

An American agent disappears after infiltrating the neo-Nazis.

Pottinger, Stan.

The Last Nazi. 2003.

Mengele's foster son and contemporary bioterror.

Silva, Daniel.

The Unlikely Spy. 1996.

Catherine Blake, a beautiful Nazi spy, works in England to uncover the details of the Allied invasion of Normandy.

Volpi Escalante, Jorge.

In Search of Klingsor. 2002.

A literary thriller featuring a search for a Nazi scientist.

Technothrillers

Technothrillers emerged in the 1980s as one of the most popular types of adventure tale. When Tom Clancy's *The Hunt for Red October* generated an interest in books that used technology to the extreme, the gadget became as important as a character. Most technothrillers feature an armed conflict between military forces; however, there are exceptions.

Until the enormous changes in Eastern Europe in the late 1980s, the enemy was usually the Soviets, and a common theme was that of the "good Russian," who in some way conveyed superior Soviet technology to the United States. More recent technothrillers use the Middle East and South America for settings. The war on drugs is also finding an important place in the plots of technothrillers. Leisure Books publishes paperbacks regularly with the technothriller designation.

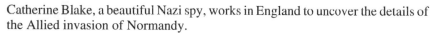

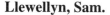

Alten, Steve.

    Goliath. 2002.

Anderson, Kevin J., and Doug Beason.

    Ignition. 1997.

Antal, John.

    Proud Legions: A Novel of America's Next War. 1999.

Ballard, Robert, and Tony Chiu.

    Bright Shark. 1992.

Berent, Mark.

    Berent, an air force pilot who served in Vietnam, uses the Vietnam War setting for his tales of good men fighting a bad war, hindered from winning by the unprincipled policy makers in Washington. Listed in original publication date order.

    Rolling Thunder. 1989. Reissued 2004.

    Steel Tiger. 1990. Reissued 2004.

    Phantom Leader. 1991. Reissued 2005.

    Eagle Station. 1992.

    Storm Flight. 1993.

Bond, Larry.

    Futuristic setting. Listed in original publication date order.

    Red Phoenix. 1989.

    Vortex. 1991.

    Cauldron. 1993.

    Dangerous Ground. 2005.

        The last mission of the USS *Memphis*, a submarine ready for the junk pile, is not what it seems.

Brown, Dale.

    Patrick McLanahan series.

        After Brown's early success with his technothriller series featuring Patrick McLanahan and crew, he wrote several prequels. The books are listed here in the order in which the action takes place, not chronologically by publication date.

    Plan of Attack. 2004.

    Air Battle Force. 2003.

    Wings of Fire. 2002.

    Warrior Class. 2001.

    Battle Born. 1999.

    The Tin Man. 1998.

    Fatal Terrain. 1997.

    Shadows of Steel. 1996.

    Day of the Cheetah. 1989.

    Storming Heaven. 1994.

    Chains of Command. 1993.

Night of the Hawk. 1992.
Sky Masters. 1991.
Hammerheads. 1990.
Flight of the Old Dog. 1987.
Silver Tower. 1988.

Buff, Joe.

Commander Jeffrey Fuller Series.

Commander Jeffrey Fuller and the nuclear submarine, USS *Challenger,* find adventures at the bottom of the ocean.

Deep Sound Channel. 2000.
Thunder in the Deep. 2001.
Crush Depth. 2002.
Tidal Rip. 2003.
Straits of Power. 2004.

Carroll, Ward.

"Punk" Reichert series.

Former fighter pilot Ward Carroll's series features Navy Lieutenant Rick "Punk" Reichert.

Punk's War. 2001.
Persian Gulf.

Punk's Wing. 2003.
Punk is training new pilots when September 11 happens.

Punk's Fight. 2004.
Punk is taken captive in Afghanistan.

Clancy, Tom.

Jack Ryan series.

While *The Hunt for Red October* has been heralded as the beginning of the technothriller trend, not all titles in the Jack Ryan series have the same emphasis on the gadgets, nor even the same emphasis on Ryan. They are listed here in the order in which events take place in the series.

Without Remorse. 1993.
Patriot Games. 1987. ▆
The Red Rabbit. 2002.
The Hunt for Red October. 1984. ▆
The Cardinal of the Kremlin. 1988.
Clear and Present Danger. 1989. ▆
The Sum of All Fears. 1991. ▆
Debt of Honor. 1994.
Executive Orders. 1996.
Rainbow Six. 1998.

> *The Bear and the Dragon.* 2000.
>
> *The Teeth of the Tiger.* 2003.
>
> Jack Ryan's son, also called Jack, and his two friends, Dom and Brian, join a vigilante organization, Henderson Associates, to fight terrorism.

Cobb, James H.

Amanda Lee Garrett series.

> Action at sea, featuring Naval Commander Amanda Lee Garrett.
>
> > *Choosers of the Slain.* 1996.
> >
> > *Sea Strike.* 1997.
> >
> > *Sea Fighter.* 2000.
> >
> > *Target Lock.* 2002.

Coonts, Stephen.

> Coonts is a former navy pilot and catapult officer.
>
> *Fortunes of War.* 1998.

Jake Grafton Series.

> Featuring Admiral Jake Grafton.
>
> > *Flight of the Intruder.* 1986. ◼
> >
> > In 1972, as the Vietnam War drags on and the commitment of Washington wanes, U.S. Navy pilot Jake Grafton flies missions in an A6 Intruder, a carrier-based attack bomber—stressed out and disillusioned, but courageous to the end.
> >
> > *The Intruders.* 1994.
> >
> > *Final Flight.* 1988.
> >
> > *Minotaur.* 1989.
> >
> > *Under Siege.* 1990.
> >
> > *The Red Horseman.* 1993.
> >
> > *Cuba.* 1999.
> >
> > *Hong Kong.* 2000.
> >
> > *America.* 2001.
> >
> > *Liberty.* 2003.
> >
> > *Liars and Thieves.* 2004.
> >
> > Featuring Tommy Carmellini, ex-burglar and CIA operative.

Coonts, Stephen, and Jim DeFelice.

> *Stephen Coonts' Deep Black.* 2004.
>
> > When a spy plane is shot down over Russia, Charlie Dean, an ex-marine sniper, teams up with a former Delta Force trooper, Lia DiFrancesca, to investigate.

Coyle, Harold.

> *Against All Enemies.* 2002.
>
> *Bright Star.* 1990.
>
> *Dead Hand.* 2001.
>
> *God's Children.* 2000.
>
> *More Than Courage.* 2003.

Sword Point. 1988.

Team Yankee. 1987.

> Lt. Col. Harry Shaddock and his elite force take on a dangerous mission to rescue POWs.

Crichton, Michael.

State of Fear. 2004.

> Radical Nick Drake is at the center of global warming hysteria, and his motives are none too pure.

DiMercurio, Michael.

Peter Vornado series.

> A former submarine commander is recruited by the CIA.

Emergency Deep. 2004.

Terrorists in a Soviet submarine.

Michael "Patch" Pacino series.

> Pacino, starts out as commander of the USS *Devilfish*, a submarine, and rises to admiral in command of the Unified Submarine Force, along the way he experiences single combat between submarines and tries to stave off World War III.

Voyage of the Devilfish. 1992.
Attack of the Seawolf. 1993.
Phoenix Sub Zero. 1994.
Barracuda Final Bearing. 1996.
Piranha Firing Point. 1999.
Threat Vector. 2000.
Terminal Run. 2002.

Grace, Tom.

Quantum. 2000.

Harrison, Payne.

Black Cipher. 1994.
Storming Intrepid. 1989.
Thunder of Erebus. 1991.

Herman, Richard, Jr.

Against All Enemies. 1998.
Iron Gate. 1997.
Power Curve. 1997.
The Warbirds. 1989.

Huston, James W.

Balance of Power. 1998.
Fallout. 2001.
Flash Point. 2000.
The Price of Power. 1999.
Secret Justice. 2004.

Shadows of Power. 2002.

Ing, Dean.

Butcher Bird. 1993.

Loose Cannon. 2003.

The Ransom of Black Stealth One. 1989.

Kent, Gordon.

Peacemaker. 2001.

Kyle, Stephen.

After Shock. 2002.

Mayer, Bob.

Dave Riley series.

Featuring Green Beret hero and Chief Warrant Officer Dave Riley.

Dragon Sim 13. 1992.

Cut-Out. 1995.

Eternity Base. 1996.

Eyes of the Hammer. 1991. Reissued 1994.

Synbat. 1994.

Z. 1997.

Pineiro, R. J.

01-01-00: A Novel of the Millennium. 1999.

Breakthrough. 1997.

Conspiracy.com. 2001.

Cyberterror. 2003.

Tom Graham, counterterrorist, computer whiz Michael Patrick Ryan, and FBI agent Karen Frost team up to battle an evil terrorist who is using the computer to control gas lines and triggering massive explosions.

Exposure. 1996.

Firewall. 2002.

Retribution. 1995.

Shutdown. 2000.

Y2K. 1999.

Poyer, David.

Dan Lenson Series.

Naval officer Lenson and the vessels and weapons of the modern navy fight for America. Titles in the series can be read in any order, bur Poyer recommends the following sequence.

The Circle. 1992.

The Med. 1988.

The Passage. 1995.

Tomahawk. 1998.

The Gulf. 1990.

   China Sea. 2000.
   Black Storm. 2002.
   The Command. 2004.

Robinson, Patrick.
 Kilo Class. 1998.
 Nimitz Class. 1997.

Stewart, Chris.
 The Kill Box. 1998.
 Shattered Bone. 1997.
 The Third Consequence. 2000.

Thomas, Craig.
 A Fine and Private War. 2002.
 <u>**Mitchell Gant Trilogy.**</u>
  Firefox. 1977. ◼
  Firefox Down! 1983.
  Winterhawk. 1987.

Weber, Joe.
 Assured Response. 2004.
 Dancing with the Dragon. 2002.
 DEFCON One. 1989.
 Shadow Flight. 1990.
 Targets of Opportunity. 1993.

White, Robin A.
 The Flight from Winter's Shadow. 1990.
 The Last High Ground. 1995.
 Sword of Orion. 1993.
 Typhoon. 2002.

Financial Intrigue/Espionage

  Paul Erdman started this subgenre in 1973 with *The Billion Dollar Sure Thing*, and since then authors have gleefully taken on the world of international banking, oil cartels, and multinational corporations as well as lesser businesses. Political chicanery is often involved, along with crooked doings among the rich and powerful. The following novels show wide variation in their plots, but money is always the prime factor. The subgenre declined in popularity in the late 1990s, but it continues to have a readership following, and a steady stream of new titles appears every year.

Davies, Linda.
 Nest of Vipers. 1995.
 Wilderness of Mirrors. 1996.

Erdman, Paul E.
 The Billion Dollar Sure Thing. 1973. ★

Finder, Joseph.

Company Man. 2005.

Paranoia. 2004.

The Zero Hour. 1996.

Frey, Stephen W.

Day Trader. 2002.

Shadow Account. 2004.

The Silent Partner. 2003.

The Take Over. 1995.

The Vulture Fund. 1996.

Morris, Ken.

The Deadly Trade. 2004.

Combining biothriller with financial.

Man in the Middle. 2003.

Patterson, James.

Black Market. 1994. Retitled and Reissued as *Black Friday* in 2004.

Reich, Christopher.

Numbered Account. 1998.

Biothrillers

With the advances in genetic engineering and the rise of terrorist activities in the 1990s, a subgenre that combines the two trends arose: biothrillers. News of gruesomely horrible diseases fueled the fire. As in technothrillers, the agent of change, in this case biological rather than technological, plays a major role, on a par with and sometimes ahead of characterization and plot. Cataclysmic disaster, narrowly averted, is a frequent theme. Terrorists who have genetically engineered a disease or stolen biological weapons often appear. Occasionally the culprit is merely science gone awry to disastrous ends.

Readers of biothrillers often also enjoy technothrillers, disaster novels, science fiction, and horror novels that deal with medicine or science gone bad.

Anderson, Kevin J., and Doug Beason.

Ill Wind. 1995.

Biological eradication of an oil spill gone wild.

Balling, L. Christian.

Revelation. 1998. Reissued 2004.

Cloning mummified DNA.

Case, John.

The First Horseman. 1998.

Will an eco-terrorist be able to unleash a biological doomsday?

The Genesis Code. 1997.

Biotechnology, ancient beliefs, and murder.

Cassutt, Michael.

Tango Midnight. 2003.
> Deadly disease on a space station.

Crichton, Michael.

Prey. 2002.
> Nanotechnology out of control starts secretly replicating and replacing humans.

Follet, Ken.

Whiteout. 2004.
> Bioterrorism.

Gerritsen, Tess.

Formerly a practicing physician, Gerritsen's more recent books are in chapter 7.

Bloodstream. 1998.
> A plague of violently irrational behavior strikes teens.

Gravity. 1999.
> A space station experiment unleashes a deadly biohazard.

Harvest. 1996.
> Some will go to any lengths to obtain organs for transplants.

Life Support. 1997.
> An upscale retirement home is experiencing an epidemic of a rare disease.

Hogan, Chuck.

The Blood Artists. 1998.
> A deadly and virulent virus turns up in Southern Carolina even after the source in Africa had been annihilated.

Iles, Greg.

The Footprints of God. 2003.
> A project to imbue a computer with human intelligence results in violence and visions.

Johansen, Iris.

And Then You Die. 1998.
> A photojournalist finds a village in which all are dead except one lone infant.

Koontz, Dean.

By the Light of the Moon. 2002.
> A mad doctor injects two strangers with nanotechnology that has surprising consequences.

Mr. Murder. 1993.
> A writer's life is devastated by someone who appears to be his exact double.

Watchers. 1987. Reissued 2003.
> Two genetically engineered animals have escaped from a top secret lab, one a veritable killing machine, the other, perhaps the only thing that can stop the killing.

Christopher Snow series.

Fear Nothing. 1998.

Due to a genetic disorder, Chris Snow can only go out after dark, so he ends up being the one to discover the danger facing the world from a troop of genetically altered monkeys.

Seize the Night. 1998.

Chris tries to save the children that he is sure are being held prisoner on a military base, where diabolical scientific experiments are being conducted.

Land, Jon.

Fires of Midnight. 1995.

An infectious disease expert finds out that new biological weapons may be what killed a mall full of shoppers.

Lynch, Patrick.

Carriers. 1995.

Will bio-warfare experts be able to determine what caused a viral outbreak in Indonesia?

Omega. 1997.

A genetically engineered antibiotic may be the only cure for a plague of common diseases run amok.

Marr, John S., and John Baldwin.

The Eleventh Plague. 1998.

Could bioterrorism be responsible for the otherwise seemingly unrelated deaths of race horses and two children?

McAuley, Paul.

White Devils. 2004.

Plagues and genetic manipulation rage out of control in Africa.

Morris, Ken.

The Deadly Trade. 2004.

Bio-weapons.

Nagata, Linda.

Limit of Vision. 2001.

Sentient nanotechnology implanted in humans may turn into a plague.

Nance, John J.

Pandora's Clock. 1995.

A plane is not allowed to land after a passenger dies from what may be a virulent engineered virus.

Scorpion Strike. 1992.

Saddam Hussein unleashes biological weapons following the Gulf War.

Nayes, Alan.

Gargoyles. 2001.

A young med student gets more than she bargained for when she agrees to be a surrogate mother.

Patterson, James.

The Lake House. 2003.

The genetically altered children from *When the Wind Blows* are back.

Maximum Ride. 2005.

When the Wind Blows. 1998.

Genetic manipulation creates flying children.

Perdue, Lewis.

Slatewiper. 2003.

When a racist gets control of a genetic engineering firm, he bioengineers a new genetic weapon.

Preston, Douglas, and Lincoln Child.

Mount Dragon. 1996.

A genetically engineered cure for the flu gone rogue.

Preston, Richard.

Cobra Event. 1997.

Bio-terrorism.

Survival

Survival is a human being's strongest drive, and it lends great force to adventure thrillers. The survival can involve escape from a burning high-rise or from the steppes of Mongolia. The main theme that the following books have in common is this: The protagonist's life is threatened by extreme danger, but through wit and dogged determination, the heroes survive. Some of these stories, particularly in the "Lone Survivor" category, have a slower pacing than other adventure stories—creating a grueling or agonizing aspect to the stories. Protagonists in this subgenre are generally of the "reluctant" variety, thrown into harm's way, but becoming heroic through their actions in the face of danger.

The Lone Survivor

One person (or sometimes a few individuals), for some reason cut off from civilization (as we know it!), resourcefully make(s) his or her (their) way out of danger.

Branon, Bill.

Spider Snatch. 2000.

A grieving mother and her unemployed former DEA agent husband go on a cruise and run afoul of a vicious drug lord.

Garber, Joseph R.

Vertical Run. 1995.

> Dave Elliott has only himself to depend on as he tries to stay alive while being stalked in a fifty-story office building.

Grell, Mike.

Sable. 2000.

> Game warden Jon Sable lost everything when poachers killed his family, but he acquired a need for vengeance.

L'Amour, Louis.

The Last of the Breed. 1986.

Matheson, Richard.

Hunted Past Reason. 2002.

> A weekend hike for writer Doug Hansen and his actor friend Doug Crowley turns into a wilderness race for survival.

West, Owen.

Four Days to Veracruz. 2004.

> A honeymooning couple escape drug dealers and are relentlessly pursued as they flee across Mexico.

Woods, Stuart.

White Cargo. 1988. Reissued in 2001.

> An entrepreneur, Wendell Catledge, goes after the drug cartel that pirated his yacht and took his wife and daughter.

Disaster

Disaster thrillers fall into several categories. The catastrophe may be natural (that is, nature's fury or an act of God) or man-made, either intentional or accidental.

Natural disasters include earthquakes, volcanic eruptions, tidal waves, meteor strikes, a new ice age, floods, plagues, aberrant behavior of bird or animal life—the only limit is the author's imagination. (Excluded from this chapter are supernatural disasters, which reside in horror.)

Man-made disasters include nuclear explosions, accidents caused by experimenting with bacteria or with humanity's biological heritage, accidents involving aircraft or ocean vessels (such as the sinking of the *Titanic*), and catastrophes caused by tampering with nature's equilibrium (for example, destroying the ozone layer); again, the range is determined by the author's imagination. Frequently, the disaster has a political link, relating this type of book to the spy/espionage subgenre. There is also a science fiction connection in the themes of apocalypse, doomsday, and colliding worlds.

The trend in the 1990s was toward narrowly averted disaster, and was paralleled in movies such as *Deep Impact* and *Armageddon*; but the complete disaster with some survivors, such as occurred in *Titanic*, was also popular. The early twenty-first century has seen a trend toward themes of reconstruction and overcoming smaller disasters, such as plane crashes and series of car wrecks.

Benchley, Peter.

Jaws. 1975. Reissued 2005. ★ 🎬

A killer shark threatens a community.

Crichton, Michael.

The Andromeda Strain. 1969. Reissued 2003. ★ 🎬

A deadly disease from space.

Jurassic Park. 1990. 🎬

Cloned dinosaurs escape on an island theme park.

Cussler, Clive.

Dirk Pitt, greatest action hero of our time, searches shipwrecks, confronts monsters, evades death, and ultimately, always saves humankind.

Atlantis Found. 1999.

Dirk Pitt battles neo-Nazis who are planning a cataclysmic event.

Trojan Odyssey. 2003.

A hurricane threatens an undersea hotel.

Valhalla Rising. 2001.

Sinking cruise ship.

Freemantle, Brian.

Ice Age. 2002.

Aging accelerated by a deadly virus.

Johansen, Iris.

Dead Aim. 2003.

A collapsing dam.

Marlow, Max.

The Burning Rocks. 1996.

Geochemical disaster.

Nance, John J.

Blackout. 2000.

Airplane accidents.

Cascadia. 2005.

Earthquake and tsunami. Developer Mick Walker is building a fancy resort on the island of Cascadia—on top of a major fault line.

Final Approach. 1990.

Plane crash.

Powlik, James.

Meltdown. 2000.

An underwater nuclear detonation endangers the arctic.

Simmons, Dan.
> *Darwin's Blade.* 2000.
>> Car wrecks.

Wiltse, David.
> *Blown Away.* 1996.
>> A serial bomber.

Male Romance

The term "male romance" is derived from the fact that adventure is considered the subgenre of male interest, just as the romance is identified for women. In this subgenre, the protagonist chooses or actively seeks adventure on land, sea, or in the air, following the old tradition of the hero who matches his strength against the powers of natural elements and enjoys the fight.

Many of these books are set in wild and primitive areas of the world. Often they feature treasure hunts or lost mines; some involve piracy; most are full of combat with villains of all sorts.

There is often a political angle to these adventures because many involve revolutionary action in non-European countries, gun-running, or mercenary activities. The story may concern the search for a friend or relative lost under strange circumstances, a ship or plane wreck, hijacking, hunting wild animals, pioneering treks, exploration expeditions, the overcoming of natural disasters, or an escape and the ensuing chase—the possibilities are limitless.

Wild Frontiers and Exotic Lands

Exotic lands and unexplored frontiers are the perfect backdrop for action-filled adventure, adding the appeal of exotic settings to exciting story lines. Many of these authors, of course, also write adventure of other types. Although this has been a rather dormant subgenre in recent years, romance authors have begun to write in this area, adding a good deal of romance, of course. The titles listed here are ones that are still circulating in public libraries.

Crichton, Michael.
> *Congo.* 1980. Reissued 2003. 🎬
>> An expedition sets out for a mysterious lost city in the depths of the Congo.

Cussler, Clive.
> **Dirk Pitt series**.
>> The adventures of underwater recovery mariner Dirk Pitt often have elements of the disaster subgenre and also political overtones, but they always take Pitt into interesting settings both above and below the sea.
>
> *The Mediterranean Caper.* 1973. Reissued 1996.
> *Iceberg.* 1975. Reissued 2000.
> *Raise the Titanic.* 1976. 🎬
> *Vixen 03.* 1978.
> *Night Probe.* 1981.

Pacific Vortex! 1982. Reissued 1985.

Deep Six. 1984.

Cyclops. 1986. Reissued with *Floodtide* in 2001.

Treasure. 1988.

Dragon. 1990.

Sahara. 1992.

Inca Gold. 1994.

Shock Wave. 1996.

Flood Tide. 1997. Reissued with *Cyclops* in 2001.

Atlantis Found. 1999.

Valhalla Rising. 2001.

Trojan Odyssey. 2003.

Forester, C. S.

The African Queen. 1935. Reissued 1984. ★

Haggard, H. Rider.

King Solomon's Mines. 1885.

English explorers seek a fabled lost empire in a remote African country.

The She series.

The Alan Quartermain series.

Jones, Ben.

The Rope Eater. 2003.

A nineteenth-century quest for an Arctic Shan-gri-la.

Preston, Douglas.

The Codex. 2003.

Three brothers seek their father's tomb deep in the rain forest, because he was buried with an ancient Mayan artifact worth billions to pharmaceutical companies.

Smith, Wilbur.

The Sunbird. 1973. Reissued 2002.

In his <u>Courtney series</u>, the Courtneys, privateers, treasure seekers, and explorers caught up in conflicts on the African continent, live life to the fullest, from Sir Francis in *Birds of Prey* (1997), a privateer fighting the Dutch in the seventeenth century, to Isabella in *The Golden Fox* (1990), caught between two men, two continents, and international terrorism in the late twentieth century. Titles are listed in the "Saga" section of the historical chapter (chapter 5).

Soldier of Fortune

The hero as picaresque soldier-of-fortune has appeared in many adventure novels over time. He is frequently an antihero, in the pay of the highest bidder or for personal gain. He is a rogue who bends and breaks the rules. He will stop at nothing to accomplish his goals. Many of the protagonists in the "Male-Action /Adventure" section, which follows, fit this mold. In recent years the soldier of fortune has turned up frequently in romance novels, with Diana Palmer writing several that feature a soldier of fortune as a romantic hero. He also appears in science fiction.

Hill, Sam.

Buzz Monkey. 2004.

Top Kiernan runs his research company from his home in an old schoolhouse, but undercover he is also a soldier of fortune working for Shaw's, "the world's leading booking agency for mercenaries, bodyguards, and probably worse."

Marcinko, Richard.

Rogue Warrior series.

The first title in the series is *Rogue Warrior,* which is not a novel but an autobiography. The first novel in the series was *Red Cell* (1994). The most recent titles are:

Violence of Action. 2002.

With Portland, Oregon, the target of nuclear armed domestic terrorists, the Rogue Warrior springs into action to save the day.

Vengeance. 2005.

Demo Dick goes up against fat-cat bureaucrats and terrorists.

Sadler, Barry.

Casca series.

An immortal warrior hires on for war after war throughout the ages after he plunges a spear into the side of Jesus Christ on the cross and must live until the second coming. The series started with *Casca: The Eternal Mercenary* in 1979, and the last one that Sadler wrote was published posthumously as *Casca: The Mongol* in 1993. Paul Dengelegi began writing the series in 1999.

Male-Action/Adventure Series

The Western has traditionally been considered an action/adventure genre, as have many detective and spy/espionage stories, all of which regularly feature series heroes. The following series are all original titles issued by paperback publishers and noted in trade parlance as action/adventure. They are specifically aimed at a male reading audience. The prototypes for plots and characters may be found in the pulp magazines that flourished before the paperbacks took over as purveyors of action/adventure in the 1940s. In these series men (and sometimes women) function as vengeance squads, martial arts experts, mercenaries, soldiers of fortune, detectives, and adventurers of almost any type. When commercially successful, these series are highly lucrative, and publishers continually experiment with them. It would be futile to list all the evanescent series, of which perhaps only two dozen may be current at any time. The following, however, are a few of the enduring ones.

Johnstone, William W.

Ashes series.

The thirty-fourth book was published in 2003. After the world as we know it is destroyed in nuclear and biological attacks, Ben Raines, a writer, puts together an army called Raines' Rebels, who go about setting the world to rights, starting with building their own homeland, the Southern United States of America, where liberals are not welcome.

Maloney, Mack.

Wingman series.

The sixteenth book was published in 1999.

Murphy, Warren, and Richard Sapir.

Destroyer series.

The 139th title was published in 2005 by Signet.

Pendleton, Don.

Mack Bolan: The Executioner series.

Mack Bolan, a larger-than-life hero who is dedicated to justice, in the first book of the series, *War Against the Mafia* (1969), goes up against those he believes killed his family. Even though Pendleton's last <u>Mack Bolan: The Executioner</u> book was *Satan's Sabbath* in 1981, he licensed the character and series name. The 318th title was published in 2005 by Gold Eagle Books.

Robeson, Kenneth.

Doc Savage series.

Currently being released by Black Mask. Doc Savage, the man of bronze, debuted in the 1930s. He is the richest and most handsome man in the world and has five of the world's top scientists for sidekicks. His headquarters are on the 86th floor of a Manhattan skyscraper One hundred and eighty-one pulp novels featuring Doc Savage were published between 1933 and 1949.

Military and Naval Adventure

The following books focus on the adventure aspects of war. Action is of major importance. Many of the titles set in the late twentieth century can fit just as easily into the technothriller category.

Twentieth Century

Beach, Edward L.

Cold Is the Sea. 1978. Reissued 2004.

Run Silent, Run Deep. 1955. Reissued 2003. ▇

Submarines and the United States after World War II.

Clancy, Tom.

The Hunt for Red October. **1984.** Reissued 1990. ★ ▇

Submarines are the central force in this U.S.–Russian political adventure that started the popular technothriller subgenre.

Fullerton, Alexander.

Nick Everard series.

Featuring young British naval officer Nick Everard during World War I

Blooding of the Guns. 1976. Reissued 2001.

Sixty Minutes for St. George. 1978. Reissued 2002.

Patrol to the Golden Horn. 1978. Reissued 2002.

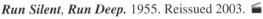

Griffin, W. E. B.

The Brotherhood of War series.

The Corps series.

Higgins, Jack.

Storm Warning. 1976. Reissued 2000.

The U.S. forces in World War II.

Monsarrat, Nicholas.

The Cruel Sea. 1951. Reissued 2000.

The British Navy in World War II.

Reeman, Douglas. (also writes under the pseudonym Alexander Kent).
The British Navy in World War II.

A Prayer for the Ship. 1958. Reissued 2005.
Twelve Seconds to Live. 2002.

Rosenbaum, Ray.

Wings of War series.

Bombers during World War II.

Falcons. 1993.
Hawks. 1994.
Condors. 1995.

Westheimer, David.

The U.S. Army and Army Air Force in World War II.

Von Ryan's Express. 1964. ★ 🎬
Von Ryan's Return. 1980.

Wouk, Herman.

The Caine Mutiny. 1951. Reissued 2003. Winner of the Pulitzer Prize. ★ 🎬
The U.S. Navy in World War II.

Historical Naval and Military Adventure

Most of the following books are published in series. Many of the naval warfare series are set during the Napoleonic Wars. The beloved and often imitated prototype is C. S. Forester's Horatio Hornblower series, which follows Hornblower's career from midshipman to admiral. These novels are rich in historical detail about life aboard ship, customs, and naval warfare. The life of Hornblower is the subject of a "biography" by C. Northcote Parkinson, *The Life and Times of Horatio Hornblower* (1971, reissued 2005), which is so authentic as to persuade the unwary that he really existed.

Cornwell, Bernard.

Richard Sharpe series.

Sharpe's adventures in the British Army from India to the Napoleonic Wars. **TVS**

Sharpe's Tiger. 1997.
Sharpe's Triumph. 1998.
Sharpe's Fortress. 1999.

Sharpe's Trafalgar. 2000.
Sharpe's Prex. 2001.
Sharpe's Rifles. 1988.
Sharpe's Havoc. 2003.
Sharpe's Eagle. 1981.
Sharpe's Gold. 1981.
Sharpe's Escape. 2004.
Sharpe's Battle. 1995.
Sharpe's Company. 1982.
Sharpe's Sword. 1983.
Sharpe's Enemy. 1984.
Sharpe's Honor. 1985.
Sharpe's Regiment. 1986.
Sharpe's Siege. 1987.
Sharpe's Revenge. 1989.
Sharpe's Waterloo. 1990.
Sharpe's Devil. 1992.

Starbuck Chronicles.

Nathanial Starbuck is a Northerner serving in the Confederate Army during the U.S. Civil War.

Rebel. 1993.
Copperhead. 1994.
Battle Flag. 1995.
The Bloody Ground. 1996.

Forester, C. S.

Horatio Hornblower series. TVS ★ 🎬

Featuring Horatio Hornblower. The titles are listed here in chronological order starting when the teenaged Hornblower joins the Royal Navy in 1793 during the Napoleonic wars and following his career as he rises through the ranks to become the commander-in-chief of the British Navy in the West Indies.

Mister Midshipman Hornblower. 1950. Reissued 1999.
Lieutenant Hornblower. 1952. Reissued 1995.
Hornblower and the Hotspur. 1962. Reissued 2003.
Hornblower During the Crisis. 1967. Reissued 1999.
Hornblower and the Atropos. 1953. Reissued 1999.
Beat to Quarters. 1937. Reissued 1999.
Ship of the Line. 1938. Reissued 1999.
Flying Colours. 1939. Reissued 1999.
Commodore Hornblower. 1945. Reissued 1986.
Lord Hornblower. 1946. Reissued 1974.
Admiral Hornblower in the West Indies. 1958. Reissued 1989.

Heyer, Georgette.

Although the following two titles are generally classified as romances and do, in fact, feature a plot that revolves around a romantic entanglement, they are known for their exquisite historical military detail.

An Infamous Army. 1937. Reissued 1998.

An excellent account of the Battle of Waterloo.

The Spanish Bride. 1940. Reissued 2005.

The Peninsular Campaign in the Napoleonic Wars.

Kent, Alexander.

Bolitho series.

Sea adventures featuring Richard and Adam Bolitho. The series starts with Richard Bolitho in 1772 at age sixteen, already a four-year veteran of the King's navy, beginning his service aboard the *Gorgon*. He is assigned to keep the shipping lanes safe from pirates. The series follows his career for over forty years, through several wars and campaigns, and to the rank of admiral. The naval adventure continues with Richard's nephew Adam, who follows in his uncle's footsteps.

Richard Bolitho, Midshipman. 1975. Reissued 1998.

Midshipman Bolitho and the "Avenger." 1978. Reissued 1990.

Stand into Danger. 1980. Reissued 1998.

In Gallant Company. 1977. Reissued 1998.

Sloop of War. 1972. Reissued 1998.

To Glory We Steer. 1968. Reissued 1998.

Command a King's Ship. 1973. Reissued 1998.

Passage to Mutiny. 1976. Reissued 2005.

With All Despatch. 1988. Reissued 1999.

Form Line of Battle. 1969. Reissued 2005.

Enemy in Sight! 1970. Reissued 1999.

The Flag Captain. 1971. Reissued 1999.

Signal—Close Action! 1974. Reissued 2004.

The Inshore Squadron. 1977. Reissued 1999.

A Tradition of Victory. 1981. Reissued 2003.

Success to the Brave. 1983. Reissued 2000.

Colours Aloft! 1986. Reissued 2000.

Honour This Day. 1987. Reissued 2000.

The Only Victor. 1990. Reissued 2000.

Beyond the Reef. 1992. Reissued 2003.

The Darkening Sea. 1993. Reissued 2000.

For My Country's Freedom. 1995. Reissued 2000.

Cross of St. George. 1996. Reissued 2001.

Sword of Honour. 1998. Reissued 2001.

Second to None. 1999. Reissued 2001.

Relentless Pursuit. 2001.

Man of War. 2003.

Lambdin, Dewey.

Alan Lewrie series.

The British Royal Navy in the eighteenth century.

The King's Coat. 1988.
The French Admiral. 1990.
The King's Commission. 1991.
The King's Privateer. 1992.
The Gun Ketch. 1993.
HMS Cockerel. 1995.
A King's Commander. 1997.
Jester's Fortune. 1999.
The King's Captain. 2000.
Sea of Grey. 2002.
Havoc's Sword. 2003.
The Captain's Vengeance. 2004.

Marryat, Frederick.

Classic sea tales set during the Napoleonic Wars, these stories have been compared to those by Patrick O'Brian.

Frank Mildmay or the Naval Officer. 1829. Reissued 2000.
Mr. Midshipman Easy. 1836. Reissued 2001.

McCutchan, Philip.

Halfhyde series.

The British Royal Navy in the Victorian era. The first book is *Halfhyde at the Bight of Benin* (1974, reissued 2004) and the sixteenth title is *Halfhyde and the Fleet Review* (1992).

O'Brian, Patrick.

Aubrey and Maturin series.

O'Brian's sea adventures are among the most popular with fans and the most historically detailed and authentic. They feature Captain Jack Aubrey and Stephen Maturin, physician. In the second title in the series, there is a meeting with Hornblower. When O'Brien died, he left behind three chapters of the twenty-first entry in the series.

Master and Commander. 1969. Reissued 1999. ▆
Post Captain. 1972.
H.M.S. Surprise. 1973. Reissued 2000.
The Mauritius Command. 1977.
Desolation Island. 1978.
The Fortune of War. 1979.
The Surgeon's Mate. 1981.
The Ionian Mission. 1981.
Treason's Harbour. 1983.
The Far Side of the World. 1984. ▆
The Reverse of the Medal. 1986.
The Letter of Marque. 1988.
The Thirteen Gun Salute. 1989.

The Nutmeg of Consolation. 1991.
The **Truelove.** 1992. Originally published as *Clarissa Oakes.*
The Wine-Dark Sea. 1988.
The Commodore. 1995.
The Yellow Admiral. 1996.
The Hundred Days. 1998.
Blue at the Mizzen. 1999. The last of the series.

Pope, Dudley.

Nicholas Ramage series.

Captain Lord Nicholas Ramage's naval story starts in 1796 and takes him through the Napoleonic Wars to 1807.

Ramage. 1965. Reissued 2000.
Ramage & the Drumbeat. 1967. Also published as *Drumbeat.*
Ramage & the Freebooters. 2000.
Governor Ramage R.N. 1973. Reissued 2000.
Ramage's Prize. 1974. Reissued 2000.
Ramage & the Guillotine. 1975. Reissued 2000.
Ramage's Diamond. 1976. Reissued 2001.
Ramage's Mutiny. 1977. Reissued 2001.
Ramage & the Rebels. 1978. Reissued 2001.
The Ramage Touch. 1979. Reissued 2001.
Ramage's Signal. 1980. Reissued 2001.
Ramage & the Renegades. 2001.
Ramage's Devil. 1982. Reissued 2002.
Ramage's Trial. 1984. Reissued 2002.
Ramage's Challenge. 1986. Reissued 2002.
Ramage at Trafalgar. 1986. Reissued 2002.
Ramage & the Saracens. 1988. Reissued 2002.
Ramage & the Dido. 1989. Reissued 2002.

Woodman, Richard.

Featuring Nathaniel Drinkwater, British Navy, in the nineteenth century.

An Eye of the Fleet. 1981. Reissued 2001.
A King's Cutter. 1982. Reissued 2001.
A Brig of War. 1983. Reissued 2001.
The Bomb Vessel. 1984. Reissued 2001.
The Corvette. 1987. Reissued 2000.
1805. 1985. Reissued 2001. Earlier published as *Decision at Trafalgar* in the United States.
Baltic Mission. 1986. Reissued 2000.
In Distant Waters. 1989. Reissued 2000.
A Private Revenge. 1990. Reissued 1999.
Under False Colours. 1999.
The Flying Squadron. 1992. Reissued 1999.
Beneath the Aurora. 1995. Reissued 2001.
The Shadow of the Eagle. 1997. Reissued 2002.
Ebb Tide. 1998. Reissued 2002.

Bibliographies

Drew, Bernard A. *Action Series & Sequels: A Bibliography of Espionage, Vigilante, and Soldier of Fortune Novels*. Garland, 1988.

Gannon, Michael B. *Blood, Bedlam, Bullets, and Bad Guys: A Reader's Guide to Adventure/Suspense Fiction*. Westport, Conn.: Libraries Unlimited, 2004.

McCormick, Donald, and Katy Fletcher. *Spy Fiction*. Facts on File, 1990.
> The bio-critical annotations list the works. The introduction is historical and critical. In the appendix, "List of Abbreviations, Titles and Jargon Used in Espionage in Fact and Fiction," the definitions are often amusing.

Special Collections

The **Gary C. Hoppenstand Adventure Fiction Collection** is housed at Bowling Green State University. It ranges from first edition classics of the late Victorian and Edwardian ages to contemporary works, including books perceived by many to fall into the genres of horror, science fiction, fantasy, and mystery.

Organizations

International Thriller Writers, Inc. (http://www.thrillerwriters.org). Organized in 2004, its first convention (Thrillerfest) is planned for 2006. It hosts a book club and offers a newsletter. The Web site also offers a list of "must read" thrillers.

Awards

The **International Thriller Writers, Inc.** has announced that awards will be given for books at its first convention in 2006 (http://www.thrillerwriters.org/awards.html, accessed June 13, 2005).

D's Adventure Picks

Deutermann, P. T.
Hunting Season. **2001.** (spy/espionage).
> A former FBI "sweeper" whose job was finding rogue agents re-enters the world of espionage when his daughter disappears on a camping trip, and with the female agent assigned to the case, uncovers a plot to bomb Washington.

L'Amour, Louis.

The Last of the Breed. **1986.** (survival).

Joe Mack, a Native American pilot, crashes over Siberia during the Cold War and must make his way to the Bering Strait while being pursued by Soviets.

Patterson, James.

Maximum Ride. **2005.** (biothriller).

The bio-engineered kids from *The Lake House* fly into danger when one is abducted by government agents, in this sequel published as a young adult novel.

Preston, Richard.

Cobra Event. **1997.** (biothriller).

A horrific fast-moving disease kills a schoolgirl, starting a race to find a bioterrorist before he unleashes a genetically engineered weapon of mass destruction on an unsuspecting populace.

Chapter 9

Romance

Essay

Denice Adkins

What Is Romance?

The couple is entwined in an unlikely position. His muscles are bulging. Her flowing dress is half off her body, but her blue eye shadow is firmly in place. Above them, in the skyline, an oxymoron flows in script and foil. You need look no further to know that this book is a romance. But this cover tells its reader more than just genre, title, and author. It tells the reader what kind of story, what level of sensuality, and what kind of ending to expect. These cover features suggest something about the genre, too—romance novels are stories of beautiful women and powerful men swept off their feet by love.

It is this emotional quality that makes the romance genre unique. Romance novels celebrate the emotional development of a love relationship. While mystery is moved by plot and horror by conflict, the action of the romance novel is internal. A man and a woman must come to admit that they love each other and form a pair bond. Beyond that focus, there may be any number of obstacles that interfere with the admission of love, and these may comprise a significant plot, but the theme of the romance novel is one of emotion.

Several romance scholars, including Pamela Regis and Margaret Ann Jensen,[1] have examined the romance "formula." In brief, it is this: The protagonists meet and realize their attraction, but something keeps them apart. This obstacle appears insurmountable. Eventually, though, it is overcome, and the hero and heroine live happily ever after. Throughout it all, the reader is able to vicariously experience the emotions of meeting someone special, being kept apart from that person, challenging the obstacle, and finally overcoming it. The reader knows that the obstacle will be overcome, which enables her to keep reading no matter how desperate the story seems.

Why Romance?

What is it that makes the romance novel so popular? What is it about this genre that hooks and keeps its readers? Studies have been conducted of the romance genre and romance readers. While the critics disagree on almost everything else, including whether or not the genre is a tool of the patriarchy, they agree on this: Romance novels make women happy. Explanations as to why this is can be found in the romance text and in the life of the reader as well.

The woman is the lead character. The romance novel revolves around a woman. She is the central character. Life (and men) revolve around her, and the novel portrays her during her courtship. This courtship is symbolic of choice; although she does not use it, the heroine has the power to reject and hurt her hero. In this stage of her life, the heroine has power. More specifically, the heroine uses her power to overcome an obstacle and improve her life. Far from passively waiting for a man to rescue her, heroines are working toward their own resolutions. These heroines are women with agency; they can make things happen in their lives, and this is what romance readers want to see.

The woman is a strong character. Although this has not always been the case historically, current romance novels feature an independent heroine who is not afraid to confront the obstacle that keeps her from true love—even if that obstacle is the hero himself! Carol Thurston provides a content analysis of romance novels in which women show strong career orientation.[2] The women portrayed here are true to their principles, and unafraid of conflict. In *Love and the Novel*, George Paizis goes on to suggest that the romance script portrays a woman's search for esteem, saying that romance novels present women overcoming their fears.[3] Romances set up a positive story line to contrast with society's negative reality.

The man surrenders to the woman. Romance is a genre of female empowerment. It is a genre in which woman, the embodiment of emotion, gets the better of man, the embodiment of rationality. In romance novels, men are forced to acknowledge their need for women, and learn that they must play the love game by women's rules: expressing their feelings and emotions. Research by Janice Radway and Lynda L. Crane suggests that readers want to see a caring, intelligent, nurturing hero.[4] While women take up the burden of work, penetrating men's domains, they want to see men take up the formerly female role of nurturing their partners.

The reader needs validation of her beliefs. The romance novel provides immense psychological reassurance to its reader. Through its formulaic nature, the romance novel assures the reader that in this world of dynamic change, it, at least, stays constant. Virtue will be rewarded. Men will be willing to look past surface attraction to see the beauty within. There will be a happy ending, regardless of how insurmountable the obstacle seems. Some critics fear that this confidence in happy endings in the face of evidence to the contrary may lead women to accept domestic abuse as a prelude to the happy ending. Readers say they enjoy the happy ending and the feeling that romance has triumphed again, but they don't confuse romance with reality.

The reader wants a predictable pleasure. One of the pleasures of reading a romance is that the reader knows more or less how the story line will be resolved. The couple will acknowledge their love and live happily ever after. But knowing the resolution is not the same thing as knowing the process by which the characters obtain that resolution. Immersion in the story line lets women look into another life. Another predictable pleasure that comes from some romance novels is a validation of women's sexual desires. Although Suzanne Juhasz suggests that women read romance because they reproduce the quest for mother love,[5] others suggest that they help women develop identities as sexual beings. The romance hero is the perfect lover, reassuring the heroine that her desire, and the desires of the readers, are right and valid.

The reader needs her own space. Radway's study of romance readers in Midwestern "Smithton" found that women used romance reading as an escape from their normal lives, and as a way to stake out some territory for themselves.[6] Reading a romance allowed women to take time away from caring for a husband and children and give that time back to themselves. In this way, reading becomes an act of resistance and a rejection, if only temporarily, of the traditional roles of wife and mother.

How Do Women Become Romance Readers?

Two forces combine to create the romance reader: heavy marketing and reader networks. Purchase opportunities are ubiquitous; romances are not found only at traditional venues such as stand-alone bookstores and public libraries. When a woman buys groceries, goes to a discount store, picks up a prescription, or visits the shopping mall, she has an opportunity to buy a romance novel. If she has a subscription to a publisher's books-by-mail programs, she goes only as far as her mailbox to find romance. The effect of this purchasing ubiquity is a $1.63 billion sales figure for romance fiction, according to the Romance Writers of America, Inc.[7]

Harlequin engaged in extensive advertising in other popular media such as television and magazines, to convince more women to try them, and in intensive market research, to find out what women wanted in a romance novel. Romance novel marketing in the 1980s attempted to create community by hosting parties at which authors and publishers met with their readers. Similarly, romance writers and fans gather at conferences, including "Celebrate Romance," the Romance Writers of America national conference, and various regional conferences.

In addition to being widely available, however, romance novels are also easily recognizable. By standardizing the appearance of romance novels, Harlequin and other romance publishers lower their costs, while readers are more easily able to identify the books. Harlequin's intensive market research also helped determine what kind of content women wanted in a romance. By standardizing content, using tip sheets for authors, and making all books the same length, readers' emotional costs in reading the book were minimized. Every book is a more or less known quantity; no book is likely to be a bad investment.

Exchanging books with other readers is another way to ward off a bad emotional investment in a book. Women share romances with relatives, friends, and colleagues, talking about the books they enjoyed and warning others off the ones they did not. Women learn romance reading from mothers and close relatives; romance forms a family identity. Jensen's Harlequin readers exchanged books with other readers, as an excuse to get out of the house.[8] Radway's Smithton readers relied on a romance bookseller to tell them which books were good, and they shared their reading experiences with the bookseller in turn.[9] From Web sites to newsgroups, romance reader communities have proliferated online as well. Romance readers have developed strong communities to share their reading experiences.

However willing romance readers are to admit their genre choice within their social networks, there is some evidence that women prefer to hide their romance reading. Besides being considered less worthy than other forms of literature, romance novels are scorned by academics and librarians for their formulaic nature, mass-market appeal, and inclusion of detailed sexual descriptions. Romance novels are further derided by feminists for showing female characters whose lives revolve around their relationships with men and who are rewarded for their beauty rather than their actions. Even in family groups, husbands and children may be resentful of time taken away from them; strangers may chide them for their reading tastes. Some romance readers use book covers or otherwise hide their reading. Reading a scorned genre can be a very solitary activity.

Development of the Romance Genre

The book acknowledged as the prototype for current romance fiction is *Pamela, or Virtue Rewarded*, written and published in 1740 by Samuel Richardson. Pamela, a servant, is threatened by her employer, Mr. B. At last, though, Mr. B. confesses his love, and Pamela's virtue is in fact rewarded with marriage. Successors to *Pamela* include Horace Walpole's gothic *The Castle of Otranto* (1764), Ann Radcliffe's *The Mysteries of Udolpho* (1794), and three novels by Fanny Burney about young women's entry into polite society (*Evelina*, 1778; *Cecilia*, 1782; *Camilla*, 1796).

In the 1800s, another novelist furthered the cause of romance: Jane Austen. Her novels, published between 1811 and 1818, include the genre classic *Pride and Prejudice*. Austen's novels showed humans with foibles and flaws and introduced the comedy of manners. Charlotte Bronte's *Jane Eyre* and Emily Bronte's *Wuthering Heights* (both published in 1847) exemplified the romantic themes of the conquering heroine and the tormented hero.

Although works of romance fiction have been published since the 1700s, and Mills & Boon in the United Kingdom had been publishing romance since 1909, the genre hit its stride in North America in 1957. Harlequin, a publisher of paperback mystery and adventure stories, started publishing romance fiction. This move was so successful that Harlequin soon started publishing romance exclusively. They presented an opportunity to other potential romance publishers to offer the romances that Harlequin did not.

Harlequin romances were "sweet," in that they did not have sexual content. The door to the hero's and heroine's bedroom was closed. The opportunity for racier romances came in the 1970s, with the women's liberation movement. Women who had control of their reproductive systems were able to engage in varied sexual activity, unfettered by fear of pregnancy and social values. In 1972, Kathleen E. Woodiwiss's *The Flame and the Flower* was published, bringing sexuality into the genre. During this period, sexual mores were caught between the traditional unschooled virgin and the modern liberated woman. Romance novels indicated the conflict through the inclusion of violent sexuality; a heroine could have sex (modern sentiment) but only if she didn't want to (traditional). Rape and humiliation were stock-in-trade. Throughout the late 1970s and early 1980s, romance readers who identified with the feminist cause encouraged publishers to experiment with consensual sexuality.

Harlequin's original method of operation was to reprint Mills & Boon romances from the United Kingdom, marketing them in the United States and Canada. Though Janet Dailey wrote American-themed romances for Harlequin, the bulk of their offerings were set in England or abroad. Silhouette, an imprint of Simon & Schuster, stepped into the void by offering romances set in the United States. Silhouette also introduced the Desire line, which featured a higher level of sensuality than the traditional Harlequin romance. Dell, Jove, Bantam, and NAL followed suit in the 1980s, greatly increasing the output of romances during this heyday of the genre. Ultimately, Harlequin bought Mills & Boon and Silhouette and was itself purchased by Torstar, the media conglomerate that owns the *Toronto Star.*

Statistics from the 1980s, 1990s, and 2000s suggest that although romance readers have one general characteristic—93 percent of all romance readers are women—they come from a variety of backgrounds. The Romance Writers of America maintain that three out of four women in the United States have read a romance novel at some point in their lives.[10] Given a broad diversity of readers, there is a corresponding diversity of interests. Some of the latest trends in the genre indicate this, with new books ranging from sweet to spicy, and acknowledging many different types of reader.

Erotica: Although the erotic romance has always been a "hot" commodity, a more recent trend is the publication of erotica for women. These novels, like those published by Kensington under the Brava imprint, are less focused on the development of the love relationship between the protagonists. They focus on the sex act itself, and push the boundaries farther than traditional steamy romances, with the protagonists participating in orgies, bondage games, and alternative sexualities. This move toward an erotica imprint has been coupled with an increased sensuality in category romances such as Harlequin's Blaze line.

Christianity: Along with the rise of the erotic romance in recent years has come the rise of the Christian-oriented romance. While developing a love relationship, protagonists in these novels are also facing spiritual crisis. These romances suggest a return to more traditional values. The bedroom door is closed again; the church door is open, and women in these novels choose more traditional roles. Harlequin's Steeple Hill line provides mainstream representation for these stories; other publishers include Multnomah Publishers and Bethany House.

Multicultural: During the 1990s, and particularly in the early 2000s, publishers developed a new awareness of multicultural audiences. Until this point, most romance heroines were white. Cultural diversity appeared, if it did, by virtue of the hero's mixed heritage. He may have been half Native American or half Arab. Blacks, Latinos, and Asians were scarcely represented in the genre; Native Americans and Middle Easterners, though represented, were seldom portrayed accurately. This changed in 1994, when Kensington developed the Arabesque line. Arabesque romances featured African American protagonists and was successful enough to be purchased by BET in 1998. Kensington less successfully developed a line of romance for Latina readers. The Encanto line, developed in 1999, folded in 2002. Genesis Publishing, a small press, produces books in the Indigo imprint.

Indigo romances feature African American protagonists; the Love Spectrum imprint features interracial couples. The Indigo After Dark imprint is a more erotic line.

Paranormal/Time Travel/Futuristic/Fantasy: Genre boundaries are stretched with these romance subgenres. Paranormal romances share features with horror novels, which are populated by ghosts, vampires, and werewolves. Futuristic and fantasy romances take elements from science fiction and fantasy novels respectively. However, in each subgenre, the romance plot generally takes precedence over the other genre. Major authors in this subgenre include Laurell K. Hamilton, Susan Krinard, and J. D. Robb (a pseudonym for Nora Roberts).

Chick Lit and Humor: The phenomenal success of Helen Fielding's *Bridget Jones's Diary* left romance publishers wondering if they'd missed something regarding the younger generation's views of romance. Harlequin's response was Red Dress Ink, an imprint dedicated to young, urban women who were living a lifestyle, not having a relationship. These heroine-dominant novels focus on careers, clothing, and empowerment. Although there is frequently a male hero partnered with this strong female heroine, the romance interest is not always resolved by marriage. However, the books do end with the heroine overcoming an obstacle and making her success on her own terms.

Judging a Book by Its Cover

The cover described in the introduction is the classic "clinch" cover, so called because the hero and heroine are clinched together. This kind of cover was the mainstay of the genre in the late twentieth century, helped along by male bookstore distributors who needed a quick way to identify romance novels. The clinch cover was in part responsible for the view of the romance genre as pornography for women, and caused many a romance reader to invest in book covers rather than be seen reading "trash." However, some readers enjoyed the vision of the hero and heroines provided by the clinch cover. A more recent adaptation of the clinch cover is the man-only cover, which shows the hero but not the heroine. Connie Mason's *The Last Rogue* features a cloaked man standing alone in sea foam.

Romance publishers have lately been experimenting with different kinds of covers. The "real estate" cover might have a picture of a castle on it, rather than the couple. The real estate cover evokes the feeling of the story without also evoking erotic overtones. Related to the real estate cover is what some call the "stuff" cover, which features fans, swords, jewelry, or other "stuff" evocative of the story line. Johanna Lindsey's *A Loving Scoundrel* is an example of a real estate cover; Mary Balogh's *Slightly Sinful* typifies the stuff cover. The stepback cover combines the respectable real estate or stuff cover with an inset clinch. Passers-by see the real estate without seeing the couple, and the reader can open to the clinch if she desires.

The cartoon cover features a cartoon-like drawing, typically of the heroine, sometimes of the couple. These are found on historical and contemporary romances, and suggest a light, humorous story. Mary Janice Davidson's *Undead and Unwed* is a good example of a cartoon cover suggesting humor. Another recent development is the "bits-and-pieces" cover. These covers show part of a woman, usually in soft lighting. Susan Krinard's *Kinsman's Oath* shows only the heroine's face, Katie McAllister's *Sex and the Single Vampire* a pair of legs.

Romance novels are popular because they present a world in which caring and emotion come from both partners. They remind women that there is a happy ending out there, even if it is just in the next novel. They demonstrate that women have power to change their own lives. As evidenced by the new trends in the genre, romances remain popular because they are moving with their demographic. The fact that these novels are the products of women with the same hopes and dreams as the reader base suggests that romance novels will be speaking to women's hearts for many years to come.

Notes

1. Pamela A. Regis, *A Natural History of the Romance Novel* (Philadelphia: University of Pennsylvania Press, 2003); Margaret Ann Jensen, "The Grand Passion of Practical People," in *Love's $weet Return: The Harlequin Story,* ed. M. A. Jensen, 140–58 (Bowling Green, Ohio: Bowling Green State University Popular Press, 1984.

2. Carol Thurston, *The Romance Revolution: Erotic Novels for Women and the Quest for a New Sexual Identity* (Urbana: University of Illinois Press, 1987).

3. George Paizis, *Love and the Novel: The Poetics and Politics of Romantic Fiction* (New York: St. Martin's Press, 1998).

4. Janice A. Radway, *Reading the Romance: Women, Patriarchy, and Popular Culture,* 2d ed. (Chapel Hill: University of North Carolina Press, 1991); Lynda L. Crane, "Romance Novel Readers: In Search of Feminist Change?" *Women's Studies* 23 (1994): 257–59.

9

5. Suzanne Juhasz, *Reading from the Heart: Women, Literature, and the Search for True Love* (New York: Viking, 1994).

6. Radway, *Reading the Romance.*

7. Romance Writers of America, Inc. *2003 Romance-Fiction Sales Statistics, Reader Demographics, and Book-Buying Habits.* 2003. Available at http://www.rwanational.org/StatiticsBrochure2003.pdf (accessed June 1, 2004).

8. Jensen, "Grand Passion."

9. Radway, *Reading the Romance.*

10. Romance Writers of America, *2003 Romance-Fiction Sales.*

Bibliography

Crane, Lynda L. "Romance Novel Readers: In Search of Feminist Change?" *Women's Studies* 23 (1994): 257–59.

Jensen, Margaret Ann. "The Grand Passion of Practical People." In *Love's $weet Return: The Harlequin Story,* ed. M. A. Jensen, 140–58. Bowling Green, Ohio: Bowling Green State University Popular Press, 1984.

Juhasz, Suzanne. *Reading from the Heart: Women, Literature, and the Search for True Love.* New York: Viking, 1994.

Kaler, Anne K., and Rosemary E. Johnson-Kurek, eds. *Romantic Conventions*. Bowling Green, Ohio: Bowling Green State University Popular Press, 1999.

Krentz, Jayne Ann, ed. *Dangerous Men & Adventurous Women: Romance Writers on the Appeal of the Romance*. Philadelphia: University of Pennsylvania Press, 1992.

Paizis, George. *Love and the Novel: The Poetics and Politics of Romantic Fiction*. New York: St. Martin's Press, 1998.

Radway, Janice A. *Reading the Romance: Women, Patriarchy, and Popular Culture*. 2d ed. Chapel Hill: University of North Carolina Press, 1991.

Regis, Pamela A. *A Natural History of the Romance Novel*. Philadelphia: University of Pennsylvania Press, 2003.

Romance Writers of America, Inc. *2003 Romance-Fiction Sales Statistics, Reader Demographics, and Book-Buying Habits*. 2003. Available at http://www.rwanational.org/StatiticsBrochure2003.pdf. Accessed June 1, 2004.

Thurston, Carol. *The Romance Revolution: Erotic Novels for Women and the Quest for a New Sexual Identity*. Urbana: University of Illinois Press, 1987.

Themes and Types

Diana Tixier Herald

There are many ways to categorize romance fiction—series fiction versus stand-alone titles, contemporary versus historical, sensual versus sweet. The categories used in this chapter reflect common reader preferences and current publishing trends—womanly romance, contemporary romance, romantic-suspense, historical, fantasy and science fiction, and ethnic romance. "Chick Lit" which is closely related to romance, is covered with "women's fiction," in chapter 14.

There is some overlap among these categories, and although single titles may arguably be put in more than one place, the categories presented here will provide choices that satisfy most romantic tastes. In the 1970s and 1980s publishers identified the subgenres on paperback spines or on hardcover dust jackets (for example, gothic, career, romantic suspense); but the trend today seems to be moving toward more general categorization. On paperbacks one is likely to find only the designations "romance," "historical romance," and "regency romance," while romance novels are often published with merely the designation "novel" or "fiction."

Beyond the categories used here to organize titles, there are other characteristics to keep in mind when advising readers. Sensuality levels are important to many romance readers. (This is why reviews in *Romantic Times* always contain sensuality ratings.) However, terminology for the levels varies, and categorizations are somewhat subjective. What one reader calls "innocent" another may call "sweet" or even "sensual." One reader may be interested in "spicy" novels, while others call it "erotic," "hot," or "sexy." One way to identify what level of sensuality a reader prefers is to ask about previous romances enjoyed and then find other titles that fit that rating. If you cannot find that information, simply ask the reader.

Another issue to consider with romance readers is series versus stand-alone titles. Some read series fiction only, some read only stand-alone, and still others read both. Again, you can determine your reader's preference by asking about previous reads or asking directly.

Keep in mind that yesterday's contemporary is tomorrow's historical. Romance Writers of America Inc. defines contemporary romances as those that have a setting after the world wars, which gives readers a choice of settings that spans more than half a century.

Women's fiction and Chick Lit are frequently included in discussions of romance, and many types that were traditionally found alongside romance, such as soap opera, mainstream womanly romance, and contemporary mainstream romance, including glitz and glamor, belong more in the women's fiction category. Many authors who gained recognition as romance writers move back and forth effortlessly between romance and Chick Lit or women's fiction.

Selected Classics

The titles below represent some of the older classics of the genre that are still available. The type or subgenre is indicated; more titles in each type as well as classics published after 1970 can be found in the categorized lists that follow. Additional titles of historic interest are mentioned in Kristin Ramsdell's *Romance Fiction: A Guide to the Genre* (Libraries Unlimited, 1999). The titles are listed in publication order.

Austen, Jane.
> *Sense and Sensibility.* 1811.
> *Pride and Prejudice.* 1813.
> *Mansfield Park.* 1814.
> *Emma.* 1815.
> *Persuasion.* 1817. (historical Regency).
> *Northanger Abbey.* 1817. (suspense, gothic parody).

Brontë, Charlotte.
> *Jane Eyre.* 1847. (suspense-gothic).

Brontë, Emily.
> *Wuthering Heights.* 1847. (suspense-gothic).

De La Roche, Mazo.
> Jalna series. (historical-saga).
>> Sixteen novels. The first novel of the series was published in 1927. The series spans 100 years in the lives of the wealthy Whiteoaks family.

Du Maurier, Daphne.
> *Rebecca.* 1938. (suspense-gothic).
>> An unnamed protagonist traveling through Europe as a companion meets and marries widower Maxim de Winter and is haunted by tales of his late wife. A sequel was published in 2001, titled *Rebecca's Tale* and written by Sally Beauman.

Galsworthy, John.
> The Forsyte Saga. (historical-saga).
>> Three volumes. The first volume, published in 1906, was reissued numerous times, most recently in 2004. The three trilogies detail the affluent Forsyte family starting in 1886. Followed by:
> A Modern Comedy. (3 volumes). (historical-saga).
> End of the Chapter. (3 volumes). (historical-saga).

Heyer, Georgette.
> Many titles. (historical-Regency).

Holt, Victoria.
> *Mistress of Mellyn.* 1960. (suspense-gothic).
> *Bride of Pendorric.* 1963. (suspense-gothic).

Kaye, M. M.

The Far Pavilions. 1978. (historical).

Described as an (East) Indian *Gone With the Wind.*

Michaels, Barbara.

Master of Blacktower. 1966. (suspense-gothic).

There are other titles.

Radcliffe, Anne.

The Mysteries of Udolpho. 1794.

Richardson, Samuel.

Pamela, or Virtue Rewarded. 1740.

Clarissa Harlowe. 1747.

Rowson, Susanna Haswell.

Charlotte Temple: A Tale of Truth. 1791.

Sabatini, Rafael.

Scaramouche. 1921. (historical).

Romance amid the French revolution.

Seton, Anya.

My Theodosia. 1941. (historical). Theodosia Burr.

Katherine. 1954. (historical). Wife of John of Gaunt.

Shellabarger, Samuel.

Captain from Castille. 1945. (historical). Sixteenth-century Mexico.

Prince of Foxes. 1947. (historical).

The King's Cavalier. 1950. (historical).

Stewart, Mary.

Madam, Will You Talk. 1955. (suspense-gothic).

The Gabriel Hounds. 1967. (suspense-gothic).

Walpole, Hugh.

The Castle of Otranto. 1764. (suspense-gothic).

The Herries chronicle. (historical-saga).

Four volumes. The first volume was published in 1930. The series follows several generations of the Herries family, starting in 1730 when they first arrive in the Lake District.

Whitney, Phyllis A.

The Trembling Hills. 1956. (suspense-gothic).

Winsor, Kathleen.

Forever Amber. 1944. (historical). Seventeenth century England.

Contemporary Romance

The contemporary romance is a "purist's" romance, focusing on the relationship between one man and one woman, with a happily-ever-after ending. Those who particularly enjoy reading stories about characters they can relate to (i.e., a character who lives in contemporary times and faces similar challenges to those they themselves face or have faced) will enjoy these titles.

The Romance Writers of America Inc. defines contemporary romance as those stories that are set in a time after World War II, which gives readers a choice of settings that spans more than half a century. Characters' occupations and station in life are varied. They can be of any ethnicity or socioeconomic class. The heroine is usually in her twenties or thirties, but more mature heroines are not unknown.

This subgenre is extremely active and volatile. Most of the following authors write prolifically, and books slip in and out of print at an alarming pace. Only a few titles are mentioned, because while it is easy to locate books by a specific author, it can be extremely difficult to locate specific titles. Peggy J. Jaegly, in *Romantic Hearts: A Personal Reference for Romance Readers.* (Scarecrow, 1997), identified many titles in this category, but there is no way to keep up with them all. As more libraries begin cataloging paperback original romances, this situation should improve, and as the large print houses and reprint publishers such as Severn House reissue paperback originals in hardcover, more are showing up in library catalogs.

When advising readers of contemporary romance, keep in mind that romance authors frequently write in more than one subgenre. Also, remember that it is a rare romance writer who does not have her (or his) own Web site. These sites usually include a list of books published and information on forthcoming titles.

Banks, Leanne. (http://www.leannebanks.com/)
> *Some Girls Do.* 2003.
> *When She's Bad.* 2003.
>> An insomniac spa owner and her new neighbor, a do-it-yourselfer who practices home improvement all through the night, are the protagonists of this humorous and sexy romp.

Brown, Sandra.
> Her older titles are frequently reissued. Her recent titles have been moving more and more into the suspense subgenre, but a list of her contemporary romances can be found online at http://www.sandrabrown.net/books/romance.html.
>
> *A Treasure Worth Seeking.* 1982. Reissued 2001.
>> Searching for her long-lost brother, Erin finds romance with a federal agent.

Crusie, Jennifer. (http://www.sff.net/people/JenniferCrusie/)
> *Bet Me.* 2004. Humorous.
>> Cal asked Min out on a date to win a bet, but found much more.

Delinsky, Barbara. (http://www.barbaradelinsky.com/)
> Delinsky's recent titles are mainstream women's fiction.

T.L.C. 1988. Reissued 2001.

> Once he tried to have her put in jail; now Dr. Brice Carlin has rescued Karen Drew from a snowy death, and together they are snowbound.

Eagle, Kathleen. (http://www.kathleeneagle.com/publications.html)

Eagle's novels feature Native American heroes and strong women in contemporary settings.

The Last Good Man. 2000.

> A famous model returns to her Wyoming home town, where she enters into a marriage of security with a childhood friend and finds true love.

Freethy, Barbara. (http://www.barbarafreethy.com/)

Some Kind of Wonderful. 2001.

> A baby left between their doors brings two apartment-dwelling neighbors together.

Hannah, Kristin. (http://www.kristinhannah.com/)

Home Again. 1996.

> A famous actor, needing a heart transplant, finds that his cardiologist is the girl he left behind.

Korbel, Kathleen. (http://www.eileendreyer.com/Eileensotherself.shtml)

Korbel is a pseudonym of Eileen Dreyer, who also writes medical thrillers. She has written twenty-two Silhouette paperback originals.

Some Men's Dreams. 2003.

> After accidentally knocking out her new boss with a thrown softball, Gen pitches in to watch his daughter and discovers a serious problem.

Krentz, Jayne Ann. (http://www.krentz-quick.com/)

Krentz is a former librarian.

Perfect Partners. 1992.

> When librarian Letty Thornquist inherits a sporting goods company, she knows she will have to learn the ropes from CEO Joel Blackstone, who is none too happy with the idea at first.

Landis, Jill Marie. (http://www.jillmarielandis.com/)

Heartbreak Hotel. 2005.

> A widow's life is changed when a suicidal motorcycle-riding author comes into her life.

Leone, Laura. (http://www.sff.net/people/laresnick/)

Leone, a pseudonym for Laura Resnick, also writes fantasy novels.

Untouched by Man. 1992. Reissued 2001.

> A shy researcher and a deep-sea diver find love off the Florida keys.

Linz, Cathie. (http://www.cathielinz.com/)

Lintz, a librarian and long-time Romance Writers of America Library Liaison, usually features military men as the heroes in her novels.

The Marine Meets his Match. 2004.

A bookseller enters into a sham marriage with a Marine to save him from the clutches of a general's daughter and finds much more than she bargained for.

Macomber, Debbie. (http://www.debbiemacomber.com)

Navy Baby. 1991. Reissued 2005.

Hannah, a preacher's daughter, grieving for her dead fiancé, loses her virginity and becomes pregnant with a sailor's baby during a one-night stand.

Phillips, Susan Elizabeth. (http://www.susanephillips.com/)

Breathing Room. 2002.

A disgraced lifestyle diva (think Martha Stewart) and a bad boy actor are thrown together in the Tuscan countryside.

Putney, Mary Jo. (http://www.maryjoputney.com)

Putney also writes historical and paranormal romances.

The Spiral Path. 2002.

An angst-filled historical film drama throws a divorcing acting couple together; they discover depths in each other they had never found during their truncated marriage.

Roberts, Nora. (http://www.noraroberts.com/)

Roberts has written more than 100 titles, many of them best sellers. As of 2005 she had more than 280 million books in print.

The Perfect Neighbor. 1999. Reissued 2002.

Cartoonist Cybil is so tired of her well-meaning neighbors setting her up on blind dates that she claims to have a date with another neighbor and then must figure out how to not look like a liar.

Seidel, Kathleen Gilles.

Please Remember This. 2002.

When Tess was still a baby, her famous fantasy-writing mother committed suicide. Now in her twenties, with an inheritance, she returns to her birthplace, where she meets a local politician who is on what may seem like a crazy quest.

Smith, Annie.

Smith, a librarian, has also written contemporary romances under the name Annie Kimberlin and is also the author of *The Romance Readers' Advisory: The Librarian's Guide to Love in the Stacks* (ALA Editions, 2000), written under the name Ann Bouricius.

Coming Home. 2002.

Sally, who has added a teenager and a rambunctious puppy to her cat-friendly household after the death of her best friend, becomes involved with Tanner, a dog trainer, in this heartwarming, cozy tale.

Spencer, LaVyrle.

Spencer has several best-selling titles; however, she is no longer writing.

Smalltown Girl. 1997. Reissued 2003.

A Nashville star returns home to care for her mom and finds love.

Wind, Ruth. (http://www.barbarasamuel.com/)

> A pseudonym of Barbara Samuel.

Meant to Be Married. 1995.

> Elias, a successful businessman, and Sarah, a famous fashion photographer, were unable to fight their feuding families to create a life together, but now, a dozen years later, they may have a second chance.

Wolf, Joan. (http://www.joanwolf.com/)

That Summer. 2003.

> Veterinarian Anne Foster returns to Virginia and the horse-racing world, where she encounters Liam, whom she knew as a teenager.

Sensuous Contemporaries

A contemporary setting and detailed descriptions of the intimate encounters between the hero and heroine may be considered soft-core pornography by some, but to the legions of their readers the vivid descriptions in these romances are merely another way of making the characters live in the reader's imagination. When readers ask for "spicy" or "erotic" romance, these authors will generally fit the bill. The stories often also include other elements such as humor or suspense. Related titles are listed in order of how the action occurs.

Andersen, Susan.

> ***Head over Heels.*** 2002.
> ***Getting Lucky.*** 2003.
> ***Hot & Bothered.*** 2004.

Blake, Jennifer.

> ***Garden of Scandal.*** 1997. Reissued 2003.

Crusie, Jennifer.

> ***Welcome to Temptation.*** 2000.

Greene, Jennifer.

> ***Wild in the Moment.*** 2004.

Howard, Linda.

> ***Mr. Perfect.*** 2001.

Leigh, Jo.

> ***A Lick and a Promise.*** 2005.

Phillips, Carly.

> ***Brazen.*** 1999. Reissued 2005.

Phillips, Susan Elizabeth.

> ***Ain't She Sweet?*** 2004.

Sweet Contemporaries

Sweet is the romance code word for "innocent" romances, in which sexual activity is not described. Kissing, hand-holding, and swooning emotional swells are about as far as things go, at least in terms of what is printed for the reader. Harlequin Romance and Silhouette Romance series are both this type. Avalon romances, frequently found as standing-order plans in libraries, also fall into this category. Readers who only want sweet romances may also enjoy the contemporary Christian romances, as well as some historical romances. These are the romance equivalent of "gentle reads" and "cozy" mysteries. The authors often change subgenres, however, and yesterday's writer of sweet romance may be today's suspense writer.

Campbell, Bethany.
> *A Little Town in Texas.* 2003.

Early, Margot.
> *Forever and a Baby.* 2000.

Linz, Cathie.
> *Cinderella's Sweet-Talking Marine.* 2004.

Macomber, Debbie.
> *The Snow Bride.* 2003.

Neels, Betty.
> Many of Neels's numerous titles are currently being re-released.
>
> *An Apple from Eve.* 1982. Reissued 2003.

Wingate, Lisa.
> *Lone Star Café.* 2004.

Romantic Suspense

Titles in the romantic-suspense subgenre (or romantic mysteries, as they are sometimes called) often blend into the mystery-suspense thriller subgenre, in which the mystery dominates the romance, making the novel of equal interest to both romance and mystery-suspense readers; or into the spy/espionage thriller subgenre in the hands of such authors as Helen MacInnes, whose novels have equal amounts of romance and espionage.

Many other types of romance have elements of suspense and mystery, and authors of romantic-suspense novels usually write in several other subgenres of romance as well. (Some of the following authors are also listed for other types of romance.) So it can be challenging to categorize these titles. However, the distinguishing feature in romantic suspense is the central role of the love relationship. Romantic-suspense novels are women's novels: Although full of adventure and suspense, neither is allowed to diminish the heroine's emotional involvement.

Mary Stewart, one of the progenitors of this subgenre, rates high in romantic appeal, but the suspenseful elements of foreign adventure involving both romantic leads is also strong—so strong that her books are of interest to men as well as women readers. Many of the following authors appear in hardcover editions as well as in paperback.

Contemporary Romantic Suspense

Contemporary romantic suspense novels are stories of love intertwined with mystery, taking place in the present. The contemporary setting makes them the most realistic of romantic-suspense novels. Related titles are listed in the order that the action occurs. Unrelated titles are listed alphabetically.

Adler, Elizabeth.
All or Nothing. 1999.
In a Heartbeat. 2000.

Aitken, Judie.
Secret Shadows. 2004.

Bradford, Barbara Taylor.
The Triumph of Katie Byrne. 2001.

Brockman, Suzanne.
The Defiant Hero. 2001.
Gone Too Far. 2003.
Hot Target. 2004.

 9

Brown, Sandra.
The Alibi. 1999.
Best Kept Secrets. 1988. Reissued 2004.
Breath of Scandal. 1991. Reissued 2001.
Charade. 1994. Reissued 2001.
The Crush. 2002.
Envy. 2001.
Exclusive. 1996. Reissued 2001.
Fat Tuesday. 1997. Reissued 2001.
French Silk. 1992. Reissued 2001.
Hello, Darkness. 2003.
Mirror Image. 1990. Reissued 2001.
Slow Heat in Heaven. 1988. Reissued 2001.
Standoff. 2000.
The Switch. 2000.
Unspeakable. 1998.
Where There's Smoke. 1993. Reissued 2001.
White Hot. 2004.
The Witness. 1995. Reissued 2001.

Cameron, Stella.
<u>**Bayou series.**</u>
French Quarter. 1998.

        Cold Day in July. 2002.

        Kiss Them Goodbye. 2003.

        Now You See Him. 2004.

Talon & Flynn series.

        Key West. 1999.

        Glass Houses. 2000.

Coulter, Catherine.

FBI series.

        The Cove. 1986.

        The Maze. 1997.

        The Target. 1998.

        The Edge. 1999.

        Riptide. 2000.

        Eleventh Hour. 2002.

        Blindside. 2003.

        Blowout. 2004.

        Point Blank. 2005.

Delinsky, Barbara.

Flirting with Pete. 2003.

Dodd, Christina.

Almost Like Being in Love. 2004.

Forster, Suzanne.

Angel Face. 2001.

Every Breath She Takes. 1999.

The Morning After. 2000.

While She was Sleeping. 2003.

Graham, Heather.

Killing Kelly. 2005.

Hooper, Kay.

After Caroline. 1997.

Amanda. 1996.

Haunting Rachel. 1998.

Shadows trilogy.

        Stealing Shadows. 2000.

        Hiding In the Shadows. 2000.

        Out of the Shadows. 2000.

Howard, Linda.

Cry No More. 2003.

Mr. Perfect. 2000.

Open Season. 2001.

To Die For. 2004.

Johansen, Iris.
 And Then You Die. 1998.
 Long After Midnight. 1997.
 The Ugly Duckling. 1996.

Jones, Pauline Baird.
 Missing You. 2002.

Krentz, Jayne Ann.
 Falling Awake. 2004.
 Light in Shadow. 2003.
 Lost & Found. 2001.
 Smoke in Mirrors. 2002.
 Soft Focus. 2000.
 Truth or Dare. 2004.

Lamb, Joyce.
 Caught in the Act. 2003.

Lowell, Elizabeth.
 The Color of Death. 2004.
 Die in Plain Sight. 2003.
 <u>The Donovans series.</u>
  Amber Beach. 1997.
  Jade Island. 1998.
  Pearl Cove. 1999.
  Midnight in Ruby Bayou. 2000.
 <u>Rarities Unlimited series.</u>
  Moving Target. 2001.
  Running Scared. 2002.
  Die in Plain Sight. 2003.

Martin, Kat.
 The Secret. 2001.

McKinney, Meagan.
 Still of the Night. 2001.

Mortman, Doris.
 Before and Again. 2003.
 Out of Nowhere. 1998.

Neggers, Carla.
 The Rapids. 2004.
 Cold Ridge. 2003.

Potter, Patricia.
 Cold Target. 2004.

Rice, Luanne.
> *The Secret Hour*. 2003.

Robards, Karen.
> *Bait*. 2004.
> *Beachcomber*. 2003.
> *Whispers at Midnight*. 2002.

Roberts, Nora.
> *Northern Lights*. 2004.
> *The Villa*. 2001.

Stuart, Anne.
> *Black Ice*. 2005.
>> An American translator in Paris discovers that her employers are really illegal arms dealers, and she ends up on the run with a dangerously sexy man.

Van Wormer, Laura.
> *The Kill Fee*. 2003.
>> Television journalist Sally Harrington seems to be a danger magnet.

Historical Romantic Suspense

A historical setting adds another dimension to romantic suspense, making this one of the most enduring romance subgenres. Readers who love old-fashioned romantic suspense by writers such as Joan Aiken, Mignon Good Eberhart, Catherine Gaskin, Velda Johnston, and Norah Lofts may wish to consult previous editions of *Genreflecting*, as many authors who wrote in this genre are no longer publishing new titles.

Historical romantic suspense continues in popularity today, with a few changes for today's readers. For example, the level of sensuality in historical romantic suspense tales varies greatly, from innocent to erotic. The Georgian era has been a popular historical setting of late.

Beauman, Sally.
> *Rebecca's Tale*. 2001.
>> A companion novel to Daphne du Maurier's classic gothic, *Rebecca*.

Camp, Candace.
> *Promise Me Tomorrow*. 2000.

Coulter, Catherine.
> *The Sherbrooke Twins*. 2004.
>> James and Jason Sherbrooke must work around their love lives to discover who is trying to kill their father.

Ferguson, Jo Ann.
> *Faire Game*. 2003.

Gilbert, Anna.
> *A Hint of Witchcraft*. 2000.
> *A Morning in Eden*. 2001.

Jordan, Nicole.
The Prince of Pleasure. 2003.

Kerstan, Lynn.
The Golden Leopard. 2002.
Heart of the Tiger. 2003.
The Silver Lion. 2003.

Quick, Amanda.
The Paid Companion. 2004.

> The Earl of St. Merryn has business of a secret nature in London, and to keep from drawing notice as a most eligible catch, he hires Elenora Lodge to masquerade as his fiancée. A romantic mystery in a Georgian setting.

Paranormal Romantic

Three genres—romance, suspense, and speculative fiction—come together to delight and engage readers in this lively subgenre. The love interest remains central, but added elements of mystery and futuristic settings add to the appeal. Psychic abilities and other paranormal aspects bring an interesting twist to these stories.

Barton, Beverly.
The Fifth Victim. 2003.

> Genny, a psychic, "sees" a brutal murder before a profiler reveals that the perpetrator kills in series of five, the first four victims at random and the fifth a psychic. Lucas, an FBI agent, falls for Genny while they seek the psycho who killed his niece and is targeting Genny.

Castle, Jayne.
Castle is a pseudonym of former librarian Jayne Ann Krentz, and is used for her paranormal fiction.

St. Helen's trilogy.
> A combination of science fiction and psychic powers.

Amaryllis. 1996.
Zinnia. 1997.
Orchid. 1998.

Hannah, Kristin.
Waiting for the Moon. 1995. Telepathy.

Howard, Linda.
Now You See Her. 1999. Psychic.

Pozzessere, Heather Graham.
If Looks Could Kill. 1997. Psychic.

Robb, J. D. (pseudonym of Nora Roberts).

Eve Dallas series.

> This best-selling series is set in the near-future and features Eve, a cop with a tortured past who marries a fabulously wealthy businessman. The first title, published in 1995, was *Naked in Death*. The twenty-third in the series was due out in 2005.

Roberts, Nora.

Key trilogy.

> Celtic mythology. Three young women meet at a mansion, where they are told they must find the keys to free the souls of three demigoddesses who have been imprisoned for centuries.

> *Key of Light.* 2003.
> *Key of Knowledge.* 2003.
> *Key of Valor.* 2004.

Gothic Romance

One of the oldest and most enduring of romance subgenres, the gothic romance, began in the late eighteenth century and was so stylish by the early nineteenth century that Jane Austen wrote *Northanger Abbey,* a parody of a gothic novel. Today, it is less popular, but it still has its devotees. Characteristically dark and atmospheric, these stories typically take place in castles or mansions set on foggy or windswept landscapes and containing shadowy hallways, locked rooms, dark secrets, and no dearth of evil-doings. Ghosts and spirits, insane relatives, and brooding heroes are likely to inhabit these forlorn landscapes.

Earlier editions of *Genreflecting* provide more detailed discussions of the gothic subgenre and contain lists of authors who, though no longer writing (indeed, the majority are no longer living), are still quite popular with readers. The titles listed below are all considered classics.

Brontë, Charlotte.

Jane Eyre. 1847. ★ 📹

> Orphaned Jane, raised by a cruel aunt and then sent off to a mean boarding school, finds happiness as a governess at Thornfield Manor, where she falls in love with her employer, Rochester. The story inspired a science fiction retelling by Sharon Shinn called *Jenna Starborn,* and the novel plays a pivotal role in the recent best seller *The Eyre Affair*.

Brontë, Emily.

Wuthering Heights. 1847. ★ 📹

> Revenge destroys any happiness Catherine and Heathcliff may have been able to find.

Du Maurier, Daphne.

Rebecca. 1938. ★ 📹

> A sequel was published in 2001, titled *Rebecca's Tale* and written by Sally Beauman.

Holt, Victoria.

Bride of Pendorric. 1963. ★

Mistress of Mellyn. 1960. ★ LP

> Taking a job as a governess in Cornwall, young Martha Leigh falls in love with Connan Tremellyn, the widowed lord of the castle.

Michaels, Barbara.

Greygallows. 1972. ★   *L P*

Master of Blacktower. 1966. Nineteenth-century Scotland. ★   *L P*

Stewart, Mary.

The Gabriel Hounds. 1967. ★

Madam, Will You Talk. 1955. ★

Whitney, Phyllis A.

Dream of Orchids. 1985. ★

The Trembling Hills. 1956. ★

Historical Romance

Historical settings can be very romantic, and when a tale of love is set against the backdrop of another time, it adds another dimension of enjoyment for readers. Simply put, historical romances are romances set in the past. But the setting contributes to a special reading experience. These are stories that take the reader to another time and place, novels that the reader can become immersed in, filled with sensory detail. Beyond that, there is a great diversity within the genre. Sometimes the stories are descriptive and atmospheric; at other times they are character-driven. Some are loosely based on historical events or characters; others simply use history as a backdrop. Historical romance (or period romance, as it is sometimes called) also varies as much in sensuality levels and authentic detail as in all the different time periods used as settings. Although some historical romances take a serious look at past people and events, using the love story to provide a reason for relating authentic historical detail, others merely use the costumes of the past to add interest to their tales of passion. Readers who enjoy the authentic details of historical romance may also enjoy historical fiction (see chapter 5). Those who revel in the exotic attire and settings may also enjoy futuristic or fantasy romances, found in the paranormal section of this chapter.

9

General Historical Romance

Any time in the past is fair game for the settings of historical romance. Listed here are novels that have retained their popularity with readers even if the time periods are not currently popular. Unique settings also are featured in this section.

Blake, Jennifer.

Dozens of historical titles published in the last thirty years. Many are set in nineteenth-century Louisiana.

Arrow to the Heart. 1993.

Challenge to Honor. 2005.

Borchardt, Alice.

Beguiled. 1998. Sequel to *Devoted.*

Devoted. 1995. Tenth-century France.

Cach, Lisa.

The Mermaid of Penperro. 2001. Nineteenth-century Cornwall.

Carr, Robyn.

Even though Carr has made the switch to contemporary women's fiction, the historicals she wrote in the 1980s are still found in public libraries.

The Braeswood Tapestry. 1984. Seventeenth century.

By Right of Arms. 1986. Fourteenth century.

The Troubadour's Romance. 1985. Twelfth century.

Cartland, Barbara.

"The Cartland formula is costume romance, fairy tales with passive heroines, men who are never less than perfection, and love that is spiritual. Although Cartland always finds a way to titillate her readers by maneuvering the lovers into bed, sex is never consummated without marriage." (Betty Rosenberg, *Genreflecting*, 2nd ed., 1986). Cartland published 623 books, all with happy endings.

Chadwick, Elizabeth.

Known for well-researched, authentic historical detail.

The Champion. 1998. Medieval France.

The Falcons of Montabard. 2004. Twelfth-century Crusades.

Lords of the White Castle. 2002. Medieval England.

The Love Knot. 1998. Medieval England.

The Marsh King's Daughter. 1999. Medieval England.

The Winter Mantle. 2003. Eleventh-century England.

Cookson, Catherine. More than 90 books, most set in nineteenth-century England.

Costain, Thomas.

The Black Rose. 1945. Medieval.

Coulter, Catherine. (http://www.catherinecoulter.com)

Coulter has written and rewritten dozens of historicals. Many of her early historical romances were republished in the early 2000s with extensive revisions.

Dodd, Christina.

Some Enchanted Evening. 2004. Nineteenth-century Scotland.

Garlock, Dorothy.

Route 66 series.

Danger and romance abound along the route from Oklahoma in hopes of a better life away from the dust bowl and the worst of the Great Depression.

With Hope. 1999.

Hope's Highway. 2004.

Mother Road. 2003.

Song of the Road. 2004.

Jones Family and Friends.

Set in and around Fertile, Missouri, in the 1920s and 1930s.

The Edge of Town. 2001.

      High on a Hill. 2002.
      A Place Called Rainwater. 2003.
      River Rising. 2005.

Gear, Kathleen O'Neal.
    Thin Moon and Cold Mist. 1995. Nineteenth-century Colorado.

Guhrke, Laura Lee.

    Breathless. 1999. Small town, early twentieth century.
    The Charade. 2000. Colonial Boston.
    Guilty Pleasures. 2004. Nineteenth-century England.

Holland, Cecelia.

    Angel and the Sword. 2000. Ninth-century France.
    Belt of Gold. 1984. Ninth-century Byzantium.
    Pillar of the Sky. 1985. England, prehistoric.
    Railroad Schemes. 1997. Nineteenth-century California.
    Soul Thief. 2002. Tenth-century England.

Holt, Victoria.
    The Devil on Horseback. 1977. French Revolution.
    My Enemy the Queen. 1978. Elizabethan England.

Jekel, Pamela.
    Natchez. 1995. Louisiana, eighteenth and nineteenth centuries.

Johansen, Iris.
    Johansen is now writing mystery and suspense fiction, but her older romantic suspense titles are still enjoyed by readers.

    The Beloved Scoundrel. 1994. Nineteenth-century England.
    Dark Rider. 1995. Nineteenth-century Hawaii and England.
    The Golden Barbarian. 1990. Nineteenth century.
    Lion's Bride. 1996. Medieval Damascus.
    The Magnificent Rogue. 1993. Sixteenth-century Scotland.
    Storm Winds. 1991. Revolutionary France.

Kaye, M. M.
    The Far Pavilions. 1978. ★
      Described as an (East) Indian *Gone With the Wind.*

Kelly, Carla.

    Daughter of Fortune. 1985. Seventeenth-century American West.

Koen, Karleen.

    Now Face to Face. 1995. Colonial Virginia. Sequel to *Through a Glass Darkly.*
    Through a Glass Darkly. 1986. Eighteenth-century England.

Laker, Rosalind.

    Circle of Pearls. 1990. Seventeenth-century England.
    Fair Wind of Love. 1988. Eighteenth-century Canada.

The Golden Tulip. 1991. Seventeenth-century Holland.

New World, New Love. 2002. Colonial America.

The Silver Touch. 1987. Eighteenth-century England.

The Sugar Pavillion. 1994. Eighteenth-century England.

To Dance with Kings. 1988. Five generations of women and French kings.

To Dream of Snow. 2004. Eighteenth-century Russia.

The Venetian Mask. 1993. Eighteenth-century Italy.

What the Heart Keeps. 1985. Edwardian era.

Macdonald, Malcolm.

Rose of Nancemellin. 2001. Early twentieth century.

Tamsin Harte. 2000. Early twentieth-century Cornwall.

Martin, Kat.

Midnight Rider. 1998. Spanish California.

Miller, Linda Lael.

Yankee Wife. 1993. Reissued 2004. Late nineteenth-century mail order bride.

Mitchell, Margaret.

Gone With the Wind. 1939.

Plaidy, Jean.

Plaidy, a pseudonym of the late Eleanor Hibbert, also wrote as Victoria Holt and Philippa Carr. Crown is currently reissuing many of her titles in the United States. She also wrote a trilogy on Lucrezia Borgia and quartets on each of the following: Catherine de Medici, Charles II, Isabella and Ferdinand, Catherine of Aragon, and the Stuarts.

Georgian saga.

Ten titles.

Victorian saga.

Six titles.

Norman trilogy.

The Bastard King. 1974.

The Lion of Justice. 1975.

The Passionate Enemies. 1976.

Plantagenet saga.

Fourteen titles.

Plain, Belva.

Crescent City. 1984. Nineteenth-century U.S. South. ★

Potter, Patricia.

Dancing with a Rogue. 2003. England.

Price, Eugenia.

Price's titles are listed in the historical fiction chapter (chapter 5), but the stories contain a good deal of romance and have a strong emphasis on relationships.

Ripley, Alexandra.

Charleston. 1981. Nineteenth-century Charleston.
From Fields of Gold. 1995. Early twentieth-century North Carolina.
On Leaving Charleston. 1984. Antebellum South.
Scarlett: The Sequel to Margaret Mitchell's Gone with the Wind. 1991.
The Time Returns. 1985. Lorenzo de' Medici, fifteenth-century Florence.

Roberts, Ann Victoria.

Morning's Gate. 1991. Early twentieth century.

Sabatini, Rafael.

Scaramouche. 1921. Romance amid the French revolution. ★

Seton, Anya.

My Theodosia. 1941. Theodosia Burr. ★
Katherine. 1954. Wife of John of Gaunt. ★

Shellabarger, Samuel.

Captain from Castille. 1945. Sixteenth-century Mexico. ★ ▆
The King's Cavalier. 1950. ★
Prince of Foxes. 1947. ★

Spencer, LaVyrle.

🏵 *The Endearment.* 1983. Mail order bride. Winner of the Rita Award.
Forgiving. 1991. 1876 Dakota Territory.
The Fulfillment. 1979. Early twentieth-century Minnesota.
🏵 *Morning Glory.* 1989. United States, 1940s. Winner of the Rita Award.
November of the Heart. 1993. Victorian era.
Twice Loved. 1984.
Vows. 1988. Nineteenth-century Wyoming.
Years. 1986. Early twentieth-century North Dakota.

Stirling, Jessica.

The Good Provider. 1988. Nineteenth-century Scotland.
The Workhouse Girl. 1997. Scotland.

Winsor, Kathleen.

Forever Amber. 1944. Reissued 2000. Seventeenth-century England. ★

Wolf, Joan.

Born of the Sun. 1989. Saxons.
Daughter of the Red Deer. 1991. Prehistoric.
The Horsemasters. 1993. Prehistoric.
The Reindeer Hunters. 1994. Prehistoric.

Woodiwiss, Kathleen E.

The beginning of the trend toward sensual romance is attributed to Woodiwiss's *The Flame and the Flower*.

The Elusive Flame. 1998.

The Flame and the Flower. 1972.
Shanna. 1977.

Frontier and Western Romance

A popular genre in the early 1990s, when it seemed that almost every romance had a cowboy, romances with an emphasis on the rugged outdoors have decreased in numbers, leaving the authors who do the subgenre the best to continue. Harlequin regularly publishes "historical Westerns." Against the dramatic backdrop of the American West, these stories combine romance with the rugged individualism and moral strength of the Western.

Barbieri, Elaine.
> *Renegade Moon.* 2003.
> *Texas Star.* 2004.
> *To Meet Again.* 2001.

Bittner, Rosanne.
> **Westward America series.**
>> *Into the Valley: The Settlers.* 2003.
>> *Into the Prairie: The Pioneers.* 2004.

Bridges, Kate.
> *The Engagement.* 2004.
> *The Midwife's Secret.* 2003.
> *The Surgeon.* 2003.

Brown, Carolyn.
> **Oklahoma Land Rush series.**
>> *Emma's Folly.* 2002.
>> *Just Grace.* 2003.
>> *Maggie's Mistake.* 2003.
> **The Promised Land Series.**
>> *Willow.* 2003.
>> *Velvet.* 2003.
>> *Gypsy.* 2004.
>> *Garnet.* 2004.

Chastain, Sandra.
> *The Mail Order Groom.* 2002.
> *The Outlaw Bride.* 2000.

Donati, Sara.
> *Dawn on a Distant Shore.* 2000.
> *Into the Wilderness.* 1998.

Garlock, Dorothy.
> *Almost Eden.* 1995. Missouri Territory.
> *Annie Lash.* 1985. Missouri Territory.

Sins of Summer. 1994. Nineteenth-century Idaho.
Wild Sweet Wilderness. 1985. Reissued 2002. Missouri Territory.

Garwood, Julie.

The Clayborne Brides. 1998.
Come the Spring. 1997.
For the Roses. 1995.

Gentry, Georgina.

To Tame a Texan. 2003.
To Tempt a Texan. 2005.

Hatcher, Robin Lee.

Chances Are. 1997. Wyoming.
In His Arms. 2001. Idaho. (Christian emphasis).

Landis, Jill Marie.

Summer Moon. 2001.

Lane, Elizabeth.
Wyoming Widow. 2003.
Wyoming Wildcat. 2003.
Wyoming Woman. 2004.

Leigh, Ana.

The Frasers series.
    Clay. 2004.
The MacKenzies series.
    Luke. 1996.
    Flint. 1996.
    Cleve. 1997. Reissued 2001.
    David. 1998. Reissued 2004.
    Peter. 1998.
    Jake. 1999. Reissued 2004.
    Josh. 2000.
    Zach. 2001.
    Jared. 2002.
    Cole. 2002.

Miller, Linda Lael.

McKettrick series. Arizona Territory.
    Shotgun Bride. 2003.
    Secondhand Bride. 2004.

Morsi, Pamela.

Sealed with a Kiss. 1998. 1890s Texas.

Osborne, Maggie.

The Bride of Willow Creek. 2001.

Foxfire Bride. 2004.

Prairie Moon. 2002.

The Promise of Jenny Jones. 1997.

Shotgun Wedding. 2003.

Pendergrass, Tess.

<u>Colorado trilogy.</u>

Colorado Shadows. 2000.

Colorado Twilight. 2001.

Colorado Sunrise. 2003.

Smith, Bobbi.

Brides of Durango. 2000.

Thomas, Jodi.

<u>The Wife Lottery series.</u>

The Texan's Wager. 2002.

When a Texan Gambles. 2003.

A Texan's Luck. 2004.

Williamson, Penelope.

Heart of the West. 1995. Montana.

Native American

Back in the 1980s, many of the romances featuring Native American heroes were of the sweet-and-savage type, featuring abductions and rapes, but times have changed and so have the books (for the most part). That being said, many readers still love the earlier type of Native American romance, in which the hero is a noble savage.

Baker, Madeline.

Apache Runaway. 1995. Reissued 2002.

Wolf Shadow. 2003.

Bittner, Rosanne.

Fifty-three titles as of 2005, all with a Western setting and most with Native American characters.

<u>Mystic Indian series.</u>

Mystic Dreamers. 1999.

Mystic Visions. 2000.

Mystic Warriors. 2001.

<u>Savage Destiny series.</u>

Sweet Prairie Passion. 1986.

In the first book in the series in the chronology of the series itself, but the last one published, Abbie meets Zeke (aka White Eagle), who is searching for his Cheyenne mother.

Meet the New Dawn. 1986.

The last in the series to feature the love of Abbie and Lone Eagle.

Eagle's Song. 1996.

A sequel set at a family reunion tells of the children and grandchildren of Abbie and Lone Eagle.

Edwards, Cassie.

As of 2005 Edwards had published seventy-eight titles, almost all romances involving Native American characters.

Fire Cloud. 2001.

Spirit Warrior. 2002.

Savage series.

Savage Heat. 1998.

Savage Moon. 2002.

Savage Thunder. 2001.

Gentry, Georgina.

To Tame a Rebel. 2003.

Scott, Theresa.

Apache Conquest. 2001.

Eagle Dancer. 2001.

Medieval

The world of castles, knights in shining armor, fair damsels, and courtly love is a natural setting for tales of romance.

Becnel, Rexanne.

Rosecliffe trilogy.

Twelfth-century Wales.

The Bride of Rosecliffe. 1998.

The Knight of Rosecliffe. 1999.

The Mistress of Rosecliffe. 2000.

Beverley, Jo.

Dark Champion. 1993. Reissued 2003.

In the early twelfth century, Imogen's castle is taken by a brutal neighbor, and she must enlist the help of a powerful man to get it back.

Lord of Midnight. 1998.

Brisbin, Terri.

The King's Mistress. 2005.

Henry Plantagenet, weary of Lady Marguerite of Alencon, determines that she will be a perfect reward for the loyal Lord Orrick of Silloth and sends her to be his wife.

Cody, Denée.

The Golden Rose. 1998.

Deveraux, Jude.

The Conquest. 1991.

Montgomery family saga.

Four truly exceptional brothers and the unique women they wed are the basis for one of the most beloved historical romance series ever. Tales of their many descendents are told in several related books. They have all been reissued several times in various formats.

Velvet Promise. 1981.

Highland Velvet. 1982.

Velvet Song. 1983.

Velvet Angel. 1983.

Gellis, Roberta.

Roselynde Chronicles. Medieval.

Original paperback series, reprinted several times, most recently in 2005 by Harlequin Signature Select. Specific titles within the series are listed in the "Saga" section of this chapter.

Graham, Heather.

The Lord of the Wolves. 1993. A Viking hero.

Kaufman, Pamela.

Shield of Three Lions. 1983. Reissued 2002.

When her family is killed by those wanting to seize their rich holdings, eleven-year-old Alix cuts her hair to disguise her gender and follows King Richard the Lion Heart to France as he heads out on crusade.

Banners of Gold. 1986.

Lady Alix is back in England following her crusade experiences, and while her husband is off at war she goes to Germany, where King Richard is held prisoner.

Lindsey, Johanna.

Joining. 1999.

When Wulfric and Milisant became betrothed as children, they formed an instant antipathy. Now as adults it is time to marry, but neither is in any hurry. Then they discover that an outside force will go to any length, including murder, to keep them apart.

Prisoner of My Desire. 1991. Reissued in 2002.

Set in 1152. Rowena is forced into marriage with a man who dies before the marriage is consummated. Then she is forced to try to become pregnant by a surrogate before the death is announced, to cement her evil stepbrothers' aspirations.

Lowell, Elizabeth.

Enchanted. 1994.

Forbidden. 1993. Reissued 2003.

Untamed. 1993.

Woodiwiss, Kathleen E.

The Wolf and the Dove. 1974. ★

Scotland

The fierce Scottish warrior has much the same appeal as the fierce Native American warrior. The rugged highland setting and frequent conflicts between clans and more frequently with the English creates an adventure-filled setting. Most are set in the eighteenth century, but the medieval era is also well represented.

Coffman, Elaine.
> **The Graham Clan series.**
>> *The Highlander.* 2003.
>> *Let Me Be Your Hero.* 2004.
>> *Born of Fire.* 2005.

Deveraux, Jude.
> *Highland Velvet.* 1982.

Faulkner, Colleen.
> *Highland Bride.* 2000. Seventeenth century.
> *Highland Lady.* 2001. Medieval.
> *Highland Lord.* 2002. Fourteenth century.

Gabaldon, Diana.
> **The Outlander series.** Eighteenth century, time travel.
>> Gabaldon calls these the <u>Old World Trilogy.</u> <u>The New World Trilogy</u>, continuing the saga of Jamie and Clare, is set in North America.
>
>> *Outlander.* 1991.
>> *Dragonfly in Amber.* 1992.
>> *Voyager.* 1994.

Garwood, Julie.
> *The Bride.* 1989. Reissued in hardcover in 2002.
>> An English bride and a Scottish laird.
>
> *Ransom.* 1999. Reissued 2003.
>> Set in Scotland while King John reigns in England.
>
> *Saving Grace.* 1993.
>> In 1206 a sixteen-year-old widow is saved from marrying a henchman of King John by instead marrying a Scottish laird.
>
> *The Wedding.* 1996. Reissued 2003.

Lamb, Arnette.
> *Beguiled.* 1996.
> *Betrayed.* 1995.
> *Highland Rogue.* 1991.

McNaught, Judith.
> *A Kingdom of Dreams.* 1989.

9

Roberson, Jennifer.

> *Lady of the Glen.* 1996. Seventeenth century, Battle of Glencoe.

Regency Romance

Perhaps the most distinctive of historical romances are those set in the Regency period. These novels are set in England in the early nineteenth century (technically the Regency period spans 1811–1821, but in terms of romance Regency readers find enjoyment in novels set in the Georgian era, which encompasses the Regency), and are epitomized by the novels of Georgette Heyer. She, in the diction of the Regency, was "The Nonpareil," and all other authors using the period are "poor drab" imitators. (For example, publishers' notes on jackets or paperback covers for years said things like "In the grand tradition of Georgette Heyer" or "The best since Georgette Heyer.)

The Regency world is one of high society and gracious formalities: the London Season of the wealthy and titled enjoying the assemblies at Almack's, the dandies in their fashionable garb. The country estate is also featured, as are the fashionable doings at Bath. Frequently, the heroine is impoverished, the daughter of a poor country parson or an orphan, but always she is a lady. Manners and dress are of utmost importance. The Regency novel features lively, sophisticated, and often witty dialogue.

The wildly successful adventure tales of Patrick O'Brian are also set during this time period, and fans of the era may well enjoy them. The Friends of the English Regency, a California association of devotees of Georgette Heyer and the Regency romance, holds an annual assemblée (at which there is period dancing in costume). They have a Web site at http://www.geocities.com/~foter/. Regency dancing has quite mysteriously become an event at some science fiction conventions.

The Beau Monde chapter of the Romance Writers of America publishes a monthly newsletter for their members and a quarterly listing of regency titles, the *Regency Reader,* that is free to libraries (http://www.thebeaumonde.com). Good Ton (http://www.thenonesuch.com) is the definitive site on the Web for Regency romance purists, with reviews, a calendar of scheduled new releases, and lots of links to all that is Regency. Recent Regency-era novels with a spicy treatment of the physical relationship between the hero and heroine are not included, and neither are Georgian titles that fall outside the specific years of the Regency.

Kristin Ramsdell's *Romance Fiction: A Guide to the Genre* (Libraries Unlimited, 1999) features extensive information on Regencies and lists many more authors and titles.

Recent trends have seen romances set in the Regency and Georgian eras becoming spicier and blending with other genres. While traditional Regencies were always of the "innocent" variety, this is no longer the case. Likewise, detection and the paranormal are no longer unknown in this formerly genteel subgenre.

Aiken, Joan.

> *The Smile of the Stranger.* 1978. ★

Angers, Helen.

> *A Lady of Independence.* 1982. ★

Balogh, Mary.

More than sixty titles. Early titles are traditional Regencies, while recent titles are much spicier than traditional Regencies.

The Bedwyn Saga. (also sometimes called the Slightly series).

The six aristocratic Bedwyn siblings find love in unexpected ways.

Slightly Married. 2003.

When Colonel Lord Aidan Bedwyn promised to protect the sister of a dying officer, he didn't know he would have to marry her to keep his word.

Slightly Wicked. 2003.

Judith Law, wanting one night of passion before settling into a dull life as a companion, convinces Lord Rannulf Bedwyn that she is an actress with worldly experience.

Slightly Scandalous. 2003.

Lady Freyja Bedwyn should have known that her brother Wulfric, the Duke of Bewcastle, would show up when she entered into a sham engagement.

Slightly Tempted. 2004.

Lady Morgan, the youngest Bedwyn, comes into her own in Brussels.

Slightly Sinful. 2004.

Lord Alleyne Bedwyn is rescued, unconscious and amnesiac, after the Battle of Waterloo, by a bevy of fallen women.

 9

Slightly Dangerous. 2004.

Wulfric Bedwyn, Duke of Bewcastle, encounters a fun-loving, impoverished widow at a country house party and finds himself acting in unpredictable ways.

Simply Quartet.

This series, related to the Bedwyn Saga, tells the tales of four young women who teach at a school secretly funded by Freyja Bedwyn.

Simply Unforgettable. 2005.

Beverley, Jo.

Spicy Regency and Georgian settings. More than twenty-five titles.

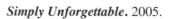

Company of Rogues.

An Arranged Marriage. 1991.

An Unwilling Bride. 1992. Reissued 2000.

Christmas Angel. 1992. Reissued 2001.

Forbidden. 1994. Reissued 2003.

Dangerous Joy. 1995. Reissued 2004.

Three Heroes. 2004. Omnibus of *The Dragon's Bride, The Devil's Heiress,* and *The Demon's Mistress.*

Hazard. 2002.

St. Raven. 2003.

Skylark. 2004.

The Malloren series.

🎗 *My Lady Notorious.* 1993. Reissued 2002. Winner of the Rita Award.

Tempting Fortune. 1995. Reissued 2002.

Something Wicked. 1997. Reissued 2005.

Secrets of the Night. 1999.

🎖 *Devilish.* 2000. Winner of the Rita Award.

Winter Fire. 2003.

A Most Unsuitable Man. 2005.

Cartland, Barbara.

Over 600 short, simple, and sweet books to her credit.

Chase, Loretta.

English Witch. 1988. Reissued with *Isabella* in 2004. (traditional).

Isabella's unsuccessful suitor finds love.

Isabella. 1987. Reissued with *English Witch* in 2004. (traditional).

When Isabella, on the shelf, goes to London to chaperone her young cousins, she finds that to her surprise two gentlemen are out to woo her.

Miss Wonderful. 2004. (sensuous).

Chesney, Marion.

Because Chesney's series were published in hardcover and well reviewed in standard library selection tools, they are usually readily available in public libraries, even titles that were published more than twenty years ago. She is now writing mysteries.

The Six Sisters series. (traditional).

A poor vicar has six daughters to marry off.

Minerva. 1982.

The Taming of Annabelle. 1983.

Deirdre and Desire. 1983.

Daphne. 1984.

Diana the Huntress. 1985.

Frederica in Fashion. 1985.

School for Manners series.

Amy and Effie Tribble help young ladies who are deemed unsuitable for marriage by fixing (or at least trying to fix) their problems.

Refining Felicity. 1988.

Perfecting Fiona. 1989.

Enlightening Delilah. 1989.

Finessing Clarissa. 1989.

Animating Maria. 1990.

Marrying Harriet. 1990.

A House for the Season series. (traditional).

The Miser of Mayfair. 1986.

Plain Jane. 1986.

The Wicked Godmother. 1987.

Rake's Progress. 1987.

The Adventuress. 1987.

Rainbird's Revenge. 1988.

The **Traveling Matchmaker series.** (traditional).

Miss Hannah Pym's travels always lead her to young people who need to find the perfect match.

Emily Goes to Exeter. 1990.
Belinda Goes to Bath. 1991.
Penelope Goes to Portsmouth. 1992.
Deborah Goes to Dover. 1992.
Yvonne Goes to York. 1992.

The Daughters of Mannerling series. (traditional).

A sextet of sisters try to regain the beloved family home.

The Banishment. 1995.
The Intrigue. 1995.
The Deception. 1996.
The Folly. 1997.
The Romance. 1997.
The Homecoming. 1997.

Poor Relations series.

A group of impoverished aristocrats band together to pool their resources and turn the home they share into a popular novelty hotel.

Lady Fortescue Steps Out. 1992.
Miss Tonks Turns to Crime. 1993.
Mrs. Budley Falls From Grace. 1993.
Sir Philip's Folly. 1993.
Colonel Sandhurst to the Rescue. 1994.
Back in Society. 1994.

Cook, Kristina.

Unlaced. 2004. (sensuous).

A hot historical set in the Regency, featuring Lucy Abbington, who only agrees to season in London to further her veterinary knowledge and becomes the talk of the ton when she finds friendship and more with Harry Ashton, the Marquess of Mandeville.

Unveiled. 2005. (sensuous).

Jane Rosemoor refuses to marry, and Hayden, Earl of Westfield, refuses to love.

Courtney, Caroline.

Even though her books were published in the 1970s and 1980s, many remain in the large-print collections of libraries and are good choices for those looking for traditional regencies.

Destiny's Duchess. 1979.
Libertine in Love. 1980.
The Masquerading Heart. 1981.

Darcy, Clare. (traditional).

Like Courtney, Darcy's traditional regencies, though long out of print, still may be found in libraries.

Allegra. 1974.

Elyza. 1976.

Letty. 1980.

Regina. 1976.

Dunn, Carola.

Crossed Quills. 1996.

The Improper Governess. 1998.

Fairchild, Elisabeth.

A Game of Patience. 2002.

Valentine's Change of Heart. 2003.

Guhrke, Laura Lee.

His Every Kiss. 2004.

Harbaugh, Karen.

Miss Carlyle's Curricle. 1999.

The Reluctant Cavalier. 1996.

Heath, Lorraine.

An Invitation to Seduction. 2004.

Love With a Scandalous Lord. 2003.

Hern, Candice.

Her Scandalous Affair. 2004.

Once trilogy.

Once a Dreamer. 2003.

Once a Scoundrel. 2003.

Once a Gentleman. 2004.

Heyer, Georgette. (traditional).

The queen of the Regency romance, Heyer published twenty-nine Regency romances not to be missed. Her witty dialogue and comedy of manners style seems to never go out of style.

Arabella. 1949.

Bath Tangle. 1955.

A Civil Contract. 1961. Reissued 2005.

Adam Deveril returns home from the Napoleonic Wars to find himself so badly in debt that he must forego marrying Julia and instead marries a rich merchant's daughter.

The Convenient Marriage. 1934. Reissued 2000.

Cousin Kate. 1968. Reissued 2000.

Frederica. 1965. Reissued 2000.

The Grand Sophy. 1950.

The Nonesuch. 1962.

The Unknown Ajax. Reissued 2005.

Kelly, Carla. (traditional).

The Lady's Companion. 1996.

Marian's Christmas Wish. 1989.
Miss Billings Treads the Boards. 1993.
Miss Grimsley's Oxford Career. 1992.
Mrs. Drew Plays Her Hand. 2003.
One Good Turn. 2001.
The Wedding Journey. 2002.
With This Ring. 1997.

Kerstan, Lynn.

Dangerous Deceptions. 2004.

Lane, Allison.

The Madcap Marriage. 2004.

Martin, Kat.

The Bride's Necklace. 2005. (sensuous).
Fanning the Flame. 2002. (sensuous).
The Fire Inside. 2002. (sensuous).
Heartless. 2001. (sensuous).

Metzger, Barbara.

She has written dozens of Regencies and is a two-time winner of *Romantic Times* Career Achievement Award.

A Debt to Delia. 2002.
The Diamond Key. 2003.
My Lady Innkeeper. 1995.

Michaels, Kasey.

The Butler Did It. 2004.

When the Marquis of Westham arrives at his London residence to spend the Season selecting a wife, he discovers that in his lengthy absence several houseguests have taken up residence in his home.

Putney, Mary Jo.

In addition to Regencies, Putney writes other best-selling historical, contemporary, and more recently, paranormal romances.

The Bargain. 1999. (sensuous).
The Diabolical Baron. 1999. (sensuous).
The Rake. 1998. (sensuous).

Quick, Amanda.

Quick, a pseudonym used by Jayne Ann Krentz, has written over twenty sexy Regency-era novels filled with suspense.

Paid Companion. 2004. (sensuous).

When Elenora Lodge's stepfather dies after losing her entire fortune, her fiancé cries off, and she is eventually hired to act the part of a jilted earl's new fiancée.

Wicked Widow. 2000. (sensuous).

> Madeline Deveridge, a misunderstood widow with a reputation for murder, enlists the help of Artemis Hunt, a strapping member of the ton and a master of Vanza, to help her rescue her abducted maid.

Robards, Karen.

Scandalous. 2001.

Ross, Julia.

Night of Sin. 2005.

The Wicked Lover. 2004.

> Twists and turns in an erotic tale of Sylvie Georgiana, the Countess of Montevrain, who disguises herself as a male to spy on Robert Sinclair Dovenby "Dove," whom she intends to destroy but instead begins to love, in Georgian England.

Smith, Joan.

Imprudent Lady. 1978. ★

> Prudence Mallow, a poor relation from the country, decides while in London to take up writing and meets a handsome rake who has penned a scandalous novel.

Lover's Vows. 1981. A theater setting.

Thornton, Elizabeth.

Almost a Princess. 2003.

The Marriage Trap. 2005.

The Perfect Princess. 2001.

Princess Charming. 2001.

Shady Lady. 2004.

Veryan, Patricia.

The Golden Chronicles Series.

> Set in the Georgian era.

Tales of the Jewelled Men Series.

Sanguinet Saga.

The Riddle Saga.

Vivian, Daisy.

A Marriage of Convenience. 1986. ★

Return to Cheyne Spa. 1988. ★

Wolf, Joan.

Golden Girl. 1999.

> A talented artist agrees to an arranged marriage because it will allow her access to great art.

Royal Bride. 2001.

Saga

The family saga romance has ties to historical romances, although there are popular examples with contemporary settings. Most of these romances span several volumes. The saga, or generational history, covers the interrelations of succeeding generations within a family, usually with emphasis on a patriarchal or matriarchal figure. The presence of this central character permeates the unfolding of future generations and thus is one of the primary appeals of the subgenre. In addition, the sheer volume of these books (or series of books) makes them especially attractive to readers who want to immerse themselves in other times. Those series in which the family relationships provide the basic plot elements are firmly in the romance tradition.

Because the genre proved so popular in the 1970s, the saga label appears in publishers' advertising and on paperback covers for single-volume novels that barely fit the definition. Some novels, such as the Poldark series, achieve the saga label through sheer number of volumes and an extensive cast of characters. Others among historical and period romances have a sequel, or sequels, without real similarity to the saga pattern.

Several themes and plot patterns are dominant in sagas. In the United States, the pattern might be an immigrant family rising to wealth and power over several generations, or the central thread may be plantation life in the Deep South, with an emphasis on master–slave relations, history from colonial times, or the movement westward. In Britain, the focus might be landed family history and relations between aristocrats and their servants or a family of any class or period or periods, changing through the generations.

Romantic sagas often do not have a happily-ever-after ending.

The historical adventure series tends to intermingle with the saga. Readers of romance sagas may also enjoy the titles listed in the "Saga" section of the Westerns chapter (chapter 6).

Although sagas are no longer published at the rate they once were, readers refuse to give up their old favorites and continue to talk about them, so even though many of the following sagas have been around for a long time, they are still circulating in libraries.

Anand, Valerie.

Anand also writes mysteries under the name Fiona Buckley.

Bridges over Time Saga.

The story of a family, the descendants of a Norman knight, Sir Ivon de Clairpont, is told through time.

The Proud Villeins. 1992. Norman England.
The Ruthless Yeomen. 1991. Fourteenth century.
Women of Ashdon. 1993. Fifteenth century.
The Faithful Lovers. 1994. Seventeenth century.
The Cherished Wives. 1994. Eighteenth century.

Bradford, Barbara Taylor.

Harte Family Saga.

A Woman of Substance. 1979. Reissued 2000. `TVM`

Hold The Dream. 1985.

To Be The Best. 1989.

Emma's Secret. 2004.

Unexpected Blessings. 2005.

Coleman, Lonnie.

Beulah Land series. `TVM`

Beulah Land. 1973.

Look Away, Beulah Land. 1977.

The Legacy of Beulah Land. 1980.

Cookson, Catherine. ★

Tilly Trotter's difficult life, starting in a Tyneside village, where she is an outcast, through life as a mistress, a wife, a move to America, and, as a widow, a return home.

Tilly. 1980. (British title: *Tilly Trotter*).

Tilly Wed. 1981. (British title: *Tilly Trotter Wed*).

Tilly Alone. 1982. (British title: *Tilly Trotter Widowed*).

Tilly Trotter: An Omnibus. 1998.

Dailey, Janet.

Calder saga.

Listed in the order Dailey recommends they be read, each volume covers the love that strikes the many Calders over several generations in the West.

This Calder Range. 1982.

Stands a Calder Man. 1983.

This Calder Sky. 1981.

Calder Born—Calder Bred. 1983.

Calder Pride. 1999.

Green Calder Grass. 2002.

Shifting Calder Wind. 2003.

Calder Promise. 2004.

Lone Calder Star. 2005.

Delderfield, R. F.

Swann family.

Set in Britain. ★

God is an Englishman. 1970.

Theirs Was the Kingdom. 1971.

Give Us This Day. 1973.

Drummond, Emma.

Knightshill saga.

A Question of Honour. 1992.

A Distant Hero. 1994.

Act of Valour. 1996.

Elegant, Robert.

Dynasty. 1977.

Mandarin. 1983.

Gellis, Roberta.

Roselynde chronicles. Medieval England. ★

Roselynde. 1978.

Desiree. 2005.

Alinor. 1978.

Joanna. 1979.

Gilliane. 1980.

Rhiannon. 1982.

Sybelle. 1983.

Graham, Winston.

Poldark series. TVM

Ten volumes. Set in Cornwall starting when Ross Poldark returns from fighting for the British against the American colonists.

Howatch, Susan. ★

The Rich Are Different. 1977.

Sins of the Fathers. 1980.

The Wheel of Fortune. 1984.

The Church of England series.

Glittering Images. 1987.

Glamorous Powers. 1988.

Ultimate Prizes. 1989.

Scandalous Risks. 1990.

Mystical Paths. 1992.

Absolute Truths. 1994.

Jakes, John. ★

Heaven and Hell. 1987.

Love and War. 1984.

North and South. 1982. TVM

Kent Family chronicles. ★

The Bastard. 1974. Reissued in 2004.

The Rebels. 1975.

The Seekers. 1975.

The Furies. 1976.

The Titans. 1976.

The Warriors. 1977.

The Lawless. 1978.

The Americans. 1980.

Johansen, Iris.

> **Wind Dancer Saga.**
>
> > *The Wind Dancer.* 1991. Renaissance Italy.
> > *Storm Winds.* 1991. Revolutionary France.
> > *Reap the Wind.* 1991.
> > *Final Target.* 2001.

McCullough, Colleen.

> *The Thorn Birds.* 1977. Australia. **TVM**

Price, Eugenia.

> **Savannah Quartet.**
>
> > *Savannah.* 1983.
> > *To See Your Face Again.* 1985.
> > *Before the Darkness Falls.* 1987.
> > *Stranger in Savannah.* 1989.

Thane, Elswyth.

> **Williamsburg series.** United States.
> > Seven volumes.

Vincenzi, Penny.

> **Lytton Family Saga.**
>
> > *No Angel.* 2003.
> > *Something Dangerous.* 2004.

Hot Historicals

Kathleen E. Woodiwiss is credited with starting the trend to sensuous historical romances with *Flame and the Flower* (1972). Now scenes of explicitly depicted love-making are requisite for some imprints. Historical detail and authenticity take a back seat to the sensuality and the plot line of sexual consummation.

Sweet-and-Savage

Characterized by clinch covers featuring a torridly embracing, scantily clad couple, this subgenre, sometimes derogatorily called the "bodice ripper," changed the face of romance forever in the 1970s. Rosemary Rogers launched the subgenre called "sweet-and-savage" in 1974 with *Sweet, Savage Love.* A reviewer succinctly epitomized the subgenre's plot in *Sweet, Savage Love* in one sentence: "The heroine is seduced, raped, prostituted, married, mistressed." Another reviewer just as tersely summed up the subgenre's characteristics: "The prose is purple, the plot thin, and the characters thinner" (referring to *The Wolf and the Dove,* by Kathleen E. Woodiwiss).

But despite panning by the critics, readers flocked to novels that offered heightened sensory detail of love-making and stories that reflected female sexual fantasy. Exotic historical settings were used lavishly, particularly those allowing for pirates, sultans, and harems. A variation of the sweet-and-savage romance was the plantation romance, with basic ingredients of miscegenation, incest, Cain versus Abel, slave uprisings, insanity, and murder. Usually they were set in the post–Civil War South, but some were set in the West Indies or in any locale in which the basic plot ingredients could seethe. Both types were loaded with sex scenes, explicit to the extent of justifying the label "soft porn."

These sultry romances had their heyday in the 1970s, mainly as paperback originals. Today, this is no longer a distinct type, as the sometimes explicit descriptions of intimate detail have become part of the standard historical romance pattern.

Readers who discovered romance in the sweet-and-savage heyday look for these titles for the nostalgic value. Because the subgenre indicated a sea change in romance fiction and society's view of women, scholars find the books of interest. Authors who specialized in this subgenre were Jennifer Blake, Shirlee Busbee, Anthony Esler, Gimone Hall, Susanna Leigh, Fern Michaels, Marilyn Ross, Jennifer Wilde, and Donna Comeaux Zide. Others who wrote in the genre. (many not exclusively) were Susannah Kells, Patricia Matthews, Laurie McBain, Natasha Peters, Janette Radcliffe. (a.k.a. Janet Louise Roberts) , Rosemary Rogers, Beatrice Small, Kathleen Winsor, and last, but not least, Kathleen E. Woodiwiss, who has said, "I'm insulted when my books are called erotic. I believe I write love stories with a little spice."

Spicy Historical

The spicy historical romance grew out of the sweet-and-savage type. It features erotic scenes, but without the violence of kidnappings and rapes so often found in its predecessor. The women are not passive victims of love, but lively and strong. Generally, the characters, both male and female, are monogamous or serially monogamous. Marriage plays an important role.

 9

Jude Deveraux's many novels involving different, far-flung members of the Montgomery family throughout history evolved from sweet-and-savage to spicy romance. Even though her early works in the <u>Velvet series</u> and <u>James River trilogy</u> featured rapes and kidnappings, the characters were not promiscuous. The women are proactive rather than reactive, as in the sweet-and-savage type.

Busbee, Shirlee.

Spanish Rose. 1986.

English pirate Gabriel Lancaster has sworn vengeance on the Delgatos, but passion has many facets when he captures Maria Delgato on a raid.

Swear by the Moon. 2001.

Even though Thea Garrett was wooed and raped by a fortune hunter when she was a teenager, she has enough wealth and power to still be received by society, but not if a blackmailer divulges her secret.

Devine, Thea.

Bliss River. 2002.

In South Africa in 1898, an aristocratic young woman is taken hostage.

Seductive. 2001.

Henley, Virginia.

Her storytelling skills have evolved, imbuing her later titles with more authentic historical detail and subtlety in the lusty passages.

Desired. 1995.

A ribald tale of a seventeen-year-old orphaned heiress who waits for the Plantagenet king to name the man she will marry.

Insatiable. 2004.

Undone. 2003.

Based on an the life of Elizabeth Gunning, who though lowborn became a duchess.

Johnson, Susan.

Again and Again. 2002.

A young lady must take a job as a governess, but finds erotic adventure.

Seduction in Mind. 2001.

A Victorian-era nude model and a renowned rogue.

Ryan, Nan.

Naughty Marietta. 2003.

Marietta Stone is sent to Texas in the care of Cole Heflin, and along the way they experience all kinds of Western and sexual adventures.

Outlaw's Kiss. 1987. Reissued 1997.

Woodiwiss, Kathleen E.

The Elusive Flame. 1998.

This sequel to *The Flame and the Flower* (1972) features Beauregard Birmingham, son of the hero and heroine, who as an adult and sea captain, in the throes of a fever attempts to rape Cerynise Edlyn Kendall, an orphan who has been thrown out on the streets.

The Reluctant Suitor. 2003.

Colton Wyndham, the new Marquess of Randwulf, returns from the Napoleanic wars to find himself enormously attracted to a woman he finds out his family had intended him to marry.

Paranormal Romance

In recent years, some unexpected settings and characters have begun to pop up in romances. Vampires, ghosts, angels, and werewolves may be a love interest in today's romance, or they might just facilitate the human lovers coming together. The time for a romance can be in the future, or in a shadowy place out of time, a parallel universe, or a magical land. The characters may be human, but may have the powers of telepathy, precognition, or other abilities classified as psionics in science fiction. Magic may work in the world instead of just in the heart. With all fiction, readers are able to stretch their imaginations, but with the paranormal romance, the reader's imagination is stretched in several directions simultaneously.

This type of story has become so popular that it has its several awards, including the Sapphire Award, the Prism Award, and the P.E.A.R.L. award, as well as a couple of monthly online newsletters, *Science Fiction Romance* (http://www.sfronline.com) and *Romantic Science Fiction and Fantasy* (http://www.romanticsf.com/).

Fantasy Romance

A major trend in the romance genre that began in the 1990s was the combination of fantasy with romance. Time travel, supernatural beings, faerie, and other fantasy tropes have been showing up frequently in romance novels. The combination of the genres is a double delight to those who love both.

Asaro, Catherine.

Asaro, a physicist and an award-winning science fiction author, has added romantic fantasy to her repertoire.

The Charmed Sphere. 2004.

> Two mages, both adrift in the intricately crafted world of Aronsdale, join forces when a neighboring kingdom threatens.

The Misted Cliffs. 2005.

> In an effort to stave off a war, Mel sacrifices herself to marry the heir of a family known for cruelty.

Beverley, Jo.

Forbidden Magic. 1998.

> A vulgar prehistoric stone statue, the sheelagh-ma-gig, has been used and passed down by generations of women to invoke a dangerous magic and is called into play in this Regency-era tale.

Carroll, Susan.

<u>St. Leger Saga.</u>

> A family gifted with magical talents, a tradition of accepting the choice of wife found by each generation's bride finder, and a legacy of ghosts combine in this enchanting series.
>
> ***The Bride Finder.*** 1998.
> ***The Night Drifter.*** 1999.
> ***The Midnight Bride.*** 2001.

Harbaugh, Karen.

Dark Enchantment. 2004.

The Devil's Bargain. 1995. Reissued in 2005.

<u>Cupid Trilogy.</u>

> ***Cupid's Mistake.*** 1997. Reissued 2005.
> ***Cupid's Darts.*** 1998.
> ***Cupid's Kiss.*** 1999.

Krinard, Susan.

The Forest Lord. 2002.

Shield of the Sky. 2004.

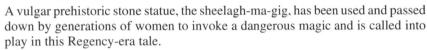

Lackey, Mercedes.
> *The Fairy Godmother.* 2004.

McReynolds, Glenna.
> *The Chalice and the Blade.* 1997.
> *Dream Stone.* 1998.
> *Prince of Time.* 2000.

Meyer, Joanne.
> *Heavenly Detour.* 2003.

O'Day-Flannery, Constance.
> *Shifting Love.* 2004.

Putney, Mary Jo.
> *A Kiss of Fate.* 2004.

Rice, Patricia.
> *This Magic Moment.* 2004.

Roberts, Nora.
> **Three Sisters Island Trilogy.**
> > Legend has it that Three Sisters Island was created by the magic of three witches escaping persecution in seventeenth-century Salem, and that at some time descendents of each of them will come together on the island. That time has come.
> >
> > *Dance Upon the Air.* 2001.
> > *Face the Fire.* 2002.
>
> **Irish Trilogy.**
> > *Heart of the Sea.* 2000.
> > *Tears of the Moon.* 2000.
> > *Jewels of the Sun.* 1999.

Wrede, Patricia C.
> *The Magician's Ward.* 1997. Magic in a Regency setting.

Wrede, Patricia C., and Caroline Stevermer.
> *Sorcery and Cecelia.* 1988. Reissued in 2003.
> > Epistolary novel set in Regency London, featuring two cousins beset by magic.

Time-Travel Romance

The books that fall into this category use time travel as a plot device for the romance. The obstacle facing the lovers is not merely one of having different backgrounds or of living in different time zones, but of living in different centuries. This is a very popular theme in paperback but is also found in hardcover. Unlike in most romances, male authors are found frequently in this subgenre. Readers of this type often also enjoy historical fiction.

Deveraux, Jude.
> *Knight in Shining Armor.* 1989.
> > Tears at a crypt bring a medieval knight into the late twentieth century.

Frank, J. Suzanne.

Chloe Kingsley, a 1990s Texan, travels through time, always somehow meeting up with her husband, another time traveler.

Reflections in the Nile. 1997.
Shadows on the Aegean. 1998.
Sunrise on the Mediterranean. 1999.
Twilight in Babylon. 2002.

Gabaldon, Diana.

The Outlander series.

Outlander is the standard against which all time-travel romances are judged. The series is so popular that the author has come out with a guide to it, *The Outlandish Companion: In Which Much Is Revealed Regarding Claire and Jamie Fraser, Their Lives and Times, Antecedents, Adventures, Companions and Progeny with Learned Commentary (and Many Footnotes) by their Humble Creator* (Delacorte Press, 1999).

Outlander. 1991.

After World War II, a nurse, visiting Scotland with her husband, walks between some standing stones and ends up in eighteenth-century Scotland.

Dragonfly in Amber. 1992.
Voyager. 1994.
Drums of Autumn. 1997.
Fiery Cross. 2001.
A Breath of Snow and Ashes. 2005.

Guhrke, Laura Lee.

Not So Innocent. 2002.

A psychic and a late nineteeth-century Scotland Yard investigator.

Howard, Linda.

Son of the Morning. 1997.

Krinard, Susan.

Twice a Hero. 1997.

Kurland, Lynn.

A Garden in the Rain. 2003.
My Heart Stood Still. 2001.
The More I See You. 1999.
The Very Thought of You. 1998.

Matheson, Richard.

Somewhere in Time. 1999. Originally published in 1975 as *Bid Time Return.*
What Dreams May Come. 1978. Reissued 2004.

Miller, Linda Lael.

Beyond the Threshold. 2002. A reissue of the novels *Here and Then* (1992) and *There and Now* (1992).

Millhiser, Marlys.

The Mirror. 1978. Reissued 1997. ★

On the eve of her wedding, a bride looks into the hideous heirloom mirror that has been passed down through her family and is transported into the past, into the body of her own grandmother on the eve of her wedding in 1900.

The Threshold. 1984.

Paranormal Beings

Creatures of the night, like vampires and werewolves, who would seem more at home in a horror novel, have made huge inroads into romance. They are the ultimate forbidden heroes.

Ashley, Amanda. Vampire.

Embrace the Night. 1995.
Midnight Embrace. 2002.
A Whisper of Eternity. 2004.

Borchardt, Alice.

Werewolf duet.

The Silver Wolf. 1999.
Night of the Wolf. 1999.

Cresswell, Jasmine.

Prince of the Night. 1995. Vampire.

Davidson, MaryJanice.

Derik's Bane. **2005.**

A werewolf falls for Morgan le Fay.

Feehan, Christine.

Dark Series.

Features Carpathians, vampire-like beings who fight vampires but turn into them if they do no not find their lifemates in time.

Dark Prince. 1999.
Dark Desire. 1999.
Dark Gold. 2000.
Dark Magic. 2000.
Dark Challenge. 2000.
Dark Fire. 2001.
Dark Legend. 2002.
Dark Guardian. 2002.
Dark Symphony. 2003.
Dark Melody. 2003.
Dark Destiny. 2004.
Dark Secret. 2005.

Hamilton, Laurell K.

Anita Blake series.

A vampire killer becomes enmeshed in the lives of vampires, werewolves, and other shapeshifters in an increasingly erotic and horror-like series. The most recent titles are found in the horror chapter (chapter 12).

Guilty Pleasures. 1994.
The Laughing Corpse. 1994.
Circus of the Damned. 1995.
The Lunatic Café. 1995.
Bloody Bones. 1996.
The Killing Dance. 1997.
Burnt Offerings. 1998.
Blue Moon. 1998.

Harbaugh, Karen.

Night Fires. 2003. Vampire.
The Vampire Viscount. 1995. Reissued 2004.

Nicholas, Viscount St. Vire, a sexy vampire, will go insane and deteriorate beyond redemption unless he is willingly embraced by a virgin, in this Regency romance.

Huff, Tanya.

Victory Nelson "Blood" series.

All titles were reissued in 2004 after originally appearing between 1991 and 1997.

Blood Price.
Blood Trail.
Blood Lines.
Blood Pact.
Blood Debt.

Klause, Annette Curtis.

Both titles are published as young adult books, but adults who find them fall in love with them.

Blood and Chocolate. 1997. Werewolf. **YA**
The Silver Kiss. 1990. Vampire. **YA**

Krinard, Susan.

Body & Soul. 1998. Ghost.
Once A Wolf. 2000.
Prince of Dreams. 1995. Vampire.
Prince of Shadows. 1996. Werewolf.
Prince of Wolves. 1994. Werewolf.
Secret of the Wolf. 2001.
To Catch a Wolf. 2003.
Touch of the Wolf. 1999. Werewolf.

Lorrah, Jean.
Blood Will Tell. 2003.

Macomber, Debbie. Angel stories.
Angels Everywhere. 2002. Includes *A Season of Angels* and *Touched by Angels.*
A Season of Angels. 1999.
The Trouble with Angels. 1999.

Miller, Linda Lael. Vampire stories.
Forever and the Night. 1993.
Tonight and Always. 1996.

Sands, Lynsay.
Love Bites. 2003.
Single White Vampire. 2003.

Shayne, Maggie.
Twilight series.
Features vampires.

Blue Twilight. 2005.
Edge of Twilight. 2004.
Embrace the Twilight. 2003.
In Twilight. 2002. Reissue of *Born in Twilight* with the novella *Beyond Twilight.*
Twilight Begins. 2004.
Twilight Hunger. 2002.
Two by Twilight. 2003. Reissue of *Twilight Vows* with the novella *Run from Twilight.*

York, Rebecca.
Witching Moon. 2003. A witch and a werewolf.

Futuristic/Science Fiction

Science fiction is often termed "futuristic" in the romance world. These tales of love set in far-flung worlds of the future may involve any of the themes often found in science fiction, including virtual reality, space travel, bioengineering, and alien races.

Asaro, Catherine.
The Veiled Web. **1999.**
Ballerina Lucia del Mar married Rashid al-Jazari, a high-tech Moroccan inventor/businessman, after they were kidnapped together, and she ends up in his family's harem where she discovers that the virtual reality and artificial intelligence projects he has been working on pose a danger.

Saga of the Skolian Empire.
This space opera romance appeals equally to fans of both science fiction and romance.

Skyfall. 2000. (prequel).
Schism. 2004.
The Last Hawk. 1997.

Primary Inversion. 1995.

Ascendant Sun. 2000.

The Radiant Seas. 1999.

Spherical Harmonic. 2001.

Quantum Rose. 2000.

The Moon's Shadow. 2003.

Catch the Lightning. 1996.

Bujold, Lois McMaster.

Shards of Honor. 1986.

Bujold's <u>Vorkosigan Saga</u> is science fiction adventure at its best, and although several of the titles in the series feature some elements of romance, readers of the romance particularly enjoy *Shards of Honor,* which takes place first in the chronology of the Vorkosigan family. It chronicles the first meeting and early relationship of Cordelia Niasmith and Aral Vorkosigan. In *A Civil Campaign* (1999), their son Miles courts his own true love in another science fiction novel that is enjoyed by romance readers.

Castle, Jayne. (pseudomym of Jayne Ann Krentz).

After Dark. 2001.

After Glow. 2004.

<u>St. Helens Trilogy.</u>

The titles in this series are listed in the "Paranormal Romantic Suspense" subsection of this chapter. All titles have futuristic settings on other planets.

Davidson, MaryJanice.

Hello, Gorgeous! 2005. A bionic woman.

Joy, Dara.

Ritual of Proof. 2002.

Krinard, Susan.

Kinsman's Oath. 2004.

Owens, Robin D.

<u>Celta.</u>

A planet settled by people with strong psionic powers is the setting for this fantasy-like science fiction series.

🏵 *Heart Mate.* 2001. Winner of the Rita Award and the P.E.A.R.L. Award.

🏵 *Heart Thief.* 2003. Winner of the Prism Award and the P.E.A.R.L. Award.

Heart Duel. 2004.

Heart Choice. 2005.

Robb, J. D. (pseudonym of Nora Roberts).

Futuristic romantic detective tales. Listed in the science fiction chapter.

Shinn, Sharon.

Jenna Starborn. 2002. Jane Eyre in space.

Ethnic Romance

In recent years African American romances have been published in greater numbers and have done extremely well in terms of sales. Ethnic readers, like all readers, enjoy books with protagonists with whom they can identify. The BET Arabesque line publishes four each month by successful authors such as Francis Ray, Shirley Hailstock, and Rochelle Alers. Beverly Jenkins writes romances with African American characters for Avon.

Unfortunately Encanto, a short-lived (1999–2002) romance line from Kensington with Latina interest romances, some published in both English and Spanish versions, did not last long.

In 2003 Signet published *Playing with Matches*, an Asian American contemporary romance anthology.

It is to be hoped that more ethnic heroes and heroines will be appearing in the future.

African American

Dana Watson, in her chapter "Romance Fiction," in *African American Literature: A Guide to Reading Interests,* edited by Alma Dawson and Connie Van Fleet (Libraries Unlimited, 2004), annotates several dozen titles by various authors.

Alers, Rochelle.

No Compromise. 2002.

> Jolene Walker, director of a center that helps abused and addicted women, is set up with Captain Michael Blanchard Kirkland, who is on leave from the Pentagon, at a glitzy Georgetown party.

Harrison, Shirley.

The Pleasure Principle. 2004.

> When accountant Natalie discovers that her former boyfriend is going to be the other godparent for her best friend Davinia's baby, she doesn't expect to fall in love with him again.

Savoy, Dierdre.

Could It Be Magic? 2003.

> Jake McKenna, raising her orphaned niece, can't support them both on what she makes as a freelance artist, so she takes a job at a magazine, where her new boss, the very formal Eamon Fitzgerald, a former lawyer, is trying to keep the family legacy solvent.

Latina

Castillo, Mary.

Hot Tamara. 2005.

Sandoval, Lynda.

Unsettling. 2004.

> Lucy Olivera may be a tough cop, but she just can't handle her fear of commitment, and she bolts from her own wedding reception.

Valdes-Rodriguez, Alisa.

The Dirty Girls Social Club. 2003.

Playing with Boys. 2004.

Native American

Native American characters appear frequently in romance novels set in the West, and readers who like the historical perspective should consult the Native American section of "Historical Romance" in this chapter.

Aitken, Judie.

Secret Shadows. 2004.

> Dr. Claire Colby, working on a Lakota reservation, resists her attraction to Dane White Eagle, who she thinks is a convicted killer released on a technicality, but he is actually an undercover F.B.I. agent on the track of drug dealers.

Topics

To find out more about the romance genre, check out the following resources.

Bibliographies and Biographies

Bontly, Susan W., and Carol J. Sheridan. *Enchanted Journeys Beyond the Imagination: An Annotated Bibliography of Fantasy, Futuristic, Supernatural, and Time Travel Romances.* Blue Diamond, 1996.
> The title says it all. Bontly and Sheridan have identified romance books that fall into the science fiction, fantasy, and supernatural areas. Unfortunately it is now quite out of date.

Bouricius, Ann. *The Romance Readers' Advisory: The Librarian's Guide to Love in the Stacks.* American Library Association, 2000.
> Bouricius, a librarian and a romance writer herself, defines the genre in which "women win," identifies subgenres, provides booklists, and gives sound readers' advisory advice.

Carpan, Carolyn. *Rocked by Romance: A Guide to Teen Romance Fiction.* Libraries Unlimited, 2004.
> Carpan includes an extensive annotated bibliography and author interviews with some of the important authors writing romantic fiction for teens.

North American Romance Writers. Edited by Kay Mussell and Johanna Tunon. Scarecrow Press, 1999.
> Essays by Judith Arnold, Mary Balogh, Jo Beverley, Loretta Chekani. (Chase) , Sue Civil-Brown. (Rachel Lee) , Judy Cuevas. (Judith Ivory) , Sharon and Tom Curtis. (Laura London) , Justine Davis, Eileen Dreyer. (Kathleen Korbel) , Kathleen Eagle, Patricia Gaffney, Alison Hart. (Jennifer Greene) , Lorraine Heath, Tami Hoag, Susan Johnson, Dara Joy, Lynn Kerstan, Sandra Kitt, Susan Krinard, Jill Marie Landis, Pamela Morsi, Maggie Osborne, Mary Jo Putney, Alicia Rasley, Emilie Richards, Paula Detmer Riggs, Nora Roberts, Barbara Samuel. (Ruth Wind) , Kathleen Gilles Seidel, and Jennifer Crusie. It also has an extensive bibliography of resources in the romance genre.

Ramsdell, Kristin. *Romance Fiction: A Guide to the Genre.* Libraries Unlimited, 1999.
> The definitive guide to the romance genre, Ramsdell's book offers users a thorough treatment of the genre, with thousands of titles described and organized in romance subgenres of contemporary, mystery, historical, regency, alternative reality, saga, gay and lesbian, inspirational, and ethnic/multicultural. Ramsdell also provides history and background notes along with thorough guidelines for readers' advisors for the genre as a whole and each of its subgenres. Information on awards, publishers, and research aids; a list of young adult romance titles; and guidelines for the core collection are some of the other features of the book. Author/title and subject indexes complete the work. An updated and expanded edition of *Happily Ever After: A Guide to Reading Interests in Romance Fiction* (Libraries Unlimited, 1987).

——. *What Romance Do I Read Next: A Reader's Guide to Recent Romance Fiction.* Gale, 1997.

Regis, Pamela. *A Natural History of the Romance Novel.* University of Pennsylvania Press, 2003.

Regis loves the genre and provides a well-executed overview and study of the genre from its earliest days to its current popularity. The romance novel is defended and defined in the first two sections. The third section covers the history of romance novels from 1740 to 1908, focusing on the impact and influence of *Pamela, Pride and Prejudice, Jane Eyre, Framley Parsonage,* and *A Room with a View.* The fourth section examines the romance novel in the twentieth century through the works of Georgette Heyer, Mary Stewart, Janet Dailey, Jayne Ann Krentz, and Nora Roberts.

Twentieth-Century Romance and Gothic Writers. 3d ed. Edited by Aruna Vasudevan and Lesley Henderson. Preface by Alison Light. St. James Press, 1994.

Hundreds of authors and their pseudonyms are listed. There are brief biographical data, a list of all published works, a statement by the author (if supplied), and a critical summation.

History and Criticism

Romance has not received the critical or scholarly interest given to many of the other genres. It is rarely the subject of academic study. It seems that the heyday for study of the genre was the early part of the 1980s, when several books were published that are now out of print. Several resources are listed in Ramsdell's *Romance Fiction: A Guide to the Genre* (Libraries Unlimited, 1999), but they are not widely available.

Krentz, Jayne Ann, ed. *Dangerous Men & Adventurous Women: Romance Writers on the Appeal of the Romance.* University of Pennsylvania Press, 1992. Reissued in mass market paperback by Harper Monogram in 1996.

Nineteen authors, beloved of romance readers, contributed essays on the appeal of their genre, the aspects of fantasy and character in the books they write, and descriptions of their readers. Many of the essays rebut feminist criticism of the genre.

Radway, Janice. *Reading the Romance: Women, Patriarchy, and Popular Literature.* University of North Carolina Press, 1984.

This classic work on genre romance examines why women in the early 1980s read romances and what this readership implied for social attitudes of women and toward women. It is of interest to scholars for a look at romance fiction in that particular time.

Review Journals

The following journals are for the devoted readership of the genre and are much more than review journals, as the annotations indicate. Their emergence parallels the genre's recent and amazing publishing activity and growth in reading audience.

Affaire de Coeur: "The Voice of the Readers and Writers of Romance Fiction." 1981– .

Six issues a year.

Provides star-rated reviews, news, and brief articles.

The Literary Times. 1988– . http://www.tlt.com
> Starting as a newsletter, it became a quarterly magazine in 1992, featuring book reviews, author profiles, and information for romance writers. In 1995 it became a Web site.

Romantic Times. 1981– . http://www.romantictimes.com.
> This publication contains reviews, annotations, excerpts from new romances, publishing and author news, biographies of romance authors, interviews, and advertisements. The name was recently changed to the *Romantic Times Bookclub Magazine* and the related convention, the Annual Booklovers Convention for Readers and Writers of Popular Fiction, was held for the twenty-second time in 2005.

The Internet is also a resource for romance reviews. Some dedicated readers review titles that are never seen by the standard library review journals. Many of the reviewers, like Nora Armstrong, are librarians who have an encyclopedic knowledge of the genre.

> **All About Romance,** http://www.likesbooks.com, is a useful resource, with sensuality ratings that really make sense, ranging from "Kisses" to "Burning." In addition to reviews, the site offers a plethora of information and features for romance readers.

> **The Romance Reader,** http://www.theromancereader.com, features reviews written by knowledgeable reviewers and organized by subgenre. It rates books using a scale of hearts and movie-like sensuality ratings.

> **Romance Reviews Today,** http://www.romrevtoday.com, publishes a list of scheduled titles along with numerous reviews.

Authors' Associations

Romance writers often do not feel comfortable within the standard authors' associations, so they have formed their own groups. Although the Romance Writers of America is some twenty years behind its British counterpart, it has been very successful, with more than 9,500 members in 2005.

> **Romantic Novelists Association** (http://www.rna-uk.org/). This British group was founded in 1960. It presents an annual award for the best romance, often having runner-up awards and a historical romance award. Its members are highly articulate apologists for the genre.

> **Romance Writers of America** (http://www.rwanational.org). The founding convention was held in Houston, Texas, in June 1981, and drew an unexpectedly large attendance of writers and fans. An award, the Rita, was established as the association's official prize for published work. The twenty-fifth annual convention was scheduled for Reno, Nevada, in July 2005. The organization also has local chapters in many communities and chapters devoted to different types of romance writing. In 2005 they had approximately 9,000 members.

Awards

The most prestigious and well-known romance awards are the "Ritas," awarded by the Romance Writers of America in several different categories. For a full listing in all of the many categories consult the RWA web site at http://www.rwanational.org/awards/awards.htm.

> **The Sapphire Award** (http://www.sfronline.com/sapphire.htm) is given for the best science fiction or fantasy romance of the year.

Paranoramal Excellence Award for Romantic Literature (http://www.
writerspace.com/ParanormalRomance/PNRpearl.htm).

The **Prism Award** (http://www.romance-ffp.com/index.htm) is given by the Futuristic, Fantasy, and Paranormal Special Interest Chapter of the Romance Writers of America.

Publishers

While romances continue to flourish in mass-market paperback (According to the Romance Writers of America, 55 percent of all paperbacks sold in the United States are romances.), more are now being published in hardcover and in trade paperback. The preponderance of genreblending is obvious in new imprints. In 2004 Harlequin ventured into fantasy with its Luna trade paperback line, while Tor, best known for science fiction and fantasy, started its Tor Romance line in mass-market paperback.

More romances, even the sex-drenched ones, are being published in large print and audio formats. This extends the lives of some titles that a few years ago would have quickly become unavailable.

D's Romance Picks

Aitken, Judie.

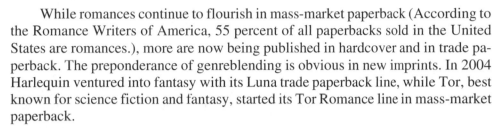

Secret Shadows. **2004.** (contemporary romantic suspense).

> A contemporary, suspenseful romance between a doctor and an undercover FBI agent set on a Lakota Reservation.

Chastain, Sandra.

The Mail Order Groom. **2002.** (historical—frontier and Western).

> A gorgeous school marm decides to marry rather than go to jail and asks her sickly pen pal to come out West to marry her, but when he is supposed to arrive it is someone else who steps off the train.

Lackey, Mercedes.

The Fairy Godmother. **2004.** (paranormal).

> When Elena escapes her wicked stepmother, it isn't to marry a prince but to become a fairy godmother. Of course nothing ever goes as planned.

Landis, Jill Marie.

Heartbreak Hotel. **2005.** (contemporary romance).

> Tracy Potter's wheeler-dealer husband was up to no good before he died, and he left her with nothing. She decides to try to make a living with all she has left, a dilapidated historical hotel with a tragic past that was left to her young son, and where a famous author comes to commit suicide and instead falls in love.

Quick, Amanda.

The Paid Companion. **2004.** (historical—Regency).

This Regency-era engagement of convenience tale is told with verve and style as a previously jilted earl hires a companion whose stepfather squandered her fortune to pose as his fiancée to keep him safe from the marriage-minded.

Roberts, Nora.

Three Sisters Island Trilogy. (paranormal).

A contemporary setting, an ancient spell, and the strong friendship that develops among three women who each find their own true love in a small island village.

Sands, Lynsay.

Single White Vampire. **2003.** (paranormal).

When Kate, an editor, goes to Toronto to persuade a reclusive romance writer to make some appearances to promote his books, she isn't expecting to find a gorgeous vampire.

Chapter 10

Science Fiction

Essay

JoAnn Palmeri

What Is Science Fiction?

Definitions of science fiction are as numerous and diverse as the alternate worlds and realities brought to life by writers in this genre. In the late 1920s editor Hugo Gernsback used "scientifiction" and then "science fiction" to describe the kind of fiction published in his magazines *Amazing Stories* and *Science Wonder Stories*. As a term "science fiction" came into common usage in the 1930s, and because (as Gary K. Wolfe points out) "science fiction gained its identity as a commercial term . . . long before literary scholarship and genre theory began attempting to define it," groups and individuals with a variety of interests and perspectives (writers and fans, publishers and media businesses, critics and academic scholars) all had a role in defining the scope of the field and articulating its boundaries.[1] The resulting competing visions of what science fiction is (or is not) can be a real challenge to those new to the genre. "Science fiction," Mary K. Chelton notes, "seems to be the most difficult genre to understand for those librarians who are not already fans."[2]

In terms of reading interests, however, some definitions are particularly useful. Science fiction is "any story that argues the case for a changed world that has not yet come into being," John Clute suggests in *Science Fiction: The Illustrated Encyclopedia*. These changed worlds are presented in terms "consistent with the language, the assumptions, and the arguments of contemporary science, or in terms that are consistent with our profound sense that human history is a continuous reality, and that changes flow from what we know of that reality."[3] For Harlan Ellison science fiction includes "anything that deals in even the smallest extrapolative manner with the future of man and his societies, with the future of science and/or its effects on us."[4] Joyce Saricks characterizes science fiction as speculative fiction in which a setting "outside everyday reality" is a crucial component, along with the story's technological and scientific aspects.[5]

All three authors key on science and the creation of alternate worlds. And because of the seeming limitless possibilities of setting, plot, and characterization inherent in the creation of alternate realities, science fiction encompasses an extraordinary diversity of titles and authors.

A Misunderstood Genre

But misconceptions and stereotypes about science fiction persist for several reasons. Film and television have represented a limited type of science fiction—accounts of alien invasion, bug-eyed monster stories, space opera, and futuristic adventure tales. These subgenres tend to feature plots weak on characterization but strong on gadgets. Narrow exposure to the genre (through only one medium or through a limited range of authors/subgenres) often leads to characterizations that miss the genre's richness and diversity. In addition to misunderstanding the genre, many persist in stereotyping the science fiction fan as a nerdish male adolescent.

Debates also continue concerning the boundaries between science fiction and the closely related genres of fantasy and horror. For example, Anne McCaffrey's works are inhabited by beings usually associated with fantasy—dragons—but she insists her stories qualify as science fiction.[6] Although the genre's ability to create alternate worlds helps explain why it remains closely linked with fantasy and horror, it differs from the others by grounding its imagined alternative worlds in a scientific worldview. "The Ground Rules . . . of science fiction are essentially those of the physical universe, although they may include rules as yet undiscovered," Wolfe says. "The ground rules of fantasy are generally said to be limited only by internal consistency and not necessarily related to experience."[7]

Kim G. Kofmel suggests that the primary response evoked in reading these genres can be used to distinguish them: Horror evokes a visceral response, science fiction an intellectual response, and fantasy an emotional response.[8] However, the lines remain blurred, partly because so much overlaps in these genres, especially given authors' efforts to appeal to multiple audiences. Today fantasy surpasses science fiction in sales and popularity, a trend that has propelled the crossover marketing trend. In addition, books are being published that appeal to a broader range of genre audiences—an example is Catherine Asaro's *Irresistible Forces*, an edited collection targeted to readers interested in both romance and science fiction.

Recent studies of the genre by Kofmel and Robinson show that science fiction readers resist labels,[9] particularly when labels are linked to assumptions about them or their interests. This may explain why some react negatively to the use of "sci-fi" rather than "SF" and why others reject the label "science fiction fan." In the final analysis, while readers are aware of the distinctions and categories of publishers and other authorities, what they emphasize is the importance of liking a book, not fitting it into a category.

The History of Science Fiction and SF Subgenres

Historical interpretations of the genre also reflect diversity and differing perspectives. Some identify Mary Shelley's nineteenth-century gothic fiction *Frankenstein* as the foundational work of the genre; others point to tales of imaginary voyages (Johann Kepler's *Somnium*) and utopian visions (Thomas More's *Utopia*) from earlier centuries as its origins. Over time many movements, subgenres, and themes have inhabited the science fiction universe. Changes in the field, from the rise and fall of subgenre, to its increasingly broad appeal, are intimately connected to wider historical and cultural developments. The emergence of science fiction as a recognizable genre in the twentieth century—and its development over the course of the century—were (and continue to be) influenced by commercial as well as cultural factors.

Many of the motifs and themes that continue to influence science fiction today were evident in the genre's "Golden Age" (late 1930s through the 1940s), in the writings of such authors as Isaac Asimov, Robert Heinlein, and Theodore Sturgeon. As in pulp magazines, much of this period literature was written by men and geared toward young male readers. It tended to be adventure-oriented, with emphasis on the technological. Early twentieth-century science fiction reflected wider cultural themes—technological utopianism and a reverence for science, but also concerns about the impact of the machine on society and the significance of evolution for human destiny. The dawn of the space age and the Cold War era brought with it exploration of encounters with beings from other worlds, including a preoccupation with the theme of alien invasion.

Beginning in the 1960s, the "New Wave" movement broadened the scope of the field by exploring the human condition within the context of the author's created world, shifting focus from the physical sciences to the sociological and human sciences. In part, this was a reaction to a perceived overemphasis on scientific and technological themes. It also reflected a broadening of the voices and backgrounds of authors (e.g., Samuel R. Delany, Philip K. Dick, Harlan Ellison, and Frank Herbert) contributing to the field at that time. In addition, changes in the status of women and the rise of feminism led women to participate more in the field, as consumers and contributors. They invigorated the field with new directions and perspectives. An exemplar is Joanna Russ's *The Female Man*.

Throughout the history of SF, artificial intelligence, robots, androids, and cyborgs have been a staple of the genre, perhaps because they provide a rich background for exploring an important question: What defines one's humanity? Shelley explores this in *Frankenstein*, as does Philip K. Dick in *Do Androids Dream of Electric Sheep?* From cyberpunk to virtual reality, science fiction has also provided a fascinating window to a near future in which computer networks dominate life in ways that readers may find jarringly realistic. William Gibson's *Neuromancer* is an archetypical example of this subgenre, elements of which have been more widely popularized in the *Matrix* films.

Even before humans had harnessed the power of the atom, writers envisioned post-apocalyptic futures (H. G. Wells, *Time Machine*). Such stories have continued to be prominent in the literature (not surprisingly, most prevalent in the 1950s and later decades of the Cold War). Reflecting late twentieth-century developments in genetics, biotechnology, and environmentalism, biological disasters and ecological catastrophes have more recently supplemented the nuclear calamity as a key cause of civilization's collapse and/or transformation (see for example, Nancy Kress's *Maximum Light*). And while most of the aforementioned works are novels, it should be noted that science fiction is a genre that encompasses a wide variety of forms—novellas, continuing series, and media tie-ins. Some of the best science fiction can be found in short stories published in magazines, anthologies, and collections.

The Science Fiction Reader

The question of why people read science fiction is intriguing (certainly it has implications for collection development and readers' advisory work). Most studies of science fiction readers neglect to address the issue. From such studies we have learned *who* is reading science fiction, *what* they are reading, and *how* these factors may have changed over time. The results of surveys conducted from a variety of perspectives over the years (general readers' studies, studies of science fiction readers, science fiction magazine polls) point to a number of trends, including increasing female readership, decreasing young male reading of science fiction magazines, and broadening of the audience receptive to the genre.[10] In fact, most studies of science fiction have focused on the genre more broadly, for example, on the phenomenon of science fiction fandom.

In contrast, Kofmel's survey of reading interests explores the questions of *why* individuals read science fiction, what they like about it, and what they get out of the experience.[11] She identifies characteristic genre themes that match reading interest. Among the most significant of these themes are other worlds, unlimited possibilities, and science and technology. Kofmel finds that readers like science fiction because of its "use of created worlds" and its "lack of limits." Since these characteristics also mark fantasy, it is not surprising many participants read both.

"One of the central, defining characteristics of science fiction lies in the way it creates worlds," Paul Kincaid notes. "We would not even recognise a work of science fiction if it did not convey some sense of otherness, some key way in which the world presented differs from the world we recognise as everyday reality."[12] The incredible variety of other worlds that can exist in science fiction is a striking feature of this genre. Varying degrees of "otherness" can be invoked by writers through story, setting, characterization and/or language. This effect takes the reader to another time and place, as in the science fiction subgenres of alternate and parallel worlds; lost worlds; space travel; and time travel, time warp.

Although science fiction authors are not constrained by the conventions of other fiction (e.g., the need to adhere to present-day realities), their created worlds are nevertheless expected to possess an "atmosphere of scientific credibility." It is this atmosphere that allows readers to engage in "the willing suspension of disbelief." For readers, the presence of science and technology distinguishes the created worlds of science fiction from those of fantasy, and it uniquely defines the genre. Science fiction incorporates science and technology into its narratives in many ways. This guide identifies some of the subgenres (or themes and types) that relate specifically to scientific or technological content.

Types, Themes, and Characteristics

The traditional means of telling readers about the science and technology content of particular works is to distinguish broadly between hard SF and soft SF. The former focuses on technology and the physical sciences (physics, astronomy, biology); the latter focuses on the social sciences (psychology, sociology). While an atmosphere of scientific credibility can be created in both, the notion of credibility has also been used as a means to distinguish between these categories. In this context, scientific credibility is equated with works that closely follow the established facts of science and technology. Since the physical sciences have traditionally been associated with the prestige and plausibility of science, it is not surprising that in some quarters these sciences are viewed as better equipped to foster an atmosphere of credibility. The New Wave movement, however, did much to bring soft SF into the mainstream.

Genre labels can repel as well as attract, Saricks emphasizes.[13] While science fiction may not be as stigmatized as it once was, stereotypes persist, and these often relate to the scientific and technological elements of the genre. With science fiction, perceptions can be shaped by views of science and technology as well as by views of the genre itself. Readers' advisors should make no assumptions about either, especially if they want to serve crossover readers, interested novices, or those who express an aversion to the genre. For example, a potential reader who equates science fiction with spaceships and computers might be surprised to find that a short story revolving around the liberation of women from menses received three major science fiction awards.[14]

When Kofmel asked her readers what they would read if science fiction did not exist, many could not identify a satisfactory substitute.[15] Although some tried, their substitutes still mirrored characterizations of science fiction: other worlds (historical fiction), problem solving (mystery), and science/technology/discovery (nonfiction).

The genre's emphasis on otherness is closely tied to a sense of disorientation one can experience when reading science fiction. Kincaid explains: "Our first exposure to science fiction . . . can be disorienting. There are words we don't know, things that don't belong in our familiar existence, events that don't make sense."[16] He points out that some readers seek that disorientation. However, this effect can be an obstacle to readers new to the genre. A case in point is the unsuccessful attempt by Kristine Rusch (former editor of *The Magazine of Fantasy & Science Fiction*) to introduce a new reader to the genre using William Gibson's cyberpunk classic *Neuromancer*. The language, Rusch emphasizes, posed too great a challenge to this beginning science fiction reader.[17]

Readers expect science fiction to challenge and intellectually provoke. As a genre driven by "what if?" questions, science fiction thrives on new and provocative ideas relating to science, technology, and society, and their interrelationships. Kofmel's study shows that some readers deliberately seek out variety of titles in the genre to see how a particular scientific or technological idea may be handled differently by different writers.[18] Readers enjoy the dizzying array of challenges to social and cultural concepts and conventions that arise during encounters with alternative realities. The genre is particularly compelling (and disturbing) when cloaking controversial issues and contemporary concerns within the context of other-worldly settings.

What distinguishes the science fiction reading experience from others is the intellectual challenge grounded in the genre's unique content. Yet the desire to be moved is not absent. The notion that science fiction evokes a "sense of wonder" in its readers is pervasive within the field. Yet this response is not purely intellectual. It is a response that captures scientists' own emotive reaction to, and aesthetic appreciation of, nature. Ultimately it speaks to an enchantment with the universe.

Anecdotal accounts abound regarding the transformative experience of becoming a science fiction reader, a behavior typically acquired in adolescence or young adulthood. Many scientists and engineers claim to have been inspired in their career choice by reading science fiction. For example, Donna Shirley, aerospace engineer and former manager of the Jet Propulsion Lab's Mars Exploration Program (who in 1997 explained the *Soujourner Truth* rover to millions of television viewers) says she found her inspiration at the age of twelve in Arthur C. Clarke's *The Sands of Mars*.[19] She later became director of the Science Fiction Museum in Seattle, where she instituted educational programs that use science fiction to promote science literacy.

Nationwide campaigns to use science fiction to promote literacy and reading (more generally) have also involved notable science fiction authors. For example, Greg Bear and David Brin founded the "Reading for the Future" project to show "teachers and librarians that science fiction inspires young readers."[20] Kofmel suggests science fiction also plays a role in affirming one's worldview and interest and views concerning science and technology.[21] Contradictions inherent in readers' own views concerning science and technology are often mirrored by contradictions in the literature.

What actually propels readers to acquire and/or continue the behavior of reading science fiction? Kofmel distinguishes two factors—those related to the texts themselves, and those related to external circumstances. The first concerns the kinds of preferences already discussed. The second concerns personal associations. A variety of social influences as well as encounters with texts (often influenced by social associations) shape how one interprets the genre and makes selections. Of particular relevance to librarians and readers' advisors is a reader's encounters with *collections* of texts.[22] In a genre with conventions learned through reading widely, such encounters may play a significant role in shaping preferences and guiding future reading experiences. This finding affirms the significance of the act of browsing and has implications for collection building and arrangement.

Selecting SF: Which Work to Recommend?

What to do when a readers' advisor identifies a patron seeking assistance as either a regular reader of science fiction or as someone new to the genre. How to guide him/her through the myriad of titles and authors available? *Genreflecting* serves as a basic guide for doing this by presenting science fiction works in terms of subgenres, themes, and types identifiable to readers (e.g., alien beings, cyberpunk, dystopia/utopia, and social criticism). Saricks and Kofmel offer supplemental approaches to help match readers' interests with particular works by suggesting strategies for characterizing reading preferences.[23] Often readers express an interest in a particular author (loyalty to authors is a well-known characteristic of science fiction readers) or a particular *type* of author (scientist/woman/African American). Using these and other expressed preferences can help identify the type of science fiction book that can best meet readers' needs.

For Saricks, matching a reader with the perfect book involves identifying the "appeal factors" of story line, frame, characterization, and pacing.[24] Two readers may be equally interested in a story about time travel (story line/frame), but one may prefer a fast-paced adventure like Michael Crichton's *Timeline*, another Jack Finney's *Time and Again*, which unfolds at a slower pace and allows the reader to more fully absorb the texture and ambience of another time and place.

Science fiction is often criticized for weak characterization, and within the genre authors tend to work out the central ideas through action and situations rather than through the characters.[25] "More than in any other fiction, in sf the imaginary setting is a major character in the story."[26] Indeed, setting is crucial to creating the otherworldliness that readers identify as essential to the genre. But science fiction readers do not overlook characterization; Kofmel's study identifies it as a highly desired element in the reading experience.[27] Saricks emphasizes science fiction's capacity to tell stories and its ability to present challenging ideas as a key to categorizing individual works for reading appeal.[28] She contrasts titles with a "storyteller focus" to those with a "philosophical focus," and suggests this as an approach to matching readers with books. For example, galactic empire series (like those of Lois McMaster Bujold) may be suitable to readers who prefer engaging stories, while more thoughtful, idea-centered works (like Mary Doria Russell's *The Sparrow*) may be appropriate for the more philosophically inclined.

While identifying appeal factors is important, recognizing the individuality of the reading experience is also essential. Two points Catherine Sheldrick Ross highlights are relevant: mood effects desired reading experience, and the meaning derived from a text is shaped in profound ways by what an individual brings to the experience.[29] Science fiction readers want to satisfy different tastes at different times. Depending on their mood, they may prefer the comfort of an established series with its familiarity of characters, or they may prefer a work that is challenging and disturbing. Different readers may also interpret the same work in different ways. While one reader might find Star Trek novels appealing because of the adventure element or because of their treatment of the relationships between characters, another reader might identify the ideas upon which the Star Trek universe is grounded as most important. The difference in response results from the different ways in which readers attach value and subscribe meaning to texts.

Works of science fiction do not always fall into neat and convenient categories. Often, a single work can fit several subgenres (e.g., Frank Herbert's classic *Dune*). Furthermore, the categories used to organize science fiction works in this guide are not necessarily comparable—some concern subject or plot elements (bio-engineering), some a distinct trend or school (New Wave), and some an overall message/theme (social criticism). Kofmel's study of readers suggests that this diversity in the ways science fiction is characterized aptly reflects how readers actually view the genre and select titles.[30]

 **10**

Kofmel identifies eight categories that reflect readers' perceptions of science fiction: purity, hybrid, heritage, relational, functional, theme, mode, and device. These categories resonate with *Genreflecting* subgenres and themes as well as with some of Saricks's appeal factors. For example, the category of "heritage" denotes works in a particular historical tradition or context, like New Wave or classic SF.[31]

In their characterization of science fiction works, readers also mention two additional aspects related to story line or plot: the purpose of a story (e.g., cautionary) and its underlying message (e.g., things-man-was-not-meant-to-know). Ultimately, what all this suggests is that readers' advisors should be particularly sensitive to diversity in the ways science fiction works can be characterized, as well as the variety of ways in which reading preferences can be expressed.

Serving the Science Fiction Reader

While this guide is primarily focused on science fiction literature, readers' advisors must keep in mind the broader nature and appeal of the genre. Recognizing the connection between print and film/video is essential (e.g., a beginning reader who enjoyed the film *Blade Runner* could be introduced to the book and to other works of Philip K. Dick). Allen Lichtenstein's study of science fiction book versus movie audiences suggests that preference for a particular format may serve as a window into reading preferences.[32] He found that those who enjoyed science fiction exclusively through books had a preference for idea-oriented stories; those who enjoyed science fiction exclusively through television/movies had a preference for adventure-oriented stories.[33] (These categories resonate with Saricks's archetypes of "philosophical focus" and "storyteller focus.")

Such oppositions may serve as a useful first-order approach in exchanges with readers, but it is good strategy to allow science fiction fans to define themselves and their interests. Even when individuals demonstrate a format preference, however, they continue to identify with science fiction more generally. By openly appreciating and clearly demonstrating familiarity with the genre, librarians invite interactions with regular readers of science fiction.

Science fiction themes and icons have become prominent features of popular culture and interest in the genre has moved well beyond dated stereotypes of the science fiction fan. Science fiction has something for a wide range of reading tastes and sensibilities—perhaps, even, those who claim to dislike it. But matching regular science fiction readers as well as novices with books is a continuing challenge for librarians, given the diversity of offerings and the reality that the science fiction universe remains an alien landscape to many. Hopefully, this chapter will help readers' advisors navigate this sometimes daunting but always intriguing landscape.

Notes

1. Gary K. Wolfe, *Critical Terms for Science Fiction and Fantasy: A Glossary and Guide to Scholarship* (New York: Greenwood Press, 1986), 108.

2. Mary K. Chelton, ed., "Introduction to 'Readers' Advising for the Young SF, Fantasy, and Horror Reader,' by David G. Hartwell," *Reference & User Services Quarterly* 42, no. 2 (2002): 133.

3. John Clute, *Science Fiction: The Illustrated Encyclopedia* (London: Dorling Kindersley, 1995), 6, 7.

4. Wolfe, *Critical Terms,* 110.

5. Joyce G. Saricks, *The Readers' Advisory Guide to Genre Fiction* (Chicago: American Library Association, 2001), 263.

6. Diana Tixier Herald, *Genreflecting: A Guide to Reading Interests in Genre Fiction,* 5th ed. (Englewood, Colo.: Libraries Unlimited, 2000), 269.

7. Wolfe, *Critical Terms,* 108.

8. Kim G. Kofmel, "Adult Readers of Science Fiction and Fantasy: A Qualitative Study of Reading Preference and Genre Perception" (Ph.D. diss., University of Western Ontario, 2002).

9. Ibid.; Michael Gerald Robinson, "Genre from the Audience Perspective: Science Fiction" (Ph.D. diss., Bowling Green State University, 2000).

10. Joe DeBolt, "Patterns of Science Fiction Readership among Academics," *Extrapolation* 19, no. 2 (1978): 112–25; Kristine Kathryn Rusch, "Editorial," *The Magazine of Fan-*

tasy and Science Fiction 88, no. 2 (1995): 5–7 and "Editorial," *The Magazine of Fantasy and Science Fiction* 89, no. 3 (1995): 5; National Science Board, *Science and Engineering Indicators—2002* (Arlington, Va.: National Science Foundation, 2002).

11. Kofmel, "Adults Readers of SF and Fantasy."

12. Paul Kincaid, "What It Is We Do When We Read Science Fiction," *Foundation* 78 (2000): 80–81.

13. Saricks, *Readers' Advisory Guide,* 277.

14. Connie Willis, "Even the Queen," Nebula (1992), Locus (1993), and Hugo (1993) awards, originally published in *Isaac Asimov's Science Fiction Magazine*.

15. Kofmel, "Adults Readers of SF and Fantasy."

16. Kincaid, "What It Is We Do," 79.

17. Kristine Kathryn Rusch, "Editorial," *The Magazine of Fantasy and Science Fiction* 87, no. 2 (1994): 5; "Editorial," *The Magazine of Fantasy and Science Fiction* 88, no. 2 (1995): 5–7; "Editorial," *The Magazine of Fantasy and Science Fiction* 89, no. 3 (1995): 5.

18. Kofmel, "Adults Readers of SF and Fantasy."

19. Donna Shirley, *Managing Martians* (New York: Broadway Books, 1999).

20. Sandy Moltz, "Forging Futures with Teens and Science Fiction: A Conversation with Greg Bear and David Brin," *VOYA: Voice of Youth Advocates* 26, pt. 1 (2003): 15.

21. Kofmel, "Adults Readers of SF and Fantasy."

22. Ibid., 183.

23. Ibid.

10

24. Saricks, *Readers' Advisory Guide.*

25. Ibid., 263.

26. Gwyneth Jones, "The Icons of Science Fiction," in *The Cambridge Companion to Science Fiction*, ed. Edward James and Farah Mendlesohn, 163–73. Cambridge: Cambridge University Press, 2003.

27. Kofmel, "Adults Readers of SF and Fantasy."

28. Saricks, *Readers' Advisory Guide.*

29. Catherine Sheldrick Ross, "Finding Without Seeking: The Information Encounter in the Context of Reading for Pleasure," *Information Processing and Management* 35 (1999): 790–96.

30. Kofmel, "Adults Readers of SF and Fantasy."

31. Saricks, *Readers' Advisory Guide.*

32. Allen Lichtenstein, "Science Fiction Book versus Movie Audiences: Implications for the Teaching of Science Fiction," *Extrapolation* 24, no. 1 (1983): 47–56.

33. Ibid., 55.

Bibliography

"Casting a Wider Spell: SF/Fantasy Players Discuss New and Better Ways of Hooking Readers—Tweaking Format, Genre, Subject." 2004. *Publishers Weekly* 251, no. 14: 27–31.

Chelton, Mary K., ed. "Introduction to 'Readers' Advising for the Young SF, Fantasy, and Horror Reader,' by David G. Hartwell." *Reference & User Services Quarterly* 42, no. 2 (2002): 133–38.

Clute, John. *Science Fiction: The Illustrated Encyclopedia.* London: Dorling Kindersley, 1995.

DeBolt, Joe. "Patterns of Science Fiction Readership among Academics." *Extrapolation* 19, no. 2 (1978): 112–25.

Herald, Diana Tixier. *Genreflecting: A Guide to Reading Interests in Genre Fiction.* 5th ed. Englewood, Colo.: Libraries Unlimited, 2000.

Herald, Diana Tixier, and Bonnie Kunzel. *Strictly Science Fiction: A Guide to Reading Interests.* Greenwood Village, Colo.: Libraries Unlimited, 2000.

Jones, Gwyneth. "The Icons of Science Fiction." In *The Cambridge Companion to Science Fiction*, ed. Edward James and Farah Mendlesohn, 163–73. Cambridge: Cambridge University Press, 2003.

Kincaid, Paul. "What It Is We Do When We Read Science Fiction." *Foundation* 78 (2000): 72–82.

Kofmel, Kim G. "Adult Readers of Science Fiction and Fantasy: A Qualitative Study of Reading Preference and Genre Perception." Ph.D. diss., University of Western Ontario, 2002.

Lichtenstein, Allen. "Science Fiction Book versus Movie Audiences: Implications for the Teaching of Science Fiction." *Extrapolation* 24, no. 1 (1983): 47–56.

Moltz, Sandy. "Forging Futures with Teens and Science Fiction: A Conversation with Greg Bear and David Brin." *VOYA: Voice of Youth Advocates* 26, pt. 1 (2003): 15–18.

National Science Board. *Science and Engineering Indicators—2002.* Arlington, Va.: National Science Foundation, 2002. NSB-02-1.

Robinson, Michael Gerald. "Genre from the Audience Perspective: Science Fiction," Ph.D. diss., Bowling Green State University, 2000.

Ross, Catherine Sheldrick. "Finding Without Seeking: The Information Encounter in the Context of Reading for Pleasure." *Information Processing and Management* 35 (1999): 783–99.

Rusch, Kristine Kathryn. "Editorial." *The Magazine of Fantasy and Science Fiction* 87, no. 2 (1994): 5.

———. "Editorial." *The Magazine of Fantasy and Science Fiction* 88, no. 2 (1995): 5–7.

———. "Editorial." *The Magazine of Fantasy and Science Fiction* 89, no. 3 (1995): 5.

Saricks, Joyce G. *The Readers' Advisory Guide to Genre Fiction.* Chicago: American Library Association, 2001.

Shirley, Donna. *Managing Martians.* New York: Broadway Books, 1999.

Wolfe, Gary K. *Critical Terms for Science Fiction and Fantasy: A Glossary and Guide to Scholarship.* New York: Greenwood Press, 1986.

Themes and Types

Diana Tixier Herald

Science Fiction contains a canon of novels and stories created throughout the history of the genre that avid readers know. Many newer stories are built on conventions that grew out of the traditions of the science fiction works that have gone before. While some of the subgenres, such as space opera, are well-established, and widely recognized as such; other categories (e.g., virtual reality, nanotechnology) are newer, seemingly less cohesive and more thematic. Still other categories represent blending of more than one genre—e.g., science fiction and romance. Nonetheless, these categories reflect distinct reading interests and preferences for SF readers, and are therefore represented in the following lists. Terms that describe historical developments in the genre, such as *cyberpunk* and *New Wave,* are of scholarly interest, but do not necessarily reflect today's reading interests. Thus, they are not used in the following schema, although they are described the preceding essay. Readers interested in New Wave literature should refer to "The Future is Bleak" and "Social Structures" categories. Cyberpunk fans should check out the "Techno SF" section.

Selected Classics

Science fiction is a genre deeply rooted in its backlist, with classic titles commonly being reissued and re-read. There are so many science fiction classics that it is impossible to do more than provide a broad sampling here. Excluded from this list are precursors of the genre, such as Mary Shelley's *Frankenstein*, and Sir Arthur Conan Doyle's *The Lost World*. Also excluded are more contemporary authors, with titles published in the 1970s and after.

These exceptions are included in the chapter essay and/or the subgenre listings, where they are tagged as classics.

Asimov, Isaac.

Numerous titles, including:

Fantastic Voyage. 1966. (techno SF—nanotechnology).
I, Robot. 1950. (techno SF—robots, cyborgs, and androids).
Foundation series.

Bester, Alfred.
The Demolished Man. 1953. (psionic powers).
The Stars My Destination. 1956. (space opera).

Bradbury, Ray.
Fahrenheit 451. 1953. (dystopias).
Martian Chronicles. 1950. (near future).
others.

Burgess, Anthony.
A Clockwork Orange. 1962. (dystopias—dark SF).

Burroughs, Edgar Rice.
Mars Series. (SF adventure).

Clarke, Arthur C.
Numerous titles, including:

Childhood's End. 1953. (dystopias—religious).
2001: A Space Odyssey. 1968. (SF adventure—exploration).

Clement, Hal.
Mission of Gravity. 1954. (time travel).

De Camp, L. Sprague.
Lest Darkness Fall. 1949. (time travel—distant past).

Delany, Samuel R.
Babel-17. 1967. (New Wave).

Dick, Philip K.
Numerous titles, including:

Do Androids Dream of Electric Sheep? 1968. (techno SF—robots, cyborgs, and androids). The movie *Blade Runner* was based on it.
The Man in the High Castle. 1962. (alternate history).

Dickson, Gordon R.
Dorsai series. (SF adventure—militaristic and war).

Farmer, Philip José.
Riverworld Saga.

Heinlein, Robert A.
Numerous titles, including:

Have Space Suit—Will Travel. 1958. (SF adventure).

Herbert, Frank.
Dune. 1965. (dystopias—social structures).

Huxley, Aldous.
Brave New World. 1932. (dystopias—dark SF).

Keyes, Daniel.
Flowers for Algernon. 1966. (bioengineering).

Le Guin, Ursula K.
The Left Hand of Darkness. 1969. (aliens).

Lewis, C. S.
Perelandra Trilogy. (aliens; Christian SF).

Miller, Walter M., Jr.
A Canticle for Leibowitz. 1961. (dystopias—religious).

Norton, Andre.
<u>Time Traders Series.</u> (SF adventure—militaristic and war).
<u>The Solar Queen Series.</u> (SF adventure—exploration).

Orwell, George.
1984. 1949. (dystopias—political).

Panshin, Alexei.
Rite of Passage. 1968. (SF adventure—space travel).

Shute, Neville.
On the Beach. 1957. (dystopias—nuclear annihilation).

Simak, Clifford D.
City. 1952. (techno SF—robots, cyborgs, and androids).

Smith, E. E. Doc.
The Skylark of Space. 1928. (space travel).

Stewart, George R.
Earth Abides. 1949. (dystopias—overpopulation and plagues).

van Vogt, A. E.
Slan. 1946. (psionic powers).

Vance, Jack.
The Dying Earth. 1950.
The Isle of Peril. 1957.
Room to Die. 1965.

Vonnegut, Kurt.
Cat's Cradle. 1963. (dystopias—ecological disasters).
Sirens of Titan. 1959. (SF humor).
Slaughterhouse Five, or, The Children's Crusade. 1968. (SF adventure—journeys through time and space—space travel).

Williamson, Jack.
The Humanoids. 1949. (techno SF—robots, cyborgs, and androids).
<u>Starchild Trilogy.</u> (with Frederik Pohl) (us and them—near future).
others.

Science Fiction Adventure

Exploration, wars, the military, and political intrigue along with fast-paced physical action are the hallmarks of science fiction adventure. They also involve strong heroes and heroines. Exploration provides a venue for looking at what may be found in previously unexplored places whether distant planets or closer to home. The thrill here is in the quest, and in unexpected discoveries.

Readers who enjoy the technical side of science fiction adventure and want to explore other genres may also enjoy political espionage novels and technothrillers.

Bova, Ben.

Venus. 2000.

A $10 billion reward to find out what happened to the missing son of a multi-billionaire sends his younger, disowned son racing to Venus to compete with others vying for the reward in a truly hostile environment.

Burroughs, Edgar Rice.

<u>Mars Series.</u> ★

A very romantic and unscientific look at John Carter's adventures on the red planet.

A Princess of Mars. 1917. Reissued in 2003.
The Gods of Mars. 1918.
The Warlord of Mars. 1919.

Card, Orson Scott.

Wyrms. 1987. Reissued 2003.

Clarke, Arthur C.

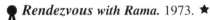 *Rendezvous with Rama.* 1973. ★

When a cylindrical vessel appears in the solar system, one planet sends explorers and another a bomb. Winner of the Hugo, Nebula, Locus,; John W. Campbell,; and British Science Fiction Awards.

Clement, Hal.

Mission of Gravity. 1954. ★

A truly alien adventurer on a high gravity world.

Crichton, Michael.

Jurassic Park. 1990. 🎬
The Lost World. 1997.

Harrison, M. John.

Light. 2004.

Two scientists working with quantum physics make choices (including murder) that will eventually lead to space travel.

Heinlein, Robert A.

Citizen of the Galaxy. 1957. Reissued 1987. ★
Farmer in the Sky. 1950. Reissued 1986. ★
Have Space Suit—Will Travel. 1958. Reissued 2005. ★

The adventurous tale of Kip Russell, a teen who wins a trip to the moon in a school contest, is still in print and popular with today's readers—from middle and high school readers to adults.

Tunnel in the Sky. 1955. Reissued 2003.

Several teens are marooned on a hostile planet.

Hogan, James P.
Outward Bound. **1999.**

> Fifteen-year-old Linc Marani, who has gotten into trouble one too many times, finds himself in a juvenile labor camp. Then a psychologist makes a mysterious offer for a trip to the Outzone.

MacLeod, Ken.
The Fall Revolution Series.

> Life after "the Deliverance," when humanity once again looks to outer space.

The Star Fraction. 2001.
The Stone Canal. 2000.

The Cassini Division. 1999.
The Sky Road. 2000.

McDevitt, Jack.
Moonfall. 1998.

McHugh, Maureen F.
🎗 *China Mountain Zhang.* 1992. Reissued 1997.

> In the twenty-second century, China dominates the world. Winner of the Hugo, Tiptree, Lambda, and Locus Awards.

Niven, Larry.
Ringworld. 1970. ★

> A world that is in the shape of a ring circling its sun is discovered. Winner of the Hugo, Nebula, and Locus Awards.

Norton, Andre.
The Solar Queen Series.

> The adventures of Dane Thorson and the crew of the *Solar Queen*, a space freighter.

Sargasso of Space. 1955. Reissued 2003 in *The Solar Queen.*
Plague Ship. 1956. Reissued 2003 in *The Solar Queen.*
Voodoo Planet. 1959.
Postmarked the Stars. 1969.
The Solar Queen. 2003. Omnibus of *Sargasso of Space* and *Plague Ship.*

Norton, Andre, and P. M. Griffin.
Redline the Stars: A New Adventure of the Solar Queen. 1993.

Norton, Andre, and Sherwood Smith.
Derelict for Trade. 1997.

Mind for Trade. 1996.

Preston, Douglas, and Lincoln Child.
The Ice Limit. 2000.

> In our day and time, a group of explorers set out to retrieve a meteorite that is buried in the ice of an island off Tierra del Fuego.

Reed, Robert.

Great Ship series.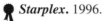
    Marrow. 2000.
    The Well of Stars. 2005. Sequel to *Marrow.*

Robinson, Kim Stanley.

Mars Trilogy.
    Red Mars. 1992. Winner of the Nebula Award.
    Green Mars. 1993. Winner of the Hugo Award.
    Blue Mars. 1996. Winner of the Hugo Award.
    The Martians. 1999.
    A companion volume to the Mars Trilogy containing stories, poems, and even the text of the planetary constitution.

Russo, Richard Paul.

    Ship of Fools. 2001.

Sawyer, Robert J.

Starplex. 1996.
    In 2094 the creators of the wormholes that have made space travel practical show up. Winner of the Aurora Award.

Sheffield, Charles.

Heritage Universe.
    Summertide. 1990.
    Divergence. 1991.
    Transcendence. 1992.
    Convergence. 1997.

Steele, Allen M.

Coyote.
    A refugee ship from Earth colonizes an alien planet.

    Coyote: A Novel of Interstellar Exploration. 2002.
    Coyote Rising. 2004.
    The colonists on the *Alabama* had fled the tyranny on Earth, but now their new home is being overrun by others from Earth who have their own agendas.

Stephenson, Neal.

Cryptonomicon. 1999. 📖
    A code ties two different generations of two families together in World War II and the present.

Swanwick, Michael.

Stations of the Tide. 1990.
    A world begins to drown under the weight of its own oceans. Winner of the Nebula Award.

Verne, Jules.

Verne is considered by many to be the originator of the SF genre.

From the Earth to the Moon. 1865. Reissued 1995. ★ ▤

20,000 Leagues Under the Sea.. 1870. Reissued 2005. ★ ▤

Space Opera

Space opera is probably the most well-defined and widely read type of SF adventure. This is romantic adventure on a grand scale, set in the spectacular arena of outer space. Interstellar travel, heroic space battles, and romance are key characteristics. Many space operas are written in series format, spanning time as well as galaxies and incorporating just about every theme found in science fiction adventure. The term was initially used derogatorily, as comparable to "horse opera" (Western) and "soap opera" (the domestic serial). Today, space opera is still sometimes maligned as simplistic or sophomoric, but it is home to many of the great adventure stories, including the still-popular Star Wars series.

Anderson, Kevin J.

Saga of the Seven Suns.

Hidden Empire. 2002.

A Forest of Stars. 2003.

Horizon Storms. 2004.

Asaro, Catherine.

Saga of the Skolian Empire.

Listed in the order events occur in the series.

Skyfall. 2000.

Schism. 2004.

The Last Hawk. 1997.

Kelric, heir to the Skolian Empire, crash lands on a restricted matriarchal planet, where he lives in the Calanya (harem) of a powerful woman.

Primary Inversion. 1995.

Sauscony Valdoria, a bioengineered fighter pilot and heir to the Skolian Empire, discovers that her soulmate may be the Aristo heir to the enemy Trader Empire and a fellow empath.

Ascendant Sun. 2000.

The Radiant Seas. 1999.

Jaibriol and Soz, scions of two warring families, find peace on an uninhabited planet until years later, when Jaibriol's empress mother discovers he still lives and abducts him. Taking their children to Earth for safekeeping, Soz returns to the Skolian Empire to fight for her family.

Spherical Harmonic. 2001.

🎗 *The Quantum Rose.* 2000.

To save her people, the beautiful ruler Kamoj Quanta Argali has agreed to marry the ruler of a more prosperous province, Jax Ironbridge. But the plan is upset when Lionstar (Vryl), an exiled prince of the Roca line of Skolian royalty, shows up and starts showing interest in Kamoj. Winner of the Nebula Award.

The Moon's Shadow. 2003.

Catch the Lightning. 1996.

Banks, Iain.

Inversions. **2000.**

The story of Vosill, a female doctor whom no one trusts except her patients; and DeWar, an assassin who trusts no one but the one he shouldn't. Conspiracy and court intrigues in the backward world of Haspidus.

Bester, Alfred.

The Stars My Destination. 1956. Reissued 1996. ★

Gully Foyle may be stranded in space, but that is not enough to stop him.

Bujold, Lois McMaster.

Vorkosigan Saga.

The adventures of the militaristic Vorkosigan family of Barrayar, and especially of son Miles, the sexiest and most powerful man under five feet tall in this or any galaxy.

Shards of Honor. 1986.

🎗*Barrayar.* 1991. Winner of the Hugo Award.

The Warrior's Apprentice. 1986.

🎗*The Vor Game.* 1990. Winner of the Hugo and Nebula Awards.

Borders of Infinity. 1989.

Brothers in Arms. 1989.

Memory. 1996.

🎗*Mirror Dance.* 1994. Winner of the Hugo Award.

Cetaganda. 1996.

Komarr. 1998.

🎗*A Civil Campaign.* 1999. Winner of the Sapphire Award.

Diplomatic Immunity. 2002.

Cherryh, C. J.

Merchanter Universe.

Set in a world of space travel, intergalactic trading, and war between the mighty Earth and Union forces. It is also known as the Alliance/Union Universe.

Heavy Time. 1991. Reissued in 2000 in *Devil in the Belt.*

Hellburner. 1992. Reissued in 2000 in *Devil in the Belt.*

Serpent's Reach. 1980.

🎗*Downbelow Station.* 1981. Reissued 2001. Winner of the Hugo Award.

Merchanter's Luck. 1982. Reissued 2002.

Rimrunners. 1989.

Tripoint. 1994.

Hamilton, Peter F.

Fallen Dragon. 2002.

> In a far future world in which pirate-like corporations exact tribute from far-flung locations, the inhabitants of Thrallspring decide to fight back.

Pandora's Star. 2004.

> In the twenty-fourth century, humans have utilized wormholes to colonize distant star systems with no trouble from aliens, until a pair of stars inside an energy barrier is found.

Homeric Space Opera Sequence.

> Space opera on an epic scale, set in the far future and featuring telepathic space dwellers called Edenists.

The Reality Dysfunction Vol. 1 Emergence. 1996.

The Reality Dysfunction Vol. 2 Expansion. 1997.

The Neutronium Alchemist No. 1 Consolidation. 1997.

The Neutronium Alchemist No. 2 Conflict. 1997.

The Naked God: Flight. 2000.

The Naked God: Faith. 2000.

Harrison, M. John.

Light. 2004. (space opera).

Herbert, Brian, and Kevin J. Anderson.

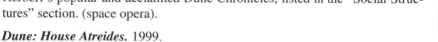

Dune prequel series.

> Rip-roaring space adventure combining battles and politics in prequels to Frank Herbert's popular and acclaimed Dune Chronicles, listed in the "Social Structures" section. (space opera).

Dune: House Atreides. 1999.

Dune: House Harkonnen. 2000.

Dune: House Corrino. 2001.

Dune: The Butlerian Jihad. 2002.

Dune: The Machine Crusade. 2003.

Dune: The Battle of Corrin. 2004.

MacLeod, Ken.

Newton's Wake. 2004.

> Set in the twenty-fourth century, this space opera skewers late twentieth-century U.S. politics.

Engines of Light series.

> Two different timelines and faster-than-light travel. (space opera).

Cosmonaut Keep. 2000.

Dark Light. 2002.

Engine City. 2003.

Reynolds, Alastair.

Reynolds is an astronomer.

Revelation Space series.

> *Revelation Space.* 2001.
>
> *Redemption Ark.* 2002.
>
> *Absolution Gap.* 2004.
>
> *Diamond Dogs, Turquoise Days.* 2005.
>
> Two novellas from a master of noir science fiction set in the Revelations Space universe.

Smith, E. E. Doc. ★

> *The Skylark of Space.* 1928. Reissued 2001.
>
> *Skylark Three.* 1948. Reissued 2003.
>
> *Skylark of Valeron.* 1949. Reissued 2003.
>
> *Skylark DuQuesne.* 1966.

Stross, Charles.

Rachel Mansour series.

> Colonel Mansour is an intergalactic weapons inspector in this space opera series.
>
> *Singularity Sky.* 2003.
>
> *Iron Sunrise.* 2004.

Militaristic

Military forces and conflicts appear frequently in SF. Here they take center stage, where warriors, weapons, and battles provide the big attraction to readers. The Honor Harrington series by David Weber and the Nicholas Seafort series by David Feintuch, with their emphasis on naval mores and traditions, share much the same appeal as historical naval adventure.

Card, Orson Scott.

Card rocketed to popularity with *Ender's Game*, a tale that starts with a six-year-old boy who proves to have the determination and ruthlessness necessary to be sent to military training and to lead human forces to victory. The sequels, starting with *Speaker for the Dead* (1986), which also won both major science fiction awards, became progressively philosophical and deep, moving far into the future and farther from the adventure aspects that made *Ender's Game* popular. In 1999 Card started a new series that dealt with the other child warriors in *Ender's Game* and what happened to them following the war. The following books are the titles in Card's saga that share the appeal of fast-paced militaristic adventure science fiction.

> ✿ *Ender's Game.* 1985. Reissued 2005. Winner of the Hugo and Nebula Awards. ★
>
> *Ender's Shadow.* 1999.
>
> *Shadow of the Hegemon.* 2001.
>
> *Shadow Puppets.* 2002.
>
> *Shadow of the Giant.* 2005.

Dickson, Gordon R.

Dorsai series. ★

> Throughout the human worlds, the Dorsai, a race of fearsome warriors, are known for their honor, independence, and rages.
>
> *Dorsai.* 1960. Reissued in 2003 with *The Spirit of Dorsai* as *Dorsai Spirit.*
>
> *Tactics of Mistake.* 1971.

Soldier Ask Not. 1967.

Lost Dorsai: The New Dorsai Companion. 1980.
A collection that includes the Hugo award-winning novella *Lost Dorsai*, the short story "Warrior," and information about Dickson's Childe Cycle, of which the Dorsai series is a part.

The Spirit of Dorsai. 1980.

Dorsai Spirit. 2003. One-volume publication of *Dorsai* and *The Spirit of Dorsai.*

Dietz, William C.

The Legion series.

Features Bill Booly and his misfit cyborg legion.

Legion of the Damned. 1993.
The Final Battle. 1995.
By Force of Arms. 2000.
For More Than Glory. 2003.

Feintuch, David.

Hope series.

This Nicholas Seafort saga has been called "Horatio Hornblower in space."

Midshipman's Hope. 1994.
Challenger's Hope. 1995.
Prisoner's Hope. 1995.
Fisherman's Hope. 1996.
Voices of Hope. 1996.
Patriarch's Hope. 1999.
Children of Hope. 2001.

Haldeman, Joe.

Forever Free. 2000.

🎗 *The Forever Peace.* 1997. Winner of the Hugo and Nebula Awards.

🎗 *The Forever War.* 1974. Reissued 2003. Winner of the Hugo, Nebula, and Locus Awards. ★

Heinlein, Robert A.

🎗 *The Moon Is a Harsh Mistress.* 1966. Reissued 1996. Winner of the Hugo Award.

🎗 *Starship Troopers.* 1959. Reissued 1998. Winner of the Hugo Award. 🎬

Hubbard, L. Ron.

Battlefield Earth: A Saga of the Year 3000. 1982. Reissued 2002. 🎬

McDevitt, Jack.

A Talent for War. 1989. Reissued 2004.

Meluch, R. M.

Tour of the Merrimack.

In the twenty-fifth century, while the U.S. battleship *Merrimack* fights against "the Hive," an alien swarm that will consume everything in its path if not stopped, a triad of hitherto unknown populated planets and a series of wormholes are discovered.

The Myriad. 2005.

Moon, Elizabeth.

Esmay Suiza series.

Once a Hero. 1997.

Rules of Engagement. 1998.

Change of Command. 1999.

Ringo, John.

A Hymn Before Battle. 2000.

Gust Front. 2001.

When the Devil Dances. 2002.

Hell's Faire. 2003.

Ringo, John, and Julie Cochrane.

Cally's War. 2004.

Ringo, John, and Michael Z. Williamson.

The Hero. 2004.

Scalzi, John.

Old Man's War. 2005.

Why is it that the Colonial Defense Forces set its minimum age requirement for recruits at age seventy-five?

Weber, David.

Honor Harrington series.

In much the same way that Horatio Hornblower rose through the ranks in the British navy, Honor Harrington rises through the ranks of the Royal Manticoran space navy.

On Basilisk Station. 1993.

The Honor of the Queen. 1993.

The Short Victorious War. 1994.

Field of Dishonor. 1994.

Flag in Exile. 1995.

Honor Among Enemies. 1997.

In Enemy Hands. 1997.

Echoes of Honor. 1998.

Ashes of Victory. 2000.

War of Honor. 2002.

At All Costs. 2005.

Students of Honor.

A follow-up to the Honor Harrington series. The next generation of officers in Star Kingdom.

The Shadow of Saganami. 2004.

Zahn, Timothy.

Cobra series.

Reissued in an omnibus edition as *The Cobra Trilogy* in 2004.

Cobra. 1985.
Cobra Strike. 1986.
Cobra Bargain. 1988.

Time Travel

Time travel is a fascinating concept, and one that provokes seemingly endless speculation on the part of SF writers, who have been writing on the theme since the nineteenth century (e.g., *The Time Machine* by H. G. Wells). Time travel can be into the past, into the future, or in both directions. In any case, the setting plays a dominant role and in this respect, it is similar to alternate and parallel worlds. The issue here usually comes down to how time travel and the ability to change the past or future affect the present.

Asimov, Isaac.

The End of Eternity. 1955. Reissued 2000. ★
Pebble in the Sky. 1950. Reissued 1990. ★

Bishop, Michael.

❧ *No Enemy But Time.* 1981. Reissued in 2000. Winner of the Nebula Award. ★

Card, Orson Scott.

Pastwatch: The Redemption of Christopher Columbus. 1996.

Crichton, Michael.

Timeline. 1999.

DeCamp, L. Sprague.

Lest Darkness Fall. 1949. Reissued 1996. ★

Leiber, Fritz.

❧ *The Big Time.* 1961. Reissued 2001. Winner of the Hugo Award. ★

Niffeneger, Audrey.

The Time Traveler's Wife. 2003.

A librarian travels back and forth in time with no control over when or where, meeting his wife when she was a young child

Norton, Andre.

Time Traders Series. ★

The Time Traders. 1958. Reissued with *Galactic Derelict* in 2000.

Galactic Derelict. 1959. Reissued with *The Time Traders* in 2000.

The Defiant Agents. 1962. Reissued with *Key Out of Time* in 2001.

Key Out of Time. 1963. Reissued with *The Defiant Agents* in 2001.

Firehand. 1994. Co-authored by P. M. Griffin.

Silverberg, Robert.

Letters from Atlantis. 1990.

Swanwick, Michael.

Bones of the Earth. 2002.

> Paleontologist Richard Leyster is exactly where he wants to be in life, when a stranger comes through his door at the Smithsonian and deposits a cooler containing a stegosaurus head on his desk, sweeping him up into a paleontological paradise of time travel and paradoxes upon paradoxes.

Vonnegut, Kurt.

Slaughterhouse Five, or, The Children's Crusade. **1968.** Reissued 2001. ★ 🎬

> Billy Pilgrim is unstuck in time. Sometimes he is in his future and sometimes in his past. Those who have read *The Time Traveler's Wife* by Niffeneger will see the parallels.

Wells, H. G.

The Time Machine. 1895. Reissued in omnibus with *The Invisible Man* (2003). ★ 🎬

Willis, Connie.

🎗 *Doomsday Book.* 1992.

> A scholar from the twenty-first century becomes trapped in the time of the plague when a computer operator miscalculates due to a future plague. Winner of the Hugo, Nebula, and Locus Awards.

🎗 *To Say Nothing of the Dog, Or, How We Found the Bishop's Birdstump at Last.* **1997.**

> When a time lagged historian from the future is sent to the Victorian era to escape Lady Schrapnell he finds love and a problem that could rend the fabric of time. Winner of the Hugo, Locus, and Awards.

Shared Worlds

Although more common in the fantasy genre, the shared world, a collaboration of authors either working together or building on the work of another author, also sometimes appears in SF. Many shared worlds are based on worlds and characters created for film or video games. As video games proliferate, we will undoubtedly see more shared world volumes. Obviously, the customs and laws, atmosphere, and inhabitants of the created universe of the shared world are the primary interests here. Often shared world stories are published in anthologies, which are edited by the originator of the world. Others are published as novels, sharing a setting or milieu with the forerunner. These books may be specially packaged and marketed by publishers.

Foundation

Second Foundation Trilogy.

World created by Isaac Asimov in which a psychohistorian, Hari Seldon, foresees the collapse of society and goes about making plans on how to shorten the Dark Ages he knows are to come. Three leading hard science fiction authors cover parts of Seldon's life not chronicled by Asimov.

Benford, Gregory. *Foundation's Fear.* 1997.
Bear, Greg. *Foundation and Chaos.* 1998.
Brin, David. *Foundation's Triumph.* 1999.

Marion Zimmer Bradley/Darkover

The Darkover series is set on a world settled ages ago by travelers from Earth. Some of the inhabitants have developed psionic powers called Laren. Bradley collaborated with several other authors on novels set on the world and edited several anthologies featuring stories set in Darkover. Anthologies edited by Bradley:

Towers of Darkover. 1993.
Red Sun of Darkover. 1987.
The Keeper's Price. 1980.
Snows of Darkover. 1994.
Renunciates of Darkover. 1991.
Leroni of Darkover. 1991.

Bradley, Marion Zimmer, and Mercedes Lackey.

Rediscovery: A Novel of Darkover. 1993.

Bradley, Marion Zimmer and Adrienne Martine-Barnes.

The Shadow Matrix. 1997.
Traitor's Sun. 1999.

Anne McCaffrey/Brainships

Space ships so complex that a human brain is required to run them are the premise of McCaffrey's *The Ship Who Sang,* in which the brain of severely handicapped Helva is implanted in a titanium scout ship, which then shares adventures with a human called a "Brawn," who accompanies her. McCaffrey collaborated with other authors to tell the stories of other Brainships (and even a city that used the same technology), each with a unique voice.

McCaffrey, Anne. *The Ship Who Sang.* 1969.
McCaffrey, Anne, and Mercedes Lackey. *The Ship Who Searched.* 1992.
McCaffrey, Anne, and S. M. Stirling. *The City Who Fought.* 1993.
McCaffrey, Anne, and Jody Lynn Nye. *The Ship Who Won.* 1994.
McCaffrey, Anne, and Margaret Ball. *Partnership.* 1996.
Nye, Jody Lynn. *The Ship Errant.* 1996.
Sterling, S. M. *The Ship Avenged.* 1997. The sequel to *The City Who Fought.*

George Lucas/Star Wars

Lucas's Star Wars films became a cultural icon for the late twentieth century. Readers couldn't get enough of Luke, Leia, and Han. The caliber of the authors writing in the Star Wars universe is stellar.

Anderson, Kevin J.
Darksaber. 1995.

Bear, Greg.
Star Wars: Rogue Planet. 2000.

Brooks, Terry.
Star Wars: Episode 1, the Phantom Menace. 1999.
> Anakin Skywalker, a nine-year-old slave on Tatooine, wins his freedom through utilization of his extraordinary talents and skills when two Jedi Knights stop on the planet for repairs.

Hambly, Barbara.
Children of the Jedi. 1995.
Planet of Twilight. 1997.

Rusch, Kristine Kathryn.
The New Rebellion. 1996.

Salvatore, R. A.
Vector Prime. 1999.

Stackpole, Michael.
I, Jedi. 1998.

Tyers, Kathy.
The Truce at Bakura. 1994.

Wolverton, Dave.
The Courtship of Princess Leia. 1994.

Zahn, Timothy.
Survivor's Quest. 2004.

Gene Roddenberry/Star Trek

It all started in 1966, with Gene Roddenberry's original television series featuring the adventures of Captain Kirk, Spock, Dr. McCoy, Scotty, Lt. Uhura, and others aboard the starship *Enterprise*. Five television series and nine movies later, Star Trek is still alive and well, not only in the hearts of dedicated Trekkers (sometimes to their chagrin called Trekkies), but in the universal consciousness of the world. The advent of e-books has been a real boon for fans of written Star Trek stories—virtually all titles are in e-print! Simon and Schuster has a comprehensive Web site for their Star Trek books at http://www.simonsays.com/content/index.cfm?sid=44 (accessed February 23, 2005). Currently they have several series going:

Star Trek: Deep Space Nine.

Star Trek: Enterprise.
Star Trek: New Frontier.
Star Trek: The Next Generation.
Star Trek: The Original Series.
Star Trek: Starfleet Corps of Engineers.
Star Trek: Stargazer.
Star Trek: Voyager.

Techno SF

Technology has always been a major theme in SF. Some of the earliest SF titles revolved around the technology of space and travel. Others, such as John Brunner's classic *Shockwave Rider* (1975), Piers Anthony's *Juxtaposition* (1982), and Neal Stephenson's *Snow Crash* (1992) focused on the power of computers. Today's popular science fiction more commonly features technology about artificial beings, artificial intelligence, nanotechnology, virtual reality, and beyond. Much of the hard SF published appears in this category, with stricter adherence to principles of physical and biological science. Scientific extrapolation based on theories not yet proven is often explored, leaving one to wonder, what technologies will tomorrow's SF explore?

High Tech

Super-sophisticated technology is the focus in the following titles. In the 1980s and 1990s high tech was most visible in cyberpunk. Now the ideas presented go far beyond what computers and technology can do today, often combining elements of artificial intelligence, self-replicating machines, and virtual reality.

Banks, Iain.

Excession. 1996. (The Culture series).

When an ancient sun disappears, then suddenly reappears in space, Diplomat Byr Genar-Hofoen is sent to investigate.

Clarke, Arthur C.

🎗 *The Fountains of Paradise.* 1979. Reissued 2001. ★

Clarke's idea of an elevator that reaches 24,000 miles into space has, like Asimov's Laws of Robotics, become part of the fabric of the genre. Winner of the Hugo and Nebula Awards.

Gibson, William.

Neuromancer trilogy.

🎗 *Neuromancer.* 1984. Reissued 2004. ★

Gibson's tale of computer cowboy Case's adventures in cyberspace is considered the novel that began the cyberpunk movement. Winner of the Hugo, Nebula, and Philip K. Dick Awards.

Count Zero. 1986.

Mona Lisa Overdrive. 1988.

Ryman, Geoff.

> *Air: Or, Have Not Have.* 2004.
>
>> A new direct-into-the-mind communication system using quantum technology is tested on villagers in a remote part of Karzistan and has a bizarre effect on a bright but illiterate young woman.

Stephenson, Neal.

> ♟ *The Diamond Age, or, a Young Lady's Illustrated Primer.* 1995. Reissued 2000.
>
>> A copy of an interactive book intended for a wealthy young neo-Victorian girl falls into the hands of a poor girl, molding her into a brilliant revolutionary. Winner of the Hugo and Locus Awards.

Robots, Cyborgs, Androids

Mary Shelley's *Frankenstein,* considered by many to be the first science fiction novel, with its monster put together from various and sundry parts and reanimated by a medical doctor, is a precursor of this subgenre.

There are three major types of artificial beings. A *robot* is a machine, usually with a somewhat human form but purely mechanical. An *android* is an artificial human, organic in composition. And a *cyborg* is a human altered with artificial parts to perform certain functions or modified to exist in conditions inimical to human life.

Asaro, Catherine.

> *The Phoenix Code.* **2000.**
>
>> Robotics expert Megan O'Flannery has her hands full with the self-aware android Aris.

Asimov, Isaac.

> *I, Robot.* 1950. Reissued 2004. ★ 🎬
>
>> Asimov's famous three laws of robotics and robots powered by positronic brains were introduced in this classic short story collection. The 2004 film bears little resemblance to the book.
>
> *The Rest of the Robots.* 1964. ★
>
>> This vintage collection is the second volume, after *I, Robot*, of Asimov's timeless robot stories.
>
> *Robot Dreams.* 1986. Reissued 2004. ★
>
> *The Complete Robot.* 1982. Reissued 1995. ★
>
>> All of Asimov's robot stories, collected in one volume.

Baker, Kage.

> **The Company series.**
>
>> Mendoza, an immortal cyborg botanist, falls in love with the same man in three different centuries.
>
> *In the Garden of Iden.* 1998.
> *Sky Coyote.* 1999.
> *Life of the World to Come.* 2004.

Dick, Philip K.
Do Androids Dream of Electric Sheep? 1968. Reissued 1996. ★ ▰ *Blade Runner*

Pohl, Frederik.
🎗 *Man Plus.* 1975. Reissued 2004. ★
Roger Torraway is adapted to work on Mars. Winner of the Nebula Award.

Simak, Clifford D.
City. 1952. Reissued 2004. ★
Dogs who pass their stories down through the generations are aided by robots.

Sterling, Bruce.
Schismatrix Plus. 1996.
Shapers go into space with genetic enhancements, while Mechanists prefer prosthetics.

Williamson, Jack.
The Humanoids. 1949. Reissued 1996.
Robots were created to serve people, but their care of people creates more problems than they solved.

Nanotechnology

Although nanotechnology has a specific definition pertaining to engineering on the atomic level (atomic constructs are measured in nanometers), it is often used in science fiction to describe situations simply involving extreme miniaturization of technology.

Bova, Ben.
<u>Moonbase Saga.</u>
Moonrise. 1996.
Moonwar. 1997.

Broderick, Damien.
Transcension. 2002.

Crichton, Michael.
Prey. 2002.
A swarm of microscopic machines escapes from the science lab, seemingly intent on killing the scientists who created them.

Goonan, Kathleen Ann.
<u>Nanotechnology Quartet.</u>
Nanotech plagues have decimated the country and turned it into a very different kind of place.

Queen City Jazz. 1994.
Mississippi Blues. 1997.
Crescent City Rhapsody. 2000.
Light Music. 2002.

Hogan, James P.

   Bug Park. 1997.

> Could the new technology that allows people to be linked into ultra-miniaturized robots for recreational adventures be enough to kill for?

McCarthy, Wil.

   Bloom. 1998.

> Earth was evacuated when the atom-sized, all-devouring Mycora showed up.

Ore, Rebecca.

   Gaia's Toys. 1995.

Schroeder, Karl.

   Permanence. 2002.

   Ventus. 2000.

> On the planet Ventus, children learn that there are three life forms: flora, fauna, and mecha. The omnipresent nanotechnology prevents the inhabitants from developing technology beyond a medieval level.

Steele, Allen M.

   A King of Infinite Space. 1997.

Virtual Reality

Virtual reality SF involves a computer-generated world in which people interact with each other and with computer-created constructs. It has elements of both cyberpunk and alternate worlds and often features game playing.

Asaro, Catherine.

   The Veiled Web. 1999.

> Lucia del Mar, adjusting to life in Rashid al-Jazari's harem, befriends an AI that Rashid created. She also tries on a virtual reality suit that infuses the body of the wearer with nanotechnology that allows touch, smell, and taste to manifest.

Gibson, William.

   Idoru. 1996.

McCarthy, Wil.

   Murder in the Solid State. 1996.

> Young scientist David Sanger ventures into virtual reality to solve the murder of which he was accused.

The Future Is Bleak

Whether an apocalyptic event strikes in the form of a nuclear bomb or comets, asteroids, or unknown life forms from space, or because of various events, including the erosion of the environment, the dwindling of resources, and the rise of strange and tremendously resistant diseases that contribute to a slow disintegration and downward spiral, these novels present a pessimistic view of the future. The defining characteristic of the titles in this category is the setting. Sometimes the natural world, which has been tampered with, becomes hazardous and threatens life as we know it. At other times, political and social changes create a different type of disaster. The pacing can be agonizingly slow or heart-stoppingly fast.

Barnes, John.

> *Mother of Storms.* 1994.
>> A nuclear blast unleashes a plague of killer hurricanes.

Benson, Ann.

> *The Plague Tales.* 1997.
>> A parallel tale about the bubonic plague, in fourteenth- and twenty-first-century England.

Brin, David.

> *The Postman.* 1985. Reissued 1997.

Brunner, John.

> *The Sheep Look Up.* 1972. Reissued 2002. ★
>> Pollution spells doom for the world.

>  *Stand on Zanzibar.* 1968. Reissued 2003. ★
>> Overpopulation spells disaster for the world as we know it. Winner of the Hugo Award.

Butler, Octavia E.

> <u>Xenogenesis trilogy.</u>
>> *Dawn.* 1987.
>> *Adulthood Rites.* 1988.
>> *Imago.* 1989.
>> *Lilith's Brood.* 2000. A one-volume compilation of all three novels in the <u>Xenogenesis trilogy</u>.

Crichton, Michael.

> *Andromeda Strain.* 1969. Reissued 2003. ★
>> A deadly microbe returns from space on a scientific probe.

DuBois, Brendan.

> *Resurrection Day.* 1999.

Frank, Pat.

> *Alas, Babylon.* 1959. Reissued 2005. ★

Harrison, Harry.

> *Make Room! Make Room!* 1966. *Soylent Green*
>> Overpopulation results in a shortage of food and other resources.

Herzog, Arthur.

> *The Swarm.* 1974. Reissued 2002.

Jensen, Jane.

Millennium Rising. 1999. Reissued as *Judgment Day.*

An international conspiracy rigs events to make it look like the end of the world is approaching, but their machinations trigger actual cataclysmic events.

Kress, Nancy.

Nothing Human. 2003.

LaHaye, Tim, and Jerry B. Jenkins.

Left Behind Series.

The last days of Earth have arrived, the Rapture, told from the evangelical Christian point of view. Titles are listed in the "Christian Fiction" chapter (chapter 13).

Leiber, Fritz.

🎖 *The Wanderer.* 1965. Reissued 2001. Winner of the Hugo Award. ★

McDevitt, Jack.

Moonfall. 1998.

A comet is headed straight for the moon.

Niven, Larry, and Jerry Pournelle.

Lucifer's Hammer. 1977. Reissued 1998. ★

When a gigantic comet slammed into the earth, it was merely the first of a series of disasters.

Pellegrino, Charles R.

Dust. 1998.

Mass extinctions of insects are the beginning of the end.

Robinson, Kim Stanley.

Forty Signs of Rain. 2004.

Global warming is on the verge of wreaking havoc on the world.

Sterling, Bruce.

Heavy Weather. 1994.

Tornadoes and typhoons caused by the greenhouse effect are wreaking havoc with the environment.

Wilhelm, Kate.

Where Late the Sweet Birds Sang. 1976. Reissued 1998. ★

Pollution and disease breed sterility. Winner of the Hugo and Locus Awards.

Zelazny, Roger.

Damnation Alley. 1969. Reissued 2004. 🎬

Dystopias and Utopias

Sometimes the very worst of worlds are those that were created by those who thought they were creating perfection. See also the following section on "Social Structures" for more nightmarish futures.

Bradbury, Ray.

Fahrenheit 451. 1953. Reissued 2005. ★

A future without books and reading.

Burgess, Anthony.

A Clockwork Orange. 1962. Reissued 2000. ★ ▬

Butler, Octavia E.

Earthseed Series.

Parable of the Sower. 1993. Reissued 2000.

 Parable of the Talents. 1998. Winner of the Nebula Award.

Hopkinson, Nalo.

Brown Girl in the Ring. 1998.

Huxley, Aldous.

Brave New World. 1932. Reissued 1998. ★ ▬

McIntyre, Vonda.

🎗 *Dreamsnake.* 1978. Audio version released 1994. ★

In a postapocalyptic world a young healer uses poisonous snakes to heal. Winner of the Hugo, Nebula, and Locus Awards.

Reed, Kit.

Thinner Than Thou. 2004.

A world in which thinness has become a religion, and a religious order takes care of those with eating disorders.

Silverberg, Robert.

The Alien Years. 1998.

Social Structures

Societal evolution and change has vast implications for individual lives. Social interactions between people, whether based on a biological, political, or religious basis, have been a suitable subject for examination in science fiction since the New Wave movement of the 1960s.

Biological

Social structures can be influenced by biology, whether it is an alien race that switches genders over time, or a world that necessitates cannibalism for humans who have made their lives in a place devoid of some necessary nutrients.

Brin, David.

Glory Season. 1993.

On a world peopled by cloned women, the social hierarchy depends on the size and wealth of ones clone clan, but vars, those born of a sexual union, are still necessary for genetic diversity in the event of disaster.

Kingsbury, Donald.

Courtship Rite. 1982. ★

The harshness of a world where cannibalism is essential also leads to a unique form of marriage among six individuals.

Le Guin, Ursula K.

The Left Hand of Darkness. 1969. Reissued 1994. ★

Gethenians are genderless except for the time each month when they can manifest one gender or the other. Winner of the Hugo and Nebula Awards.

Religious

Spiritual beliefs, moral codes, and religious fervor have tremendous impact on society and its inhabitants. Science fiction, with its ethic of looking at hard questions in an open way, finds the effects of religion on social structures a fertile area.

Atwood, Margaret.

Handmaid's Tale. 1985. 📖

Blish, James.

🎗 *A Case of Conscience.* 1958. Reissued 2000. ★

A priest visiting an alien world questions how a society can seem so perfect and have no concept of sin or God. Winner of the Hugo Award.

Heinlein, Robert A.

🎗 *Stranger in a Strange Land.* 1961. Reissued 1991. ★

Valentine Michael Smith, the son of two members of a doomed Mars expedition, is brought to Earth, where he starts a religion. Winner of the Hugo Award.

Herbert, Frank.

Dune Chronicles.

This popular series was later extended by Herbert's son, Brian Herbert, and Kevin J. Anderson, with an emphasis on the space opera aspects of the original title. When the Atreides family is attacked by the Harkonens, Paul and his mother flee to the desert, where they join the Fremen. When Paul leads them to take back their planet, he becomes the center of a new religion.

🎗 *Dune.* 1965. Winner of the Hugo and Nebula Awards. ★ 🎬
Dune Messiah. 1969. Reissued 1994.
Children of Dune. 1976. Reissued 1991.
God Emperor of Dune. 1981. Reissued 1991.
Heretics of Dune. 1984. Reissued 1996.
Chapter House Dune. 1985. Reissued 1996.

Lewis, C. S.

Perelandra Trilogy. ★

Linguist Dr. Elwin Ransom is abducted by aliens and examines the conflicts between science and ethics.

Out of the Silent Planet. 1943. Reissued 1996.

Perelandra. 1943. Reissued 1996.

That Hideous Strength. 1945. Reissued 1996.

Marley, Louise.

The Terrorists of Irustan. 1999.

On the planet Irustan, women's roles are clearly delineated by religion.

Russell, Mary Doria.

Children of God. 1998.

🎗 *The Sparrow.* 1996. Winner of the James Tiptree Jr. Award.

Sawyer, Robert J.

Calculating God. 2000.

An alien paleontologist comes to Earth looking for information on extinction events because "the primary goal of modern science is to discover why God has behaved as he has and to determine his methods."

Shinn, Sharon.

Samaria series.

On the planet Samaria the population depends on genetically engineered angels to intercede with the god Jovah to mitigate the violent weather. Listed in chronological series order.

Angelica. 2003.

The Archangel. 1996.

Angel Seeker. 2004.

Jovah's Angel. 1997.

The Alleluia Files. 1998.

Simmons, Dan.

Hyperion series.

A party of pilgrims sets out to find the Shrike, who many believe is a god.

🎗 *Hyperion.* 1989. Winner of the Hugo Award.

The Fall of Hyperion. 1990.

Endymion. 1996.

The Rise of Endymion. 1997.

Stewart, Ian, and Jack Cohen.

Heaven. **2004.**

The Church of Cosmic Unity is full of violent missionary zeal.

Zelazny, Roger.

🎗 *Lord of Light.* **1967.** Reissued 2004.

A band of men who control the technology on a colony planet have made themselves virtually immortal and expect to be treated like Hindu gods. Winner of the Hugo Award.

Alternate and Parallel Worlds

One question that is asked over and over again in science fiction is "what if?" What if every decision that dictates a different outcome creates a new world where the other path is taken? In this scenario the number of worlds grows exponentially. What if we could travel back and forth between these worlds? Novels set in parallel worlds look at that question. If the change happened sometime in the past, the alternate world would end up with a different history than ours. Alternate history explores what may have happened through time in a world that followed a different path than ours.

Parallel Worlds

Parallel earths and parallel universes are worlds that exist simultaneously with our Earth, conceived, perhaps, along a spatial fourth dimension. (In some worlds of fantasy, characters can be transported out of one parallel universe and into another.) This theme has been used by many science fiction authors in addition to those in the following list, as well as by authors of the mainstream novel (e.g., Vladimir Nabokov).

Hopkinson, Nalo.

Midnight Robber. 2000.

> When Tan Tan's father kills someone in a duel, they flee their high-tech planet for its alternate universe twin, where Tan Tan feels she is being taken over by the mythical Robber Queen.

Reed, Robert.

Cosmic Event Agency series.

> Microscopic wormholes connect billions of worlds, but when anyone travels through, he or she is reborn into the body of a member of the dominant species.

Beyond the Veil of Stars. 1994.

Beneath the Gated Sky. 1997.

Sawyer, Robert. J.

Neanderthal Parallax.

> Two sets of scientists working in two parallel worlds at the same time on completely different projects have created a temporary passage. In the world Ponter Boddit is from, Neanderthals are the dominant species and have pretty much bred criminal tendencies out of their gene pool. Sawyer's exquisite world building creates a world with complex familial relationships and culture.

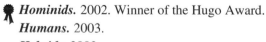 *Hominids.* 2002. Winner of the Hugo Award.
Humans. 2003.
Hybrids. 2003.

Alternate History

Alternate history tells the stories of what could have happened if some event in history had diverged from the path we know and as a result caused that time's future to experience events that differ from the events we know.

Birmingham, John.

<u>**Axis of Time Trilogy.**</u>

In 2021 a wormhole experiment takes several ships on a UN mission and flings them backward through time to World War II, where mores about race and gender are very different.

Weapons of Choice. 2004.

Dick, Philip K.

The Man in the High Castle. 1962. Reissued 1992. Winner of the Hugo Award. ★

DuBois, Brendan.

Resurrection Day. 1999.

Gingrich, Newt, and William R. Forstchen.

Grant Comes East. 2004.

Turtledove, Harry.

The Guns of the South: A Novel of the Civil War. 1992.

<u>**The Great War.**</u>

The Great War: American Front. 1998.

The Great War: Walk in Hell. 1999.

The Great War: Breakthroughs. 2000.

<u>**Worldwar series.**</u>

World War II is interrupted by a fleet of lizard-like beings from outer space.

Worldwar: In the Balance: The Alternate History of Alien Invasion. 1994.

Worldwar: Tilting the Balance. 1995.

Worldwar: Upsetting the Balance. 1996.

Worldwar: Striking the Balance. 1996.

Wilson, Robert Charles.

Darwinia. 1998.

Earth's Children

The children of Earth in future generations may or may not remember their roots, but they are our descendants no matter what new abilities they have acquired or how they have been transformed through science. Beings in these stories are recognizable as humans, but with significant differences.

Bioengineering

The dynamic field of bioengineering is a particularly rich field for SF writers to explore. DNA, genetics, cloning, mapping the human genome, and anything else one may never have imagined that take biology to another level are fodder for this type of science fiction. Sometimes the bioengineering imbues the character with extended abilities, while at other times tampering with the genome creates disaster.

Atwood, Margaret.

Oryx and Crake. 2003.

A near-future world turned into a bio-wasteland.

Budz, Mark.

<u>Biopunk series.</u>

After an ecocaust has decimated the world as we know it, some people are selected to colonize an asteroid.

Clade. 2003.
Crache. 2004.

Bujold, Lois McMaster.

Falling Free. 1988. Reissued 2004.

To work in a gravity-free environment, Quaddies are bioengineered with four arms and no legs, which works perfectly until artificial gravity is invented. Winner of the Nebula Award.

Cannell, Stephen J.

Runaway Heart. 2003.

Private Investigator Jack Wirta, following up leads on some genetically modified corn that will kill off butterflies, discovers a government project to engineer a creature to replace combat troops.

Cook, Robin.

Chromosome 6. 1997.

Kress, Nancy.

Nothing Human. 2003.

With humanity dying off, aliens genetically alter a group of fourteen year olds and take them onto their ship, until the teens rebel.

Lethem, Jonathan.

Gun, with Occasional Music. 1994.

A private investigator in a world where bioengineering runs rampant deals with a trigger-happy kangaroo and other oddities.

McAuley, Paul.

White Devils. 2004.

Genetic engineering gone hideously wrong in a near future devastated by disease.

Mitchell, Syne.

The Changeling Plague. 2003.

Looking for a cure for his cystic fibrosis, a wealthy patient turns to an in illegal viral treatment that infects everyone he encounters.

Moon, Elizabeth.

The Speed of Dark. 2003.

Lou, a bioinformatics specialist who has a gift for pattern analysis and is autistic, does not like that his employer wants all autistic employees to undergo an experimental process that will make them "normal." Winner of the Nebula Award.

Nissenson, Hugh.

The Song of the Earth. 2001.

Born in 2037, Johnny Baker was meant to be an artist from the very beginning, which just happened to be in a test tube.

Patterson, James.

Flying Children series.

The subjects of a top secret government project are children who have been genetically engineered to fly.

When the Wind Blows. 1999.
The Lake House. 2003.
Maximum Ride. 2005.

A stand-alone novel published for young adults, from the children's point of view.

Rucker, Rudy.

Frek and the Elixir. 2004.

This wild and crazy story is set a thousand years in the future, when bioengineering is everything. Biodiversity is way down because of the biosphere collapse, but it doesn't really matter because bioengineering can make just about anything. Aliens, cartoons that jump off the screen, and strange little people are just a fraction of the inventiveness in this bizarre (in a really good way) book.

Scarborough, Elizabeth Ann.

Cleopatra series.

A new technology allows DNA from one person, even someone dead for centuries, to be implanted in another, allowing the subject access to the personality and thoughts of the donor.

Channeling Cleopatra. 2002.
Cleopatra 7.2. 2004.

Sterling, Bruce.

Distraction. 1998.

Oscar Valparaiso is a political spin doctor in a United States gone, bad but he is also the result of illegal Columbian bioengineering.

Wells, H. G.

The Island of Dr. Moreau. 1896. ★

Wilson, F. Paul.

Sims. 2003.

There is a new kind of slavery in the world, sims, a combination of humans and chimpanzees created by the SimGen corporation and bred specifically for that purpose.

Zettel, Sarah.

Kingdom of Cages. 2001.

The planet Pandora is the only one where humans aren't dying off, and the secret may turn up in the genes of Chena Trust.

Psionic Powers

The powers of precognition, telepathy, clairvoyance, telekinesis, and teleportation displayed by characters in science fiction make current research in parapsychology seem crude. Science fiction authors invented the term *psionics* (psychic electronics) to describe these powers of the mind.

Barnes, John.

Candle. 2000.

A telepathic linkage of humankind, despite creating peace, may be actually controlling those it is supposed to be serving.

Clough, Brenda W.

Barbarossa series.

Rob Lewis has the ability to control minds and make people do what he wants them to do.

How Like a God. 1997.
Doors of Death and Life. 2000.

Foster, Alan Dean.

Pip and Flinx Adventures.

Flinx, a former street urchin, has a flying snake and telepathic abilities.

The Tar-Aiym Krang. 1972.
Bloodhype. 1973.
The End of the Matter. 1977.
Orphan Star. 1977. Reissued 2003.
For Love of Mother Not. 1983.
Flinx in Flux. 1988.
Mid-Flinx. 1995.
Reunion. 2001.
Flinx's Folly. 2003.
Sliding Scales. 2004.

Gould, Steven.

Davy Rice Duology.

Davy Rice can teleport away from danger or to wherever he wants to go.

Jumper. 1992. Reissued 2002.
Reflex. 2004.

Lethem, Jonathan.

Girl in Landscape. 1998.

Thirteen-year-old Pella Marsh moves with her family to a ruined planet, where she is able to telepathically move into the bodies of local indigenous life forms, called household deer, and wander at will.

McCaffrey, Anne.

Dragonriders of Pern series.

After Pern was colonized, the settlers discovered that, because of irregular orbits, a neighboring planet periodically came close to Pern, and "Thread," a filament that would fly from the other planet, would burn through anything organic. Telepathic flame-throwing dragons were bred to fight the "Thread."

Dragonflight. 1968.
Dragonquest. 1968.
The White Dragon. 1978.
Moreta, Dragonlady of Pern. 1983.
Dragonsdawn. 1988.

The Renegades of Pern. 1989.
All the Weyrs of Pern. 1991.
The Chronicles of Pern: First Fall. 1993.
The Dolphins of Pern. 1994.
Dragonseye. 1996.

The Girl Who Heard Dragons. 1985.
Masterharper of Pern. 1998.

McCaffrey, Anne, and Todd McCaffrey.

Dragon's Kin. 2003.

McCaffrey, Todd.

Dragonsblood. 2005.

Harper Hall Trilogy.

McCaffrey also wrote this trilogy for teenagers, set on Pern.

Tower and the Hive series.

Primes use their psi-abilities to teleport people and cargo through space.

The Rowan. 1990.

Damia. 1992.
Damia's Children. 1992.
Lyon's Pride. 1994.
The Tower and the Hive. 1999.

Murphy, Pat.

The Falling Woman. 1987. Reissued 1993.

An archeologist who can see into the past falls into the world of ancient Mayan magic. Winner of the Nebula Award.

Schmitz, James H.

The Witches of Karres. 1966. Reissued 2004.

A captain rescues three little girls, buying them out of slavery, and while trying to take them to their home planet, he discovers that they have powerful psionic powers.

The Complete Federation of the Hub.

Telzey Amberdon is not only a talented telepath, she is also a xenotelepath, able to communicate with aliens.

Telzey Amberdon. 2000. Includes the novels *The Universe Against Her* (1964) and *The Lion Game* (1973).

T'NT Telzey & Trigger. 2000.

Stories featuring Telzey Amberdon and Trigger Argee.

Trigger and Friends. 2001.

A new collection of classic Trigger Argee stories.

The Hub: Dangerous Territory. 2001.

van Vogt, A. E.

Slan. 1946. Reissued 1998. ★

A mutant minority develops psionic abilities, enhanced bodies, and super intelligence, but being found a slan is a death sentence.

Aliens

One of the richest areas in science fiction, and a type that usually appears in no other genre, is the type featuring aliens. "First contact" is a situation ripe with possibilities for drama. Exactly what alien life looks like is a question often probed, along with how humans will respond to and interact with aliens, and whether aliens pose a threat to humankind or are benevolent.

Anderson, Poul.

Starfarers. 1999.

Brin, David.

Uplift Storm Trilogy.

Brightness Reef. 1995.

Infinity's Shore. 1996.

Heaven's Reach. 1998.

Cherryh, C. J.

Cherryh is one of today's most popular science fiction/fantasy authors. She is renowned for her ability to create truly alien aliens.

Faded Sun Trilogy. Reissued in Omnibus edition, 2000.

The remaining humanoid Mri on Kesrith lose their home when the Regul surrender the planet to the humans.

Kesrith. 1978.

Shon'jir. 1978.

Kutath. 1979.

Foreigner Series.

Foreigner: A Novel of First Contact. 1994.

Invader. 1995.

Inheritor. 1996.
Precursor. 1999.
Defender. 2001.
Explorer. 2002.
Destroyer. 2005.

Clarke, Arthur C.

Childhood's End. 1953. Reissued 2001. ★

Haldeman, Joe.

Camouflage. 2004.

Heinlein, Robert A.

The Star Beast. 1954. Reissued 1987.

Lummox, a family pet, is huge, voracious, and has an unearthly ancestry.

Kress, Nancy.

Cosmic Crossfire series.

With Earth dying, human colonists go to a distant planet, where they find primitive humanoid aliens who do not seem to be indigenous to the planet. The colonists end up being drawn into a war between alien species.

Crossfire. 2003.
Crucible. 2004.

Probability series.

Literary hard science fiction that revolves around a war between humans and an alien race.

Probability Moon. 2000.
Probability Sun. 2001.
Probability Space. 2002.

Lichtenberg, Jacqueline.

Alien Vampire series.

Those of My Blood. 1988. Reissued 2003.
Dreamspy. 1989. Reissued 2004.

Like, Russel.

After the Blue. 1998.

After aliens unwittingly bring a devastating plague to New Jersey, they try to rectify the wrong, in this hilarious parody.

McCaffrey, Anne.

Freedom Trilogy.

Freedom's Landing. 1995.
Freedom's Choice. 1997.
Freedom's Challenge. 1998.

McCaffrey, Anne, Elizabeth Ann Scarborough, and Margaret Ball.

   <u>**Acorna Series.**</u>

   McCaffrey, Anne, and Margaret Ball.

   Acorna: The Unicorn Girl. 1997.

   Acorna's Quest. 1998.

   McCaffrey, Anne and Elizabeth Ann Scarborough.

   Acorna's People. 1999.

   Acorna's World. 2000.

   Acorna's Search. 2001.

   Acorna's Rebels. 2003.

   Acorna's Triumph. 2004.

Moon, Elizabeth.

   Remnant Population. 1996.

Niven, Larry, and Jerry Pournelle.

   Footfall. 1985. Reissued 1997.

      Aliens attack Earth.

Pohl, Frederik.

   <u>**Heechee Saga.**</u> ★

      Gateway. 1977. Winner of the Hugo, Nebula, and Locus Awards.
      Beyond the Blue Event Horizon. 1980.
      Heechee Rendezvous. 1984.
      The Annals of the Heechee. 1987.
      The Gateway Trip. 1990.
      The Boy Who Would Live Forever: A Novel of Gateway. 2004.

Sawyer, Robert J.

   Calculating God. 2000.

   Factoring Humanity. 1998.

   Illegal Alien. 1997.

   Starplex. 1996.

Silverberg, Robert.

   The Alien Years. 1998.

   The Longest Way Home. 2002.

   A Time of Changes. 1971. Winner of the Nebula Award.

Simak, Clifford D.

   Way Station. 1963. Reissued 2004. ★

      Enoch Wallace, a hermit, hides a galactic transfer station in his home that is a stopping-off
      place for traveling aliens. Winner of the Hugo Award.

Slonczewski, Joan.

The Children Star. 1998.

On Prokaryon, a planet heavily laced with arsenic, a small religious order of both humans and AIs strives to create a colony with orphaned children rescued from a plague-ridden planet. The highly structured ecosystem indicates that there must be intelligent life on the planet, but what could it be? The aliens not only have a totally different biological basis than humans, with triple-strand DNA, but live at a totally different pace.

Tepper, Sheri S.

The Companions. 2003.

Jewel manages to take several condemned dogs to the planet Moss with her, where they help unravel a mystery discovered by her late mother on the planet Mars that indicates humans are not the only sentient species with a connection to dogs.

Traviss, Karen.

City of Pearl. 2004.

Cavanagh's Star is claimed by three different alien societies.

Vinge, Vernor.

 A Deepness in the Sky. 1999. Winner of the Hugo Award.

 ***A Fire Upon the Deep.*** 1991. ★

The Blight, a mind-destroying virus, is spreading throughout the universe. When an alien race blames humanity for the virus and follows through with an attack, Pham Numan manages to escape and sets out to find two young children who may hold the key to stopping the Blight before it's too late. Winner of the Hugo Award.

Wells, H. G.

The War of the Worlds. 1898. ★ 🎬

White, James.

Sector General series.

A hospital station in space takes care of a huge diversity of aliens.

Hospital Station. 1962.
Star Surgeon. 1963.
Major Operation. 1971.
Ambulance Ship. 1979.
Sector General. 1983.
Star Healer. 1985.
Code Blue: Emergency. 1987.
The Genocidal Healer. 1992.
The Galactic Gourmet. 1996.
Final Diagnosis. 1997.
Mind Changer. 1998.
Double Contact. 1999.

Genreblending

Genreblending between science fiction and other genres continues to grow. There have always been combinations putting science fiction and fantasy together. Mystery in a science fiction setting is also not new. The most remarkable trend in genreblending may be science fiction blended with romance.

Romantic Science Fiction

The trend toward genreblending marries SF and romance. The future offers an exciting backdrop to romance; romantic elements add a new dimension of excitement to SF. Although throughout the history of SF, action and adventure focusing on male heroes have prevailed, the rise of female authors and characters in the genre has in recent years added a new emphasis on relationships. Romances that are most clearly science fiction are the romances referred to as "futuristics" by romance readers. The proportions of science and romance vary greatly from title to title, but publishers in both genres seem eager to promote the blend. Generally, the characters involved are of human ancestry. Romance is also one of the standard elements in space opera; and readers who enjoy romantic SF may find additional titles in that section to enjoy.

Asaro, Catherine.

> *The Phoenix Code.* 2000.
>
> *Sunrise Alley.* 2004.

Bujold, Lois McMaster.

> **Vorkosigan Saga.**
>
> Although the entire series has a good deal of romance, the two listed here in particular have plenty to satisfy even romance fans. They are published as science fiction.
>
> *Shards of Honor.* 1986.
>
> 🏵 *A Civil Campaign.* 1999. Winner of the Sapphire Award.

Lee, Sharon, and Steve Miller.

> **Agent of Change Sequence.**
>
> Also referred to as the <u>Liaden Universe</u>, this space opera has a strong romantic element. The books are published as science fiction.
>
> *Conflict of Honors.* 1988. Reissued 2002.
>
> *Agent of Change.* 1988. Reissued 2002.
>
> *Carpe Diem.* 1989. Reissued 2003.
>
> *Plan B.* 1999. Reissued 2003.
>
> *Pilots Choice.* 2001. This omnibus edition of *Local Custom* and *Scout's Progress* is a prequel to *Agent of Change.*
>
> *I Dare.* 2002. Reissued 2003.

Maverick, Liz.

> *The Shadow Runners: 2176.* 2004.
>
> > The dystopian future and nonstop action calls to mind classic adventure movies like *Mad Max* and *Tank Girl*. Published as romance.

O'Shea, Patti.

The Power of Two: 2176. 2004. Published as romance.

Owens, Robin D.

Celta Series.

The planet Celta was settled by Wiccans with psionic powers. The world building in this series makes Celta come alive in much the same way Pern, Darkover, and Witch World have become part of the science fiction fabric. Published as romance.

Heart Mate. 2002.

Heart Thief. 2003.

Heart Duel. 2004.

Heart Choice. 2005.

Tyers, Kathy.

Firebird Trilogy. (Christian).

Firebird. 1987. Reissued 1999.

Fusion Fire. 2000.

Crown of Fire. 2000.

Science Fiction Mysteries

The combination of science fiction and mystery is an established tradition that produces galactic policemen and private eyes—human, alien, and mechanical. Detection became popular in science fiction novels in the 1950s following Clements's 1949 novel *Needle*, in which an alien detective comes to Earth and must inhabit a human body to catch a malign entity who has taken over the body of a young boy's father.

Asimov, Isaac.

Elijah Baley & R. Daneel Olivaw series.

This classic series pairs a robot and human detective.

The Caves of Steel. 1954. Reissued 1991.

The Naked Sun. 1957. Reissued 1991.

The Robots of Dawn. 1983. Reissued 1994.

Bester, Alfred.

🎗 *The Demolished Man.* 1953. Reissued 1996.

The very first Hugo award winner features Lincoln Powell, a telepathic cop-hunting a man who will murder to avoid "psychic demolition." Winner of the Hugo Award.

Carroll, Jerry Jay.

Inhuman Beings. 1998.

A private detective is offered a small fortune by a celebrity psychic to find the aliens she is sure exist on Earth.

Dietz, William C.

Sam McCade series.

Wise-cracking, cigar-chomping Sam McCade is an interstellar bounty hunter with a spaceship called *Pegasus.*

Galactic Bounty. 1986. Reissued 2004. Originally titled *War World.*

Imperial Bounty. 1988. Reissued 2004.

Alien Bounty. 1990. Reissued 2005.

McCade's Bounty. 1990. Reissued 2005.

Gould, Steven.

Blind Waves. 2000.

Patricia Beeman, a busy underwater salvage operator, stumbles across a horrifying sight that sends her into hiding as she tries to evade the powerful INS while seeking answers to the mystery she found at the bottom of the ocean, in a world menaced by rising sea levels.

Gresh, Lois H., and Robert Weinberg.

The Termination Node. 1999.

If she has any hope of surviving, a hacker on the run from both authorities and assassins must discover what is was she triggered.

Hamilton, Peter F.

Greg Mandel series.

Featuring a biologically enhanced psychic detective.

Mindstar Rising. 1993. Reissued 1997.

A Quantum Murder. 1994. Reissued 1998.

The Nano Flower. 1995. Reissued 1999.

McDevitt, Jack.

Alex Benedict and Chase Kolpath series.

In the distant future, an adventurous antiquarian and his beautiful brilliant assistant fall into mysteries.

A Talent for War. 1988. Reissued 2004.

When his archaeologist uncle dies suddenly, Alex is sucked into a mystery involving a long-dead war hero.

Polaris. 2004.

Sixty years after the crew of the *Polaris* disappeared B la the *Marie Celeste*, their personal belongings start turning up and being sold for profit.

Seeker. 2005.

Robb, J. D. (pseudonym of romance writer, Nora Roberts).

Eve Dallas series.

Set in the twenty-first century. The star of this series is supercop Eve Dallas, a New York police lieutenant who is married to a billionaire.

Naked in Death. 1995.

Glory in Death. 1995.

Immortal in Death. 1996.

Rapture in Death. 1996.

Ceremony in Death. 1997.

Vengeance in Death. 1997.

Holiday in Death. 1998.

Conspiracy in Death. 1999.
Loyalty in Death. 1999.
Witness in Death. 2000.
Betrayal in Death. 2001.
Seduction in Death. 2001.
Reunion in Death. 2002.
Purity in Death. 2002.
Portrait in Death. 2003.
Imitation in Death. 2003.
Divided in Death. 2004.
Visions in Death. 2004.
Survivor in Death. 2005.
Origin in Death. 2005.

Shetterly, Will.

Chimera. 2000.

Max Maxwell, a tough-talking P.I., finds himself stuck with a beautiful new client after losing a poker hand, which wouldn't be bad except that he discovers
that she is really a jaguar chimera disguised as a real human. Her mentor, a famous scientist, has been killed, and she is the prime suspect.

Shinn, Sharon.

Wrapt in Crystal. 1999.

The priestess of two very different religious orders have been targeted by a serial
killer, and it is up to Cowen Drake to find and stop the killer.

Stableford, Brian.

Inherit the Earth. 1998.

Nanotechnology and life extension are at the heart of a thriller in which the son
of a legendary inventor is targeted by extremists.

Swann, S. Andrew.

Moreau series.

Moreaus are second-class citizens because they are descended from animals.
The series features two private investigators, Nohar Rjasthan, of genetically altered tiger stock, and Angelica Lopez, descended from a rabbit.

Moreau Omnibus. 2003. Includes *Forests of the Night* (1993), *Emperors of the*
Twilight (1994), and *Specters of the Dawn* (1994).
Fearful Symmetries: The Return of Nohar Rajasthan. 1999.

Vinge, Joan D.

Tangled Up in Blue. 2000.

Hegemonic Police officer Nyx LaisTree, the sole survivor of a massacre in a
warehouse, is exposed as one of the infamous Nameday vigilantes and stripped
of his badge but not his need for justice.

Vinge, Vernor.

Marooned in Realtime. 1986. Reissued 2004.

> Fifty thousand years in the future, one of only 300 humans left is murdered, and it is up to the sole cop left in the world to find the culprit.

Williamson, Jack.

The Silicon Dagger. 1999.

> When his investigative journalist brother is murdered in a small Kentucky town, Clay Barstow goes in and uncovers a secret high-tech plot.

Wolfe, Gene.

Free Live Free. 1985. Reissued 1999. 📖

Humor in Science Fiction

Humor is so subjective that there can be no guaranteed funny reads, but there are some readers who have found the following tales humorous in varying degrees.

Adams, Douglas.

Hitchhiker's trilogy.

> *The Ultimate Hitchhiker's Guide* (2000) is an omnibus edition of the five titles in the "trilogy." Arthur Dent is off on a universe of wacky adventures featuring incredibly odd characters when he finds out at the last minute that Earth is slated for destruction because it is in the path of a construction project.

The Hitchhiker's Guide to the Galaxy. 1979. Reissued 2004. 🎬
The Restaurant at the End of the Universe. 1980. Reissued 1995.
Life, the Universe and Everything. 1982. Reissued 2005.
So Long, and Thanks for All the Fish. 1984. Reissued 1999.
Mostly Harmless. 1982. Reissued 2000.

Asprin, Robert.

Phule series.

> Featuring Willard Phule, who is an officer in the Galactic Alliance and a filthy rich thrill seeker (and his butler, Beeker).

Phule's Company. 1990.
Phule's Paradise. 1992.

Asprin, Robert, with Peter J. Heck.

A Phule and His Money. 1999.
Phule's Me Twice. 2001.
No Phule Like an Old Phule. 2004.

Brown, Fredric.

Martians Go Home. 1955. Reissued in 2002 in the omnibus *Martians and Madness: The Complete SF Novels of Fredric Brown*.

Brust, Steven.

Cowboy Feng's Space Bar and Grille. 1990. Reissued 2003.

Harrison, Harry.

Bill, the Galactic Hero. 1965. Reissued 2001.

Recruiters will go to any lengths to meet their quotas.

Moore, Christopher.

Fluke: Or, I Know Why the Winged Whale Sings. 2003.

Niven, Larry.

Rainbow Mars. 1999.

Hanville Svetz, living in a polluted and grim thirty-first century and working for the Institute for Temporal Research, travels to the past, with unexpected results.

Pratchett, Terry.

Bromeliad series.

Four-inch-tall aliens have made a home on Earth after being stranded here.

Truckers. 1989. Reissued 2004.

Diggers. 1990. Reissued 2004.

Wings. 1990. Reissued 2004.

Rankin, Robert.

The Hollow Chocolate Bunnies of the Apocalypse. 2004.

Robinson, Spider.

Callahan Stories Series.

Callahan's Crosstime Saloon. 1977. Reissued 1999. Winner of the Campbell and Skylark Awards.

Time Travelers Strictly Cash. 2001.

Callahan's Secret. 1986. Reissued 2002.

The Callahan Chronicles. 1997. An omnibus edition of the first three titles in the series.

Callahan's Lady. 1989. Reissued 2001.

Callahan's Legacy. 1996.

The Callahan Touch. 1993.

Callahan's Key. 2000.

Willis, Connie.

Sophisticated wit appears in all her works.

Bellwether. 1996. 📖

Could it be that one person is unknowingly starting trends and fashion?

Uncharted Territory. 1994. Reissued 2000.

Planetary surveyors experience the dark side of political correctness in this satirical novella.

Science Fantasy

The combination of science fiction and fantasy is sometimes called science fantasy. Readers who like both genres will often enjoy the combination of the two or novels that are SF but have a fantasy "feel" to them because of science or religion that appears to be magic or the presence of mythical creatures.

Chambers, Stephen.

Vel Chronicles.

Hope's End. 2001.

Vel is targeted by the secret police of the planet Hera, city Hope. As an unregistered child, he is on the run after his father is murdered and his mother commits suicide, leaving him a note saying that he is the rightful heir to the throne. SF with fantasy trappings in what has the feel of a medieval world.

Hope's War. 2002.

Egan, Doris.

Ivory.

The Complete Ivory. 2001. Omnibus of the three following titles.

Theodora, an anthropology scholar from a technological planet, is fascinated by the way magic is used on Ivory.

The Gate of Ivory. 1989.
Two-Bit Heroes. 1992.
Guilt-Edged Ivory. 1992.

Grimsley, Jim.

The Ordinary. 2004.

A technologically advanced race wants to establish trade through a gate with the inhabitants of a world where the inhabitants believe in magic.

Jones, Diana Wynne.

Deep Secret. 2000.

Parallel worlds, a science fiction convention, and magids, who are supposed to keep it all in order.

Kirstein, Rosemary.

Steerswoman series.

Steerswomen acquire and disseminate knowledge in a medieval fantasy world that is orbited by spacecraft. It has been called a perfect example of Arthur C. Clarke's Third Law: "Any sufficiently advanced technology is indistinguishable from magic."

The Steerswoman's Road. 2003. Omnibus of *The Steerswoman* and *Outskirter's Secret.*
The Lost Steersman. 2003.
The Language of Power. 2004.

Topics

Well-established as a genre, science fiction has been written about from scholarly as well as writing and publishing perspectives. There are many sources in which to explore this genre and its rich history. A few suggestions follow.

Anthologies

An effective way to become acquainted with the characteristics of authors in the science fiction genre, and particularly with the work of new authors, is through anthologies. Both the theme anthologies and the critical and historical collections may have stories from all periods and often suffer from repetition of much-anthologized pieces. The short story is a very popular form in both science fiction and fantasy. Although the following listing of anthologies is long, it is by no means exhaustive.

The essential reference tool for contending with the massive number of short stories is William G. Contento's *Index to Science Fiction Anthologies and Collections* (G. K. Hall, 1984), for those published before 1984. Contento and Charles N. Brown are the authors of *The Locus Index to Science Fiction 1984–2003* (Locus Press, 2004). In addition to indexing science fiction, fantasy, and horror short stories published in those years, it also indexes books and magazines.

Ashley, Mike, ed. *The Mammoth Book of Science Fiction*. Carroll & Graf Publishers, 2002. Includes stories by Brian W. Aldiss, Mike Ashley, Stephen Baxter, Eric Brown, Mark Clifton, Philip K. Dick, Greg Egan, H. Chandler Elliott, Peter F. Hamilton, Colin Kapp, Damon Knight, Geoffrey A. Landis, John Morressy, Frank Lillie Pollock, Robert Reed, Keith Roberts, Kim Stanley Robinson, Eric Frank Russell, Robert Sheckley, Clifford D. Simak, Michael Swanick, George C. Wallis, and Connie Willis.

Card, Orson Scott, ed. *Masterpieces: The Best Science Fiction of the Century*. Ace, 2001. Includes stories by Brian W. Aldiss, Isaac Asimov, Greg Bear, Gregory Benford, Octavia E. Butler, Arthur C. Clarke, Philip K. Dick, William Gibson, Joe Haldeman, Robert A. Heinlein, Ursula K. Le Guin, Anne McCaffrey, Frederik Pohl, Mike Resnick, Kim Stanley Robinson, Pamela Sargent, Robert Silverberg, Clifford D. Simak, John Varley, and Roger Zelazny.

Dozois, Gardner, ed. *Best of the Best: 20 Years of the Year's Best Science Fiction*. St. Martin's, 2005.
Includes stories by Stephen Baxter, Greg Bear, William Bigson, Terry Bisson, Pat Cadigan, Ted Chiang, John Crowley, Tony Daniel, Greg Egan, Molly Gloss, Eileen Gunn, Joe Haldeman, James Patrick Kelly, John Kessel, Nancy Kress, Ursula K. Le Guin, Ian R. MacLeod, David Marusek, Paul McAuley, Ian McDonald, Maureen F. McHugh, Robert Reed, Mike Resnick, Geoff Ryman, William Sander, Lucius Shepard, Robert Silverberg, Brian Stableford, Bruce Sterling, Charles Stross, Michael Swanwick, Steven Utley, Howard Waldrop, Walter Jon Williams, Connie Willis, and Gene Wolfe.

Ellison, Harlan, ed. *Dangerous Visions.* Doubleday, 1967 and *Again, Dangerous Visions.* Doubleday, 1972.
  Groundbreaking anthologies that continue to be read.

Pohl, Frederik, ed. *The SFWA Grand Masters Volume 1.* Tor, 1999; *The SFWA Grand Masters Volume 2.* Tor, 2000; and *The SFWA Grand Masters Volume 3.* Tor, 2001.

Anthology Series

For decades the anthology series played an important role in science fiction publishing. Many libraries still have the old anthology series on their shelves, and they continue to be used. Most of the series have now been discontinued for a number of years. For a more comprehensive listing of anthology series, consult earlier editions of *Genreflecting*.

The Best from Fantasy and Science Fiction. The twenty-fourth and last series was published in 1982, but there were fortieth, forty-fifth, and fiftieth anniversary editions published by St. Martin's Press in 1989, 1994, and 1999.

L. Ron Hubbard Presents Writers of the Future. Number 20 was published in 2004.

Nebula Awards. 1965– . Number 33 was published in 1999. In 2000 the title was changed to Nebula Awards Showcase. *Nebula Awards Showcase 2004,* edited by Vonda N. McIntyre, was published in 2004.

Science Fiction: The Best of . . . . Edited by Karen Haber and Jonathan Strahan. *Science Fiction: The Best of 2004* was published as an electronic book in 2005.

Starlight. Edited by Patrick Nielsen Hayden. 1996– . Number 3 was published in 2001.

The Year's Best Science Fiction. Edited by Gardner Dozois. Number 21 was published in 2004.

Year's Best SF. Edited by David Hartwell. Number 9 was published in 2004.

Encyclopedias

The following encyclopedias contain extensive bibliographical, historical, and critical material.

Clute, John. *Science Fiction: The Illustrated Encyclopedia.* DK Publishing, 1995.
  Although not exactly an encyclopedia, this lavishly illustrated browsing book does an outstanding job of placing science fiction in a historical context.

Clute, John, and Peter Nicholls. *The Encyclopedia of Science Fiction.* St. Martin's Press, 1995.
  The essential guide to science fiction lists trends, authors, titles, terminology, and much more in narrative and pictures. It has 4,360 entries. Alphabetical arrangement of themes, biography, and other topics, with many cross-references. Historical and critical, with extensive bibliographical material. Biographical listings for many little-known authors. Many of the articles are extended critical essays.

Gunn, James, ed. *The New Encyclopedia of Science Fiction.* Viking-Penguin, 1988.
  Summaries, criticism, and bibliographical and historical information on people, books, topics, trends, and films in science fiction.

Review Journals

Most of the magazines and fanzines of science fiction contain reviews. There are, however, a few other outstanding sources of reviews.

Locus. 1968– . http://www.locusmag.com
> Published monthly, it lists all SF and fantasy published in English. Seven accomplished reviewers discuss not only book-length fiction but also short stories. Author interviews, news of events and personalities, bibliographies, and the highly respected Locus Poll also make it very useful.

New York Review of Science Fiction. 1988– . http://www.nyrsf.com/
> Edited by David Hartwell and Kathryn Cramer, it features essays and articles in addition to reviews.

VOYA: Voice of Youth Advocates. 1978– . http://www.voya.com/
> A bimonthly that reviews books for young adults and has remarkably good coverage of science fiction, fantasy, and horror paperback originals. VOYA annually publishes a list of the best science fiction, fantasy, and horror of the year for young adults.

Associations

European Science Fiction Society. Formed in 1972, it has a membership of fans from several European countries and meets at an annual convention.

Science Fiction and Fantasy Writers of America (http://www.sfwa.org/). The association was founded in 1965. It sponsors the annual Nebula Awards for several categories of science fiction writing. The group's motto is "The Future Isn't What It Used to Be."

Science Fiction Research Association (http://www.sfra.org/). Has an academic and research orientation but is open to all.

SF Canada (http://www.sfcanada.ca/). Formerly called the Speculative Writers' Association of Canada. Open to published authors.

Conventions

Fans and writers form many associations and hold innumerable conventions, usually combining science fiction and fantasy, and often adding horror and the supernatural. "Con" is usually part of the conference name. They are listed in science fiction magazines and on the Internet. Locus Online at http://www.locusmag.com/Conventions.html (accessed February 25, 2005) does an exceptionally good job of listing "cons."

World Science Fiction Convention ("WorldCon"). The first was held in 1939; the sixty-second was held in Boston, in 2004. The membership of WorldCon awards the annual Hugo Awards.

Awards

Awards are generally reported in the various science fiction magazines soon after the results are announced. For a comprehensive listing of awards up to 1990, consult *Reginald's Science Fiction and Fantasy Awards: A Comprehensive Guide to the Awards and Their Winners,* by Daryl F. Mallett and R. Reginald (Borgo, 1991). Currently the easiest way to find award information is on the World Wide Web.

Award Web (http://www.awardweb.info).

Locus Index to Science Fiction Awards (http://www.locusmag.com/SFAwards/index.html).

The following are the best-known major awards for science fiction:

Arthur C. Clarke Award. Awarded for the best British science fiction novel from the previous year.

Aurealis Award. Australian science fiction, fantasy, and horror award.

Compton Crook Award. Awarded by the Baltimore Science Fiction Society for the best first novel of science fiction (including fantasy).

Ditmar. Australian science fiction award.

Hugo. Awarded at World Science Fiction Conventions. Named after Hugo Gernsback, it is voted on by members of the annual WorldCon; in other words, the winner is selected by readers of science fiction. One of the most prestigious awards, it is a reflection of fan opinion.

James Tiptree, Jr., Award. Named for Alice Sheldon, who wrote under this male pseudonym, this award is presented for science fiction and fantasy that looks at gender in a different way. The James Tiptree, Jr. Award is "given to the work of science fiction or fantasy published in one year which best explores or expands gender roles."

Locus. Is awarded as a result of a poll taken among the subscribers to *Locus.*

Nebula. Awarded by the Science Fiction and Fantasy Writers of America. The winners are selected by a vote of the members of the organization. A prerequisite of membership is the publication of a work of science fiction, fantasy, or horror by the candidate. Membership in SFWA is open only to published authors in the field, making this prestigious award a writers' award that reflects high literary merit.

Philip K. Dick Award. Awarded to a science fiction or fantasy book published in paperback. It is administered by the Philadelphia SF Society.

Prix Aurora Award. Given to the best in Canadian science fiction and fantasy.

Sapphire Award (http://members.aol.com/sfreditor/bestsfr.htm). Given to the Best SF Romance of the Year. Sponsored by the *SF Romance Newsletter.*

D's Science Fiction Picks

D's Science Fiction Picks

Bujold, Lois McMaster.

A Civil Campaign. 1999. (space opera/SF romance).

Both Miles and his clone brother Mark are courting the women of their dreams, as preparations for the royal wedding advance.

Moore, Christopher.

Fluke: Or, I Know Why the Winged Whale Sings. **2003.** (humor).

Outrageously hilarious tale of whale researcher Nate Quinn, who discovers a bizarre secret about a humpback whale he is stalking as he tries to puzzle out the meaning of whale song. A dreadlocked rasta white boy from New Jersey, an accomplished underwater photographer with a saucy school teacher girlfriend, and a mysteriously pale research intern whose credentials don't check out round out the likeable cast, along with the whaley boys, who must be read to be believed. It is a combination of Carl Hiaasen-like hilarity and absurd science fiction.

Sawyer, Robert. J.

Hominids. **2002.** (parallel worlds).

Scientists working in a nickel mine far below the earth are shocked when someone appearing to be a Neanderthal with a high-tech device imbedded in his arm appears within their large globe of heavy water. Two sets of scientists working in two parallel worlds at the same time on completely different projects have created a temporary passage. In the world Ponter Boddit is from, Neanderthals are the dominant species and have pretty much bred criminal tendencies out of their gene pool. Sawyer's exquisite world building creates a world with complex familial relationships and culture. Men and women live apart. Individuals can have partners of both sexes, living with the same sex partner for the majority of the month and the other sex partner for four days, when "two become one.

Schmitz, James H.

The Witches of Karres. **1966.** Reissued 2004. (psionic powers).

Captain Pausert, a young space trader, rescues three young sisters, Maleen, the Leewit, and Goth, from slavery to return them to their home and discovers that they have powerful talents. One is precognitive, one can teleport, and one can communicate with anybody or anything. Together they can instantly transport the *Venture* to another location. Classic light fun with fast-paced encounters with pirates, spies, and aliens.

Vinge, Vernor.

A Deepness in the Sky. **1999.** (aliens).

A civilization of spider-like sentients has been found when ships from a trading culture and those from a slaver culture converge on a planet that orbits a bizarre OnOff star that forces the inhabitants into hibernation for years at a time. Three disparate cultures comes to life through brilliant characterizations.

Chapter 11

Fantasy

Essay

John H. Timmerman

Although fantasy is often described as an escapist genre, fantasy literature actually attempts nothing less than to engage our reality in new and startling ways. When the fantasy story opens, we discover that this alternative world is not altogether different from our own. The failures and victories, virtues and vices, joy and suffering, all somehow correspond to the reality of who we are. By looking outward, we learn to look inward.

Since fantasy has to evoke another world clean and whole—this place the reader lives in for the length of the reading—the books, or series of books, are often long. Stephen R. Donaldson's <u>Chronicles of Thomas Covenant, the Unbeliever</u>, evokes a world called simply The Land over six long books, with a new quartet planned for release. Erin Hunter's <u>Warriors Series</u> stretches over six volumes. Anne McCaffrey's notable <u>Dragonriders of Pern</u> includes over a dozen books. In such works, lengthy and compelling, we learn about not just an alternative world but also an entire and parallel world history, complete with its myths and values, villains and heroes.

Furthermore, fantasy tends not to jerk us abruptly, by means of scientific mechanisms, from our world to the fantasy world. This is the way of science fiction, or what is sometimes called "extrapolative fiction." Different authors come to mind when we think of science fiction—from Jules Verne and H.G. Wells to Ray Bradbury and Isaac Asimov. Science fiction uses a means—from a space vehicle to a time warp—to thrust us into a hypothetical world. In fantasy we arrive at a re-created world not altogether different than our own. Surely the inhabitants differ. But so too do the inhabitants of Guatemala from, say, Greenland. Or those of Watts from those of Beverly Hills.

Nor, finally, is fantasy understood as allegory. Repeatedly, fantasy authors have drawn a very firm line between their work and allegory. Allegory tends to have a meaning predetermined by the author. The success of the work lies in whether the reader can decipher enough signs and symbols to find that meaning. It is very much like the rational solving of an intricate puzzle. Fantasy, on the other hand, is nonrestrictive, freeing the reader to make individual claims about this "other world." In fantasy, meaning is *appropriated* by the reader rather than given by the author.

Definition

Excluding related kinds of literature helps narrow our definition of the fantasy genre. Perhaps the early pioneer of modern fantasy, J. R. R. Tolkien, gave us the clearest definition of the fantasy genre itself in his "On Fairy-Stories" (In *The Tolkien Reader*, Ballantine, 1966). Tolkien sees two elements at work: First, the creation of an internally consistent secondary world (the "subcreation") and second, the use of Faerie (the use of magic and enchantment). This world is accessed by the narrative skill of the author and the imaginative willingness of the reader.

This definition is brief but serviceable, simply because fantasy has branched into so many variations. One solid, uncomplicated trunk is necessary to hold them in place. Common suborders of fantasy include, the animal story (Richard Adams, *Watership Down*), the beast fable (Walter Wangerin Jr., *The Book of the Dun Cow*), the heroic quest (Lloyd Alexander, *The Chronicles of Prydain*; J. R. R. Tolkien, *The Lord of the Rings*), wizardry (John Bellaires, *The Face in the Frost*, Ursula LeGuin, A Wizard of Earthsea series), religious/metaphysical (Orson Scott Card, *Seventh Son*), and sword and sorcery (Fritz Leiber, The Fafhrd and the Gray Mouser series), Clearly, the genre has emerged in creative diversity as it has in popularity.

The essential question of this essay is this: Wherein lies fantasy's deep and rich appeal to the readers of our time? The essential roots of fantasy dig way down into the earliest soil of literature itself. Perhaps around a fire in a cave, perhaps atop a hill ringed by stones, perhaps in a hunting lodge, people told stories. Those stories told about fears encountered and how they were overcome. They told of foreign peoples and divine beings. They spoke of heroes, those who conquered and those who died trying. In this way the stories explored mysteries. That is why we call them *myths*, a word with the same etymological root as mystery. They were told in order to discover humanity's place in an often mystifying and threatening world. Our question is why the stories, ever made new, continue to appeal to our age of technological comfort, in which mysteries have been largely obliterated. Now, if they still remain, they throb like a primitive drum within our spirit.

Appeal and Characteristics

To speak of people's favorite authors, tabulate the startling sales figures of fantasy literature, and recognize its increasing diversity does little to explain just why it appeals to modern readers. These facts only indicate that it does and, consequently, that our central question merits probing. It's as if modern society has an ache in its heart, a deep longing for directions and satisfaction, that fantasy somehow assuages. To answer the large question of why fantasy appeals to modern readers, one has to ask, simultaneously, how fantasy functions. This question basically defines the genre of fantasy itself and is distinguished by traits that collectively shape the definition. These are the (1) use of story, (2) use of common characters, (3) evocation of another world, (4) conflict of good and evil, and (5) use of a quest. Each of these shapes part of fantasy's unique appeal to modern readers.

Story

Story works to free the imagination, allowing it to live for a time in another world. We would also likely agree that in our postmodern age there is a hunger for story. We seem tied to the immediate, nailed to routine, imprisoned in demands. Thus, story is seen as liberation.

Because of its use of powerful story, fantasy works have also grown in popularity with children and young adult readers. An entire branch of the genre has responded to this craving. In the modern tradition, this phenomenon may be traced to L. Frank Baum's *The Wonderful Wizard of Oz* (1900) and C. S. Lewis's The Chronicles of Narnia. By the end of the twentieth century, the industry was in full swing, evidenced by J. K. Rowling's Harry Potter series, Hilari Bell's Farsala Trilogy, Anne McCaffrey's Dragon series (initiated with *Dragonflight* in 1968), and Piers Anthony's popular Xanth Series. Repeatedly, such works demonstrate the human craving for story, one in which genuine dangers (physical and metaphysical) are encountered and order is restored.

The essential quality to fantasy story, then, is to create a world and characters so believable, a plot so urgent, and a conflict so daunting that the reader cannot part with it. This is simply because the reader imaginatively lives the story and thereby participates in its making and meaning.

Character

Story, a "make-believe" tale that nonetheless may bear crushing relevance, lies at the heart of fantasy. If, however, story is to bear relevance, to be applicable to the everyday lives of the readers, to open insight as to how one should then live, these relevances, applications, and insights must arise through characters immediately living the story. Story offers lessons in experience, and those lessons we obtain by the experiences of the characters. Fantasy has thereby developed characters generally bearing specific traits.

The characters of fantasy are largely people or beings of a common nature. They might be any one of us in the tale—and that is precisely the point. We are not asked to stand on the outside and survey this tale from a detached perspective; we are asked to enter into it so that the story becomes ours. Thus we find characters quite like us. Granted, they may not always be human characters, or they may be persons of royalty or wizardry, but they are like us.

Furthermore, the common character is often naïve; that is, he or she retains a certain innocence and is disinterested in terms of worldly or political allegiances. The common character is naïve in the sense of not having become cynical, hard-bitten, or spoiled by the world about her. He or she retains the child-like trait of wonder, the willingness to engage adventure. Often the primary characters of fantasy are children, although this is certainly not a prerequisite for the genre. It is only because the authors see in children the willingness to wonder, which we adults so often lose.

The point of fantasy is not to provide tidy morals, but to provide growth by experience, the same growth experienced by the naïve character. In fantasy we learn not morals but lessons on life's way. It is necessary, therefore, that the reader clearly recognizes this in the characters of the story. The characters may be called to be heroes, but first of all to be human, to recognize the human situation for what it is, and what possibly can be done about it.

Another World

One might expect an essay on fantasy to begin with this most immediately associated term. But the quality of story and plausibility of character are the requisite precursors to make the other world an apparently real one. What, then, makes this fictional world apparently "real"?

First, the world of fantasy is not a dream world, a never-never land, but a world in which characters confront the same terrors, choices, and dilemmas we confront in our world. The reason for creating such a world is to confront more openly and daringly a spiritual reality too often ignored in our world of system and fact. Perhaps it is the case that when these "realities of the human heart" are devalued in our daily life, one must look to another world where such realities may be restructured and be given credibility and value.

Second, this world is "evoked," or called forth clean and whole. It is simply provided for us, and we have to cross the threshold to it in our minds. Usually we are simply there in this other world from the first line. This immediacy is opposed, for example, to the nineteenth-century notion of "suspension of disbelief," with which we enter the work pretending for a time that this might be real. In fantasy, given a certain groundwork, the story *is* real.

Third, the world of fantasy should not be considered an escapist world, but a world in which we live. There is always this reciprocating action in fantasy, an interchange between two worlds. One of E. Nesbit's stories is entitled, all in one word, "Whereyouwanttogo" and ends "Whereyoustartedfrom." Precisely: We leave the road of life for a time not to lose the road, but to find the road more certain.

Essential Conflict: Good and Evil

Although exceptions are bound to exist in a genre as diverse as fantasy, the conflict between good and evil, and the often attendant use of magic and the supernatural, remains essential, defining traits of the genre. In fantasy literature there is usually a keen recognition of forces of good and evil, a sense of right and wrong, but also a driving necessity to act upon it. It may be the case, however, that in the human struggle of the character to act upon choices between good and evil the distinction may become blurred. Often he or she does not know for certain if the action is correct *until* he or she has acted.

Fantasy is keenly aware of the terror of life as well as the joy of life. But like the fairy tale, fantasy does hold forth as one of its central points the belief that the end of a successful story is joy. It is not a joy separate from sorrow, but a joy distilled from the experience of agonizing choice and painful awareness of the errors in human decision making. Only through such decisions and the actions attendant upon them may the often hazy edges of good and evil be clarified.

The Quest

Ancient literature and mythology frequently based the action of a story on a quest. In place of the quest, modern literature has often provided an adventure. The distinction lies at the heart of fantasy. If the fantasy hero must act, he or she must often seek long and desperately for a basis for action. The question that this hero pursues is different from an adventure in several significant ways. In the first place, an adventure may lead anywhere. Jack Kerouac's *On the Road* is an adventure; the road takes the rider out, but the rider has no precise goal. The quest is always *toward* something, although that something often becomes clear only with the seeking of it. Second, the adventure may be undertaken for any number of reasons—boredom with one's present situation, wanderlust, dissatisfaction with things as they are.

The quest, however, is always a spiritual or religious undertaking. The quest hero is appointed or ordained to his or her mission, and its end has spiritual significance. Third, the adventure may be merely a whimsical frolic. In contrast, the quest is always a grave, serious undertaking. It is often life-threatening, marked by a sense of struggle, of imminent or immediate danger in which the character must call upon all of his or her will and power to push on.

Fantasy provides not a hiding place but a point from which the reader can begin anew. The author invites the reader to probe an inner nature, to grow in experience, to resolve oneself to new directions. The quest provides a basis for such exploration.

Quests are pursued only when grave events threaten the well-being of a society. In ancient literature as well as modern fantasy, no quest is pursued for the sheer fun of it. The qualification is important, since an adventure is often undertaken simply because the status quo has become torpid in its uneventfulness, and the adventurer is motivated by little more than accentuated ennui. In the quest, the threat to the status quo often makes the hero long for the routine, and frequently the quest is pursued in order to recover that state.

Resolution

It seems, finally, that fantasy literature possesses one additional quality that cannot be neatly categorized. Again, although exceptions exist, much of the appeal in modern fantasy resides in its optimism for humankind. The human spirit may be maligned, but it will endure. It may be tested, but it will be found worthy. In an age acutely pessimistic about the human race, fantasy remains adamant in its belief that all life is worthy. There may be bad people around us—fantasy never denies that—but somehow even the feeblest of creatures can individually confront them. Fantasy believes the confrontation with evil in any of its multifaceted variations is worth the risk, the sorrow, the pain, for the struggle will come to an end, and at that end lies joy: "They both laughed. Laughed—the Mountains rang with it!" (J. R. R. Tolkien, "Leaf by Niggle") .

Bibliography

To list the central works in the fantasy tradition is a task far beyond the scope of this brief essay. Several leading twentieth-century authors are mentioned in the course of writing. The following includes several of the seminal critical studies that have helped define fantasy as we now know it.

Atteberry, Brian. *The Fantasy Tradition in American Literature.* Bloomington: Indiana University Press, 1980.

_____. *Strategies of Fantasy.* Bloomington: Indiana University Press, 1992.

Bettelheim, Bruno. *The Uses of Enchantment: The Meaning and Importance of Fairy Tales.* New York: Vintage, 1977.

Clute, John, and John Grant. *The Encyclopedia of Fantasy.* New York: St. Martin's, 1997.

Manlove, C. N. *Modern Fantasy: Five Studies.* Cambridge: Cambridge University Press, 1976.

Matthews, Richard. *Fantasy: The Liberation of the Imagination.* New York: Twayne Publishers, 1997.

Rabkin, Eric S. *The Fantastic in Literature.* Princeton: Princeton University Press, 1976.

Shippey, T. A., ed. *McGill's Guide to Science Fiction and Fantasy Literature*, 4 vols. Pasadena, Calif.: Salem Press, 1996.

Timmerman, John H. *Other Worlds: The Fantasy Genre.* Bowling Green, Ohio: Bowling Green University Popular Press, 1983.

Tolkien, J. R. R. "Leaf by Niggle." In *The Tolkien Reader.* New York: Ballantine, 1966.

———. "On Fairy Stories." In *The Tolkien Reader.* New York: Ballantine, 1966.

Themes and Types

Diana Tixier Herald

Fantasy rocketed to popularity with the Harry Potter phenomenon in the 1990s, resulting in a boom in fantasy publishing and reading. The <u>Lord of the Rings</u> movies also have played a part, with readers seeking out the books after seeing the movies and wanting more. Many titles that were long out of print have been reissued. Because fantasy is currently so popular, genreblends with romance, horror, and science fiction are also common. Titles listed here are representative rather than comprehensive because of the vast numbers.

Fantasy novels are frequently written as series, and it is not uncommon to see several series within a series. Titles of subseries are indicated by ***<u>boldface italic and underscoring.</u>***

Selected Classics

Adams, Richard.
>   *Watership Down.* 1972. (bestiary—uncommon common animals).

Baum, L. Frank.
>   *The Wonderful Wizard of Oz.* 1900.

Bradbury, Ray.
>   *The October Country.* 1955. (dark fantasy).
>   *Something Wicked This Way Comes.* 1962. (dark fantasy).

Bradley, Marion Zimmer.
>   *The Mists of Avalon.* 1984. (Arthurian legend).

Brooks, Terry.
>   **<u>The Shannara Series.</u>** (epic).

Donaldson, Stephen R.
>   **<u>The Chronicles of Thomas Covenant, the Unbeliever.</u>** (parallel worlds).

Kurtz, Katherine.
>   **<u>The Deryni Saga.</u>** (alternate worlds).

Le Guin, Ursula K.
>   *The Lathe of Heaven.* 1971. (parallel worlds)
>   **<u>The Earthsea series.</u>** (epic).

Leiber, Fritz.
>   **<u>Fafhrd and the Grey Mouser series.</u>**

Lewis, C. S.
>   **The Chronicles of Narnia.**

Tolkien, J. R. R.
>   *The Hobbit.* 1937. (epic).
>   **The Lord of the Rings trilogy.** (epic).

Epic/Sword and Sorcery

The best-selling and most widely recognized subgenre of fantasy is the epic, many of which qualify as traditional "sword and sorcery" titles, and the best known of those is Tolkien's Lord of the Rings trilogy. The distinguishing characteristics of the epic are its heroic protagonist(s); the story following a series of adventures or deeds often of a symbolic nature, usually a quest; and the story's sweep over time. Many epics take years or even decades to unfold as the authors create fully developed worlds rich with history and religious, political, and social systems. Series of titles are common, sometimes with consecutive series and series within series. The order of the books is often important to readers, so when new titles in the series have been published in the last decade, all titles in a series are listed here.

Baird, Alison.
>   **Dragon Throne.**
>>   *The Stone of the Stars.* 2004.
>>   *The Empire of the Stars.* 2004.
>>   *Archons of the Stars.* 2005.

Bakker, R. Scott.
>   **The Prince of Nothing.**
>>   *The Darkness That Comes Before.* 2004.
>>   *The Warrior-Prophet.* 2004.

Berg, Carol.
>   **The Bridge of D'Arnath.**
>>   *Son of Avonar.* 2004.
>>   *Guardians of the Keep.* 2004.
>>   *The Soul Weaver.* 2005.
>   **The Books of the Rai-kirah.**
>>   *Transformation.* 2001.
>>   *Revelation.* 2001.
>>   *Restoration.* 2002.

Brooks, Terry.
>   In the 1970s readers of Tolkien's Lord of the Rings were demanding more great reads along the same lines, and Terry Brooks and his Shannara series fulfilled that need. This epic tale of a land torn by war, peopled by humans, elves, dwarves, trolls, and gnomes, has strong heroes who fight great evil. Brooks suggests that the best order for reading the books is publication order.

The Shannara series.

The Original Shannara Trilogy. ★

The Sword of Shannara. 1977. Reissued 2002.

The Elfstones of Shannara. 1982.

The Wishsong of Shannara. 1985.

Heritage of Shannara.

The Scions of Shannara. 1990.

The Druid of Shannara. 1991.

The Elf Queen of Shannara. 1992.

The Talismans of Shannara. 1993.

Shannara Prequel Trilogy.

The First King of Shannara. 1996. Prequel to the Shannara series. Only one title has been issued to date.

Voyage of the Jerle Shannara.

Ilse Witch. 2000.

Antrax. 2001.

Morgawr. 2002.

High Druid of Shannara.

Jarka Ruus. 2003.

Tanequil. 2004.

Straken. 2005.

Dart-Thornton, Cecilia.

Bitterbynde.

The Ill-Made Mute. 2001.

The Lady of the Sorrows. 2002.

The Battle of Evernight. 2003.

Douglass, Sara.

The Wayfarer Redemption.

The Wayfarer Redemption. 2001.

Enchanter. 2002.

Starman. 2002.

Sinner. 2004.

Drake, David.

Lord of the Isles.

Lord of the Isles. 1997.

Queen of Demons. 1999.

Servant of the Dragon. 1999.

Mistress of the Catacombs. 2001.

Goddess of the Ice Realm. 2003.

Duncan, Dave.

> **King's Blades.**
>
> > *Chronicle of the King's Blades.*
> >
> > > *Impossible Odds.* 2003.
> > >
> > > *Paragon Lost.* 2002.
> > >
> > > *The Jaguar Knights.* 2004.
> >
> > *Tales of the King's Blades.*
> >
> > > *The Gilded Chain.* 1998.
> > >
> > > *Lord of the Fire Lands.* 1999.
> > >
> > > *Sky of Swords.* 2000.

Eddings, David, and Leigh Eddings.

> (Even though Leigh is not listed as coauthor of the early books, it has been reported that she is.)
>
> **Belgariad Series.**
>
> > *Pawn of Prophecy.* 1982. Reissued 2004.
> >
> > *Queen of Sorcery.* 1982. Reissued 2002 in the omnibus *The Belgariad Volume 1.*
> >
> > *Magician's Gambit.* 1983. Reissued 1997. Reissued 2002 in the omnibus *The Belgariad Volume 1.*
> >
> > *Castle of Wizardry.* 1985. Reissued 2002 in the omnibus *The Belgariad Volume 2.*
> >
> > *Enchanter's End Game.* 1986. Reissued 2002 in the omnibus *The Belgariad Volume 1.*
> >
> > *Belgarath the Sorcerer.* 1995.
> >
> > *Polgara the Sorceress.* 1997.
>
> **Malloreon series.**
>
> > *Guardians of the West.* 1987. Reissued 2005 in the omnibus *The Malloreon Volume One.*
> >
> > *King of the Murgos.* 1988. Reissued 2005 in the omnibus *The Malloreon Volume One.*
> >
> > *Demon Lord of Karanda.* 1988. Reissued 2005 in the omnibus *The Malloreon Volume One.*
> >
> > *Sorceress of Darshiva.* 1989. Reissued 2005 in the omnibus *The Malloreon Volume Two.*
> >
> > *The Seeress of Kell.* 1991. Reissued 2005 in the omnibus *The Malloreon Volume Two.*
>
> **Ellenium series.**
>
> > *The Diamond Throne.* 1989.
> >
> > *The Ruby Knight.* 1990.
> >
> > *The Sapphire Rose.* 1992.
>
> **Tamuli Series.**
>
> > *Domes of Fire.* 1993.
> >
> > *The Shining Ones.* 1993.
> >
> > *The Hidden City.* 1994.

Farland, David.

> **The Runelords.**
>
> > *The Sum of All Men.* 1998.
> >
> > *Brotherhood of the Wolf.* 1999.
> >
> > *Wizardborn.* 2001.
> >
> > *The Lair of Bones.* 2003.

Feist, Raymond E.

The World of Midkemia.

Riftwar Saga.

Magician. 1982. Reissued 2003. It has also been issued in two volumes as *Magician: Apprentice* and *Magician: Master.*
Silverthorn. 1985. Reissued 1993.
A Darkness at Sethanon. 1986. Reissued 1994.

Serpentwar Series.

Prince of the Blood. 1989. Reissued 2004.
The King's Buccaneer. 1992.

The Empire Sequence. Written with Janny Wurts.

Daughter of the Empire. 1987.
Servant of the Empire. 1990.
Mistress of the Empire. 1992.

Serpentwar Saga.

Shadow of a Dark Queen. 1994.
Rise of a Merchant Prince. 1995.
Rage of a Demon King. 1997.
Shards of a Broken Crown. 1998.

The Riftwar Legacy.

Krondor, the Betrayal. 1998.
Krondor, the Assassins. 1999.
Krondor Tear of the Gods. 2001.

Conclave of Shadows.

Talon of the Silver Hawk. 2003.
King of Foxes. 2004.
Exile's Return. 2005.

Foster, Alan Dean.

Kingdoms of Light. 2001.

Gemmell, David.

Dates listed are for the U.S. editions; Gemmell's books were originally published in Great Britain.

Drenai series.

Legend. 1994. Also published as *Against the Horde.*
Waylander. 1995.
The King Beyond the Gate. 1995.
Quest for Lost Heroes. 1995.
Waylander II: In the Realm of the Wolf. 1998.
The First Chronicles of Druss the Legend. 1999.
The Legend of Deathwalker. 1999.
Winter Warriors. 2000.
Hero in the Shadows. 2000.
White Wolf. 2003.
Swords of Night and Day: A Novel of Skilgannon the Damned. 2004.

Sipstrassi series. (also called the Stones of Power series).

Ghost King. 1996.

Last Sword of Power. 1988.

Wolf in Shadow. 1997. Also published as *The Jerusalem Man* (1988).

The Last Guardian. 1997.

Bloodstone. 1997.

Riganti Series.

The Sword in the Storm. 2001.

Midnight Falcon. 2001.

Ravenheart. 2001.

Stormrider. 2002.

Goodkind, Terry.

Sword of Truth series.

Wizard's First Rule. 1994.

Stone of Tears. 1995.

Blood of the Fold. 1996.

Temple of the Winds. 1997.

Soul of the Fire. 2000.

Faith of the Fallen. 2001.

The Pillars of Creation. 2002.

Naked Empire. 2003.

Chainfire. 2005.

Greenwood, Ed.

Band of Four.

Band of Four Original Series.

The Kingless Land. 2000.

The Vacant Throne. 2001.

A Dragon's Ascension. 2002.

The Dragon's Doom. 2003.

Band of Four Chronicle of Aglirta.

The Silent House. 2004.

Haydon, Elizabeth.

Rhapsody.

Rhapsody: Child of Blood. 2000.

Prophecy: Child of Earth. 2001.

Destiny: Child of the Sky. 2001.

Symphony of the Ages.

Requiem for the Sun. 2002.

Elegy for a Lost Star. 2004.

Hearn, Lian.

Tales of the Otori.

Across the Nightingale Floor. 2002.

Sixteen-year-old Takeo is captured by Lord Otori as he flees from his village of the Hidden after it is annihilated by Lord Iida. He learns the skills of artists, scholars, and warriors when Lord Otori adopts him and names him his heir.

Grass for His Pillow. 2003.
Brilliance of the Moon. 2004.

Hobb, Robin.

The Farseer series.

Assassin's Apprentice. 1995.
Royal Assassin. 1996.
Assassin's Quest. 1997.

The Liveship Traders.

Ship of Magic. 1999.
Mad Ship. 2000.
Ship of Destiny. 2000.

Tawny Man.

Fool's Errand. 2002.
Golden Fool. 2003.
Fool's Fate. 2004.

Jordan, Robert.

The Wheel of Time series.

The Eye of the World. 1990.
The Great Hunt. 1990.
The Dragon Reborn. 1991.
The Shadow Rising. 1992.
The Fires of Heaven. 1993.
Lord of Chaos. 1994.
Crown of Swords. 1996.
The Path of Daggers. 1998.
Winter's Heart. 2000.
Crossroads of Twilight. 2003.
New Spring. 2004.

Kerr, Katharine.

Deverry Series.

Deverry Original series.

Daggerspell. 1986.
Darkspell. 1987.
The Bristling Wood. 1989.
The Dragon Revenant. 1990.

Deverry: The Westlands series.

A Time of Exile. 1991.
A Time of Omens. 1992.

Days of Blood and Fire. 1993.

Days of Air and Darkness. 1995.

Deverry: Dragon Mage series.

The Red Wyvern. 1997.

The Black Raven. 2000.

Fire Dragon. 2001.

Keyes, Greg.

Kingdoms of Thorn and Bone.

The Briar King. 2003.

The Charnel Prince. 2004.

Le Guin, Ursula K.

The Earthsea series. ★

A Wizard of Earthsea. 1968. Reissued 2004.

The Tombs of Atuan. 1971. Reissued 2004.

The Farthest Shore. 1972. Reissued 2004.

Tehanu. 1990. Reissued 2004.

Tales of Earthsea. 2001. Reissued 2004.

The Other Wind. 2001. Reissued 2004. Winne of the World Fantasy Award, 2002.

Leiber, Fritz.

Fafhrd and the Gray Mouser series.

These are not novels; they are connected short stories and novellas detailing the adventures of the massively heroic barbarian Fafhrd and thief, sorcerer, and swordsman the Gray Mouser. The first story was published in 1939. The following are collections. The order they are listed is the order the Gregg Press editions of 1977 used.

Swords and Deviltry. 1970. Reissued 2003 with the subtitle "Book 1 of the Adventures of Fafhrd and the Gray Mouser."

Swords Against Death. 1970. Reissued 2003 with the subtitle "Book 2 of the Adventures of Fafhrd and the Gray Mouser."

Swords in the Mist. 1968. Reissued 2004 with the subtitle "Books 3 & 4 of the Adventures of Fafhrd and the Gray Mouser."

Swords Against Wizardry. 1968. Reissued 2003.

The Swords of Lankhmar. 1968. Reissued 1986.

Lustbader, Eric Van.

Pearl Saga.

The Ring of Five Dragons. 2001.

The Veil of a Thousand Tears. 2002.

Mistress of the Pearl. 2004.

Martin, George R. R.

Song of Ice and Fire.

When Eddard, Lord of Winterfell, serving as Guardian of the North for the Seven Kingdoms, goes to the capital as the King's Hand, the family is thrust into the political machinations of the evil queen. The seasons of undetermined length, sometimes lasting for years, and a menacing presence beyond a giant frozen wall to the north betide a dire future.

A Game of Thrones. 1996.

A Clash of Kings. 1999. Locus Poll winner.

A Storm of Swords. 2000. Locus Poll winner.

Micklem, Sarah.

Firethorn. 2004.

Modesitt, L. E., Jr.

Corean Chronicles.

Legacies. 2002.

Darkness. 2003.

Scepters. 2004.

Alector's Choice. 2005.

Recluce series.

The Magic of Recluce. 1991.

The Towers of the Sunset. 1992.

The Magic Engineer. 1994.

The Order War. 1995.

The Death of Chaos. 1995.

Fall of Angels. 1996.

Chaos Balance. 1997.

The White Order. 1998.

Colors of Chaos. 1999.

Magi'i of Cyador. 2000.

Scion of Cyador. 2000.

Wellspring of Chaos. 2004.

Ordermaster. 2005.

Newcomb, Robert.

The Chronicles of Blood and Stone.

The Fifth Sorceress. 2002.

The Gates of Dawn. 2004.

The Scrolls of the Ancients. 2004.

Reichert, Mickey Zucker.

Legend of Nightfall. 1993.

The Return of Nightfall. 2004.

Reimann, Katya.

Tielmaran chronicles.

Wind from a Foreign Sky. 1996.

A Tremor in the Bitter Earth. 1998.

Prince of Fire and Ashes. 2002.

Resnick, Laura.

The Chronicles of Sirkara.

The setting is Sileria.

In Legend Born. 1998.

In Fire Forged.

The White Dragon. 2003.

The Destroyer Goddess. 2004.

Russell, Sean.

Swan's War.

The One Kingdom. 2001.

The Isle of Battle. 2003.

The Shadow Roads. 2004.

Shinn, Sharon.

Twelve Houses series.

Mystic and Rider. 2005.

Tolkien, J. R. R.

The Hobbit. 1937. Reissued 2003. ★

The Lord of the Rings trilogy. ★ 🎬

Originally published in 1954 as a three-volume set, these titles have gone through numerous reissues. The popularity of the movies has renewed interest in the classic series.

The Fellowship of the Ring. 1954. Reissued 2004.

The Two Towers. 1954. Reissued 2003.

The Return of the King. 1954. Reissued 2003.

West, Michelle.

The Sun Sword.

The Broken Crown. 1997.

The Uncrowned King. 1998.

The Shining Court. 1999.

The Sea of Sorrows. 2001.

Riven Shield. 2003.

The Sun Sword. 2004.

Williams, Tad.

Shadowmarch Trilogy.

Shadowmarch. Volume 1. 2004.

Wolfe, Gene.

The Wizard Knight.

An elf queen transforms a teenager from our world into a grown man of heroic proportions and sends him on a quest to find a sword.

The Knight. 2004.

The Wizard. 2004.

Saga, Myth, and Legend

Many readers come to fantasy through a love of the tales that are part of the heritage of civilization. Here are the stories that are based on the myths and legends of our ancestors. Our own world is always involved, even if most of the action takes place in a distant land such as the Norse Niflheim or Celtic Summerlands. Titles in the category of saga, myth, and legend are always connected to human cultural traditions.

This section is presented in four parts, the first being "Arthurian Legend," which deals with Arthur and Merlin as well as with other figures related or connected to the "once and future king". The other three sections deal with three culturally diverse groupings (Celtic, Nordic, and Asian) that are currently popular. Many other fascinating cultures have been the basis for fantasy, including Native American, African, Greek, and Roman; however, books in these areas have not been published recently in significant numbers, although they do appear occasionally.

Arthurian Legend

Tales of the heroic King Arthur and those surrounding him abound. Arthurian legends are steeped in historical and cultural heritage. The amount of magic can vary widely. Arthurian fantasy ranges from magic-filled high fantasy to historical fiction extrapolated from archaeological and anthropological research.

Attanasio, A. A.

The Serpent and the Grail. 1999.

Borchardt, Alice.

Tales of Guinevere.

The Dragon Queen. 2001.

The Raven Warrior. 2003.

Bradley, Marion Zimmer.

The Mists of Avalon. 1984. Reissued 2000. ★

Bradley, Marion Zimmer, and Diana L. Paxson.

Priestess of Avalon. **2000.**

The last book in the series that started with *The Mists of Avalon* was completed by Paxson after the death of Marion Zimmer Bradley.

Cochran, Molly, and Warren Murphy.

Arthur Blessing series.

The Forever King. 1992.

The Broken Sword. 1997.

The Third Magic. 2003.

Written by Molly Cochran. Warren Murphy is not listed as a coauthor on the final book in the series.

David, Peter.

Arthur Penn.

Satirical series set in contemporary New York.

Knight Life. 2003.

One Knight Only. 2003.

Holdstock, Robert.

Merlin Codex.

A unique blend of the Merlin legend and Greek mythology.

Celtika. 2003.

The Iron Grail. 2004.

Lawhead, Stephen R.

Avalon: The Return of King Arthur. 1999.

McKenzie, Nancy.

The Tale of Guinevere and King Arthur.

The Child Queen: The Tale of Guinevere and King Arthur. 1994.

Queen of Camelot. 1994.

The High Queen: The Tale of Guinevere and King Arthur Continues. 1995.

Grail Prince. 2003.

Prince of Dreams. 2004.

Miles, Rosalind.

Guenevere series.

This feminist take on the legend looks at the clash between the Roman invaders of Britain and the matriarchal society living there.

Guenevere: Queen of the Summer Country. 1998.

Knight of the Sacred Lake. 2000.

The Child of the Holy Grail. 2001.

The Tristan and Isolde Novels.

Isolde, Queen of the Western Isle. 2002.

The Maid of the White Hands. 2003.

The Lady of the Sea. 2004.

Paxson, Diana L.

Hallowed Isle.

The Book of the Sword. 1999.

The Book of the Spear. 1999.

The Book of the Cauldron. 1999.

The Book of the Stone. 2000.

Radford, Irene.

Merlin's Descendants.

Guardian of the Balance. 1999.

Guardian of the Trust. 2000.

Guardian of the Vision. 2001.

Guardian of the Promise. 2003.
Guardian of the Freedom. 2005.

Stewart, Mary.

The Merlin Sequence. Reissued 2003.

The Crystal Cave. 1970.
The Hollow Hills. 1973.
The Last Enchantment. 1979.
The Wicked Day. 1983.

Whyte, Jack.

Camulod Chronicles.

The lack of magic and the meticulous historical research make this series appealing to fans of historical fiction as well as to fantasy readers.

The Skystone. 1996.
The Singing Sword. 1996.
The Eagle's Brood. 1997.
The Saxon Shore. 1998.
The Fort at River's Bend. 2000.
The Sorcerer: Metamorphosis. 2000.
Uther. 2001.
The Lance Thrower. 2004.

Zettel, Sarah.

The Two Ravens Saga.

In Camelot's Shadow. 2004.

Celtic

Ireland, Scotland, Isle of Man, Cornwall, and Wales were the home of the Celts as far back as the fourth century B.C. Their mythology often deals with the goddess and the fertility of fields and flocks.

Eickhoff, Randy Lee.

Ulster Cycle.

The classic Irish legend featuring heroes, tricksters, and bawdy relationships is retold.

The Raid. 1997.
Cuchulainn and a cattle raid.

The Feast. 1999.
Three heroes go on an epic quest.

The Sorrows. 2000.
The Destruction of the Inn. 2001.
He Stands Alone. 2002.
Cuchulainn's tale from birth, through becoming a warrior, to a battle with underworld spirits.

   The Red Branch Tales. 2003.

Marillier, Juliet.
   <u>Seven Waters Trilogy.</u>
   At the time when the druidic beliefs of caring for the forest, the islands, and the spirit of the land are being replaced by Christian beliefs, strong young women face epic challenges.

   Daughter of the Forest. 2000.
   Son of the Shadows. 2001.
   Child of the Prophecy. 2002.

Osborne-McKnight, Juilene.
   I Am of Irelaunde: A Novel of Patrick and Osian. 2000.
   Daughter of Ireland. 2002.
   Bright Sword of Ireland. 2004.

Nordic

Vikings, berserkers, and their mythology have been a popular setting for fantasy novels of late. A warrior culture and harsh environment make this type of fantasy appealing to readers who enjoy adventure as well as myth and legend.

Anderson, Poul.
   Mother of Kings. 2001.
   War of the Gods. 1997.

Burgess, Melvin.
   Bloodtide. 2001.
   Post-apocalyptic world based on Norse mythology.

Gaiman, Neil.
    *American Gods.* 2001.
   A horrific novel set in contemporary times, but with connections to Norse mythology. Winner of the Hugo, Nebula,; and Bram Stoker Awards and the Locus Poll.

Kay, Guy Gavriel.
   The Last Light of the Sun. 2004.

Marillier, Juliet.
   <u>Children of the Light Isles.</u>
   Wolfskin. 2003.
   Eyvind, a Viking warrior in the eighth century and one of the elite Wolfskins, travels to the Light Isles on a raid and is faced with an enormous dilemma between honoring a blood oath and doing what he feels is right.

Foxmask. 2004.

> When Thorvald sets out on a quest to find his real father, he does not know that Creidhe, the woman who loves him and the daughter of a loving marriage between a Viking warrior and a Celtic woman, has stowed away on his ship.

Asian

Exotic lands of the fabled East provide a wealth of little-known myth and legend to create unique and unusual fantasy novels. Readers who enjoy the Asian setting may also enjoy Lian Hearn's epic fantasy <u>Tales of the Otori</u>, listed in the "Epic/Sword and Sorcery" section of this chapter.

Alexander, Alma.

Secrets of Jin-Shei. 2004.

> In a magical Chinese kingdom, eight young women are bound by a secret language.

Banker, Ashok K.

Ramayana.

> Prince Rama is the protagonist in this retelling of the Ramayana, an ancient Hindu saga. Only the first volume has been published in the United States. The others are from the United Kingdom.

> *Prince of Ayodhya.* 2003.
> *Armies of Hanuman.* 2005.
> *Demons of Chitrakut.* 2005.
> *Bridge of Rama.* 2005.

Johnson, Kij.

The Fox Woman. 2000.

> Based on a Japanese legend. A fox becomes a young woman to win the desire of her soul.

Fudoki. 2003.

> A woman warrior and philosopher started out as a small tortoise shell cat.

Fairy Tales

Retelling of fairy tales and traditional folktales, often with a new twist, has been a growing trend for more than a decade. Some of the stories told in the following novels are familiar, while others may seem new but give the reader a sense that they have been told before. Readers who enjoy fantasy with the flavor of fairy tales and folktales may also want to check out collections and compilations of the original stories. They are often shelved in the nonfiction sections in the children's and adult areas of libraries, places that fantasy readers may not think to visit without the suggestion of a readers' advisor.

An overview of the last 150 years of the short form of fairy tale can be found in *The Oxford Book of Modern Fairy Tales,* edited by Alison Lurie (Oxford University Press, 1993).

Sometimes the classic fairy tale is elaborated upon, extended, or reworked, with the characters developed beyond stereotype (or archetype, if you will) and given human backgrounds and motivation. Sometimes the tale is retold from the antagonist's or a minor character's viewpoint. In other books, familiar fairy tales are used as jumping-off points: The original premise remains, but it is used only as a springboard into something entirely different, taking the hero or heroine into a different century or situation.

Card, Orson Scott.

Enchantment. 1999.

> In the waning days of the Soviet Union, a young boy running through a forest sees a beautiful woman sleeping on a pedestal surrounded by a chasm. As an adult he returns to free her with a kiss and ends up in the tenth century, battling Baba Yaga and other evils.

Ferris, Jean.

Once upon a Marigold. 2002. **YA**

> A child found wandering in a forest is raised by a troll and falls in love with a princess living under a curse.

Lackey, Mercedes.

The Fairy Godmother. 2004.

> Elena, born in the wrong time to be saved by a Prince Charming, flees her wicked stepmother and becomes a fairy godmother-in-training.

Lee, Tanith.

White as Snow. 2000.

> An adaptation of "Snow White."

Maguire, Gregory.

Confessions of an Ugly Stepsister. 1999.

> Cinderella's stepsister.

Mirror, Mirror. 2003.

> Snow White's stepmother.

Wicked: The Life and Times of the Wicked Witch of the West. 1995.

> The life story of the wicked witch from *The Wizard of Oz.*

Medeiros, Teresa.

A Kiss to Remember. 2001.

> A romance-fantasy blend with a male sleeping beauty.

Pattou, Edith.

East. 2003. **YA**

> Based on "East of the Sun, West of the Moon."

Pierce, Meredith Ann.

Treasure at the Heart of the Tanglewood. 2001.

> A young woman's metamorphosis makes the seasons change.

Humorous

Humor plays a major role in fantasy. Often full of topical "in jokes," occasional satire, and parody, such books present more humor to the well-read.

Anthony, Piers.

Xanth series.

Books in this series are full of puns and plays on words. There are far too many to list here, and a new one seems to be published every year. The first three (which are considered by most readers to be the best) are:

🎗 *A Spell for Chameleon.* 1977. Winner of the August Derleth Fantasy Award.
The Source of Magic. 1979.
Castle Roogna. 1979.
Pet Peeve. 2005. The 29th title.

Asprin, Robert.

The M. Y. T. H. series.

Many of the titles are being reprinted.

Baker, Kage.

The Anvil of the World. 2003.

Jones, Diana Wynne.

Howl's Moving Castle. 1986. 🎬 **YA**

A seventeen-year-old is turned into a seventy-year-old and becomes housekeeper for a wizard who lives in a wandering castle.

Moore, John.

Heroics for Beginners. 2004.

This tongue-in-cheek parody of sword-and-sorcery novels is a laugh-out-loud romp. It is a great choice for readers of Pratchett and Asprin as well as those who liked the humorous twist Lackey put on fantasy archetypes in *The Fairy Godmother.*

The Unhandsome Prince. 2005.

Pratchett, Terry.

Discworld series.

This classic series about a flat world riding on the backs of four elephants perched on the back of a turtle continues to gain adherents.

The Color of Magic. 1983.
Eric: A Discworld Novel. 1990.
Reaper Man. 1991.
Lords and Ladies. 1992.
The Light Fantastic. 1986.
Sourcery. 1988.
Guards! Guards! 1989.
Small Gods. 1992.

Men at Arms. 1993.

Wyrd Sisters. 1988.

Moving Pictures. 1990.

Pyramids: The Book of Going Forth. 1989.

Witches Abroad. 1991.

Strata. 1981.

Mort. 1987.

Equal Rites. 1987.

Soul Music. 1995.

Interesting Times. 1994.

Feet of Clay. 1996.

Maskerade. 1995.

Jingo. 1998.

Hogfather. 1996.

The Last Continent. 1998.

Carpe Jugulum. 1998.

The Fifth Elephant. 2000.

The Truth. 2000.

Thief of Time. 2001.

Nightwatch. 2002.

Monstrous Regiment. 2003.

Going Postal. 2004.

The Amazing Maurice and His Educated Rodents. 2001.

The Wee Free Men. 2002. Locus Poll winner. **YA**

A Hat Full of Sky. 2004. **YA**

Rankin, Robert.

The Hollow Chocolate Bunnies of the Apocalypse. 2004.

Toys and nursery rhymes come to life.

A Bestiary

Animals and other creatures play a large role in fantasy. Almost every fantasy has some kind of nonhuman being in it, whether it is a major character with a speaking role, or mere window dressing in the form of a cat soaking up some sunshine. Fantasy in this category ranges from animal fables in which humans play no role and the characters are sentient beasts, to books with an emphasis on the relationship between humans and animals. The preponderance of magic workers in fantasy brings with it animal familiars, who may facilitate the magic of humans or even work magic of their own. Communication between humans and animals is a frequently occurring theme.

Dragons

In fantasy fiction, dragons, which have been depicted in many different ways around the world and throughout history, are often portrayed as telepathic creatures.

Bertin, Joanne.

<u>**Dragonlords series.**</u>

Immortals can shift from human to dragon form.

The Last Dragonlord. 1998.
Dragon and Phoenix. 2000.

Dickson, Gordon R.

<u>**The Dragon and the George series.**</u>

The Dragon and the George. 1976. Reissued 1987.
The Dragon Knight. 1990.
The Dragon on the Border. 1992.
The Dragon at War. 1992.
The Dragon, the Earl, and the Troll. 1994.
Dragon and the Gnarly King. 1997.
The Dragon in Lyonesse. 1999.
The Dragon and the Fair Maid of Kent. 2000.

Hambly, Barbara.

<u>**Dragonsbane series.**</u>

Dragonsbane. 1985. Reissued 1987.
Dragonshadow. 1999.
Knight of the Demon King. 2000.
Dragonstar. 2002.

Kerner, Elizabeth.

<u>**The Tale of Lanen Kaelar.**</u>

Song in the Silence. 1997.
Lesser Kindred. 2000.
Redeeming the Lost. 2004.

Lackey, Mercedes.

<u>**Joust.**</u>

Joust. 2003.
Alta. 2004.

McCaffrey, Anne.

<u>**Pern series.**</u>

Although McCaffrey contends, and even presents evidence to prove, that her works are science fiction, dragon-loving fantasy fans claim the books set on the planet Pern as their own. The titles are listed in the science fiction chapter (chapter 10).

Norton, Andre, and Mercedes Lackey.

<u>**Halfblood chronicles.**</u>

The Elvenbane. 1991.
Elvenblood. 1995.
Elvenborn. 2002.

Paolini, Christopher.

> *Eragon.* 2003.
>
> *Eldest.* 2005.

Radford, Irene.

> **Dragon Nimbus.**
>
> > *Glass Dragon.* 1994.
> >
> > *The Perfect Princess.* 1995.
> >
> > *The Loneliest Magician.* 1996.
>
> **The Dragon Nimbus History.**
>
> > *The Dragon's Touchstone.* 1997.
> >
> > *The Last Battlemage.* 1998.
> >
> > *The Renegade Dragon.* 1999.
>
> **Stargods.**
>
> > *The Hidden Dragon.* 2002.

Walton, Jo.

> ✿ *Tooth and Claw.* 2003. Winner of the World Fantasy Award.

Watt-Evans, Lawrence.

> **Obsidian Chronicles.**
>
> > *Dragon Weather.* 1999.
> >
> > *The Dragon Society.* 2001.
> >
> > *Dragon Venom.* 2003.

Weis, Margaret.

> **Dragonvarld trilogy.**
>
> > *Mistress of Dragons.* 2003.
> >
> > *The Dragon's Son.* 2004.

Uncommon Common Animals

Animals from our world—ordinary creatures such as rabbits, ants, dogs, cats, skunks, and horses—may not seem to fit the fabric of fantasy, but in these stories they take on special characteristics. The animals range from the mundane and ordinary to sentient members of complex societies.

Adams, Richard.

> *Watership Down.* 1972. Reissued 2001. ★ 🎬
>
> > A world of sentient rabbits.

Beagle, Peter.

> *Dance for Emilia.* 2000.
>
> > A possessed, dancing cat.

Hunter, Erin.

> **The Warriors.** YA
>
> > Clans of warrior cats battle for domination of the forest.

Into the Wild. 2003.
Fire and Ice. 2003.
Forest of Secrets. 2003.

Rising Storm. 2004.
A Dangerous Path. 2004.
The Darkest Hour. 2004.

Warriors: The New Prophecy.

Midnight. 2005.
Moonrise. 2005.

Jacques, Brian.

The Redwall series. YA

Small woodland creatures battle evil in this fantasy adventure; popular with all ages.

Redwall. 1986.

Mossflower. 1988.
Mattimeo. 1989.
Mariel of Redwall. 1991.
Salamandastron. 1992.
Martin the Warrior. 1993.

The Bellmaker. 1994. Reissued 2004.
Outcast of Redwall. 1995.
Pearls of Lutra. 1996.
The Long Patrol. 1997.

Marlfox. 1998.
The Legend of Luke. 1999.
Lord Brocktree. 2000.
The Taggerung. 2001.

Triss. 2002.
Loamhedge. 2003.
Rakkety Tam. 2004.

King, Gabriel.

The Golden Cat. 1999.
The Wild Road. 1998.

Lackey, Mercedes.

Valdemar series.

Lacky has written several series about the magical world of Valemar and the Heralds, who have telepathic contact with their horse-like Companions. She lists the more than two dozen titles in both chronological and publication order at http://www.mercedeslackey.com/text/1mlchron.shtml.

Murphy, Shirley Rousseau.

The Catswold Portal. 1993. Reissued 2005.

Shapeshifting cats.

Joe Grey, Cat Detective series.

> Very un-fantasy-like except for the fact that the cats talk and solve mysteries.

Tolkien, J. R. R.

> *Roverandom.* 1998.

> > A dog, transformed into a toy, searches for the wizard who cursed him.

Wangerin, Walter.

> *The Book of the Dun Cow.* 1978. Reissued 2003.

> > Barnyard animals.

World of Faerie

Although not a large subgenre, the world of Faerie has influenced much of fantasy, and its conventions frequently pop up in many types of literature and popular media. This is not a world inhabited by delicate-winged, Tinkerbell-like creatures, but rather one where dwells a strange and mysterious race with powers that seem magical to mere humans. Plots in this subgenre almost always involve the conflict between humans and the elven inhabitants of Faerie, who seem to have a proclivity for falling in love with each other. Tales of changelings also abound.

Readers fond of this subgenre may also enjoy urban fantasy, in which the worlds of Faerie and humans collide, the idea being that a place exists side by side with our world that has different rules of nature and where time passes at a different rate.

Augarde, Steve.

> *The Various.* 2004.

> > In this book for all ages, a young girl sent to stay with an uncle for the summer finds and frees a winged horse who has been trapped in an outbuilding.

Datlow, Ellen, and Terri Windling, eds.

> *The Green Man: Tales from the Mythic Forest.* 2002.

> > Short stories dealing with the world of faerie.

Gaiman, Neil.

> *Stardust.* 1998.

Holdstock, Robert.

> **Mythago Cycle.**

> > Ryhope Wood is an enchanted world in which mythic images come to life.

> > ✿ *Mythago Wood.* 1984. Reissued 2003 Winner of the World Fantasy Award.
> > *Lavondyss: Journey to an Unkown Region.* 1988. Reissued 2004.
> > *The Hollowing.* 1994. Reissued 2005.
> > *Gate of Ivory, Gate of Horn.* 1997. Reissued 2001.

Hoyt, Sarah A.

> **Shakespeare series.**

> > *Ill Met by Moonlight.* 2001.

>>> *All Night Awake.* 2002.

>>> *Any Man So Daring.* 2003.

Lackey, Mercedes, and Roberta Gellis.

> ### The Scepter'd Isle.

>> *This Scepter'd Isle.* 2004.

>> Henry VIII.

>> *Ill Met by Moonlight.* 2005.

>> The evil Unseleighe Sidhe try to keep Elizabeth from becoming queen.

McNaughton, Janet.

> *An Earthly Knight.* 2004. **YA**

>> Based on Scottish ballads.

Shinn, Sharon.

> *Summers at Castle Auburn.* 2001.

>> The young Coriel, illegitimate daughter of a noble and a wise woman, finds that things she thought were terrific—hunting for Aliora, the elven-like fey creatures used as slaves, and the gorgeous crown prince who is betrothed to her half-sister—are not exactly as great as they seemed.

Snyder, Midori.

> *Hannah's Garden.* 2002. **YA**

Windling, Terri.

> *The Wood Wife.* 1996. Reissued 2003.

Urban Fantasy

Drugs, racism, gangs, and other scourges of modern life are evident in this subgenre, the fantasy equivalent of science fiction's cyberpunk. Here magic and technology share a place in gritty, dangerous cities, where a rift between our world and the world of Faerie has occurred. Readers of urban fantasy should also check the "Shared Worlds" section later in this chapter for the <u>Borderlands series.</u>

Black, Holly.

> *Tithe, a Modern Faerie Tale.* 2002. **YA**

Brust, Steven, and Megan Lindholm.

> *The Gypsy.* 1992. Reissued 2005.

Bull, Emma.

> *War for the Oaks.* 1987. Reissued 2004.

Cunningham, Elaine.

> ### Changeling Trilogy.

>> A faerie detective.

>> *Shadows in the Darkness.* 2004.

de Lint, Charles.

> <u>**Newford Series.**</u>
>
> > Many of de Lint's novels are set in the fictional city Newford. The titles listed here are in chronological order, but each titles stands alone quite well. Newford has also been the setting of several of de Lint's short stories.
> >
> > *Trader.* 1997. Reissued 2005.
> > *Someplace to Be Flying.* 1998.
> > *The Onion Girl.* 2001.
> > *Spirits in the Wires.* 2003.
> > *The Blue Girl.* 2004. **YA**

Gaiman, Neil.

> *Neverwhere.* 1997. Reissued 2003. **TVS**
> Gritty London setting.

Rusch, Kristine Kathryn.

> *Fantasy Life.* 2003.

Shetterly, Will.

> <u>**Bordertown.**</u> Both titles reissued in 2004.
>
> > *Elsewhere.* 1991.
> > Runaway Ron ends up in Bordertown.
> >
> > *NeverNever.* 1993.
> > Ron, now transformed into a wolf-boy, comes of age as he discovers what life is really about.

Spencer, Wen.

> *Tinker.* 2003.
>
> > Tinker, an inventor and girl genius, saves an elven lord who is chased into her salvage yard by a pack of wargs. Winner of the Sapphire Award.

Windling, Terri, and Delia Sherman, eds.

> *The Essential Bordertown.* 1998.
> Shared-world short stories set in Bordertown.

Alternate and Parallel Worlds

Other fully developed worlds, whether our own transformed by a difference in history or that can be traveled to from our world, are featured in this subgenre. Sometimes the alternate world is a fully fleshed-out one that has no relation to our own but rather has its own fully developed history and rules. Alternate and parallel worlds are also found in science fiction.

Alternate History

Due to a divergence someplace in time, the worlds presented are very different from the world we know. Alternate history is an area that is most frequently claimed by science fiction, but many titles fit in the fantasy arena as well as or better than in science fiction.

Barnes, Steven.

Slavery and Freedom.

A young Irish slave is brought to a North America ruled by those who came from Africa.

Lion's Blood. 2002.
Zulu Heart. 2003.

Bear, Greg.

Dinosaur Summer. 1998.

Brust, Steven, and Emma Bull.

Freedom and Necessity. 1997.

A magical, mysterious romp through mid-nineteenth-century England.

Card, Orson Scott.

Chronicles of Alvin Maker.

In this alternate nineteenth-century North America, hexes and spells work, and the states never became a union. It is American history with a twist and echoes of the life of Joseph Smith, the founder of Mormonism.

Seventh Son. 1987.
Red Prophet. 1988.
Prentice Alvin. 1989.
Alvin Journeyman. 1995.
Heartfire. 1998.
The Crystal City. 2003.

Dalkey, Kara.

Genpei. **2001.**

Twelfth-century Japan.

Blood of the Goddess.

Sixteenth-century India.

Goa. 1997.
Bijapur. 1998.
Bhagavati. 1998.

Douglass, Sara.

The Troy Game.

Hades' Daughter. 2003.
Gods' Concubine. 2004.
Darkwitch Rising. 2005.

Goldstein, Lisa.

Alchemist's Door. 2002.

Sixteenth century.

Hickman, Tracy, and Laura Hickman.
> <u>The Bronze Canticles.</u>
>> *Mystic Warrior.* 2004.
>> *Mystic Quest.* 2005.

Kay, Guy Gavriel.
> *The Last Light of the Sun.* 2004.
> *The Lions of Al-Rassan.* 1995.
> *The Sarantine Mosaic.* 1999.

Robinson, Kim Stanley.
> *The Years of Rice and Salt.* 2002.

Sargent, Pamela.
> *Climb the Wind: A Novel of Another America.* 1999.

Turtledove, Harry.
> The prolific and most widely known author of alternative histories often has a technological emphasis that places many of his tales in science fiction, where several of his titles are listed.

Parallel Worlds

In the following works, characters travel from one world to another. The conflict in the story often arises from being a stranger in a strange land.

Barker, Clive.
> <u>Abarat.</u>
>> Miserable in Chickentown, Minnesota, Candy Quackenbush finds a lighthouse in the middle of the fields and ends up in the darkly magical land of Abarat, where each island is in a different time, and the evil Lord Carrion pursues her.
>>
>> *Abarat.* 2002.
>> *Days of Magic, Nights of War.* 2004.

Donaldson, Stephen R.
> <u>The Chronicles of Thomas Covenant, the Unbeliever.</u>
>> *First Chronicle.*
>>> *Lord Foul's Bane.* 1977. Reissued 1987.
>>> *The Illearth War.* 1977. Reissued 1987.
>>> *The Power That Preserves.* 1977. Reissued 1987.
>> *Second Chronicle.*
>>> *The Wounded Land.* 1980. Reissued 1987.
>>> *The One Tree.* 1982. Reissued 1987.
>>> *White Gold Wielder.* 1983. Reissued 1987.
>> *Last Chronicle.*
>>> *The Runes of the Earth.* 2004.

Fforde, Jasper.

<u>**Thursday Next series.**</u>

In a world where literature is of major importance, Special Operative Thursday Next solves a series of literary mysteries, in this series filled with humor and wit.

Eyre Affair. 2002.
Lost in a Good Book. 2003.
The Well of Lost Plots. 2004.
Something Rotten. 2004.

Funke, Cornelia.

Inkheart. 2003.

This lengthy book, featuring a protagonist who is such a powerful reader that characters step out of the pages for him, was written for young adults, but adults will also enjoy the story.

Inkspell. 2005. ▮

Grimsley, Jim.

The Ordinary. 2004.

Jones, Diana Wynne.

The Merlin Conspiracy. 2003. ▮

In a very complex tale of parallel worlds, two teens from a land called Blest team up with a teen who has traveled from our world to fight a diabolical political plot.

King, Stephen.

<u>**The Dark Tower series.**</u>

The Gunslinger. 1982. Reissued 2003.
The Drawing of the Three. 1987. Reissued 2003.
The Waste Lands. 1991. Reissued 2003.
Wizard and Glass. 1997.
Wolves of the Calla. 2003.
Song of Susannah. 2004.
The Dark Tower. 2004.

Le Guin, Ursula K.

The Lathe of Heaven. 1971. Reissued 2003. ★ 🎬
George Orr's dreams become reality.

Marley, Louise.

The Glass Harmonica. 2000.

A young woman from the future sees one from the past with the help of music.

Modesitt, L. E., Jr.

<u>**The Spellsong Cycle.**</u>

The Soprano Sorceress. 1997.
The Spellsong War. 1998.
Darksong Rising. 1999.

> *The Shadow Sorceress.* 2001.

Pullman, Philip.

His Dark Materials.

> Lyra, her daemon Pantalaimon, and Will have far-ranging adventures as they travel through several different worlds experiencing all kinds of dangers and meeting a myriad of people who affect their lives.

> *The Golden Compass.* 1996. (film in production for release in 2007).
> *The Subtle Knife.* 1998.
> *The Amber Spyglass.* 2000.

Rosenberg, Joel.

Keepers of the Hidden Ways series.

> *The Fire Duke.* 1995.
> *The Silver Stone.* 1996.
> *The Crimson Sky.* 1998.

Guardians of the Flame.

> *The Sleeping Dragon.* 1983.
> *The Sword and the Chain.* 1984.
> *The Silver Crown.* 1985.
> *The Heir Apparent.* 1987.
> *The Warrior Lives.* 1988.
> *The Road to Ehvenor.* 1991. Reissued 2004.
> *The Road Home.* 1995.
> *Not Exactly the Three Musketeers.* 1999.
> *Not Quite Scaramouche.* 2001.
> *Not Really the Prisoner of Zenda.* 2003.

Twelve Hawks, John.

> *The Traveler.* 2005.

Zettel, Sarah.

Isavalta.

> *A Sorcerer's Treason A Novel of Isavalta.* 2002.
> *The Usurper's Crown.* 2003.
> *The Firebird's Vengeance.* 2004.

Alternate Worlds

Fully realized worlds with distinct political and cultural histories are found throughout the fantasy genre. All of the following titles feature complex worlds, and perhaps because of this, they tend to appear in multivolume series.

Bell, Hilari.

The Farsala Trilogy.

> Three teens, a highborn deghass, her bastard brother, and a scheming peasant are caught up in a world at war.

Fall of a Kindgdom. 2004. Published as *Flame* in 2003. **YA**

Rise of a Hero. 2005. **YA**

Bradley, Marion Zimmer.

Darkover series.

Brust, Steven.

World of Dragaera.

Phoenix Guards.

The Phoenix Guards. 1991.

Five Hundred Years After. 1994.

The Viscount of Andrilankha.

The Paths of the Dead. 2002.

The Lord of Castle Black. 2003.

Sethra Lavode. 2004.

Vlad Taltos series.

Jhereg. 1983.

Yendi. 1984.

Teckla. 1987.

Taltos. 1988.

Phoenix. 1990.

Athyra. 1993.

Orca. 1996.

Dragon. 1998.

Issola. 2001.

Carey, Jacqueline.

Kushiel's Legacy.

A world filled with eroticism and pain.

Kushiel's Dart. 2001.

Kushiel's Chosen. 2002.

Kushiel's Avatar. 2003.

Clarke, Susanna.

🏅 *Jonathan Strange & Mr. Norrell.* 2004.

This Hugo Award winner is set in an alternate England where magic, long in decline, is revived by two very different men.

Clayton, Jo.

Drums of Chaos series.

Drum Warning. 1996.

Drum Calls. 1997.

Drum into Silence. 2002.

This posthumous conclusion to the Drums of Chaos series was coauthored and finished by Kevin Andrew Murphy.

Dorsey, Candas Jane.

  Black Wine. 1997. 📖

Elliott, Kate.

  <u>Crown of Stars series.</u>

    Kings Dragon. 1997.
    Prince of Dogs. 1998.
    The Burning Stone. 1999.
    Child of Flame. 2000.
    The Gathering Storm. 2003.

Kurtz, Katherine.

  <u>The Deryni Saga.</u> ★

    Encompasses several trilogies.

  <u>*The Legends of Camber of Culdi series.*</u>

    Camber of Culdi. 1976.
    Saint Camber. 1978.
    Camber the Heretic. 1981.

  <u>*The Heirs of Saint Camber series.*</u>

    The Harrowing of Gwynedd. 1989.
    King Javan's Year. 1992.
    The Bastard Prince. 1994.

  <u>*The Chronicles of the Deryni.*</u>

    Deryni Rising. 1970. Reissued 2004.
    Deryni Checkmate. 1972.
    High Deryni. 1973.

  <u>The Histories of King Kelson series.</u>

    The Bishop's Heir. 1984.
    The King's Justice. 1985.
    The Quest for Saint Camber. 1986.
    King Kelson's Bride. 2000.
    In the King's Service. 2003.

Nix, Garth.

  <u>The Old Kingdom.</u>

    Sabriel. 1995. Winner of both the Best Fantasy Novel and Best Young Adult Novel in the 1995 Australian Aurealis Awards. **YA**
    Lirael. 2001.
    Abhorsen. 2003.

Rowling, J. K.

  <u>Harry Potter series.</u> **YA**

    The series that originally started as one for children has developed a life of its own and has had a major impact on the world of fantasy fiction.

Harry Potter and the Sorcerer's Stone. 1998. Originally published in England under the title *Harry Potter and the Philosopher's Stone.*

Harry Potter and the Chamber of Secrets. 1999.

Harry Potter and the Prisoner of Azkaban. 1999. Winner of the Whitbread Award and the Locus Poll.

Harry Potter and the Goblet of Fire. 2000. Winner of the Hugo Award.

Harry Potter and the Order of the Phoenix. 2003.

Harry Potter and the Half-Blood Prince. 2005.

Scott, Melissa, and Lisa Barnett.

Point of Dreams. 2001.

Point of Hopes. 1995.

Volsky, Paula.

The Grand Ellipse. 2000.

Religion-Based Alternate Worlds

The role of religion in shaping an alternate world is a growing theme in fantasy fiction today, although mythology has long been popular. This more recent type delves into how religion affects individual lives, as well as society as a whole.

Bujold, Lois McMaster.

Chalion.

The Curse of Chalion. 2001.

Paladin of Souls. 2003. Winner of the Hugo and Nebula Awards and the Locus Poll.

The Hallowed Hunt. 2005.

Carey, Jacqueline.

The Sundering.

Banewreaker. 2004.

Godslayer. 2005.

Douglass, Sara.

The Crucible.

The Nameless Day. 2005.

The Wounded Hawk. 2005.

Hambly, Barbara.

Sisters of the Raven. 2002.

Gangsters and a new religious cult have cornered the market on water in the Slaughterhouse, the district just outside the city walls that houses the poor.

Lindskold, Jane.

The Buried Pyramid. 2004.

In an Indiana Jones–like adventure turned to fantasy, a young American, her uncle, and his hieroglyphs teacher are locked into a buried pyramid and escape through passages to the shores of a Nile that shouldn't be there, where they help Ra travel the dangers of night so the sun can rise again.

Shinn, Sharon.

 <u>**Samaria series.**</u>

 The Archangel. 1996.

 Jovah's Angel. 1997.

 The Alleluia Files. 1998.

 Angelica. 2003.

 Angel-Seeker. 2004.

Strauss, Victoria.

 The Burning Land. 2004.

 The adherents of the sleeping god Arata, who has many aspects, have finally reclaimed Galea and overthrown the Caryaxists, who desecrated and destroyed temples and monasteries, forcing the Aratists into exile or prison over a period of eighty years. Gyalo, a young priest and strongly talented shaper, is sent on an expedition into the Burning Lands to discover what happened to the Aratists who were exiled there.

Shared Worlds

Shared world novels are those that are written by various authors, set in a world conceived and developed by another individual or group. Sometimes they arise organically from a novel or series so beloved that it achieves a life of its own, such as Norton's <u>Witch World</u> and Bradley's <u>Darkover</u>. Shared worlds are not necessarily initially conceived in books. They may have their genesis in television or movies or games, either computerized or not.

The introduction of shared world stories, in which an imaginary world is created by an editor, author, or group and is then used as a background by several authors, has resulted in the publication of several series. As in any set of works created by committee, there is bound to be some variation in quality, but the following series have been popular.

The shared worlds seem to be particularly popular in series based on role-playing games, movies, television shows, and even computer games. A growing trend in shared world universes has been for the setting and characters to appear in several different venues: novels, graphic novels, comics, games, and the Internet.

 <u>**Bordertown.**</u>

 This quintessential shared world series basically created the urban fantasy. Locus called it "the finest of all shared worlds." This is a world in which our world and that of Faerie meet in a gritty city where runaways from both worlds meet.

 Bull, Emma.

 Finder. 1994. Reissued 2004.

 Shetterly, Will.

 Elsewhere. 1991. Reissued 2004.

 NeverNever. 1993. Reissued 2004.

 Windling, Terri, and Delia Sherman, eds.

 The Essential Bordertown: A Traveller's Guide to the Edge of Faerie. 1999.

Darkover.

The late Marion Zimmer Bradley's world of <u>Darkover</u> has proven to be popular enough to work its way into a shared world universe. She edited several anthologies of stories set in the world she created. This is a world in which some of the descendants of human colonists have developed telepathic powers called *laran*.

DragonLance.

Role-playing-game based, this series continues to thrive. Margaret Weis and Tracy Hickman became best-selling authors with their many series set in the world of Krynn. A list of titles is available at http://www.wizards.com/default.asp?x=books/dl/ bibliography.

Forgotten Realms.

Role-playing-game based, this series also continues to thrive. It is a series of fantasy worlds filled with elves, dwarves, dragons, wizards, and all things magical.

Magic Time.

When all things mechanical or electronic stop working and people start morphing into other creatures, it is obvious that huge changes are taking place in the world.

Zicree, Marc Scott, and Barbara Hambly.

Magic Time. 2001.

Bohnhoff, Maya Kaathryn.

Angelfire. 2002.

Zicree, Marc Scott, and Robert Charles Wilson.

Ghostlands. 2004.

Thieves' World-Sanctuary Series.

The creation of Robert Lynn Asprin and Lynn Abbey in 1978, all books were published between 1979 and 1990. While many shared world series are based on games, a game was created based on the <u>Thieves' World series</u>. A graphic novel series was also created. Among the contributing authors were Lynn Abbey, Poul Anderson, Robert Lynn Asprin, Robin Wayne Bailey, Marion Zimmer Bradley, John Brunner, C. J. Cherryh, Christine DeWeese, David Drake, Diane Duane, Philip José Farmer, Joe Haldeman, Vonda N. McIntyre, Chris Morris, Janet Morris (who has done separate novels on <u>Thieves' World</u>: *Beyond Sanctuary*, *Beyond Wizard-Wall*, and *Beyond the Veil*), Andrew Offutt, Diana L. Paxson, and A. E. van Vogt. The first six volumes (original paperbacks) were gathered into two volumes by Science Fiction Books in Sanctuary: *Thieves' World*, *Tales from the Vulgar Unicorn*, *Shadows of Sanctuary*, and *Cross Currents: Storm Season, The Face of Chaos, Wings of Omen*. Volumes 7–10 in the series are long out of print, and even though some libraries still list them in their catalogs, the physical copies are missing. Those titles are *The Dead of Winter, Soul of the City, Blood Ties, Aftermath, Uneasy Alliances,* and *Stealer's Sky*.

The series was reborn in this century with *Sanctuary* (2002) by Lynn Abbey, followed by *Turning Points* (2002), which features stories by Mickey Zucker Reichert, Andrew Offutt, Diana L Paxson, Selina Rosen, Dennis L McKiernan, Robin Wayne Bailey, Jody Lynn Nye, Lynn Abbey, Jeff Grubb, and Raymond E. Feist. *Enemies of Fortune* (2004) features stories by C. J. Cherryh, Mickey Zucker Reichert, Dennis L. McKiernan, Jody Lynn Nye, Lynn Abbey, Selina Rosen, Andrew Offutt, Robin Wayne Bailey, Jane Fancher, Jeff Grubb, Steven Brust, Diana L. Paxson, and Ian Grey.

Valdemar

Mercedes Lackey made the world of Valdemar so fully developed and enticing that others wanted to write stories set there. *Sword of Ice: And Other Tales of Valdemar* (1999), edited by Mercedes Lackey and John Yezeguielian, includes eighteen stories by Mickey Zucker Reichert, Larry Dixon, Tanya Huff, Michelle Sagara, and others.

Dark Fantasy

Defining dark fantasy is as difficult as defining fantasy itself. It is very strongly linked to horror. Both genres scare or terrify, but in dark fantasy the emphasis is on the magic and often on the conflict between good and evil, while in horror the emphasis is simply on terrifying the reader. Like horror, dark fantasy tends to be very atmospheric. Many titles included in this section also appear on horror lists, and readers who enjoy the titles listed here may also want to consult the "dark fantasy" section in the horror chapter (chapter 12). Many authors who are known for writing horror have been recipients of major fantasy awards for their dark fantasy titles.

Bellaires, John.

> *The Face in the Frost.* 1969. Reissued 2000.
>
>> Wizard Prospero's strange dreams and glimpses of strange beings out of the corner of his eye may be connected to a mysterious book written in cipher, which his friend Roger Bacon is seeking.

Bradbury, Ray.

> *The October Country.* 1955. Reissued 1999. ★
>
> *Something Wicked This Way Comes.* 1962. Reissued 1999. ★

Brooks, Terry.

> <u>The Word and the Void Trilogy.</u>
>
>> *Running with the Demon.* 1997.
>>
>> *Knight of the Word.* 1998.
>>
>> *Angel Fire East.* 1999.

Gaiman, Neil.

> *Coraline.* 2002. Winner of the Hugo and Nebula (Novella) Awards and the Locus Poll for Young Adults. **YA**

Hamilton, Laurell K.

> <u>Merry Gentry series.</u>
>
>> *A Kiss of Shadows.* 2002.
>>
>> *Seduced by Moonlight.* 2004.

Hoffman, Nina Kiriki.

> *Past the Size of Dreaming.* 2001.
>
> *A Red Heart of Memories.* 1999.

McKillip, Patricia A.

> *Ombria in Shadow.* 2002. Winner of the World Fantasy Award.

McMullen, Sean.

    <u>Moonworlds saga.</u>

        Voyage of the Shadowmoon. 2002.

        Glass Dragons. 2004.

Meiville, China.

    Iron Council. 2004.

    🏵 *Perdido Street Station.* 2001. Winner of the Arthur C. Clarke and British Fantasy Awards.

    🏵 *The Scar.* 2002. Winner of the Locus Poll and the British Fantasy Award.

Zicree, Marc Scott.

    <u>Magic Time.</u>

        A shared world series created by Zicree and listed in the "Shared Worlds" section of this chapter.

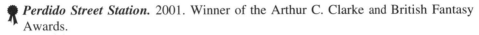

Romantic Fantasy

    Fantasy and romance are a match seemingly made in fairyland. The early twenty-first century saw many popular and successful combinations of the two genres. Tor, a publisher long known for fantasy and science fiction, has added a romance line called Tor Romance that features romance with strong fantasy and/or paranormal themes. Harlequin, a publisher that means romance to many, has come into the fantasy field in a major way with its Luna line. While time travel romance, so popular in the 1990s, is waning, romance blended with fairy tales and paranormal powers is blossoming. The Romance Writers of America award the Prism Award, while the *Science Fiction Romance Newsletter* (which also includes fantasy) awards the Sapphire Award. Readers will find many titles that combine fantasy and romance in the romance chapter (chapter 9).

Smith, Deborah.

    Alice at Heart. 2002.

        Alice, an ugly duckling with webbed feet who has not grown into a swan, is taking a frigid winter swim in Lake Riley, high in the Georgia Appalachians, when she has a vision of a diver far away—drowning.

Tower, S. D.

    The Assassins of Tamurin. 2003.

        Her loyalty cemented by wraiths from the Quiet World who will torture her to death if she betrays the Despotana, Lale is sent out in the world to earn the skills of an actress in the high theater, where she learns that she looks almost exactly like the Sun Lord's late wife.

Topics

The resources listed here are intended to broaden the reader's knowledge of the genre.

Anthologies

Anthologies are of particular importance because they showcase a broad range of styles and types. Many of the anthologies offer insightful essays, historical information, and informative commentary on trends and authors. The following is merely a sampling of what is available. A more extensive list of anthologies is included in *Fluent in Fantasy* (Libraries Unlimited, 1999), which also lists selected short story collections by individual authors.

Friesner, Esther, ed. *Chicks in Chainmail.* Pocket, 1995.
   A wildly popular, humorous anthology featuring swordswomen and other formidable females.

———. *Did You Say Chicks?* Baen, 1998.
   Short stories about sword-wielding warrior women by Elizabeth Moon, Jody Lynn Nye, Margaret Ball, Harry Turtledove, Esther Friesner, and others.

Griffith, Nicola, and Stephen Pagel, eds. *Bending the Landscape: Fantasy.* White Wolf Publishing, 1997.
   Gay and lesbian fantasy by Mark Shepherd, Holly Wade Matter, Kim Antieau, Mark W. Tiedemann, Simon Sheppard, J. A. Salmonson, Don Bassingthwaite, Ellen Kushner, Tanya Huff, Robin Wayne Bailey, and others.

Scarborough, Elizabeth Ann, and Martin H. Greenberg. *Warrior Princesses.* DAW, 1998. Stories by Anne McCaffrey, Jane Yolen, Elizabeth Moon, and more.

Silverberg, Robert, ed. *The Fantasy Hall of Fame: The Definitive Collection of the Best Modern Fantasy Chosen by the Members of the Science Fiction and Fantasy Writers of America.* HarperPrism, 1998.
   Thirty stories first published between 1939 and 1990, selected by the membership of the Science Fiction and Fantasy Writers of America, offer a sampling of classic fantasy. The voting criteria are explained and the ranking of the stories is listed. The fifteen stories receiving the most votes were "The Lottery," Shirley Jackson; "Jeffty Is Five," Harlan Ellison; "Unicorn Variations," Roger Zelazny; "Bears Discover Fire," Terry Bisson; "That Hell-Bound Train," Robert Bloch; "Come Lady Death," Peter S. Beagle; "Basileus," Robert Silverberg; "The Golem," Avram Davidson; "Buffalo Gals, Won't You Come Out Tonight," Ursula K. Le Guin; "Her Smoke Rose up Forever," James Tiptree, Jr. (not included in the anthology); "The Loom of Darkness," Jack Vance; "The Drowned Giant," J. G. Ballard; "The Detective of Dreams," Gene Wolfe; "The Jaguar Hunter," Lucius Shepard; and "The Compleat Werewolf," Anthony Boucher. The collection also includes sixteen runners-up.

—————. *Legends: Short Novels by the Masters of Modern Fantasy.* Tor, 1998.
Stories by Stephen King, Terry Pratchett, Terry Goodkind, Orson Scott Card, Robert Silverberg, Ursula K. Le Guin, Tad Williams, George R. R. Martin, Anne McCaffrey, Raymond E. Feist, and Robert Jordan are a great introduction to current popular fantasy novelists.

—————. *Legends II: Short Novels by the Masters of Modern Fantasy.* DelRey, 2003.
Stories by Robin Hobb, George R. R. Martin, Orson Scott Card, Diana Gabaldon, Robert Silverberg, Tad Williams, Anne Mccaffrey, Raymond E. Feist, Elizabeth Haydon, Neil Gaiman, and Terry Brooks.

Williams, A. Susan, and Richard Glyn Jones, eds. *The Penguin Book of Modern Fantasy by Women.* Penguin USA, 1997. Winner of the World Fantasy Award. Thirty-eight stories written since 1941. Introduction by Joanna Russ. Authors included are Elizabeth Bowen, Shirley Jackson, Leigh Brackett, Daphne du Maurier, Leonora Carrington, Zenna Henderson, Muriel Spark, Anna Kavan, Anne McCaffrey, Joan Aiken, Hilary Bailey, Kit Reed, Josephine Saxton, Christine Brooke-Rose, Kate Wilhelm, Joanna Russ, P. D. James, James Tiptree, Jr., Margaret Atwood, Fay Weldon, Joyce Carol Oates, Vonda N. McIntyre, Lisa Tuttle, Tanith Lee, Ursula K. Le Guin, Angela Carter, Mary Gentle, Janet Frame, Zoe Fairbairns, Octavia E. Butler, Candas Jane Dorsey, Suniti Namjoshi, Suzy McKee Charnas, Carol Emshwiller, Lynda Rajan, L. A. Hall, Ann Oakley, and Lucy Sussex.

Anthology Series

Fantasy: The Best of . . . Edited by Jonathan Strahan and Karen Haber. I Books, 2004–
.

Nebula Awards Showcase. Roc, 2000– .
Nebula Awards Showcase 2004, edited by Vonda N. McIntyre, was published in 2004.

Nebula Awards: SFWA's Choices for the Best Science Fiction and Fantasy of the Year. Harcourt Brace, 1966–1999.
This annual anthology included short pieces and excerpts of nominations for the year as well as essays. Editors have included Connie Willis, Pamela Sargent, James Morrow, George Zebrowski, Michael Bishop, Jack Dann, Poul Anderson, Ursula K. Le Guin, James Blish, Lloyd Biggle Jr., James Gunn, Kate Wilhelm, Joe Haldeman, Brian Aldiss, Roger Zelazny, Clifford D. Simak, Isaac Asimov, Jerry Pournelle, Marta Randall, Robert Silverberg, Samuel R. Delany, Gordon R. Dickson, Frederik Pohl, Frank Herbert, and Damon Knight. The name was changed to *Nebula Awards Showcase* in 2000.

Year's Best Fantasy. Edited by David G. Hartwell and Kathryn Cramer. Eos, 2001– .

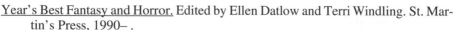

Year's Best Fantasy and Horror. Edited by Ellen Datlow and Terri Windling. St. Martin's Press, 1990– .
The twelfth annual collection was published in 1999, the numbering continuing from the previous title, *Year's Best Fantasy.*

Bibliographies and Biographies

Ashley, Michael, and William G. Contento. *The Supernatural Index: A Listing of Fantasy, Supernatural, Occult, Weird, and Horror Anthologies.* Greenwood, 1995.
  More than 21,000 stories by over 7,700 authors in more than 2,100 anthologies are indexed.

Barron, Neil, ed. *What Fantastic Fiction Do I Read Next? A Reader's Guide to Recent Fantasy, Horror and Science Fiction.* Gale, 1998.
  Noncritical, it lists books released in the specified time span of 1989–1997. Characters, settings, and key worlds are indexed.

Hall, Hal W., ed. *Science Fiction and Fantasy Reference Index, 1985–1991: An International Author and Subject Index to History and Criticism.* Libraries Unlimited, 1993.
  Definitive listings of secondary materials.

———. *Science Fiction and Fantasy Reference Index, 1992–1995: An International Subject and Author Index to History and Criticism.* Libraries Unlimited, 1997.
  Definitive listings of secondary materials.

Hawk, Pat. *Hawk's Science Fiction, Fantasy & Horror Series & Sequels.* Hawk's Enterprises, 2001.
  The title says it all.

Herald, Diana Tixier. *Fluent in Fantasy: A Guide to Reading Interests.* Libraries Unlimited, 1999.
  The first readers' advisory tool focusing solely on fantasy, this is the definitive guide to the genre. The book describes thousands of fantasy titles and categorizes them into fifteen subgenres (e.g., sword and sorcery, humor, shared world, dark fantasy). It also includes a historical background of the genre, tips for readers' advisors, a recommended core list for libraries, and lists of resources. Award winners and titles that appeal to teens are noted, and there are author/title and subject indexes.

Mediavilla, Cindy. *Arthurian Fiction.* Scarecrow, 1999.
  Over 200 Arthurian novels are annotated, with an emphasis on books for young adults.

Encyclopedias

Clute, John, and John Grant. *The Encyclopedia of Fantasy.* St. Martin's Press, 1997.
  The first, only, and definitive encyclopedia of fantasy. This is a must-have for every serious fantasy collection. It has over a million words in 4,000 entries. Everything you ever wanted to know about fantasy from the dawn of time to 1995 is included. Not only covering the written word, it also takes on movies, television, art, and live performances that are fantasy based. Awards and conventions are listed, as are themes and motifs.

History and Criticism

In addition to the following works, material on fantasy can be found in some histories and criticisms of science fiction.

Buker, Derek M. *The Science Fiction and Fantasy Readers' Advisory: The Librarian's Guide to Cyborgs, Aliens, and Sorcerers.* ALA Editions, 2002.

Hall, Hal W., ed. *Science Fiction and Fantasy Reference Index, 1985–1991: An International Author and Subject Index to History and Criticism*. Libraries Unlimited, 1993.

MacRae, Cathi Dunn. *Presenting Young Adult Fantasy Fiction*. Twayne, 1998. Discusses what young adults really read and why, but because in fantasy young adults and adults read the same things, this is a book for all serious fantasy collections. Biographies of Terry Brooks, Jane Yolen, Barbara Hambly, and Meredith Ann Pierce provide more in-depth fantasy analysis.

Magill, Frank N., ed. *Survey of Modern Fantasy Literature*. Salem Press, 1983. 5 vols.

Sobczak, A. J., and T. A. Shippey, eds. *Magill's Guide to Science Fiction and Fantasy Literature*. Salem Press, 1996. 4 vols. *Volume 1. The Absolute at Large—Dragonsbane; Volume 2. Dream—The Lensman Series; Volume 3. Lest Darkness Fall—So Love Returns; Volume 4. Software and Wetware— Zotz!*

Organizations and Conventions

The British Fantasy Society (http://www.britishfantasysociety.org.uk). Established in 1971 and sponsors the annual FantasyCon. FantasyCon 2005 was held from September 30 to October 2, 2005 at the Quality Hotel in Bentley, Walsall. BFS also provides a list of recommended books, consisting of novels and anthologies nominated for the British Fantasy Awards.

The Mythopoeic Society (http://www.mythsoc.org/). Devoted to the study, discussion, and enjoyment of myth and fantasy literature. The Society holds an annual conference called Mythcon. The 305th annual conference was held at the University of Michigan in 2004.

Science Fiction & Fantasy Writers of America (http://www.sfwa.org/). Founded in 1965 by Damon Knight, who also served as the first president. Originally the Science Fiction Writers of America, the name was changed to include fantasy in 1992, better reflecting the intertwined relationship of the two genres. Membership is open only to writers of published science fiction or fantasy.

The Tolkien Society (http://www.tolkiensociety.org/). The society was founded in 1969 to further interest in the works of J. R. R. Tolkien.

World Fantasy Convention (http://www.worldfantasy.org). The Web site lists upcoming conventions. The 2005 World Fantasy Convention was scheduled for Madison, Wisconsin. Attendance at the convention is limited to 850 people, but supporting memberships are also available. Members nominate for the World Fantasy Awards, but a panel of judges makes the final decisions.

Awards

The most up-to-date and comprehensive information on fantasy awards can be found at the Locus Web site: http://www.locusmag.com/SFAwards/index.html (accessed April 5, 2005). The following is a listing of fantasy awards that continue to be given. The winners are listed in *Fluent in Fantasy* (Libraries Unlimited, 1999), as are the winners of now-defunct awards.

August Derleth Award (http://www.britishfantasysociety.org.uk/info/bfsawards.htm). The British Fantasy Award, often referred to as the August Derleth Award, is selected by members of the British Fantasy Society and attendees of the annual FantasyCon. The close relationship between fantasy and horror is indicated by the number of horror novels awarded this fantasy prize. Several of the books that have received this award are covered in the horror chapter (chapter 12).

Locus Awards. Readers of *Locus* are annually given a chance to select their favorites in a magazine poll. Because *Locus* is to science fiction, fantasy, and horror what *Billboard* is to music and *Variety* to acting, the poll really reflects what serious readers of fantasy like. The poll has been taken annually since 1971. Ballots are only accepted from subscribers, and results are published in the July or August issue. An online resource listing nominees, winners, and results is at http://www.locusmag.com/ SFAwards/Db/Locus.html (accessed April 5, 2005). Poll results are given in the categories of SF novel, fantasy novel, young adult novel, horror/dark fantasy novel, first novel, novella, novelette, short story, collection, anthology, nonfiction, art book, editor, magazine, book publisher/imprint, and artist. In 1994 and 1990, dark fantasy was not listed as a category even though horror was. Although the poll has been conducted since 1971, the best fantasy novel category first appeared in 1980. Prior to that, fantasy was included in the novel category.

Mythopoeic Award (http://www.mythsoc.org/awards.html). The Mythopoeic Award is given at the annual Mythcon. The winner is chosen by a committee of Mythopoeic Society members. In 1992 the society divided the fantasy award into categories of fantasy for children and for adults.

Sidewise Awards (http://www.uchronia.net/sidewise/). "The Sidewise Awards for Alternate History were conceived in late 1995 to honor the best 'genre' publications of the year. The award takes its name from Murray Leinster's 1934 short story 'Sidewise in Time,' in which a strange storm causes portions of Earth to swap places with their analogs from other timelines."—Sidewise Award Web site.

William L. Crawford Memorial Award (http://wiz.cath.vt.edu/iafa/iafa.awards.html). A panel of judges awards this prize at the International Association for the Fantastic in the Arts annual convention for the best first fantasy published during the previous eighteen months.

World Fantasy Award (http://www.worldfantasy.org/awards/). Members of the annual World Fantasy Convention may nominate, but the winners are selected by a panel. The panel also awards the World Fantasy Life Achievement Award to an individual.

Online Resources

Online resources specific to fantasy are listed here. Additional listings of sites that group fantasy with science fiction are listed in the science fiction chapter (chapter 10).

Feminist Science Fiction, Fantasy, & Utopia, http://www.feministsf.org/femsf (accessed April 5, 2005).

Fluent in Fantasy, http://www.sff.net/people/dherald/ (accessed April 5, 2005), features hyperlinks to all sites listed in the book of the same title as well as listing new sites of interest to fantasy readers.

International Association for the Fantastic in the Arts, http://ebbs.english.vt.edu/iafa/ iafa.home.html (accessed April 5, 2005).

Reader's Robot Fantasy Page, http://www.tnrdlib.bc.ca/fa-menu.html (accessed April 5, 2005).

Recommended Fantasy Author List, http://www.sff.net/people/Amy.Sheldon/ listcont.htm (accessed April 5, 2005).

D's Fantasy Picks

de Lint, Charles.

The Onion Girl. **2001.** (urban fantasy).

Jilly Coppercorn, Newford's favorite artist, is struck down in a hit-and-run accident, leaving her in a coma in this world but allowing her to wander in the spirit world, or dreamlands. Her physical injuries are not the only ones that are keeping her down; ancient hurts done to her are also playing a role.

Gaiman, Neil.

American Gods. **2001.** (saga, myth and legend).

Just before his long-anticipated release from prison, Shadow discovers that his wife has been killed in an automobile accident, along with a friend who was to have been his employer. Upon his release, he meets the mysterious, charismatic Wednesday, who introduces him to the old gods, who are on the verge of war with the new gods.

Lackey, Mercedes.

The Fairy Godmother. **2001.** (fairy tales).

As an apprentice fairy godmother, it is Elena's duty to fight to prevent the bad things that come with "Tradition" as well as guiding the folks involved in the better parts along. Her life takes a curious turn when, disguised as a crone to test three questing princes, she loses her temper at Prince Alexander, who acts like an ass, so she turns him into one. Unwilling to let a defenseless donkey wander the woods alone, she takes him home and puts him to work transforming his life.

Moore, John.

Heroics for Beginners. **2004.** (humorous).

Prince Kevin Timberline and Princess Rebecca, the Ice Princess, who are madly in love, are more than dismayed to learn that all Kevin's carefully orchestrated moves to win the approval of the council of Lords have been in vain. He has been thrust aside in favor of whoever can retrieve the Ancient Artifact before it can be put to use in the Diabolical Device (a weapon of mass destruction). "Borrowing" a book titled *The Handbook of Practical Heroics* from the palace library, Kevin sets out to beat more heroic knights to it. Not being a timid stay-at-home miss, Becky, armed with a sword and wearing a chainmail bustier, decides to follow Kevin and act as his comic sidekick as he faces Lord Voltmeter (He who must be named), evil minions, and Valerie, Voltmeter's sexy Evil Assistant.

Nix, Garth.

Lirael. **2001.** (alternate worlds).

Instead of committing suicide on her fourteenth birthday when she doesn't receive the future Seeing ability shared by all adult Clayr, Lirael becomes a librarian in the vast warren of a library that not only houses books but also guards monstrous dangers and arcane magic.

Pattou, Edith.

East. **2003.** (fairy tales).

> With her family facing ruin, adventurous Rose agrees to go with a great white bear to live in a distant land, but when she makes a horrible mistake she must travel East of the Sun and West of the Moon to rectify her error.

Chapter 12

Horror

Essay

Dale Bailey

My love of horror fiction, like that of most horror readers, sprang up in secret and was nourished on the sly—in the gaudy paperbacks I secreted inside the sober classics assigned by my high school English teachers, and during late-night reruns of *The Night Stalker*, a 1970s-era television shocker featuring a new supernatural menace every week. Even as a child, I sensed that there was something faintly sordid about horror as a genre—a suspicion reinforced by the disdain of my teachers when they discovered my secret addiction to paperbacks like *They Thirst* (in which vampires overrun Los Angeles), and confirmed when I became a horror novelist. "What makes an otherwise normal husband and father, a college professor of English, write horror fiction?" a local National Public Radio host recently asked in the teaser spots for an interview about my novel *House of Bones,* and it wasn't hard to hear the barely suppressed assumption that an interest in horror fiction is somehow abnormal.

Even the most perceptive writing about the field echoes this idea. In *Danse Macabre*, Stephen King, the most successful purveyor of contemporary horror fiction, writes:

> *We all have a postulate buried deep in our minds: that an interest in horror is unhealthy and aberrant. So when people say, "Why do you write that stuff?" they are really inviting me to lie down on the couch and explain about the time I was locked in the cellar three weeks.*[1]

Mark Edmundson begins his study of the genre, *Nightmare on Main Street*, with a similar moment of subterranean self-examination:

> *A penchant for horror films didn't fit in particularly well with my self-conception. I think of myself as an upbeat type. . . . Horror films were for misanthropes, for people who lived in the cellars of their own minds and never wanted to come out.*[2]

After screening films such as Tobe Hooper's 1974 drive-in classic *The Texas Chainsaw Massacre,* I've found myself entertaining similar doubts. Surely an interest in horror, with its standard fare of graphic slaying and flaying, can't be entirely healthy. Yet in my choices as a teacher and a critic, as a writer of fiction, even as a consumer looking for a quickie beach read or a Friday-night movie rental, I find myself constantly gravitating to the genre. Why?

This is a crucial question for all popular genres, of course, but a particularly acute one for horror for two reasons. First, horror is alone among popular genres in the problems of definition it poses. And second, unlike most other categories of commercial writing, horror is often seen as symptomatic of some personal pathology on the part of its consumers. Nor are these unrelated issues.

Definition

Genres of popular fiction are usually understood in terms of content—the romance focuses on matters of the heart, the mystery on the causes and consequence of crime, and so on. Because horror fiction, however, seeks to inspire a unique emotional state in its reader—fear—it is more properly seen in light of what it *does* than what it *is*. In *Danse Macabre,* King establishes a hierarchy of related emotions that the genre engages. Terror, a purely psychological variety of fear, is at the top, followed by horror, which includes a physical dimension, and the gross-out, a state of outright physical revulsion. Because these emotions are more central to the genre than the means the narrative uses to achieve them, horror tends to erode generic boundaries, exploiting the materials of other commercial categories to achieve its own effects.

Many readers, of course, continue to identify the genre with matters of content, associating it, for example, with monsters and the supernatural—with tales of vampires, werewolves, hauntings, and demonic possession. Yet horror often omits such elements. Norman Bates, of Robert Bloch's *Psycho,* is a kind of werewolf to be sure—as are Thomas Harris's Hannibal Lecter and the dozens of other less-celebrated serial killers who populate the genre—yet his divided nature is presented in purely psychological terms. There is nothing supernatural about him at all. In other cases, more conventional horror elements are integrated with materials from other genres—as in William Hjortsberg's exercise in hard-boiled supernatural noir, *Falling Angel,* or Laurell K. Hamilton's series of vampire romances starring the recurring character of Anita Blake. Such cross-genre exercises may employ only a handful of horror's conventional elements—its interest in physical and emotional violence, its reliance on suspense in plotting, its use of ruined and isolated settings, its atmosphere of moral gloom and physical decay, its Manichean vision of a world divided between powers of darkness and light—but they share horror's overriding interest in frightening the reader.

The Horror Reader

This interest in disrupting the reader's emotional equilibrium may well account for the fact that an interest in horror is often seen as deviant. Finding pleasure and entertainment in terror, the logic runs, is psychologically aberrant. Such thinking, however, fails to distinguish genuine terror from the illusory fear experienced within the secure frame of a clearly fictional world—a tamer variation of the kind of safe thrill-seeking that makes roller coasters so appealing. It also fails to take into account the unique demographics of horror's primary readership. Obviously, different genres appeal to different groups of readers. The romance audience, as Janice Radway makes clear in *Reading the Romance,*[3] is made up almost entirely of women. Anecdotal evidence suggests that Western and spy fiction have a similarly exclusive appeal to men; and while other publishing categories—science fiction, perhaps, and especially mystery fiction—appeal more broadly to both genders, even those populations may split along gender lines in their preference for subcategories such as drawing room mysteries and hard-boiled noir.

In *Danse Macabre,* King points out that horror movies typically draw a teenage demographic. Carol Clover refines this observation, noting in *Men, Women, and Chainsaws* that adolescent males "hold pride of place" in such audiences.[4] Though there is little formal research specifically focused on such reading populations, critic John Cawelti argues that "horror seems especially fascinating to the young and relatively unsophisticated parts of the public."[5] My own observations in the genre—gathered over two decades as a reader, critic, and writer, at conventions, at book signings, and in conversations with writers, editors, publishers, and booksellers—also suggest that horror fiction appeals primarily to men between the ages of twelve and thirty.

Horror's perennial popularity may well be rooted in its ability to address that population's specific emotional needs. Adolescence is a time of considerable emotional, physical, and sexual upheaval. It is also a time of enormous instability in personal identity. Caught between the circumscribed freedoms of childhood and the potentially onerous responsibilities of adulthood, teenagers find themselves uniquely situated. The freedom of adolescence promises rewarding change and development; however, its restrictions create tremendous frustrations. In short, adolescents—no longer children, but not yet fully adults—experience the best, and the worst, of both conditions. In *The Philosophy of Horror,* Noël Carroll argues that monsters are "creatures that transgress categorical distinctions such as inside/outside, living/dead, insect/human" and so on.[6] If so, it's easy to see why teenagers, themselves caught between the categorical conditions of childhood and adulthood, find horror fiction so fascinating. In its misunderstood monsters, they see distorted reflections of themselves. What's more, horror's lowly status in adult culture gives it an additional attraction—the same subversive charge enjoyed by any number of adolescent interests, from skateboarding to gangster rap.

This appeal to the issues of adolescence is obvious in many horror novels, ranging from near-classics such as King's *Carrie* (in which Carrie's awakening telekinetic powers are explicitly linked to menstruation and her anxiety about the onset of adult sexuality) to more recent paperback originals like Simon Clark's *Blood Crazy* (in which British teenagers face an outbreak of homicidal violence among their parents). However, even horror novels that don't explicitly address adolescent issues often do so implicitly. It's easy to read horror's concern with bodily integrity and transformation, for example, in terms of the sweeping physiological changes of adolescence. Similarly, horror's often reactionary depiction of sexuality—especially the misogynistic fantasies that equate sexual gratification with violent punishment—encode the sexual guilt occasioned by a culture that simultaneously exploits and condemns teenage sexuality.

Some students of the genre—among them psychoanalyst Ernest Jones[7]—have gone so far as to argue that horror's appeal lies specifically in its ability to speak to our most deeply repressed sexual desires. By dressing those desires in nightmare imagery, Jones argues in *On the Nightmare,* the horror tale enables us simultaneously to fulfill and repudiate them. Yet Jones's analysis, as persuasive as it seems, does not apply universally. It fails, first of all, to account for any number of horror texts that resist even the most ingenious psychosexual analysis. It also fails to explain the nature of horror's cyclical appeal to adult readers outside its core adolescent demographic—and there is, clearly, a pattern of such cyclical appeal. While other genres enjoy periods of heightened popularity (take the Western's predominance in the 1930s, 1940s, and 1950s), once they wane, they rarely regain the energy they enjoyed at their peak (witness the Western's failure to achieve renewed cultural prominence). Horror, however, in keeping with one of its most popular conceits, has a penchant for rising from the grave to enjoy renewed periods of popularity—in the 1950s, in the early 1970s, in the 1980s, and again at the turn of this century—with audiences that extend well beyond its core of adolescent readers.

If we expand Jones's thesis to include broader cultural anxieties as well as specifically sexual fears, however, the cyclical nature of horror fiction's appeal becomes clearer. Horror seeks to unsettle. Its core audience—adolescents—is by nature unsettled: ill at ease with their place in the world and uncomfortable in their own skin. During periods of social, political, and economic turmoil, when the unsettling conditions of adolescence become endemic—during periods when we're all a little unsettled and chafing inside the envelope of our own skins—horror transcends that core audience to achieve more universal appeal. In the 1950s, for example, horror novels such as Robert Heinlein's *The Puppet Masters* and Jack Finney's *The Body Snatchers* reflected contemporary anxiety about the Cold War. The recession of the 1970s saw a rash of horror novels with a distinctly economic subtext, among them Robert Marasco's *Burnt Offerings* and Stephen King's *The Shining*. And many critics have linked the surge of vampire fiction in the 1980s to cultural anxiety about the AIDs epidemic.

In short, horror purges us of our most troubling fears, both personal (especially for its core adolescent audience) and cultural (during those periods when it attracts a larger adult audience). And so it is that horror stories typically begin with the eruption of chaotic forces into a previously ordered existence, and conclude with the restoration—however tentative—of that order. Working inside the fictive—and therefore emotionally unthreatening—framework of popular genre, horror first invokes, and then resolves, the things that frighten us most.

Origins of the Genre

A look at the origins of the genre reinforces this model of horror's appeal. While there has always been an interest in horrific material—consider Odysseus's encounter with the Cyclops—most historians agree that horror as a discrete genre finds its beginnings in Horace Walpole's 1764 novel, *The Castle of Otranto.* Walpole subtitled his book "A Gothic Story," thus associating it with his interest in the architecture of the Middle Ages, and inadvertently naming the genre to which his novel would give rise. However, Walpole could hardly have imagined the long-term popularity and influence that his slim book—inspired by a dream and composed in a mere two months—would enjoy. By the turn of the nineteenth century, <u>Otranto</u> had spawned a host of successful imitators—some of them, notably Ann Radcliffe and M. G. "Monk" Lewis, so popular that Jane Austen explicitly parodied the new genre in *Northanger Abbey.*

Indeed, a reader versed in gothic fiction but unfamiliar with Walpole's role as progenitor might dismiss his book as a compendium of gothic clichés. Set in a sprawling medieval castle, the plot—such as it is—revolves around Prince Manfred's attempts, in collusion with a corrupt church, to maintain his illegitimate grasp on power. Arrayed against him are a variety of vengeful supernatural forces, virtuous elements of his own family, and the rightful heir to the castle. An atmosphere of gloom, decay, and menace (often specifically sexual, Jones would note) pervades the tale; many of its most memorable set pieces, including a darkened pursuit through the labyrinthine bowels of the castle, continue to echo through contemporary horror fiction. The strangely compelling figure of Manfred—a tortured over-reacher, railing against fate and monstrous even to himself—provides a template for gothic villain-heroes ranging from the titanic literary archetypes of the romantics (including Shelley's Prometheus and Melville's Ahab) to the mad scientists of Michael Crichton's *Jurassic Park* and a thousand B movies.

Such a synopsis tempts us to attribute the genre's popularity to sensationalism alone. Viewed in the context of its revolutionary age, however, *Otranto,* like the imitators that followed, seems to express the anxieties of an increasingly democratic era. Wicked priests and malign aristocrats populate the gothic novels of the late eighteenth and early nineteenth centuries; as Mark Edmundson writes, these villain-heroes "figure church and state, the forces that weigh too hard upon society, that need renovation."[8] In short, the early gothic novels mounted subversive attacks on the presiding European powers of the day—a conclusion in keeping with Leslie Fiedler's observation that "most gothicists were not only avant-garde in their literary aspirations, but radical in their politics; they were, that is to say, anti-aristocratic, anti-Catholic, and antinostalgic."[9]

A survey of the nineteenth-century icons of British gothic fiction confirms this model of horror fiction's attractions. By the end of the Victorian era, *Otranto*'s influence had spread well beyond the narrow constraints of explicitly gothic novels to impact writers as diverse as the Brontë sisters, Charles Dickens, and Wilkie Collins. It had also given rise, however, to a growing body of direct antecedents to contemporary horror. Three of those works—Mary Shelley's *Frankenstein* at the beginning of the century, and Robert Louis Stevenson's *The Strange Case of Dr. Jekyll and Mr. Hyde* and Bram Stoker's *Dracula* at its close—have achieved archetypal status, establishing tropes that remain at the genre's heart. While many of today's readers come to these texts indirectly, through their seemingly endless film adaptations, a re-reading of the novels themselves highlights the degree to which each reflects the cultural anxieties of its era. *Frankenstein,* with its seminal portrayal of the Faustian scientist, distills the fears of an increasingly technological culture on the verge of industrialization. In its depiction of a respectable middle-class life derailed by atavistic urges, *Jekyll and Hyde*—published less than forty years after Darwin's *Origin of Species* shook Victorian piety to its foundations—grapples with the spiritual implications of evolutionary theory. Similarly, Stoker's sexually charged narrative in *Dracula* reflects a passionate late-Victorian debate over the proper social, sexual, and professional roles of women.

A similar division is evident in American literature. During the mid-nineteenth century, gothic was the primary mode of American fiction, notably in the work of Nathaniel Hawthorne, Herman Melville, and—most crucially for the development of modern horror fiction—Edgar Allan Poe. Following the rise of realism in the aftermath of the Civil War, however, the American gothic split into two streams. While gothic overtones continued to infuse the work of early twentieth-century writers working in the realistic mode (especially William Faulkner), another group of writers, working outside the mainstream in cheaply published pulp magazines, quietly began building a new commercial genre, horror, on the foundation of Walpole's gothic. Their chief venue was *Weird Tales,* their central figure a reclusive New Englander named H. P. Lovecraft. It's almost impossible to overestimate Lovecraft's influence on the field. Through his editorial services and voluminous correspondence, he shaped two generations of horror writers. Despite its limitations, his critical survey, "Supernatural Horror in Literature," remains required reading for every student of the genre. And his much-imitated fiction—especially the cycle of short stories known as the Cthulhu Mythos—established yet another of the genre's abiding motifs: a "cosmic horror" of the enormous vistas in time and space described by early twentieth-century physicists.

In this sense, Lovecraft, like his British predecessors of the previous century, expresses the zeitgeist of an unsettled age: filled with the wasteland imagery that marks the works of his modernist contemporaries, his fiction echoes the existential crisis of the Lost Generation. Despite a veneer of supernaturalism, Lovecraft's worldview is essentially scientific, his heroes impotent pawns at the mercy both of their own atavistic Darwinian histories and an array of ancient extraterrestrial forces, the Elder Gods of the Cthulhu Mythos.

The boom-and-bust cycles of horror fiction in the six decades since Lovecraft's death have also generally conformed to the repression-anxiety model. Many works from the horror boom of the 1950s, such as Richard Matheson's *The Shrinking Man,* highlight the anxieties of the post-Hiroshima nuclear world. The unsettled period of the late 1960s and early 1970s produced another surge in popularity, this time marked by such milestones as Ira Levin's *The Stepford Wives,* which grapples with the burgeoning feminist movement, and William Peter Blatty's *The Exorcist,* a terrifying depiction of a possessed adolescent that, as King argues in *Danse Macabre,* mirrors parental anxieties about the unrest on America's Vietnam-era campuses. Other books from the period—most notably John Farris's *The Fury* and, in 1980, King's own *Firestarter*—describe vast conspiracies that reflect growing American distrust of the federal government following Watergate.

Perhaps the most significant development of this period, however, was the unprecedented expansion—and subsequent collapse—of horror publishing following Stephen King's commercial success. Before King ascended the best-seller lists in the mid-1970s, most book-length horror fiction—even by established masters of the genre—was published and marketed in the mainstream. In the early 1980s, however, hoping to capitalize on King's success, bookstores began to shelve horror in a separate section, and publishers started channeling newer writers into imprints devoted specifically to the field. In short, the process begun almost sixty years previously by the founders of *Weird Tales* finally reached its fruition: No longer merely a fictive mode, horror was suddenly, indisputably, a commercial publishing category. This expansion energized the careers of a growing class of best-selling horror writers (including Clive Barker, Dean Koontz, Robert McCammon, Anne Rice, and Peter Straub), created opportunities for other crucial talents who might otherwise have languished in obscurity (among them, Dennis Etchison and Thomas Ligotti), and fed the growth of important movements within the genre (most notably, perhaps, splatterplunk, which carried the depiction of violence to graphic extremes).

However, it also had negative long-term consequences. As publishers fed an ever-growing number of titles into the pipeline, horror writers found it increasingly difficult to sustain serious literary careers (as had figures ranging from Sheridan Le Fanu in the mid-1800s to Shirley Jackson a century later), and readers found themselves more and more often unable to discover quality fiction amid the mountains of dreck. Unsurprisingly, perhaps, the boom collapsed. By the mid-1990s, all but a few publishers had canceled their horror imprints. The few horror titles published were once again finding their way back into the general fiction racks at most bookstores, and many of the writers who had clotted the genre during the previous decade had moved on.

Subgenres

Despite this commercial contraction, horror fiction continues to thrive. Even a cursory survey of contemporary horror will highlight not only the field's breadth of theme, motif, and approach, but its continuing penchant for deploying the materials of other popular genres to achieve its own emotional effects.

Apocalypse: Apocalyptic stories describe the end of the world, with a special focus on the various trials survivors face as they work to rebuild civilization. Horror stories set in such venues often employ tropes associated with science fiction. However, they tend to shift the narrative focus away from the scientific causes and consequences of the disaster in favor of an emphasis on the clash between good and evil in the post-apocalyptic setting. Stephen King's *The Stand,* for example, begins by depicting the ravages of a plausibly extrapolated strain of flu virus, but soon shifts its focus to the clash between two bands of survivors: one associated with the saintly figure of Mother Abigail, the other with a clearly Satanic figure known as Randall Flagg. Other examples of the subgenre include Robert R. McCammon's *Swan Song,* Stewart O'Nan's *A Prayer for the Dying,* and Tim Lebbon's *The Nature of Balance.*

Cosmic horror: Written in the tradition of H. P. Lovecraft, cosmic horror often employs his pantheon of ancient and malevolent alien beings know as the Old Ones. Lovecraft's works are available in a variety of inexpensive editions, but a good place to start is *The Best of H. P. Lovecraft.* Later additions to the subgenre—such as Fred Chappell's *Dagon*—often build directly upon Lovecraft's legacy. Others—such as T. E. D. Klein's *The Ceremonies*—reflect Lovecraft's vision of human impotence in the face of an incomprehensible and almost certainly hostile universe, but do not employ his mythology. Additional works in the cosmic horror tradition include Michael Shea's *The Colour Out of Time,* Brian Lumley's works (especially *The Caller of the Black, Beneath the Moors, The Burrower's Be-*

neath, and the <u>Titus Crow series</u>), Ramsey Campbell's *Cold Print,* Elizabeth Hand's *Waking the Moon,* and my own first novel, *The Fallen.*

Dark fantasy: Distinguished from mainstream horror by its reduced emphasis on explicit violence, dark fantasy typically comes in one of two varieties. The first variety explores the horrific potential of human encounters with surviving remnants of ancient myths and belief systems. The second exploits the horrific possibilities of intersections between our own reality and the fantastic secondary worlds more often associated with J. R. R. Tolkein and his imitators. Examples of the first approach include Ramsey Campbell's *The Darkest Part of the Woods,* Neil Gaiman's *American Gods,* Elizabeth Hand's *Mortal Love,* James Herbert's *Once,* and Robert Holdstock's <u>Mythago Wood series.</u> Clive Barker's *Weaveworld,* Sean Stewart's *Resurrection Man,* and Stephen King's <u>Dark Tower series</u> are examples of the second approach.

Demonic possession/invasion: Tales of demonic possession focus on attempts to repel Satanic powers as they invade everyday reality. William Peter Blatty's *The Exorcist,* which describes the possession of a teenage girl by a demonic spirit who may be Satan himself, is by far the most important such novel. Another variety of such tales focuses on the fulfillment of biblical prophecy of the end times, as signaled by the birth of a Satanic messiah figure. Examples of this variety include Ira Levin's *Rosemary's Baby* and the best-selling <u>Left Behind series,</u> an explicitly evangelical sequence of novels by Tim LaHaye and Jerry B. Jenkins.

Ghosts: Almost certainly the most common kind of horror story, ghost stories focus on disembodied spirits that linger after death. Such spirits may be malevolent or benevolent, and ghost stories often range in tone from horrific to nostalgic. Examples include Richard Adams's *The Girl in a Swing,* Stewart O'Nan's *The Night Country,* Alice Sebold's *The Lovely Bones,* Chet Williamson's *Ash Wednesday,* and a number of Peter Straub's novels, including *Julia, If You Could See Me Now,* and *lost boy, lost girl.* Straub's *Ghost Story* explicitly reimagines some of the classic ghost stories most central to the American tradition (including "The Turn of the Screw"). Despite the title, however, it is not in fact a conventional ghost story.

Haunted houses: Although haunted house stories often overlap significantly with ghost stories, they can usually be distinguished from ghost stories by their emphasis on the house as a locus of supernatural incursion. Examples include Shirley Jackson's *The Haunting of Hill House,* Stephen King's *The Shining,* Bentley Little's *The House,* Robert Marasco's *Burnt Offerings,* Susie Moloney's *The Dwelling,* Anne Rivers Siddons's *The House Next Door,* Chet Williamson's *Soulstorm,* and my own *House of Bones.* Mark Z. Danielewski's *House of Leaves* is an important, if not wholly successful, attempt to reimagine the subgenre.

Monsters: Perhaps no other subgenre of horror fiction is so diverse. Monster stories include tales of animals run amuck (often through the interference of human science; animal-human transformation; and the incursion into everyday reality of aliens, extinct species, or supernatural beings. Though monsters usually pose a threat to humanity and may be actively maligned, they are also often, like Frankenstein's monster, profoundly misunderstood figures intended to arouse the reader's sympathy. Whatever their provenance and intentions, however, they inevitably provoke dread and fascination in their human observers. Kirsten Bakis's *Lives of the Monster Dogs* is a literary treatment of deliberate scientific tampering with animals; Dean Koontz's *Watchers* and Michael Crichton's *Jurassic Park* treat the question of scientific tampering in thriller terms. James Herbert's <u>Rats</u> sequence and Guy N. Smith's series of <u>Killer Crab</u> novels describe giant, carnivorous manifestations of their eponymous beasts. *The Relic,* by Douglas Preston and Lincoln Child, focuses on a mysterious monster lurking in the bowels of the American Museum of Natural History, while Richard Laymon's *The Beast House* attaches a monster story to the protocols of the haunted-house tale. Tom Piccirilli's *A Choir of Ill Children* focuses on the monstrous potential of human deformity; Robert R. McCammon's *Stinger* borrows the conventions of science fiction to describe the depredations of an extraterrestrial monster in an isolated Texas town. The werewolf myth has provided an especially fertile subject for horror writers interested in monsters. Such tales include Michael Cadnum's *St. Peter's Wolf,* Robert R. McCammon's *The Wolf's Hour,* S. P. Somtow's *Moon Dance,* Whitley Strieber's <u>Wolfen</u>, Thomas Tessier's *The Nightwalker,* and Jack Williamson's *Darker Than You Think.*

Psychological horror/serial killer: With the possible exception of vampire stories, serial killer novels are probably the single most popular subgenre of horror fiction. Though serial killer novels invariably blur the lines between horror, mystery, and suspense, those variations that fall into the horror genre tend to emphasize violence and gore over police and detective work. Prominent examples include Robert Bloch's *Psycho,* Dennis Cooper's *Frisk,* Bradley Denton's *Blackburn,* Bret Easton Ellis's *American Psycho,* Thomas Harris's <u>Hannibal Lecter series</u> (including *Red Dragon, The Silence of the Lambs,* and *Hannibal*), Jack Ketchum's *The Girl Next Door,* Michael Slade's *Ghoul,* and Joyce Carol Oates's *Zombie.* Serial killers play significant roles in a number of novels by Peter Straub, including *The Throat, The Hellfire Club,* and *lost boy, lost girl.*

Short stories: There is a thriving small-press market for short horror fiction. <u>The Year's Best Fantasy & Horror</u>, edited by Ellen Datlow and Kelly Link and Gavin Grant, and *The Mammoth Book of Best New Horror,* edited by Stephen Jones, provide solid annual coverage of the field. David Hartwell's *The Dark Descent* and *Foundations of Fear* provide a comprehensive introduction to the field's classics, while anthologies such as Kirby McCauley's *Dark Forces* and Al Sarrantonio's *999* provide collected work by some of horror's leading contemporary writers. Many theme anthologies focus on specific subgenres, such as Ellen Datlow's *The Dark* (ghost stories) and *The Mammoth Book of Zombies, The Mammoth Book of Werewolves,* and *The Mammoth Book of Vampires,* all edited by Stephen Jones.

Splatterpunk: In the mid-1980s, the term splatterpunk was applied to an ideologically unified group of horror writers who sought to bring a newly explicit treatment of violence to the genre. Though the movement disintegrated fairly quickly, the splatterpunks profoundly influenced contemporary horror writers, who tend to be far more graphic than their predecessors in depicting violence. Because it has more to do with its treatment of material than with any particular theme or motif, splatterpunk draws upon many of horror's subgenres. Examples include Clive Barker's *The Books of Blood,* Poppy Z. Brite's *Exquisite Corpse,* Joe R. Lansdale's *Act of Love,* David J. Schow's *The Shaft,* and John Skipp and Craig Spector's *The Scream. Silver Scream,* edited by David J. Schow, along with

Splatterpunks: Extreme Horror and *Splatterpunks II: Over the Edge,* both edited by Paul Sammon, provide concise introductions to the subgenre's short fiction.

Vampires: The vampire has become the most popular subgenre of horror fiction—virtually a publishing category in itself. Bram Stoker's *Dracula* remains the single most important vampire novel ever written—the defining text from which the whole subgenre springs—and traditional vampire novels in Stoker's manner continue to be written: Michael Cadnum's *The Judas Glass,* Stephen King's *'Salem's Lot,* and Lucius Shepard's *The Golden* are crucial examples. Roderick Anscombe's *The Secret Life of Laszlo, Count Dracula,* Marie Kiraly's *Mina,* Fred Saberhagen's *The Dracula Tape* (the first in a series), Dan Simmons's *Children of the Night,* and Peter Tremayne's *Dracula Unborn* (the first in a trilogy) variously sequel, reimagine, or otherwise embroider Stoker's narrative. The vampire motif has also proved very receptive to cross-genre influence. Perhaps the most fertile strain of such cross-genre hybrids finds its roots in the intersection of horror and romance fiction pioneered by Anne Rice in *Interview with the Vampire* and its sequels. Other examples of the form include Nancy Kilpatrick's *Child of the Night,* Michael Romkey's *I, Vampire,* and Chelsea Quinn Yarbro's long-running series about the vampire Saint-Germain, which begins with 1978's *Hotel Transylvania.* Suzy McKee Charnas's *The Vampire Tapestry,* Richard Matheson's *I Am Legend,* George R. R. Martin's *Fevre Dream,* and Whitley Strieber's *The Hunger* employ elements of science fiction to offer us rationalized vampires.

In *Bloodlist* and its sequels. P. N. Elrod synthesizes vampire fiction and hard-boiled noir in the Raymond Chandler mode; in *Vampire$,* John Steakley merges the vampire tale with the protocols of the action-adventure novel. Like Rice's *The Vampire Lestat,* S. P. Somtow's *Vampire Junction* and its sequel, *Valentine,* place vampires in the context of the rock music industry, a theme later explored in Poppy Z. Brite's *Lost Souls.* Barbara Hambley's *Those Who Hunt the Night* gives us a vampire mystery set in the Victorian era. In *The Black Castle* and its sequels, Les Daniels also imbeds the vampire tale into strongly realized historical settings, while F. Paul Wilson's *The Keep* inserts the vampire motif into the universe of the World War II thriller.

Dozens of other vampire novels—many of them long-running series—draw upon or combine conventions from multiple genres. Jack Butler's *Nightshade* is a science fiction vampire Western. Nancy Collins combines action-adventure, vampires, and fantasy tropes in the <u>Sonja Blue series</u>, beginning with *Sunglasses After Dark.* With *Guilty Pleasures,* Laurell K. Hamilton launched her long-running <u>Anita Blake, Vampire Hunter series</u>, which includes elements of romance, erotica, fantasy, and adventure. In the sequence beginning with *Anno-Dracula,* Kim Newman rewrites Stoker's narrative, lovingly re-creates Victorian London, and compiles a detailed alternate history of the twentieth century that borrows tropes and techniques from science fiction. And this summary—as long, complex, and necessarily inexact as it is (many of the novels listed above fit in more than one of the subcategories)—merely scratches the surface. Readers have a seemingly endless thirst for vampire fiction, while writers possess apparently endless ingenuity in transfusing new energy into what should by all rights be an exhausted blood line.

Witchcraft: Tales of witchcraft focus on the manipulation of malign supernatural powers by human beings—and vice versa. Examples include Graham Joyce's *Dark Sister,* Fritz Leiber's *Conjure Wife,* Anne Rice's *The Witching Hour* (first in a series), and Peter Straub's *Shadowland.* John Updike gives the theme a literary treatment in *The Witches of Eastwick.*

Zombies: Once associated strongly with the voodoo tradition of Caribbean folklore, the zombie tale now draws almost all of its cultural power from George Romero's 1968 film, *Night of the Living Dead,* which focused on the depredations of a worldwide plague of cannibalistic zombies. In *Book of the Dead* and *Still Dead: Book of the Dead II,* anthologies edited by John Skipp and Craig Spector, a variety of short story writers explore Romero's concept. Further variations on the theme include Brian Keene's *The Rising,* J. Knight's *Risen,* and Phillip Nutman's *Wet Work.*

Conclusion

As the scope and diversity of subgenres available to the contemporary horror writer suggests, the field remains vibrant at every level of literary accomplishment. Indeed, after a decade of retrenchment and contraction, horror seems to be enjoying a period of renewed popularity, perhaps energized by the specter of international terrorism and the financial pressures of an increasingly global economy. Many of the best-selling writers from the 1980s—including King, Koontz, Rice, and Straub—continue to produce compelling fiction. With their Leisure paper-back-original imprint, Dorcester Publishing provides a thriving commercial venue for a variety of newer writers, including Douglas Clegg, Tim Lebbon, Brian Keene, and Edward Lee, who are reworking many of the traditional tropes of the genre. And as the barriers erected by category publishing in the 1980s continue to erode, an influx of fresh talent has arisen to blur the margins between horror and the mainstream. A number of new writers who began their careers in traditional genre venues—among them Graham Joyce (*The Toothfairy*), Glen Hirshberg (*The Snowman's Children*), and Caitlín R. Kiernan (*Murder of Angels*)—have slowly been expanding their reputations beyond the borders of horror. Others, who began their careers as traditional literary writers—most notably perhaps Stewart O'Nan (*A Prayer for the Dying*), Michel Faber (*Under the Skin*), and Joyce Carol Oates (*Haunted: Tales of the Grotesque*)—have increasingly worked horror tropes and motifs into fiction published in the mainstream. The ongoing viability of both career paths is evidence that horror fiction today continues to speak to us in vital and important ways. No doubt it will continue to do so as long as we live in anxious and uncertain times.

12

Notes

1.   Stephen King, *Danse Macabre* (New York: Berkley, 1981), 89.

2.   Mark Edmundson, *A Nightmare on Main Street: Angels, Sadomasochism, and the Culture of Gothic* (Cambridge, Mass.: Harvard University Press, 1997), ix–x.

3   Janice Radway, *Reading the Romance: Women, Patriarchy, and Popular Literature* (Chapel Hill: University of North Carolina Press, 1984).

4.   Carol J. Clover, *Men, Women, and Chainsaws: Gender in the Modern Horror Film* (Princeton, N.J.: Princeton University Press, 1992), 6.

5. John Cawelti, *Adventure, Mystery, and Romance: Formula Stories as Art and Popular Culture* (Chicago: University of Chicago Press, 1976), 52.

6. Noël Carroll, *The Philosophy of Horror: Or Paradoxes of the Heart* (New York: Routledge, 1990), 43.

7. Ernest Jones, *On the Nightmare* (London: Liveright, 1971).

8. Edmundson, *Nightmare on Main Street,* 54.

9. Leslie Fiedler, *Love and Death in the American Novel* (New York: Stein and Day, 1966), 137.

Bibliography

Bailey, Dale. *American Nightmares: The Haunted House Formula in American Popular Fiction.* Bowling Green, Ohio: Bowling Green State University Popular Press, 1999.

Barron, Neil, ed. *Horror Literature: A Reader's Guide.* New York: Garland, 1990.

Carroll, Noël. *The Philosophy of Horror: Or Paradoxes of the Heart.* New York: Routledge, 1990.

Cawelti, John. *Adventure, Mystery, and Romance: Formula Stories as Art and Popular Culture.* Chicago: University of Chicago Press, 1967.

Clover, Carol J. *Men, Women, and Chainsaws: Gender in the Modern Horror Film.* Princeton, N.J.: Princeton University Press, 1992.

Edmundson, Mark. *A Nightmare on Main Street: Angels, Sadomasochism, and the Culture of Gothic.* Cambridge, Mass.: Harvard University Press, 1997.

Fiedler, Leslie. *Love and Death in the American Novel.* New York: Stein and Day, 1966.

Jones, Ernest. *On the Nightmare.* London: Liveright, 1971.

King, Stephen. *Danse Macabre.* New York: Berkley, 1981.

Lovecraft, H. P. *Supernatural Horror in Literature.* New York: Dover Publications, 1927 [1973].

Radway, Janice. *Reading the Romance: Women, Patriarchy, and Popular Literature.* Chapel Hill: University of North Carolina Press, 1984.

Themes and Types

Diana Tixier Herald

In the past decade or two, the horror genre has undergone such transformation that fans from the boom years of the 1980s would have a hard time understanding the appeal of most of the current releases that feature vampires, werewolves, and ghosts. Nowhere is the genreblending as pervasive as it is between horror and romance. Although some types of erotica have long been part of horror, a new trend has placed many fairly bloodless and sometimes comedic romantic capers into the horror camp. Thus, while the overarching categorization of "vampires," "werewolves," and the like remains the same, the content of these categories is diverse enough to warrant subcategories to distinguish the "vampire romances" from "vampire sleuths" and "traditional vampires." In some the historical setting, or the canvas of world events at the time, plays a vital role.

Selected Classics

Horror classics are plentiful and span centuries, with the genre's popularity waxing and waning over the years. The most recent boom occurred in the 1980s and 1990s, and thus, to keep the list of horror classics manageable, we cover only classics published before that time, although a number of newer titles have certainly reached cult status and the popularity levels of older classics. Classics are also tagged as such in the following subgenre lists.

Bierce, Ambrose.

Numerous short stories, particularly "An Occurrence at Owl Creek Bridge," and the nonfiction.

The Devil's Dictionary. 1911.

Blatty, William Peter.

The Exorcist. 1971. (Satanism and demonic possession).

Bloch, Robert.

Psycho. 1959. (psychological horror).

Bradbury, Ray.

The October Country. 1955. (occult and supernatural).
Something Wicked This Way Comes. 1963. (occult and supernatural).

Derleth, August.

Dwellers in Darkness. 1976. (cosmic paranoia).
The Lurker at the Threshold. 1945. (cosmic paranoia).

Farris, John.

The Fury. 1976. (occult and supernatural).

Jackson, Shirley.

The Haunting of Hill House. 1959. (haunted houses).

James, Henry.

The Turn of the Screw. 1897. (ghosts).

King, Stephen.

King is not only one of the most successful horror writers of all time, but also one of the most successful writers of our times.

'Salem's Lot. 1975. (vampires).
The Shining. 1977. (haunted houses).
The Stand. 1978. (apocalypse).

Leiber, Fritz.

Conjure Wife. 1953. (witches and warlocks).

Levin, Ira.

Rosemary's Baby. 1967. (Satanism and demonic possession).

Lovecraft, H. P.

At the Mountains of Madness. 1964. (cosmic paranoia).
The Dunwich Horror. 1945. (cosmic paranoia).
others.

Matheson, Richard.

I Am Legend. 1954. (vampires).

Poe, Edgar Allan.

Short stories include "The Telltale Heart," "The Mask of the Red Death," "The Pit and the Pendulum," "The Cask of Amontillado," and others.

Rice, Anne.

Interview with the Vampire. 1976. (vampires).

Shelley, Mary Wollstonecraft.

Frankenstein; or, the Modern Prometheus. 1818. (monsters, medical horror).

Stevenson, Robert Louis.

"The Strange Case of Dr. Jekyll and Mr. Hyde." 1886. (monsters).

Stoker, Bram.

Dracula. 1897. (vampires). The vampire story that started it all.

Monsters

Monstrous creations, usually of a freakish nature—taking unnatural form from any of the elements (water, earth, air), plants, or animals—abound in horror fiction. The predominant forms are vampires and werewolves, listed after the following books about monsters in general.

Bakis, Kirsten.

Lives of the Monster Dogs. 1997.

Clegg, Douglas.

The Halloween Man. 1998.

Crichton, Michael.

Jurassic Park. **1990.** Reissued 1997.

This adventure-filled tale deals with the horror that can be created by reconstituting dinosaurs from DNA.

Herbert, James.

Domain. 1985.

Rats. 1989. Reissued 2003.

Mutant animals in London after a nuclear attack.

Koontz, Dean.

Watchers. **1987.**

A genetically engineered monster escapes from a secret laboratory.

Laymon, Richard.

<u>The Beast House Chronicles.</u>

The Cellar. 1980. Reissued 1987.

The Beast House. 1986.

The Midnight Tour. 1986.

McCammon, Robert R.

Stinger. 1988.

Piccirilli, Tom.

A Choir of Ill Children. 2003.

Preston, Douglas, and Lincoln Child.

Relic. 1996.

Shelley, Mary Wollstonecraft.

Frankenstein; or, the Modern Prometheus. 1818. ★

Also considered science fiction (e.g., androids, mad scientist). Forrest J. Ackerman's *World of Science Fiction* (General Publishing Group, 1997) devotes thirty pages to discussion of the 250 editions of this book and to the countless spin-offs, from movies to toys.

Smith, Guy N.

<u>Crabs series.</u>

Night of the Crabs. 1976.

Killer Crabs. 1978.

Origin of the Crabs. 1979.

Crabs on the Rampage. 1981.

Crabs' Moon. 1984.

The Human Sacrifice. 1988.

Stevenson, Robert Louis.

The Strange Case of Dr. Jekyll and Mr. Hyde. 1886. Reissued 2003. ★ 🎬 *Dr. Jekyll and Mr. Hyde*

The drug and psychological aspects of the story were also influential in science fiction.

Vampires

Ever popular with readers, these blood-sucking denizens of the night are also frequently romantic heroes. The following listing demonstrates the wide variety to be found in vampire novels today, with sections for vampire romance and vampires with mystery and suspense following the general vampire novels.

Anscombe, Roderick.

Secret Life of Laszlo Count Dracula. 1994.

A tale of bloodlust without supernatural elements.

Banks, L. A.

The Vampire Huntress Legend Series.

A sexy series featuring an African American Buffy-like slayer, her band of sidekicks, and a powerful vampire cabal.

Minion. 2003.
Awakening. 2004.
The Hunted. 2004.
The Bitten. 2005.

Bradbury, Ray.

From the Dust Returned. 2001.

Brite, Poppy Z.

Lost Souls. **1992.** Reissued 2002.

A teen named Nothing begins to understand why he feels different from the others when he finds out that his father is a vampire. Intense homoeroticism, intense violence.

Cacek, P. D.

Night Players. 2001.
Night Prayers. 1998.

Cadnum, Michael.

The Judas Glass. 1996.

Charnas, Suzy McKee.

The Vampire Tapestry. 1980. Reissued 1993. ★

Collins, Nancy A.

Sonja Blue series.

Dark and violent.

Sunglasses after Dark. 1989. Reissued 2000.
In the Blood. 1992. Reissued 2004.

Paint It Black. 1995. Reissued 2005.

A Dozen Black Roses. 1996.

Darkest Heart. 2000.

Dead Roses for a Blue Lady. 2002.

A collection of stories featuring Sonjia Blue.

Elrod, P. N.

Jonathan Barrett series.

The Gentleman vampire.

Red Death. 1994. Revised and expanded 2004.

Set in pre-Revolutionary War America.

Death and the Maiden. 1994. Revised and expanded 2004.

Featuring Jonathon Barrett, Tory loyalist and vampire.

Death Masque. 1994. Revised and expanded 2004.

Jonathon returns to England, hoping to find Nora Jones.

Dance of Death. 1994. Revised and cxpanded 2004.

A four-year-old boy who strongly resembles Jonathon Barrett puts a new twist into the story.

Farren, Mick.

Nosferatu series.

The Time of Feasting. 1996.

A colony of nosferatu living on New York's Lower East Side.

Darklost. 2000.

The vampire clan moves to L.A.

More Than Mortal. 2001.

Victor Rehnquist, thc lcader of the vampire group, is called to England.

Underland. 2002.

Rehnquist is recruited by the Feds to help fight Nazis who escaped Germany and are living in Antarctica, scheming to take over the world.

Fox, Andrew.

Jules Duchon series.

Fat White Vampire Blues. 2003.

Blood can be very fattening—Jules Duchon, a New Orleans vampire, knows only too well.

Bride of the Fat White Vampire. 2004.

Can vampire Jules Duchon pull himself together from 187 white rats to reclaim the love of his afterlife from the dead?

IIambly, Barbara.

Those Who Hunt the Night. 1988.

Someone's been killing the vampires of London.

Hendee, Barb, and J. C. Hendee.
Half-vampires, half-elves, in a medieval setting.

Dhampir. 2003.
Sister of the Dead: A Novel of the Noble Dead. 2005.
Thief of Lives. 2004.

King, Stephen.
'Salem's Lot. 1975. Reissued 1999. ★ 🎬

Knox, Elizabeth.
Daylight. 2003.
Another sensuous vampire tale.

Kostova, Elizabeth.
The Historian. 2004.

Laymon, Richard.
🎗 *The Traveling Vampire Show.* 2000. Winner of the Stoker Award.
In 1963, three teens sneak into an adults-only vampire show. Graphic sex and violence.

Lumley, Brian.
<u>Necroscope.</u>
Necroscope. 1988.
Vamphyri. 1988.
The Source. 1989.
Deadspeak. 1990.
Deadspawn. 1991. Reissued 2003.
Blood Brothers. 1992.
The Last Aerie. 1993.
Bloodwars. 1994.
Necroscope: The Lost Years. 1996.
Necroscope: Resurgence. 1996.
Invaders. 1999.
Defilers. 2000.
Avengers. 2001.

Martin, George R .R.
Fevre Dream. 1982. Reissued 2004.

Matheson, Richard.
I Am Legend. 1954. Reissued 1995. ★

Mosiman, Billie Sue.
<u>The Vampire Nation Series.</u>
Red Moon Rising. 2001.
Malachi's Moon. 2002.
Craven Moon. 2003.

Newman, Kim.

Anno-Dracula. 1993.

The Bloody Red Baron. 1995.

Judgment of Tears. 1998.

Rice, Anne.

<u>The Vampire Chronicles.</u>

Interview with the Vampire. 1976. Reissued 1997. ★ 🎬

Louis tells, in his own words, the tale of his life, both living and undead, and of Lestat, who made him a vampire.

The Vampire Lestat. 1985.

Queen of the Damned. 1988. 🎬

Tale of the Body Thief. 1992.

Memnoch the Devil. 1995.

The Vampire Armand. 1998.

Merrick: A Novel. 2000.

Blood and Gold, or, the Story of Marius. 2001.

Blackwood Farm. 2002.

Blood Canticle. 2004.

<u>New Tales of the Vampires.</u>

Pandora. 1998.

Vittorio the Vampire. 1999.

Saberhagen, Fred.

<u>Dracula series.</u>

The Dracula Tape. 1977. Reissued 1999.

Dracula attempts to set the record straight.

A Matter of Taste. 1990. Reissued 1993.

A Question of Time. 1992. Reissued 1993.

Séance for a Vampire. 1994. Reissued 1997.

A Sharpness on the Neck. 1996. Reissued 1998.

A Coldness in the Blood. 2002.

Simmons, Dan.

Children of the Night. 1993.

Does vampirism hold the cure for cancer and AIDs?

Somtow, S. P.

Valentine. 1992.

Vampire Junction. 1984.

Starring Timmy Valentine, an ageless, vampire rock star.

Sosnowski, David.

Vamped. 2004.

In a world dominated by vampires, where humans are raised on farms, Martin Kowalski ends up as the foster father of a human child.

Steakley, John.

> *Vampire$.* 1990. ★
>
>> A modern-day pack of manly vampire slayers.

Stoker, Bram.

> *Dracula.* 1897. Reissued 2005. ★ ▄
>
>> The original novel, like its hero, has never died, and has produced bloodthirsty progeny in novels, stage plays, and motion pictures.

Strieber, Whitley.

> *The Hunger.* 1981. Reissued 2001. ★ ▄
>
> *Last Vampire.* 2001.
>
> *Lilith's Dream: A Tale of the Vampire Life.* 2002.

Wilson, F. Paul.

> *The Keep.* 1981. Reissued 2000. ★ ▄
>
>> In a remote castle in 1941, German soldiers are being found dead and bloodless, one by one, each morning.
>
> *Midnight Mass.* 2004.
>
>> Wilson describes the vampires in this novel as "soulless, merciless, parasitic creatures we all knew and loved" (http://www.repairmanjack.com/books/midnight.html).

Yarbro, Chelsea Quinn.

> <u>Saint-Germain series.</u>
>
>> The adventures of vampire Count Ragoczy Saint-Germain through the centuries and across the world.
>
> *Hotel Transylvania.* 1978. Reissued 2002.
>
> *The Palace.* 1978. Reissued 2002.
>
> *Blood Games.* 1979. Reissued 2004.
>
> *Path of the Eclipse.* 1981.
>
> *Tempting Fate.* 1981. Reissued 2001.
>
> *Darker Jewels.* 1993.
>
> *Better in the Dark.* 1993.
>
> *Mansions of Darkness.* 1996.
>
> *Writ in Blood.* 1997.
>
> *Blood Roses.* 1998.
>
> *Communion Blood.* 1999.
>
> *Come Twilight.* 2000.
>
> *A Feast in Exile.* 2001.
>
> *In the Face of Death.* 2001.
>
> *Night Blooming.* 2002.
>
> *Midnight Harvest.* 2003.
>
> *Dark of the Sun.* 2004.

Vampire Romance

A romantic and sensual undertone has always been a part of vampire literature, but many of today's horror authors push it further. In these stories, vampires are attractive, romantic, and oh-so-sexy. Many of the novels are light in tone, even funny.

Davidson, MaryJanice.

Betsy Taylor series.

When Betsy Taylor wakes up in a cheap, tacky coffin, she discovers that she is now a vampire who doesn't burn in sunlight, can fight the urge to feed, and is not repulsed by religious articles; this may make her the prophesied Queen of the Vampires.

Undead and Unwed. 2004.

Undead and Unemployed. 2004.

Undead and Unappreciated. 2005.

Undead and Unreturnable. 2005.

Feehan, Christine.

Dark Series.

Dark Prince. 1999.

Dark Desire. 1999.

Dark Gold. 2000.

Dark Magic. 2000.

Dark Challenge. 2000.

Dark Fire. 2001.

Dark Guardian. 2002.

Dark Symphony. 2003.

Dark Melody. 2003.

Dark Destiny. 2004.

Dark Secret. 2005.

Kenyon, Sherrilyn.

A Dark-Hunter.

Fantasy Lover. 2002.

Night Pleasures. 2002.

Night Embrace. 2003.

Dance with the Devil. 2003.

Kiss of the Night. 2004.

Night Play. 2004.

Stroke of Midnight. 2004.

Seize the Night. 2005.

12

McKinley, Robin.

Sunshine. 2003.

Sands, Lynsay.

> <u>Argeneau series.</u> Comedic.
>> *Single White Vampire.* 2003.
>> *Love Bites.* 2004.
>> *Tall, Dark, and Hungry.* 2004.

Sizemore, Susan.

> <u>The Primes Universe.</u>
>> *I Burn for You.* 2003.
>> *I Thirst for You.* 2004.
>> *I Hunger for You.* 2005.

> <u>Laws of the Blood.</u>
>> *The Hunt.* 1999.
>> *Partners.* 2000.
>> *Companions.* 2001.
>> *Deceptions.* 2002.
>> *Heroes.* 2003.

Vampire Mystery/Suspense

Vampires, with their keen senses and familiarity with the night, fit perfectly into the dark worlds of mystery and suspense.

Dedman, Stephen.

> *Shadows Bite.* 2001.
>> A missing body that turns up headless, a sinister cult, and vampires in contemporary Los Angeles thrust Mage Magistrale and Charlie Takumo into an action-packed adventure.

Elrod, P. N.

> <u>Jack Fleming series.</u>
>> *The Vampire Files.* 2003. An omnibus of the first three titles in the series.
>> *Bloodlist.* 1990.
>> *Lifeblood.* 1990.
>> *Bloodcircle.* 1990.
>> *Art in the Blood.* 1991.
>> *Fire in the Blood.* 1991.
>> *Blood on the Water.* 1992.
>> *A Chill in the Blood.* 1998.
>> *The Dark Sleep.* 1999.
>> *Lady Crymsyn.* 2000.
>> *Cold Streets.* 2003.

Hamilton, Laurell K.

> <u>Anita Blake series.</u>
>> Anita Blake is a vampire hunter involved with werewolves and shapeshifters in an increasingly dark and erotic series.

>> *Guilty Pleasures.* 1993.

Laughing Corpse. 1994.
Circus of the Damned. 1995.
Lunatic Café. 1996.
Bloody Bones. 1996.
Killing Dance. 1997.
Burnt Offerings. 1998.
Blue Moon. 1998.
Obsidian Butterfly. 2000.
Narcissus in Chains. 2001.
Cerulean Sins. 2003.
Circus of the Damned. 2004.
Incubus Dreams. 2004.

Harris, Charlaine.

Southern Vampire series.

Sookie Stackhouse, a telepathic waitress, becomes involved with mysteries involving not only vampires but also witches, shapeshifters, and serial killers.

Dead until Dark. 2001.
Living Dead in Dallas. 2002.
Club Dead. 2003.
Dead to the World. 2004.
Dead as a Doornail. 2005.

Huff, Tanya.

Huff also writes fantasy and SF.

The Blood series.

Also called the <u>Victory Nelson series</u>. A combination of horror, detection, and romance.

Blood Price. 1991.
Ancient forces of chaos have been loosed on Toronto.

Blood Trail. 1992.
Innocent Canadian werewolves are being killed.

Blood Lines. 1993.
A mummy feeds on the unwary.

Blood Pact. 1993.
Vicki's mom's body disappears from a funeral home.

Blood Debt. 1997.
Wraiths play a deadly nightly game.

Henry Fitzroy and Tony Foster series.

A spin-off of the <u>Blood series</u>.

Smoke and Shadows. 2004.
Smoke and Mirrors. 2005.

James, Dean.

> Even though Simon Kirby-Jones, a gay historian and mystery author, is also a vampire, the series is really more cozy mystery than horror. Titles are listed in the crime chapter (chapter 7).

Werewolves

Werewolves are the most common of shapeshifters. They run the gamut from clever, thoughtful, and essentially good to mindless, slavering beasts. Like vampires, the tales about them are often romantic.

Adams, C. J., and Cathy Clamp.

> *Hunter's Moon.* 2004.
>
>> Horror combined with romance.
>
> *Moon's Web.* 2005.

Armstrong, Kelley.

> *Bitten.* 2001.
>
>> Elena Michaels, born a werewolf, tries to make it as a human journalist in Toronto, but how long can she resist the call of the wild?
>
> *Stolen.* 2003.
>
>> Further adventures of the sexy Elena Michaels, werewolf.

Borchardt, Alice.

> *Night of the Wolf.* 1999.
>
>> In ancient Rome, Maeniel's desire for the beautiful Imona transforms him from werewolf to human.
>
> *The Silver Wolf.* 1998.
>
>> Regeane, female shapeshifter and werewolf, in eighth-century Rome.
>
> *The Wolf King.* 2001.
>
>> On the brink of Charlemagne's attack on Rome, Maeniel undertakes a mission that threatens his relationship with Regeane, his shapeshifter followers, and all of humanity.

Cacek, P. D.

> *Canyons.* 2000.
>
>> A Denver tabloid reporter's life is saved by a werewolf, and she finds herself in the middle of a conflict between opposing packs of werewolves.

Cadnum, Michael.

> *Saint Peter's Wolf.* 1991.

Davidson, MaryJanice.

> *Derik's Bane.* 2004.
>
>> Comedic romance involving a werewolf who thinks he is supposed to kill a woman who is the reincarnation of Morgan le Fay.

Handeland, Lori.

> Wisconsin werewolves offer danger, suspense, and romance.

Blue Moon. 2004.
Hunter's Moon. 2005.

Hayter, Sparkle.
Naked Brunch. 2003.

Comedic romantic mystery. What's a girl to do when she is told she has "lycan-thropic morphic disorder?"

McCammon, Robert R.
The Wolf's Hour. 1989.

Somtow, S. P.
Moon Dance. 1989.

Strieber, Whitley.
Wolfen. 1978. 🎬

Tessier, Thomas.
The Nightwalker. 1981. Reissued 1989.

Williamson, Jack.
Darker Than You Think. 1948. Reissued 1999.

York, Rebecca.
Werewolf romances.

Crimson Moon. 2005.
Edge of the Moon. 2003.
Killing Moon. 2003.

The Occult and Supernatural

The occult embraces all mysterious things beyond human understanding. The term is also used to describe those sciences, often appearing in horror literature, that involve knowledge and use of the supernatural. The supernatural encompasses things existing or occurring outside humanity's normal experience. A supernatural event cannot be explained by any known force of nature. Accompanying a belief in supernatural forces is the belief that these forces intervene to control nature and the universe and that they are above ordinary nature. Naturally, then, it follows that supernatural beings and powers exist that are active in the ordinary world.

Armstrong, Kelley.
Women of the Otherworld.

Werewolves, witches, sorcerers, and demons.

Bitten. 2001.
Elena Michaels, the only female werewolf in the world, is the protagonist of the first two titles in the series, which are also listed in the werewolf section of this chapter.

Stolen. 2003.

Dime-Store Magic. 2004.

Paige Winterbourne, an apprentice witch, is the protagonist of the second two titles.

Industrial Magic. 2004.

Haunted. 2005.

Eve Levine finds a bargain she made carries right over into death, and now she must play the role of a bounty hunter in the afterlife.

Bradbury, Ray.

The October Country. 1955. Reissued 1999. ★

Something Wicked This Way Comes. 1963. Reissued 1999. ★ ▀

Brite, Poppy Z., and Christa Faust.

Triads. 2004.

Homosexuality, racism, and a ghost.

Cacek, P. D.

The Wind Caller. 2004.

You'll never say "it's only the wind" again.

Campbell, Ramsey.

🎀 *Hungry Moon.* 1986. Winner of the British Fantasy Award.

🎀 *Incarnate.* 1983. Winner of the British Fantasy Award.

Midnight Sun. 1991.

The creeping horror of a species of snow that gluttonously devours people.

The Overnight. 2005.

Dank darkness overwhelms a chain bookstore in a new mall.

Clegg, Douglas.

The Hour Before Dark. 2002.

A trio of siblings, who had practiced a strange form of mind control growing up, are reunited in the family home on an isolated Massachusetts island after their father is slaughtered.

Due, Tananarive.

The Between. 1995.

Hilton James, a middle-class African American family man living in Miami, is beset by terrifying dreams that are either symptoms of a supernatural ability or the early stages of schizophrenia.

My Soul to Keep. 1997.

Mortal and immortal forces face off when an immortal tells his mortal wife his secret and tries to convert her and his daughter.

Everett, Percival.

American Desert. 2004.

Darkly comic tale of a decapitated man, reanimated.

Farris, John.

Phantom Nights. 2005.

> In 1952, a murdered nurse continues to communicate with a mute boy.

Fury Series.

> *The Fury.* 1976. Reissued 2000. ★ 🎬
>
> Two children, Gillian and Robert, possess powerful psychic talents that make them targets.

> *The Fury and the Terror.* 2002.
>
> Psychic bioengineering, secret government agencies, and an evil First Lady.

> *The Fury and the Power.* 2003.
>
> A psychic is the target of malevolent forces that want to harness her paranormal talents.

Herbert, James.

Others. 1999

> While working on a case, private investigator Nicholas Dismas, who suffers from bizarre birth defects, finds a diabolical doctor who may have been responsible for his deformities and for the tormented souls he sees in his mirror.

Irvine, Alexander C.

A Scattering of Jades. 2002.

> P. T. Barnum, a Mayan deity, a bereaved father, and the possible end of the world.

Keene, Brian.

The Rising. 2004.

> Zombies.

King, Stephen.

From a Buick 8. 2002.

> A haunted car instead of a house.

Koontz, Dean.

Life Expectancy. 2004.

> On the day he is born, Jimmy Tock's dying grandfather predicts five days that will be terrible for Jimmy.

Odd Thomas. 2003.

> Twenty-year-old Odd sees and talks to ghosts, and can also see the malevolent bodachs who presage imminent violence.

Little, Bentley.

The Policy. 2003.

> Those who do not buy unlikely types of insurance from a creepy insurance salesman find themselves in terrible situations.

Lumley, Brian.

Harry Keogh: Necroscope and Other Weird Heroes! 2003.

Khai of Khem. **1981.** Reissued 2003. ★
> An ancient Egyptian setting.

Martinez, A. Lee.

Gil's All Fright Diner. 2005.
> The Earl of Vampires and the Duke of Werewolves stop at a diner and end up helping fend off a zombie attack, in this comedic horror romp.

Piccirilli, Tom.

A Choir of Ill Children. 2003.
> Conjoined triplets, an accusing witch, and a swampy wasteland.

The Deceased. 2000.
> A long-dead writer shapes reality in Maelstrom mansion, the site of a gruesome multiple murder.

🎗 *The Night Class.* 2001.
> A college student experiences stigmata after a murder occurs in his room. Winner of the Stoker Award.

Saul, John.

Midnight Voices. 2002.
> When Ryan and Laurie move into their new stepfather's apartment, they hear menacing voices in their nightmares and find much to arouse their suspicions of the strange inhabitants of the building.

Thurlo, David, and Aimée Thurlo.

Lee Nez series.
> A Native American vampire who is also a New Mexico state policeman faces shapeshifting skinwalkers and other dangers.

> *Second Sunrise.* 2002.
> *Blood Retribution.* 2004.

Waggoner, Tim.

Necropolis. 2004.
> Zombies, werewolves, and a cyber-vampire.

Witches and Warlocks

Witches often appear in the historical romance, but usually as secondary characters. In the following books, the witch and the warlock are presented as real, existing in the present as well as in the past, and they may be practitioners of either white or black witchcraft.

Joyce, Graham.

🎗 *Dark Sister.* 1999.
> Originally published in Great Britain in the early 1990s, this is the tale of an unfulfilled housewife who finds what she thinks is an herbalist's journal when cleaning a chimney, but discovers that she can now perform witchcraft and has unloosed a stalking evil. Winner of the British Fantasy Award.

Leiber, Fritz.

Conjure Wife. 1953. Reissued 1977. ★

Behind every great man may be a witch.

Rice, Anne.

Lives of the Mayfair Witches.

Family dynasty of witches.

The Witching Hour. 1990.

Lasher. 1993.

Taltos. 1994.

Straub, Peter.

Shadowland. 1980. Reissued 2003.

Two New England school boys experiment with magic.

Updike, John.

The Witches of Eastwick. 1984.

Three small-town New England witches in the 1960s. "A wicked entertainment with lots (and lots) of sex."—*The New Republic*

Cosmic Paranoia

Sometimes called "weird tales" and categorized as fantasy, the mythology created by H. P. Lovecraft, with its malevolent life force, nightmares, monsters, and "The Great Old Ones," has had an important influence on horror literature. This list includes the works of Lovecraft and some of his followers.

Bailey, Dale.

The Fallen. 2002.

Campbell, Ramsey.

Cold Print. 1985. ★

Derleth, August.

Derleth was so enamored of the Cthulhu mythos and such a good friend of Lovecraft, that when Lovecraft died, Derleth founded Arkham House for the express purpose of keeping the Cthulhu stories alive, while allowing other authors to expand upon the mythos.

 12

Dwellers in Darkness. 1976. ★

The Lurker at the Threshold. 1945. Reissued 2003. ★

Quest for Cthulhu. 2000. Omnibus contains *The Mask of Cthulhu* (1958) and *The Trail of Cthulhu* (1962).

Hand, Elizabeth.

Waking the Moon. 1995.

Klein, T. E. D.

The Ceremonies. 1984.

Koontz, Dean R.
Phantoms. 1983. Reissued 2002. ★ 🎬

Lovecraft, H. P.
At the Mountains of Madness. 1964. Reissued 2005.
The Call of Cthulhu and Other Weird Stories. 1999. Edited with an introduction and notes by S. T. Joshi.
The Case of Charles Dexter Ward. 1965. Reissued 1987.
The Dunwich Horror. 1945. Reissued with other stories in *The Dunwich Horror and Others* (1984). 🎬
The Lurker at the Threshold. 1945. Reissued 2003. Cowritten with August Derleth.
Tales of H. P. Lovecraft: Major Works. 2000. Selected and introduced by Joyce Carol Oates.

Lumley, Brian.
Beneath the Moors and Darker Places. 2002.
The Caller of the Black. 1971.

Dreamlands series.
    Hero of Dreams. 1986.
    Ship of Dreams. 1986.
    Mad Moon of Dreams. 1987.
    Iced on Aran. 1990.

Titus Crow series.
    Titus Crow Volume 1. 1997. Omnibus of:
        The Burrowers Beneath. 1974.
        The Transition of Titus Crow. 1975.
    Titus Crow Volume 2. 1997. Omnibus of:
        The Clock of Dreams. 1978. Reissued 1994.
        Spawn of the Winds. 1978. Reissued 1995.
    Titus Crow Volume 3. 1997. Omnibus of:
        In the Moons of Borea. 1979. Reissued 1995.
        Elysia: The Coming of Cthulhu. 1989.

Pelan, John, and Benjamin Adams.
The Children of Cthulhu: Chilling New Tales Inspired by H. P. Lovecraft. 2002.

Turner, Jim, ed.
Cthulhu 2000: A Lovecraftian Anthology. 1999.
    Includes, among others, "The Barrens," by F. Paul Wilson; "Pickman's Modem," by Lawrence Watt-Evans; "Shaft Number 247," by Basil Copper; "The Adder," by Fred Chappell; "Fat Face," by Michael Shea; "The Big Fish," by Kim Newman; "H.P.L.," by Gahan Wilson; "The Shadow on the Doorstep," by James P. Blaylock; "Lord of the Land," by Gene Wolfe; "The Faces at Pine Dunes," by Ramsey Campbell; "On the Slab," by Harlan Ellison; and "Views of Mt. Fuji, by Hokusai," by Roger Zelazny.

Eternal Lovecraft: The Persistence of HPL in Popular Culture. 1998.
    Eighteen short stories by Stephen King, Robert Charles Wilson, Fritz Leiber, Gene Wolfe, Harlan Ellison, Nancy A. Collins, and others.

Wooding, Chris.

   The Haunting of Alaizabel Cray. 2004.

Ghosts

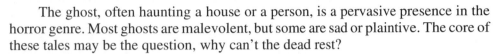

   The ghost, often haunting a house or a person, is a pervasive presence in the horror genre. Most ghosts are malevolent, but some are sad or plaintive. The core of these tales may be the question, why can't the dead rest?

Adams, Richard.

   The Girl in a Swing. 1980.

Ansa, Tina McElroy.

   <u>Lena McPherson.</u>

   Baby of the Family. 1989. ★

      Lena, a young African American girl, born in the 1950s, converses with ghosts.

   The Hand I Fan With. 1996.

      Lena's psychic abilities may mean that she will never find a living man to love.

Barker, Clive.

   Coldheart Canyon. 2001.

      The ghosts of Hollywood greats are held prisoner in a canyon near an evil room where each imported, hand-painted tile was imbued with evil.

Harper, M. A.

   The Year of Past Things: A New Orleans Ghost Story. 2005.

      A haunted relationship.

James, Henry.

   The Turn of the Screw. 1897. Reissued 2004. ★ ◼ 📖

Michaels, Barbara.

   Ammie, Come Home. 1968. Reissued 2005. ◼ *The House That Would Not Die*

      Romantic suspense.

O'Nan, Stewart.

   The Night Country. 2003.

      Reflections a year after three teenagers were killed in an accident by both the living and the dead.

Sebold, Alice.

   🎗 *The Lovely Bones.* 2002. 📖

      A murdered teenager keeps an eye on those she left behind. Winner of the Stoker Award.

Straub, Peter.

   Ghost Story. 1980. Reissued 1989. ★

   If You Could See Me Now. 1977. Reissued 2000.

   In the Night Room. 2004.

   Julia. 1975. Reissued 2000.

Haunted Houses

A house possessed is only a little less terrifying than a mind possessed. Haunted houses have long been a staple in the horror genre. What town does not feature a haunted house as a Halloween fund-raising project? The following tales tell of dealings with homes or lodgings that display malevolence.

Anson, Jay.
> *The Amityville Horror.* 1977. Reissued 2005. ▪
>> This nonfiction story is enjoyed by some horror fans.

Bailey, Dale.
> *House of Bones.* 2003.

Bonansinga, Jay.
> *Oblivion.* 2004.
>> An ex-priest is asked to exorcise a malevolent presence from the White House.

Campbell, Ramsey.
> *Nazareth Hill.* 1997.
>> A haunted apartment complex.

Clegg, Douglas.
> **Harrow trilogy.**
>> A Hudson Valley mansion converted into a prep school is filled with malevolent energy.
>
> *Mischief.* 2000.
> *The Infinite.* 2001.
> *Nightmare House.* 2004. The third in the series is set first in time.

Danielewski, Mark Z.
> *House of Leaves by Zampanò.* 2000.

Due, Tananarive.
> *The Good House.* 2003.
>> Angela Toussaint wants to sell the home her African American family has lived in for four generations in Sacajawea, Washington. The house seems to be a source of evil that seems bent on destroying her life.

Herbert, James.
> *Haunted.* 1988. Reissued 2000.
> *The Magic Cottage.* 1987.

Jackson, Shirley.
> *The Haunting of Hill House.* 1959. ★ ▪
>> Four people and a haunted mansion.

King, Stephen.
> *The Shining.* 1977. Reissued 2001. ★ ▪
>> In an isolated Rocky Mountain hotel, a writer, the father of a psychic son, is being driven insane by forces of evil.

Little, Bentley.

The House. 1999.

Marasco, Robert.

Burnt Offerings. 1973. ▰

Moloney, Susie.

The Dwelling. 2003.

> 362 Belisle Street selects its next victims from those to whom a realtor shows it.

Palahniuk, Chuck.

Lullaby. 2002.

> Helen Hoover Boyle is a witch who makes her living reselling haunted houses. She meets Carl Streator, a man who also knows the culling song, a song that results in death.

Saul, John.

Black Creek Crossing. 2004.

Siddons, Anne Rivers.

> Siddons also writes romances.

The House Next Door. 1978. Reissued 1995.

Simmons, Dan.

A Winter Haunting. 2002.

> Dale returns to his boyhood home forty-one years after his best friend was killed there when they were both eleven years old. Now, deeply depressed, he hears strange things and finds scary messages on his computer.

Straub, Peter.

🎗 *lost boy lost girl.* 2003.

> The secret to teenaged Mark's disappearance and his mother's suicide may lie in an abandoned house. The sequel, *In the Night Room* (2004), is listed in the "Ghosts" section of this chapter. Winner of the Stoker Award.

Williamson, Chet.

Soulstorm. 1986.

Demonic Possession and Exorcism

The control of an innocent mind by a demon or ghost, or domination by a psychotic person, is a most terrifying theme. Belief in possession is widespread, and many religions have rituals for exorcising evil spirits.

Blatty, William Peter.

The Exorcist. 1971. ▰

> This is the standard that all other possession stories are judged against.

Bloch, Robert.

Lori. 1989.

A college student returns home to discover her house has burned, her parents are dead, and she is a dead ringer for a woman in a photo in a yearbook from the year she was born.

Coyne, John.

The Piercing. 1978.

Stigmata and sexuality.

The Searing. 1980.

Farris, John.

Son of the Endless Night. 1985.

On a trip to Colorado a young man stumbles across a strange ceremony in the woods, during which he becomes possessed and then murders his fiancée. Even though it is twenty years old, this book is still found in libraries and has a fan following.

Mitchell, Mary Ann.

Drawn to the Grave. 1997.

An updated telling of the Bluebeard story, through the eyes of the next victim.

Strieber, Whitley.

Unholy Fire. 1993.

Are priests being possessed by demons?

Satanism, Demonology, and Black Magic

Worshipping the devil, pacts with the devil, raising the devil, haunting by demons, transmigration of souls, magicians, and black magic: The diversity of topics in this category is frightening.

Blish, James.

Black Easter. 1969.

Demons are released from hell to prey on the world.

Campbell, Ramsey.

Obsession. 1985. ★

Teens mail a chain letter. Some twenty years later, they must deal with the consequences.

King, Stephen, and Peter Straub.

The Talisman. 1984. Reissued 2001.

Thirteen-year-old Jack Sawyer enters into a bizarre realm on a quest to save his mother's life.

Levin, Ira.

Rosemary's Baby. 1967. Reissued 2003. ★ ▦

A young woman's dream life turns into a nightmare after she is unknowingly impregnated by Satan.

Straczynski, J. Michael.
>*Demon Night.* 2003.

Apocalypse

A horror is unleashed that is so terrible the world could be destroyed. The apocalypse is also a popular subgenre in Christian fiction.

Alten, Steve.
>**Domain.**
>>*Domain.* 2002.
>>*Resurrection.* 2004.

BeauSeigneur, James.
>**Christ Clone Trilogy.**
>>*In His Image.* 1997.
>>*Birth of an Age.* 1997. Reissued 2003.
>>*Acts of God.* 1998. Reissued 2004.

Grant, Charles L.
>**Millennium Quartet.**
>>The Four Horsemen of the Apocalypse sweep across the planet.
>>
>>*Symphony.* 1997.
>>*In the Mood.* 1998.
>>*Chariot.* 1999.
>>*Riders in the Sky.* 1999.

King, Stephen.
>*The Stand.* 1978. Reissued 2001. A "complete and un-cut" version was published in 1990. ★

Koontz, Dean.
>*The Taking.* 2004.
>>The world as we know it comes to an end in the glowing fog of fungus-like aliens who reanimate the dead.

LaHaye, Tim, and Jerry B. Jenkins.
>**Left Behind Series.**
>>Listed in the Christian fiction chapter, 13.

Lebbon, Tim.
>*The Nature of Balance.* 2000.
>>One night the world changes when people dream of falling and end up as bloody pulp. The few survivors attempt to negotiate a world where everything seems to be mutating.

Long, Jeff.

Year Zero. 2002.

A plague from year 00 C.E. is unleashed on the world, and the only way to halt its progress may be to clone the dead from the first century.

McCammon Robert R.

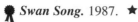 *Swan Song.* 1987. ★

Following a nuclear holocaust, a group of survivors band together. Winner of the Stoker Award.

O'Nan, Stewart.

A Prayer for the Dying. 1999.

Just after the Civil War, diphtheria and fire decimate the population of Friendship, Wisconsin.

Reaves, Michael.

Hell on Earth. 2000.

Splatterpunk style. A visceral, bloody, and violent tale involving an orphan who was raised by sorcerers, an angel, and a shapeshifting demon.

Medical Horror and Evil Science

Evil doctors, sometimes mad, and hospitals in which unnatural medicine is practiced can be found in this horrifying subgenre. Science run amok, with deadly consequences, is also a popular theme.

Braver, Gary.

Elixer. 2000.

Gray Matter. 2002.

Could there be any connection between dead children with mysterious holes in their sculls and a new process to increase the intelligence of developmentally disabled children?

Cook, Robin.

Cook's terrifying novels are also considered "medical thrillers" (See "Adventure," chapter 8).

Coma. 1977. Reissued 2002. 🎬

Toxin. 1998.

A heart surgeon's daughter is struck by e-coli, which sends him on a rampage against those responsible.

<u>Dr. Laurie Montgomery and Dr. Jack Stapleton series.</u>

Chromosome 6. 1997.

Marker. 2005.

Vector. 1999.

Crichton, Michael.

Prey. 2002.

A swarm of microscopic machines has escaped from a top secret facility and is taking the place of people in this science fiction-horror blend.

David, James F.
> *Fragments.* 1997.
>> A psychologist melds together the minds of five idiot-savants, but a sixth mind, the spirit of a woman raped and murdered, joins them and takes over.

> *Ship of the Damned.* 2000.

Gerritsen, Tess.
> *Bloodstream.* 1998.
> *Gravity.* 1999.
> *Life Support.* 1997.
> *The Surgeon.* 2001.

Koontz, Dean.
> *Watchers.* 1987. Reissued 2003. ▰
>> A genetically engineered monster escapes from a secret laboratory.

Koontz, Dean, and Kevin J. Anderson.
> **Dean Koontz's Frankenstein.**
>> A biotech magnate has created a New Race, but not all of them are perfect, including one who becomes a serial killer in his attempt to assemble a perfect woman from the parts of many whom he has killed.

> *Prodigal Son.* 2005.

Palmer, Michael.
> *Fatal.* 2002.
>> Could a vaccination be the cause of several bizarre deaths?

> *Natural Causes.* 1994.
>> Dr. Sarah Baldwin suddenly loses several patients who had been taking an herbal supplement she prescribed.

Shelley, Mary Wollstonecraft.
> *Frankenstein; or, the Modern Prometheus.* 1818. Reissued 2004. ★ ▰

Psychological Horror

Many of the horror stories currently being published involve terrors of the mind. Fears often do have an explicable cause, however deranged the mind from which the horror emanates. Serial killer stories fall into this category.

Bloch, Robert.
> *Psycho.* 1959. Reissued with *Psycho House* and *Psycho II* in omnibus (1993). ★ ▰

Campbell, Ramsey.
> *The Count of Eleven.* 1992.
> *Nazareth Hill.* 1997.
> *Silent Children.* 2000.

Cooper, Dennis.
> *Frisk.* 1991.
>> A homoerotic horror tale in which death and desire meet in an intensely violent explosion.

David, James F.
> *Before the Cradle Falls.* 2002.

Denton, Bradley.
> *Blackburn.* 1993.

Dobyns, Stephen.
> *The Church of Dead Girls.* 1997. Reissued 2001. 📖
>> A town spins out of control as a series of girls are murdered, in this tale of terror.

Ellis, Bret Easton.
> *American Psycho.* 1991. Reissued 2000. 🎬
>> Patrick Bateman is young, handsome, prosperous, and a serial killer.

Gerritsen, Tess.
> *The Apprentice.* 2002.

Harris, Thomas.
> **Hannibal Lecter.**
>> The creepiest serial killer ever.
>> *Red Dragon.* 1981. Reissued 2000. 🎬
>> 🎖 *The Silence of the Lambs.* 1989. Winner of the Stoker Award. 🎬
>> *Hannibal.* 1999. 🎬
>> Erudite cannibal Hannibal Lecter goes up against FBI Agent Clarice Starling.

Ketchum, Jack.
> *The Girl Next Door.* 2003.

King, Stephen.
> 🎖 *Misery.* 1987. Winner of the Stoker Award. 🎬

Koontz, Dean.
> *False Memory.* 1999.

Krabbé, Tim.
> *The Vanishing.* 1993. 🎬

Masterton, Graham.
> *The Chosen Child.* 2000.

Oates, Joyce Carol.
> 🎖 *Zombie.* 1995. Winner of the Stoker Award.

Saul, John.
> *The Manhattan Hunt Club.* 2001.

Straub, Peter.

> *The Hellfire Club.* 1996.

> *lost boy lost girl.* 2003. Winner of the Stoker Award.

> *The Throat.* 1993. Reissued 1999. Winner of the Stoker Award. Part of the <u>Blue Rose Trilogy</u>.

Dark Fantasy

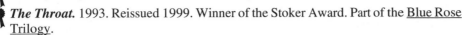

A hint of evil, a touch of magic, and a dark look at the world combine to create fantasy with a surrealistic feeling that shades into horror. These are moody, atmospheric tales that pull the reader in like quicksand. Dark fantasy is a subgenre that rests evenly between horror and fantasy. Readers who like dark fantasy should also consult the dark fantasy section of the fantasy chapter.

Campbell, Ramsey.

> *The Darkest Part of the Woods.* 2003.

> > A forest is haunted by an ancient evil and a family has been destroyed in its darkness.

Dedman, Stephen.

> <u>The Art of Arrow Cutting.</u>

> > *The Art of Arrow Cutting.* 1997.

> > A photographer becomes the target of three supernatural beings out of Japanese mythology when he receives a key from a woman who later is found dead.

> > *Shadows Bite.* 2001.

Gaiman, Neil.

> *American Gods.* 2001. Winner of the Stoker Award.

Hand, Elizabeth.

> *Mortal Love.* 2004.

> > Three entwined stories from three different times twist and writhe with art and insanity.

Herbert, James.

> *Once.* **2003.**

> > Thom Kindred has paranormal experiences when he goes to Castle Bracken to recuperate from a stroke.

12

Joyce, Graham.

> *The Tooth Fairy.* 1998. Winner of the British Fantasy Award.

> > As it turns out, the tooth fairy is not very nice.

King, Stephen.

> <u>The Dark Tower series.</u>

> > *The Gunslinger.* 1982. Reissued 2003.

> > *The Drawing of the Three.* 1987. Reissued 2003.

The Waste Lands. 1991. Reissued 2003.

Wizard and Glass. 1997.

Wolves of the Calla. 2003.

Song of Susannah. 2004.

The Dark Tower. 2004.

King, Stephen, and Peter Straub.

Black House. 2001.

Meiville, China.

Iron Council. 2004.

♠ *Perdido Street Station.* 2001. Winner of the Arthur C. Clarke and the British Fantasy Awards.

♠ *The Scar.* 2002. Winner of the Locus Poll and the British Fantasy Award.

Powers, Tim.

Earthquake Weather. 1997.

Expiration Date. 1996.

Last Call. 1992.

> In a bizarre poker game involving Tarot cards, Scott Crane must face down his father, the Fisher King.

Stewart, Sean.

Resurrection Man. 1995.

Zicree, Marc Scott.

Magic Time.

> A shared world series. A secret government project unleashes a force that stops everything electrical and starts many people mutating into strange and different forms, including a dragon and a young woman who begins to visibly shine with an interior light.

Zicree, Marc Scott, and Barbara Hambly.

Magic Time. 2001.

Bohnhoff, Maya Kaathryn.

Angelfire. 2002.

Zicree, Marc Scott, and Robert Charles Wilson.

Ghostlands. 2004.

Topics

To find out more about this genre, check out the following resources.

Grand Masters

Selected by the World Horror Convention, these are the "Grand Masters" of this genre, in reverse order beginning with 2004.

Jack Williamson
Chelsea Quinn Yarbro
Charles L. Grant
Ray Bradbury
Harlan Ellison
Ramsey Campbell
Brian Lumley
Peter Straub
Dean Koontz
Clive Barker
Anne Rice
Richard Matheson
Stephen King
Robert Bloch
F. Paul Wilson

Stephen King

Stephen King was arguably the best storyteller of the twentieth century. He won a well deserved National Book Award Medal for Distinguished Contribution to American Letters, a World Fantasy Lifetime Achievement Award, and a Horror Writers' Association Lifetime Fantasy Award as well as numerous other awards. King's first novel was published in 1973, and he quickly became *the* name defining the contemporary horror genre. Always best sellers, his novels led the rise in popularity of the horror genre in literature. They have been made into movies and television miniseries, and many of them are also available in audio format. Other authors whom readers of King often enjoy include Dean Koontz and Robert R. McCammon.

Short Stories

The short story has been popular in horror from the beginning. It wasn't until Stephen King roared onto the scene that its popularity in the horror genre was surpassed by the novel form.

459

Anthologies

The large number of horror anthologies indicates both the popularity of such collections and the significance of the short story in the genre. There are several inveterate anthologists; the listings here are but a selection from their volumes. Other horror stories can be found in anthologies listed for science fiction and fantasy, and some authors from those fields appear in the following anthologies. One of the interesting facts about horror anthologies is that libraries seem to hang onto them forever. Even when they are not reprinted, anthologies published long ago can still be found on library shelves.

🎗 Chizmar, Richard, and Robert Morrish, eds. *October Dreams*. Cemetery Dance, 2000. Winner of the International Horror Guild Award.

🎗 Chizmar, Richard, ed. *Night Visions 10*. Subterranean Press, 2001. Winner of the International Horror Guild Award.

Massey, Brandon, ed. *Dark Dreams: A Collection of Horror and Suspense by Black Writers*. Dafina Books. 2004.

🎗 Monteleone, Elizabeth, and Thomas Monteleone, eds. *Borderlands 5*. Borderlands Press. 2003. Winner of the Stoker Award.

🎗 Pelan, John, ed. *The Darker Side*. Roc. 2002. Winner of the Stoker Award.

Annual Anthologies

The Year's Best Fantasy and Horror. Edited by Ellen Datlow and Terri Windling. St. Martin's Press.
The first annual collection was published in 1988, and it was edited by Ellen Datlow and Terri Windling until the seventeenth annual collection, when Kelly Link and Gavin J. Grant replaced Windling. In addition to collecting outstanding stories, the anthologies also offer an overview of the year in the genre.

The Mammoth Book of Best New Horror. Edited by Stephen Jones. Carroll & Graf.
The fifteenth annual edition was published in 2004.

Bibliographies

Ashley, Michael, and William Contento. *Supernatural Index: A Listing of Fantasy, Supernatural, Occult, Weird, Horror Anthologies*. Greenwood, 1995.
Indexes over 2,100 anthologies containing more than 21,000 stories by over 7,700 authors, published between 1813 and 1994.

Burgess, Michael, and Lisa R. Bartle. *Reference Guide to Science Fiction, Fantasy, and Horror*. 2d ed. Libraries Unlimited, 2002.
A critical guide to reference sources and research tools.

Fonseca, Anthony J., and June Michele Pulliam. *Hooked on Horror: A Guide to Reading Interests in Horror Fiction*. Libraries Unlimited, 1999.
This ultimate guide to advising the horror reader classifies approximately 1,000 works into thirty subgenres (e.g., psychological horror, technohorror, splatterpunk). Award winners are listed, and a comprehensive guide to bibliographies, history, criticism, organizations, and conferences important in the genre is included. There is also a thorough index to horror short stories.

_____. *Hooked on Horror: A Guide to Reading Interests in Horror Fiction*. 2d ed. Libraries Unlimited, 2003.
> This is really more of a second volume or a supplement to the first edition, as it repeats very little of what was in the first edition.

Jones, Stephen, and Kim Newman, eds. *Horror: The 100 Best Books*. Carroll & Graf, 1999.

Spratford, Becky Siegel, and Tammy Hennigh Clausen. *The Horror Readers' Advisory: The Librarian's Guide to Vampires, Killer Tomatoes, and Haunted Houses*. American Library Association, 2004.

Encyclopedias

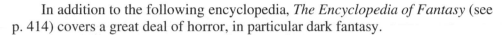

In addition to the following encyclopedia, *The Encyclopedia of Fantasy* (see p. 414) covers a great deal of horror, in particular dark fantasy.

Sullivan, Jack, ed. *The Penguin Encyclopedia of Horror and the Supernatural*. With an introduction by Jacques Barzun. Viking, 1986.
> An exemplary encyclopedia of awesome text and abundant, fearful illustrations that covers literature, art, film, radio, television, music, and illustration. There are fifty-four theme essays, listed alphabetically, with names (authors, artists, composers, actors, film directors) and film titles. All entries are signed, and the list of contributors is impressive. All of the theme essays (and, indeed, all the entries) are engrossing reading. A few of the theme essays indicate specific significance to genre fiction, although the whole work is, of course, relevant: "Definitions: Horror, Supernatural, and Science Fiction"; "Detection and Ghosts"; "The Devil, Devils, Demons"; "Frankenstein: The Myth"; "Ghosts"; "Horror and Science Fiction"; "Mad Doctors"; "Occult Fiction"; "Poltergeists"; "Possession"; "Vampires"; "Werewolves"; "Zombies." The work is invaluable for readers' advisors as a critical guide to authors, their works, and types of fiction within the genre. Of particular use is the lengthy essay "Writers of Today," a critical roundup of current authors, each listed with a cross-reference within the main alphabet. Jacques Barzun's introduction, "The Art and Appeal of the Ghostly and Ghastly," undoubtedly will become a classic in the literature.

History and Criticism

The definitive history and criticism of the horror genre are yet to be written. Until they are, the following books may be used for background on various aspects of the genre.

12

Bleiler, E. F., ed. *Supernatural Fiction Writers: Fantasy and Horror*. Scribner's, 1985. 2 vols.
> Brief biography and criticism of 148 authors.

_____. *Supernatural Fiction Writers: Contemporary Fantasy and Horror*. Charles Scribner's Sons, 2003. 2 vols.
> Essays on 116 authors, including analysis and criticism.

Bloom, Clive, ed. *Gothic Horror: A Reader's Guide from Poe to King and Beyond*. St. Martin's Press, 1998.

Bloom, Harold. *Classic Horror Writers*. Chelsea House Publishers, 1994.
> Biographical, bibliographical, and critical analysis of a dozen early writers of horror, including Ann Radcliffe, Edgar Allan Poe, Ambrose Bierce, Robert Louis Stevenson, and Bram Stoker.

Cox, Greg. *Transylvanian Library: A Consumer's Guide to Vampire Fiction*. Borgo, 1993.
> Includes chapters such as "History of the Vampire," "In the Wake of Dracula," "The Vampire Meets the Atomic Age," "Return of the Heroic Vampire," and "The Heroic Vampire Triumphs." It also contains author, title, subject, publisher, and character indexes.

Joshi, S. T. *The Weird Tale*. University of Texas, 1990.
> The fantastic writings of Arthur Machen, Lord Dunsany, Algernon Blackwood, M. R. James, Ambrose Bierce, and H. P. Lovecraft are surveyed.

King, Stephen. *Danse Macabre*. Everest House, 1979.
> These essays in history and criticism of the horror novel and film are personal and often anecdotal, albeit at the same time sharply critical and interpretative. Recommended reading for those who are *not* fans of the genre.

Lovecraft, Howard Phillips. *Supernatural Horror in Literature*. With a new introduction by E. F. Bleiler. Dover, 1973.
> Essential reading as definition, history, and criticism.

Review Journals

Horror is most often reviewed with science fiction and fantasy.

Locus. 1968– . http://www.locusmag.com
> Published monthly, it provides excellent coverage for horror along with its science fiction and fantasy reviews.

Necropsy: The Review of Horror Fiction. 2001– . http://www.lsu.edu/necrofile/reviews
> Several new titles are covered in each issue. It focuses solely on horror. The Web site also offers links to other horror literature sites.

Conventions

World Horror Convention. The first (annual) was held in Nashville, Tennessee, in 1991. The 2005 convention was held in New York. Information on locations and the current convention's Web site is at www.worldhorrorsociety.org (accessed April 12, 2005).

HWA Annual Conference and Stoker Banquet. A weekend-long professional conference for members of the Horror Writers Association culminates in presentation of the Stoker Awards at a banquet.

Organizations

The Horror Writers Association (http://www.horror.org/). Formerly the Horror Writers of America; has awarded the Bram Stoker Awards annually since 1987. In 2005 it had 819 members.

The International Horror Guild (http://www.ihgonline.org/). Founded in 1995 by Nancy A. Collins. It awards the International Horror Guild Award annually in several categories. The gargoyle-shaped statuettes are awarded at the World Horror Convention.

World Horror Society (http://www.worldhorrorsociety.org/index.html). The purpose of the Society's Web site is to provide information and direction for planning and executing the annual World Horror Convention.

Online Resources

Horror Writers Association, http://www.horror.org/ (accessed April 12, 2005). Not only does the site provide award information, it also has a section specifically for librarians, and the most comprehensive list of horror literature–related sites online.

Horror World (formerly called Masters of Terror and Horror Fiction), http://www.horrorworld.org/ (accessed April 12, 2005). Provides bibliographic information on over 400 authors, reviews, a top 100 listing, and links to other horror-related Web sites.

D's Horror Picks

Davidson, Mary Janice.

Undead and Unappreciated. **2005.** (vampire romance).

According to the *Book of the Dead,* Betsy the Queen of the Vampires will team up with the Spawn of Satan to achieve world domination.

Feehan, Christine.

Dark Secret. **2005.** (vampire romance).

Colby finds the handsome Rafael De La Cruz threatening but irresistibly attractive. When an ancient and powerful vampire, who had been one of Rafael's childhood friends centuries ago, surfaces on the ranch, Colby and Rafael combine forces to try to survive.

Koontz, Dean.

Watchers. **1987.** (monsters, medical horror).

A genetically engineered monster escapes from a secret laboratory, but fortunately so does a genetically enhanced dog, who helps thwart the monster.

 12

Wooding, Chris.

The Haunting of Alaizabel Cray. **2004.** (cosmic paranoia).

A young woman bereft of memories is taken to wych hunter Thaniel who along with Cathaline tries to keep the dank, dark streets of London safe from the wide variety of wych-kin who menace its inhabitants. As a diabolical plan by the Fraternity is unearthed, the true extent of the peril facing humanity comes into focus.

Chapter 13

Christian Fiction

Essay

Erin A. Smith

Christian fiction includes a variety of genres—romances, "classics," biblical fiction, historicals, Westerns, fantasy, science fiction, tales of spiritual warfare, mysteries, and thrillers. These various genres can be meaningfully discussed under the rubric of Christian fiction, because they all reflect a Christian worldview and include serious consideration of the evolving relationship between the protagonist and God. Although there are Catholic, Quaker, Mennonite, Mormon, and Christian fictions whose theology is not orthodox, increasingly "Christian fiction" is used as a synonym for evangelical fiction. The category does not include spiritual or new age fiction (e.g., James Redfield's best-selling *Celestine Prophecy* [1994]) sometimes grouped with it under the amorphous label of "inspirational fiction."

Christian fiction was so prominent a part of mainstream publishing from the nineteenth century through the 1950s that there was little need for a separate category to name it. As mainstream publishing grew increasingly secular in the 1960s and 1970s—including blasphemous language, frank depictions of sex, and explorations of drinking and drug use—Christian fiction as a self-conscious genre category with a distinct, evangelical literary market emerged in opposition.

Christian Ambivalence about Fiction

Christians did not always embrace fiction with enthusiasm; Puritans in Europe and America distrusted its effects profoundly. They distinguished between Truth (the Bible, histories) and lies (which included all types of fiction). The novel got more bad press than any other genre in the late eighteenth and early nineteenth centuries. First, reading novels was a waste of time better spent in study, prayer, and service. Second, even wholesome, moral novels worked on the emotions rather than reason, arousing passions that would unfit readers for their duties in life. Third, some novels represented immoral acts and unwholesome characters that might serve as bad examples. At best, fiction was a self-indulgent waste of time; at worst, a corrupting influence.

Increasingly some clergy and lay leaders argued that *godly* fiction had the potential to bring Christian faith to people who did not attend church or those who might find reading the Bible or published sermons too difficult or tiresome. Many clergy decided it was best to appropriate fictional forms for Christian ends, rather than wage a losing battle for the attention of their congregants against the ubiquitous and immensely popular novels of the day. The nineteenth-century rapprochement between faith and fiction was an illustration of the tensions in evangelical culture between a desire for moral purity and a desire to be a transforming presence in the world.[1]

Some kinds of fiction had long been classics in Christian homes. John Bunyan's *Pilgrim's Progress* (1678) offered generations of readers an allegorical tale of an ordinary Christian's journey to the celestial city and the hazards and difficulties that beset him on his way. Between 1785 and 1850, an increasing number of writers turned from writing tracts and treatises about questions of theology to writing engaging stories that reached and delighted a much wider audience. Women—who had been excluded from public theological debate—found fiction a particularly useful way to enter the marketplace of religious ideas.

The Nineteenth-Century Rapprochement between Faith and Fiction

Jane Tompkins describes the sentimental or domestic fiction written by the wives and daughters of clergymen in the 1850s as having "designs" on the world, seeking to transform society by evoking the right kind of emotions in the hearts of Christian readers.[2] Susan Warner's best-selling *The Wide, Wide World* (1850) was a sermon wrapped up in a young woman's coming-of-age tale, a story whose message of self-sacrifice and submission to the will of God was continuous with the ubiquitous evangelizing tracts of the period. Harriet Beecher Stowe claimed divine inspiration for *Uncle Tom's Cabin* (1852), a novel targeted to women that argued slavery was a gross violation of Christian principles and the sanctity of the family. These sentimental stories evoked tears of sympathy and moved the reader's heart into closer alignment with the teachings of Jesus. Other popular titles were Maria Cummins's *The Lamplighter* (1854), Augusta Wilson's *St. Elmo* (1867)—in which a fallen man is redeemed by the love of a Christian woman—and Elizabeth Stuart Phelps Ward's *The Gates Ajar* (1868), which offered readers a vision of heaven.

Ministers themselves also turned to fiction. Well-known titles included Joseph Holt Ingraham's New Testament novel, *The Prince of the House of David* (1855) and Henry Ward Beecher's *Norwood* (1868), which was serialized in a best-selling periodical. The American Sunday School Union (ASSU), founded in 1824, had an immense publishing arm that produced innumerable tracts, periodicals, and moral tales with a strong Christian message designed to socialize a new generation into evangelical beliefs and culture. Stories like these brought Christian doctrine into closer connection with daily life by illustrating domestic piety, visualizing heaven in everyday terms, allowing readers to imaginatively enter the stories of the Bible, and advocating social reform on Christian principles.

Biblical Fiction

Biblical fiction includes tales based on the Bible (Old Testament or New Testament) or on the experience of Christ's earliest followers, often Christian martyrs in the Roman Empire. Initially, authors shied away from writing biblical fiction, because of belief that the Bible was sacred and inviolable.[3] However, best-selling titles have appeared from the 1830s into the present day, including such books as William Ware's *Julian* (1841) and Joseph Holt Ingraham's *Prince of the House of David* (1855) and *Pillar of Fire* (1859). The best-selling novel of the nineteenth century was Lew Wallace's epic, *Ben-Hur: A Tale of the Christ* (1880), which made the world Jesus inhabited much more vivid and real to millions of readers. Henryk Sienkiewicz's *Quo Vadis* (1895), another epic about the persecution of early Christians, was a publishing phenomenon. biblical fiction's popularity persisted. Lloyd C. Douglas's *The Robe* (1942) was a blockbuster best seller both upon its initial release and after the release of the 1953 film. Many contemporary book clubs enjoyed Anita Diamant's *The Red Tent* (1997), which retells scripture from the point of view of the women given only passing mention in the Bible.

Social Gospel Novels

Liberal Protestants published roughly 100 social gospel novels around the turn of the twentieth century. These were popularizations of the ideas of ministers like Washington Gladden, Richard Ely, and Walter Rauschenbusch, who argued that Christians could bring about the kingdom of God here on Earth by remaking social and economic institutions according to Christian principles. By far the best known is Charles Sheldon's *In His Steps: What Would Jesus Do?* (1897), which was originally delivered as a series of Sunday evening sermons. In it, a minister, an author, a singer, a businessman, a newspaper editor, and others resolve to support each other in first asking what Jesus would do, before making any business or personal decisions. Harold Bell Wright, one of the five most popular writers of the early twentieth century, made his name with wholesome fiction (*The Shepherd of the Hills* [1907], *The Calling of Dan Matthews* [1909]) and originally sold through a mail-order book company specializing in religious books. Wright's *That Printer of Udell's* (1903) showed how the founding of an institutional church transformed life for the better in an ordinary Western town.

The Postwar Explosion of Evangelical Publishing

Although religion was less prominent on best-seller lists after 1915, an occasional blockbuster religious novel like Lloyd C. Douglas's *The Robe* (1942) or the works of Agnes Sligh Turnbull, Taylor Caldwell, and Grace Livingston Hill testified to its continuing importance to many readers. After World War II, however, "Christian fiction" increasingly meant books published by self-described evangelical publishers who defined themselves in opposition to mainstream literature. As self-consciously literary writers represented worlds in which God was absent or irrelevant and placed increasing emphasis on formal experimentation and high style,

13

evangelical audiences continued to seek out simple stories that celebrated family values, faith in God, and happy endings. The gap between mainstream and Christian booksellers is perhaps most evident in the fact that the best-selling book of the 1970s, Hal Lindsey's *The Late, Great Planet Earth* (1970), an account of life after Armageddon, never appeared on any best-seller list, because its sales were almost entirely through evangelical Christian bookstores and mail order rather than trade bookshops.

Since the 1970s, growth in evangelical, Christian publishing has been remarkable, often twice as fast as overall growth in the publishing industry. Evangelical publishing is a separate media enterprise with a purposely didactic mission. Members of the Evangelical Christian Publishers' Association (ECPA) want to sell books, but they also want to save souls. Their titles counter mainstream media pushing self-gratification and pleasure with messages about Christian love and sacrifice. ECPA titles must exclude profanity and explicit sexuality, and they embrace a theological stance that places a divine Jesus at the center of everyday life. Presses such as Zondervan, Warner, Bethany House, Thomas Nelson, Tyndale House, and Crossway distribute books mostly through Christian bookstores (members of the Christian Booksellers' Association or CBA) or through book clubs. The roughly 2,500 CBA stores service a public of three to ten million regular customers.[4] However, since the 1990s, some of these companies have been acquired by secular media conglomerates, and chain bookstores such as Barnes & Noble and Borders or discount retailers like Sam's Club, Wal-Mart, and Costco increasingly carry evangelical titles. In 1999, the ECPA and the CBA began awarding Christy prizes to recognize and encourage excellence in Christian fiction.

Christian Romances

The category of "Christian fiction" was moribund in the 1970s when evangelical publishers began to produce "clean" fiction with a strong Christian message. Janette Oke's *Love Comes Softly* (1979) was the first big seller, and Christian romances that placed earthly love in service to the greater love of Jesus rapidly came to be some of the biggest sellers at Christian bookstores. Romances were the first major genre of Christian fiction, and they continue to be the most popular. Ninety percent of those purchasing evangelical fiction are women, and they are overwhelmingly purchasing romances promising a good story, a fast-moving plot, likable characters, traditional moral values, and a happy ending.[5] The ECPA reports that the market share of Christian romance has grown 25 percent per year since 2001.[6] Subgenres include the prairie romances celebrating old-fashioned, pioneer virtues that made Oke famous; historical romances; contemporary romances; "problem" romances exploring the faith and hard work necessary to achieve and maintain a Christian marriage; and romances that include adventure, suspense, or Western elements. Although the average shopper at Christian bookstores is a forty-two-year-old married, white woman with children,[7] publishers are increasingly targeting younger—sometimes single—women in their twenties and thirties with "Christian chick lit" modeled after secular best sellers like *Bridget Jones's Diary*. Harlequin started a new line of Christian romances targeting these younger readers in 2004 under the Steeple Hill Café imprint.[8]

Diversifying the Field and Bringing in the Men

"Gentle reads" continue to dominate the field of Christian fiction. These include Christian romances and also more literary, general fiction like the best-selling crossover <u>Mitford Series</u> by Jan Karon, which was introduced in 1994 by Christian publisher Chariot Victor, but moved to mainstream Penguin in 1996. Nevertheless, the field has broadened considerably to include many more genres since the mid-1980s. In 1986, Frank Peretti wrote the first best-selling novel of spiritual warfare, *This Present Darkness.* The armies of angels and demons that clashed in the sky over a small, unassuming university town made clear that the contest over souls between Christians and New Age mystics, feminists, and other "modern" gurus was a holy war. This exciting and often violent genre brought many male readers to Christian fiction.

The field has diversified to include almost every imaginable genre. Linda Hall's *Island of Refuge* (1999) represents contemporary Christian mysteries/thrillers; science fiction and fantasy includes the works of Stephen Lawhead, Orson Scott Card, Mary Doria Russell, James BeauSeigneur, and Frederick Buechner. Brock and Bodie Thoene made names for themselves writing historical fiction; they join Stephen Bly and others in re-imagining Westerns as Christian territory.

Apocalyptic Fiction

Most attention in recent years has been directed to novels about the Rapture—when Jesus returns to take the true Christians to heaven, leaving nonbelievers behind to suffer through a painful period of tribulation under the rule of the anti-Christ. Tim LaHaye's and Jerry B. Jenkins's best-selling <u>Left Behind</u> novels, which began appearing in 1995, grew into a sales empire for evangelical publisher Tyndale House, including twelve novels, children's editions, comic book versions, calendars, greeting cards, CDs, and computer software. The twelve books of the <u>Left Behind</u> series have sold over 42 million copies, with every book since number five spending time at the top of the *New York Times* best-seller list (which does not count sales from CBA bookstores).[9] This immense crossover success to readers outside the ECPA fold calls into question the self-definition of evangelical publishers as separate from and opposed to a corrupt and degraded mainstream.

Evangelical Readers

As Amy Johnson Frykholm argues in her ethnographic study of readers of the <u>Left Behind series</u>, individuals do not encounter Christian fiction as solitary readers. Most encounter it as part of family, friendship, and faith networks.[10] For example, readers of <u>Left Behind</u> novels are often introduced to the series by an adult child, a spouse, or a friend. Some buy or borrow the books in order to fully participate in the conversations going on about the stories in their extended families, their church choir, or their Bible study class. In this way, reading cements them into a particular faith community and feeds relationships with people they love and care about.

13

Reading Christian fiction is a way to affirm and maintain one's religious faith. Like Bible study, daily devotional reading, prayer breakfasts, church services, listening to Christian radio stations, or reading materials from James Dobson's Focus on the Family, Christian fiction reminds believers to practice their faith daily and operates as a kind of ritual rehearsal of their membership in this larger, evangelical community. In addition, much Christian fiction is based on the Bible or illustrates points of doctrine in an accessible, material way. For example, many Left Behind readers find the Book of Revelation difficult to read and understand, but Left Behind books illustrate a particular interpretation of the text in an engaging, narrative framework. Christian fiction helps readers understand difficult scripture and allows them to visualize incidents in the Bible, making them seem more "real."

Independent of their particular theological positions, many readers choose to read evangelical Christian fiction because it is "clean"—free of offensive language, overt expressions of sexuality, drinking or drug use, etc. A Christian novel, then, will not present readers with images of immorality that might corrupt their thinking or behavior. On a deeper level, readers choosing Christian fiction ensure that they will not encounter ideas that might challenge or contradict their particular worldview. Every Christian novel takes for granted that Jesus is divine, died and was resurrected for our sins, and ought to be the center of our moral and spiritual lives. These stories promise to reinforce readers' principles, values, and beliefs, rather than inviting doubt, struggle, or mental conflict over alternative ideas.

The Uses of Evangelical Fiction

Although the world of evangelical fiction is somewhat insular, it is nonetheless also a powerful critique of mainstream society. This fiction positions religion and family as central, rather than money or personal ambition. Often, it is critical of materialism, worldly codes of conduct about sex, and the pleasure seeking at the center of secular life. As such, it offers support to readers who might feel embattled or isolated in the larger world, because their coworkers and neighbors have made more conventional, secular lifestyle choices.

Although modern, feminist ideas about men's and women's changing roles are making their way into evangelical fiction, it often maintains an ideal of male supremacy and female domesticity. For many women, the importance evangelical fiction places on the home as the center of religious life and the mother/wife as the keeper of that sacred space gives respect to the culturally devalued caring work most of them do every day. One of the most common characters in Christian fiction is the long-suffering wife/mother whose faith ultimately brings a wayward husband or child back into the fold.

Above all, Christian fiction provides a secure, privileged space for believers. In these narrative spaces, God is in complete control of the world; believers have privileged access to knowledge and emerge victorious (in this world or the next); and historical and current events are placed in a larger, religious framework that gives meaning to everyday life. For people feeling overwhelmed by the complexity and speed of modern life and lacking a sense of control over larger events in the world, Christian fiction promises stability, meaning, and ultimate triumph.

Reading Christian fiction in public places is also a way of "witnessing" to non-evangelicals, a casual, nonthreatening way to invite discussion about faith and convert nonbelievers. Although Tyndale House publicity for the <u>Left Behind</u> touts the many conversions brought about by the novels, research indicates that books like these are much more successful at affirming and maintaining the beliefs of those already embracing an evangelical worldview.[11] Like much Christian fiction, <u>Left Behind</u> novels require that readers possess knowledge of the language, assumptions, and worldview invoked without much explanation in the books. For example, one reader complained that the "Protestant-ese" in the <u>Left Behind</u> series made it difficult for him to understand.[12]

Mainstream Neglect of Christian Fiction

The standards by which Christian fiction is judged differ significantly from mainstream literary standards. Christian books are valued not (or not only) because of their style, aesthetics, or form, but because of their effects on readers. Candy Gunther Brown argues that nineteenth-century evangelicals had a "functionalist" approach to language that deemed whatever words induced readers to promote their own and others' progress in holiness sacred.[13] Frykholm describes the "life-application method" of reading characteristic of contemporary evangelicals. As with reading scripture, readers look for a take-home message in Christian fiction to immediately apply to their own lives.[14] Questions of aesthetics or historical context are irrelevant, if a book brings individuals closer to Jesus, inspires them to moral action on behalf of others, or moves the community of Christian pilgrims closer to sanctification.

In part because Christian fiction is imagined not as literature, but as religious outreach, mainstream media outlets largely ignore it. Secular newspapers and periodicals do not review Christian fiction, and many of the best-loved Christian novels in history were uniformly panned by literary critics. For example, a 1946 *Publishers Weekly* article about the history of best sellers in America characterized Harold Bell Wright—a publishing legend for the immensely popular wholesome, Christian novels he wrote in the early twentieth century—by arguing, "No critic has ever damned Wright with even the faintest of praise." Millions of ordinary readers read and loved Wright's books anyway. His flowery language, sentimental appeals, and happy endings that critics scorned made it easier for Christian readers to see the designing hand of God at work in the world.[15]

Although "Christian fiction" has become almost synonymous in our own day with evangelical Christian fiction (published by members of the ECPA and sold in CBA stores), it is important to remember that there are other kinds of Christian fiction. For example, Catholic fiction has a long history in America, and its canon might include writers such as G. K Chesterton, Evelyn Waugh, Graham Greene, Flannery O'Connor, and Andrew Greeley. Mormon fiction sells well in Utah. There are Quaker and Mennonite fictions. Some evangelicals write Christian fiction that does not receive the ECPA stamp of approval, because it represents explicit sex or cursing, or because its theology is not orthodox. There are also immensely popular Christian fictions that might be dismissed as heretical for their representations of sacred figures, church history, or doctrine. For example, Nikos Kazantzakis's *The Last Temptation of Christ* (1960) angered many, because it included a scene in which Jesus has erotic fantasies. Dan Brown's best-*selling The Da Vinci Code* (2003) is a mystery/thriller centered on the ancient heresy that Jesus was married to Mary Magdalene, who bore a child and continued his bloodline into the present day. This modern-day grail quest is also a critique of the suppression of women's sacredness and power by the Catholic Church. Like many popular Christian books from the past, texts like these arouse controversy among believers, offending some, but providing others with stories and frameworks for building and maintaining a personal and a collective faith.

Notes

1. Candy Gunther Brown, *The Word in the World: Evangelical Writing, Publishing, and Reading in America, 1789–1880* (Chapel Hill: University of North Carolina Press, 2004).

2. Jane Tompkins, *Sensational Designs: The Cultural Work of American Fiction, 1790–1860* (New York: Oxford University Press, 1985).

3. David S. Reynolds, *Faith in Fiction: The Emergence of Religious Literature in America* (Cambridge, Mass.: Harvard University Press, 1981), 123.

4. John Mort, *Christian Fiction: A Guide to the Genre* (Greenwood Village, Colo.: Libraries Unlimited, 2002), 2.

5. Ibid., 4–5.

6. Joshua Kurlantzick, "The New Bodice-Rippers Have More God and Less Sex," *New York Times,* September 21, 2004, B1–2.

7. Mort, *Christian Fiction,* 5; Colleen McDannell, *Material Christianity: Religion and Popular Culture in America* (New Haven, Conn.: Yale University Press, 1995), 256.

8. Kurlantzick, "The New Bodice-Rippers."

9. Sales figures quoted in Ira J. Hadnot, "New Take on Rapture Puts Authors in Apocalyptic Feud," *Dallas Morning News,* November 6, 2004, 1G, 4G.

10. Amy Johnson Frykholm, *Rapture Culture: Left Behind in Evangelical America* (New York: Oxford University Press, 2004).

11. Ibid., 159.

12. Ibid., 72.

13. Brown, *Word in the World,* 4.

14. Ibid., 111.

15. Erin A. Smith, "Melodrama, Popular Religion, and Literary Value: The Case of Harold Bell Wright," *American Literary History* 17, no. 2 (summer 2005): 217–43.

Bibliography

Blodgett, Jan. *Protestant Evangelical Literary Culture and Contemporary Society.* Westport, Conn.: Greenwood, 1997.

Brown, Candy Gunther. *The Word in the World: Evangelical Writing, Publishing, and Reading in America, 1789–1880.* Chapel Hill: University of North Carolina Press, 2004.

Frykholm, Amy Johnson. *Rapture Culture: Left Behind in Evangelical America.* New York: Oxford University Press, 2004.

Gutjahr, Paul C. *An American Bible: A History of the Good Book in the United States, 1777–1880.* Stanford, Calif.: Stanford University Press, 1999.

Hadnot, Ira J. "New Take on Rapture Puts Authors in Apocalyptic Feud." *Dallas Morning News,* November 6, 2004, 1G, 4G.

Hall, David D. *Worlds of Wonder, Days of Judgment: Popular Religious Belief in Early New England.* Cambridge, Mass.: Harvard University Press, 1989.

Kurlantzick, Joshua. "The New Bodice-Rippers Have More God and Less Sex." *New York Times,* September 21, 2004, B1–2.

McDannell, Colleen. *Material Christianity: Religion and Popular Culture in America.* New Haven, Conn.: Yale University Press, 1995.

Mort, John. *Christian Fiction: A Guide to the Genre.* Greenwood Village, Colo.: Libraries Unlimited, 2002.

Reynolds, David S. *Faith in Fiction: The Emergence of Religious Literature in America.* Cambridge, Mass.: Harvard University Press, 1981.

Smith, Erin A. "Melodrama, Popular Religion, and Literary Value: The Case of Harold Bell Wright." *American Literary History* 17, no. 2 (summer 2005): 217–43.

Tompkins, Jane. *Sensational Designs: The Cultural Work of American Fiction, 1790–1860.* New York: Oxford University Press, 1985.

Themes and Types

Diana Tixier Herald

Christian fiction, as read as a genre in the twenty-first century, comes out of the trend started in the 1980s with the romantic series written by Janet Oke. The titles in this chapter, for the most part, appeal to readers who are looking for affirming reads with a Christian view. The readership is far larger than the evangelical Christians. In fact several titles, particularly in the historical section, are written by writers of other traditions such as Anita Diamant and Orson Scott Card.

The chapter is organized with "Classics" first, providing a glimpse into the long tradition of Christian fiction, particularly in mainstream appeal prior to the late twentieth century. "Contemporary," a section dealing with life as it is now, and analogous to mainstream fiction, follows. One of the latest trends in Christian fiction, as in fiction in general, is Chick Lit which is covered in the "Christian Romance" section. Novels with an emphasis on relationships are in the "Christian Romance" and "Gentle Reads" sections. Page-turning excitement follows, with "Mysteries/Thrillers" and "Speculative," which includes fantasy, science fiction, and apocalyptic tales. The "Historical" and "Westerns" sections feature lessons of the past conveyed through the stories of people who, although living in different eras, have much in common with today's readers.

Selected Classics

Because Christianity has historically been the dominant religion in the West, much of Western classic literature is imbued with Christian values and themes. Thus, readers who enjoy Christian fiction may enjoy other classic titles as well. The authors and titles below are those that have been recognized for their overt Christian themes. More detail is given on most of the titles and authors in the subgenre listings that follow, or in the preceding essay.

Bunyan, John.

Pilgrim's Progress. 1678.

Caldwell, Taylor.

A prolific, best-selling author, Caldwell wrote in a number of genres, particularly biblical fiction and stories in the speculative range. Although most of her titles have slid out of print, many are still available in libraries or can be purchased online.

Cummins, Maria.

The Lamplighter. 1854. (historical).

A young orphan girl comes of age, finding faith.

Douglas, Lloyd C.

The Robe. 1942. (historical).

Hawthorne, Nathaniel.

> *The Scarlet Letter.* 1850. (historical).

Hill, Grace Livingston. (romance, gentle reads).

> A prolific writer, Hill produced more than a hundred books in the late nineteenth and early twentieth centuries. Although written as contemporary romances, they are decidedly inspirational, and can be read today as historical Christian romance. In recent years, her works have been reissued by the evangelical publishers as a series of collections.

Ingraham, Joseph Holt.

> *Prince of the House of David.* 1855. (biblical).
> *Pillar of Fire.* 1859.

Lewis, C. S.

> *Till We Have Faces.* 1956. Reissued 1998.
> **Chronicles of Narnia.** (fantasy). Fantasy for all ages.

MacDonald, George. (fantasy)

> A Scottish preacher, poet, and storyteller who lived in the nineteenth century, MacDonald wrote in a number of genres, but always with a spiritual slant. He is best remembered for his fantasies.

Oke, Janette.

> Canadian writer Oke has written many titles, but is most known for her "prairie romances."
>
> *Love Comes Softly.* 1979. (historical romance).

Sheldon, Charles.

> *In His Steps: What Would Jesus Do?* 1897. (social gospel, historical).

Sienkiewicz, Henryk.

> *Quo Vadis?* 1895. (historical).

Stowe, Harriet Beecher.

> *Uncle Tom's Cabin.* 1852.
>> One of the most important American novels ever written, this dramatic moral tale, written as a contemporary story, may now be read as historical fiction.

Wallace, Lew.

> *Ben-Hur: A Tale of the Christ.* 1880. (historical).

Warner, Susan.

> *The Wide, Wide World.* 1850 (coming of age).

Wilson, Augusta.

> *St. Elmo.* 1866. (romance).

Wright, Harold Bell. (social gospel).

> *The Shepherd of the Hills.* 1907.
> *The Calling of Dan Matthews.* 1909.
> *That Printer of Udell's.* 1903.

Contemporary Christian Fiction

Titles in this section are the equivalent of mainstream fiction—stories of everyday people coping with the complexities of contemporary life—but with Christian themes and a message of redemption through Christian faith.

Alcorn, Randy.

🎗 *Safely Home.* 2002.

An American businessman rediscovers his faith when he goes to China and sees persecution. Winner of the Gold Medallion Award.

Carlson, Melody.

Finding Alice. 2003.

A college senior survives the onset of schizophrenia.

Jackson, Netta.

The Yada Yada Prayer Group series.

A wildly diverse group of women, from different faiths, coming together in prayer (and via e-mail), finding friendship and mutual support.

The Yada Yada Prayer Group. 2003.
The Yada Yada Prayer Group Gets Down. 2004.
The Yada Yada Prayer Group Gets Real. 2005.

Morris, Michael.

A Place Called Wiregrass. 2002.

Samson, Lisa.

The Living End. 2003.

🎗 *Songbird.* 2003. Winner of the Christy Award.

Tatlock, Ann.

🎗 *All the Way Home.* 2002. Winner of the Christy Award.

Whittington, Brad.

Welcome to Fred. 2003.

Christian Romance

Christian faith and romantic desire have proved a compelling combination for readers, and many of these titles have achieved best-seller status. Indeed, this has traditionally been one of the most popular areas of publishing and reading in the Christian fiction arena. The category has become so popular that Harlequin, long known for publishing secular romances, now has an imprint, Steeple Hill, for Christian romance.

Contemporary

Contemporary stories are more realistic to some readers, and therefore more believable. They readily allow readers to conjecture—this could happen to me.

Alexander, Hannah.

Hideaway series.

Romantic suspense set in Hideaway, Missouri.

Hideaway. 2003. Winner of the Christy Award.
Safe Haven. 2004.

Blackston, Ray.

Flabbergasted. **2003.**

A romance with a male point of view.

Gunn, Robin Jones.

Wildflowers. 2001.

Hatcher, Robin Lee.

Hart's Crossing.

Legacy Lane. 2004.
Veterans Way. 2005.

Henderson, Dee.

Uncommon Heroes series.

Suspenseful romances featuring Navy SEALS, FBI agents, and pilots.

True Devotion. 2000.
True Valor. 2002.

True Honor. 2002. Winner of the Christy Award.
True Courage. 2004.

Hill, Patti.

Like a Watered Garden. 2005.

Kingsbury, Karen, with Gary Smalley.

Redemption Series.

The continuing saga of the Baxter family.

Redemption. 2002.
Remember. 2003.
Return. 2003.
Rejoice. 2004.
Reunion. 2004.

Lewis, David.

Coming Home. 2004.

Raney, Deborah.

🎀 *Beneath a Southern Sky.* 2001. Winner of the Rita Award.

🎀 *Playing by Heart.* 2003. Winner of the Rita Award.

Roper, Gayle.

Seaside Seasons Series.

Spring Rain. 2001.

Summer Shadows. 2002.

🎀 *Autumn Dreams.* 2003. Winner of the Rita Award.

Winter Winds. 2004.

Warren, Susan May.

The Deep Haven Series.

🎀 *Happily Ever After.* 2003. Winner of the American Christian Romance Writer's Award.

Tying the Knot. 2003.

🎀 *The Perfect Match.* 2004. Winner of the Rita Award.

Wick, Lori.

Sophie's Heart. 1995. Reissued 2004.

Christian Chick Lit

Like its secular counterpart, Christian Chick Lit is romantic and completely up to date. The protagonists contend with the challenges that face many young women involving conflicts at work and finding love. The tales are hip, funny, and often feature fashion. However, overt sexuality is absent from Christian Chick Lit, where the protagonists may think about sex, but they rely on their faith to help then stay on a righteous path. Because they follow this path, marriage and motherhood may soon follow, evolving into what is being called Mommy Lit.

Christian Chick Lit was the topic of a Faithful Reader Round Table at which several authors writing in the genre had an opportunity to share their opinions (http://www.faithfulreader.com/features/0411chicklit/chicklit.asp).

Baer, Judy.

Whitney Blake series.

The major difference between Bridgette Jones and Whitney Blake is that Whitney is an evangelical Christian.

The Whitney Chronicles. 2004.

Billerbeck, Kristin.

Ashley Stockingdale series.

"All I want is a nice Christian guy who doesn't live with his mother . . . and maybe a Prada handbag . . . "

What a Girl Wants. 2004.

Will Ashley, a thirty-something patent attorney in Silicon Valley, find him?

13

She's Out of Control. 2004.
Will he pop the question?

With This Ring, I'm Confused! 2005.
Is it finally going to happen for Ashley?

Gunn, Robin Jones.

Sisterchicks Mommy Lit series.

About pairs of friends (or sisters) who reconnect in mid-life for far-flung adventures. While they were not written as Chick Lit, they were immediately adopted by fans of the genre.

Sisterchicks on the Loose! 2003.
Sisterchicks Do the Hula! 2003.
Sisterchicks in Sombreros! 2004.
Sisterchicks Down Under. 2005.
Sisterchicks Say Ooh La La! 2005.

Walker, Laura Jensen.

Phoebe Grant series.

Dreaming in Black & White. 2005.
Dreaming in Technicolor. 2005.

Historical Romance

Historical romances of the Christian variety often have a nostalgic tone, hearkening back to simpler, more innocent times, when life may have been hard, but the issues were clear-cut; and always, faith pulled you through. This is the genre that brought Christian fiction to the attention of many readers' advisory librarians in the 1980s with the works of Janette Oke and June Masters Bacher.

Hatcher, Robin Lee.

 The Shepherd's Voice. 2000.
Depression-era Idaho. Winner of the Rita Award.

Lewis, Beverly.

Abram's Daughters.

Just barely historical fiction because the stories take place in the post–World War II era, this saga of an Old Order (Amish) family with four courting-age daughters appeals to readers of historical romance.

The Covenant. 2002.
The Betrayal. 2003.
The Sacrifice. 2004.
The Prodigal. 2004.
The Revelation. 2005.

Oke, Janette.

Oke's tales of prairie romance deal with life on the western frontier of Canada. She has penned more than seventy books, many of them best sellers, and is credited with starting the popularity of Christian fiction as we know it today.

Canadian West Series.

When Calls the Heart. 1983. Reissued 2005.

A young schoolteacher on the Canadian prairie frontier falls in love with a member of the Royal Canadian Mounted Police.

When Comes the Spring. 1985. Reissued 2005.
When Breaks the Dawn. 1986. Reissued 2005.
When Hope Springs New. 1986. Reissued 2005.

Peterson, Tracie.

Heirs of Montana.

Set in the world of ranching in Montana in the 1870s and 1880s.

To Dream Anew. 2004.
The Coming Storm. 2004.
The Hope Within. 2005.

Peterson, Tracie, and Judith Miller.

Lights of Lowell.

A Southern belle finds her perceptions changing after entering into a loveless marriage in Lowell, Massachusetts in the 1840s.

A Tapestry of Hope. 2004.
A Love Woven True. 2005.
The Pattern of Her Heart. 2005.

Snelling, Lauraine.

Dakotah Treasures.

A pair of sisters leave their New York home to claim their inheritance in the Dakotah territories of the late nineteenth century.

Ruby. 2003.
Pearl. 2004.
Opal. 2005.

Gentle Reads

Gentle reads offer comfort and affirmation to readers. These stories contain no explicit sex, violence, or bad language to upset or unnecessarily excite readers. Instead they are warm and soothing, sometimes funny, often sentimental stories about the lives of gentle people, coping with day-to-day problems in a Christian manner. The characters and their relationships provide the core of these stories. Often they are set in small towns.

Cramer, W. Dale.

Bad Ground. 2004.

Hill, Grace Livingston. ★

Hill lived from 1865 to 1947, but her books found a new audience with readers looking for good stories sans sex or violence. She wrote more than a hundred books during her writing career.

Brentwood. 1937. Reissued 2004.

A young woman is reunited with her family.

Kerry. 1931. Reissued 2001.
More Than Conqueror. 1944. Reissued 2001.
Rainbow Cottage. 1934. Reissued 2003.
Sunrise. 1931. Reissued 2000.

Karon, Jan.

<u>Mitford Series.</u>

This tremendously popular series is as soothing as a bowl of chicken soup, and as sweet as milk and cookies after school. It even has its own cookbook. Its appeal extends beyond the evangelical Christian audience. The residents of this charming village are generally loveable. At the center of the stories is Father Tim, the Episcopal rector.

At Home in Mitford. 1994.
A Light in the Window. 1995.
These High, Green Hills. 1996.
Out to Canaan. 1997.
A New Song. 1999. Winner of the Gold Medallion Award.
A Common Life. 2001.
In This Mountain. 2002.
Shepherds Abiding. 2003.
Light from Heaven: The Final Mitford Novel. 2005.

Mysteries/Thrillers

In the Christian suspense story, lines between good and evil are clearly drawn, and faith and prayer support the protagonists, helping them bring the investigation to a successful conclusion.

Alger, Mike.

Snow Storm. 2002.

Blackstock, Terri.

<u>Cape Refuge Series.</u>

Cape Refuge. 2002.
Southern Storm. 2003.
River's Edge. 2004.
Breaker's Reef. 2005.

Brouwer, Sigmund.
> *The Lies of Saints: A Nick Barrett Mystery.* 2003.

Bunn, T. Davis.
> 🎗 *Drummer in the Dark.* 2001. Winner of the Christy Award.
> *Elixir.* 2004.
> *The Lazarus Trap.* 2005.

Dekker, Ted.
> *Obsessed.* 2005.
>> After receiving a dead woman's papers, a real estate developer in the 1970s starts on a treasure hunt that leads back to the holocaust in Poland.

> 🎗 *Thr3e.* 2003.
>> Winner of the Christy and Gold Medallion Awards. Kevin Parson, a seminary student, receives threatening phone calls commanding him to publicly confess or a bomb will be set off. Unfortunately Kevin is mystified.

Hall, Linda.
> *Island of Refuge.* 1999.

LaHaye, Tim.
> <u>Babylon Rising.</u>
>> Archaeologist Michael Murphy confronts evil as he searches for biblical antiquities.
>
>> *Babylon Rising.* 2003. Cowritten with Greg Dinallo.
>> *The Secret on Ararat.* 2004. Cowritten with Bob Phillips
>> *The Europa Conspiracy.* 2005. Cowritten with Bob Phillips

North, Oliver, with Joe Musser.
> 🎗 *Mission Compromised.* 2002. Winner of the Gold Medallion Award.

Peretti, Frank
> *Monster.* 2005.

Singer, Randy.
> *Directed Verdict.* 2002.

Wise, Robert L.
> <u>Sam and Vera Sloan series.</u>
>> *The Dead Detective.* 2002.
>> *Deleted!* (2003.

Speculative

Fantasy worlds, with their heroes and their quests, their magnificent and miraculous worlds, provide a wonderful venue for the Christian message, as the classic fantasy and science fiction author C. S. Lewis has shown.

But what does the future hold for Christians? What obstacles and trials will they face? How will they cope with technology and increasing challenges to their faith? This subject became very popular around the turn of the millennium, when many Christian authors turned to the visionary Book of Revelations and offered interpretations of its prophesies in SF stories.

Fantasy

Fantasy usually deals with the conflict of good versus evil. In Christian fantasy, faith, rather than magical powers, imbues the hero with the strength needed to triumph.

Hancock, Karen.

> **Legends of the Guardian-King.**
>> *The Light of Eidon.* 2003.
>> *The Shadow Within.* 2004.

Ingermanson, Randall.

> **City of God Series.** (time travel).
>> *Retribution.* 2004.

Johnson, Shane.

> *The Last Guardian.* 2001.
>> In 1975 T. G. Shass, in possession of an artifact he has no memory of obtaining, journeys to an alternate world filled with horrors, where he must defeat evil to make way for salvation to change the world.

MacDonald, George.

> *The Complete Fairy Tales.* 1999.
>> Written individually in the late nineteenth century, MacDonald's allegorical tales were eventually published as a collection.

> *Lilith.* 1895.
>> A moral allegory.

Plass, Adrian.

> *Ghosts: The Story of a Reunion.* 2003.
>> A Christian widower, haunted by nightmares and ghosts, accepts an invitation to a reunion from a friend of his late wife, where he must face his fears and ghosts head on.

Wangerin, Walter, Jr.

> *The Book of the Dun Cow.* 1978.
>> An animal allegory.

> *Crying for a Vision.* 1994. Reissued 2003.

Science Fiction

Science fiction is not a genre traditionally thought of in the context of Christian fiction, but as the interest in Christian novels has grown, so has the variety showing that concepts of faith can be conveyed in just about any setting or time period.

Beauseigneur, James.

   <u>Christ Clone trilogy.</u>

      In His Image. 1998.

      Birth of an Age. 1997.

      Acts of God. 1998.

David, James F.

   Judgment Day. 2005.

      God grants a faster-than-light spaceship to a religious group, which then begins a mass exodus to another planet.

Gansky, Alton.

   Dark Moon. 2002.

      An astronomer is called in to help when a mysterious stain appears across the moon, wreaking chaos across the world.

Hancock, Karen.

    *Arena.* 2002.

      Callie Hayes volunteers for a psychology experiment and is thrust into a terrifying alien world in the midst of a battle between good and evil. Winner of the Christy Award.

Ingermanson, Randall.

   Transgression. 2000.

      Virtual reality time travel

Ingermanson, Randall, and John Olson.

   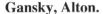 *Oxygen.* 2001. Winner of the Christy Award.

Moser, Nancy.

   Time Lottery. 2002.

Olson, John, and Randall Ingermanson.

   The Fifth Man. 2002.

Russell, Mary Doria.

   The Sparrow. 1996.

   Children of God. 1998.

Apocalyptic Fiction

Apocalyptic fiction hit the secular best-seller lists as well as the Christian best-seller lists when the <u>Left Behind series</u> featuring Rayford Steele, who is one of those "left behind" when Rapture happens and people all over the world, even up in the plane he was piloting at the time, disappear. At the turn of the millennium, this was the best known type of Christian fiction.

Hanegraaff, Hank, and Sigmund Brouwer.

   The Last Disciple. **2004.**

      Is it possible that the Apocalypse really happened nearly 2000 years ago?

Jenkins, Jerry B.

Underground Zealot.

Following an apocalyptic war, the world's governments outlaw religion as a way of keeping peace. Paul Stepola is an agent for the NPO (National Peace Organization) who becomes a Christian.

🎗 *Soon.* 2003. Winner of the Christy Award.
Slenced. 2004.
Shadowed. 2005.

Lalonde, Peter, and Paul Lalonde.

Apocalypse. 2001.

Could the forces of evil fake Rapture?

Wise, Robert L.

Tribulation Survival Series.

Wired. 2004.
Tagged. 2004.

Left Behind

The Left Behind series is to Christian fiction as Harry Potter is to fantasy—but bigger. When Rapture comes, those who are not "Christians" are left behind and face what happens as the Antichrist claims the world. The original series by Tim LaHaye and Jerry B. Jenkins spawned a series for young readers and has turned into a franchise universe with new series by other authors dealing with the same apocalypse but from a militaristic or political angle. There are even graphic novels and a series for kids. There have been many imitators.

LaHaye, Tim, and Jerry B. Jenkins.

Left Behind series.

Left Behind. 1995. Reissued 2005
Tribulation Force. 1996.
Nicolae. 1997.
Soul Harvest. 1998.
Apollyon. 1999.
Assassins. 1999.
The Indwelling. 2000.
The Mark. 2000.
Desecration. 2001.
The Remnant. 2002.
Armageddon. 2003.
Glorious Appearing. 2004.

Before They Were Left Behind.

A prequel series looking at the lives of those who will play roles in the Left Behind series.

The Rising. 2005.

Hart, Neesa.

   <u>Left Behind—Political Series.</u>

      End of State. 2003.

      Impeachable Offense. 2004.

      Necessary Evils. 2005.

Odom, Mel.

   <u>Left Behind—Military Series.</u>

      Apocalypse Dawn. 2003.

      Apocalypse Crucible. 2004.

      Apocalypse Burning. 2004.

Historical

Historical fiction for Christian readers has much the same appeal as it does for other readers. The major difference is that a relationship with God plays a central role.

Austin, Lynn.

   <u>Refiner's Fire.</u>

      Set during the Civil War.

      ✿ *Candle in the Darkness.* 2002. Winner of the Christy Award.

      ✿ *Fire by Night.* 2003. Winner of the Christy Award.

      A Light to My Path. 2004.

Bergren, Lisa Tawn.

   <u>Northern Lights Series.</u>

      Norwegian immigration to North America in the 1880s.

      The Captain's Bride. 1998.

      Deep Harbor. 1999.

      Midnight Sun. 2000.

Cavanaugh, Jack.

   <u>Book of Books series.</u>

      Those who translated the Bible into the vernacular.

      Glimpses of Truth. 1999.

      John Wycliffe.

      Beyond the Sacred Page. 2003.

      William Tyndale.

   <u>Songs in the Night.</u>

      World War II Germany.

 13

      While Mortals Sleep. 2001.

      His Watchful Eye. 2002.

      Above All Earthly Powers. 2004.

Pella, Judith.

Daughters of Fortune.

Written on the Wind. 2002.

Somewhere a Song. 2002.

Toward the Sunrise. 2003.

Homeward My Heart. 2004.

Rivers, Francine.

 The Last Sin Eater. 1998.

This winner of the Gold Medallion Award is about Appalachia in the 1850s.

Sprinkle, Patricia.

Job's Corner Chronicles.

When her mother dies, eleven-year-old Carley is sent to live with her uncle, who is a minister with firm convictions on racial equality.

The Remember Box. 2001.

Carley's Song. 2001.

Thoene, Bodie, and Brock Thoene.

The Zion Legacy.

The first three are set in Israel in 1948, and then the action moves back to the first century.

Jerusalem Vigil. 2000.

Thunder from Jerusalem. 2000.

Jerusalem's Heart. 2001.

The Jerusalem Scrolls. 2001.

Stones of Jerusalem. 2002.

Jerusalem's Hope. 2002.

Biblical

These stories use the characters or motifs of Bible stories and extrapolate, offering more detail or different viewpoints on events.

Card, Orson Scott.

Women of Genesis.

Sarah. 2000.

Rebekah. 2001.

Rachel & Leah. 2004.

Diamant, Anita.

The Red Tent. 1997.

Edghill, India.

Wisdom's Daughter: A Novel of Solomon and Sheba. 2004.

Hendricks, Obery M.

Living Water. 2003.

New Testament setting.

Morris, Gilbert.

    <u>Lions of Judah series.</u>

        Heart of a Lion. 2002.

        No Woman So Fair. 2003.

        The Gate of Heaven. 2004.

        Till Shiloh Comes. 2005.

Rivers, Francine.

    <u>Sons of Encouragement.</u>

        The Priest. 2004.

        The Warrior. 2005.

Shott, James R.

    <u>People of the Promise.</u>

        Leah. 1990. Reissued 1999.

        Joseph. 1992. Reissued 2000.

        Hagar. 1992. Reissued 2000.

        Esau. 1993. Reissued 2001.

        Deborah. 1993. Reissued 2001.

        Othniel. 1994. Reissued 2002.

        Abigail. 1996. Reissued 2002.

        Bathsheba. 1995. Reissued 2003.

Tenney, Tommy.

    Hadassah: One Night with the King. 2005.

        The story of Esther.

Wangerin, Walter.

    🏵 *Paul: A Novel.* 2000.

        A fictional biography of the apostle Paul. Winner of the Golden Medallion Award.

Westerns

    Westerns seem like a natural fit for Christian fiction. The conflict of good versus evil is inherent in the genre, and in traditional Westerns there is little sex or cursing.

Bagdon, Paul.

    Stallions at Burnt Rock. 2003.

13

Bly, Stephen.

    Friends and Enemies. 2002.

    Last of the Texas Camp. 2002.

    🏵 *The Long Trail Home.* 2001. Winner of the Christie Award.

    The Outlaw's Twin Sister. 2002.

    The Next Roundup. 2003.

Rogers, R. William.
>*Toward a New Beginning.* 2001.

Thoene, Brock, and Bodie Thoene.
>**Saga of the Sierras.**
>>*The Man from Shadow Ridge.* 1990. Reissued 2002.
>>*Riders of the Silver Rim.* 1990.
>>*Gold Rush Prodigal.* 1991.
>>*Sequoia Scout.* 1991.
>>*Cannons of the Comstock.* 1992. Reissued 2002.
>>*The Year of the Grizzly.* 1992.
>>*Shooting Star.* 1993.
>>*Flames on the Barbary Coast.* 1991.

Topics

Reference and Resources

Aue, Pamela Willwerth, ed. *What Inspirational Literature Do I Read Next?* Gale Group, 2000.

DeLong, Janice, and Rachel Schwedt. *Contemporary Christian Authors: Lives and Works.* Scarecrow Press, 2000.

Mort, John. *Christian Fiction: A Guide to the Genre.* Libraries Unlimited, 2002.

Walker, Barbara J. *Developing Christian Fiction Collections for Children and Adults: Selection Criteria and a Core Collection.* Neal Schuman, 1998.

Review Journals

Christian Book Previews, http://www.christianbookpreviews.com/

Christian Library Journal. http://www.christianlibraryj.org/
Online journal featuring reviews. As of May 2005 the last issue posted was December 2004.

Organizations

American Christian Fiction Writers (http://www.americanchristianfictionwriters.com/) started as the American Christian Romance Writers in 2002, the 650 member organization changed its name in December of 2004 to be more encompassing.

Evangelical Christian Publishers Association (http://www.ecpa.org/). Information for publishers and aspiring writers. This is the place to find the evangelical best sellers.

Awards

ACFW Book of the Year Award. American Christian Fiction Writers presents an annual award in several categories, including long contemporary romance, long historical romance, contemporary novella, historical novella, contemporary women's fiction, and historical women's fiction. With the organization's name change in 2004 it is probable that the categories will change.

Christy Awards. Beginning in 2000, winners in six categories of fiction are announced at the Christian Booksellers Association annual meeting.

Gold Medallion Award. Awarded by the Evangelical Christian Publisher's Association starting in 1978. Even though awards are made in several categories, only one fiction title a year is honored.

Rita Award. Among the many categories for which the Romance Writers of America award an annual Rita is "Inspirational Romance." The first one in 1995 was to *An Echo in the Darkness* by Francine Rivers

D's Picks

Alger, Mike.

Snow Storm. **2002.** (mystery-thriller).

A Reno weatherman is drawn into a mystery involving a cocaine cartel when someone tries to assassinate him. His Christian beliefs sustain him on his quest to solve the mystery.

Blackston, Ray.

Flabbergasted. **2003.** (contemporary romance).

Jay Jarvis, an up-and-coming young stockbroker, has just started a new job in Greenvillle, South Carolina. Asking his realtor where he can find the singles scene, he is told that in Greenville the singles meet at church. Trying out North Hills Presbyterian church, he sees a gorgeous girl and decides to join the singles group that is planning a trip to Myrtle Beach to get close to her. Quirky good fun and a gentle romance from a male point of view.

Russell, Mary Doria.

The Sparrow. **1996.** (science fiction).

Alternating between the hope-filled days when extraterrestrial music is discovered by Jimmy Quinn and the Jesuit order swings into action outfitting an expedition to the planet Rakhat and the slow drawing out of the horrible outcome from the sole tortured and vilified survivor of the expedition, this fully captivates the reader.

Chapter 14

Emerging Genres

Diana Tixier Herald

Genres are constantly changing, with new trends coming into play, new genres co-alescing, new subgenres rising, and old themes and subgenres fading away. Often genre trends reflect demographic changes and transformations on the social level. Certainly this is the case with the two genres covered in this chapter. Women's fiction could be viewed as a more contemporary and realistic version of traditional romance, where lovers don't neces-sarily get married and live happily ever after; where mature women discover support in fe-male friendship and success in their own inner strength.

Chick Lit, which might be considered the kid sister of women's fiction, certainly speaks to the swelling demographics in young adult female populations, and it portrays a world in which young women juggle the demands of career and relationships in new and nontraditional ways.

Other publishing and reading trends are not necessarily reflected within the boundaries of traditional genres. For example, graphic novels, which are arguably only an alternative format, have become extremely popular, particularly among teen readers. Readers' advi-sors have begun considering recreational nonfiction as a genre. In the near future, we will undoubtedly be seeing more definition and description in this arena. For the time being, these are trends that can be observed, but it would be premature to pronounce them full-fledged genres, and impossible to draw on the rich histories of their evolution.

In the meantime, let's take a look at two interesting and rather recent developments (or at least, developments recently recognized by publishers) in reading interests—women's fiction and Chick Lit.

Women's Fiction

It may seem odd to categorize "women's fiction" as a genre, let alone as an "emerging genre." After all, women have been writing novels about women's lives and relationships for a long time. However, in the last decades of the twentieth century, as women's roles underwent tremendous transformations, a new type of book struck a chord with readers. Like romance, these stories centered on the lives of women, and also like romance, they presented women as caring, warm, funny individuals, coping with life's many changes. However, the romantic interest was not central to the story. Instead, the women in these books often faced life's challenges with the help of a small, supportive group of usually female friends.

Although not formally a genre in the way that "romance" and "crime" have become, this body of literature has widely become known as "women's fiction," because it is generally by, about, and for women. The designation is beginning to turn up in publishers' catalogs and in book jacket blurbs. You won't find a "women's fiction" shelf at your local bookstore, nor are there "women's fiction" writer and fan organizations (yet). However, it is interesting to note that a small group of retail bookstores cater specifically to female readers. (For example, Women and Children First, in Chicago). Harlequin's mainstream imprint, Mira, calls them "Relationship novels."

It might be said that women's fiction has its roots in the earliest published novels written by women—for example, Jane Austen, whose spirited heroines transcended the traditional roles of their times; or we may look to early twentieth-century writers for beginnings. Such authors as Virginia Woolf (*Mrs. Dalloway*) and Kate Chopin (*The Awakening*) helped redefine the roles of women with their work. A history of women's fiction as a genre has not yet been published, and it is not within the scope of this work to create one at this time. What is more important for today's readers' advisor is to understand the genre's characteristics and appeal to readers.

Women's fiction is all about relationships, and thus it is related to romance and to Chick Lit. Like romance, it is about women's relationships, and its appeal is emotional, but women's fiction does not have the tight focus on the romantic interest, and "happily ever after" endings are not required. In fact, many titles have themes of "after the divorce" or "making it on my own." It is similar to Chick Lit in that it takes this broader focus on women's lives and emphasizes friendship and humor, but the protagonists are more mature women, well into their lives, often with grown children, rather than young singles searching for fulfillment. The tone ranges from humorous (Lorna Landvik), to bittersweet (Maeve Binchy), to melodramatic (Terry McMillan).

For purposes of this guide, women's fiction consists of the stories about a woman or (most commonly) a small group of women who care about each other and lend each other strength as they face adversity as they celebrate the joys of life. Whether women's fiction is a subgenre of romance fiction, as some romance publishers would have us believe, or romance fiction is in fact a subgenre of women's fiction is a question we will not attempt to answer at this time. Certainly, a case could be made for either statement.

Readers who enjoy their women's fiction on the humorous side often also enjoy very personal nonfiction such as Bailey White's collections of essays and the advice dispensed in Jill Connor Browne's <u>Sweet Potato Queens</u> guides.

Since many of the contemporary authors of women's fiction started out in the romance genre, readers may find earlier books by their favorite authors among long contemporary romance novels. Those who enjoy the sense of collegiality, the close-knit friendships, may enjoy some of the books called gentle reads. Mainstream novels featuring female protagonists often hold appeal for readers of women's fiction.

The titles that follow are a small sampling from this developing genre.

Alvarez, Julia.
How the Garcia Girls Lost Their Accents. 1991.

Berg, Elizabeth.
The Art of Mending. 2004.
The Pull of the Moon. 1996
The Year of Pleasures. 2005.

Binchy, Maeve.
A Circle of Friends. 1991.
Night of Rain and Stars. 2004.

Bradford, Barbara Taylor.
Unexpected Blessings. 2005.

Chamberlain, Diane.
Her Mother's Shadow. 2004. A sequel to *Kiss River*.
Kiss River. 2003.
The Courage Tree. 2001.

Chiaverini, Jennifer.
<u>Elm Creek Quilts Series.</u>
Started in 1999 with *The Quilter's Apprentice*.

Cleage, Pearl.
Babylon Sisters. 2005.
What Looks Like Crazy on an Ordinary Day. 1997.

Delinsky, Barbara.
An Accidental Woman. 2002.

Fielding, Joy.
Fielding is best known for her romantic suspense.

Grand Avenue. 2001.
Four mothers, all with daughters the same age, establish a friendship that lasts for decades when they all live on Grand Avenue.

Flagg, Fannie.
Fried Green Tomatoes at the Whistle Stop Café. 1987. Reissued 2000. ▪

Fowler, Karen Joy.
The Jane Austen Book Club. 2004.

Hannah, Kristin.
Between Sisters. 2003.
The Things We Do for Love. 2004.

Keyes, Marian.
The Other Side of the Story. 2004.

Landis, Jill Marie.
Lover's Lane. 2003.

Landvik, Lorna.
Angry Housewives Eating Bon Bons. 2003.
> The five women of Freesia Court's unofficial book group find mutual support gets them through forty eventful years.

Patty Jane's House of Curl. 1995.
Welcome to the Great Mysterious. 2000.

Lipman, Elinor.
The Dearly Departed. 2001.
Isabel's Bed. 1996.
The Pursuit of Alice Thrift. 2003.

Macomber, Debbie.
<u>A Good Yarn.</u>
> A cancer survivor opens a yarn shop in Seattle that creates a connection among several women, who become friends.

The Shop on Blossom Street. 2004.
A Good Yarn. 2005.

McMillan, Terry.
A Day Late and a Dollar Short. 2001.
Waiting to Exhale. 1992. ▪
> Savannah, Bernie, Gloria, and Robin, four African American women living in Phoenix, provide community and support for each other as they look for love.

Naylor, Gloria.
Women of Brewster Place. 1982. ▪
> Seven African American neighbors support each other.

Pilcher, Rosamunde.
Winter Solstice. 2000.

Rice, Luanne.
> *Beach Girls.* 2004.
> *Firefly Beach.* 2001.
> *The Perfect Summer.* 2003.
> *Safe Harbor.* 2003.

Roberts, Nora.
> *The Villa.* 2001.

Samuel, Barbara.
> *The Goddesses of Kitchen Avenue.* 2004.
> *Lady Luck's Map of Vegas.* 2005.
> *No Place Like Home.* 2002.
> *A Piece of Heaven.* 2003.

Smith, Haywood.
> **The Red Hat Club.**
>> A group of fifty-something sorority sisters meet for tea and adventures.
>
>> *The Red Hat Club.* 2003.
>> *The Red Hat Club Rides Again.* 2005.

Steel, Danielle.
> *The Ranch.* 1997. Reissued 2005.
>> After more than twenty years apart, three college roommates, Mary Stuart, Tanya, and Zoe, reunite at a ranch in Wyoming to reconnect and share their heartaches and joys.

Thayer, Nancy.
> **The Hot Flash Club.**
>> When four women between the ages of fifty-two and sixty-two meet at a retirement party, they discover that each has the resources to solve one of the other's problems.
>
>> *The Hot Flash Club.* 2003.
>> *Hot Flash Club Strikes Again.* 2004.

Trollope, Joanna.
> *Marrying the Mistress.* 2002.
> *Other People's Children.* 1999.
>> Three women wrestle with stepfamilies.

Weiner, Jennifer.
> *Little Earthquakes.* 2004.
>> Four new mothers' lives entwine.

Wells, Rebecca.
> *Divine Secrets of the Ya-Ya Sisterhood.* 1998.
> *Ya-Yas in Bloom.* 2005.

White, Bailey.

Quite a Year for Plums. 1998.

> The women of a small Georgia town worry and gossip about Roger and his budding romance.

Resources

As of yet there is no guide to the genre of contemporary women's fiction. Joyce Sarick, in *The Readers' Advisory Guide to Genre Fiction* (American Library Association, 2001) has a chapter titled "Women's Lives and Relationships" in which she discusses the genre that is now commonly referred to as women's fiction. There are a number of scholarly publications on the literary works of women writers, for example, *Twentieth Century American Women's Fiction* by Guy Reynolds (Palgrave, 1999). Some articles of interest may also be found online. Of particular note is Lisa Craig, *Women's Fiction vs. Romance: A Tale of Two Genres,* available at http://www.writing-world.com/romance/craig.shtml (accessed June 8, 2005).

D's Women's Fiction Picks

Hannah, Kristin.

Between Sisters. **2003.**

> Now she is a successful attorney, but at age sixteen Meghann Dontess had pretty much raised her younger half-sister, Claire. When their mother abandoned them to go to Hollywood, she took Claire to the father she had never known. Estranged since then, Meghann becomes involved in Claire's life again in a short visit to prepare for Claire's wedding (to a country singer) that turns into much more.

Lipman, Elinor.

Isabel's Bed. **1996.**

> An unlikely friendship grows between the flamboyant femme fatale Isabel, who was in bed with her rich boyfriend when he was shot by his wife and Harriett, fleeing the aftermath of a breakup, who answers Isabel's ad for a ghost writer.

Samuel, Barbara.

Lady Luck's Map of Vegas. **2005.**

> Web designer India, age forty and newly pregnant, promised her dying father that she would take care of her mother. So when Eldora, her mother, a former Vegas "show girl" determines that she must go to Las Vegas and search for India's schizophrenic twin Gypsy along the way, she hits the road. As she ponders what to do about her pregnancy and her gorgeous Irish boyfriend, Eldora divulges family secrets.

Chick Lit

The genre that gained widespread recognition with the advent of *Bridget Jones's Diary* in 1998 has grown by leaps and bounds, but whether it will continue to flourish and actually solidify into a lasting genre remains to be seen. Whatever the case, right now it's huge. Several publishers have started imprints to feature Chick Lit. Harlequin's is Red Dress Ink, Ballantine's XYZ Group, Pocket's Downtown Press, and Kensington's is Strapless. Among the PublishersWeekly.com's book types (listed on a pull down menu), only three of about two dozen are specifically related to fiction—mystery, romance, and chick lit—indicating that they think it is a newsworthy type.

It seems there are nearly as many descriptions of the genre as there are titles in it. Generally the stories feature a young woman (or group of young women), usually in their twenties or thirties, with relationship or career issues, and the stories are told with wit and humor. In fact, if women's fiction can be said to be "all about relationships," Chick Lit might be said to be "all about attitude and relationships." The tone is both humorous and upbeat, with lots of dialogue, usually of the witty, confidential, and gossipy variety. (In fact, this genre has also been referred to as "gossip lit.") Often the stories are told in the first person, but whatever the case, the voice of the author is important. Readers usually identify strongly with the characters in the books. These books are sexy, smart, sassy, and very trendy. As the genre has evolved, so have the situations. Some of the protagonists are now married or young mothers (Mommy Lit). This diversification as well as hybrids with mystery and paranormal are also indications of the genre's strength and durability.

The genre is too young to really have any "classics," and you won't see a "Chick Lit" label on these books, nor will you see them grouped together on a shelf at the bookstore, but they are usually unmistakable because of their packaging. Bright, candy-colored covers sport images of high heels, lips, rhinestone sunglasses, and other fashionable iconography.

Readers who enjoy Chick Lit tend to reflect qualities of the women featured in the books—young twenty- to thirty-year olds, working to succeed in careers and relationships. Chick Lit is also very popular with young adult readers, with many authors (such as Louise Rennison and Ann Brashares) writing specifically for them. Those titles are covered in *Teen Genreflecting*, 2d ed. (Libraries Unlimited, 2004) and are therefore not included here.

Readers of Chick Lit may also enjoy contemporary humorous romances. The paranormal romances by MaryJanice Davidson that feature Betsy Taylor, "the Queen of the Vampires," are actually very much Chick Lit, featuring a group of supportive friends and high-dollar shoes along with vampires and werewolves. Readers who like the sassy brashness of the characters and the drop-dead-gorgeous men will also enjoy the <u>Stephanie Plum</u> mysteries by Janet Evanovich. Some readers may also enjoy Christian Chick Lit, which features smart and fashion-conscious young women without the sex and cursing. Again, the titles below offer a sampling of the genre.

Bank, Melissa.
The Girls' Guide to Hunting and Fishing. 1999.

Burley, Charlotte, and Lyah LeFlore.
Cosmopolitan Girls. 2004.
African American protagonists.

Cabot, Meg.
Boy Meets Girl. 2004.
Every Boy's Got One. 2005.

Castillo, Mary.
Hot Tamara. 2005.
Latina protaganist.

Coburn, Jennifer.
Reinventing Mona. 2005.
The Wife of Reilly. 2004.

Dunn, Sarah.
The Big Love. 2004.

Fielding, Helen.
Bridget Jones's Diary. 1998.

Frankel, Valerie.
The Girlfriend Curse. 2005.

Gold, Emma.
Easy. 2003.

Grazer, Gigi Levangie.
Maneater. 2003.

Green, Jane.
Bookends. 2000.
The Other Woman. 2005.

Holden, Wendy.
Farm Fatale. 2002.
The Wives of Bath. 2005.

Hwang, Caroline.
In Full Bloom. 2003.
A Korean American protagonist.

Kauffman, Donna.
The Cinderella Rules. 2004.

Keltner, Kim Wong.
The Dim Sum of All Things. 2004.
A Chinese American protagonist.

Kinsella, Sophie.
> *Can You Keep a Secret?* 2004.
> <u>Shopaholic series.</u>
>> *Confessions of a Shopaholic.* 2001.
>> *Shopaholic Takes Manhattan.* 2002.
>> *Shopaholic Ties the Knot.* 2003.
>> *Shopaholic and Sister.* 2004.

Kwitney, Alisa.
> *The Dominant Blonde.* 2002.

Matthews, Carole.
> *Bare Necessity.* 2003.

Maxted, Anna.
> *Being Committed.* 2004.
> *Getting Over It.* 2000.

McLaughlin, Emma, and Nicola Kraus.
> *The Nanny Diaries.* 2002.

Mendle, Jane.
> *Kissing in Technicolor.* 2004.

Nichols, Lee.
> *Tales of a Drama Queen.* 2004.

Senate, Melissa.
> *See Jane Date.* 2001.

Shapiro, Laurie Gwen.
> *The Matzo Ball Heiress.* 2004.
>> Jewish protagonist.

Swain, Heather.
> *Luscious Lemon.* 2004.

Sykes, Plum.
> *Bergdorf Blondes: A Novel.* 2004.

Townley, Gemma.
> *Little White Lies: A Novel of Love and Good Intentions.* 2005.

Valdes-Rodriguez, Alisa.
> *The Dirty Girls Social Club.* 2003.
>> The lives and loves of six Latinas who met at Boston University.
>
> *Playing with Boys.* 2004

Weiner, Jennifer.
> *Good in Bed.* 2001.
> *In Her Shoes.* 2003.

Weisberger, Lauren.

The Devil Wears Prada. 2004.

Williams, Tia.

The Accidental Diva. 2004.

African American protaganist.

Resources

Authors on the Web—Chick Lit Roundtable (http://www.authorsontheweb.com/features/0402-chicklit/chicklit.asp). A discussion of Chick Lit by those who write it.

" "Chick Lit 101." ***Baltimore City Paper On Line Edition.*** Available at http://www.citypaper.com/special/story.asp?id=5972.

Chick Lit USA (http://www.chicklit.us). This Web site, an online British Chick Lit store, provides much more than lists of books, including a definition of Chick Lit and a glossary of terms used in British Chick Lit.

Romance Writers of America Chick Lit Chapter (http://www.chicklitwriters.com/). Information for writers and readers of Chick Lit

D's Chick Lit Picks

Cabot, Meg.

Boy Meets Girl. **2004.**

Told in the form of journal entries, instant messages, e-mail, and notes on receipts and menus. Both Kate, a homeless (couch surfing) human resources manager and Mitch, an unconventional lawyer who is defending her in a lawsuit and who also happens to be the brother of her persistent ex, spring vividly to life with their hilariously complicated lives.

Holden, Wendy.

Farm Fatale. **2002.**

Moving to a cottage in the picturesque village of Eight Mile Bottom because it is her boyfriend's dream, Rosie, an illustrator, finds everything she could ever want—a book contract and true love—if only she could get rid of the boyfriend.

Author/Title Index

Blue Girl, The, 400
Blue Highways, 212
Blue Horizon, The, 75
Blue Horse Dreaming, 98
Blue Mars, 328
Blue Moon, 303, 441, 443
Blue Twilight, 304
Bluefeather Fellini, 123
*Bluefeather Fellini in the Sacred
      Realm,* 123
Blues Detective, The, 140, 144, 145
Bly, Stephen, 128, 489
Body & Soul, 303
Body Double, 194
Body in the Bath House, A, 181
Body Language, 193
Body of a Girl, 191
Body of David Hayes, The, 162
Body of Lies, 194
Body Snatchers, The, 422
Boggs, Johnny, 94, 97, 106, 114
Bohnhoff, Maya Kaathryn, 409, 458
Bold Sons of Erin, 185
Bolitho series, 248
Bomb Vessel, The, 250
Bond, Larry, 225, 230
Bond, Michael, 177
Bondurant, Matt, 227
Bone Collector, The, 160
Bone Game, 124
Bones of the Buffalo, 96
Bones of the Earth, 336
Bonesetter's Daughter, The, 50, 72
Bonfiglioli, Kyril, 195
Bonner, Cindy, 119
Bonner Family Saga, 68
Bontly, Susan W., 308
*Book Clubs: Women and the Uses of
      Reading in Everyday Life,*
      7, 9, 13, 14
Book Discussions for Adults, 18
Book of Books series, 487
Book of Eleanor, The, 63
Book of the Cauldron, The, 388
Book of the Dead, 429, 463
Book of the Dun Cow, The, 372, 398,
      484
Book of the Spear, The, 388
Book of the Stone, The, 388
Book of the Sword, The, 388
Bookends, 500
Booklist, 90
Booklover's Mystery series, 177
Books of Blood, The, 427
Books of the Rai-kirah, The, 378
Books That Made a Difference, 47,
      51
Boot Hill, 131
Booth, Stephen, 153
Bootlegger's Daughter, 171
Bopp, Richard E., 19
Borchardt, Alice, 275, 302, 387, 442
Border Dogs, 103
Border Line, 95
Border Lords, 99
Border Showdown, 129
Border trilogy, The, 124
Border Trumpet, 106

Borderlands, 5, 460
Borderlands, 399
Borders of Infinity, 330
Bordertown, 400, 408
Borges, Jorge Luis, 141
Borland, Hal, 107
Born in Twilight, 304
Born of Fire, 285
Born of the Sun, 279
"Both a Woman and a Complete
      Professional': Women
      Readers and Women's
      Hard-boiled Detective
      Fiction" 144, 145
Boucher, Anthony, 412
Bound by Blood, 116
Bounty Man, 129
Bourdieu, Pierre, 14
Bouricius, Ann, 266, 308
Bourne Identity, The, 222
Bourne Legacy, The, 222
Bourne Supremacy, The, 222
Bourne Ultimatum, The, 222
Bova, Ben, 326, 341
Bowen, Elizabeth, 413
Bowen, Gail, 172
Bowen, Peter, 159, 175
Bowen, Rhys, 153, 180
Bower, B.M., 83
Bowie, 115
*Bowling Alone: The Collapse and
      Revival of American
      Community,* 9, 13, 14
Boy Meets Girl, 500, 502
Boy Who Would Live Forever, The,
      356
Boyarin, Jonathan, 14
Boyle, Alistair, 164
Boys from Brazil, 217, 229
Brackett, Leigh, 116, 413
Bradbury, Ray, 323, 345, 371, 377,
      410, 431, 434, 444, 459
Bradford, Barbara Taylor, 269, 294,
      495
Bradford, Richard, 122
Bradley, Marion Zimmer, 337, 377,
      387, 405, 409
Bradshaw, Gillian, 59
Brady, John, 155
Braeswood Tapestry, The, 276
Brainships, 337
Brand, Max, 35, 83, 88, 92, 101,
      104, 112, 132, 134
Brandon, Jay, 198
Brandvold, Peter, 102
Branon, Bill, 239
Brashares, Ann, 499
Brass Eagle, 223
Braun, Lilian Jackson, 173
Brave Bulls, The, 107
Brave Cowboy, The, 122
Brave New World, 324, 345
Braver, Gary, 454
Bravo, The, 48
Brazen, 267
Brazos, The, 130
Breaker, The, 192
Breaker's Reef, 482

Breaking Even, 116, 129
Breakthrough, 161, 234
Breakthroughs, 349
Breath of Scandal, 269
Breath of Snow and Ashes, A, 301
Breathing Room, 266
Breathless, 277
Brentwood, 482
Bretheren, The, 198
Brett, Simon, 169
Brewer, Steve, 166
Briar King, The, 384
Bridal Wreath, The, 56
Bride Finder, The, 299
Bride of Pendorric, 262, 274
Bride of Rosecliffe, The, 283
Bride of the Fat White Vampire, 435
Bride of the Morning Star, 126
Bride of Willow Creek, The, 281
Bride, The, 285
Bride's Necklace, The, 291
Brides of Durango, 282
Bridge, The, 162
Bridge of D'Arnath, The, 378
Bridge of Rama, 391
Bridges over Time, 72, 293
Bridges, Kate, 280
Bridget Jones's Diary, 258, 468, 499, 500
"Brief History of Readers' Advisory, A,"
      15
Brig of War, A, 250
Bright Captivity, 74
Bright Shark, 230
Bright Star, 232
Bright Sword of Ireland, 390
Brightness Reef, 354
Brightwell, Emily, 180
Brilliance of the Moon, 383
Brin, David, 318, 321, 322, 337, 343,
      345, 354
Brisbin, Terri, 283
Bristling Wood, The, 383
Bristow, Gwen, 53
Brite, Poppy Z., 427, 428, 434, 444
Brockman, Suzanne, 269
Broderick, Damien, 341
Broken Arrow, 94
Broken Crown, The, 386
Broken Hearts Club, The, 160
Broken Prey, 193
Broken Ranks, 117
Broken Sword, The, 387
Bromeliad series, 363
Brontë, Charlotte, 256, 262, 274
Brontë, Emily, 256, 262, 274
Bronze Canticles, The, 402
Brooke-Rose, Christine, 413
Brooks, Bill, 102, 114
Brooks, Geraldine, 70
Brooks, Terry, 338, 377, 378, 410, 413,
      415
Brother Cadfael, 63
Brother Wind, 58
Brotherhood of the Wolf, 380
Brotherhood of War series, The, 246
Brothers in Arms, 330
Brouwer, Sigmund, 483, 485
Brown Girl in the Ring, 345

Subject Index

Dates are listed chronologically at the beginning of the index.

kangaroo, 350
Kansas, 116, 120, 121, 127, 158
    territory, 120
Karzistan, 340
Katharine of Aragon, 66
Kellogg grant, 11
Kennedy, President, 46
Kent, 154
Kentucky, 362
kidnappings, 63, 69, 117, 118, 159,
    162, 192, 199, 205, 304
King Charles I, 66
King John, 63, 285
King Richard, 63, 284
King Tutankhamen, 60
kings, 278
Kiowa, 94, 96, 175
Korean, 140
Korean American, 500

La Malinche, 59
labeling, 34, 36
laboratories, 433, 455, 463
ladder approach, 15
Lake District, 263
Lakota, 124, 307, 311
land grant, 109
land rush, 280
landscape, 86
Langum Prize, 68, 78
laran, 337, 409
Las Vegas, 173, 498
Latinos, 140, 257, 306, 500, 501
lawmen, 86, 91, 102, 129
lawyers, 148, 170, 502
Lee, John D., 118
Lee, Robert E., 71
Left Coast Crime conference, 78
legal thrillers, 36, 141, 147, 170,
    189, 197
legends, 387, 388
Leigh , Robert D., 17
Leisure Books, 134, 229
lesbians, 139–40, 150, 174, 308, 412
Lewis and Clark expedition, 46, 69,
    70, 71
librarians, 3, 5, 7–13, 15–17, 19–20,
    23, 26, 28, 33–39, 66, 73,
    76, 91, 125, 133, 147, 178,
    208, 211, 219, 242, 255,
    264–67, 266, 268, 273, 276,
    286, 288–91, 293, 308, 335,
    366, 391, 409, 414, 417,
    452, 460,
libraries, 3, 5, 7–13, 15–17, 19–20,
    23, 33–39, 66, 73, 76, 91,
    125, 133, 147, 219, 242,
    255, 264, 268, 276, 286,
    288–91, 293, 366, 391, 409,
    414, 452, 460
libraries and genre fiction, 33
library education, 12, 18–21, 34
life forms, 342, 352
Lincoln, Abraham, 45, 71
linguist, 346
Linsford. Roundup, 134
listening skills, 36

literary, 7, 13–14, 19, 26–27, 31–32,
    43, 44, 47– 49, 52–53,
    64–65, 70–71, 74, 76, 78,
    85–88, 98, 100, 105, 108,
    111, 119–20, 122–24, 127,
    139, 142, 147, 217, 227–31,
    313, 328, 350, 355, 362–67,
    368, 403, 406, 423, 425,
    426, 428–33, 449, 456, 465,
    467, 469, 471–76, 497
literary criticism, 49, 142
literary terms, 26
literature, 403
little person, 166
locked rooms, 274
London, 14, 28–29, 76, 78, 132, 152,
    172, 179–80, 182, 184, 186,
    188, 192, 204, 217, 224,
    273, 286, 288–91, 291–94,
    300, 308, 320, 322, 400,
    428–34, 433, 435, 463
London Detection Club, 138
lone survivor, 239
Los Angeles, 61, 140, 147, 150, 157,
    164, 165, 169, 172, 174,
    177, 189, 419, 440
lost city, 242
Lost Dutchman mine, 102
lost mines, 101, 210, 242
Louis VII, 63
Louisiana, 57, 70, 158, 165, 275,
    277
Louisiana Purchase, 71
Love Spectrum, 258
Lowell, 481
Ludlow massacre, 119
Luna, 33
Luong, 155
lycanthropic morphic disorder, 443

Ma, Yo Yo, 8
machines
Madrid, 156
Magazine of Fantasy & Science
    Fiction, 317
Magdalene, 60
Maggody, 150
magic, 364, 410
magical powers, 484
mail order bride, 112, 135, 278, 279
mail-order book company, 467
Maine, 166, 184
mainstream fiction, 31, 36, 87–88,
    113, 122, 140, 257, 261,
    265, 317, 348, 424, 426,
    429, 465, 467–75, 475, 477,
    494
Majorca, 156
male point of view, 478
male romance, 210, 215, 216, 217,
    218, 242
male supremacy, 470
Malice Domestic, 204
Manchester, 195
Manichean vision, 420
Mansfield, Jayne, 181
mansions, 274, 446, 450
marines, 266

Marlowe, Christopher, 224
marriage, 63, 118, 144, 210, 256, 258,
    265, 266, 276, 284, 288, 292,
    311, 346, 391, 468, 479, 481
Mars, 159, 318, 324, 326, 328, 341, 346,
    357, 363
Marseilles, 188
Mary, Queen of Scots, 66, 183
Maryland, 69, 166
Massachusetts, 68, 144, 145, 158, 166,
    172, 174, 444
Masters of Terror and Horror Fiction, 463
Masterson, Bat, 116
matriarchal, 293, 329, 388
Mayan, 243, 353, 445
Mayan artifact, 243
McCarthy, Joe, 181
mechanical, 340, 359, 409
Mechanists, 341
medical examiner, 165, 170
medical horror, 454
medical suspense, 191
medical thrillers, 265, 454
medicine, 75
medicine show, 114
medieval, 47, 53, 72, 178, 183, 186, 276,
    277, 283, 284, 285, 295, 300,
    342, 364, 423, 436
medieval English, 72
medieval fantasy, 53
medieval knight, 300
medieval mysteries, 183, 186
Mennonite, 465, 471
mercenaries, 244
Merlin, 387, 388, 389, 403
meteorite, 327
Metis, 175
Mexican, 59, 71, 92, 104, 106, 125
Mexican border, 92
Mexican War, 71
Mexico, 59, 60, 76, 111, 118, 135, 164,
    206, 240, 263, 279
Mexico City, 175
Miami, 171, 193, 198, 444
Michelangelo, 64
Michigan, 48, 159, 166, 415
microscopic, 341, 454
Mid-Continent Public Library Readers'
    Advisory page, 36
Middle Ages, 61, 422
Middle East, 215, 229
Middle Easterners, 257
midlist fiction, 36
midwife, 184
Milan, 227
militaristic and war, 212, 324, 325, 330,
    332, 335, 486
militaristic science fiction, 212
military, 55, 59, 105, 117, 168, 198, 206,
    216, 218, 229, 238, 248, 265,
    325, 332
military adventure, 245
military historical, 218
military police, 168
Mills & Boon, 256, 257
Milwaukee, 3, 4, 16, 23
miners, 92
mines and mining, 101, 369

miniaturization, 341–46
ministers, 466, 488
Minnesota, 14, 159, 166, 174, 180, 279, 402
Mira, 494
mirror, 302
misogynistic, 421
missionary, 119
Mississippi Valley, 57
Mississippi, 14, 51, 57, 145, 166
Missouri, 70, 122, 159, 166, 276, 280, 478
    territory, 280
Mix, Tom, 115
mob violence, 103
Mohawk Valley. *See*
mommy lit, 479, 480, 499
moms, 169, 266, 441
Mongolia, 239
Monroe, Marilyn, 181
monsters, 241, 314, 340, 420, 421, 426, 427, 432, 433, 447, 455, 463
Montana, 92, 102, 103, 107, 108, 110, 123, 126, 127, 158, 159, 166, 171, 282, 481
    territory, 102, 103
Montfort, Simon de, 63
mood, 25, 27, 82, 88, 319
moon, 326, 344, 485
moral codes, 346
morals, 374
Morgan le Fay, 302, 442
Mormon Battalion, 118
Mormons, 118, 401, 465, 471
Moroccan, 304
Morton Grove Library, 34
Moscow, 156, 225
Mossad, 222
motherhood, 479
mothers, 135, 255, 495, 497, 499
motifs, 315, 414, 424, 429, 488
motorcycle-riding, 265
Mount Vesuvius, 60
Mountain Meadows massacre, 118
mountain men, 91, 98–100, 109–10, 112, 117, 128, 134
movie stars, 169
movies. *See* films
Mozart, Wolfgang, 64
Muir, John, 115
mule-train, 101
multiculturalism, 44, 49
Multnomah, 134, 257
murder, 32, 46, 65, 104, 141, 150, 178, 181–83, 187–88, 192, 197, 205, 227, 236, 273, 284, 292, 326, 342, 359, 446
Murieta, Joaquin, 114
music, 31, 84, 403, 416, 428, 461, 492
musician, 107
mutant, 354, 433
mutating, 453, 458
mutism, 445
Mycora, 342
Myrtle Beach, 492

mysteries, 19, 25, 27, 31, 32, 32, 34, 37, 47, 53, 53, 63, 65, 70, 84, 89, 102, 123, 125, 137–40, 142–44, 149–50, 160, 162–63, 168–70, 172, 176–78, 180–86, 188–89, 197, 202–205, 207, 223, 227, 251, 256, 268–71, 273, 277, 288, 293, 308, 317, 357, 359–64, 372, 398, 403, 420–25, 427–32, 434, 440–47, 465, 469, 472, 475, 482, 492, 499
Mystery Readers International, 203, 204
Mystery Writers of America, 176, 203, 204
Mythcon, 415, 416
mythic, 87, 398
mythical, 82, 86, 152, 348, 364
mythology, 274, 375, 389, 390, 407, 425, 447, 457, 461
Mythopoeic Society, 415, 416
myths, 61, 84, 90, 181, 371, 372, 387, 426

Naiad, 139
NAL, 257
nanotechnology, 237, 238, 323, 339, 341, 342, 361
Napoleon, 64
Napoleonic wars, 47, 246–51, 290
Nashville, 162, 167, 175, 266, 462
National Peace Organization, 486
Native American detectives, 140
Native American leuths, 175
Native Americans, 57, 87, 94, 113, 116, 122–24, 175, 205, 252, 257, 265, 282–85, 285, 307, 387, 446
natural disasters, 208, 212, 242
natural world, 343
nature, 85
Navaho, 175
Navajo Tribal Police, 157, 160, 175
naval adventure, 245, 246, 248, 250
Navy SEALS, 478
navy, 234
Nazis, 208, 217, 228–31, 241, 435
Neanderthals, 57, 348, 369
near future, 66, 274, 315, 323, 325, 350, 493
Nebraska, 47, 53, 108, 132
Neo-Victorian, 340
Netherlands, 63, 156
Nevada, 84, 101, 110, 127, 310
new age fiction, 465, 469
New Amsterdam, 185
New England, 447
New Jersey, 166, 206, 355, 369
New Mexico, 53, 70, 84, 90, 109, 112, 122, 123, 128, 131, 133, 135, 160, 166, 178, 206, 446
New Orleans, 6, 64, 158, 184, 435, 449
New South Wales, 67
New Testament, 466, 467, 488

new wave, 315, 317, 319, 324, 345
new world, 48, 278, 285, 324
New York, 48, 68, 150, 160, 166, 183, 204, 224, 360, 481.
New Zealand, 67
Newford, 400, 417
newsgroups, 78, 256
newspaperman, 101
Niflheim, 387
nightmares, 446, 447, 484
Nile, 301, 408
nineteenth century, 5, 15, 20, 48, 49, 54, 66–67, 69–70, 73, 82–83, 91, 96, 100, 108, 134, 138, 142, 152–54, 178–79, 183, 186, 210, 243, 250, 274–82, 286, 301, 314, 374, 401, 423–29, 465–71, 471, 481
ninth century, 57, 61, 277
Nisei, 157, 175
Noah's ark, 61
noir, 149, 162, 168, 332, 420, 421, 428
nonfiction, 15, 16, 26, 35, 50, 92, 317, 391, 416, 493
Norman England, 293
Normans, 55
Norse, 387, 390
North America, 7, 82, 94, 256, 285, 401, 487
North Carolina, 14, 22, 52, 70, 161, 171, 259, 260, 279, 309, 429, 430
North Dakota., 72, 279
northern plains, 57
Northumberland, 73
Norwegian, 174, 229, 487
nostalgia, 45
Notre Dame, 172
NoveList, 19, 34, 176
novella anthology series, 132
novels of the West, 86, 87, 88
nuclear, 231, 240, 241, 244, 315, 325, 342, 343, 424, 433, 454
nuclear annihilation, 325
nuclear detonation, 241
nuns, 172
nurses, 301, 445
NYPL, 17

Oakland, 164, 175
occult, 32, 64, 178, 431, 443
Office for Research & Statistics, 8
office temp, 169
Ohio, 14, 68, 71, 161, 167
Ohio valley, 68
oil spill, 236
Oklahoma, 72, 93, 161, 276, 280
Old Testament, 467
O'Malley, Grace, 66
one-armed, 167
one-eyed, 228
online resources, 78, 134, 205, 416, 463
Ontario, 151, 320, 322
open questions, 27
Oprah's book club, 10
Orange County, 157
Orchid Beach, 157
Oregon Trail, 92, 122
organ transplants, 237, 265
organization, 34

Ramses II, 60
ranch story, 86
Random, Inc., 36
range wars, 109
rapture, 344, 469, 472, 473, 485, 486
rats, 183, 435
read-alikes, 39
readers' advisory, 9, 12, 16–23,
        25–29, 33–37, 40, 38,
        87–88, 90–91, 176,
        202–203, 211, 308, 318–24,
        266, 391, 414, 461, 498,
    adult, 19
    classes, 34
    history of, 15–23
    interview, 25–29, 211
    services, 8, 17, 19, 35
    techniques, 35
Readers Advisory Committee of the
        Reference and User
        Services Association's, 18
Reading for the Future, 318
reading interests, 3, 26, 33, 35, 38,
        174,308, 313, 493
reading journal, 35
reading patterns, 26
reading plans, 35
reading preferences, 27, 318–24
real estate developer, 483
reanimated, 340, 444
Reconstruction, 69, 116
recruiters, 363
Red Dress Ink, 258, 499, 493
Red River, 130
reference interviews, 26–27
reference sources, 19, 40, 460, 491
reference work, 17
regency era, 179, 300
regency romance, 54, 78, 261–64,
        286–94, 299–300, 303, 308,
        311
regional/national characteristics, 139
relationship novels, 494
religion, 5, 49, 134, 139, 140, 325,
        345–51, 357, 361, 364, 372,
        407–12, 451, 465–96
Renaissance, 18, 63, 64, 66, 79, 227,
        296
reprints, 37, 134, 138, 219
research, 8, 12–13, 19, 22, 44, 46,
        50, 77, 202, 254
researchers, 265, 369
restaurant critic, 177
Restoration England, 186
retired homicide detective, 168
retirement home, 237
revenge story, 86
review journals, 207, 309–13, 462,
        463, 491
reviewers, 45, 204, 296, 310, 367
reviews, 19, 35–36, 43, 133, 309–13,
        367, 462, 491
Revolutionary war, 48, 49, 56,
        68–69, 73, 75, 184, 435
Rhodesia, 75
Richard III, 46, 51, 63
rising sea levels, 360
robotics, 340

robots, 315, 323, 324, 325, 340, 341,
        342, 359
Rocksburg, 161
Rocky Mountains, 57, 98, 451
rogues, 141, 195, 239, 243, 251, 298
role-playing, 408, 409
Roman, 54, 56, 59, 100, 147, 172,
        176, 187, 387, 388, 467
Roman Britain, 56, 59
Roman Catholic, 147, 172
romance, 6, 25, 28, 31–38, 45, 47,
        53–55, 57, 64–66, 71–72,
        78, 82–84, 86, 89, 120–21,
        125, 139, 193–95, 208, 210,
        224, 242, 244, 248,
        253–312, 314, 358–64, 368,
        377, 392, 415, 420–25, 428,
        431, 434, 439–47, 446, 451,
        465, 468–73, 475– 480,
        491–99, 497, 499
romance covers
    cartoon, 258
    clinch, 258, 296
    real estate, 258
    stepback, 258
romance formula., 253
romance readers, 45, 254, 256, 257,
        305, 358
romance writers (character), 169,
        178
Romance Writers of America, 78,
        255, 257, 259, 260, 264,
        286, 310, 311, 415, 492,
        502
    Library Liaison, 265
romantic fantasy, 299, 415
Romantic Novelists Association,
        310
romantic SF, 299, 358
romantic suspense, 148, 261,
        268–76, 277, 305, 311, 449,
        478, 495
Rome, 155, 442
    ancient, 54, 59, 60, 181, 187,
        442
Roosevelt, Eleanor, 169
Roosevelt, Teddy, 115
Rosenberg, Betty, 12, 18, 23, 33, 91,
        96, 276
Route 66, 72, 276
Royal Canadian Mounted Police,
        151, 481
Royal Navy, 247, 249
Royals, 63, 65
runaways, 408
rural, 98, 149, 150, 158
RUSA, 18, 20, 22
Russia, 56, 64, 76, 156, 210, 229,
        232, 245, 278
Russian revolution
rustlers, 94, 108

Sacajawea, 97
saga, 54, 61, 65–66, 68, 72–74, 76,
        78, 84, 88, 95, 109, 114,
        120, 125–128, 243, 262,
        278, 284–87, 287, 292–96,
        296, 299, 304–305, 308,

        324, 329–34, 332–37, 341, 356,
        358, 377, 381, 384, 387, 389,
        391, 406, 478, 480, 490
Sagebrush, 134
sales figures, 372
Salisbury Plain, 76
Salt Lake City, 78
salvage yard, 400
Sam's Club, 468
San Antonio, 114, 135, 167, 198
San Francisco, 54, 119, 164, 171, 174,
        175, 181, 182, 213
Santa Ana, 44
Santa Barbara, 164
Santa Fe, 160, 206
Sarandon, Susan, 8
Saskatchewan, 172
Satan, 182, 245, 426, 452, 463
Satanic, 425, 426
Satanism, 431, 432, 452
satire, 393
Savannah, 70
Saxons, 55, 279
Scandinavia, 56
schizophrenia, 444, 477
scholarly materials, 40
scholars, 6, 10, 19, 32, 82, 139, 143, 253,
        297, 309, 313, 383
scholarship, 3, 6, 7, 12, 124, 313, 322
school shooting, 154
schools, 4, 8, 18, 45–48, 68, 77, 287, 326,
        419, 447, 482
    boarding school, 274
    prep school, 450
schoolteachers, 120, 169, 172, 369, 481
    schoolmarms, 94, 311
science, 316
science fantasy, 363, 369
science fiction, 10, 31–34, 36–38, 53, 84,
        92, 113, 188, 204, 207, 218, 225,
        236, 240, 244, 251, 258, 261,
        273–76, 286, 298, 299, 304–305,
        308, 310–14, 313–75, 377, 395,
        400, 402, 415, 414–21, 421, 425,
        427–32, 433–38, 454, 460,
        462–67, 465, 469, 483–88
science fiction adventure, 325
Science Fiction and Fantasy Writers of
        America, 367
science fiction mysteries, 359
Science Fiction Reader, 316
Science Fiction Research Association,
        367
science fiction romance, 299, 415
science run amok, 454
scientific investigation, 139
scientists, 76, 144, 229, 245, 317, 318,
        326, 341, 342, 348, 361, 369,
        423, 433
scope, 38
Scotland Yard, 152, 153, 182, 301
Scotland, 48, 67, 110, 152, 153, 154, 169,
        182, 275, 276, 277, 279, 285,
        301, 389
Scotsman, 65
Scottish laird, 285
sea, 232
sea adventures, 54, 208, 249

About the Contributors

Denice Adkins is Assistant Professor, School of Information Science and Learning Technologies, University of Missouri, Columbia. Her research interests include Latino fiction, and she teaches readers' advisory and reference services.

Dale Bailey is a popular and acclaimed horror writer. He is also author of *American Nightmares: The Haunted House Formula in American Popular Fiction* (Bowling Green State University Popular Press, 1999). He is Instructor of American Literature at Lenoir Rhyne College, Hickory, North Carolina.

R. Gordon Kelly is Professor, American Studies, University of Maryland, College Park. His publications, focusing on the relationship between literature and society, include *Mystery Fiction and Modern Life* (University Press of Mississippi, 1998) and *Mother Was a Lady: Self and Society in Selected American Children's Periodicals, 1865–1890* (Greenwood Press, 1974).

Melanie A. Kimball is Assistant Professor, School of Informatics, Department of Library and Information Studies, University at Buffalo, State University of New York. Her research and writing focuses on the history of public libraries as cultural and social institutions, children's services in public libraries, and children's literature.

JoAnn Palmeri has a Ph.D. in the history of science and is a master's candidate at the School of Library and Information Studies, University of Oklahoma, Norman. Most recently, she was Visiting Assistant Professor in the History of Science Department at the University of Oklahoma, where she taught a class on science and popular culture. Palmeri has contributed as editor and author to several encyclopedias on the history of science. Her research focuses on popular science, and she is interested in reading habits related to fiction as well as nonfiction.

Catherine Sheldrick Ross is Professor and Dean, School of Information and Media Studies, University of Western Ontario, London, Ontario, Canada. Known for her research in adult reading interests, Ross is a widely published author. Her books include *Conducting the Reference Interview* (Neal-Schuman, 2002) and *Reading Matters: What the Research Reveals about Reading, Libraries, and Community* (Libraries Unlimited, 2005).

Erin A. **Smith** is Associate Professor, American Studies and Literature and Associate Director, Gender Studies, University of Texas at Dallas. She is the author of *Hard-boiled: Working Class Readers and Pulp Magazines* (Temple University Press, 2000), and she is working on a book about twentieth-century American religious best sellers and their readers.

John H. **Timmerman** is Professor of English, Calvin College, Grand Rapids, Michigan. He is author of more than twenty books, primarily in American literature, including *Other Worlds: The Fantasy Genre* (Bowling Green State University Popular Press, 1983).

Connie Van Fleet is Professor, School of Library and Information Studies, University of Oklahoma, Norman. A longtime proponent and teacher of readers' advisory, and a widely published author, Van Fleet is coeditor of *Reference User and Services Quarterly* and coauthor of *African American Literature: A Guide to Reading Interests* (Libraries Unlimited, 2004).

About the Author and Editor

Diana Tixier Herald is an author, readers' advisory consultant, workshop presenter, and speaker. She started her career as an avid reader long before she ever saw the inside of a classroom and usually reads in excess of 400 books a year. At age ten she started working as a library volunteer and has since been a bookseller, a library assistant, a library director, and head of a public library popular materials center. Her Master of Arts in Librarianship and Information Management was earned at the University of Denver.

Today she lives on the edge of a canyon at 7,000 feet altitude with her husband in a sustainable house they built from recycled materials. She also runs the nonprofit Center for Adolescent Reading, and is the author of several other readers' advisory guides, including *Teen Genreflecting*, 2d ed., *Fluent in Fantasy*, and *Strictly Science Fiction*.

Wayne A. Wiegand is F. William Summers Professor of Library and Information Studies and Professor of American Studies at Florida State University. He is co-editor of *Library Quarterly* (University of Chicago Press) and Executive Director of Beta Phi Mu (the International Library and Information Science Honor Society). An internationally known authority on library history, Wiegand is author of five books (three of which have won the G.K. Hall Awards given by the American Library Association for "outstanding contribution to library literature"), editor or coeditor of five others, and author of more than fifty scholarly articles (many of which have won awards for exemplary research). He has lectured widely to audiences across the world on subjects ranging from "library as place" to "the social nature of reading."

Wiegand has received numerous awards for his publications and for distinguished professional activities, including the Herbert Putnam Award, the Justin Winsor Award, and the ALISE Research Paper Award.